MW00653078

THE SHOCK OF WAR

To Herb Plambeck
for the wonderful things
he has done for the
Second Infantry Division

Loyally,
Ele Lemen P. Wakefield
(Mrs. John P.)

THE SHOCK OF WAR
VOLUME 2

Unknown Battles That Ruined
Adolph Hitler's Plan for a Second *Blitzkrieg*
in the West, December-January, 1944-45.

J. C. Doherty

Vert Milon press, Alexandria, VA

Volume 2 Copyright: J.C. Doherty, 1996. All rights reserved, including translations into other languages.

Library of Congress Catalogue Number 95-60258 (Volumes 1 and 2).

Publishing history: First Edition, Volume 1 (ISBN 0-9613980-4-3), 1994; Second Edition, Volume 1, 1995; Volume 2, 1996 (ISBN 0-9613980-5-1).

COVER PHOTO: Two American soldiers take cover in back of an M-4 medium tank in anticipation of an enemy assault from somewhere. (U.S. Signal Corps photo)
MAPS based on author's designs.

VERT MILON press,
Box 332, Alexandria, VA 22313

Acknowledgements

During the five years required to research and write the two volumes of <u>The Shock of War</u>, the author received help and encouragement from some three hundred individuals, most of whom participated in the battles and other events described. They sent letters enclosing "war stories," submitted to interviews, and sent diaries and other personal records, mementos, and photographs. (See Documentation sections of this volume and the previous one.)

Also several individuals whom we named in the Preface, Volume 1, made a major contribution, directly or indirectly, to Volume 2. Principal among these is Lisa Wagoner whose word-processing skills, infinite patience, and capacity to keep working cheerfully on a task that never seemed to end were crucial to the production of <u>The Shock of War</u>. Without her participation, it never would have been done.

Also deserving the author's gratitude in connection with the preparation of Volume 2 are the following:

Lionel P. Adda, a veteran of "D" Company, 393rd Infantry Regiment, brought his talent for precision of language and concern over detail to the arduous task of proofreading the manuscript. The author's wife, Josephine Kristan Doherty, also took the time to proof the ms. of both volumes.

J.R. McIlroy, Thor Ronningen, and Richard Byers, 99th Division Association, answered many questions and did their best to provide needed information.

Charles E. Lamkin, W.J. Osterkamp, and Raymond R. Ritter supplied information on the 99th Recon Troop battle with 3rd *Panzergrenadier* Division. (Narrative X, Part 1)

Colonel Charles Biggio, Jr. (Ret.) straightened out the artillery parts, although the author alone is responsible for what appears in Narrative VI. Colonel Biggio also sent a copy of an informative interview with the commander of 3rd *PzGD*.

Jett Johnson, Goldthwaite, TX, son of an officer in the 393rd Infantry, sent a valuable collection of letters his father wrote from the front.

John W. Rue supplied information and a photograph on the officers of the 394th Infantry.

Dr. Richard B. Tobias, formerly of the 393rd Medical Detachment, who studied medicine after the war, straightened out the parts of this volume dealing with the work of medical personnel.

Roy W. Holmes, formerly of the 146th Engineer Combat Battalion, which received a Presidential Unit Citation for the battles around Höfen and Mützenich (Volume 1, Narrative II), reminded us of how vital was the contribution of detached battalions such as his in contributing to the outcome of battles.

Colonel James W. Love (Ret.), former commander of the 38th Infantry Antitank Company, answered inquiries and supplied information on the post-war careers of 2nd Infantry Division officers and the combat in the dual towns. (Narrative VIII)

Colonel Steve F. Phillips, Jr. (Ret.) did the same for the officers of the 26th Infantry Regiment.

Edward L. Farrell, former operations officer of the 38th Infantry, was kind enough to read the chapter on the dual towns battle and comment at length thereon.

Arthur L. Chaitt, executive director, Society of the 1st Division, answered questions and suggested sources of information.

John F. Votaw, Cantigny 1st Division Foundation, Wheaton, IL, was helpful in uncovering post-war career information on officers of the 1st.

Roma Danysh, Army Center of Military History, Washington, DC, made available center materials and introduced the author to colleagues who also were helpful.

The Documentation sections of both volumes include lists of published works consulted in preparing The Shock of War. In connection with writing Volume 2, the author found much useful matter in MacDonald, A Time for Trumpets; Cole, The Ardennes, Battle of the Bulge; Cavanagh, Krinkelt-Rocherath, The Battle for the Twin Villages, and Dauntless, A History of the 99th Infantry Division; Hamilton, Final Years of the Field Marshal, 1944-1976; Luther, Blood and Honor, The History of the 12th SS Panzer Division, Hitler Youth, 1943-45; and Meyer, Kriegsgeschichte der 12 SS Panzerdivision, Hitlerjugend.

The author is grateful to the latter for permission to quote extensively from his Kriegsgeschichte and to the Taylor Publishing Company, Dallas, TX and members of the 99th Infantry Division Association for the same with regard to Dauntless, one of the better division histories of World War II. As with Volume 1, Bill Meyer, editor of The Checkerboard, newspaper of the 99th Infantry Division Association, has allowed the author unlimited use of material appearing in its columns, an invaluable resource.

✠　　　✠　　　✠　　　✠　　　✠

Contents

Maps

THE STORY SO FAR

On December 16, 1944 with enemies closing in on the *Reich* from east and west, Adolph Hitler, *Führer* of the German nation and supreme commander of the still formidable German armed forces, the *Wehrmacht*, let loose twenty-five infantry and armored divisions supported by nearly one thousand warplanes, eight hundred tanks, and thousands of artillery, rocket, and mortar tubes against the unsuspecting U.S. 1st Army in eastern Belgium and Luxembourg. This powerful aggregation of armed force was organized into three armies, two of them *Panzer* armies.

Hitler's objective was no less than the seizure of the great Belgian port and Allied supply center of Antwerp, one hundred miles from the front line held by 1st Army south of Aachen, Germany. When the attacking German forces reached this objective, they were to wheel north and pin the Canadian 1st and British 2nd armies against the North Sea, thus splitting them away from their American allies to the south.

The success of this astounding plan depended on the success of the newly formed 6th *SS Panzer* Army. This army consisted of four *Waffen SS* armored divisions and an assortment of infantry divisions (given the honorific title *Volksgrenadier*), a large but ill-trained parachute division of Hermann Goering's *Luftwaffe*, several corps of artillery and rocket-throwing machines, and attached units of heavy tanks, tank destroyers, assault guns, antiaircraft guns, and pioneers. Sixth *SS Panzer* also was to receive ample air coverage and support.

On *Null Tag* (zero day, December 16, 1944), two of the armored divisions, the 1st *SS*, "*Leibstandarte Adolph Hitler*," and 12th *SS*, "*Hitlerjugend*," were to rush through the breach created by the infantry in the line held by the U.S. 1st Army's 5th Corps between Monschau, Germany and Losheim, Belgium, fourteen airline miles to the south, and strike for the Meuse River in the vicinity of Liege, Belgium, their initial objective. This was the *Schwerpunkt*, the point of maximum force of the entire German counteroffensive in the West. The armored divisions of 6th *Panzer* Army were to lead the way to Antwerp. Standing in their way were only two American infantry divisions, the 99th and the 2nd and a mechanized cavalry squadron.

After one of the most punishing artillery and rocket bombardments laid by the Germans in World War II on their enemies, two regiments of the 99th Division were struck at dawn December 16 by elements of three *Volksgrenadier* (infantry) divisions, the 326th, 277th, and 12th; and a regiment of paratroops from the 3rd *Fallschirmjäger* Division.

Faced with their first serious combat of the war, the young and

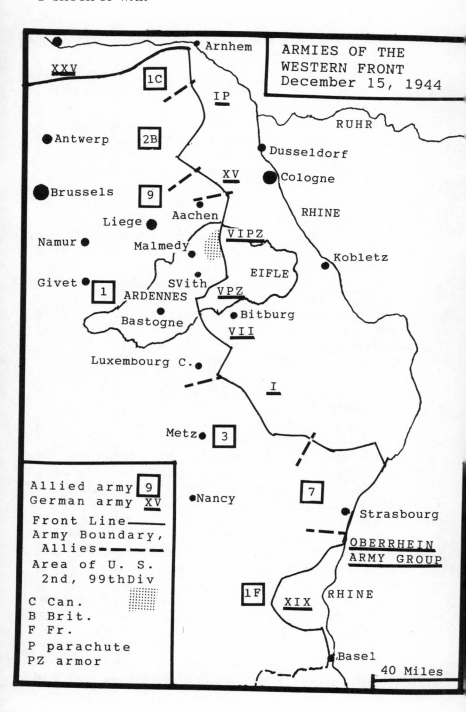

ARMIES OF THE
WESTERN FRONT
December 15, 1944

XXV

1C

IP

RUHR

Antwerp

2B

Dusseldorf

XV

Cologne

Brussels

9

RHINE

Liege

Aachen

Namur

Malmedy

VIPZ

Kobletz

Givet

1

SVith

EIFLE

ARDENNES

VPZ

Bastogne

Bitburg

VII

Luxembourg C.

I

Metz

3

Nancy

7

Strasbourg

OBERRHEIN
ARMY GROUP

Allied army 9
German army XV
Front Line
Army Boundary,
  Allies
Area of U. S.
  2nd, 99thDiv

C Can.
B Brit.
F Fr.
P parachute
PZ armor

1F

XIX

RHINE

Basel

40 Miles

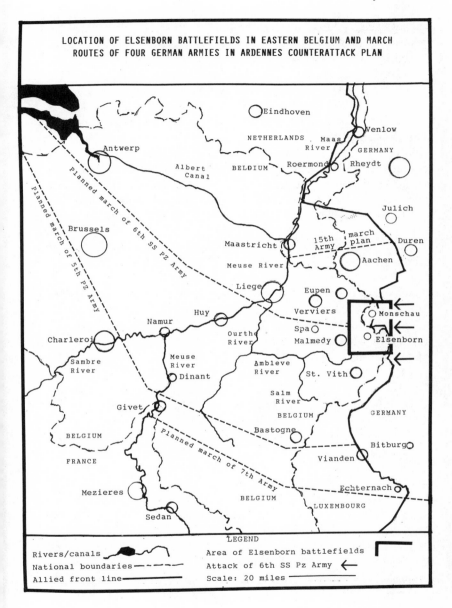

LOCATION OF ELSENBORN BATTLEFIELDS IN EASTERN BELGIUM AND MARCH
ROUTES OF FOUR GERMAN ARMIES IN ARDENNES COUNTERATTACK PLAN

Eindhoven

NETHERLANDS   Maas   Venlow
River   GERMANY

Antwerp   Roermond   Rheydt

Albert   BELGIUM
Canal

Julich

Planned march of 6th SS Pz Army

Brussels   Maastricht   15th   march   Duren
Army   plan

Meuse River   Aachen

Liege   Eupen

Huy   Verviers   Monschau

Namur   Spa   Elsenborn

Planned march of 5th Pz Army   Ourthe   Malmedy
River

Charleroi

Sambre   Meuse   Ambleve
River   River   River   St. Vith

Dinant

Salm
River

Givet   BELGIUM   GERMANY

Bastogne

BELGIUM   Bitburg

FRANCE   Vianden

Planned march of 7th Army

Mezieres   Echternach

BELGIUM

Sedan   LUXEMBOURG

LEGEND

Rivers/canals   Area of Elsenborn battlefields
National boundaries – – – –   Attack of 6th SS Pz Army ⟵
Allied front line ————   Scale: 20 miles ——

inexperienced soldiers of the 99th held at great cost to themselves for some thirty hours, until noon Sunday, December 17. They were buttressed by two battalions of the 2nd Division.

The five narratives of Volume 1 and their contents:

I: THE HEARTBREAK CROSSROADS. A large-scale attack early in December by U.S. 5th Corps (Major General Leonard T. Gerow) to seize several strategically important dams on the headwaters of Germany's Roer River south of Duren. This brought the 2nd Infantry Division into the 99th's sector of the front line before the German counterattack in the Eifel-Ardennes region erupted. The 2nd Division 9th RCT (regimental combat team, Colonel Chester L. Hirschfelder) supported by the 99th Division 395th RCT (Colonel Alexander J. MacKenzie) on the right initiated the 5th Corps attack on the right flank.

II: THE GERMANS STUMBLE. The 3rd Battalion, 395th Infantry Regiment, 99th Division (Lieutenant Colonel McClernand Butler) and the attached 38th Cavalry Reconnaissance Squadron (Lieutenant Colonel Robert E. O'Brien) fought to a standstill two regiments of the 326th *Volksgrenadier* Division (Major General Erwin Kaschner) at Monschau-Mützenich and thereby protected Eupen, Belgium, headquarters of General Gerow's 5th Corps, from being overrun by the 6th *SS* Army's 67th Infantry Corps (Lieutenant General Otto Hitzfeld).

III: TODESWALD. A battle in thick conifer woods along the German-Belgian border southeast of Liege. The 3rd and 1st Battalions, 393rd Infantry Regiment (Lieutenant Colonel Jack Allen and Major Matthew Legler) and the 2nd Battalion, 394th Infantry Regiment of the 99th Division fought to hold back three regiments of the 277th *Volksgrenadier* Division (Colonel Wilhelm Viebig) from reaching the vital Elsenborn high plateau seven miles to the west. Six hours after the German attack began, *Panzergrenadiers* and *Panzerjäger* of the 12th *SS Panzer* Division (*SS* Colonel Hugo Kraas) came in to reinforce the 277th. General Gerow sent the 3rd Battalion, (Lieutenant Colonel Paul Tuttle) 23rd Infantry Regiment, 2nd Division to help the 393rd Regiment (Lieutenant Colonel Jean D. Scott) stem the tide.

IV: AT GROUND ZERO. At the epicenter of the German offensive, the 1st and 3rd battalions of the 394th Infantry Regiment (Lieutenant Colonel Robert H. Douglas and Major Norman A. Moore) and the fifty-man reconnaissance platoon of the 394th (Lieutenant Lyle J. Bouck) tried to stand fast against an assault from several directions by elements of three German divisions; 12th *Volksgrenadier* (Major General Gerhard Engle), 3rd *Fallschirmjäger* (parachute) Division (Major General Walter Wadehn), and 1st *SS Panzer* (*SS* Colonel

Wilhelm Mohnke, *Kampfgruppe* Joachim Peiper) along the northern reaches of the historic Losheim Gap.

V: THE AMERICAN BATTLE LINE DECONSTRUCTS. Swift march of the armored *Kampfgruppe* Peiper along the open right flank of the 99th Infantry Division and the fall of the major supply town of Büllingen. Fierce battle at the villages of Hünningen and Mürringen flanking the vital east-to-west road to Malmedy and the Meuse River Valley in which a second 23rd Infantry battalion participated (1st Battalion commanded by Lieutenant Colonel John M. Hightower). Withdrawal of the survivors of the five battered infantry battalions of the 99th Division and two attached battalions of the 2nd Division. Perilous situation of three regiments of 2nd and 99th division soldiers trying to break contact with the enemy after an attack at the Heartbreak Crossroads in the German West Wall (Narrative I) as armored and infantry enemy columns moved across both their right and left flanks and threatened to encircle them.

Principal army, corps, and division commanders who play a prominent role in Volume 1 are:

U.S. Lieutenant General Omar N. Bradley, 12th Army Group; Lieutenant General Courtney H. Hodges, 1st Army; Gerow, 5th Corps; Major General Walter E. Lauer, 99th Division; Major General Walter M. Robertson, 2nd Division.

German Field Marshal Gerd von Rundstedt, commander of all German armies on the Western Front; Field Marshal Walter Model, Army Group B, responsible for leading the counteroffensive; *SS* General Josef ("Sepp") Dietrich, 6th *SS Panzer* Army; *SS* Lieutenant General Hermann Priess, 1st *SS Panzer* Corps; Lieutenant General Otto Hitzfeld, 67th Infantry Corps.

☩   ☩   ☩   ☩   ☩

At the opening of Volume 2, the situation is as follows: The eight artillery battalions of the 99th and 2nd divisions are withdrawing to the Elsenborn high plateau or repositioning and engaging in the critical battles raging across the front: at the dual towns (Rocherath-Krinkelt); Hünningen-Mürringen; Wirtzfeld; and Monschau-Mützenich.

The 2nd Division headquarters troops, plus armor, antiaircraft, antitank and infantry hastily scraped together, are preparing for a defense at Wirtzfeld north of Büllingen to block *Kampfgruppe* Peiper's expected attack from the south against Elsenborn on the heights.

General Robertson, the 2nd Infantry Division commander, is moving to carry out the difficult assignment of extracting his soldiers and those of the 99th Division from the Wahlerscheid crossroads pocket while holding the German columns at bay long enough for a buildup of American men and guns on the Elsenborn heights, the most suitable terrain between the Meuse and the German-Belgian border for a defense against the rampaging columns of 1st *SS Panzer* Corps. The keystone of Robertson's escape route is the dual towns of Rocherath-Krinkelt where armor and infantry forces are gathering for a major battle.

NUMBERED UNITS AND NAMED COMMANDERS	
American	German[*]
1st Army (Hodges)	6th *SS Panzer* Army (Dietrich)
C/S (Keane)	C/S Kraemer
5th Corps (Gerow/Huebner)	1st *SS Panzer* Corps (Priess)
	C/S (Lehmann)
1st Infantry Division (Andrus)	1st *SS Panzer* Division (Mohnke)
16th Infantry Regiment (Gibb)	*Kampfgruppe* Peiper
3rd Battalion (Horner)	12th *SS Panzer* Division (Kraas)
18th Infantry	12th *SS Pz* Regiment, 25th and
26th Infantry (Seitz)	26th *PzGrenadier* regiments
1st Battalion (Murdoch)	operating in three *Kampf-*
2nd (Daniel)	*gruppen*: Müller, Kuhlmann,
3rd (Corley)	Krause
	3rd *Fallschirmjäger* Division
2nd Infantry Division (Robertson)	(Wadehn)
ADC (Stokes)	5th, 6th, 9th (von Hoffman)
9th Infantry Regiment	regiments
(Hirschfelder/Ginder)	12th *Volksgrenadier* Division
1st Battalion (McKinley)	(Engle)
2nd (Higgins) and 3rd	27th *Füsilier*, 48th (Osterhold),
38th Infantry (Boos)	89th regiments
1st Battalion (Mildren)	277th *Volksgrenadier* Division
2nd (Norris)	(Viebig)
3rd (Barsanti)	150th *Panzer* Brigade (Skorzeny)
23rd Infantry (Lovless)	Special *Fallschirmjäger* Battalion
1st Battalion (Hightower)	(von der Heydte)
2nd, 3rd (Tuttle)	

[*]Divisions moved from one corps to another in course of campaign.

American	German
9th Infantry Division (Craig)	2nd *SS Panzer* Corps (Bittrich)
47th Infantry Regiment	2nd *SS Panzer* Division*
39th Infantry Regiment	9th *SS Panzer* Division
	3rd *Panzergrenadier* Division
99th Infantry Division (Lauer)	(Denkert)
ADC (Mayberry)	8th and 29th *PzGd* regiments
393rd Infantry Regiment (Scott)	103rd *Panzer* Battalion
1st Battalion (Legler)	
2nd (Peters)	67th Infantry Corps (Hitzfeld)
3rd (Allen)	326th *Volksgrenadier* Division
394th Infantry (Riley)	(Kaschner)
1st Battalion (Douglas)	89th *Volksgrenadier* Division
2nd (Legare/Kriz)	246th *Volksgrenadier* Division
3rd (Moore)	(Körte)
395th Infantry (MacKenzie)	
1st, 2nd battalions	
3rd (Butler)	

Refer to sections in Documentation, Volumes 1 and 2, that list supporting and attached artillery, armor, antitank, engineer, antiaircraft, etc. units that worked with the infantry of both sides. Each of the divisions in the above tables also included artillery, engineer, signals, etc., as described many times in these pages. The artillery units are identified in the Documentation. (See also division emblems inside back cover, this volume and Index to names.)

---

* 2nd and 9th *SS* divisions did not participate in Elsenborn battles.

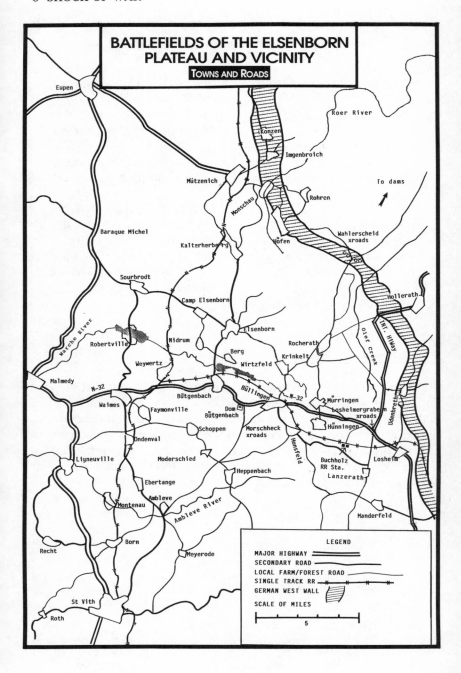

BATTLEFIELDS OF THE ELSENBORN
PLATEAU AND VICINITY
TOWNS AND ROADS

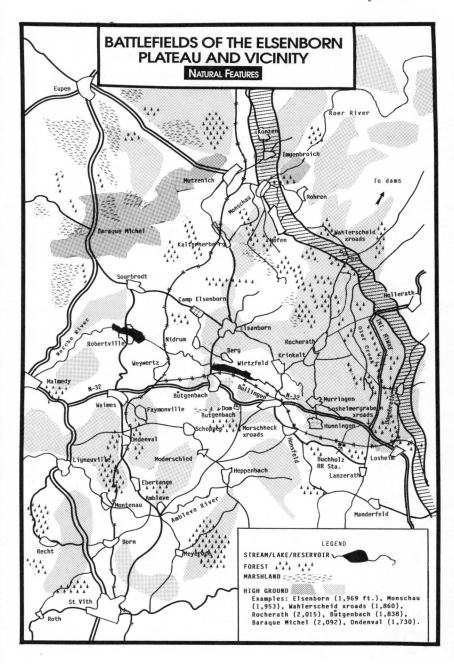

BATTLEFIELDS OF THE ELSENBORN PLATEAU AND VICINITY
Natural Features

LEGEND

STREAM/LAKE/RESERVOIR

FOREST

MARSHLAND

HIGH GROUND
Examples: Elsenborn (1,969 ft.), Monschau (1,953), Wahlerscheid xroads (1,860), Rocherath (2,015), Bütgenbach (1,838), Baraque Michel (2,092), Ondenval (1,730).

KEY TO NARRATIVE VI

CONTENDERS: U.S. Artillery battalions of the 99th Infantry Division (Brigadier General Frederick H. Black, division artillery commander); same for 2nd Infantry Division (Brigadier General John H. Hinds). Cannon companies of three infantry regiments of each division, one company per regiment. Batteries of four separate artillery battalions; three antiaircraft artillery battalions, including one with 90mm high-velocity guns, a company of heavy (4.2-inch) mortars. German. Artillery regiments of 326th, 277, and 12th *Volksgrenadier* divisions and of 12th *SS Panzer* Division. Batteries of two 6th *SS* Army artillery corps attached to 1st *SS Panzer* Corps and four *Werfer* (rocket-throwing) regiments. Also, one artillery corps and two *Werfer* regiments with 67th *Infanterie* Corps. Heavy howitzer and mortar batteries of 6th *SS Panzer* Army.

LOCATION: On December 15, one battalion of 99th Division light field artillery in place east of Mürringen; a second, east of Krinkelt; a third plus some separate batteries, north of Rocherath; the division's medium battalion, east and north of Krinkelt, close to one of the light battalions. Their orders after the initial German attack December 16 have one light battalion holding its place east of Krinkelt; another displacing northwest of Krinkelt; the third plus the batteries assigned by the 5th Corps, to the Elsenborn area; the medium battalion pulling back to the Wirtzfeld area.

On December 15 the 2nd Division medium artillery battalion is east of the Kalterherberg-Elsenborn road; one light battalion is north of Wirtzfeld and southeast of Elsenborn; a second, southeast of Kalterherberg and west of Wahlerscheid; a third, west of the Wahlerscheid-Rocherath road. Their orders after the German attack are to hold their positions, then to displace as necessary to maintain support of the 2nd Division's Rocherath-to-Wirtzfeld defense line screening the withdrawal road, dual towns-Wirtzfeld-Elsenborn heights. The 2nd Division's artillery is then to displace to a triangular area whose three points are Elsenborn on the north, Bütgenbach on the south, and Weywertz on the west. The attached batteries assigned by 5th Corps join the artillery build up in the Elsenborn defenses.

The huge array of *Wehrmacht* division, corps, and army howitzers, long guns, mortars, and *Nebelwerfer* machines are spread through the forests and across the fields east of the 6th *SS Panzer* Army zone of attack from the Roer River headwaters south to the West Wall east of Krewinkel, three miles south of Losheim. As the German infantry attack develops, the division and corps guns and *Werfer* tubes displace to new positions to the west to support the advancing infantry and armor.

ISSUE: On *Null Tag*, the German artillery and rocketry have a triple mission: One, breaking up the U.S. main line of resistance and driving off the 99th

Infantry Division holding this line to open the way for German ground attacks toward Eupen, the Elsenborn ridge, and across the Losheim Gap in the south. Two, suppressing the American artillery holding positions described above by bombarding their howitzer pits, ammunition caches, battery command bunkers, fire direction centers, battalion command posts, service centers and motor parks. Three, bombarding towns and villages serving as major supply and command centers of corps and division such as the dual towns, Büllingen, Elsenborn, Bütgenbach, Wirtzfeld, Malmedy, and Eupen.

The American artillery must hold batteries in position to keep up rapid rates of fire against the attacking German infantry while displacing other batteries to better-protected locations from which to perform new and rapidly changing fire missions, then withdraw safely to positions west and south of Elsenborn.

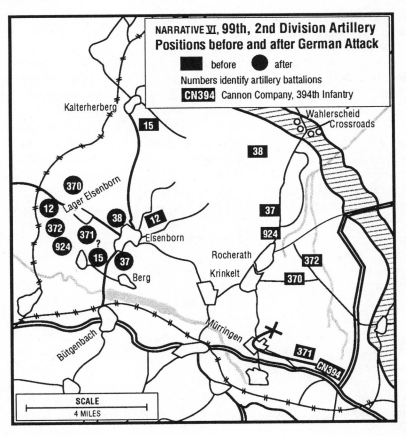

NARRATIVE VI, 99th, 2nd Division Artillery Positions before and after German Attack

■ before ● after

Numbers identify artillery battalions

CN394 Cannon Company, 394th Infantry

Kalterherberg

Wahlerscheid Crossroads

15

38

370

Lager Elsenborn

12

37

372
371
924

38

12

924

15 37

Elsenborn

Rocherath

372

Berg

Krinkelt

370

Mürringen

371

CN394

Bütgenbach

SCALE
4 MILES

SIXTH NARRATIVE: THE HOWITZERS' WAR

Part 1: Fight Like Infantry, Shoot Like Tankers

The nexus of killing power at the front in both German wars was roughly the same, although more advanced and sophisticated in the second than in the first, obviously: Infantry stood at the main line of resistance and in reserve positions behind and protected the light and medium howitzers and firing and command superstructure of the field artillery, whose 105 and 155mm rounds executed the fundamental task of destroying the enemy mass.

With the deconstruction of the American battle line from Hollerath on the north to Lanzerath on the south during the four fatal days and nights, December 16-20, (Volume 1, Narratives II-V), the infantry-artillery nexus at the center and south of the 99th-2nd Division sector is twisted and cracked and in danger of falling to pieces altogether.

Each of the 2 infantry divisions includes 4 battalions of light and medium truck or tractor-drawn howitzers, 48 cannons total, plus 3 cannon companies of 6 guns each, one company to each infantry regiment. These add another 18 howitzers for a total of 66.

Because of the U.S. 5th Corps operation early in December 1944 to break through the West Wall at Wahlerscheid crossroads and march east to the headwater dams of the Roer River, General Gerow's headquarters has put a 4.5-inch rocket battalion, three medium howitzer battalions, and a battalion of twelve self-propelled 155mm rifles each riding on a Sherman tank chassis into the attack to add gravitas to the artillery power on the 2nd-99th front.

However, only the 155mm rifles are self-propelled. The remainder of this arsenal must be hauled into and out of position. Once in the firing pits, they must be turned from one direction to another by man and truck or tractor. This is usually an acceptable task but during the crisis of the 1st *SS Panzer* Corps attack, a never-ending labor under fearful danger and extreme pressure.

Infantry divisions along the Western Front also are normally accompanied by a full battalion of automatic antiaircraft weapons; quad fours (i.e. four coaxial .50caliber machine guns) and 37mm diameter fast-firing guns. Each of the two divisions has such a battalion attached to it. The continuous presence of the V-1 robot bombs parading across the skies over the borderland ground they occupy (Volume 1, Narrative IV, Part 1) has also brought out an uncommon amount of additional American antiaircraft artillery, including the big 90mm (diameter), high-velocity long rifles.*

As with the rest of the 99th and 2nd divisions, the four artillery battalions of each plus their 5th Corps attached artillery battalions are concentrating on the drive to the Roer River dams on December 15.

At the far south of the 99th's main line of resistance, Colonel Riley's 394th Regiment is backed by one battalion of 105mm howitzers. These are dug into pits in the sloping fields a mile or so east of Mürringen.

In the center, another 105mm battalion is backing the two ill-fated infantry battalions of Lieutenant Colonel Jean D. Scott's 393rd Infantry. Their gun pits and dugouts are east of Krinkelt, in the snow-splattered, barren winter fields. The guns are pointed toward the woods where the infantrymen overlook the international highway and the outposts of the German West Wall. They are putting down fire in advance of feints and diversionary attacks.

---

* Artillerymen of the American Army in World War II fashioned a highly efficient killing machine from the raw material of their howitzers and long guns and the fifteen different types of shot and shell that they fired. At the same time, to do so required them to put in place a technically advanced and complex battlefield structure. From the liaison officers and teams of forward observers at the front of the infantry line to the artillery battalion commanders in their dugouts or stone-walled headquarters back in some village three or four miles away, the artillerymen operated with a network of land lines, switchboards, radio nets and receiving-transmitting sets, fire direction centers, gun pits, crew dugouts, ammunition pits, vehicle parks, repair facilities, a fleet of little Piper cubs for target spotting.

Each artillery battalion of 509 to 518 soldiers had one headquarters, one service, and three firing batteries. Each of the latter had four howitzer sections (one cannon each), and a wire section. Each battery also was armed with four .50caliber machine guns.

A light (105mm) howitzer battalion usually worked closely with one infantry regiment, delivering shell fire as needed. The six little 105s of the regiment's cannon company filled in the gaps and responded quickly to the inevitable crisis need for immediate shooting in specific places. The howitzermen depended totally on an efficient and hardworking fleet (train) of trucks, drivers, and handlers to go back to the ammunition dumps, as they were called, and bring up a never-failing supply of explosive steel, phosphorous, smoke, and the rest.

In addition to the four artillery battalions "organic" to each U.S. Infantry Division, the U.S. Army in Europe also brought to the battlefield large numbers of artillery battalions available to army group, army, and corps commands to attach to infantry and armor divisions as the situation demanded. They delivered the additional weight of howitzer and gun power at the front that amazed and disconcerted the *Wehrmacht* from top to bottom.

The artillery units that participated in the events of Narrative VI are identified in the Documentation. So many battalions participated that to refer to each by their numbered designation would merely confuse the reader and drag down the narrative.

The rest of the 99th Division artillery power is north and northwest of Rocherath, putting smoke and explosive steel in front of the 395th Regimental Combat Team as its riflemen move through the dense, hilly woods toward the trenches, log bunkers, and mortar digs of the German West Wall line there. It is a considerable power: twelve 105mm and twenty-four 155mm tubes including an attached battalion, plus a chemical mortar (4.2-inch) company.

Artillery of the 2nd Division and attached battalions are north of Rocherath and east of Elsenborn. Their mission is to work with commanders of the 9th and 38th infantry and their captains to make it possible for their men to overcome the machine-gun and mortar-armed fortress of cement pillboxes and bunkers that the Germans have rooted around the Wahlerscheid crossroads. (Volume 1, Narrative I, Part 1)

In thick, wet snow the 2nd Division mediums (155s) have moved to Elsenborn, and the battery crews have dug gun pits and sleeping holes alongside the road to Kalterherberg and put an observation post in Höfen. The long 155mm diameter rifles of the tracked artillery gun battalion that will try later to level the pillboxes (Narrative I) are in firing positions nearby. Of the 2nd Division's three light howitzer battalions, two are west of the 99th batteries along the Rocherath-Wahlerscheid road backing the 9th and 38th infantry regiments. All of the division's power is being applied to breaking through the West Wall at Wahlerscheid. General Robertson's light artillery battalion that usually works with his 23rd Infantry is also in the Wahlerscheid attack.

In sum, on December 15, 1944 the ground east of Elsenborn and south of Kalterherberg bristles like a porcupine's back with howitzer tubes and antiaircraft guns. And the little towns there are filled with the American command, control, and supply centers for the guns.

The *Luftwaffe* reconnaissance aircraft, which have been droning away in the cloudy skies since the beginning of December, have been able to pinpoint many of the American artillery positions in the snowy fields. Spies have identified artillery headquarters, fire direction centers, and supply facilities in the towns. Some of the destruction visited upon the artillerymen of the 99th and 2nd divisions by the pre-dawn bombardment on *Null Tag* has been described. (Volume 1, Narrative III, Part 1) The 1st *SS Panzer* Corps and its division gunners seem to know where to drop their 105, 150, and 170mm diameter shells, even to reach back with heavier ordnance to pummel Elsenborn heights and points farther west.

For the forty minutes or so during which the enemy gunners have walked their fire west beyond the 99th Infantry's main line of resistance to the artillery digs and command posts, no one is safe, not the humblest ammunition-handlers, not the battalion commanders. One informs the 99th Division artillery chief that his men are "nervous and a little punch drunk from the concussions...about fifteen or (more) enemy batteries of 105 and 170mm (6.8-inch diameter) guns fired at us."

So many shells come at the 2nd Division's 155 base at Elsenborn before dawn on *Null Tag*, the officers in charge believe they are under attack by *Panzers* mounting fearsome 88mm, high-velocity rifles. They send out bazooka teams in the dark to hunt down the nonexistent monsters, only to learn the next day what is really happening.

And the German gunners do not call off their beatings after the initial *Schlag* of fire and steel. They keep up their bombardment throughout the three days and nights of the fighting in the cockpit east of the Elsenborn heights. Their reconnaissance aircraft, forward observers, troop leaders, NCOs, and reconnaissance tanks identify targets of opportunity for them: convoys of howitzers moving out, artillery crews making a last stand with a few howitzers, bunkers, communication centers, etc.

At Büllingen the rear-echelon soldiers are dragged out of their houses and barns by the sound and fury of the pre-dawn bombardment. One 2nd Division combat engineer comes tumbling out of bed to stand in the street "seeing and hearing the flashes and distant thunder of incoming artillery," from large-caliber guns, apparently. The big shells explode around and about Büllingen lighting up the thick pre-dawn darkness and illuminating the fog. "The whole company turned out," wrote the engineer, "we had never seen anything like that."

The dual towns (Rocherath-Krinkelt) base for so many 99th front line units, take a persistent pounding from the German guns. A forward observer with General Lauer's mediums has been relieved for a few days from his front line duties and is occupying one of the stone houses in Krinkelt, site of his artillery battalion's HQ. He is jolted out of sleep by a sentinel who is screaming that the town is being bombarded.

The lieutenant is a soldier of the front rather than the rear (echelon) and is blasé about the commotion. He goes back to sleep—for a few minutes. The sound of shells whistling and whispering above the house he is sleeping in "and bursting all around, like a New Year's celebration," wakes him good and proper. At the doorway, he peers out to "see flashes and hear outbursts and screaming shells from every nook and corner of the little town....(I) proceeded to the cellar, which provided ample protection but was cold as ice."

In the rear-echelon Belgian towns and villages, cellars and stout walls save uncounted American lives. However, the artillerymen manning the howitzers spread across the fields and forest clearings don't have cellars and stone walls. And with 144 American howitzers in the field, plus the long 155mm rifles, the German gunners have plenty to shoot at. But some American batteries receive more attention than others do, and some endure the bombardment better. And some that are not hit before dawn on *Null Tag* are hit early the next day (December 17).

"A terrific artillery barrage (lasting) for a good while," remembers a 99th Division artilleryman whose 155mm battery is half a mile down a slope from the center of Krinkelt. When the initial gunschlag ends about 6:15 a.m. on *Null Tag*, he crawls out of a bunker near the howitzers and counts twenty fresh holes and patches of black in the snow made by the exploding shells. Nearby some headquarters soldiers of a battery are sleeping in a tent above ground next to a half-completed dugout they are working on. A shell explodes by the side of the tent, spraying jagged, hot steel through the canvas. An officer dies, five other soldiers, including the battery commander, are wounded.

The 105mm battalion of the 99th Division operating with Colonel Scott's 393rd Infantry has dug its pits and dugouts in the fields east of Krinkelt near the 155s. Four gun crews (and their guns) endure incoming "mail" (as soldiers call enemy shell fire) for nearly an hour. As a forward observer team prepares to go up to the front to help with the 277th *Volksgrenadier* attack against "I" Company in the forest, their lieutenant takes a shell fragment in the head. It appears an awful wound because it bleeds so copiously but is not fatal.

Another howitzerman remembers a shell coming down on the makeshift steps leading to the dugout where he and his fellows are hunkered down waiting out the attack. It blows off the door and blows out his eardrums but does no other damage. The soldier believes it "a miracle" that all escape. "You could hardly take a step in the entire battery (four guns) without stepping in a shell hole. There were also a lot of duds lying around. The German ammo (ammunition) wasn't too good."

Artillerymen of the 99th and 2nd divisions are as ignorant of enemy intentions as are other soldiers in the Monschau-to-Losheim sector. Their officers have received the same top-down information (or misinformation) that has been distributed to their counterparts in the infantry regiments and battalions. Brigadier Generals Frederick H. Black and John H. Hinds, artillery commanders of the two divisions, know as little as do Major Generals Lauer and Robertson of how much the *Wehrmacht* is investing in the action that has begun before dawn on December 16 and what its leaders expect to gain in exchange.

The sporadic batterings of December 16-17 damage a few of the howitzers but not so severely that they can't be repaired. (Remarkable, given the punishment so many American batteries have taken.) However, the complex network of land lines connecting the various components of the artillery system—forward observers, battalion liaison officers, fire direction centers, batteries, commanders' digs, etc.—has been devastated.

A shell has hit the building in Wirtzfeld where General Hinds' communication center is located, cutting up seven outgoing lines. They are no sooner repaired than another large-caliber shell crashes outside the window, wrecks the switchboard and renders all headquarters' lines useless. Hinds orders all of his wire crews out to trace down and repair breaks in lines to the 2nd Division artillery battalions. They work in the open most of the time, thus must enter life and limb in the grim lottery of what soldiers call harassing fire, i.e. occasional explosive rounds coming down willy-nilly that may hit you and then again may not.

Hinds' artillery command post moves to Elsenborn after noon December 17. This complicates the work of the 2nd Division Signal Company wiremen, who keep going without pause for eighteen hours, riding jeeps and light trucks over icy roads, with exploding shells near and far, grubbing around in snowy, mucky ground for wire connections, raising rickety poles, pulling bits and pieces of wire from the snow-heavy fir branches, cutting and reconnecting frazzled lines with hands that ache from the cold.

Every artillery space and battery has its own nasty wire problem, smaller but no less unpleasant than that of the general's men. The lineman for a battery in the 99th Division and a companion volunteer to repair the line going to their battalion headquarters. "We were out all day and night (December 16) and the morning of the 17th. We came in only long enough to get something to eat and more wire to repair breaks. There were loose ends of wires everywhere. Some we could get no response on the other end; others, from another outfit....We would find our break, splice the wire, only to find it out again either in front or behind us."

Everywhere the artillery's second communication system—SCR 300 and 610 radios, are going into service, a necessary but not always satisfactory alternative. The sets often fail. Also the artillery's radio networks may be broken into by the clever Germans, who use them to transmit confusing nonsense or to learn American positions and intentions. The confusion and mistakes of a shifting battleground result in usable radios left behind. The commander of a 99th Division artillery battery remembered "the Germans have captured plenty of American equipment." The proliferation of signals going through the air is itself a burden, a cause of confusion.

The American attack to the northeast and the Roer River dams is still going forward on the morning of December 16 in spite of all. (Volume 1, Narrative I, Part 2) Therefore, after the pre-dawn enemy bombardment dies away, the light and medium cannons of the two divisions laboring in the Wahlerscheid operation continue to blast explosive shells at the West Wall in the Monschauwald.

To the west of Colonel Allen and Major Legler's 393rd Infantry battalions in the Todeswald (Volume 1, Narrative III), the regiment's cannon company continues to fire what its men believe is a close-support mission to add shell weight to the "demonstrations" to divert the Germans. They "stay and stay," as one of the gunners puts it, even when they can see *Panzers* prowling up ahead in the woods.

As *Null Tag* moves along, however, it becomes clear to these and other 99th Division gunners working with the infantry in the forests along the international highway and at Losheimergraben that the mud soldiers they are supporting are no longer trying to divert the enemy with demonstrations but instead are at risk of being annihilated.

General Black, Lauer's artillery commander, orders some of the mediums (155s) in the Wahlerscheid operation to start putting shells into the woods south of Hollerath along the international highway where the 277 *Volksgrenadiers* are striking at the 393rd Infantry, thus adding to the gun power of the light artillery there.

Forward observer (FO) teams of the artillery battalions are jeeping down the rutted, muddy forest roads to the 393rd and 394th regiment positions to direct howitzer fire at the onrushing *Volksgrenadiers*. Theirs is a dangerous and frustrating task. The riflemen and machine gunners are being driven west deeper into the dense forest away from the international highway. This makes it nearly impossible for the artillery-observers to direct their howitzers back in the fields to shoot. As one puts it, "No forward observer can hit what he can't see, and we (were) in a big (sic) part of the forest."

After noon December 16, the riflemen and machine gunners they are with are beset by enemy infesting this forest. "The night of the 16th, the Germans surrounded the company," remembered the FO just quoted. At dawn the captain calls his surviving noncoms together for a desperate council of war. While the little group is talking quietly in a clearing in the trees, a sniper's rifle cracks. A sergeant dies with a bullet in his head. The captain tells the artillerymen to clear out; they can do no more for him and his men.

The artillery radio nets crackle with pleas for howitzer fire, but too many add up to nothing but frustration: fading signals, garbled directions, rejected targets. Yet the gunners manage to get off some rounds that come down here and there to hurt Germans and save Americans. The 99th Division cannoneers stand and deliver until nightfall on *Null Tag*, sending some sixty-five hundred rounds against the Germans coming across the international highway and at Losheimergraben crossroads and to clear the way in the West Wall for the 395th Regimental Combat Team as well, which is still pushing eastward.

Simultaneously, the two little six-howitzer (105mm) cannon companies of the 393rd and 394th Infantry regiments are adding their weight of steel to the struggle of the division's artillerymen to keep the German infantry away from their infantry. Immediately after the bombardment, the men of the 394th's Cannon Company come out of their bunkers and go to work, sending some 220 rounds of high explosive shell at General Engle's 12th Division *Volksgrenadiers* attacking the 1st Battalion east of Losheimergraben. They keep up some harassing fire during the night but wait for the dawn to reveal more of what the shooting, American and German, is all about.

As the screeching, booming, fiery night of December 16 gives way to the awful Sunday of December 17, Kaschner's 326th *Volksgrenadiers* push ever harder at the Höfen-Monschau Gatepost; Viebig's 277 *Volksgrenadiers*, Engle's 12th *Volksgrenadiers*, and the armor-infantry columns of 12th and 1st *SS Panzer* and the 3rd *Fallschirmjäger* divisions begin marching through, and around, and over the five 99th and two 2nd division infantry battalions south of Wahlerscheid crossroads and north of Lanzerath. (Volume 1, Narrative II-V)

The American cannoneers in the howitzer pits now come face to face with: One, an artilleryman's worst nightmare—lots of tracked, armored enemy guns and infantry moving upon him with hostile intent. Two, his most difficult challenge—firing the cannons in several different directions simultaneously and without dependable information from the FO teams up front.

Cannon Company (394th) endures both within scarcely an hour on December 17. In the morning, the company is asked to shift its tubes 90 degrees and start sending shells south to Honsfeld. The steel gun trails are frozen solid. Before the gunners can make the change, they must hack the trails out of the icy ground. One gun section must cut down trees to make a new space in the air for the rounds from their howitzer to take flight.

Not long after noon, beyond the open space to the front of these cannoneers, a storm of rockets come in on the infantry they are supporting. This is followed closely by the unmistakable ripping sound of German machine pistols and the repetitive hammering of their machine guns. A regimental staff officer comes racing by and shouts at their captain to get his men and howitzers moving west. They let loose one last salvo toward the woods, a "189 with charge one." The shells are set to explode within six hundred feet of the nearly erect tubes. Then they connect the little howitzers to their trucks and run.

For most of December 17, the battalion of twelve 105s firing in support of Colonel Allen and Major Legler's beleaguered riflemen and machine gunners (393rd Infantry) stands its ground to the east of Krinkelt. One battery of four howitzers sends off six hundred rounds, even though by mid-afternoon enemy shooters with sniper rifles are moving around them in the fields trying to pick off the crews. At dark they are told to pull the howitzers from their pits and move them a mile west of Krinkelt.

Another battery is located in a field west of the forest when Allen's infantry run past, dead beat and dejected. The machine gun-machine pistol fire grows louder. Soon the 2nd Division men come running by as well. The artillerymen have orders to stand by their guns in the field, which is about a third of a mile west of the forest edge near the road to Rocherath.

The hammering, ripping, and popping noise of gunfire in the woods stops. Then silence, followed shortly by a sight to fret their hearts: hundreds of long grey coats, black helmets, splinter camouflage jackets, billed cloth caps milling out of the woods and coming toward them along the road. The distant figures carry *Maschinengewehre, Maschinen-pistolen, Gewehre, Panzerfäuste*, with here and there the flash of a bayonet fixed upon a rifle barrel. Some in the frightening crowd also have armed themselves with American M-1 rifles, carbines, and light machine guns picked up in the forest.

The battery of howitzermen load high explosive shells and depress their guns to ground level for barrel sighting. They make ready with such small arms as they have: .50caliber machine guns taken from the trucks, carbines, pistols. As the German attackers close to bullet range, the blessed order comes down to the four crews: save yourselves, take the guns if possible. They do both, just barely, with the aid of their trucks and drivers, plus animal effort impelled by fear.

A lieutenant commanding an antitank 57mm gun platoon and his sergeant, who have escaped from the savage battle around Legler's 1st Battalion command post, stumble upon a battery of light howitzers. The tubes are not elevated. They are flat out, parallel to the ground. And they are sending shells "over open sights at five hundred yards" toward a brace of onrushing *Panzers*. "Their tubes were red hot," said the lieutenant. "When a 155 (AN: 105, actually) has to fire over open sights, you know it's all about over."

In the dark and confusion constantly stirred and thickened by the smoke of exploding shells and rockets and made even more fearful by fog and night-obscured images of men and machines moving about, some howitzermen get separated from their guns altogether and are baptized instant infantry.

A group of twenty led by a lieutenant from the battalion of mediums attached to the 99th is sent out to help one of their batteries being hassled by a German patrol. They return to their own battery the next day (December 17) only to be sent out again by truck. This time they are to rescue the battalion command post in Krinkelt. The lieutenant remembers, "I was twenty-three years old, had no infantry training, and (this was) my fourth day of combat." It is a false alarm. Nonetheless he and his band of howitzermen are ordered to go southwest along a road, dig in and prepare to fight as mud soldiers. Unlike mud soldiers, however, they are armed only with carbines and .45caliber pistols.

After noon December 16 the 2nd Division artillery commanders receive word that the attack beyond Wahlerscheid crossroads, which is their reason for being where they are, has been "temporarily" suspended. They find this a strange, inexplicable development, especially since the division's infantry has finally pushed through the fearsome fortress at the crossroads. Soon after light the next day (December 17), ominous things begin to happen, the news of which moves from south to north across the 2nd Division artillery command posts, eventually reaching the battery commanders in their bunkers by the howitzers.

At 7:00 a.m. General Hinds, the division artillery chief, receives an unnerving phone call from General Lauer's 99th Division headquarters. It is a junior-level staff officer. He wants "the loan" of some tank destroyer guns. The request disturbs Hinds. The manner of making it—way out of the normal procedure and command channels— more so. The general said later this was "the first information we had that the German armored attack (was) in the rear of our command post and some (seven miles) in the rear of our leading elements" (at Wahlerscheid). He notifies Robertson and organizes a pick-up defense of the 2nd Division command post and his own, both of which are in Wirtzfeld.

As will be seen, General Robertson's plan is to use the dual towns, Rocherath and Krinkelt, as a chokepoint, to delay the march of

Hitlerjugend, 12th *SS Panzer* Division. The 2nd Division commander must look to the artillerymen for the hitting power that will determine whether the infantry and armor can hold off the enemy long enough to make the plan succeed. Of signal importance is bringing to bear enough shell power to keep *Kampfgruppe* Peiper, 1st *SS Panzer* Division, away from Bütgenbach south of Elsenborn and *Hitlerjugend*, away from the dual towns long enough to put defensive lines in place. Thus from early Sunday December 17, the 2nd Division howitzer battalions, the antiaircraft and long 155mm rifles, and such 99th Division and attached artillery battalion guns as are still up and shooting will be carrying heavy water.

The 2nd Division battalion of 105s shooting for the 99th moves in the night December 18 amidst exploding shells and striking rockets. It takes up a position near Elsenborn to put rounds in front of Krinkelt-Rocherath, under siege by the 12th *SS Panzer* Division. This battalion manages to keep its light howitzers firing from *Null Tag* on. But its forward observer teams, who are out in front trying to spot targets for the guns, lose seven team leaders (of seventeen).

General Robertson's 105mm battalion emplaced in clearings in the Monschauwald northeast of the dual towns is preparing to provide shell fire to support the division's 38th Regiment. They receive little counter-battery fire on *Null Tag*. But early the next day (December 17) General Hinds orders them to get clear of their increasingly dangerous and exposed positions. Drawn by trucks, the 105mm guns lurch and bump over cart tracks made nearly impassable by the snowy muck, ford a creek or two and are on new ground by dark. The battalion will shoot 4,500 shells in the battle with *Hitlerjugend* Division for the dual towns. (Narrative VIII)

As these two 2nd Division light howitzer battalions move to safer places from which to help fight the battle of the dual towns, a heavy additional weight is laid on the third. This battalion normally works with the 23rd Infantry. However, during the Wahlerscheid action, this regiment has been in reserve. Its artillery comrades are lending a hand (or a gun) to supplement the fires against the Germans defending the crossroads. Their cannons are operating from pits in the forest clearings a half mile north of Rocherath.

As the 1st *SS Panzer* Corps presses the attack and the situation of the Americans turns dangerous in the extreme on the morning of December 17, these twelve howitzer crews are required to adjust their guns to hit new and widely scattered targets. At 7:30 a.m. one battery of four cannons receives an order to smother the front of the 2nd Division command post at Wirtzfeld with explosive steel to keep enemy armor away. To do so the battery must go into a new position.

The howitzers are connected to their two-and-one-half-ton trucks. They lurch down a logging road, up a slope, and over an ice-crusted creek. Takes little imagination to view the scene: the cumbersome trucks, swaying tubes on awkward carriages bouncing and reeling behind over the spongy, uneven ground; loaders, ammo handlers, NCOs, even a few lieutenants, hovering around, pushing, steadying, and shoveling slushy mud, wading through icy water, while keeping a wary eye and ear for falling shells and *Luftwaffe* attacks.

For most of December 17 the twelve howitzers of the battalion shoot over Wirtzfeld as the 2nd Division headquarters withdraws northwest to Elsenborn. They bombard the *Grenadiers* attacking Mürringen-Hünningen. They mix their fires with those of other batteries in the battle for the dual towns. And after dark when the howitzers with the 9th Infantry Combat Team move west, as previously described, this same group of cannoneers take over their shooting missions until they relocate. All of this is accomplished because the battalion "(maintained) an extremely high rate of fire, which taxed the (battalion) fire direction center personnel and the gun crews to the limit of physical endurance," wrote General Hinds afterward.

Remaining to be accounted for in the saga of Robertson's artillery in the battle December 16-20 east of Elsenborn heights are the 2nd Division medium howitzers (155mm) and the powerful long rifles attached to them. The day before *Null Tag*, a snow storm has blown over the barren slopes east of Elsenborn. The weather then turns warm, and the thick mat of snow becomes a thick mat of slush over the soft ground. It is in this environment that the 2nd Division mediums are embedded, three and four hundred yards east of Elsenborn—eleven 155mm howitzers in all (The twelfth is being repaired.).

Closer to the town are four 90mm antiaircraft guns assigned to shooting down V-1 flying bombs. With the crisis of the 1st *SS Panzer* Corps attack, they are integrated into the medium howitzer defense force to go into action against ground targets.

Not far away, spread out and well camouflaged are the tracked 155mm long guns that tried and (failed) to blast holes in the Wahlerscheid pillboxes and bunkers. (Volume 1, Narrative V, Part 2)

The 90s and 155s are operating at the command of a 2nd Division artillery fire direction center. Forward observers of the medium howitzer battalion are spread around as never before in the 2nd Division's campaigns: several in and around the dual towns; one on a rise overlooking German-occupied Büllingen; one, miles to the north with Colonel Butler's 99th Division infantry.

These nineteen pieces, as they are called, shoot nonstop from 8 a.m. on December 17th to afternoon of the 19th. The eleven 155mm howitzer crews endure three days of constant pressure to move trails and relay their guns as the ground battle across the slopes and valleys east of the heights moves now one place, now another. All the while, the 155 long rifles prowl around on their Sherman tank chassis, seeking better shooting places, avoiding counter-battery fire, shadowy prehistoric shapes in the night and fog.

Seven "provisional" pick-up crews of cooks, clerks, truck drivers, dog robbers (senior officers' servants) work ceaselessly in the dark, in the muck and cold, under falling artillery shells to keep the communications wires in repair and functioning. And almost everyone in the battalion comes down to the gun pits and helps work the big howitzers: loading the one hundred pound shells, moving the guns, relieving men too exhausted to go on, unloading ammo trucks, deafened all the while by the terrifying voices of their own cannons and the even more terrifying voices of the 90mm long rifles behind them, which sound off with a "crack" like a glacier splitting asunder.

Keeping the ammunition pits by the howitzers replenished under these chaotic conditions is a brave and onerous task comparable to working the guns—and just as important. During the four-day period of crisis December 16-19 in front of the Elsenborn high plateau, three ammunition supply trains (i.e. several big two-and-one-half-ton and four-ton trucks) are in constant motion from ammunition dumps west and south of Elsenborn, across the slippery, deteriorating roads over the heights and to the batteries.

These trains are supplemented by pick-up drivers and ammo handlers operating vehicles scrounged hither and yon. Some bear 99th Division markings and have been left behind or abandoned as undrivable. Caches of 99th ammunition also are found by 2nd Division artillerymen and brought to the guns.

The soldiers operating the trains are determined. At one rear echelon dump, the lieutenant in charge refuses to let a 2nd Division officer load his trucks, telling him he is over his allotment of shells. The officer unholsters his .45caliber automatic pistol, points it at the hapless fellow, and gets the load of shells he came for.

In spite of all, so rapidly are the guns being fired that from time to time at this battery or that, the shell supply runs thin, and the crews have to slow their pace until a truck emerges out of the dark or fog bringing more. The exec of the 155mm battery remembered, "We did run dangerously low on ammo a number of times...(but) each time we got really low and started to worry, one of the trains (trucks) would roll in with another batch." His four howitzers have limitations on how fast they can be fired, however: One round per minute if, as here, the tubes must be kept going hour after hour. "There were so many requests for fire support (during the three days) that priorities had to be assigned." And these keep changing due to the volatile conditions of the battlefield.

Part 2: Harrowing Journeys

At 5:30 a.m. on *Null Tag* the 2nd Division artillery battalions were located north of the target zones of the 1st *SS* Corps infantry and armor. Their batteries have been able to hold their place and work their howitzers for the first thirty-six hours of the fighting in the cockpit between Elsenborn and Rocherath-Wahlerscheid. Not so the gunners of the 99th Division. Some of their batteries have endured attacks by enemy infantry from the early afternoon of *Null Tag*, as we have seen. Howitzers of the two light artillery battalions firing in support of the 393rd and 394th regiments at, respectively, the Todeswald and the Fatal Triangle are located in front of the strongest enemy infantry assaults of the day, and the division's mediums more so. The latter are working from positions in fields east of Rocherath in front of the light howitzers to support the 395th Regimental Combat Team (not the by-the-book location for these cumbersome cannons).

Under attack, artillerymen embrace roads as infantrymen do holes in the earth to make survival possible. With Herculean muscling and engine-destroying demands on their big trucks and tractors, it is possible to move the howitzers cross country in snow and muck. Nonetheless, really serious artillery "displacement" requires road space. The 99th Division howitzer crews and drivers must now fight for every inch of it with the crowding, pushing, often panic-impelled vehicles of scores of fighting and rear-echelon units. To abandon his howitzer and retreat on foot, which under the circumstances would be the safe and sensible thing to do, is the ultimate loss, not to say disgrace, for the artilleryman. Some 99th cannoneers suffer this fate.

By daylight December 17 General Black, Lauer's artillery chief, is getting sporadic, often garbled, and usually ephemeral intelligence on what is happening to his howitzers. It is clear, however, that one, he will have to move his headquarters away from Bütgenbach on the *Panzer*-endangered N-32 high road that goes west to Malmedy; and two, his battalions will have to get away from the onrushing enemy without at the same time abandoning Lauer's infantry in the Todeswald and at Losheimergraben crossroads.

For the lieutenant colonel in charge of the 99th Division's mediums (155s) close to where Colonel Allen's 3rd Battalion (393rd) men are waging their lonely war in the Todeswald, conditions are deteriorating fast. He takes it upon himself in the late night of December 16 to start his cannons moving out without an order to do so. He heads the battalion for Wirtzfeld, where he hopes to find a new and safer place to shoot from.

The three gun batteries (twelve cumbersome pieces) take turns departing in leap-frog fashion, with two covering the third and maintaining some defensive fires, as they are called, against the 12th *SS Panzer* Division (*Hitlerjugend*) soldiers now swarming into the woods. They leave behind in Rocherath, where the command post has been located, a big gun-pulling tractor, a trailer, and a truck plus some machine guns, tools, and two supply men who don't know their mates are leaving.

The landscape of low, hilly fields and marshes covered with patches of snow is filmed over with icy mist and fog. The first cannons to clear the area lurch and bounce over a poor road that skirts the northern edge of Rocherath. With some cross-country movements as well, they get about half the way to Wirtzfeld when enemy rocket and artillery fire finds them. The exploding steel damages a jeep that is carrying soldiers hurt by counter-battery shelling on *Null Tag*. It takes some flying splinters, and a few of the wounded are wounded a second time.

The big howitzers stay only long enough in the fields near Wirtzfeld for a section to send some shots after *Kampfgruppe* Peiper's *Panzers* outside Büllingen and to watch the dueling aircraft. (Narrative VII, Part 3) Then at 4:30 p.m. December 17, all four batteries are ordered to move again, this time to a location on the north side of Elsenborn.

In the fields around Mürringen, three firing batteries of 99th Division 105s are trying to bombard the infantry of General Engle's 12th *VG* Division coming through the forest east of Losheimergraben crossroads to attack Colonel Douglas' 1st Battalion (394th). Early on December 17, they receive a "march order" to pull their cannons and displace to Krinkelt three miles to the north. The journey is a short but tortuous one, as enemy shell and rocket fire comes down near and far and *Luftwaffe* aircraft circle around in the sky looking for prey.

By afternoon these howitzers have mostly found places. Their cannoneers are again in the business of firing east and south at the attacking enemy: the three gun batteries located due west of the center of Krinkelt in some open fields. Headquarters Battery stays put, is now between the guns and the infantry, an unusual location. Certainly the headquarters men consider it unusual. Back at Camp Maxey (Volume 1, INTRODUCTION), their training led them to believe they would always be behind—well behind—the howitzer batteries up front banging away over the heads of the infantry. Yet here they are, east of the howitzers with nothing between them and the onrushing enemy save a deteriorating infantry line.

Their gun battery crews are hard at it throughout the afternoon of December 17 chopping and mucking out a semblance of gun pit and command dugout in the grey winter light over the fields below the Elsenborn heights. As they work, they are witness to unnerving spectacles of retreat. One of the battery executive officers remembered long after the war, "Infantry and artillery personnel were in complete disarray and wandering back through my position."

Disheartening errors happen. As the night closes in, the nervous Headquarters Battery men occupy a picket line of shallow holes they've made in front of the position. They are spooked by the sound of gunfire somewhere out there in the dark close by. They are technicians, not infantry soldiers, and experience many shallow fears wanting instance. A 99th Division artillery major approaches the line in the dark, leading some men of the battalion fire direction center home to headquarters where they hope to find food, safety, and a place to sleep. Challenged, the officer fails to give the right password or his password goes unheard. A nervous sentinel fires his carbine. The major dies, three of his party are wounded.

In their hasty digs west of Krinkelt, the other battery commanders of this battalion wonder what to do. The ominous rising and falling spouts of light in the dual towns carry across to their positions in the icy muck and splotches of snow covering it. Their radios bring only garbled messages and pleas for artillery from somewhere out there to the east in the black and limitless Todeswald.

Nearby are a dozen or so vehicles bearing automatic weapons. They belong to an antiaircraft artillery battalion operating with the 99th Division. The AAA men have a base in a house in Krinkelt. At 7:30 p.m. December 17, they burn their papers. "A half hour later, small arms and machine gun fire to the rear of the command post gave evidence of the oncoming German infantry," remembered one. They load up with all deliberate speed and start moving west in their halftracks, trucks, jeeps, toward a ford over a stream at the base of the Elsenborn rise.

For the batteries of 99th Division artillery nearby, it is a fateful move. The commander of one battery and his men watch the night erupt around them. They watch the AAA halftracks lurch on to the road going west toward the Elsenborn heights. They watch the dual towns a half mile to the east ignite, smolder, smoke, then repeat the cycle hour after hour, while the sound of shell fire, rockets, machine guns,

Panzerfäuste, high-velocity tank-destroying guns fill the night with bedlam. (Narrative VIII) The battery commander has no orders to go west. He has little capacity to shoot at Germans either; ammunition running low, targets chancy and as likely to be American as enemy. "Very late in the evening," remembered one of his men, "he decided to take action before it was too late, but by then, it was too late."

His four howitzers sit on ground that is a huge porridge of icy muck engulfing the axles of the gun carriages. In the misting dark illuminated by the fires and explosions nearby, the men grind their trucks into the muck, attach the cannons, then winch the whole ponderous load of death machinery up to the road. "Everyone was spurred on by the infernal scene across the valley (in the dual towns). Most of the men had never heard a battle much less seen one," remembered one of the artillerymen.

They have escaped from one peril only to couple with another. The road they use is nothing more than a farmer's wagon track of gravel over mud. It is also a writhing, lurching, clotted mass of jeeps, trucks, gun wagons, and towed howitzers, with escaping soldiers hanging from every handhold and others walking rapidly alongside in the melting snow and muck. The battery crews wedge their vehicles and four howitzers on to the road, nevertheless. A minor triumph, but a futile one. They scarcely move a hundred yards when the entire grim parade is halted. The gun wagons of the antiaircraft men who departed before sit by a bridge over a stream. They are immobile, sunk to the tops of the tracks in a wallow of watery muck.

The 99th Division artillery vehicles following on now have no place to go. The road is blocked. The way round the halftracks is over icy marshland and creek bed, which would instantly swallow up the heavy trucks and howitzers connected to them. The drivers, cannoneers, ammo handlers have no choice but to abandon the lot.

A few of the soldiers race around in the black killing their machinery so the onrushing enemy can make no use of it. They explode thermite grenades in the howitzer tubes; drain the radiators of the trucks, then run the engines full throttle. With the howitzermen of another battery whose guns and trucks also sit immobile on the road, they start walking west in a misty, cold rain toward Elsenborn. It is close to midnight Sunday, December 17. In all, some three hundred 99th Division artillerymen make the march on foot: sans vehicles, sans howitzers, sans spirit. "A sad bunch of artillerymen," remembered one.

This battalion, which just forty-eight hours previous was well ensconced and deadly to the enemy in its deep gun pits around Mürringen and in front of Krinkelt, giving steady fire to support

Colonel Riley's 394th infantrymen, leaves eight of its twelve 105mm cannons behind on the battlefield, half of its trucks, nearly seven hundred rounds of ammunition. It's human losses are two killed outright, twelve missing (Blown apart by a hostile shell or rocket or bagged by the Germans and sent east—that's usually what "missing" means.), and thirteen wounded and evacuated.

As described before, a battery along the forest road to Rocherath delivering fire in front of the 393rd and 23rd infantry battalions in the Todeswald moves its guns and trucks out just before the *SS Panzergrenadiers* get to them. It is attacked by the 12th *SS* Division's mobile antitank guns. German artillery working with 12th *SS* also puts shells down on the little convoy. Some of these are packed with phosphorous that upon explosion spray chunks of burning metal over the American artillerymen.

However, the four gun crews make it to Krinkelt where they join the general bedlam lit by explosions, flares, tracer bullets, and burning buildings and machines. Every few minutes a barrage comes down. The howitzermen jump from their vehicles and hunt for shelter. In the fiery dark, gun sections get separated, move by themselves in the stream of alien traffic, find another group of their battalion's trucks and guns, join them, lose them, find others.

A second battery (four howitzers) of the same artillery battalion has been located close to Krinkelt from the start, with its command post in a house there. As things grow ominous and the enemy gunners and rocketeers in the eastern reaches of the borderland keep up their fiery barrages, rumors spread that German armor is prowling around behind the battalion's gun positions, fire direction center, and headquarters.

The battery commander prepares to get his men and cannons ready to confront the attacking *Hitlerjugend Panzergrenadiers*. One of his men is not enthused. "(The lieutenant) said the battery was not retreating. He was going out to look for gun positions...for direct fire on the German infantry. (I) did not agree with this tactic at all. (I) wanted to go west and fast."

He soon gets his wish. The battery is ordered to connect its howitzers, pack its equipment, and prepare to start moving toward Wirtzfeld. Other bits and pieces of the battalion come through the streets to join them. The whole parade of artillery vehicles start their escape from Krinkelt, but they can't escape the enemy gunners, who punish them as harshly as they do their companions moving back from the fields west of this town.

The soldier who wants to go west fast remembered German shells falling. "I hit the street hard, with my nose in the mud." Fifteen or twenty rounds explode among the convoy's vehicles, damaging some, killing a soldier, injuring more. The battalion, now shrunk to a sort of chaotic convoy, manages to get on to the all-weather road that goes south to Bütgenbach. But when the vehicles and cannons move into enemy space north of Büllingen, they encounter a new menace: high-velocity 88 and 75mm rounds from *Panzer* guns of 1st *SS Panzer* Division (*Leibstandarte AH*). The drivers go north up a poor but less jammed road to Wirtzfeld and the Elsenborn heights.

Another of Lauer's light artillery battalions is also sore beset. At the start of the German attack, they are dug in along the road between Rocherath and Wahlerscheid crossroads. Their battalion commander does not get the signal to pull the guns and move west until after dark on December 17. They don't clear the area until close to 9 p.m. In sight of Rocherath, the vehicles of one of the batteries are forced to run from a *Panzer* but not before taking hits. These disable a truck and kill and injure men. One is the battery first sergeant whose face and eyes are lacerated cruelly.

The battery has more misfortune ahead. After finally escaping the *Panzer* guns, they push their way down the muddy farm road clotted with traffic toward Elsenborn heights and are soon stymied by the same block at the creek crossing encountered by other 99th artillerymen (above). The crews and drivers try to get round the stopper of immobile machines at the creek by moving on to the snow-splattered, marshy fields and fording it. Their gun-dragging trucks go a few yards then sink to the hubs and will go no further, no matter how desperately the crews shove, push, and grind the motors. It is close to midnight. The sight and sound of battle in the dual towns just a few hundred yards to the east overwhelm all. The men give up, abandon everything and start hiking west.

The two other gun batteries (eight howitzers total) of this battalion escape intact, but the Headquarters and Service batteries do not fare as well. Service Battery disappears in the disastrous attack by *Kampfgruppe* Peiper on Büllingen. (Volume 1, Narrative V, Part 3) The men of Headquarters Battery try to muscle their vehicles down the road to Rocherath but are thwarted by traffic, return to their old position, wait until the grey dawn arrives, then move cross country.

The battalion of mediums (155mm) assigned by 5th Corps to Lauer's division draw a good hand in the deadly game of hold and withdraw that the Americans are playing across the slopes and forests east of the Elsenborn plateau. They occupy space just northeast of Krinkelt where they have been shooting for the 393rd and 395th infantry regiments.

As the battle line begins to give way about noon December 17, the range they are shooting at grows shorter and shorter until it is down to scarcely more than a half mile. It is obvious to all that they either pull their big cannons and move or be taken. They move, merging their vehicles with the traffic crawling through Krinkelt and on down the wretched road to Wirtzfeld. For whatever blessed reason, the hostile artillery and rocket fire, prowling enemy patrols, and viscous traffic do not seem to do this collection of twelve big guns and tractors much harm, although the batteries become separated.

If these 155 medium howitzer crews draw a good hand, Colonel Riley's 394th Infantry Cannon Company (105s) draws a frightful one. After shooting at the infiltrating *Volksgrenadiers* in the Honsfelderwald west of Losheimergraben December 17, the company bumps its trucks and six little cannons down a corduroy road out of the forest to the N-32, which is alive with fleeing men and machines. Sporadic shelling, sniper fire, and an occasional hostile aircraft sweeping over them make the going not only snail-like but also hazardous.

The Cannon Company parade goes into the town of Mürringen where it makes a wrong move. Instead of following the mass of 99th men and machines heading for Krinkelt, a mile and a half to the north, Cannon Company moves northeast toward a treeless hill overlooking the Todeswald.

Here the cannon soldiers find four deep circular pits. These have been made for the 90mm (diameter) rifles of an antiaircraft gun battalion that has gone west a few hours before. They also find crude troop shelters. These are better than nothing but no protection as fighting holes against infantry or as bunkers against exploding artillery shells or mortar bombs.

The officers and men are disturbed. The position is exposed, obviously out front. Enemy infantry is about to emerge from the woods at any time. This is no place for cannoneers with six little 105 howitzers and personal weapons that are mostly light .30caliber carbines and .45caliber pistols. Also, the company commander orders the cannons emplaced in the existing pits. Because of their depth, this makes firing the howitzers difficult.

Cannon Company goes to work preparing for what may come. Remembered one lieutenant, "Everyone was in a state of uneasiness. (The position) was contrary to any instruction we ever had. We had to keep (the men) calmed down because of the nervous condition they were getting into."

As they fear, bad things now begin to happen. About midnight December 17 the radio connection with Colonel Riley's 394th Infantry headquarters goes out, leaving the company isolated in the dark, cold night, angry with blasts and blows of artillery and rocketry near and far. Two soldiers returning with food rations are shot at by what is obviously a *Panzer* gun. An American soldier wanders into the perimeter from out of nowhere, says he is lost, then after a while disappears (perhaps one of Colonel Skorzeny's mischief makers in American uniform). A squad of Colonel Hightower's 2nd Division 23rd Infantry digging a position nearby when the cannoneers arrive remove themselves to a safer place.

Suddenly one of the crews manning a cannon is struck by what appear to be German paratroops (AN: probably 12th *VGD* soldiers), who fire machine guns into their shelter, then grenade it. Several Americans are wounded; the rest give up. An unequal battle erupts round the other gun pits.

A truck roars out of the dark from west of the Cannon Company position and stops. Soldiers emerge and start shooting up the company command post. The captain and his handful of headquarters men shoot back, but can see no targets, only flashes of gunfire emerging from round the vague shape of the truck. The Americans throw grenades, which seem to hurt some of the attackers because they cry out in pain, an awful sound in the night.

No matter. Cannon Company is being dismembered. In desperation, a gun lieutenant and two of his soldiers attach a howitzer to a truck, drag it out of the deep pit, and start shooting flat out at the shadowy enemy as though their stubby little cannon were an antitank gun. A few rounds go wild, but one hits the truck and scatters the *Grenadiers* around it. Another crew also have dragged their cannon from a pit and brought it into the battle. Its fiery explosions so near, dangerous, and unexpected stun the enemy soldiers. They pull back, seek places to hide, lick their wounds, and regroup.

Daylight December 18 reveals the little battleground to be without the lines that separate hostile fighting men. The cannoneers not captured, wounded, or dead have organized themselves into squad-size hedgehogs of defense anchored on their command post and howitzers. The company is shelled by a 2nd Division battery working with Hightower's men at Hünningen.

The captain sends an officer by jeep to find out whether the Germans are west of them, at their backs. He returns to report they are. The captain searches for a road they can use to escape. There is one, still apparently free of enemy. The American shells exploding willy-nilly are a danger and add to the company's treacherous state.

But the exploding steel also holds their enemy off long enough to permit Cannon Company's officers to organize a march group of undamaged vehicles and surviving men. Seven wounded are loaded on a three-quarter ton truck; equipment and men on other trucks and jeeps. Forty men will try to walk out. There is neither time nor safety to connect the cannons. They are thermited and abandoned. Everyone knows what a perilous enterprise this is, but to stay is to die or surrender. A rear guard of fifteen men and five officers, including the captain, take on the suicidal mission of trying to keep the Germans off the column until it can escape.

Disaster strikes immediately. In some fir trees at the top of the slope about two hundred yards distant, hidden by the shadows of the forest and fog, is a large group of Germans. Also there are the Cannon Company prisoners they have taken in the battle. The Germans watch as the parade of trucks, jeeps, and walking men prepare to move along the road at the bottom of the slope. Methodically they set up their mortars and emplace their light machine guns. A Cannon Company soldier remembered, "When the escape column…came roaring up the dirt road below, it was raked from front to back with devastating fire while the American prisoners watched in horror."

The lead truck is hit by a mortar bomb and collapses on the road, effectively stopping the motion of all. The walking men scatter and burrow into the muck alongside the road. Riders leap from the vehicles as the bullets and jagged chunks of exploding mortar bombs whine all around. Some men die; others take wounds that by and by will bring death. A medical corpsman with the wounded in the three-quarter ton truck climbs on the hood, removes his helmet with its red cross upon a white background, and waves it around, screaming at the same time to stop the shooting, he has wounded men. A German machine gunner kills him.

The Americans have scarcely more than a few M-1 rifles and carbines to fight back with. In despair, the Cannon Company's first (senior) sergeant signals to the *Grenadiers* on the rise that he will surrender the men in the column if they will stop the carnage. The enemy guns go silent as the survivors of the column, who have been cringing on the ground or inside the vehicles, come forward hands high.

The wounded not killed in the ambush lie suffering in the truck, as do men hurt in the destruction of the column and spread around near the road. The German troop commander orders his soldiers to take the wounded who can walk, and leave the others behind. They will lie throughout the day and icy night as the morphine wears off and the pain comes followed by death's mercy for some.

By the close of this tragic day for the 394th Infantry cannoneers, only twenty have been able to escape into friendly hands. Ironically, some of them get away because as the rear guard they haven't been struck down in the ambush of the march column. It is the end of a proud company of 110 men and their 6 howitzers.

Ten miles to the west (as the shell flies) at about the same time, an officer of the 99th Division's battalion of mediums stops at the division artillery headquarters now at Camp Elsenborn to give General Black, 99th Division artillery chief, intelligence on the battle as he knows it and the fate of his battalion. Black is cheered to learn his mediums have survived. But he has little time to savor the news; he is preoccupied with the catastrophe that has struck the 99th Division and his artillery. When the harsh reckoning is made in a few days, Black will find he has lost a dozen howitzers and many light and heavy trucks.* A total of 207 of his artillerymen will be casualties (killed, wounded, missing).

General Hinds, the 2nd Division's artillery chief, has gone to the command post of his own 155mm battalion at Elsenborn. The diligent wire teams of the artillery have put in place a working wire net among the division's howitzer battalions and are keeping it up in spite of the endless counter-battery and harassing fire from German gunners. This makes it possible for Hinds to be on the battle scene controlling his cannons in the cockpit battle and to supervise their move to positions behind the Elsenborn heights for the crucial defense of that sector during the last days of December 1944.

The 155s are scheduled for departure to positions west of Elsenborn on December 19. Two of the firing batteries can't disengage because their power is still needed in the Rocherath-Krinkelt melee now coming to a climax. (Narrative VIII) Finally, they do go, but the third battery, the one that has taken such a dramatic part in the shooting of the previous two days (above), stays awhile, continuing to beat down on *Hitlerjugend's* men and *Panzers*. It is dark when they hitch up their big cannons to the prime movers and plow a way out through the muck covered with wide patches of soggy snow.

The two batteries that have departed before dark are set upon by *Messerschmidt* 109s with their ample machine guns and belly bombs. One bomb hits off to the side, damaging a tractor and hurting a few artillerymen. Given what has happened to all and everyone over the previous three days, this scarcely causes a man in the long column to light a cigarette to steady his nerves.

---

* A few of these vehicles will turn up later in the 2nd Division motor pools and two or three of the guns found and dragged back by 2nd Division artillerymen.

The 2nd Division's three light howitzer battalions have similar experiences. The last one to leave the field west of Rocherath for the Elsenborn heights and the village of Nidrum beyond it suffers a machine gunning by what one man in the convoy describes as "German training planes" (probably the slow but lethal dive-bombing *Stukas*). The convoy includes a few of the 105mm howitzers and trucks left behind by the 99th Division during the melee.

Thus ends the saga of the American artillerymen and their antiaircraft companions in the four days of ferocious shooting and harrowing escapes from the hills, fields, and towns east of the Elsenborn plateau. The saga is not complete, however, without a brief but painful coda: The confusion, exigent danger to guns and gunners, death and injury of so many artillery forward observers, impossible demands on the gun crews, loss of wires and radio signals, ignorance of who and where the enemy is, and many other destructive factors have made it inevitable that some—indeed a lot—of the American shellfire has killed and injured Americans.

The slaughter at the creek south of the dual towns (Volume 1, Narrative V, Part 6) has not been an isolated incident, nor is the shelling of 394th Infantry Cannon Company. Some of Major Norman A. Moore's 3rd Battalion (394) soldiers after the Buchholz-Losheimergraben fighting also take wounds and deaths under American shellfire while trying to find their way back to American lines.

The commander of the 2nd Division Headquarters Company remembered at Wirtzfeld "noticing several shells land that came in from our own artillery. I wondered how come our own are throwing shells in our own area and quite near (our) aid station. I was told by someone that the artillery had to just about turn their guns around and drop their shells just ahead of us to keep the enemy from another attack. I heard about similar incidents as to the artillery having to 'turn about' on other sectors."

Soldiers are at dreadful risk as they mush through the snow and muck trying to reach the safety of the American defenses hastily put together and connected loosely, or not at all, with their cooperating artillery. Some are intermixed with enemy and even if not are impossible to discern and identify as American troops in the black and fog. Second Division commanders have exhorted their men to take care, hold fire until sure of their targets: dangerous and difficult for the 2nd's infantry in their improvised holes, sometimes impossible for the cannoneers. The horror of soldiers killing their fellow soldiers by mistake always pullulates like foul carrion crows whenever, as in the borderland forests of eastern Belgium, a well-organized battle line is shattered and anarchy is loosed upon the military metropolis that is the infantry division at war.*

---

* After the Gulf War in 1990 to rid Kuwait of Sadam Hussein, journalists and editors of such newspapers as THE WASHINGTON POST made much of "friendly fire" killing American soldiers. A well-meant concern, no doubt, but revealing an abysmal ignorance of the pitiless realities of the modern battlefield.

WE WERE THERE

A Reluctant Truck Driver

"About two or three miles down this road, we came upon one of our battalion service company trucks off in a ditch leaning over on its side. It was a two-and-one-half-ton spare parts truck with no winch. The captain drove by and stopped (the jeep) and said to me, 'You get out and bring that truck in...' I really did not want to do this and I said to him, 'Are you telling me or are you asking me?' He said, 'I'm telling you.' I said, 'Well, that's the only damn way I'm gonna do it.'

"I really thought the Germans were close to us and might appear any time or certainly a German patrol would probably be in the vicinity. I got out, went back to the truck, opened the door, and there was the driver and I think two other men....He said that he had tried to get (the truck) out and couldn't. I don't know why he just continued to sit there.

"I made him try again but to no avail. About this time a few trucks from some other outfit started by. I asked them to give me a pull. They said, 'Hell, no. We are getting out of here. If you want a ride, get on, but we're leaving.'"

"A couple more trucks came by and I asked them the same thing and I got the same answer. I told the driver of our truck, 'We will try one more time to get out, and if we don't we're going to burn this truck and catch a ride or walk out.'

"(It's) a little vague in my mind but I think I got behind the wheel, and after cowboying (sic) the truck back and forth, it finally jumped back on the road. I told the driver of the truck to get behind the wheel and drive. He said, 'Lieutenant, I can't see a damn thing at night driving black out. I just can't drive.' I said, 'O.K. I'll do the driving.'

"By this time, there was no traffic or personnel along the road. It was a lonesome feeling....I was afraid to light a match or even have the glow of a cigarette. I would not turn on the blackout lights for fear of being seen. We crept along at a snail's pace. It seemed forever until we finally came (through the American front line)."

Ezra B. Trice, motor officer, Battery "B,"
776th Field Artillery Battalion, 99th Division

An Unpleasant Way to Save Some Lives

"...the lieutenant decided we should go back for supplies. We started down the road and came to a spot in the woods where we ran into a bunch of small arms fire. He ordered the jeep to turn around and we went back to the front.

"After a half hour or so (the lieutenant) said that we should go back again. We got to the same spot and there was more small arms fire. This time we jumped out of the jeep, took cover, and returned the fire.

"In a matter of minutes, we heard the words, 'comrade, comrade.' Out of the woods came four young boys. Granted they were in uniform, though the oldest was maybe twelve years of age. (AN: More likely, they were sixteen and seventeen. The *Heer* and *Waffen SS* put few boys of twelve into the Ardennes offensive; but many teenagers.)

"We were trying to talk to them when (the lieutenant) drew his pistol and said, 'I'm going to kill all of them.' I pulled my pistol, flipped the safety, and pointed it at him as I said, 'Go ahead and start shooting, but you'll be the next to die.'

"He said he was an officer and would have me court marshalled. I told him to do what he had to do, but if he shot one of the boys I would kill him. He put his pistol back and (so did I). We put the four boys on the hood of the jeep and took them with us. Prisoners were a dime a dozen at that time so we had no trouble dropping them off at a prisoner-of-war site.

"Of course, when we got back to (our artillery) battery, the lieutenant did press charges. The officers we had were a pretty good group, but they did have a problem on their hands because I did not deny the charges. However, cool heads prevailed and after a short time, a week or so, I was busted back to private. There was no court marshal. The jeep driver (who was with us) was transferred out."

Jack Press, member of artillery forward observer team, Battery "A," 370 Field Artillery, 99th Division

"I Could Not Have Done One More Thing"

"We heard a lot of rumors that day (December 16), knew something was afoot, didn't seem right, but you couldn't put your finger on it. Did a lot of firing, couldn't understand why we did so much, and we had a lot of artillery coming in. Couldn't understand that either.

"I got a call. Operator told me Major Younger wanted to talk to me. He says, 'Ryals, how long will it take you to be ready to fire (toward the south)?' Realizing that such a wide deflection would be required in relaying the guns, (AN: adjust guns to new directions and elevations) I told him 'Well, I say about 10 tomorrow morning.' He said Ryals 'We got to do better than that,' and I said 'Are you pulling my leg? Is this some kind of joke?' And he said, 'No I'm not joking Ryals. You have those guns ready to fire in twenty minutes, you hear me?'" (AN: four 155mm howitzers)

"I didn't answer him. I didn't think there was any possible way we could relay those guns, pull them out of the pits. First thing I did was call battalion...and roust out everybody they could send me and also send me all the prime movers (tractors) they could. ...Everybody fell to and came down on the guns. We jerked them out of the pits and got out trying to relay 'em. Snow had turned to slush, really sloppy. And there was so much firing going on, deafening, a very difficult job.

"You looked down the draw toward Mürringen (AN: He probably means Wirtzfeld.) and you could see the tanks firing....The flame would snake out from one side, then it would snake out from the other side....There was a lot of talk about we'd better get the hell out of here, find a better position. We were getting so many fire calls (AN: requests for artillery support), I said we'll stay here till they blow us out, because up front they're needing this fire, and we're going to give it to 'em. We fired in directions that were over half a circle; the only direction we didn't fire in was to the rear."

"That night (December 17-18) to me was the night of all nights as far as World War II was concerned. I felt that if I could get through this night without screwing up or making a bad mistake that the rest of my life would be anticlimactic. I think others shared this feeling....I could not have done one more thing than I had to do that night. I doubt that any field artillery battery of the U.S. Army was ever called upon to do more than ('C') Battery did that night."

Andrew B. Ryals, Jr., executive officer, Battery
"C," 12th Field Artillery, 2nd Division

A Howitzer Crew Turns Away from their Doom

"I was in my usual number one position on the right side (of the howitzer) waiting for fire commands from the command post when I saw our infantry (AN: 393rd Infantry, 3rd Battalion) running out of the woods on our right front. They were running hard for the high ground at Krinkelt. They had run about three hundred yards when there appeared a much larger group of black helmets and uniforms.

"I was already talking to Lieutenant Whipf (battery executive officer)...asking when we were going to get out of there. He said he was on his knees begging Colonel Brinley (the artillery battalion commander) to give the order, and he would let me know whether to take the gun or not. By this time, we could hear a tank (AN: probably a *Jagdpanzer IV*) coming up the draw in front of us and had put an armor-piercing shell in the chamber, pointing the muzzle in the direction of the sound. I was still hanging on to the phone and the lanyard. About that time, the phone rang and Whipf said, 'March orders, take the guns.'"

"I have never seen a crew move so fast. One problem: I couldn't get the projectile (shell) out of the gun, so I aimed it in the direction of the Germans standing in the trees. By that time Carter had the truck in the gun pit and we hooked up. I remember jumping in the back of the truck with the phone still in my hand. I cut the phone wire as we were moving out. This was the fastest march order on record and none too soon.

"In the next few hours, we found out what war was really like. I didn't think we were going to make it into Krinkelt. That tank and the (German) artillery were firing at the truck column all the way up the hill.

"Fortunately, the rounds were falling just a little short. The white phosphorous was really frightening. A small piece landed on the back of my hand. I didn't notice it until it burned through my glove. It took forever to heal up. I still have the scar.

"Krinkelt was utter bedlam. The streets were all clogged up with traffic and the Germans were throwing all the artillery they could muster in there. We were moving a few feet at a time, (then) we would jump off the truck and lay beside the road. It seemed like everything was on fire."

Jack Denhart, first gunner, "A" Battery,
370 Field Artillery, 99th Division

Incoming Mail for an American Artillery Battalion

"I decided to spend the night...at the battery executive post near the (four) howitzers....My executive officer and his crew were operating in a pyramidal tent because the bunker they were digging alongside had not yet been completed."

"At about 5:30 next morning (AN: *Null Tag*, December 16), I was awakened by the sound of incoming shell bursts. There was no mistaking these sounds. They seemed to be landing just a few yards away."

"Lieutenant Mount, who had been sleeping next to me on my right quickly rose to a sitting position and exclaimed, 'What's that?' These were his last words because an instant later there was a deafening explosion and I realized our tent had been hit by an artillery shell.

"I felt a sharp pain in my right leg. I knew I had been hit. Fortunately I found that I could get up and stand on my leg. Lieutenant Frankboner, who was also lying close to me, was seriously wounded..."

"I reached for the field phone to call battalion for medical assistance, but all lines were dead...the wires cut by the shells....I went over to where Lieutenant Mount lay. He had been hit on the top of the head...and was probably already dead. Corporal Brill had a nasty wound on his left elbow and Private Wilkie had been hit in the right foot..."

"One of the cannoneers...agreed to try to get to the battery switchboard despite the large number of shells that continued to fall on our position....He relayed the message to headquarters about our urgent need for medical help."

"Captain William H. Nickell, the battalion surgeon, arrived. ...He had Frankboner removed from the tent to the nearby unfinished (bunker) for the relative safety it afforded from the German shells..."

"He proceeded to operate. Frankboner's right foot had been blown off by shell fragments. It was the doctor's task to treat the mangled stump, including some ligaments, stop the bleeding, and bandage the wound. This surgery was carried out by flashlight with the tools available in the doctor's medical bag."

Carl T. Smith, commander, Battery "A,"
372nd Field Artillery, 99th Division

KEY TO NARRATIVE VII

CONTENDERS: At Wirtzfeld, Belgium: <u>U.S.</u> 2nd Infantry Division head-quarters units, an infantry company of 23rd Regiment, a platoon each of Sherman tanks and tracked M-10 tank destroyers and a company of towed 3-inch diameter antitank guns, sections of antiaircraft automatic weapons, 2nd and 99th division artillery batteries. (Major General Walter T. Robertson, Brigadier General John H. Hinds, Lieutenant Colonel Matt Konop.) <u>German</u> An armored reconnaissance patrol of six *Panzer IV* tanks, the same number of armed troop carriers, and several platoons of *Panzergrenadier* infantry. (*Kampfgruppe* Peiper)

At Rocherath-Krinkelt (dual towns): <u>U.S.</u> 38th Infantry moving in (Colonel Francis H. Boos); 9th Infantry (Colonel Chester J. Hirschfelder) moving through to south of Krinkelt; assorted 99th Division units and subunits packing and moving, passing through toward Elsenborn heights, or staying in dual towns to work with the 38th Infantry in the coming battle. Two companies and one platoon of M-10 tank destroyers (including a recon company); one company of towed antitank guns; all moving into dual towns. A company of Sherman tanks. <u>German</u> A *Kampfgruppe* of 12th *SS Panzer* Division including battalions of *Panzergrenadiers* and companies of *Jagdpanzers* and *Panzer IVs* and *Vs* (*SS* Major Siegfried Müller) in Krinkelterwald east of towns.

In Rocheratherwald: <u>U.S.</u> companies of 38th Infantry, 395th Regimental Combat Team of 99th Division (Colonel Alexander J. MacKenzie). <u>German</u> A regiment of 277th *VGD* (Colonel Wilhelm Viebig). Company of 326th *VGD*.

ISSUE: With the deconstruction of the American battle line in the borderland forests after noon on Sunday, December 17, the 2nd and 99th division fighters east and south of the Elsenborn heights are in danger of being enveloped and destroyed by the attacking armor and infantry columns of 1st *SS Panzer* Corps. The crunch points are the towns Wirtzfeld and Rocherath-Krinkelt (dual towns). <u>Significance</u>: If one or both of these points should be lost, the escape routes for the American troops leading to the Elsenborn heights will be overrun and filled with hostile soldiers and guns. This outcome would put at hazard the U.S. 5th Corps' (General Leonard T. Gerow) plan to use the heights as a barrier to hold back the tide of 6th *SS Panzer* Army on the north shoulder of the Ardennes-Eifel breakthrough sector.

LOCATION: A curving emergency defense line devised by General Robertson that begins southeast of Elsenborn, continues along the southern outposts of the Wirtzfeld defenses, then northeast in front of the dual towns and on north into the thick fir forest (Rocheratherwald) south of Wahlerscheid crossroads. Wirtz-feld is 2.5 miles southeast of Elsenborn, one mile west of Rocherath-Krinkelt. These two adjoining towns are southwest of the 395 RCT positions in the Rocheratherwald, the northern end of Robertson's line.

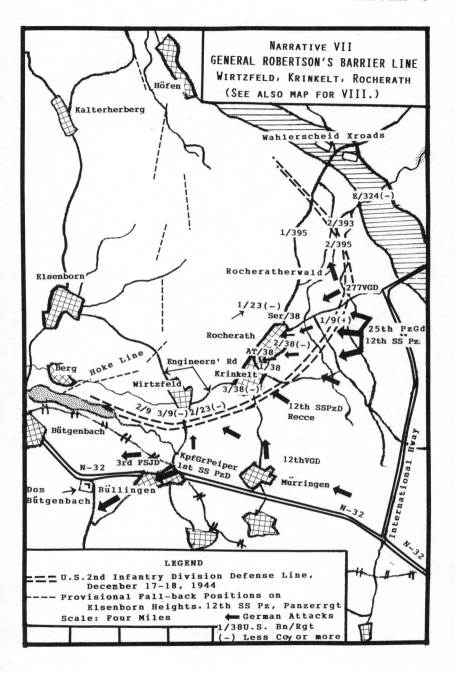

NARRATIVE VII
GENERAL ROBERTSON'S BARRIER LINE
WIRTZFELD, KRINKELT, ROCHERATH
(SEE ALSO MAP FOR VIII.)

Höfen

Kalterherberg

Wahlerscheid Xroads

E/324(-)

2/393

1/395

2/395

Rocheratherwald

277VGD

Elsenborn

1/23(-)

Ser/38

1/9(+)

25th PzGd
12th SS Pz

Rocherath

2/38(-)

Berg   Hoke Line   Engineers' Rd   AT/38
                                                1/38

Krinkelt

Wirtzfeld

3/38(-)

2/9 3/9(-) 2/23(-)

12th SSPzD
Recce

Bütgenbach

3rd FSJD   KpfGrPeiper
             1st SS PzD   12thVGD

N-32

Dom
Bütgenbach   Büllingen   Mürringen

N-32

International Hwy

N-32

LEGEND

═══ U.S. 2nd Infantry Division Defense Line,
       December 17-18, 1944
---- Provisional Fall-back Positions on
       Elsenborn Heights. 12th SS Pz, Panzerrgt
Scale: Four Miles   ← German Attacks

1/38 U.S. Bn/Rgt
(-) Less Coy or more

SEVENTH NARRATIVE: TO HOLD RUIN AT ARM'S END

Part 1: The High Commands React

The first twenty-four hours of mayhem in the Eifel-Ardennes region following the German attack before dawn on December 16 has produced decidedly mixed reactions among the commanders in the two camps, American and German.

Field Marshal Gerd von Rundstedt visits his *Führer* late on *Null Tag* at the War Lord's enormous underground bunker in the Taunus Hills north of Frankfurt, Germany to brief him on the day's victories and defeats. The weather has behaved splendidly i.e. it is dark and dismal over the Eifel-Ardennes. The shock and surprise inflicted on the American enemy have been total. Deep penetrations have been made by General Hasso von Manteuffel's 5th *Panzer* Army and the left wing of Sepp Dietrich's 6th *SS Panzer* Army. The flank guard in the action, General Eric Brandenberger's 7th *Infanterie* Army, has been able to punch holes in the American main line of resistance in the south above Echternach, Luxembourg.

Yet the crafty, eagle-beaked old field marshal is pessimistic. No enthusiast for the whole show anyway, von Rundstedt believes the events of the day are ominous. Dietrich's staff has been unable to impose order on the 6th *SS Panzer* Army's traffic to the front, in part because the roads assigned are worse than expected; in part because they can't cope with the complex scheduling of marching men, horses, armor, guns, supply vehicles.

The infantry of this army is charged with the task of pushing aside the *Ami* forces in the borderland of eastern Belgium (i.e. the 99th's six battalions). It has not yet fulfilled its mission, is behind schedule, and has entangled some of the 12th *SS Panzer* Division in the battle. This, the *Führer's* chosen power to lead the armored march west to the Meuse River, remains bogged in the borderland forest and the clotted traffic on the rural roads into Belgium.

At Monschau-Höfen, the 326 *Volksgrenadier* Division has succeeded not at all in penetrating the front of two small American forces there, an infantry battalion and a cavalry squadron. (Volume 1, Narrative II) This has upset a vital element of the 6th Army plan to reach Eupen, Belgium after noon of *Null Tag* and begin building the infantry line along the northern edge of the Ardennes. This is crucial to keep the American infantry and armor away from the columns of 12th and 1st *SS Panzer* divisions (*Hitlerjugend* and *Leibstandarte Adolph Hitler*.)

The War Lord's manic optimism does not allow for such negative thinking. He dismisses von Rundstedt, who returns to his own headquarters in a castle a few miles away. He is resigned to his fate as a figurehead and notable persona who adds weight to the Ardennes-Eifel counteroffensive but an officer with only a pro forma command role. Hitler's opinion is that *Null Tag* has gone remarkably well. Dietrich's left wing (*Kampfgruppe* Peiper and 2nd *SS Panzergrenadier* Regiment) is moving inexorably west in the Amblève River Valley. On their left, Manteuffel's 5th *Panzer* Army is moving rapidly on St. Vith and Bastogne.

As to Dietrich's right wing, 12th *SS Panzer* Division, it is only a matter of time before this most treasured formation with its twenty thousand stalwart men and boys and enormous amount of armor (not all that enormous in reality) will slice through the enemy and be on their way to the Meuse—and beyond. "Everything has changed in the west," Hitler tells the commander of his Army Group G, south of the breakthrough area. "Success, complete success, is now in our grasp."

His commander for the Eifel-Ardennes offensive, Field Marshal Walter Model, occupies the large, ornate hunting lodge of a German manufacturer in a wooded valley of the Eifel Mountains. Early on December 17 the difficult but determined little field marshal has a visitor, Albert Speer, *Reichminister* for Armaments and Supply. Speer has chosen to roam the front, doing what he can to expedite the forward movement of vital supplies, especially the precious "Otto" (gasoline).

He finds Model in a rare good mood. All three of the armies in the attack report ruptures in the American main line of resistance and penetrations into the rear echelon of the four U.S. infantry divisions (99, 106, 28, 4) and one armored combat command struck *Null Tag* morning. True, the vital right wing of Dietrich's 6th *Panzer* Army, *Schwerpunkt* of the entire counteroffensive, is lagging behind schedule. But the schedule (three days to reach the Meuse River) was considered unrealistic from the beginning by the field commanders and accepted only because handed down from on high (i.e. Hitler's headquarters—*OKW*). However, Model is a realist and has the gravest of doubts whether his Army Group B attack columns can advance beyond the Meuse. He hopes to persuade Hitler to accept the consolation prize of destroying the U.S. 1st Army as an alternative.

The sector assigned to Dietrich's right wing troubles Model: the Monschau-Hohes Venn-Eupen triangle on the north where much was planned and little has been accomplished. General Kaschner's 329 *VGD* has not run over the Americans at the Monschau-Höfen Gatepost as was expected. Colonel von der Heydte's *Fallschirmjäger* are only now going aloft. *Hitlerjugend* Division's tracked troop-carrying vehicles and armor apparently are entangled on the roads and forest trails west of Hollerath, Germany. And according to spies and reconnaissance aircraft pilots of the *Luftwaffe*, the Americans are moving troops, guns, and armor un-impeded from the Aachen area south toward Elsenborn, Malmedy, and St. Vith.

The three generals commanding Model's armies in the counter-offensive are influenced, as might be expected, by the opposition their troops have encountered on *Null Tag* and how successfully they have overcome it. Brandenberger is satisfied with the progress of his 7th Army on the extreme south. His troops have breached the *Ami* line in dozens of places. Manteuffel has not met the unrealistic time-distance numbers set by *OKW*. Nevertheless, 5th *Panzer* Army's men and tanks have made good progress over rough terrain, are about to bag two regiments of a U.S. infantry division (the 106th), and have the road junction of St. Vith, Belgium well in their sights.

Only in Sepp Dietrich's camp in the early morning hours of Sunday December 17 do the harsh realities of *Null Tag* raise the troubling specter of failure. Although the War Lord's favorite among the three armies and his designated power to carry the battle swiftly to the River Meuse and beyond, Dietrich's Sixth *SS Panzer* has been saddled with the worst sector of the breakthrough front. It is scarcely wider than twenty-five miles; served by few paved, all-weather roads; thick with high, forested hills, marshy fields, and deep ravines, confining small rivers, streams, and creeks flowing every which way. A less desirable terrain for men, horses, vehicles, tanks, armored gun platforms to storm across can scarcely be imagined.

"(It was) extremely difficult country for the combined attack of the *Panzers* (and the infantry)," Fritz Kraemer, 6th *Pz Armee* chief of staff, said after the battle. He also has been surprised by the hedgehogs of resistance the Americans have thrown together to thwart and frustrate the German infantry assault teams.

As dawn breaks on bloody Sunday, December 17, Kraemer is determined that the front on the north flank of 6th *SS Panzer* Army be opened up. Meaning, of course, that the 12th and 277 *Volksgrenadier* divisions push across the heights of Elsenborn; the 326th *VG*, break through to Eupen and get behind the enemy gathering on the heights; *Hitlerjugend*, move its two armored strike columns west over *Rollbahn* B and C along the right flank of *Kampfgruppe* Peiper to the Meuse River.

The leaders of 6th *SS Panzer* Army seem unconcerned about the presence of the U.S. 2nd Infantry Division on the northern wing of their breakthrough front. They know an American infantry and armor force is west of the heights in and around the Belgian Army's Camp Elsenborn. Spies have told them so. (Volume 1, Narrative I) What they don't seem to know is that these are merely some of the supply and maintenance troops and equipment of the 2nd Division, its armor auxiliaries, and its reserve regiment. The main power of the division is up north in the Monschauwald trying to muscle its way through the West Wall at the Wahlerscheid crossroads. And just as ominous for the cause of *Hitlerjugend*, General Gerow has already ordered the 2nd Division to send two battalions from its reserve regiment (the 23rd) to Lauer's beleaguered troops.

As the commander of 1st *SS Panzer* Corps, *SS* General Priess knows that his betters up the chain of command to the War Lord himself will hold him accountable for the failures of the *Volksgrenadiers* in the wooded hills and marshy valleys east of the Elsenborn heights. The unsatisfactory unfolding of events on *Null Tag* east of the international highway pushed him into the decision to turn the attack over to *Hitlerjugend's* commander; place the 277th *VGD* under the latter's command; temporarily pass the lead in the 12th *SS Panzer* Division sector to a heavied-up *Kampfgruppe* that will attack over the dual towns, Rocherath-Krinkelt.

After dawn December 17, General Priess learns that *Kampfgruppe* Peiper has taken Büllingen, well behind the 99th Division main line of resistance. He believes 12th *SS Panzer* (*Hitlerjugend*) should be able to push through to Elsenborn and Bütgenbach without hurtful opposition from the already tired and sorely punished fighters of the 99th Division. *Luftwaffe* General Dietrich Peltz, CO of the 2nd *Jagdkorps*, has assured 6th *Panzer* Army that his pilots will be out in force over the Elsenborn heights. Priess has reason for optimism after a day of frustration and unsatisfactory results.

Closer still to the first day's amphitheater of bloody struggle east of the Elsenborn plateau, commanders of the three *Volksgrenadier* divisions (326, 277, 12) assigned the task of running through the 99th Division battle line are less sanguine. They maintain the professional soldier's mandatory optimism, but it is tempered by realism and shadowed by fatalism. General Kaschner (326) and Colonel Viebig (277) are concerned over the inadequate training their men and boys have received. The inevitable results of this have been amply proven in the first day of marching and fighting. All three commanders fret over the severe casualties among their junior officers and non-commissioned officers. In too many assault companies they have been forced to get up front, do the blood letting and take it as well.

Kaschner early on Sunday December 17 is being pushed by his chief, General Hitzfeld, 67th Infantry Corps commander, to remove the Americans at the Monschau-Mützenich Gatepost and get to Eupen. He is beginning to wonder whether it is doable; however, Hitzfeld has promised to send a detachment of tracked assault guns, which should help. (They don't. Volume 1, Narrative II, Part 3)

Viebig is the only higher commander in the 1st *SS* Corps who frets over the *Ami* troops in the woods south of Wahlerscheid crossroads and their potential for driving in the flank of the German columns moving toward Rocherath-Krinkelt. However, his attention is focused on Mac-Kenzie's 395th Regimental Combat Team. He seems unaware that just north of these men in the woods are two regiments of the steely 2nd Division.

Also, Viebig is preoccupied with operational problems: throughout *Null Tag*, his horse-drawn guns and supply wagons have been ensnarled in the traffic along the rural roads east of the international highway. Also the *Sturmgeschütze* (assault guns) have not mixed in the battle as promised to wear down the enemy. Communications with his regimental commanders and theirs down the line to subordinates have constantly failed. Messengers are carrying the communication load in the 277 *VGD*. Messengers have a way of getting shot or hit by exploding artillery rounds.

General Engle's 12 *VGD* infantry has become snagged at the Losheim-ergraben crossroads by a battalion of the 99th Division. (Volume 1, Narrative IV, Part 2) His view of things is colored by the pressure he is getting from Priess and Dietrich to do his job and clear the cross-roads. Nevertheless, Engle has no reason to despair. He commands the most effective infantry in Dietrich's Army. Some of his assault companies already are moving on Buchholz, and Hünningen and Mürringen on the N-32.

Hugo Kraas, the *SS* colonel running *Hitlerjugend*, intends to drive rapidly through Rocherath-Krinkelt before "the Camp Elsenborn group," as he believes the 2nd Division to be, can move in to engage. Here, once again, a leading 1st *SS Panzer* Corps officer seems unknowing about the location and potential threat of Robertson's 2nd Division. (See also Volume 1, pps. 291-92)

Saturday December 16 is a busy day for General Dwight D. Eisenhower, the commander in chief of all the Allied power in the struggle to breach the German defenses along the Western Front and bring down the *Nazi Reich*. In the morning he attends the wedding of his orderly, in the afternoon meets with American 12th Army Group (9th, 1st, 3rd armies) commander, Lieutenant General Omar N.

Bradley, at his headquarters in a Versailles hotel. The two generals discuss the agonizing subject of where and how to find replacements for the shockingly large number of American infantrymen being killed, wounded, sickened with disease and cold, and CE'd (combat exhausted) along the Western Front. (Volume 1, INTRODUCTION)

As they mull over their options for keeping up the rifle strength of the American divisions, they are utterly unaware that Adolph Hitler's reinvigorated and rearmed legions are that very hour engaged in a massive attack across seventy miles of the American front line with the intention of vaulting the River Meuse and marching on the vital port of Antwerp, Belgium. The meeting is coming to a close when a colonel enters the room and hands a note to British General Kenneth W.O. Strong, Eisenhower's intelligence chief. The Germans are making trouble along the front of the U.S. 8th Corps, 1st Army. Shortly, another message arrives informing the assembled generals and their staffs and aides that it may be serious trouble. No less than eight enemy divisions have been identified as participating in the action.

Bradley is simply nonplussed. He responds that Field Marshal von Rundstedt, who is in command of all German forces on the Western Front, must be trying to fake U.S. 1st Army out of its attack to seize the Roer River dams. It is the standard response that day at all echelons, from the American battalion command posts upward to the command stratosphere where Bradley dwells.

General Eisenhower does not share this opinion. He does not believe the German Army is engaged in an insignificant "spoiling action" to distract U.S. 1st Army or any of his other armies along the Western battle line. He believes something serious is up. He knows what others in the room do not know.

Strong has been increasingly uneasy over German intentions. His fears are based on the ULTRA intercepts and other intelligence sources. Eisenhower is aware of Strong's interesting if nonspecific estimates. The SHAEF commander also is privy to MAGIC decodes of the most secret Japanese communications, including messages between the Japanese ambassador in Berlin and his betters in Tokyo.* These are

---

* Early in the war, the British devised a method of reading *Wehrmacht* messages sent in code by radio, and they designed some extraordinary machinery to help them do it. This "ULTRA" code-breaking system, which was centered at Bletchley Park in Buckinghamshire, England enabled SHAEF and Allied army group and army commanders to learn in advance their enemy's intentions, plans, and directed moves on land, in the air, and at sea. By the autumn of 1944, Hitler and some of his staff officers began to suspect their enemy was finding a way to listen in. He ordered radio silence in the weeks before the

despatched "eyes only" from the Pentagon to Eisenhower. Hitler has informed the ambassador that the *Wehrmacht* will launch a counter-offensive against the Americans in the West before the end of the year, details unspecified.

The Supreme Commander doesn't even bother to put a call through to Lieutenant General Courtney Hodges, whose soldiers are in direst peril by midnight of *Null Tag*, before he instructs Bradley to immediately call Generals Patton (3rd Army) and Simpson (9th Army). They are to send, respectively, the 10th and 7th armored divisions to General Middleton, commander of U.S. 8th Corps and Hodges' subordinate.

However, Eisenhower seems not to realize what a risk he is running by not sending at least as much power, whether armor or infantry, to General Gerow's 5th Corps sector north of the Losheim Gap where the 99th and 2nd infantry divisions are in as much danger of being annihilated as is 8th Corps—and with more potentially destructive consequences for the Allied cause.

Following the afternoon meeting, Generals Eisenhower and Bradley and companions relax with a good dinner and a bridge game. They call it a day about midnight. Before they can retire, a watch officer with the ULTRA unit housed in a stable near the Supreme Commander's villa asks to see General Strong. Bletchley Park has just transmitted an urgent message: General Peltz, leader of *Luftwaffe Jagdkorps II*, is preparing a major air operation for December 17 intended to give cover for the attacks of the 5th and 6th German *Panzer* armies. The two generals are informed immediately. The effect on Eisenhower's slumbers that night has been lost to history; Bradley, who has been plagued that fall by colds and fatigue, does not sleep well.

The next morning, he is off to his headquarters in Luxembourg City still disbelieving an enemy on the verge of collapse has risen from the misty forests of the Eifel-Ardennes to challenge the American power there and put at risk two full corps of his mighty army group. Bradley has been heard to say he would welcome localized attacks by a few enemy divisions to get them out of their steel and concrete pillboxes in the villages and forests, out of their well-prepared trenches behind the mine fields and force them to fight in the open where his big guns and swarms of fighter-bombers can go to work on them. (Volume 1, INTRODUCTION) However, from the reports received at SHAEF, this

---

Ardennes offensive. However, the *Luftwaffe* did not adhere strictly to the order, nor did the German railways personnel responsible for moving the troops into the Eifel region prior to the action. "MAGIC" was the code name for the American system of intercepting and decoding messages sent by Japanese military and diplomatic officials.

appears to be something else, a major assault with objectives unknown and bringing out the *Luftwaffe* in force on the Western Front for the first time since the *Wehrmacht* attacked the Western Allies in 1940.

Whatever plans and preparations the 12th Army Group commander may (or may not) have had in mind before December 16, to counter such an attack, the lack of concern around Bradley's headquarters in Luxembourg City during most of *Null Tag* indicates his staff knew little about them.

As reports come in that the troops of U.S. 5th and 8th corps are being attacked by enemy assault teams. Brigadier General Edwin L. Sibert, Bradley's G-2, at first considers these as merely "spoiling attacks" to throw off the Allied schedule for breaking through the West Wall into the plains of the Rhine. And with their chief in Versailles conferring with Eisenhower and no concrete plan for bringing up reinforcements, 12th Army Group staff can offer little but calming words for the embattled field commanders under the metastasizing German guns.

Null Tag for 1st Army commander Courtney Hodges and his chief of staff, General Keane, has been confusing. The sketchy reports of his division commanders telephoned or telegraphed to the Hotel Brittanique in Spa, Belgium do not give them the impression a crisis is upon them. Hodges' own liaison officers with the infantry divisions up front seem calm and matter of fact in their reports, which go directly to him, reinforcing the once-again idée fixe in his camp that the enemy is just trying to draw men and guns away from the U.S. 5th Corps attack toward the headwater dams of the Roer River.

General Alan W. Jones, commander of the doomed 106th Division in line south of the 99th Division, seems a bit excited in his reports. But he and his men are new to the front. And his information seems so uncertain and imprecise as to the size and vectors of the German attacks that Hodges' staff has trouble with them.

Still and all, it appears Jones' barely established regiments, which have come on line December 10, are in some trouble and need help. To confuse matters more, the infantry division on Jones' right flank (28th) is telling Hodges' staff late in the afternoon of *Null Tag* "the situation is well in hand," in spite of the German power that has driven in their outposts and is cracking their line. And to compound the confusion, earlier in the day, Hodges' staff people at Spa received a transcript of the famous "hour of destiny" order of the day to German troops found on a prisoner and sent up the chain of command. (Volume 1, p. 29)

General Hodges does move, if cautiously and confusedly. He sends Combat Command "B" of the 9th Armored Division to Middleton's 8th

Corps sector. He tells Major General J. Lawton Collins, his 7th Corps commander, to alert the 1st Infantry Division and an armored combat command for movement to the Elsenborn plateau. He orders a battalion of combat engineers to General Lauer's dreadfully undermanned southern flank.

The 1st Army commander is restricted and confined in his decisions on *Null Tag* by the bad fortune that his own commander, General Bradley, is unavailable for advice and consultation. In fact, General Hodges will not even talk with Bradley by telephone until the morning of bloody Sunday December 17 when German columns have ruptured the front of five 1st Army divisions.

Soon after noon on *Null Tag*, December 16, General Hodges receives the urgent message from General Gerow, CO of 5th Corps, referred to before. (Volume 1, p. 295) Gerow asks him to call off the march of the 2nd Division through the West Wall at Wahlerscheid. Hodges refuses. General Hodges has just been informed that the 2nd Division has opened a wide hole in the impregnable pillbox-bunker line in front of the Wahlerscheid crossroads. (Volume 1, Narrative I, Part 2) To withdraw these men and give up the advantage this success brings—Hodges can't accept this.

Until the night of December 16, the march to the high dams of the Roer River headwaters has been another ghastly blood letting: twelve hundred battle casualties in the U.S. 8th and 78th divisions on the north wing; six hundred in the 2nd and 99th on the south wing. To allow Gerow to signal General Robertson to withdraw, abandon the bloody gains at Wahlerscheid and go back to where the two divisions started (Rocherath-Krinkelt) is just too much to contemplate: the Hürtgenwald all over again, the endless, pointless slogging, backing and filling, local successes soon rolled over and obliterated by larger disasters. Hodges and his chief of staff can not bring themselves to give the order.

And of course the other factor in their deliberations is the absence of definitive intelligence on German intentions available to them. The 1st Army chief staff officer for intelligence (G-2), Colonel Benjamin A. Dickson, has spent many hours lately agonizing over what these intentions are. At a briefing December 14 for General Hodges and his staff, Dickson startled one and all with the pronouncement that the German 6th *SS Panzer* Army was about to strike through the Ardennes. Their mission was to recapture Aachen, Germany (or the little that is left of it), the *Führer's* favorite symbol of everlasting resistance. None of the other staff officers present seemed moved. Dickson has the reputation of being impetuous. And his written intelligence assessment December 15 contained no such dire prediction.

In the morning of the 16th, the Americans around Wahlerscheid crossroads continue to extend their positions farther to the northeast, deeper into enemy territory. Meanwhile on both flanks German assault columns—infantry, armor, cannons, rocket machines—are pushing west to encircle them. Two 2nd Division rifle battalions have moved through the break in the West Wall at Wahlerscheid crossroads. At mid-morning they stand a half mile beyond in the woods close to the all-weather highway needed for the second stage of the march to the Roer River dams.

Shortly after noon, Robertson receives a call from his chief, General Gerow, who informs him what 5th Corps officers are learning and his own plea to General Hodges to call off the 2nd-99th division attack. Robertson's subordinates begin to sound alarms as well. Around noon on *Null Tag*, he also learns of Hodges' transfer of the U.S. 9th Armored Combat Command B to the 8th Corps. This CC was programmed as the armored spearhead of the drive beyond Wahlerscheid to take the dams. Robertson wonders what is going on. He orderes his two regimental commanders (9th, 38th) to stand in place.

Late on December 16, General Huebner, acting deputy commander of 5th Corps, shows up at the farm house in Wirtzfeld that is the 2nd Division commander's forward command post. He is troubled mightily. The enemy all across the Ardennes front seems to be on the move. The U.S. cavalry south of Lauer's troops are in retreat. Lauer's power is engaged in a ferocious fight in the forests east and south of the dual towns. The German artillery and rocketry keeps pounding and pounding at the rear echelon emplacements. As he takes his leave, Huebner tells Robertson to be cautious and circumspect.

The 2nd Division commander needs no urging.

Part 2: A Full Soldier

At first light in Eupen Sunday, December 17, General Gerow receives word that the *Panzers* are rampaging around the vital 2nd Division supply center of Büllingen, far in the rear of the 99th Division front line. His own headquarters city, Eupen, is a mere ten miles west of the battle at the Monschau Gatepost. The small force there may be overwhelmed at any moment. An unknown number of paratroopers have come down in the hills and marshes of the Hohes Venn just a few miles away. (Volume 1, Narrative II) And ruin is aborning along the wide and long sector held by the 99th and 2nd divisions. A sketchy plan to use the Elsenborn heights as a fall-back position devised by Gerow's staff in the event of an enemy attack south of Wahlerscheid crossroads now takes on an importance out of all proportion to the thought and time put into it.

In Spa, fifteen miles south of Eupen, Hodges remains ambivalent. He is still reluctant to yield up the gains at Wahlerscheid crossroads. Yet, as we know (Volume 1, p. 295), he grants General Gerow some leeway: The 5th Corps commander may call off the attack beyond the crossroads and order the 2nd and 99th division troops out of the woods, but only if he believes this to be absolutely necessary. Gerow does, of course, and has since early afternoon of the previous day. (In short, the 1st Army commander tells the 5th Corps commander to shoulder the weight of the decision—and its consequences.)

The retreat to the heights of Elsenborn of all friendly forces in the valleys below and in the Rocheratherwald and the re-establishment of a defensive line to hold the rampaging Germans will require a display of battlefield leadership to test the mettle of an Alexander the Great. No matter. The task must be tried, and a full soldier assigned to it who is on the bloody scene, up front, in control, and aware of all the monsters he and his men are facing. That soldier can only be Major General Walter M. Robertson, CO of the 2nd Division.

At his command post on the morning of the 17th, General Robertson receives three messages:

A representative of General Lauer informs him that the Germans are getting through the 99th's main line of resistance. Gerow's headquarters tells him the same. Shortly thereafter the 5th Corps commander himself comes on the phone to give Robertson the message he has been waiting for with increasing disquiet since noon on *Null Tag*. He is to clear the Wahlerscheid sector of all troops and as many arms and as much equipment as they can bring with them. Robertson will also need to find ways of shoring up the critical strong points still held by the troops of the 99th Division, his own 23rd Infantry and 2nd Division Headquarters people, and the disparate armor and artillery serving with the two divisions. These critical places include the roads east and south of the dual towns, Krinkelt-Rocherath, and the strong points Hünningen, Mürringen, Wirtzfeld.

Then when all this is in hand and the surging enemy temporarily held off, Robertson is to clear the valleys and move everyone and everything west to the Elsenborn heights. "I was authorized to use my own judgement," Robertson wrote dryly after the battle.

The 2nd Division leader's later report on the conversation does not indicate whether he and Gerow discussed a previous plan or any details thereof. Probably not. Time, a vital part of Robertson's diminishing capital, is flying by and any details of a plan for withdrawal to the heights of Elsenborn worked out at corps in the quiet and safety of an office in Eupen is now quite irrelevant under the harrowing, chaotic, battlefield conditions confronting Robertson. He is on his own, faced with what John Eisenhower, the Supreme Commander's son, will later describe as "probably the most complex maneuver encountered by a division commander in World War II."

Gerow's best help to Robertson has been to prevail on General Hodges to free him from pursuing the Wahlerscheid operation and to impress on the 1st Army commander and his chief of staff that the deconstructing American positions east and south of the line Kalter-herberg-Elsenborn-Bütgenbach need their attention and concern as much as does Troy Middleton's 8th Army Corps front to the south.

The 5th Corps commander has no reinforcements to send to Robertson. The U.S. 78th Division fighting through the villages and farm lands around the Simmerath—Vossenach sector in Germany, as the northern arm of the Roer River dams operation, is entangled in a costly battle with the 272 *Volksgrenadier* Division. The combat command of tanks and armored infantry programmed for the "exploitation" phase of that operation has been moved to Middleton's crumbling front.

The experienced fighters of the U.S. 9th Infantry Division are moving in to harden Gerow's defenses east of Eupen. Eventually they will relieve the infantry and cavalry there. However, they will be several days in coming. They also will be too far to the north to screen the 2nd and 99th division soldiers as they withdraw from the Wahlerscheid salient and the other exposed places in the east-of-Elsenborn battle pit.

General Robertson will have to perform his duty with the power he has in hand. He will need to manage the formations at his disposal in such a way that they take turns screening and protecting each other from being run over by the enemy until all can escape to the Elsenborn heights. He cannot expect any reinforcements. The 2nd Division and what is left of the 99th Division are it. They save themselves or they perish.

Robertson and his chief of staff, Colonel Ralph Zwicker, have spent several hours the night of December 16-17 in the 2nd Division forward command post at Wirtzfeld putting together a plan of escape. As occasionally happens on the battlefields of the world (or did before the high-tech modern age), a general and his aides studying maps around a rough table in some lowly farm house in some totally unknown village create a plan that will save or lose an army.

As he worked, Robertson still believed that the 99th Division was holding the southern flank along the N-32 highway and that his critical supply center at Büllingen remained safe. He has talked by phone with his regimental commanders in the Wahlerscheid operation, Colonels Francis H. Boos (38th Infantry) and Chester J. Hirschfelder (9th Infantry), to ascertain the position of their battalions and obtain their views on how quickly and safely they can disengage.

The plan Robertson and his little command group finally completed sometime early on Sunday, December 17 has three parts, interlocking and supporting each other:

One, Colonel Boos' regiment, which has taken the point in the march to the Roer River dams beyond the West Wall, will withdraw and establish itself in the dual towns. Hirschfelder's regiment will man defensive positions south and west of the towns. The 9th Regiment mission: protect the lifeline supply and escape route from Wirtzfeld to Krinkelt and the southern approaches to it. Armor with the 2nd Division in the Wahlerscheid operation will act as a rear guard and meld into the streams of foot going south.

Two, General Lauer's 395th Regimental Combat Team, which has been doing flanking work for the 2nd Division in its attack at Wahlerscheid crossroads will remain in the Monschauwald north of Rocherath. Its mission: to fight off enemy attempts to get round the left flank of Boos' regiment in the dual towns or mount an attack from the north simultaneously with *Hitlerjugend's* from the east.

Three, A company of 2nd Division engineers will go to work on the road Elsenborn-Wirtzfeld-Krinkelt, the lifeline over which defenders of the dual towns will obtain supplies and ammunition and eventually use to make their escape to the Elsenborn heights. Robertson is not sanguine about this road. "(It) had never been completed and had about a thousand yards of bottomless mud," he wrote.

In sum, the 2nd Division commander and his officers and Colonel MacKenzie's 395th Regimental Combat Team leaders will spread a long line of fighters and fighting machines from the fields and forests north of the dual towns, on around their southern and eastern edges, then west to Wirtzfeld and then around that village north to Elsenborn on the heights.

The fulcrum to lever the plan to success is, of course, the dual towns, Rocherath-Krinkelt. If *Hitlerjugend* and its companion 277th *Volksgrenadier* Division swiftly overrun these two adjoining towns, large numbers of 2nd and 99th troops out front to the north, east, and south will be trapped. Robertson's plan will fail.

Following the session at his forward command post, the 2nd Division commander manages a few hours of sleep. He awakens to grim news. *Panzers* are in Büllingen, the division's base on the main supply road. The entire right (south) flank of the 99th Division is being driven in by *Kampfgruppe* Peiper, General Engle's 12th *Volksgrenadier* Division, and a few battalions of the 3rd *Fallschirmjäger*. Wirtzfeld is at urgent and immediate risk.

Colonel Riley's 394th Infantry command post at Mürringen, reinforced by Colonel Hightower's 1st Battalion, 23rd Infantry, (Volume 1, Narrative V, Part 5) has yet to fall. Yet it can't be long before the besieged soldiers there also will need to be moved out. If Wirtzfeld goes and the enemy keeps driving northwest and gains the Elsenborn plateau, all of the American defenses, command centers, supply dumps, and road nets east of a line Malmedy-Eupen will be in peril, and 6th *SS Panzer* Army's northern wing will be on the move to the Meuse.

The 2nd Division commander need only go outside the front door of his farm house in the village at dawn December 17 to sense how threatening is the situation. First *SS Panzer* cannoneers are bombarding it with big rounds—up to ten inches in diameter—that shock the senses and drive fear deep into the heart as they explode, bringing down buildings and washing jagged steel fragments up and down the streets. Off to the south, can be heard the screech-bang of high-velocity *Panzer* guns being fired and the characteristic urgent hammering sound of German *Maschinengewheren*. Overhead V-1 flying bombs clatter across the sky. Enemy aircraft appear and disappear in and out of the thick, grey cloud mat of early morning.

At 7:30 a.m. Robertson receives a message from General Lauer's headquarters in Bütgenbach that they are leaving for the Belgian Army camp two miles west of Elsenborn. Lauer later explained, "My staff felt at the time and so did I that it was dangerous for our division headquarters to remain on this exposed flank, which we expected would be overrun momentarily."

It is a precipitous leave taking by some accounts. A soldier-clerk in the 99th's headquarters remembered he and his fellow clerks were about to eat Sunday breakfast, "Pancakes with a fresh egg on top. We heard the sound of machine gun fire. We didn't know if it was ours or theirs or anything else, so we just kept on eating. Within minutes, however, the division chaplain's assistant burst in the door and said, 'The forward echelon has been overrun. General Lauer sent me back to tell you to get out the best you can.' ...(The major) told us to pack up the records...he somehow got a couple of trucks. We loaded them with the boxes containing the records...and the trucks left for Elsenborn (camp).''*

---

* The assistant operations officer of the 99th Division (G-3) denied there was anything precipitous about the evacuation of Bütgenbach by General Lauer and his headquarters troops. He was ordered at daylight December 17 to take an advance party to Camp Elsenborn while "the remainder of the command post was packing and loading and preparing to join us (there). (This) leap-frog technique was standard practice." (Bishop,

Lauer's departure leaves Robertson in an ambiguous position. He is now the only senior commander up front in the hurly burly of the battlefield. Yet many of the troops still caught up in the battle are Lauer's men: MacKenzie's 395th Combat Team in the woods north of Rocherath; battalions of the 99th Division west of the international highway, around Losheimergraben, drifting into Mürringen. Two companies of 99th Division combat engineers in the Monschauwald. Also, two of Robertson's own battalions (1st and 3rd, 23rd Infantry) are attached to Lauer's division and under the latter's command. Robertson has no authority to order the leaders of these disparate forces to do anything.

How Robertson is to influence this large number of officers and men who are the responsibility of a headquarters now moving to Camp Elsenborn, distant from the scene of battle and in only intermittent control of them by radio and messenger, is another nightmare Robertson has awakened to early Sunday morning. He will have no more communication with Lauer or the 99th Division staff for the rest of bloody Sunday, December 17.

The next day, Monday, December 18, General Gerow, the 5th Corps commander, will finally clarify this ambiguous command situation. As soldiers term it, Lauer will be subordinated to Robertson. The latter will be in charge of all American troops in the cockpit east and south of Elsenborn; General Lauer will organize the new main line of resistance on the Elsenborn high plateau. In this task Lauer will receive no little help from Gerow's staff and liaison officers and from Robertson's officers, as described further on.[*]

---

quoted in Cavanagh, Dauntless, p. 127. Documentation, this volume) Well, this officer was present and in a position to know. However, other testimony points to a most hurried displacement west to the Belgian Army camp, with much material including vehicles left behind and the tactically vital post of Bütgenbach virtually abandoned.

[*] In a report written soon after the battle, General Robertson made a characteristically sober and realistic appraisal of the 99th Division's experience in the borderland forests, December 16-18. "(Their) defensive positions had no depth, and the enemy drove armor and infantry down the roads, isolating groups, which then formed islands of resistance deep in the woods. In these positions, they were preventing the enemy from free use of roads, but nearly all of these groups had lost liberty of action and were...being surrounded and cut to pieces."

General Lauer, as might be expected, was more effusive in his appraisal. "During the 16, 17, and most of the 18th (of) December, the 99th Division carried the full brunt of the entire German attack while stretched out on a twenty-two mile front....It was the 99th Division alone which stopped the German breakthrough and saved the 2nd Division

As the 2nd Division leader prepares to leave his headquarters in Wirtzfeld in his command car to visit the officers who will lead the difficult maneuver, he totals up his assets:

Colonel Boos' 38th Infantry is intact. However, two battalions are far out on the Wahlerscheid salient, ten road miles from Rocherath and seven airline miles from the heights of Elsenborn through wooded hills, over pastures and marshes covered with snow, veined with icy creeks.

The 9th Infantry Regiment, taken down severely by the struggle to overcome the West Wall fortress at the crossroads, has dropped back to the forest southeast of Höfen.

Two of the 2nd Division's 23rd Infantry battalions (1st, 3rd) are assigned to General Lauer's command and are about to do heavy and hazardous duty in the Todeswald and at Hünningen. The third is in the Wirtzfeld defense.

Robertson will soon take in hand MacKenzie's combat team (1st and 2nd battalions, 395th Infantry, and 2nd Battalion, 393rd). He believes he can depend on these riflemen, machine gunners, mortarmen, and armor-fighting infantry to do their duty in the Rocherath-Krinkelt battle. He rates them as 80 percent effective. Although new to the killing grounds, they have done well in supporting the 2nd Division assault on the Wahlerscheid crossroads. However, he has no purchase on the two companies of Lauer's combat engineers somewhere out there in the Monschauwald on the left wing of the 395th. They appear to have been swallowed up in the hilly woods.

Robertson expects his own engineers to play a central role in the gathering campaign for survival. One company will work on the long forest road south from the Wahlerscheid crossroads to Rocherath. They will clear it of slush and boggy places so the howitzers, trucks, tanks and tank destroyers, and walking infantry can keep moving south to the dual towns. They also will do more lethal work: placing explosive mines on the shoulders and road bed, hiding them with snow, brush, logs, tree limbs.

A second company will bend their backs and grind down their heavy equipment logging and relogging the muck and slush of the vital road across the fields and marshes from Krinkelt to Wirtzfeld and beyond to the Elsenborn heights.

The third 2nd Division engineer company has been pummelled and

---

from being cut off, surrounded, and destroyed." General Lauer makes only one reference to the 2nd Division commander in his book(Battle Babies, loc. cit.) on the 99th's campaigns in Western Europe in 1944-45: a footnote on page 63 in which Robertson's name is spelled incorrectly.

scattered by *Kampfgruppe* Peiper at Büllingen. (Volume 1, Narrative V, Part 2) Those who escaped have been ordered to join their comrades in the Wirtzfeld road work, or take up a foxhole in one of the hasty defense lines put down here and there along the south flank.

Robertson also has in hand two companies of tracked, long-gunned tank destroyers (M-10s) and three companies of Sherman (M-4) tanks.

Lauer's two battered regiments (393 and 394) still clinging to the borderland forest line and the Losheimergraben crossroads early Sunday morning must be considered both asset and liability. They have suffered serious losses in men and material: half the fighters gone in the two battalions of Colonel Scott's 393rd Infantry; a third or more in the three battalions of Colonel Riley's 394th. Yet before the battle is over, some of these survivors who escape the forests east of the Elsenborn heights will stand and fight with the 2nd Division men at the dual towns.

On the other side of the ledger, the moving pools of 99th Division stragglers and organized units passing the hastily dug foxholes and machine gun pits of the 2nd Division's infantry battalions will make heartbreaking difficulties for the soldiers manning the dual towns-Wirtzfeld line. In the presence of the specters and shadows in the night and fog do Robertson's fighters shoot or do they wait? Drifting fogs against the grey landscape meld friend and foe in daylight; after dark they become one and can only be identified if challenged and questioned. Adding to the fears and frustrations of the 2nd's infantry are the occasional Skorzeny masquer or a *Landser* with one of the German units attacking wearing bits and pieces of American uniforms they have picked up on the battlefield.

Robertson also weighs his assets against the enemy's up and down the long front east of the Elsenborn high plateau. The scales do not show a favorable balance. Not at all:

—A *Volksgrenadier* division (Kaschner's 326th) about to overwhelm, or so he believes, Americans at Monschau-Mützenich in the north.

—Another (Viebig's 277th) pushing through the woods along the international highway.

—The 12th *Panzer* Division *Hitlerjugend* showing up to join in the mayhem east of the dual towns and beginning to bring its armor to bear in the battle as well.

—A third *Volksgrenadier* division (General Engle's 12th) about to overwhelm the brave 99th men at the Losheimergraben crossroads and already bringing under attack the southern rampart villages of Hünningen and Mürringen flanking the N-32.

—What appears to be a mighty *Panzer* force of the 1st *SS Panzer* Division (*Kampfgruppe* Peiper) even now threatening Robertson's own forward command post at Wirtzfeld.

To the 2nd Division's leaders early on December 17 this enemy threat along the N-32 highway south of Wirtzfeld must be accounted even more menacing than that east and south of the dual towns. It is the "key to the battle in German hands." (Volume 1, Narrative V, Part 3) If *Kampfgruppe* Peiper and the *Fallschirmjäger* storming through the 99th Division's right wing after midnight December 16 should march on Bütgenbach just west of Büllingen on the N-32 then pivot to the north and get behind the Elsenborn heights, it will matter not at all how bravely and doggedly the 2nd Division clings to the dual towns. The American soldiers east of the heights will be trapped.

The town of Bütgenbach, four miles northwest of Büllingen on the N-32, late Sunday morning, December 17, has scarcely any defenders. When Lauer and his staff departed, they took all their division headquarters units with them, leaving only a few lowly staff officers to close out the command post. A mile to the southeast at a farm estate called Domaine Bütgenbach, a few Stuart (light) tanks of the tank battalion working with the 2nd Division stand vigil. Each is armed with a 37mm (diameter) cannon and a .50caliber machine gun. The Stuarts are no match at all for a German *Panzer IV* or *Panther* tank. Later in the morning, a company of twelve 3-inch tank-fighting long guns will deploy in the area. Like the Stuarts, they are vulnerable to infantry assault teams armed with *Panzerfäuste*.

Yet Robertson can not consider trying to extend his line of men and guns west of Wirtzfeld to protect the southern approach to Bütgenbach. The demands upon his fighters elsewhere are too overwhelming. Tactically important though it be, Bütgenbach is well to the south and west of the lifeline road that is Robertson's preoccupation. Still, the gaping underside of the Bütgenbach position can not but be another weight on his mind. The 2nd Division CO hasn't much time this Sunday morning for literary allusions, but he is learning in full measure the meaning of King Claudius' lament that, "when troubles ('sorrows,' actually) come, they come not single spies but in battalions."

At 6:53 a.m. December 17, the telephone rings next to the cot of Colonel Matt Konop, the division headquarters commandant and commander of special troops. Robertson is on the other end of the line. He orders Konop to call out his HQ security force (a platoon) for the last ditch defense of Wirtzfeld. He informs the general that most of these men have been pressed into carrying out the wounded at the Wahlerscheid crossroads killing ground. No matter, says Robertson, "gather everyone and everything you can get your hands on" and put them into the line.

Shortly, Robertson also confers with Brigadier General John H. Hinds, his artillery commander, whose headquarters is a few houses away in Wirtzfeld. Hinds is to organize the foxhole and gun line protecting the village from the south and make certain that communications are in place with 2nd Division howitzers a few miles to the north.

Robertson has ordered the 2nd Battalion of Colonel Lovless' 23rd Infantry (The other two are still attached to Lauer's division.) to march post haste from Elsenborn to Wirtzfeld. But so stretched are the 2nd Division ranks that he decides one of the battalion's three rifle companies must be sent to the dual towns, leaving only two companies—two hundred or so rifle soldiers—to start digging against the expected onslaught of enemy tanks and mechanized infantry from Büllingen.

The pre-dawn telephone call to Konop has energized that officer to engage in a round of telephoning and face-to-face meetings all over Wirtzfeld as he puts together his motley provisional rifle company—orderlies, clerks, typists, military police, supply soldiers, cooks, bakers, etc. They gather all the lethal weapons they can lay their hands on—machine guns, M-1 rifles, carbines, grenades, grenade launchers, bazookas—and start digging holes and pits in the frigid soil around Wirtzfeld. These soldiers are not used to either digging or shooting. But in the 2nd Division, everyone is expected to be on call to fight.

The lieutenant of the 2nd's military police platoon appears with twenty men. Seventeen are his; three are clerks or orderlies. The MPs carry .45caliber automatic pistols; the others carry carbines. Konop wonders what good they will be against *Panzers* and *Panzergrenadiers* armed with machine guns, machine pistols, and automatic rifles, but keeps his own counsel.

General Hinds puts in a call to the CO of the big M-10 tank-destroying machines with their long 3-inch guns that are under control of the 2nd Division. Shortly after dawn, several of them lumber south to Wirtzfeld, elbowing out of the way the traffic streaming west and north from the front. The tank battalion commander whose men and machines are in Robertson's command also will send four of his Shermans.

Hinds instructs some of his artillery commanders to raise teams of two men armed with bazookas and send them immediately by jeep. A half dozen antiaircraft gun wagons, quad four .50caliber machine guns mounted on vehicles, are in the vicinity. Hinds brings them into the hasty defense.

Within a few hours, General Robertson hopes to have soldiers of his 23rd Infantry and Colonel Hirschfelder's 9th Infantry cemented into the Wirtzfeld defense. The scratch force of headquarters men, newly baptized bazookamen from the artillery, and tank-fighting guns will have to hold until then.

Sunday morning, December 17 they are out busily digging holes in the slush-covered fields south of Wirtzfeld and throwing up parapets and stringing wire. They notice silhouettes moving on a fog-covered ridge a half mile to the south. Six *Panzer IV* tanks, and at least as many big halftracked troop carriers each filled with a dozen or more *Panzergrenadiers* of 1st *SS Panzer* Division are crawling up the road from Büllingen and heading straight for them.

The *Panzer IVs* and the eager young *Panzergrenadiers* do not have a pleasant journey to Wirtzfeld. As they emerge from the fog, climbing the rise south of the village, and making the sharp turn toward the odd collection of American power, Hinds' artillery forward observer phones the howitzers to attack the enemy column with overhead fire. Some of the rounds fall short. Two artillerymen in the outpost spotting for the howitzers are wounded. Their switchboard is smashed by a shell.

So traumatized by the shelling is the forward observer lieutenant, he can no longer function and must be relieved by Hinds. The 2nd Division artillery commander now takes charge of the artillery post in front of Wirtzfeld. He sends orders through his radio operator to the fire direction center, calling targets and exhorting his gunners in vivid terms to stop dropping rounds on his position.

As the *Panzers* continue their march up the long slope north of Büllingen, the gunners in the big open turrets of the American M-10s load and fire, sending round after round at the *Panzer* column grinding and lurching up the road. The *Panzer* commanders by turn halt their tanks to strike back, their own long guns spitting forth, aiming on the muzzle blasts of the Americans. The M-10s bear a powerful and accurate gun but offer no overhead protection to their crews. Although none takes a destructive hit, exploding shells hurt individual crew members as the fragments ricochet around the crew compartments and pierce the lightly armored sides.

The probing column of Colonel Peiper's *Kampfgruppe* brings with it too few *Panzers* (six). They are moving into a trap, as well, unable to disperse across the muddy, snow-covered fields, constricted, and confined. And insufficient *Grenadiers* in the troop carriers follow to overrun the M-10s, automatic weapons, and foxhole line manned by Robertson's instant infantry.

A *Panzer IV* takes an armor-piercing round in its guts, smolders a while, spewing grey smoke, then blows up with a roar. No one emerges. A second lurches to a halt, machine guns still running on but now a wounded animal waiting for the end. Several M-10 tank destroyers go after it with explosive shells and their .50caliber machine guns. The *Panzer* is soon burning.

To the *SS* crews of the surviving armored machines, their comrades' distress is simply a reason to fight more determinedly. They keep coming and they keep shooting, with both the big 75mm diameter rifle up front and the two .30mm machine guns, in hull and turret respectively. Gunners riding with the *Panzergrenadiers* also are working machine guns and light cannons mounted on the troop carriers. The instant infantrymen of the American defense are being hurt. A medical officer and his men manning an improvised aid station wonder whether they will be able to find sufficient litter-carrying jeeps or ambulances to move the wounded out of the melee.

Yet the young *SS* soldiers riding the half wheeled, halftracked armored personnel carriers are open to far worse hurt. General Hinds notices the guns of the American antiaircraft crews seem strangely silent. Accustomed to shooting at hostile aircraft, these men, according to Hinds, "hesitated (to open fire) because they could not believe their eyes when they saw Germans so close." They soon get over their amazement, prodded by the general, and add their murderous .50caliber bullet fire to all the rest coming down on the luckless young Germans in the troop carriers.

To add to their terror, the 2nd Division howitzers have the range at last and are dropping round after round of explosive shells on the road where the now disorganized *Panzers* and *Panzergrenadiers* are milling forward, trying to find a soft place in Robertson's line that they can drive through. Two more *Panzer IVs* go up, dreadfully, blazing away in the grey morning fog like isolated sacrificial pyres out on a moor, disgorging an occasional apparition, a black-clad crewman.

After clearing out of the dual towns and vicinity the night of December 16-17, the 99th Division's medium howitzer battalion displaced to Wirtzfeld. (Narrative VI, Part 1) When the fight south of the village boils up after daylight, the battalion commander orders one of his big guns to go into firing position on the south side and add its considerable shell power to the ordnance being hurled at the little *SS Kampfgruppe*. After a harrowing journey over slick roads, the crew and their big gun arrive. They adjust for direct firing at the *Panzers*, which are in clear sight a third of a mile away, and let fly several rounds only to be informed the tanks they are shooting at already have been put out of action. It is a grievous disappointment to the gun crew.

In spite of the death of most of their *Panzers*, the *Panzergrenadiers* quit their vehicles, form skirmish lines, and try to make a fight of it. They are beset from all directions by bullet and shell. Some try to surrender, not always successfully. (If the Americans don't shoot them down, their own NCOs may.) Fearful confusion engulfs the young soldiers. They see their end in the bloody, mangled bodies of their comrades. The two *Panzer IVs* still up and moving and the troop carriers make a run for it back down the slope. The *Panzergrenadiers* still on their feet fade into the fog.

Hinds sums it up in laconic military style: "The soft ground made it difficult for the German tanks to leave the roads with the result that our tank destroyers and artillery destroyed enough of them to block the roads. The .50caliber multiple mounts (AAA guns) took care of the German infantry, which followed the tanks in open halftracks."

Two companies of the 23rd Infantry's 2nd Battalion have arrived. They are digging the mandatory holes and dugouts in the cold, mucky ground to heavy up the provisional infantry line. Their introduction to the Wirtzfeld front comes by way of a short but lethal flurry of artillery falls, enemy or American. This kills a few of them and wounds more for a quick loss of twenty men, half of one rifle platoon.

Some of these soldiers also are caught up in the exchange of shots between the Wirtzfeld "provisionals" and the *Leibstandarte* armor and infantry patrol. A platoon of the 2nd Battalion infantry riding Sherman tanks and accompanied by three of the M-10 tank destroyers rushing to the Wirtzfeld battleground come upon a *Panzer IV*, an armored car, and a troop carrier full of *Panzergrenadiers*. The tank-riding infantry leap to the ground and watch from ditches, gullies, and shell holes, as the three American destroyers with their long 3-inch guns work over the German armor. Within minutes the armored car is a burning wreck, the *Panzer IV* has been disabled and is smoldering, and the *Panzergrenadiers* are fleeing for their lives or giving up.

This little war with the enemy concluded, the American tankers find themselves in one with their friends. The landscape early Sunday morning around Wirtzfeld is grey and suffused with fog, ideal for mistakes to be made. A Sherman resembles the *Panzer IV* in size if not shape and armament. The four Shermans clank and grind along a muddy, narrow farm road from the northeast into the space being defended by the scratch force of soldiers and machines assembled in front of Wirtzfeld.

The American antiaircraft gunners are spooked. They start shooting at the Shermans, which retaliate with their 75mm rifles and machine guns. A few of the high explosive shells slam against trees near some tank destroyer crews. The shell fragments hit several men. When 2nd

Division soldiers run over to help, the machine gunners in the four American tanks shoot at them too. A cease fire comes quickly when both sides realize whom they have been trying to kill. But men have been hurt and some die.

Part 3: Stonewall's Spirit Moves

Preoccupied this early Sunday morning with trying to put in place the many building blocks of his massive escape plan, General Robertson can give only passing attention to the fierce little battle taking place not far from his command post. His lieutenants—Konop, Hinds, and the others—and the men in the holes and at the guns of the fighting machines will do what he has asked of them he has no doubt.

The 2nd Division commander assumes these *Panzers* and *Panzer* infantry are merely the prologue to what will be a huge drama of blood and fire as *Leibstandarte Adolph Hitler* (1st *SS*) tries to march north and west to capture Bütgenbach and Elsenborn, linch pins of U.S. 5th Corps' gathering defense along the heights. Robertson is receiving accumulating intelligence of the power that has gathered in Büllingen and along the roads to the southeast of it. He believes this force will try to strike through his improvised defenses in front of Wirtzfeld to seize the Elsenborn heights. He has done what he can to shore up his scratched-together force of men, armor, and guns at Wirtzfeld. All else in his opinion is pointless fret and wasted spirit.

Robertson and Zwicker have worked out who the leaders of the 2nd Division command group will be that the general expects to put together and manage the many crucial elements of his plan of defense, withdrawal, and re-establishment on the Elsenborn heights.

—Colonel P. G. Ginder, a spare regimental commander assigned to the 2nd, will be responsible for hardening the defense south of Wirtzfeld, then leading all men there to Berg and Nidrum a few miles to the west when the battlefield situation permits.

—Hirschfelder will direct the march south out of the Monschauwald of his 9th Regiment men and those of the 38th Regiment, as well as the many guns and armored and other machines still intermingled with them.

—Brigadier General John H. Stokes, Robertson's assistant division commander, will direct the defense of the dual towns. His orders are to stop *Hitlerjugend* long enough for the withdrawal to be carried off.

—Colonel Jay Lovless, whose 23rd Infantry is scattered far and wide on and below the Elsenborn heights, will organize the 2nd Division's new main line of resistance in front of Berg, south of Elsenborn.

The 2nd Division commander's task this chaotic Sunday morning, December 17, is to insure these officers know what to do and get about the business of doing it.

Before Robertson leaves Wirtzfeld he tells Konop and Zwicker to start moving his command post back to Camp Elsenborn that afternoon, barring unforeseen disasters.

He receives a message that the 394th Infantry (99th Division) command post at Mürringen and his own 2nd Battalion, 23rd Infantry (Hightower), which is attached, are being struck by a large force of enemy infantry that has armored assault guns working with them. (Volume 1, Narrative V, Part 5) Robertson sends a message to his assistant commander, Stokes. He wants the 38th Infantry reserve—the 3rd Battalion whose commander is Lieutenant Colonel Olinto Barsanti—to take a position on the south side of Krinkelt to guard against a German attempt to push north from Mürringen.

Therefore, as he starts on his journey north, Robertson must face the reality that he may be able to allocate only two battalions of Colonel Francis Boos' 38th Infantry to the east side of Rocherath-Krinkelt.

The 2nd Division commander intends to spend the remainder of daylight December 17 driving the lifeline road connecting Wirtzfeld with the dual towns and the latter with Wahlerscheid crossroads, counseling with his captains, exhorting his men. As a Virginian intent on soldiering from his early days, he no doubt has spent much time studying the tactics, leadership methods, and battlefield practices of Thomas (Stonewall) Jackson, the fearsome, bible-quoting, right hand of Robert E. Lee.

Jackson, who died in 1863 as a result of a wound at the battle of Chancellorsville, believed in riding into the smoke and fire of battle, showing himself, and making his voice heard by officers and men alike. If he was going to ask men to die, he would show them by deed he was willing to die alongside of them. God was with him, he believed, and would not desert him or his troops. (He was wrong on both counts, but this in no way diminished the legend he left behind.) Robertson resembles Jackson not at all with one exception: He shares with the Confederate general the spirit of how a field commander should behave in a crucial engagement. And he proceeds to behave just so.

About 9 a.m., with the detritus of the battle south of Wirtzfeld still in the air (odd bursts of machine gun fire, artillery shells and rockets falling about, nervous friendly troops taking pot shots at unfamiliar vehicles), the 2nd Division commander climbs into his command car and moves east along the road to the dual towns. He passes teams of his "A" Company engineers and their groaning trucks and bulldozers. The logs and timbers they are putting down keep sinking into the two or three feet of soupy, snowy muck that they work in and need to be topped and topped again.

Robertson's vehicle receives some priority, as might be expected, both along the road and driving through the dual towns. The scene there is chaotic. The infantry line three miles to the east is disintegrating. Convoys of the 99th Division support and supply platoons and companies, howitzer batteries ordered to displace, antiaircraft gun wagons and their support and service vehicles, jeep-bearing litters and ambulances over-loaded with wounded—all and more are grinding through the streets, milling about in confusion, or stalled along squares and in farm yards. Some of the officers managing the marchers in this bizarre parade are hunting for someone to tell them what to do, where to go. All the while General Viebig's 277 *VGD* artillery gunners and those of 12th *SS Panzer* Division and 1st *SS Panzer* Corps and a *Werfer* brigade are putting down harassing fire on the two towns, adding to the chaos and dread.

Rocherath and Krinkelt are the location of important supply and command facilities for the 99th Division infantry and artillery. They are heavy with trucks and jeeps. Later in the day, the troops manning these facilities will try to merge their vehicles into the westward moving traffic as their front line companies withdraw from the woods along the international highway. However, when Robertson passes through at midmorning, they remain mostly in place, but stressed and confused, burning papers they don't want the Germans to find, loading for departure at any moment.

The general can waste little time on the condition of traffic and the random confusion in Krinkelt and Rocherath. His immediate destinations are the headquarters of the three regiments in the Monschauwald to the north that he is depending on to keep open the escape route and buy time for the Elsenborn defenses to solidify. At 10:30 a.m. his command car stops in front of Colonel Hirschfelder's 9th Regiment command post. It is in a stone house on the northern edge of Rocherath hard by the road to Wahlerscheid crossroads.

The colonel is in agony due to the pleurisy burning around his ribs. Nevertheless he stands tall in the presence of his commanding officer as they discuss in a low key, matter-of-fact manner the hazardous maneuver he must lead: withdrawing the two 2nd Division infantry regiments and all their impedimenta in the teeth of an enemy marching against them. Robertson can see that the tough old soldier is on his feet and ready and able to essay his critical command task in the Monschau woods, the pain be damned.

Departing Colonel Hirschfelder's CP about 11 a.m., Robertson's vehicle proceeds to weave its way in and out of the columns of trucks and soldiers on foot. The general, sometimes standing, sometimes sitting, exhorts the drivers and men trudging in the snow and muck alongside to keep up the pace. Now and then, he will leave the jeep to engage one of his battalion, company, or armored unit commanders, always repeating how important their assignment is, what it means to the American troops in the woods and the dual towns and beyond.

The road from Wahlerscheid crossroads to Rocherath is narrow, ill-surfaced, hemmed in on both sides most of the way by the tall, black evergreens now thick with clouds of snow. Along this road, violent little storms of artillery and rocket fire come down at random, exploding in the trees and on the road, forcing riders to leap from their vehicles and walking soldiers to make themselves small in the snow and muck.

Robertson can't make it easier or less harmful for any of them. But his presence among them impresses even the most hapless and forlorn soldier: an unimposing officer, wearing round, steel Army-issue spectacles on his undistinguished features, a bulky officer's trench coat, ugly Shoepacs on his feet, mud splattered, whipped by the winds, endangered by the exploding shells and rockets—one with all of them in this.

No task is beneath Robertson if it will keep the columns moving, maintain the schedule, expedite building the Rocherath-Krinkelt defense. A supply sergeant with "K" Company of the 38th Regiment recalls seeing the general along the Wahlerscheid road, standing on the center line, moving traffic along, telling drivers where to deliver their loads of troops, spare ammunition, heavy weapons, and what to do when they arrive there.

The captain of "L" Company, 23rd Infantry, whose men have escaped the disaster inflicted on the other two companies in the Todeswald (Volume 1, Narrative V, Part 4), leads his men up to the edge of Krinkelt where his scouts encounter Robertson. "Our first friendly contact since we left the woods," remembered the captain. He tells the captain he is herewith attaching "L" Company to Boos' regiment for the defense of the dual towns, orders the captain to report to Boos' command post, and collars a nearby 38th Infantryman to lead the way.

Along the road, the 2nd Division CO comes across an officer of an antiaircraft unit, who later recounted his impressions. "He wanted to know the type of guns we had, number of men, equipment, morale, etc. and where he could reach me. Talking to General Robertson that afternoon was a calming inspiration." (sic)

In Krinkelt he visits his second in command, General Stokes, responsible for the defense of the dual towns. It is afternoon with the shadows of the winter day already lengthening, the clouds thickening, and the mist turning to a nasty, cold rain. It is at Stokes' command center, we can assume, that Robertson receives the first big good news since the *Wehrmacht* struck *Null Tag* morning. He learns the 26th Regiment of the Spartan U.S. 1st Infantry Division has arrived in Camp Elsenborn, checked in with General Lauer, and been despatched to the hills south of Bütgenbach astride the N-32.

To increase the general's momentary satisfaction, the 16th Infantry of this division has been ordered to extend the 5th Corps' defense line west to Waimes, Belgium, and should start arriving within three or four hours. Two shell-backed, steel-fanged regiments to anchor the southern flank of the Elsenborn heights position of the Americans if, that is, they can be emplaced in time for the inevitable enemy assaults. The nagging fear at the back of Robertson's mind all the while he has been going about his business this day that this flank is wide open is eased somewhat.

He also is informed that the fearsome armored *Kampfgruppe* Peiper whose combat patrol attacked his command post shortly after dawn that day at Wirtzfeld has yet to open a drive in a northwest direction (through Wirtzfeld to the Elsenborn plateau), as he and all his officers expected. And mirabile dictu the *Kampfgruppe* may be dragging its long armored anaconda of a body toward the southwest instead.

Robertson leaves Stokes' CP and once again is on the road to make sure the last of the 9th Regiment infantrymen are moving rapidly south, and Colonel Boos' two 38th Regiment battalions (1st, 2nd) have been able to shake loose of the enemy patrols slipping out of the forests east of the West Wall to harass them and also are moving rapidly toward Rocherath. The 2nd Division commander also intends to find Colonel MacKenzie's 395th Combat Team, 99th Division, command post and make certain he understands how vital it is to protect the northern flank of the 38th Infantry. It is late afternoon. Robertson has had scarcely more than three hours sleep since dawn *Null Tag*, thirty-three hours previous.

As his jeep moves along the streets of Krinkelt and adjoining Rocherath on the north, it moves through a landscape of chaos and disorder more disturbing to the general than that of a few hours before when he first drove through the two towns. The enemy's pre-assault barrage is in full cry. Artillery shells explode, rockets crash, and the high-velocity *PAK* (antitank) guns of the Germans send 75 and 88mm rounds streaking in. Men are shouting directions and orders above the din or crying for help. All is obscured by the smoke of exploding ordnance and burning buildings.

From time to time as Robertson's command car moves north past the Rocherath Barracks toward Wahlerscheid crossroads, the grey and lowering sky will whistle and screech. The eerie noise is followed by frightening explosions in the woods flanking the road. Robertson and his two-man crew (driver, radio man) seem impervious to the danger. So seem most of the drivers and walkers going south. They flatten themselves or take shelter next to a vehicle until the sound and smoke of the concussion blow off, then stoically, doggedly go back to it, plodding in the slush to where they know not.

Robertson finds MacKenzie in a hunting lodge in the forest east of the road from Rocherath. He is impressed by the colonel, a tall Scot with an unhandsome face who shows a willingness to do what he can to help the 2nd Division troops defend the dual towns.

Satisfied with the hasty meeting that winter afternoon, Robertson also is shocked by some news MacKenzie gives him. The colonel's radio operators are monitoring transmissions on the 99th Division radio net. He has learned thereby that the fall-back defense line in the woods east of Rocherath at the Jans Bach (creek) has collapsed. (Volume 1, Narrative V, Part 4) The survivors of the 393rd Infantry's 3rd Battalion and the 23rd Infantry's 3rd Battalion are moving back to Rocherath in some disorder pursued by swarms of *Panzergrenadiers* and *Jagdpanzers*.

No icy night falling upon MacKenzie's command post along the forest road could have chilled Robertson's blood more swiftly than this news. He gambled that the American position astride the forest road would stand at least until Colonel Boos' 1st and 2nd battalions and armor were in place and ready. Now, it seems, this crucial gatepost to the dual towns is gaping wide. Yet Boos' riflemen are still several miles up the Wahlerscheid road to the north. Their rear guard has only just shaken free of enemy patrols lunging at them from the woods and broken emplacements of the West Wall. Robertson bids the 395th Infantry colonel a hasty goodby and good luck. He orders his driver to point the car south again to the dual towns and dodge through the parade of men and vehicles until told to stop.

Part 4: A Race to the Panzer Line

They soon come upon the tail of the 9th Infantry's 3rd Battalion, which consists of "K" Company and a platoon of machine gunners, the

rear guard of the column, destined to follow the rest of its battalion
already several miles to the south to buttress the Wirtzfeld defense line.
Robertson is about to give them another destiny. He tells his driver to
stop and hunts down the "K" Company captain. The general can spend
little time informing the young, respectful, but confused company
commander of his mission and his fate. Robertson points out some
coordinates on his map where he wants "K" Company to go. Here is
located a barren crossroads the locals call Lausdell where stand a few
forlorn farm buildings on a low hill a thousand yards east of Rocherath.

The general returns to his vehicle and leads the captain and his little
headquarters group to the position, which overlooks the road coming
west from the Krinkelterwald. Already in the gathering gloom friendly
soldiers, some without weapons, can be seen running across the fields
headed willy-nilly for Rocherath, obviously pursued by some frightful
thing. Robertson promises to send the captain reinforcements. The
captain turns to organizing his men for their ordeal, while Robertson
goes hunting down more reinforcements, as he promised. He is like a
debtor beset by creditors, each threatening ruin unless paid in full. Yet
he does not possess the assets to buy off even one who presses his case
hard enough:

To divert men and guns from Barsanti's line (3rd Battalion-38th) on
the south edge of Krinkelt may mean a collapse there if the Germans
strike in force from Mürringen.

To message Colonel Ginder at Wirtzfeld to pull troops there and
send them running the mile east to the dual towns may open that
vulnerability wide.

To order Colonel Boos to rejuggle his two 38th Infantry battalions
coming down from the Wahlerscheid crossroads in order to divert some
of this power to the Lausdell sector may render it impossible for him
to establish an in-depth defense inside the dual towns.

To order Colonel MacKenzie to move a battalion or more of his
99th Division infantry down the Wahlerscheid road to Lausdell would
endanger the left (north) flank of General Stokes' defense.

As the indefatigable 2nd Division leader moves rapidly around the
assembling battleground in the dimming light of late Sunday afternoon,
December 17, amid the chaos, he is doing sums of life and death,
survival and destruction, what combinations of soldier sacrifice and in
what order will produce salvation for the American side.

Robertson proceeds to honor his pledge to the lonely "K" Company
captain and his men just outside Rocherath on the Wahlerscheid road.
He stops the trucks of the 9th Infantry, 3rd Battalion Ammunition and
Pioneer Platoon. The men sit shivering, tired, cold, hungry, and more

than a little scared and confused.

No matter. Robertson must now deliver their fates to God. He explains to the lieutenant in charge what he wants: His men are to leave their trucks, march cross country east a mile or so to the Lausdell position. There they will report to the "K" Company captain and do what he tells them to buttress his little force. The A/P Platoon is armed with M-1 rifles, a few tommy guns and grease guns (These are the American equivalent, if they can be so called, of the Germans' *Machinenpistole.*), a few bazookas and jeeps equipped with machine guns. They set out, fearful, resigned, and cursing their lot.

This deed done, Robertson climbs into his car once again and once again directs his driver to go north on the road to Wahlerscheid, which he just came down less than an hour before. He is hunting more men to reinforce "K" Company. Two miles north of Rocherath, he encounters a column of infantry moving rapidly south. It is the 1st Battalion of the 9th Infantry, commanded by a twenty-eight year old lieutenant colonel named William D. McKinley, a descendent (and namesake) of the twenty-fifth president of the U.S. The 1st also happens to be one of the battalions that took part in the brutal, bloody attack at Wahlerscheid a few days previous. (Volume 1, Narrative I) Because of a delay in getting free of the German patrols in the forest, McKinley's men are only now on the road south, several hours behind the march schedule of their regiment.

Robertson has not recorded his feelings that grey afternoon in the snowy forest as he realizes it is McKinley's already severely punished battalion he will use as a stop gap against the enemy armor and infantry east of Rocherath. He has no choice. McKinley's men are in hand on the scene. They must be used to allow the 38th Infantry sufficient time to come into the dual towns and get their guns and armor in position to block *Hitlerjugend*. (Soldiers who must send other soldiers to their deaths do not have the luxury of "feelings.")

He confers with McKinley, his captains and lieutenants, drawing them around him alongside the road. The riflemen, machine gunners, mortarmen and other soldiers of the battalion wait in the slush under the cold drizzle. They smoke. They eat the last crumbs of some boxed ration preserved from the day before yesterday. They listen to the ominous war sounds of the gathering night beyond the already dark forest.

Nearby are some trucks belonging to MacKenzie's 395th Infantry. Robertson confiscates these to move McKinley's troops. All climb aboard, and the parade, led by Robertson in his jeep, moves into Rocherath, then east along the road to Lausdell. Here they stop, and

Robertson gives McKinley final instructions.

The young lieutenant colonel is a West Point-trained professional soldier schooled in the Normandy, Brittany, and Wahlerscheid blood letting. The vicissitudes, unfairness, and gross oppressions of the battlefield are givens with him. Orders are to be obeyed and missions accomplished regardless of what went before or what impediments now lie in the way. But he is also a compassionate man, who loves his soldiers, offers up his flesh to the guns with them, and tries to make the miseries and terrors they face bearable when this is possible, which in the Old Army 2nd Infantry Division it often is not.

He is now duty bound to order these men of the 1st Battalion, who have survived the mayhem and gross miseries of trying to get through the Wahlerscheid forts, to take up positions in an unfamiliar place and combat an enemy of unknown power and dimension. Five days before, at the start of the offensive in the Monschauwald to breach the West Wall, McKinley commanded 38 officers and 678 men in his rifle, machine gun, mortar, pioneer, and tank-fighting formations. As they leave the 395th Infantry trucks and start for Lausdell, he commands 22 officers and 387 men. The difference between the first numbers and the second is the result of the deaths, wounds, frozen feet, and exhaustions the battalion endured at the pillbox line in the woods.

As they move into the fields covered with patches of snow at the northeastern edge of Rocherath, neither McKinley nor his soldiers know the size, kind, or intentions of the enemy forces in the forest to the east. They are to hold at Lausdell against whatever enemy power emerges along the road from the Krinkelterwald until receiving an order to withdraw. Nothing more—nothing less.

Later McKinley's aides will write, "Upon arrival at (Lausdell) road junction, the full meaning of (our mission) became clear.... 'K' Company, a section of machine guns from 'M' Company, and a thirty-man group from Headquarters Company of the 9th Regiment...were digging in. Streams of men and vehicles were pouring down the forest roads through the junction in wild confusion and disorder...the stragglers echoed each other with remarks that their units had been surrounded and annihilated. One of our own (2nd Division) battalions from the 23rd Infantry (3rd Battalion) had also been engulfed..."

McKinley's soldiers have experienced the death and suffering of their comrades for nearly a week in a brutal battle. They now go to work digging in the earth and emplacing their guns as night falls December 17 because their chief, McKinley, orders them to. They are angry, cursing their fate and the soldiers going by who, they believe, have been unable to stand up to some Germans in their first fight.

McKinley's men, of course, can not know what has happened in the past thirty-four hours in that shadowy, fog-obscured woods off to the east: First, the massive bombardment of the 3rd Battalion (393rd Infantry) at dawn on *Null Tag*; then the confused fighting up and down the dark corridors under the fir trees, the battalion's rifle platoons outnumbered and cut into small hedgehogs of resistance; finally, the appearance of the *Jagdpanzers* to resolve matters, their machine guns and long, high-velocity rifles spraying bullets and hot steel all round. (Volume 1, Narrative III)

McKinley places two of his companies, "A" and "B" on the Lausdell defense line to integrate them and their guns with those of "K" Company busily digging and timbering (to the extent they can find stray timbers). The diggers use the soldier's entrenching tool (a kind of midget shovel that folds at the handle) and real shovels brought with them or found at one of or another of the abandoned 99th Division artillery emplacements in the area. They also make good use of these dugouts, pits, foxholes.

McKinley locates his command post in an abandoned log bunker nine hundred feet north and west of Lausdell crossroads where the riflemen are making their foxholes behind hedges bordering the farm fields. Nearby in another abandoned, logged-over digging is his artillery liaison officer, who is busy trying to make his SCR610 (radio) function. McKinley places his "C" Company nearby as a reserve. "C" has been reduced to little more than a platoon of thirty-six riflemen by the carnage at Wahlerscheid, but this is all he has for a reserve. A few M-10 armored and tracked 3-inch (diameter) guns have come up. He locates them on a rise commanding the road leading to Rocherath. He also emplaces his heavy .30caliber machine guns on slightly elevated places to cover the roads and paths across the fields. His battalion wire section men work like ants in a colony, running telephone lines back and forth.

General Robertson has instructed McKinley to gather up the 393rd and 23rd regiment soldiers passing by as they leave their last-gasp struggle in the woods. The young lieutenant colonel and his officers find this difficult. Few are coming back in organized groups. Even a full squad (twelve) of soldiers armed and under command of a noncommissioned officer is seldom seen. The 3rd Battalion of 393rd Regiment has been ripped badly, many of its officers and NCOs killed, captured, or missing, leaving the surviving soldiers leaderless. Colonel Tuttle's 3rd Battalion, 23rd Regiment has lost half of two companies and the third has struck for Rocherath on its own. All in all, McKinley and his valiants can not look to these tired, hungry, and battle-weary soldiers for reinforcement. Few are willing to stand and grapple once again with the beast that has just mauled them in the woods. (And only those who were in their boots that awful Sunday long ago may judge them for that.)

The dirty, yellowish, winter twilight has thickened into black night across the fields and marshes east of Rocherath as McKinley meets one last time with his captains in his log bunker to go over all their hasty preparations: machine guns in place; riflemen positioned to screen their automatic weapons and protect each other; the forest road from the east, cart tracks, and paths down the slope in front of them covered by their gun muzzles; light and heavy mortars in place and ready to work with the rifles; communication wire laid; ammunition by the guns; antitank rocket launchers (bazookas) distributed; artillery fires plotted to the captains' satisfaction.

It is a remarkable accomplishment this tired, sorely tried battalion of infantry at half strength has achieved in a few hours in a hostile and unfamiliar environment. After McKinley dismisses his captains, they are scarcely back with their companies for fifteen minutes (about 6:30 p.m., December 17) when *Hitlerjugend's* power starts rolling upon them in the foggy dark.

While McKinley's battalion is working to put in its defensive line at Lausdell, the two battalions of Colonel Boos' 38th Infantry selected by Robertson to be the hard armature of the Rocherath-Krinkelt defense are struggling to leave the Monschauwald and move south to the dual towns. Lieutenant Colonel Frank T. Mildren's 1st Battalion is in the lead; Lieutenant Colonel Jack Norris' 2nd Battalion is following. Its "E" Company acts as a rear guard to keep the enemy infantry patrols coming out of the West Wall from getting on the flanks of the march column and perhaps cutting it in two or three pieces.*

Each of the two 38th Regiment battalions have sectors on the east side of the two towns that they will be responsible for defending. Both commanders have been told by Boos of the urgency of their missions. Neither have a clear idea of the details: The size and kind of enemy they face. How they are to be resupplied. How they are to feed their men. How long the siege will last before they are to go west to the Elsenborn heights if, in fact, they are to go west.

---

* Norris' operations officer recalled that "G" Company pulled (as soldiers express it) the rear guard detail. The records indicate otherwise. However, given the wild and hazardous situation, riflemen of several different companies might have been bringing up the rear. They were aided immensely by the presence of tanks.

Both battalions are behind schedule in moving into the towns. Shortly after noon, the rear guard (Company "E") is struck in the forest just south of the Wahlerscheid crossroads by a large German patrol probing south (probably from General Kaschner's 326th *Volksgrenadiers*). A vicious little battle erupts, with "E" Company riflemen concealed by trees, picking off the *VG* soldiers one by one. More *Grenadiers* come up. By 1:30 they have pushed into the company's hasty picket line. Rapid shooting and bombing by the light (60mm) mortars drive them off, finally. But "E" Company has let blood, is disorganized momentarily, and delayed in moving south.

Mildren's 1st Battalion begins moving at 3:00 p.m., the colonel and his headquarters people and one rifle company in the lead walking and riding trucks and jeeps. At Rocherather Baracken (barracks), Mildren encounters the 38th Infantry's executive officer, who tells him where to put his men and guns: along a wide defensive arch east and northeast of the southernmost town, Krinkelt, to tie in with Colonel Barsanti's 3rd Battalion on the right and Norris' men on the left, west of McKinley's battalion.

Mildren's HQ party and "A" Company move on. As their two following rifle companies ("B" and "C") pass over the road, off to the east some 1st *SS Panzer* Corps rocket men have maneuvered their machines with the big tubes loaded with blunt-nosed rockets into position. They let fly with a roar of fire and the wild moaning characteristic of these death machines in action. The rockets descend with a rush on the crossroads at Rocherath Baracken just as Mildren's soldiers are passing by. The fiery explosions and jagged pieces of hot metal spread death and awful wounds in "C" Company and among some of the "D" Company mortar crews, who are trudging along with the riflemen, carrying their heavy tubes, bipods, and base plates.

Medical corpsmen in the march set to, administering first aid to the dead and dying and finding litter bearers to carry them into Rocherath, where they hope to find a functioning battalion (medical) aid station. Survivors of the rocketing find their way into Rocherath. They are spread hither and yon and are finally incorporated into Norris' 2nd Battalion as it enters the town from the north. The disaster at the Baracken has taken away almost a quarter of Mildren's power.

Mercifully, Norris' men experience no such destruction from the air as does the 1st Battalion. They reach their destination by 7:00 p.m. However, it has been a frightening and miserable journey in the dark for the riders and walkers: the tall trees overhead, dripping gobs of snow; cat eye lights of vehicles winking in the darkness; off to the south, buildings already on fire in Rocherath; and bullet fire, including streams of tracers, glowing like giant fireflies as they arc across the roads and streets, houses and barns that the battalion will use to build their hasty positions. The battle has started, but these principal players are yet observers only. "There was an eerie sense of an enemy moving in on three sides," a battalion historian wrote about the scene.

The three battalions of MacKenzie's 395th Combat Team, after dark are moving in columns through the opaque woods north of Rocherath. Their officers try to keep companies and platoons together in some kind of order according to some kind of plan. MacKenzie wants the 2nd Battalion (393rd Infantry) to occupy a low ridge line about a mile northeast of Rocherath overlooking the Lausdell cockpit. His 1st Battalion (395th) will hold the road between Wahlerscheid and Rocherath down which all the 2nd Division traffic has moved that day. His 2nd Battalion (395th) will occupy the woods between the other two battalions.

The mission seems possible, at least against a comparable number of enemy foot soldiers. But MacKenzie's power is plagued by serious problems: It has been placed under Boos' command in Rocherath; yet Lauer's 99th Division headquarters in Camp Elsenborn is operating on the assumption the 395th RCT is still taking orders from them. His officers are befuddled by the Rocheratherwald, with its deep recesses of snowy woods, dark even in daylight, plunging hillsides, and marshy ravines, where hunters' trails, fire breaks and logging roads may simply peter out in the forest yet are the only means of travel. They have no way of knowing the strength or intentions of the Germans who are in the forest also, prowling about, shooting and making noise. And to add to it all, their men are low on ammunition, having discarded some of it to lighten their loads.

The day before, as the 277th *Volksgrenadiers* pressed hard upon Lieutenant Colonel Allen's 3rd Battalion, 393rd Infantry in the Todeswald northwest of the international highway, General Lauer sent two companies of his combat engineers up the forest paths on their left (north) flank to give some protection.

In the confusion that followed the early German attacks, the engineers, dug in and ready for action far to the east, are forgotten. They have not been able to find friendly troops to work with. They have lost communication with 99th Division headquarters to the west. "For two days and two nights, we sat on the side of a hill waiting for an attack. We could hear fighting on both sides of us and our rear and we couldn't figure out what was going on," one of the engineers wrote afterward.

Finally, their battalion commander orders them out of the woods.

It is a welcome but not easy command to obey. They stumble through the endless stands of conifers toward a valley below the Elsenborn plateau that will take them to their base. On the way they are shot at by infiltrating Germans and by Americans mistaking them for Germans, lose their way, become separated. A few join up with MacKenzie's men.

Robertson stays in the dual towns Sunday afternoon, December 17 long enough to assure himself that Boos' two battalions are clearing the Monschauwald and moving into their positions and sufficient American armor has come down from the woods and east from Wirtzfeld to harden the position. He also is adamant in insisting that the 2nd Division artillery and that of 5th Corps working with it be prepared to deliver a hecatomb of explosives on the German attackers. And he has discussed with both Stokes and Boos and the armor captains means of supplying ammunition and food to their fighters.

How serious a problem will be treating and removing American wounded none can predict; all know it will be pretty dreadful. The regiment's doctors and their helpers will simply have to cope.

At dark Robertson's little team—the general, his driver, his radio operator—move west out of Krinkelt, past the busy 2nd Division engineers slaving away on the soupy swales of the road to Wirtzfeld and Elsenborn, weaving in and out of the bulky vehicles pushing and shoving down the road. They drive into Wirtzfeld, which they departed nearly eight hours before.

The grim determination of the early morning round his command post has abated. A battalion of infantry and two companies of wheeled tank destroyer guns and antiaircraft weapons wagons are in position around the village. And it appears the German high command does not intend to send against them the fifteen-mile-long anaconda of armor and troop carriers bearing armed-to-the-eyes young SS infantry that overwhelmed Büllingen at dawn that morning.

The departure schedule of 2nd Division headquarters that Robertson established is being adhered to, in spite of the sporadic artillery fire and aerial bombing endured by the soldiers at Wirtzfeld throughout the day and the traffic cluttering the miserable slush-filled cart tracks and paths up the long rise to Elsenborn. The general arrives about 7:00 p.m. Sunday night at the Belgian Army building at Camp Elsenborn where his relocated headquarters is being put together. He finds the switchboard up and running and puts through a call to his chief, General Gerow, at Eupen. The two officers review dangers and options. Robertson later summarized his side of the conversation:

"I told (General Gerow) the only practicable solution was to attempt to stabilize on the line which I was then occupying (i.e. Wahlerscheid-Rocherath-Krinkelt-Wirtzfeld). There were a number of units in advance of this line, which had been fighting all day long (the 17th) and whose location and situation was undetermined. I discussed the situation...and arrived at the following decision: We would hold and fight on the position that I had designated. All units in advance of this line would be withdrawn through (it), reorganized and sent to the rear for (use) as reserves."

Around midnight, December 17, Robertson meets at Camp Elsenborn with the 99th's General Lauer and Colonel Clarence E. Beck, operations officer of the U.S. 1st Infantry Division. His summary of the meeting in matter-of-fact soldier's prose cannot convey the emotions, tension, uncertainties that must have been bubbling away behind all their soldierly facades:

Lauer, the flamboyant, proud 99th Division leader who has tried to cope as elements of six German divisions* battered at his men, has no certainty that his division still exists, yet maintains his usual attitude of bluff optimism and aggressiveness.

The stoic, professional Robertson whose fate it is to try to save tens of thousands of embattled men and get them back to build a new defense line that will decide the survival of 5th Corps and probably 1st Army.

The cool, experienced Beck, who refuses to believe things are so bad the 1st Division can not set them right.

Robertson briefly noted the results, "It was generally agreed...that rather than attempt any immediate withdrawal...the course of action I directed was all that was possible under the conditions..."

Nevertheless, and in spite of Lauer's optimism, Robertson must face up to the harsh realities of the battlefield. Although MacKenzie's men north of Rocherath can play a part in the defense of the dual towns, the survivors of Lauer's other battalions will need to be relieved long enough to reorganize, rearm, and recover their balance.

There is some evidence General Lauer does not agree. The following morning (December 18) his headquarters will radio to Colonel Riley, commander of the 394th Infantry, that he is to move his regiment to a position south of Krinkelt, join with Colonel Scott's 1st and 3rd battalions (393rd Infantry), and coordinate the defense of the town with Colonel Boos. They are not to withdraw to the Elsenborn heights. This message will be somewhat late in coming: What remains of Riley's

---

* 1st and 2nd *SS Panzer*; 3rd *Fallschirmjäger*; 326th, 277th, 12th *Volksgrenadier*.

power will already be well on their way west by then, well past Krinkelt, in fact. And Scott's two battalions will be scattered far and wide not only by the fighting in the Todeswald but also by the grim misfortunes of the journey west to the plateau. (Volume 1, Narrative V)

Bloody Sunday for General Robertson has been a whirlwind of action under fire surrounded by the mud soldiers of his division such as few general officers ever experience. The day has brought him some sorrows: The grim necessity of pushing McKinley's young heroes once more into a place some will never leave alive. The attrition in his camp caused by the incessant German shelling, rocketing, and bombing. The disintegration of the barrier line west of the international highway under the swarming German tide of armor and men. It also has brought him some joys that for his cause are more decisive:

—The Wirtzfeld's garrisons' repelling the *SS* armored combat patrol.

—Movement of *Kampfgruppe* Peiper off to the southwest away from his front.

—Arrival at Bütgenbach of General Huebner's 1st Division.

—Remarkable stand of Lieutenant Colonel McClernand Butler's 3rd Battalion (395th Infantry) and attached cavalry and artillery at the Monschau-Höfen Gatepost against the German 326th *Volksgrenadier* Division.

—Race to the dual towns between the 2nd Division infantry and the *Hitlerjugend Panzers*, won by the infantry—just.

Yet Robertson knows for all its high drama, Bloody Sunday has been a day of preparation only. The German enemy is diligent, persistent, determined. By nightfall he has learned more about what they intend, how much *Wehrmacht* ground and air power has been invested in their offensive, the length of the American line in the Ardennes-Eifel they have struck through, their success in the Losheim Gap and the Schnee Eifel, the role of the *Waffen SS* and its leaders—Dietrich, Priess, Kraemer, etc.—in the battle facing the American forces building upon the Elsenborn heights. Before trying to snatch a few hours of sleep in the early hours of December 18, Robertson knows the new day will bring his men and those of the 99th Division even more death, wounds, sorrow, and despair. It is the way of the cross borne by fighting soldiers in battle. He also knows for some it will be a day of testing and triumph they will remember proudly all their lives, another reality of war.

WE WERE THERE

War Comes to the 2nd Division Service Troops

"Two German fighter-bombers came in low and (each) dropped a five-hundred pound bomb and strafed the area. This is one hell of a place to be, right on top of an ammo dump. (AN: An ammunition resupply facility south of Elsenborn, Belgium.)"

"I can see the pilots very clearly. They dropped their load right smack on our battalion motor pool in Elsenborn. I can see the shock waves from the explosions, the flash and then the terrific thud of the bombs exploding."

"I jumped up on the .50caliber machine gun, which was mounted on the ring (AN: Device bolted to the cab to allow a machine gun mounting.) of a nearby two and a half ton truck and started to return fire on the airplanes, with no apparent effect. Somebody screamed at me to come off the gun as I would be drawing attention to our position and the planes would return and give us a going over. I jumped down from the truck and crawled into a nearby hole."

"Company 'B' (2nd Division engineers) has lost a few trucks, and I've just learned the (fighter-bombers) killed most of our motor pool personnel, wiped them out: Miller, Conatsa, Colby, Wonderly, Graham, and Sergeant O'Reilly, who had cleared the fallen trees from the supply road forward a few days ago, all dead. (AN: The road he refers to is that going from Rocherath to Wahlerscheid described in Volume 1, Narrative I.)

"It's really breaking loose now, all hell. We've got the 612th Tank Destroyer Battalion (AN: 3-inch long guns towed by trucks) and the 462nd Antiaircraft Artillery Battalion (.50caliber machine guns and 37mm diameter rifles) spread all over this field around the ammo dump. The noise is terrific and every kind of gun is firing at something."

"No casualties have been reported except for the motor pool. Headquarters and Service Company (2nd Division Engineer Battalion) was caught flat footed....We're pulling bodies out of the shed where the motor pool was when the bombs dropped (on them). Arms, legs, guts, heads. It's terrible. I think we found Conatsa's torso."

"On Tuesday (December 19) the 702nd Ordinance Company (AN: light arms maintenance company of the 2nd Division) was hit by a buzz bomb (V-1 flying bomb). Forty men were wounded. 'Blow job' Hunter, our air compressor truck driver, was just killed in Elsenborn. 'Beak' Grayon was killed yesterday."

Raymond E. Konrad, ammunition handler, Headquarters and Service Company, 2nd Division Engineer Combat Battalion

The Shooting Gallery at Wirtzfeld

"A spray of light machine gun bullets whiz by us into the ground and over the top of the trees. Surely it fell on the command post (AN: General Robertson's 2nd Division forward CP in Wirtzfeld). A tank destroyer fires at the German tank and hits it—tank blazes and swerves to the right and stops. Sergeant Brown and Private Taylor fire .50caliber bullets at (the tank). Again a blaze and explosion. Tank destroyer fires again.

"Lieutenant Juneau comes down the road at high speed, arrives, and tells me other (enemy) tanks on the way. I send him back to take charge of guns (at that location). Another tank appears on the road following the tracks of the first. It fires in our direction. Tank destroyer fires at tank and misses, its shot landing several hundred yards past in the field.

"I tell (our) gunners to 'give it to 'em.' A 57mm gun (AN: wheeled, light, high-velocity antitank gun probably with 2nd Division headquarters defense force) from our main line of resistance fires and makes a bulls eye (AN: presumably on the tank the destroyer missed). One of our .50caliber machine guns fires and ignites (the tank).

"Moments later, another vehicle appearing to be a halftrack appears, and without further formality our .50caliber machine gun opens up and ignites it. Three enemy vehicles (to our front) now are burning.

"Minutes pass. We wait for more. Firing is heard farther south of the hill four hundred yards to our front. Several artillery shells land on our left flank and hit a small house near the church (in Wirtzfeld)....minutes pass, and no more (enemy) tanks.

"Lieutenant Juneau comes back to report that three tanks have been knocked out. A rifleman jumped from (one of the enemy) vehicles and started running (toward the American line) but one of his men got him."

"Casualties are coming in from tank destroyer unit. A medic gets wounded by rifle or machine gun fire and limps into the aid station. Infantry troops take positions and start shooting and get fired upon by machine gun or tanks plus heavy guns. Casualties are increasing."

> Matt F.C. Konop, 2nd Division
> Headquarters Company commander

Deadly Misunderstandings

"About morning of 17th (December), we got news, 'Saddle up, we were heading out.' Heading on south to Wirtzfeld. We arrived on that morning about 11 o'clock. The Germans were coming in from the south, from Büllingen. We went on and occupied the high ground south of Wirtzfeld in between there and Büllingen.

"An artillery shell landed about two feet from me or less. Two men in front of me were wounded and one back of me, and the (shell) landed right by me and I didn't get scratched. I had a slight headache after that, though."

"Late that evening, we moved (south) and took up positions just outside Büllingen. We had no contact on our right at all, open right flank."

"On the evening of the 18th, it was getting dark, and we saw a group (of soldiers) coming in. They were just out in the open, out in the open, and come a running. The word was passed down, 'Don't shoot at 'em, don't shoot at 'em.' And they kept coming a running. About seventeen men, and the patrol leader came up to the head, and they were Germans. He told us to hold up our hands because he thought we wanted to surrender. After (we saw that) they were Germans and they went by, we thought they wanted to surrender. But (the German patrol leader) recognized we weren't going to surrender. He turned around (and started firing) with the machine gun he had on him. Then we just wiped out the others. (Our) artillery was zeroed in out there. And that was the end of that. We heard 'em moaning out there that night, but we didn't fool with 'em. During the night other Germans got 'em out. A German medic came in there with a white flag. That was the end of it, except for sniper fire."

"We had one man turn green on us. He just said, 'This is it.' The only one. Lieutenant Duckworth ran him off, said 'Get out of here, I don't need you.' He almost shot the (man). He was the only one I ever saw direct quit."

Hodges T. Homan, rifleman, Company "F", 23rd Infantry, 2nd Division

"More Tanks and Germans than You Have Ever Seen"

"Early on the morning of December 17, Technical Sergeant Campbell called all the NCOs together and told us to be ready to move out on a moment's notice. Enemy paratroopers had landed behind our lines. The Germans had hit the 99th Division and broken through their lines in several places. He said we would have to fight our way back to Wirtzfeld, where (2nd) division headquarters was set up."

"(It) was cold, bitter cold. As we were going down the road to Rocherath about seven miles to our rear...we would double time for awhile. Then we would walk for awhile. We came under long-range enemy artillery fire. We moved off the road to the east side into the woods. The artillery stopped after a fifteen minute barrage."

"We moved on toward Rocherath, arriving there about noon (December 17). The 1st Battalion (9th Infantry) was deployed north and east of Rocherath to protect a crossroads. The rest was sent on south and west of Rocherath-Krinkelt to Wirtzfeld to stop an enemy force moving from Büllingen.

"Our battalion (2nd) was the extreme right flank of the 2nd Division....There was so much confusion that no one knew where we were or where anyone else was....We took positions behind a bushy hedge. We intended to hold there as long as we could....We all had the feeling that we were the only Americans left."

"Our lieutenant had orders not to fire on troops approaching until we could identify them because some 99th Division men would be coming through our lines. It was extremely cold and fog began to gather and get thicker as night came on.

"About an hour before dark, we heard troops and a vehicle coming down the road to our front. We could see they were Americans. The lieutenant had me stop them so he could talk to the officer in command. He was a major from the 99th Division. He was in a jeep with about two hundred infantry troops walking with him. Our lieutenant asked him to stop and help us defend our position...

"The major said, 'Lieutenant, you'd better get the hell out of here. All of us put together couldn't stop the *Krauts*. Get your men out of here while you can. The next troops you see will be Germans and man, they have more tanks and Germans than you have ever seen. We're going to the rear while we can.'"

> Nobel Perryman, sergeant and squad leader,
> Company "G," 9th Infantry, 2nd Division

A Rapid Journey from Frying Pan to Fire

"My battalion was out in front. We had passed through the 9th Infantry, and we had passed through the rest of the 38th, and we were getting right to the edge of the woods. (AN: east of the Wahlerscheid crossroads) All of a sudden, I got this call from regiment, 'Hold everything and withdraw.' I couldn't understand this because it still wasn't dark. I had been told at Benning (AN: Fort Benning, GA infantry training center) you could only withdraw when you were in contact with the enemy if you had a lot of smoke (AN: artillery smoke shells to hide the retrograde movement). We didn't have any smoke, or anything else."

"When I got this call, I couldn't believe it, but obviously it was there, and they knew more than I did.... We withdrew and tried to come back into Rocherath-Krinkelt. I told the executive officer to go ahead and lead (the battalion) down (the road). We sent an advance party on down. We were to occupy a defense line to the east of Rocherath. I wanted to see that I got everybody out so I said I'll follow and pass through the line.

"I've never gone through an evening like that. It started to get dark. 'A' Company managed to get down and into position. 'C' and 'D' came under *Neblewerfer* fire (AN: enemy ground-to-ground rockets) coming down that road. I'd never seen such fire like that. My Headquarters Company commander, the only one who had been with me since Normandy, was hit and the (rocket fragment) tore a good part of his chest out. We had no way to evacuate him or anything else. We put him in a barn there. His name was Arringdale. I'll never forget."

"It was dark when my exec (executive officer) finally met me and told me he only managed to get one company into position. But the positions we were directed by regiment to go into were already occupied by the (German *Hitlerjugend* Division) with their tanks."

"I didn't have a battalion. I had 'A' Company. Half my 'C' Company was attached to Jack Norris, the 2nd Battalion (commander). And 'D' Company (heavy machine guns and mortars.) was half lost. We had the heavy machine guns except for (those with) 'B' Company. They were all decapitated.

"This was the biggest shock that ever happened. To come down there in the dark and all of a sudden here came a lieutenant running back and said 'We've lost everything.' He was <u>running</u>. My exec grabbed him by the arm and he said 'We're lost, we're lost.'"

"We incorporated some 99th Division (soldiers). A friend of mine walked into my command post. He was out of the 99th. He said he had fifty or sixty men. He said we'd like to join your defense force. The rest of them were going hell bent for Elsenborn, but this fellow brought 'em in and organized and helped me win a battle at the right corner up in front of Rocherath. I wish I could remember his name."

> Frank T. Mildren, lieutenant colonel and
> commander, 1st Battalion, 38th Infantry,
> 2nd Division

KEY TO NARRATIVE VIII

CONTENDERS: <u>U.S. in Rocherath/Krinkelt</u>. Sector commander for the defense of the dual towns, Brigadier General John H. Stokes, assistant CO of the 2nd Infantry Division. 38th Infantry Regiment, 2nd Division (Colonel Francis H. Boos) and its three rifle battalions: 1st (Lieutenant Colonel Frank T. Mildren); 2nd (Lieutenant Colonel Jack Norris); 3rd (Lieutenant Colonel Olinto M. Barsanti). 9th Infantry Regiment, 1st Battalion (Lieutenant Colonel William D. McKinley) and "K" Company of this regiment. 23rd Infantry Regiment, 1st Battalion (Lieutenant Colonel John M. Hightower) and Company "L" of this regiment. 2nd Combat Engineering Battalion and other 2nd Division units including artillery liaison and forward observer teams, medical, signals, reconnaissance, supply. Five platoons of medium tanks, a company of M-10 tank destroyers plus the TD recce company, and a company of 3-inch (diameter) antitank guns on wheeled carriages. 2nd and 99th division and 5th Corps artillery and a company of heavy (4.2-inch) mortars in support. <u>In forest north of Rocherath</u>. 395th Regimental Combat Team (Colonel Alexander J. MacKenzie) of 99th Division and two companies of division's combat engineering battalion. <u>South of Krinkelt and Wirtzfeld</u>. Second and 3rd battalions of the 9th Infantry; 2nd Battalion of the 23rd Infantry.

<u>German in Rocherath/Krinkelt</u>. *Kampfgruppe* Müller (*SS* Major Siegfried Müller) consisting of three battalions of 25th *SS Panzergrenadier* Regiment and four companies of tanks (*Panzerkraftwagen*) and two *Panzerjäger* companies (tank destroyers) of 12th *SS Panzer* Regiment, plus engineers, reconnaissance troops, mobile artillery, and rocket launchers, all units of 12th *SS Panzer* Division (*Hitlerjugend*) (*SS* Colonel Hugo Kraas). Third *Panzergrenadier* Division (Major General Walter Denkert). <u>In forest north of Rocherath</u>. Battalions of 277th *Volksgrenadier* Division (Colonel Wilhelm Viebig). <u>South of Krinkelt</u>. 12th *VGD* (Major General Gerhard Engle).

ISSUE: *Kampfgruppe* Müller will attempt to move rapidly through the dual towns—Rocherath/Krinkelt, seize the four miles of road Krinkelt-Wirtzfeld-Elsenborn. The 2nd Division and its allies will attempt to stop them until American troops east and south of these towns withdraw to the Elsenborn heights and U.S. 5th Corps defenses along the heights are hardened against further German attacks. <u>Significance</u>. The most crucial battle of the Elsenborn campaign. First *SS Panzer* Corps must overrun the Americans holding back its northern (right) wing to bring the 12th *SS Panzer* Division abreast of 1st *SS Panzer* Division and break loose the 1st *SS* Corps infantry to reach blocking positions on the Eupen-to-Liege line.

LOCATION: Fields and forests between Rocherath and Wahlerscheid crossroads. Area of Rocherather Baracken (Barracks), Lausdell crossroads, respectively one half mile north and east of the dual towns, Rocherath-Krinkelt and other passageways between the Krinkelterwald and the dual towns. The streets and environs of these two towns. The 1 mile of undeveloped farm road from Krinkelt to Wirtzfeld and the 2.5 miles from the latter to Elsenborn. The open country south of the Krinkelt-Wirtzfeld segment of this road.

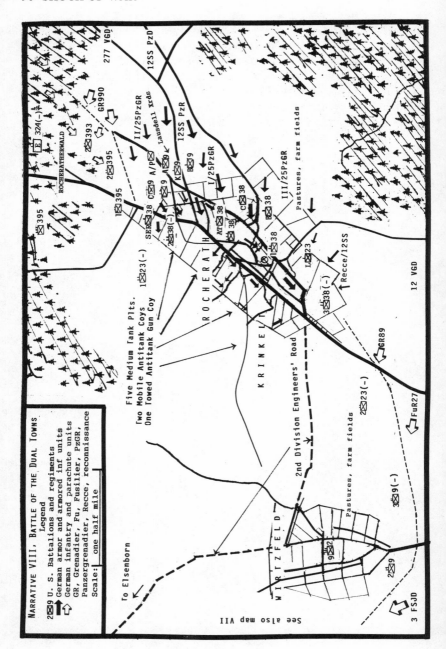

NARRATIVE VIII, BATTLE OF THE DUAL TOWNS
Legend

2🔲9 U. S. Battalions and regiments
⇧ German armor and armored inf units
   German infantry and parachute units
   GR, Grenadier, Fu, Fusilier, PzGR,
   Panzergrenadier, Recce, reconnaissance
   Scale: one half mile

Narrative VIII: MORTAL ENGINES, IMMORTAL MEN

Part 1: The Weight of Warriors, The Tyranny of Circumstances

Twelfth *SS Panzer* Division, *Hitlerjugend*, came late to the violent stage of Germany's interminable drama of death and destruction. In July 1943 a cadre of young NCOs and junior officers from the 1st *SS Panzer* Division, *Leibstandarte Adolph Hitler*, were detailed, as soldiers put it, to start building the new formation. The raw material were volunteers from the Hitler youth organization, which shaped and indoctrinated a whole generation of young Germans. "The *Hitlerjugend* Division will fight (fanatically)," Hitler is alleged to have said. "The enemy will be struck with wonder."

By June 1, 1944 *Hitlerjugend* Division, 20,500 strong were in Normandy ready to take on the invading Allied forces. The seventeen and eighteen year olds of the *Hitlerjugend* did indeed fight with ferocity and determination. They delivered serious punishment to the Canadians and British in the mammoth killing fields around Caen. They were a factor in keeping open the Falaise gap long enough to allow many other Germans to escape. They also suffered huge losses. Within a month of June 6th, D Day, the division had taken 4,500 casualties and was down to 37 tanks. By October 1, 1944, it was down another 4,500 boys and men.[*]

The survivors crossed the Rhine and assembled around Minden and Osnabrück, southeast of Hanover, Germany. Refitting, restocking, and replacing men and guns started immediately. A new commanding officer, *SS* Colonel Hugo Kraas, was appointed. He had been a regimental commander with *Leibstandarte Adolph Hitler*. A huge assembly of men and death machines was gathering across this part of Germany. Four *SS Panzer* divisions, including *Hitlrjugend*, were at the core of it.

SS General "Sepp" Dietrich former commander of the 1st *SS Panzer* Corps in Normandy (1st and 12th *SS*) had recently come on the scene

---

[*] While putting on a performance in Normandy that amazed and impressed friend and foe, a few of *Hitlerjugend's* soldiers also executed Canadian prisoners they had captured. Thereafter, the Canadians, like other Allied soldiers, made little distinction between "good" *Hitlerjugend* troops and "evil" ones. Field Marshal Bernard Law Montgomery personally "ate out," as soldiers put it, one of the division's officers who had been captured and delivered into his presence. A Canadian military court recommended that two *HJ* field grade officers, *SS* Majors Siegfried Müller and Gerhard Bremer be brought to trial for atrocities committed by their troops in Normandy. Both these officers played an active role in the attacks on the 99th, 2nd, and 1st divisions in the Elsenborn battles. Headcount of 20,500 is from p. 254 of Luther, Doc., Biblio., this volume.

to lead the assembling forces. And a new army, 6th *Panzer*, had been created for Dietrich as well, which would be built of the assembling power. He and his chief of staff, *SS* Major General Fritz Kraemer, would not be told its mission until well into *OKW's* planning for *Wacht am Rhein*.

Hitler ordered that the four *SS* divisions of 6th Army should be brought up to the old strength in armor and guns, halftracks, and trucks. Of course, at this stage of the war this was impossible to do.

Twelfth *SS Panzer* received only enough armor to add to the few tanks brought back from France and Belgium to make up about one half the number called for, 105 machines instead of 215. Of this, 37 were the sturdy but outdated *Panzer IVs*, 41 were *Vs* (*Panthers*), 22 *Jagdpanzer IVs*. Five were light tanks used to observe for the artillery. (See also footnote, p. 115.) Later, another twenty or so *Jagdpanthers* armed with high-velocity 88mm guns would be attached to Kraas' *Panzer* regiment.* He said after the Elsenborn Battles that such a mixed bag of *Panzers* in the regiment "considerably weakened (it). The commitment of the *Panzer* regiment was to prove very difficult—tactically as well as technically..."

Even though *OKW* raided other fronts for trucks to support the attack plan code named *Wacht am Rhein* (German forces in Italy yielded up some one thousand.), 12th *SS Panzer* Division would start its march to the Meuse River without sufficient trucks for transporting men, equipment, and supplies and only half the towing machines needed. Only 75 percent of the vehicles expected were on the scene at the beginning of the offensive. Also the equipment that did arrive was a parade of mismatched machines, some of which were worse for wartime wear. However, 12th *SS* would also bring 131 armed troop carriers (*Schützenpanzerwagen*) and 16 armored recon cars (*Panzerspäwagen*) to the struggle.

The *Führer* also ordered that the four *SS* divisions of Dietrich's army be well stocked with eager young soldiers in numbers comparable

---

* The German military developed and produced several new types of armored fighting vehicles (AFVs) to save scarce raw materials and labor and meet changing demands of the battle fronts. These included the tank-hunting *Jagdpanzer IVs* and *Vs*, which travelled on respectively a *Panzer IV* and a *Panther* chassis. They carried powerful high-velocity long guns, housed in a fixed mount, which saved the weight of a tank turret. The *Jagdpanzer IV* weighed 26 tons, the *V*, 45 tons. Also the line of tracked, armored assault guns (*Sturmgeschütze*) was expanded for close-in infantry support and a speedy, lethal little tank destroyer, the *Hertzer* was introduced. All of these AFVs except the *Hertzer* appeared on the Elsenborn battlefields of December-January 1944-45.

to those called for in the original tables of organization. This too was impossible. When *Hitlerjugend* departed its training area near Hanover, 17,488 men—fighters and supports—filled its ranks. Officers and NCOs were another matter. The number of officers to run the division was down by 32 percent; the number of NCOs, by 33 percent. And at the higher levels, the officers did not exhibit the skill and acumen in military matters prevalent in the regular *Heer* (army) formations. "They lacked the necessary staff experience and abilities," as a student of the *Waffen SS* put it.

And the soldier numbers were deceiving. These were not the fresh-faced, well-indoctrinated, determined boys of *Hitlerjugend* before the slaughter in Normandy. These were former *Luftwaffe* ground troops and *Kriegsmarine* (navy) who scarcely knew how to load a machinepistol, veterans returned to the division from hospitals, draftees and volunteers from *SS* replacement training centers. Too many of the draftees were middle-aged men and civilian police personnel who had to be weeded out.

To be sure, young enthusiasts, some as young as fifteen turned up wanting to serve. During the short training period, one of them wrote to the home folks, "Today was our big day....The *Reichsjugenführer* (national youth leader) spent many long hours with us. Early in the morning, with the fog still covering everything, we marched with our companies to the troop training ground where the entire regiment and the training battalion got into formation. The ground was (covered) with armor and heavy guns that we had brought along. The fog lifted and beautiful sunshine lit the landscape of the training ground."

Idealism, including the naive Hitler Youth kind, butters no parsnips, however. And the month of November plus a week or so in December simply did not provide sufficient time to train thousands of men and boys to cope with the complexities and horrors of modern warfare. "(They) could not be trained in battalions or regiments nor in cooperation with tanks, heavy weapons, and artillery," wrote a *HJ* officer later. Precious fuel could not be wasted on tank training exercises.

Hitlerjugend arrived at an assembly area around Hellenthal, Germany during the second week of December, a few miles north of Hollerath and a few miles east of the Wahlerscheid crossroads. (Volume 1, Narrative I) Colonel Kraas did not learn of his divisions's vital role in the Ardennes offensive until December 11. He and other senior commanders expected to bear the weight of leadership in carrying out Hitler's plan were called into his still mesmerizing presence and given a pep talk. Kraas was forbidden, however, to tell subordinate commanders of *Hitlerjugend* Division of its mission until the morning of

December 14. This was less than forty-eight hours before they were expected to lead their men and armor across treacherous ground in bitter cold and ice against powerful and well-armed enemies to the banks of one of Europe's largest rivers. Colonel Kraas believed his soldiers were not ready for an offensive of such overwhelming scope and ambition. He said so to his *Führer* (or so he would assert after the War).

Yet on the eve of *Null Tag*, Kraas seemed more hopeful. Although short one half of the *Panzers* called for, their crews were led by experienced officers and noncoms. The same was true of his artillery regiment. His *Panzergrenadier* (infantry) component—two regiments of men armed with rifles, machine pistols, machine guns, mortars, and *Panzerfäuste*, riding a variety of halftracks and plain trucks, overflowed with men and boys never in battle before. However, they would be led by officers and noncoms with the blood and gunpowder of old battles clinging to them.

After arriving in their assembly area, Kraas and his staff pore over maps and *OKW* and 6th Army intelligence assessments. These contain both fact and fiction: The U.S. 99th Infantry Division, although inexperienced, is deeply entrenched south of Hollerath in front of the international highway. (Not true; it is holding scattered strong points.) The U.S. 2nd Infantry Division is far back, behind the Elsenborn Ridge, in reserve. (Not true, as we know.) The terrain is not friendly: mucky ground with many rivers and streams running from north to south. (All too true.)

As they mull over the plan of attack—a devastating artillery barrage to open things up, a rush of thousands of *Volksgrenadiers* and *Fallschirmjäger* across the international highway and through the defenses of the neophyte 99th Division, then the march of their division's *Kampfgruppe* through its dying remnants—Kraas and his officers are optimistic. "The success of our mission seemed possible," he said afterward.

As previously described (Volume 1, Narrative III), Dietrich's 6th *SS Panzer* Army has drawn five of the eight armor routes (*Rollbahnen*) west assigned the two *Panzer* armies in the attack. They are concentrated in a narrow space of scarcely ten miles, from Losheim in the south to Hollerath in the north. The three routes labeled A, B, and C are the provenance of Colonel Kraas' division; D and E, of 1st *SS Panzer* Division.

Early in the game, the troop carriers and few armored fighting vehicles (AFVs) with them moving over Route A north of Rocherath become bogged in the impassable woods and mucky fields. On the left flank of *Hitlerjugend's* attack, the powerful combination of 26th *SS*

Panzergrenadier Regiment plus much of the *Panzer* Regiment's armor programmed for route C are still struggling over the icy, precipitous roads, through the viscous military traffic trying to reach their start line.

Most damning of all, as we know, the *Volksgrenadiers* of 277th and 12th divisions and the *Fallschirmjäger* south of Bütgenbach-Waimes have not accomplished their missions by midday December 17. They have not cleared the way for the *Panzers* of *Hitlerjugend* to leap forward. Road conditions, confusion among the field commanders, the stubborn stand of those 99th Division infantrymen who make defensive hedgehogs and hold fast to them. These and more force the commander of 1st *SS Panzer* Corps, *SS* Lieutenant General Herrmann Priess, to plan anew.

As we have seen (Volume 1, Narrative IV, Part 2) after noon of *Null Tag*, Priess had ordered Kraas to get some of his *Jagdpanzers* and *Panzergrenadiers* into the wild and confused combat in the Todeswald west of Hollerath. The dual towns, Rocherath and Krinkelt, now take on central importance in the 12th *SS Panzer* Division plans. The pivotal towns at and near the entrance to the N-32 for the *Panzers*, i.e. Losheimergraben crossroads and Mürringen, remain in the possession of the Americans even as late as Sunday afternoon, December 17. Therefore, the initial *Schlag* by *Hitlerjugend* to break its armor loose will have to come at the dual towns west of the borderland forest, Priess decides. In effect *Rollbahn A* and *B* are combined at the starting gate: the critical *Rollbahn C* will be put aside for the moment. (A most egregious mistake.)

By early Sunday, December 17, Field Marshal Walter Model and his staff at the headquarters of German Army Group B are becoming increasingly vexed about the situation on the enemy's 99th Division front. The Army Group B commander who, be it recalled, is running *Wacht am Rhein* in the field, wants matters put straight. *Hitlerjugend* Division is to get its armor and infantry carriers on to the N-32. The right wing is to link up with von der Heydte's paratroops. The infantry divisions of 1st *SS Panzer* Corps are to take hold of the Elsenborn plateau and march to Eupen, as the *Führer's* plan calls for.

In the American camp, General Robertson's power assigned the mission of holding the dual towns, Rocherath-Krinkelt, until the 99th and 2nd division troops and material can be got out of the sack east of Elsenborn plateau is not insignificant:

Four battalions of 2nd Division infantry.

The 38th Infantry Antitank Company and Service and Headquarters companies.

Two platoons of "L" Company, 23rd Infantry, and "K" Company, 9th Infantry.

Stragglers and displacees of the two 99th Division regiments that fought in the woods, at Losheimergraben crossroads, at Mürringen-Hünningen, and elsewhere who volunteer (or are volunteered) to stand and fight with Robertson's soldiers.

A company of the 2nd Combat Engineering Battalion.

Artillerymen separated from their batteries or observing for them.

Members of antiaircraft artillery crews left behind after their battalions displace westward.

Second Division support troops (wiremen, vehicle drivers, etc.) working in the battle zone and taking part in the shooting.

Medical corpsmen and aid station personnel from both 2nd and 99th divisions. Thirty-eighth Infantry Cannon Company working as litter bearers as well as fighters.

There are also, of course, Colonel MacKenzie's three battalions of 99th Infantry a few miles to the north of Rocherath in the woods to fight off enemy attacks if these should develop.

Robertson's two long suits in the defense of the dual towns are the armor and tank fighting guns his officers have been able to gather and move there:

—Five platoons of the Sherman medium tank battalion that has been with the 2nd Division off and on since Normandy.

—Two companies of a tank destroyer battalion. One is armed with twelve M-10 destroyers bearing a long, high-velocity three-inch diameter gun riding on a Sherman tank chassis. The other is a reconnaissance company—armored cars and halftracks. Before the battle ends, another M-10 platoon will join the fight. Total AFVs in Robertson's command: 40 to 45.

—A company of 3-inch diameter tank-fighting long guns riding on rubber tires, hauled by halftracks, which have been present before in various of our narratives. The gun crews working as riflemen will also supplement Colonel Boos' infantry line here and there if and when their weapons are destroyed.

And then there is the artillery. Some one hundred 105 and 155mm (diameter) howitzers and long guns of 2nd, 99th, and 5th Corps-assigned battalions. However, not all of the batteries will be in a position to attack the *Hitlerjugend* troops and armor. Some will have been put out of action; others will be moving west. (Narrative VI)

The order that comes down to *SS* Colonel Kraas from *SS* General Priess, his corps commander, after noon December 17 is to "destroy the enemy still defending Rocherath and Krinkelt, then advance to Elsenborn."

Priess apparently is willing to allow Kraas to make a heavy investment of men and machines at the start of this operation, which originally was considered a walk over for *Hitlerjugend*. One entire *Panzergrenadier* regiment—some three thousand men and boys—is now programmed for the attack on the dual towns plus the tank destroyer (*Panzerjäger*) battalion of the division, some twenty *Jagdpanzer IVs*, each weighing 28 tons and bearing a high-velocity 75mm diameter gun and two .30caliber machine guns as well. They will go in as the first wave; *Panzer IVs* and *Panthers* (*Vs*) will follow if needed.

Kraas' infantry and armor will be supported by plenty of artillery, too: An artillery regiment (105 and 150mm cannons), some of them mounted on tracked and armored vehicles, will support the attack on the dual towns, as will the division's mortars. And their power will be added to by cannons and heavy mortars of 6th Army. PAK (antitank) guns riding a *Panzer* chassis also will be on the field.

Kraas has ordered a forward command post for himself and staff to be fashioned out of a West Wall bunker just west of Hollerath along the road his *Panzergrenadiers* and *Panzers* will follow on their way to the front.

Rocherath and Krinkelt together spread a mile north to south and a half mile east to west. Typical of borderland villages and towns, they are made up of a Gasthaus, a few shops, farm buildings, homesteads, and farm yards alongside the streets, with hedged fields all around. Rocherath is about the size of Krinkelt but less compact and with more open space. So elongated is the area that the two towns occupy, soldiers holding one neighborhood may not even know their comrades are in a life and death struggle in another. This towns offer countless places for ambushing men and machines, many *cul de sacs*, numerous little unpaved lanes and cart tracks doubling back on themselves.

Near the line separating them stands the pride and joy of the populace, a large, stone Roman Catholic church with a massive bell tower and spire that can be seen for miles across the fields all the way east to the Todeswald and west to Elsenborn, three miles away. Older houses and house-barn combinations are constructed of stone with walls to last the ages. Newer ones are also well walled but constructed of brick.

To tank soldiers, these boring construction details are not boring at all but matters of survival. Determined infantry soldiers can turn such sturdy buildings into good imitations of pillboxes. Little groups of shooters can lurk behind the windows in these thick walls and strike at tanks with machine guns, rifle grenades, bazookas, do-it-yourself gasoline bombs, aimed from a variety of directions. And barns and accessory farm buildings can be used to hide an enemy tank or tank destroyer as a cluster of coral hides a moray eel that will strike out at an unsuspecting prey swimming by.

Yet all these harsh realities of the little urban battlefield *Hitlerjugend Panzermen* are about to enter upon may be less of a threat than is their own ignorance. Not only do they assume Rocherath-Krinkelt are garrisoned by the 99th Division soldiers, who have just been driven from the woods and are fought out, but also that these towns are of insignificant size. In the initial armored assault, the commander of a company of the *Hitlerjugend* tank destroyer battalion will use a map that gives him the impression Krinkelt is "a very small village with a church, a cemetery, and just a house or two." An indication of just how ill prepared *Hitlerjugend* is to assault the dual towns, for all its weight of armor, guns, and men and boys.

Part 2: A Night on Fire

Lieutenant Colonel William D. McKinley, commanding officer of the 1st Battalion, 9th Infantry, is operating out of an abandoned artillery bunker described previously. The "K" Company captain's headquarters is in a farm house a few hundred yards to the southeast. McKinley's rifle companies "A" and "B" flank "K" Company, with two platoons of the latter slightly forward. Heavy machine guns (water-cooled .30s) occupy such high ground as can be found covering the roads from the woods a mile to the east. The late afternoon of December 17 is dark, the ground covered with an inch or so of snow, the air sharp, and the fog impenetrable in places, ghostly light in others.

McKinley's men and those of 3rd Battalion's "K" Company and Ammunition and Pioneer platoon don't know what to expect. Their orders are to stand against whatever enemy comes down the roads from the forest to the east and hold their ground until ordered to do otherwise. They have the infantryman's premonition of savagery and horror. They also have his determination not to dwell on it, not to die a hundred deaths before the real one comes to claim him.

McKinley has passed the word down the line to his men to take care with their trigger fingers lest they kill or wound 99th and 2nd division soldiers still coming west from the battle under the fir trees in the Todeswald. (Volume 1, Narrative III, Part 3) They have brought no antitank mines with them but are supplied with a dozen by the lieutenant in charge of three tank destroyers (M-10s) that have moved on to the fields nearby. The big machines are a blessed sight to the soldiers gouging muddy holes and dugouts from the icy ground.

Since McKinley and his men moved in, his artillery liaison officer has been trying to seduce his dormant SCR610 radio into transmitting and receiving. Suddenly, almost on the cusp of the enemy attack, it crackles to life, putting him in communication with the howitzer power that General Robertson has programmed to back the five infantry companies.

At 6:30 p.m., riflemen of Company "B" watch as four large vehicles and a gaggle of walking men appear shrouded in night and fog and pass by along the road into Rocherath. McKinley's men are at a loss how to react. The apparitions may be friendlies escaping the woods— or they may be the enemy. The machines and men are indeed the enemy: Four of 12th *SS Panzer* Regiment's tank destroyers (*Jagdpanzer IVs*) accompanied by infantry of *Hitlerjugend's* 25th *Panzergrenadier* Regiment. Thus the opening shot in the battle for the dual towns is not a shot at all but a drive by in the night.

McKinley's soldiers in the hastily made slit trenches and foxholes along the rifle line now are alert and at their guns, knowing as well as they know the miseries of the icy night that the armored machines and their foot guard of *Panzergrenadiers* will be followed by lots more of both.

At 8:00 p.m. the "B" Company men again hear the ominous sound of squealing bogies and turning tracks. This time they don't wait. A sergeant and a lieutenant go into the arena carrying some of the antitank mines scrounged from the destroyer crews and spread them across the road. Men on the infantry line armed with bazookas insert rockets in the tubes and watch.

The first German tank destroyer to take shape in the dark rolls over a mine, which wrecks the track-wheel assembly and bogs it down on the road. The same for the machine following. The two crippled *Jagdpanzer* make a neat road block, forcing the others in the column to disperse across the fields. They lurch about, their drivers and commanders confused by the opposition, or so it seems to the Americans.

Company "B" men with bazookas leave their holes and go out into the dark to hunt down the monsters. One team (two men) fires four rockets at a *Panzer*. Either they miss or their hits are ineffective. The low-slung machine squats in the field flaying McKinley's infantry line with exploding steel and a steady stream of machine gun fire as well, the latter laced with flashing tracer rounds.

Something must be done. Two soldiers of "B" Company and two of "D," the battalion heavy weapons company, drain gasoline from an abandoned American halftrack into "jerry" (five gallon) cans. They creep up on a *Panzer*, slosh gasoline over the chassis and crew compartment, activate a thermite grenade, and hurl it at the machine, which explodes in fire. As the four black-clad crewmen scramble from the hatches, they are shot dead.

A hundred or more *Panzergrenadiers* have come up to work with the armor, some on foot, some trying to navigate through the night in their big, awkward halftracks, over the cow paths and cart tracks. Like the *Panzer* crews, they, too, seem unfocused, disoriented by the strange terrain, ignorant of their enemy's size, location, or nature. McKinley's machine gun line to the rear and on the flanks of his companies keeps hammering bullets in their general direction. Some *Grenadiers* are hit.

They also are confronted with a more murderous threat: McKinley's captains have asked for howitzer fire moving from a few yards in front of their foxholes and slit trenches all the way east to the edge of the Todeswald. Shortly, the sky sings and whispers with the shells going over. The Lausdell crossroads and all the area around to the east erupt with hundreds of explosions. They tear crimson-stained, smoking holes in the dark and spray jagged chunks of steel at the young Germans slogging across the fields.

Not all the artillery fire orders go over the radio accurately. Not all of the howitzers deliver as desired. Some of the shells fall short, exploding among McKinley's soldiers. Others go wild or fall on empty woods and fields. Given the circumstances—the opaque night shot through with fog, the distant guns, the shaky radio transmissions, the desperation of the captains and their men—that the American artillery does so much damage to the enemy in spite of all is something of a miracle.

McKinley's Company "A" also is lashing at *Hitlerjugend's* tank destroyers. Its command post is in an abandoned 99th Division dugout about half way to the "K" Company farmhouse west of the Lausdell crossroads. The "A" Company soldiers have dragged straw from the barn to line their muddy, icy foxholes and slit trenches. As they struggle with the smelly stuff, men on outposts hear the sound of tracks clanking and bogies squealing.

They scramble down to the road into Rocherath where they stand like spectators at a parade as the *Panzers* and *Panzergrenadiers* go by in the dark. One American remembers, "What followed made no sense. The German infantrymen passed by, scarcely looking in our direction. Some were laughing and joking. One with a very foul breath leaned over and looked in my face as he passed. Then tanks passed, splashing (us) with mud and slush. One of the tank commanders standing in the open hatch gave us the vulgar middle finger gesture as he passed (by)."

The playful *Hitlerjugend Panzermen* do not stay playful for long.

The *Panzer* commanders direct their drivers to steer off the road and turn off their engines. They are one hundred and fifty feet to the rear of "A" Company's foxhole line. For a short while they just sit. Then, as one, the machines suddenly come to life, laying a volley of high explosive shells and tracer-laced machine gun fire across the rear of "A" Company. A vicious little battle foams up. Several "A" Company soldiers are killed straight off by the machine gun fire.

The captain sends a messenger to "D" Company to get their heavy (81mm) mortars in the fight and use their radio to call in artillery fire as well. The cloudburst of death and destruction rocks and holes the *Jagdpanzers*, one of which bursts into flame. The rain of shells sends the *Grenadiers* around them scrambling for holes, depressions, ditches, places in the muck and snow to shelter from the explosions. But others continue to fire their machine guns and assault rifles at McKinley's heavy machine gunners on a rise nearby. With the burning *Panzer* illuminating the dark landscape, "A" Company shooters are able to see to fire back. The *Grenadiers* panic. Some hide. Some race for cover. Some burrow into the snow while working their guns—or trying to—at the same time.

Two *Jagdpanzers* take revenge. They methodically work up and down the American rifle line, grinding across the soft earth with their steel treads that reach down with the slashing force of mammoth chain saws to the riflemen crouching in their foxholes and dugouts. They lurch themselves out of the muddy holes to flee before this horror only to be shattered by the machine guns of the *Panzers*.

Other "A" Company men run off, their rifles and hand grenades useless against the armored machines, to find a depression or fold in the earth where they can hide until the *Panzers* move on.

Company "K" and the A/P Platoon, operating as riflemen, in the center of McKinley's line are attacked by two *Jagdpanzers*. The commanders bring them down the hill into a depression below the farmhouse where the company's captain has his command post. (As soldiers say, they are in defilade.) They proceed to send high-explosive rounds and machine gun fire at "K" Company, the explosions lighting up the dark ground around their holes, the tracer fire spitting overhead.

Another *Panzer* lumbers into the farmyard at the crossroads and goes after the barn where a few of the "I" Company, 23rd Infantry Regiment, men who escaped the debacle in the Todeswald a few hours before (Volume 1, Narrative V, Part 4) are sleeping the sleep of the utterly exhausted. The twenty-two year old company commander is jolted awake by one of his men, who shouts, "Capn,' the sonsabitches have hit us again." They escape out the rear window of the building as rounds from the *Panzer* gun ignite the hay they've been sleeping on. As they pick their way across the hedgerow toward Rocherath, the barn blazes up in the night.

By ten p.m. Sunday night, December 17, the battlefield at Lausdell is lit by dozens of large and small torches: burning *Panzers* and the barn; abandoned American equipment; flares fired by the Germans; artillery explosions here, there, and everywhere; tracer streams etching the black. By these garish lights, McKinley's soldiers can see shapes and silhouettes of men and machines moving out of the woods, over the fields, on the roads and tracks, trying to get around them.

Their bazooka teams go hunting, knowing that behind every hedgerow, down every shallow ravine lurk *Panzergrenadiers* waiting with their machine pistols to put paid to this dangerous game. One of the hunters, a "K" Company soldier, damages a tank destroyer. As he goes after another, a German machine gunner ends the game for him.

An hour or so before midnight, even more of the lumbering, fogenshrouded shapes of *Jagdpanzer IVs* emerge from the woods to the east accompanied by walking and riding *Panzergrenadiers*. This new force coming into the fiery-bloody fray spells doom for McKinley and his valiants. His artillery officer screams into his radio that all possible shellfire must be put down immediately on the fields east of Lausdell. He gets no response and in despair "reaches out for God to take him by the hand."

God does, apparently, for within minutes the sky above the killing ground sings and whistles with a river of shells that descend in a cascade of explosive, fiery steel all across the Lausdell-to-Todeswald road, clear up and into the forest. The young Germans and their machines can do nothing but put space around themselves at the line where the Todeswald meets the open fields in order to escape the swarm of flying steel and the crushing force of the explosions.

After the bombardment, silence descends on the cold, dark scene lit by burning pyres of battlefield trash where so many young Americans and Germans have just died in the embrace of agony and terror. It is midnight. McKinley messages Colonel Boos at his command post near the northeast corner of Rocherath: "We have been strenuously engaged, but everything is under control at present."

The blood and flesh of McKinley's 1st Battalion soldiers are buying time to enable General Stokes and Colonel Boos and his 38th Infantry officers to put into motion General Robertson's plan to use Rocherath and Krinkelt as a breakwater to delay the 1st *SS Panzer* Corps' march west. It will be a close thing. In the dual towns, after dark December 17 the weather adds to the murkiness of things: fog; frost and snow under foot; air shot through with bursts of sleet, an all-round dismal opacity of landscape and spirit in the two towns and the nearby fields.

Two companies of Colonel Mildren's 1st Battalion have been filing into the towns since late afternoon in platoons and squads, severed from their formation and its leader by the afternoon's confusion. (Narrative VII, Part 4) Shortly after dark arrives, Mildren telephones Boos that the two rifle companies are still trying to find their way into the defensive line assigned them at the center of the dual towns, east of the church.

As to the 2nd Battalion commanded by Jack Norris, Colonel Boos wrote later, "It was the last element of the 2nd Division to disengage from the attack (at Wahlerscheid) and withdraw, closed in (i.e. entered) at 11 p.m. and moved into defensive positions under great difficulty..."

These two battalions (1st, 2nd, 38th Infantry), confused and fragmented though they be, are carrying the weight of General Robertson's hope and plan to screw his 2nd Division power to the Rocherath and Krinkelt sticking point until the mass of the 2nd and 99th divisions is able to escape west to the Elsenborn plateau.

Boos' regiment is moving into the positions laid out by Robertson that day:

—Service Company, working as riflemen, on the northeast flank near the Baracken (barracks).

—Colonel Norris' 2nd Battalion on their right, with companies in the buildings and fields on the eastern border of Rocherath, a third of a mile west of McKinley's command post at Lausdell.

—Colonel Mildren's 1st Battalion on Norris' right (south) covering the other gateways to Krinkelt from the forest, and blocking the main north-south road through the dual towns.

—Next in line to the south, on the right flank of the dual towns defense, three platoons of Company "L," 23rd Infantry Regiment, the soldiers that General Robertson encountered and sent to Boos' command post early on December 17, and Colonel Barsanti's 3rd Battalion, 38th Infantry. They will defend the southern border of Krinkelt and cover the road to Mürringen, which will fall to the enemy this night.

—Crews of the little 57mm tank-fighting guns of the 38th Infantry have been in the dual towns since the 2nd Division's Wahlerscheid operation began December 13. They will move into front-row positions at points of entrance facing east.

Some of these units are not up to strength. Both 1st and 2nd battalions (38th) are only about 65 percent effective by Robertson's estimate. (About six hundred men each.)

In the best of times and under ideal conditions, this long, curving line would be difficult to make secure against a large and determined foe equipped with armor. In the late afternoon of December 17, the gloomy day darkening to night, enemy shell and rocket fire flashing and crashing all around, men and machines moving this way and that on the slushy streets and farm tracks, the task is Herculean.

Colonel Mildren, his staff, and most of his Headquarters Company are in place across the open space around the church at the border dividing Rocherath from Krinkelt. Company "A" is located south of the square on the battalion's right flank. Companies "B" and "C" (or what is left of them) are scattered about among the defensive hedgehogs in Rocherath.

Jack Norris' 2nd Battalion is working its way after dark down the forest road and parallel fire breaks and logging trails to reach their assigned position at the northeast side of Rocherath. Soon after all finally arrive about 11:00 p.m. Sunday night, Colonel Boos orders Norris to reposition one full rifle company ("G") to protect his regimental headquarters from marauding enemy. This leaves only two 2nd Battalion rifle companies ("E," "F") up front.

In regimental reserve on December 16, Colonel Barsanti's 3rd Battalion on the right (southern) flank of the dual towns' hedgehog has been blessed with time to make a strong defense. Its main line of resistance (MLR) is anchored on stout stone-walled houses and barns; out front in the direction of the enemy are foxholes and communications trenches for the pickets. (Antipersonnel mines can not be put about because retreating friendlies may be hurt by them.)

One heavy machine gun platoon (four guns) is working with Company "I," to give protection against infiltrators coming up a draw in the field that leads to the center of Barsanti's position; the other machine gun platoon is with Company "K" covering another draw—this one, grown over with fir trees—on the left. Barsanti's six heavy (81mm) mortars are in pits and shell holes directly behind, on the southern edge of Krinkelt.

About 3:30 Sunday afternoon a platoon of "I" Company digging on the edge of Krinkelt is spotted by a roving *Luftwaffe* pilot. Like a hawk on hares, he swoops down and over the little group, depositing a 500-pound bomb. A few men are killed straight off; many more damaged by blast and bomb fragments.

After dark the 3rd Battalion gives up another platoon of its rifles. This one from Company "K." They are moved to the vicinity of some 57mm tank-fighting guns near Colonel Boos' headquarters in Rocherath to give their crews some protection from enemy foot soldiers.

As this platoon is positioning itself around the three guns in the icy mud, an ominous squealing of running wheels, and clanking of tracks is heard. In the dark whirling with wisps of fog, the riflemen see four large vehicles of some kind moving toward them. Each seems to be armed with a gun as long as the machine itself.

These are the four *Jagdpanzers* of the 12th *SS Panzer* Regiment's tank destroyer element that slipped through McKinley's foxhole line. Arriving at the outskirts of Rocherath, the commander of the little combat team orders his destroyers to halt. He sends a patrol into the streets of the town to discern the size and preparations of the *Amis* there.

He assumes the remainder of his *Panzerjäger* company will follow him in. However, they are nowhere to be seen. He also has lost radio contact. Nonetheless in the dark and silence, the tank destroyer captain decides, bravely but foolishly to "promptly (engage) the unsuspecting enemy."

Some of the *Hitlerjugend* armored infantry ride the decks of the *Jagdpanzers*, others dog trot beside the large, beetling machines. The patrol comes up on the open ground around the church that marks the boundary of the two towns. "The first sign of the enemy came in the form of infantry (small arms) fire from in front of the church. I moved forward toward the church with the remaining guns (*Panzers*) close behind me," remembered the *SS* captain leading the patrol.

One of the *Jagdpanzers* gets an idling American M-10 tank destroyer in its sights. The *Ami* starts moving slowing and cautiously toward it in the dark. A quick armor-piercing shot from the long *Panzer* gun drives straight through the armored side of the M-10, stopping it dead and killing several crew.

Colonel Mildren, the 1st Battalion commander, finds himself after nightfall, December 17, occupying Krinkelt's abattoir, which is across the wide, open space surrounding the big church. It is under the guns of his enemy's four death machines. His rifle and machine gun soldiers are scattered (or scattering) from north to south across Rocherath. The troops available to save his command post from being overrun and obliterated consist of his headquarters staff, service people, truck drivers, a few antitank and pioneer soldiers.

This little force is fattened by sixty 99th Division rifle soldiers passing through, whose leader, a lieutenant, has volunteered them. Mildren is delighted. The reinforcements have mixed feelings, but take their place with the 1st Battalion's men in buildings near the church.

The *SS* infantry working with the *Jagdpanzers*, mottled camouflage smocks over uniforms, some wearing billed caps, others steel helmets with a camouflage cloth cover, move boldly about. They seem indifferent to the bullet fire coming at them from the buildings in the neighborhood of the church. Punctuating their shouts and orders with bursts from their

Maschinenpistolen, backed up by their vicious *Maschinengewher 42s*, and *Panzerfäuste*, they storm into buildings, driving a few of Mildren's men and those of other units as well on to the streets and lanes. Some black troops serving with a Quartermaster battalion and trapped in Krinkelt when the fighting starts are among the prisoners taken.

But the Germans also encounter hard and unyielding opposition, unexpected and unforeseen. The gunfire from windows, doorways, basements is lethal. The abattoir occupied by Mildren and his headquarters people is armed and fighting, its windows serving as rifle ports. And his men are on the streets as well, sniping from doorways, trying to knock down the running, milling-about *Panzergrenadiers*.

Colonel Mildren, now sorely tried and, he thinks, facing the imminent annihilation of his CP, orders an officer to send a radio message to General Stokes in Rocherath that "tanks" are overrunning him and to send armor. Three Shermans arrive. The *Panzer* captain detects engine noise around the enormous bulk of the church. One of the American tanks emerges from the dark and comes rushing at him, going backward. The captain's gunner sends a high-velocity, armor-piercing round into it. The American tank smokes up, the hatches fly open, and two of the crew fly out, hitting the ground running. The other three are trapped down in their dead, iron womb, suffocating in the smoke, as the fire creeps toward them.

Another Sherman is moving in the dark, illuminated in the flickering rising and falling light of flares, shell explosions, and its now violently burning running mate. A shot explodes from a *Panzer* that goes into the hull, chops up the crewmen.

The third Sherman is hit, smokes up, then bursts into fire.

The terror of battle turns some men catatonic, others manic. In the dark around Mildren's abattoir, one of his sergeants goes hunting the *Panzers*. He is carrying thermite grenades, which produce a fierce fire and sulfurous smoke, and with a lucky hit can ignite a tank. He hurls one of the grenades at the shadowy shape of a *Jagdpanzer* outlined against the light of the burning *Ami* tank. Bullet fire flashes from somewhere in the dark, killing him.

Mildren's sergeant major (the 1st Battalion's highest noncommissioned ranker) takes a bazooka and goes out after the *Panzers*. The up-front ball turret machine gun of one chatters and flashes. He too dies.

Another soldier removes a .30caliber light machine gun from a jeep and goes prowling among the houses, hunting *Panzergrenadiers* to shoot. Going after human rather than armored prey makes for better odds. He survives for the moment at least.

The eastern borders of the dual towns are a mile long and pierced by many roads and tracks. McKinley's diminishing 1st Battalion at Lausdell crossroads can only try to staunch the flood where they stand. Where they do not stand, more *Panzergrenadiers* and *Jagdpanzers* are getting through to challenge the outer defensive line of Colonel Boos' 38th Infantry. Colonel Kraas has invested two battalions of *Panzer-grenadiers* in the fight along this line. And on the southeast of Krinkelt, his armored reconnaissance battalion (infantry backed by light armor, mainly *Schützenpanzerwagen* (halftracks) armed with machine guns and 75mm short cannons) are to run over Colonel Barsanti's 3rd Battalion and turn the 38th Infantry defenses from the south.

During the battle against the *Hitlerjugend* armored and infantry combat group round the church yard and nearby crossroads late Sunday, December 17, Mildren and his staff have been out of contact with companies "B" and "C" and machine gunners, mortarmen, and other 1st Battalion troops. Enemy action in the woods beyond Wahlerscheid crossroads and on the road south have cut deeply into their numbers. "C" has been halved, to scarcely more than a hundred fighters; "B" has been taken down a third. (Narrative VII, Part 4)

A platoon of "C" Company riflemen have joined 38th HQ and Antitank company soldiers in throwing together a roadblock across a main road into Rocherath from the east. The little defensive barrier consists of two small antitank guns (57mm), some light (.30caliber) machine gunners, and riflemen spread around in holes in the earth and behind walls and barricades.

Along a hedgerow facing east about a hundred yards from the barricade a half dozen Company "C" riflemen scrape shallow slit trenches for themselves in the wet snow. The "C" Company captain has his command post in one of three houses near the junction of two important roads. Next to the captain's CP is a house occupied by his soldiers. Directly across the street a third house also shelters men of this company.

The dogged, stoic pickets laboring in the icy ground to deepen their slit trenches see in the strobe-like flashes of exploding shells and rockets the gross shapes of *Panzers* down field a quarter of a mile or so. The squat, compact machines are accompanied by a swarm of *Panzer-grenadiers*. How many the Americans can only guess. However, the number is irrelevant. They are teamed with the armor and are heading straight for the half-finished slit trenches of the "C" Company riflemen. They drop their entrenching tools and run toward the nearest house to sound the alarm.

In the three houses occupied by "C" Company, men are bedding down for the night on the floors or, if lucky, in the owners' beds. Rung out utterly and wanting only oblivion for as long as allowed, they have dropped like stones into a pool of sleep. A soldier from the field nearby comes stumbling into the first house screaming *Panzers*. Another throws a grenade at a *Panzer* in the dark, then fires a volley from an automatic rifle at the *Panzergrenadiers* sprawled on the deck.

The tank commander fires off a bright flare. His clanking, lurching machine stops and turns its long gun on the house, blowing holes in the wall, stunning the occupants, opening the way for the *Hitlerjugend* infantry to enter and take everyone prisoner. They are lined up outside before the muzzles of the German machine pistols and rifles, the scene lit by shell explosions and falling flares.

An *SS* noncommissioned officer talks to the prisoners in English, trying to elicit information. His comrades watch. He is unsatisfied by the answers, angry, impatient. One of his prisoners tries to put on a show of friendliness, proffering cigarettes in a trembling hand. A mistake. The pathetic gesture seems to infuriate the *Hitlerjugend* soldiers. The American is knocked down pleading for his life and shot dead. The NCO tells the prisoners he will have all of them shot if they don't speak up. The captured "C" Company men stay silent. Two *Panzergrenadiers* seize three of the prisoners and march them away behind the house, out of sight of the others. Shots and screams. They are seen no more.

Three other *Amis* from the house are walked a few yards down the road to the east, then brought back, ordered to stand face forward against a wall. A knot of *Hitlerjugend* soldiers nearby take random shots at them, like boys playing a prank. The Americans go down. Two lie motionless as though dead; the other cries out for mercy. An officer delivers it in the form of a burst from his machine pistol. Artillery rounds come in, crashing all around, driving the *Panzergrenadiers* off. The one American of the three who has not been hurt tries to help his wounded comrade, who has bloody holes in an arm and a leg. "He said leave him there. Moving would hurt him too much. I gave him some fresh snow. The only thing I had for water."

In the house across the muddy, gravely road, are more soldiers of "C" Company. The machine gun fire and tank gun explosions have jerked them from their sleeping bags just in time to hide beneath the windows as two *Jagdpanzer IVs* lumber up to the house, stop, and send two high-explosive shells into the building. The rounds do damage, bringing down bricks and mortar, tearing away window frames. But the men sheltering there stay put and wait for what they believe will be the inevitable assault by *Hitlerjugend* infantry.

Other *Panzergrenadiers* are moving about bagging stray Americans and herding them into the basement of the farmhouse that has been captured. They sit or stand about in the ill-lit basement, wondering whether their lives will soon end at the muzzle of a *Hitlerjugend's* machine pistol. However, the *Panzergrenadier* lieutenant seems more interested in changing their *Zeitgeist*. In harsh but correct English, he berates the Americans for fighting their true friends (i.e. the Germans) while their Satanic enemy (i.e. the Soviets) are about to take over all of Europe. The politically innocent Americans are simply nonplussed. They have no idea what the fellow is talking about.

Bored with the effort to enlighten these *Dummköpfe*, the *SS* officer orders three of them to go out and shout to their comrades holding the house across the street to surrender. They are to say that all the American prisoners held in the basement will be killed otherwise. Having no choice, the prisoners do. But the only response they get is friendly fire directed at the house from which they have just emerged.

The *SS* lieutenant is bluffing, nor does he seem to want to engage the obviously armed and determined Americans across the street until daylight arrives. "During the rest of the night there was no action. The artillery fire kept houses blazing. Smoke billowing over the town added to the confusion caused by the mist and light rain that fell intermittently throughout the battle," remembered a "C" Company officer.

Shortly after midnight, a messenger from the company command post slips into the basement. He tells a sad tale. The CP has been struck by the same *Jagdpanzers* that caused such grief earlier. Their long guns and machine guns have crushed and scattered the platoon occupying the CP. The company commander is gone, whether to seek reinforcements or escape the German armor's punishment he can not say. Company "C" now consists of the men still holding this one house and the few still on the streets of Rocherath or in the hedgerows working with the 38th Infantry HQ and Antitank companies. One hundred and seventy men and officers down to maybe fifty total.

Colonel Mildren's Company "B," has found its way to a farm field about three hundred yards southeast of "C" Company's three ill-starred houses. However, the captain has second thoughts about the position: too far out front and exposed. So he orders his long-suffering riflemen and machine gunners to pull back toward Rocherath and dig anew.

They set to it for the second time this night, scraping at the snow-covered muck, scratched and sandpapered by the wind. They are angry that they must dig places for themselves tortured all the while by the cold and wet even though not more than a football field away are stout stone houses and barns.

They have scarcely started when the black sky overhead sighs and whistles and mortar bombs and artillery rounds come down to explode among them. Simultaneously, they are raked by machine gun and rifle fire from their front and flank.

The noise of ordnance is so overwhelming, they don't hear the sound of tracks and road wheels nearby. *Jagdpanzers* are on the road running across the company's left (north) flank. *Hitlerjugend* foot troops are running beside the squat machines or riding the decks. Soon more of them come charging out of the dark into the center of the company position. They split the two up-front "B" Company platoons and get into the reserve area behind. Company "B" is being broken apart.

The young Germans, confident, hopped up with high spirits, fire their machine pistols and assault rifles willy-nilly in the dark, killing and wounding some "B" Company riflemen trying to defend themselves, forcing others to throw down their guns and give up. An NCO remembered, "With the exception of seven men, the third platoon on the left was wiped out as a fighting force. All but the seven (were) listed as either killed or missing. They were not heard of again."

The survivors clear out of the position, picking up odds and ends of other American units caught up in the clamors of the night as they go, and head for Mildren's command post south of the church common. They are soon part of the confused and unfocused fighting around the church.

Along the southern border of Krinkelt, Colonel Barsanti's two rifle companies have fashioned a hard defensive line across the road to Mürringen, 1.5 miles to the south. Close to 10 p.m. Sunday, troop carriers of Colonel Kraas' 12th *SS* Reconnaissance Battalion come up the road from Mürringen. It is a probe in force, supported by a *Panzer* or two. Barsanti's "K" Company is covering the road, a platoon of shooters on each side. The 2nd Division artillery forward observer signals for a barrage on the hostile force, as do observers for the mortars working with the battalion.

As the flurry of violence comes down on the surprised young *Hitlerjugend*, the "K" Company riflemen and machine gunners send bullet fire into the column. It disintegrates. The *Schützenpanzerwagen* (troop carriers) lurch away over the fields; the tanks disappear; the infantry surviving and able to move, do so with dispatch.

Directly north of Rocherath on both sides of the road to Wahlerscheid, Colonel MacKenzie's 99th Division soldiers (395th Regimental Combat Team) have put out rifle and machine gun pickets. The 1st Battalion, 395th Infantry is astride the road two and a quarter miles north of Boos' command post. The 2nd Battalion, 393rd Infantry is closer in, along the top of the heights overlooking the Lausdell battleground, a mile to the south. The 2nd Battalion, 395th is between the two. These dispositions have been messaged to Boos' command post. Their accuracy, however, is open to question since the infantry companies that make up this force are caught in the darkest, most impenetrable forest imaginable. To compound their confusion, MacKenzie's RCT is in Lauer's command but is attached to the 38th Infantry.

Colonel Wilhelm Viebig's 277th *Volksgrenadier* Division, which has been placed under *SS* Colonel Kraas, leader of *Hitlerjugend*, is also north of the dual towns. Viebig seems more worried about MacKenzie's men falling on his *Volksgrenadiers* than the reverse. His division has suffered unexpected losses in the Todeswald. Kraas' killing machines have preempted the roads through this woods and over the fields to Lausdell and the dual towns. This has made it impossible for him to bring up his artillery, supply, or the few *Sturmgeschütze* tracked assault guns he has been alloted. On the night of December 17, Viebig has a depleted two battalions in the woods pushing confusedly against Mac-Kenzie's RCT.

A soldier of Colonel Ernst C. Peters' 2nd Battalion, which is part of MacKenzie's force in the Rocheratherwald, remembered, "We existed as separate, almost isolated battle groups. Minor fire fights developed in almost any direction we moved. There was confusion, but no panic. Lack of dependable knowledge was the basic cause of confusion: Where were friendly forces? How far away? Were they aware of us? How was the battle going further south and what was to be the effect on us? Where were the Germans in force and what were their plans?"

Colonel Peters' 2nd Battalion, 393rd column breaks through the dense woods at a low ridge line where the forest meets the fields just north of Lausdell Sunday night about the time McKinley's 1st Battalion, 9th Infantry, is fighting off *Hitlerjugend's Panzers* and *Panzergrenadiers*. Strung out across the ridge line, they are mesmerized spectators of the fiery, smoky, crashing mayhem that has engulfed McKinley's battalion.

In every man's mind is the specter of being ordered down the snowy hills, across the fields, and into this caldron of death and destruction being stirred round and round by McKinley's fighters and the guns, armor, and infantry of *Hitlerjugend*. But the wings of this malign fate merely brush across the column, then pass on. The 2nd Battalion moves through the dark to bivouac a mile away on the western edge of the Monschauwald woods.

For all their brave and determined efforts this terrible, incendiary night of December 17-18, the armored crews and foot soldiers of *Hitlerjugend* have not even gained a beachhead in the dual towns.

True, the little *Panzer Kampfgruppe* reached the grounds and streets around the stone church at the center of the two towns. A few *Jagdpanzers* and accompanying infantry breached the eastern border of Rocherath with lethal thrusts at Mildren's "C" and "B" companies. And on the southern (left) flank, some machines and troops of the division's recon-naissance battalion briefly engaged Barsanti's 3rd Battalion. Yet none of these aggressions has changed the tactical situation one whit.

Colonel Kraas and his *Kampfgruppe* leader, *SS* Major Siegfried Müller, expected their power to push through Rocherath-Krinkelt by early evening and be on the way to Wirtzfeld, Elsenborn, and the west. They expected their men and boys would meet only badly mauled survivors of the 99th Division there. Instead, the U.S. 2nd Infantry Division reinforced with armor and tank-fighting guns is in the dual towns. The hated and feared American howitzer batteries are in the battle also, a destructive power only too evident in the broken bodies and immobilized *Jagdpanzer IVs* strewn about the fields east of Rocherath. Pursuing a badly wounded young wolf, the hunter has blundered into a den of angry wolverines.

Long after the war, the operations officer of *Hitlerjugend* sum-marized its night's work: "Only three antitank guns (AN: *Jagdpanzer IVs*. The number should be four, we believe.) and approximately one platoon of *Grenadiers* entered the village. (Rocherath)...The 2nd Bat-talion of the 25th Regiment got tied down east of Rocherath together with the second company of the antitank battalion."

"Their attack got stuck in very heavy artillery fire. The attempt to circumvent (sic) the enemy by a northern encirclement also failed because of the American's superior forces, leading to the loss of several tank destroyers. The commander of the *Panzerjäger* company and of his third platoon were killed."

"Some of (the *Panzergrenadier*) battalion and accompanying *Jagd-panzer IVs* broke into the northern part of Rocherath. But they could not maintain their positions."

In spite of the appearance of armored might made by the little *Panzerjäger* task force that shot up Mildren's space around the church, killed the Sherman tanks, bagged some Americans and made them pris-oners, the commander by midnight has decided that he and his men better clear out of Rocherath and Krinkelt.

The *Panzer* captain fears that if they remain in Rocherath after dawn they will be done for. "So we left the position and took up a new one about three hundred meters to the east of the outskirts of the village.

We had scarcely reached the new position when a hail of enemy shells started to come over....Our prisoners crawled under our *Panzers* to find shelter. So did our infantry..."

The hours from 4 p.m. to midnight Sunday December 17 were critical hours for Kraas, Müller, and their armored crews and foot soldiers. In the dual towns, General Stokes and Colonel Boos were still struggling to bring all the 2nd Division troops south from the Monschauwald. These hours would have been the time for *Hitlerjugend* to strike with its full armored and infantry power, including the fearsome *Panzer V Panther* tanks.

It did not happen. Perhaps could not have happened, given the entanglements of the division's vehicles along the forest roads and fire breaks in the Todeswald east of the dual towns; the confusions of the night; poor communication and control in *Hitlerjugend*; lack of meaningful intelligence on their enemy.

In the event, Kraas and Müller suspend operations about midnight (except for the inevitable artillery harassments against the towns). By morning, no doubt, conditions for attack will be more opportune: better intelligence on the enemy power there, the 12th *SS Panzer* Regiment's *Panzer IVs* and *Vs* on line, the *Panzergrenadiers* fully mustered and in hand.

A sound appraisal of the situation, but fatally wrong, as are so many sound appraisals in warfare. The *Hitlerjugend* commanders have gifted their opposite numbers with time to mass their forces and prepare for a battle on the streets of Rocherath-Krinkelt. Time, in short, to create a labyrinth of infinite danger for the *HJ* tanks and tank destroyers and the crews they carry.

About 2 a.m., December 18 Colonel Boos sends a message to General Robertson: "My 3rd Battalion (Barsanti) still holding steady. First Battalion (Mildren) disorganized, no dependable force....Enemy holds church...infiltrated with tanks and infantry on east part of Rocherath. Know nothing of the 395th Regimental Combat Team (MacKenzie) situation. All wire out. Traffic jammed on road....My 2nd and 3rd battalions are in good shape. First Battalion is of little help....Action quieting. Believe we can hold." The colonel exaggerates Mildren's situation. His 1st Battalion, as will be seen, still has plenty of teeth to bare to the enemy. The big church is still in American hands also.

Part 3: "An Absolute Death Trap for Armor"

During the dark early hours of Monday, December 18, American artillery east of the Elsenborn heights has kept up a steady flow of

shells that illuminate the Krinkelterwald (Todeswald) woods line a mile
and a half east of Lausdell crossroads with rising and falling fiery,
smoky light. The gunners are trying to prevent Major Müller's *Kampfgruppe* of *Panzers* and *Panzergrenadiers* from mustering for a march
on the dual towns after daylight. Occasionally the cry can be heard of
a *SS* soldier wounded in the earlier fight lying in the fields lost to his
comrades.

Sleep is a blessing McKinley's 1st Battalion soldiers can not afford.
Land lines need repair. Bullets for rifles and machine guns and rockets
for bazookas hauled in. Slit trenches and holes dug deeper or re-dug,
having been collapsed by artillery shells and the chain-saw effect of the
Jagdpanzer IV treads.

The artillery pounding that their enemies are taking a mile to the
east gives heart to McKinley's night-watching soldiers in their icy holes
along the picket line at Lausdell. They yearn to hope: The shell fire
may kill and wound so many Germans that they will not move against
McKinley's position in the morning. Or what remains of 1st Battalion,
"K" Company, and the other 9th Infantry soldiers with them may be
withdrawn to the dual towns to strengthen Colonel Norris' 2nd Battalion. Or *something* will happen to free them from more of the terrors
they have endured this night.

It is not to be. Colonel Boos and General Stokes in the early hours
of December 18 continue to grapple with the task of putting in place a
defense. For Boos to allow McKinley to withdraw his little force before
the line on the border of the towns is firm would be to hazard catastrophe.

Boos is well aware he may be condemning Colonel McKinley's
troops at Lausdell crossroads to destruction. Just before dawn the 38th
Infantry commander talks with McKinley by way of a newly laid wire
connecting their headquarters (a farmhouse in Rocherath; a wet, log
bunker a half mile to the east). McKinley is told that Lieutenant Colonel
Jack Norris, the 2nd Battalion commander, 38th Infantry, has authority
to release the troops holding Lausdell crossroads when Norris believes
his own battalion is in place on the edge of Rocherath behind
McKinley.

It is cold comfort to McKinley. It means the dawn will find his men
still in their icy holes at Lausdell awaiting the *coup de grâce* that will
without doubt be administered by an enemy power that outnumbers
them in every way.

Dawn December 18 comes on grey and dismal at the crossroads.
Dirty grey clouds dip low and sheets of ground fog drift over the fields
to obscure the Krinkelterwald to the east. A thaw is turning the snow
cover to mush. Smoke from smoldering and burning buildings and
vehicles in the dual towns floats in the heavy air.

The three rifle companies on McKinley's MLR (main line of resistance) stand as they did, although taken down by the carnage of the night before: "K" is in the center, its command post in a farmhouse; "A" on the right flank; "B" on the left. The few remaining men of "C," which is McKinley's reserve, are a football field away in ground holes and dugouts near the colonel's own.

The three American tank destroyers still occupy their positions on a rise nearby. However, their crews know and the infantrymen know (although without having much sympathy) that if Colonel Kraas sends in *Panther* tanks they will devour these machines. With no place to hide in this wide open space, they are fatally vulnerable to the ferocious long gun of the *Panzer V Panther*.

The second battle of the Lausdell crossroads begins about 6:45 a.m. December 18. *Panzer* guns and armored howitzers start firing from behind the fog off to the east. They have come up during the night to within killing range of the Americans. *SS* Major Müller, the leader of the *Kampfgruppe* investing the dual towns has no intention of wasting a large number of his men and machines on McKinley's diminished band. Nor does he have any intention of leaving them as a thorn in the side of his *Kampfgruppe* as it goes forward into Rocherath and Krinkelt.

He sends a company of twelve *Panther*[*] tanks accompanied by clean-up crews of *Panzergrenadiers* to dispense with the pesky Americans at Lausdell once and for all. About 7:00 a.m., Monday, December 18, five of the huge machines, clamorous harbingers of blood and death, come lumbering out of the fog.

---

[*] Details on tanks participating in the battle for the dual towns:

Panzerkraftwagen (tank) *IV* weighed 24.6 tons, was 19.4 feet in length, 10.8 feet in width, stood 8.10 feet high, was armed with a 75mm high-velocity long gun mounted in a revolving turret, one machine gun in the front hull, and one in the turret, maximum thickness of armor, 80mm. However, this was supplemented by spaced armor protecting the turret and side plates or steel mesh protecting the sides of the hull.

Comparable numbers for the *Panzer V Panther*: 44.10 tons, 22.7, 11.3, and 9.10 feet. Armed with a 75mm high-velocity long gun, one machine gun in the front hull, one in turret. Maximum armor 120mm (turret), also supplemented by side plates.

Comparable numbers for their rival in the dual towns armor battle, the U.S. M-4 Sherman: 32.5 tons, 19.4, 8.7, and 9 feet. Armed with a 75mm short gun plus 1 machine gun in front hull, 1 in turret, and 1 attachable to turret for antiaircraft work.

See also footnote, p. 92 for details on other armored and tracked guns in this battle. Eyewitness accounts and even official reports tend to refer to both tanks and tank destroyers as "Tigers" (*Panzer VIs* and *VIIs*) or *Panthers*. Although no *Panzer VIs* or *VIIs* took part in the dual towns battle, some twenty *Panthers* (*V*) did. However, these were outnumbered by *Panzer IVs*, *Jagdpanzer IVs*, tracked *PAK* guns, lightly armored half-tracked troop carriers, mobile artillery and antiaircraft guns.

They push around the burnt-out hulks of the *Jagdpanzer IVs* of the night before, lumber up to the 1st Battalion and "K" Company picket line of foxholes and dugouts. There they open the muzzles of all their weapons: long gun, coaxial (turret) and hull machine guns. McKinley's riflemen crunch themselves to the mucky bottoms of their holes as the whoosh of *Panzer* cannon fire and rush of machine gun bullets sweep over them.

A few men are hit, holed by bullets or torn apart by exploding shells. But with heartbreaking courage others try to fight back with rifle grenades and bazookas, seeking a vulnerable place in the monsters' armored skins or underpinnings to get a shot that will blow off a track, damage a road wheel, or crush a vital motor part. The bazookamen immobilize two of the five machines. The crews stay closed up in their armor cocoons, firing their guns, waiting for the *Panzergrenadiers* to save them from the riflemen's inevitable revenge as they emerge.

The fields and hedgerows of the Lausdell crossroads are obscured by early morning fog. Neither friend nor foe can be sure how much damage he is doing to his enemy. The three surviving *Panthers* already have rumbled off toward Rocherath before McKinley's men even know it. From the high ground in the rear and on the flanks of McKinley's main line of resistance, the battalion's heavy machine gunners are trying to find and kill the young *SS Panzergrenadiers* now moving here, there, and everywhere in the fog.

About midmorning the remaining seven of the twelve *Panthers* in this company come lurching and clanking out of the fog into McKinley's perimeter. The three American M-10 tank destroyers are still on the field covering his men. The big open turret of one swings round and propels six three-inch diameter armor-piercing rounds at the rampaging *Panzers*. No hits are observed. And with that, the little contingent of American tank destroyers takes its leave. McKinley's men now are on their own, except for the artillery off to the west.

They are like Stone Age hunters suddenly surrounded by large numbers of rampaging mastodons. The big German tanks stomp across their space. They repeat the maneuver of the *Jagdpanzers* the night before: grinding the wide tracks with the big sharp cleats into the holes and trenches where the soldiers hide. The carnage is kept down because the American foxholes are widely spaced and spread around the fields. The fog clouds the periscopes of the tank drivers. The tank commanders want to get on with the main task that morning of taking Rocherath and Krinkelt.

Another presence on the battlefield motivates them as well: McKinley's captains and his artillery liaison officer in desperation are bringing shell fire straight down on Lausdell crossroads. As at the Höfen Gatepost (Volume 1, Narrative II, Part 3), it is the ultimate violence against the enemy, based on the not-always certain hope that your men can shelter in their slit trenches and dugouts while the enemy armor and soldiers out in the open are chopped up by the violent explosions and flying metal.

Eight battalions of 105 and 155mm howitzers and long guns a few miles to the west lay a blanket of fire and steel upon the fields around Lausdell crossroads as do the heavy mortars. The bombardment hurries off the *Panzers* that are taking apart McKinley's line and kills and wounds untold numbers of *Panzergrenadiers*. One of *Kampfgruppe* Müller's *Panthers* is riding under the bombardment with the commander's hatch open. Fatal. A shell comes through the open hatch and explodes, blowing apart the machine and all of its five-man crew. The other *Panthers* escape, moving off toward Rocherath.

The lieutenant of the "A" Company Weapons Platoon (light mortars and machine guns) has his command post in a hutment half sunk in the earth. He sends one of his soldiers out to take a message to a mortar section. The man is hit by shell fragments before he goes a hundred yards. Two explosions destroy another hutment, killing several of the occupants. A wounded soldier recalls, "We had no cover, the (American) shells were dropping in all over us."

Between the *Panthers* and the American guns, McKinley's little power is being destroyed this grey and somber morning. All but the most steely of his men are afflicted by that frost on mind and spirit that immobilizes the stoutest soldier who survives a ferocious battle only to face more of the same without surcease or relief.

On the left of McKinley's rifle line, first one, then another despairing soldier tried beyond his limits rises from his foxhole and goes running for the Rocherather Baracken north of the town. In all, eight men decide they have had enough. McKinley intercepts them. He admonishes first one, then another as they come by not to desert their comrades, not to fail them all, not to go back on him. They are suffused with fear, the smell of their own death in their nostrils, but they respect McKinley, and all eight go back into the caldron. How many of them die or are bagged by the enemy is lost in the final chaos of the 1st Battalion's stand.

At last Colonel McKinley receives a call at midmorning, December 18, from Norris that he may bring 1st Battalion and "K" Company out at 1 p.m. What McKinley is thinking is not known, probably nothing except how to extract the remnants of his men without losing more. Yet somewhere in the inner recesses of his soldier's mind he must have given fleeting place to the thought: It is too late for my riflemen and my machine gunners, too late for my fighters.

McKinley's captains receive the order to withdraw amid a chaotic scene. As the ground fog starts to lift, they see *Panzergrenadiers* swarming over the foxholes and dugouts of their few surviving men, letting go with blasts from rapid-fire *Maschinenpistolen*, forcing them to throw their weapons on the ground and climb out of their holes and other diggings. Those too damaged by bullet or shell fire to obey are ignored or dispatched. Either way they die, the former slowly, numbed by cold as their life flows from their wounds; the latter swiftly, war's terminal anesthetic freeing soldiers from the pain, fear, and misery of the battlefield for good.

The finally triumphant *Hitlerjugend Grenadiers* have some *Panzers* with them, machines that have come up in the second wave to reinforce the march on the dual towns. These now take under fire the few riflemen and machine gunners still holding out and the rear area elements of the 1st Battalion: command posts, mortar crews, supply people, drivers.

In the basement of the farmhouse that has been at the center of McKinley's front line, the "K" Company captain watches as a *Panzer* clanks into the farmyard and starts prowling around. The captain knows it's only a matter of minutes before the tank commander orders his gunner to blow the house down. He sends a man out with a piece of white sheeting on a stick. A *Panzergrenadier* officer takes the surrender and orders his men to march the captain and his men off to Germany.

Colonel McKinley sends a lieutenant from his bunker up the hill to the northwest where four Shermans have appeared as though a gift from God. The tank platoon leader in charge agrees to bring his machines into the dying battle to help the remaining soldiers of 1st Battalion make their escape from the German armor.

Instead of charging in, to stand with guns blazing, certain death in a head to head engagement with the *Panzers*, the lieutenant parades two of his four Shermans out where the Germans can see them coming and conceals the other two in a draw nearby. Five *Panzers* take the bait and go lumbering and clanking after the decoys. The gunner of the lieutenant's tank in defilade stops one with a single shot in the side (it is probably a *Jagdpanzer IV*), then does the same to another with three shots. The other three German machines back off, no doubt their commanders have decided that killing a few fleeing *Ami* infantrymen is not worth the hazard.

The tank and artillery counterattacks, give McKinley's few survivors a chance to get away. The fate of Company "K" has been described.

Few men of McKinley's Company "A" remain to leave the field. His Company "B" on the left, taken down by more than half in the battle, extracts itself along the road by emplacing rear-guard fighters. They keep the *Panzergrenadiers* at bay while what is left of the company make their way out.

Some "D" Company machine gunners, who have been firing from a shell hole, dismantle their gun and go hopping across the fields, using other shell holes as places to rest. "All up hill," remembered one, "We would run for a while, then jump into an artillery hole and go again. We did that about four times before reaching the top of the hill (a third of a mile from where they started)."

A "C" Company rifleman watches as the *Panzergrenadiers* "(take) our men, with their hands behind their heads as prisoners back to their lines. We were sure we were going to be captured, but we decided to run for it, then regroup. (But) we ran straight toward the enemy, then turned left along a fence row, and into the woods. All the time they were firing at us with small arms."

McKinley is one of the last to go. As his few surviving fighters rush by, he grasps each by the hand, his heart swelling with admiration, gratitude, and reverence.

McKinley's soldiers (1st Battalion, 9th Infantry) and those of Company "K" and the Ammunition and Pioneer Platoon (both units, 3rd Battalion, 9th Infantry) have been the precious gold General Robertson has had to pay to buy time for his officers to prepare the defense of the dual towns. Under direct orders from Robertson, the survivors assemble in a barn in Rocherath to be given their first hot meal in three days and a place to sleep out of the snow, muck, cold, and ubiquitous terror.

In the barn McKinley counts 217 officers and men. Most of them are mortar crewmen, a few machine gunners, headquarters men, vehicle drivers, here and there, a rifle soldier. Company "K" (3rd Battalion) walked across the snow-covered fields around Lausdell crossroads and started digging twenty hours ago. It consisted of about one hundred and seventy men. Assembled in the barn in Rocherath after noon December 18 are the survivors: twelve men, pale, gaunt, and bruised under the wet grime of the field. Scarcely 10 percent of the rifle soldiers who fought the battle of Lausdell crossroads have come back. The rest died, were wounded, were taken by *Hitlerjugend*, or disappeared forever in the blast of an exploding shell.

Yet in warfare, no misery, horror, or sacrifice ever plumbs the ultimate depths; always another descent is waiting to be made. The Lausdell battle, intent and murderous as it has been, and the pitched

battles in the two towns the night of December 17-18 are mere preliminaries to the clash of World War II armored dinosaurs in Rocherath
and Krinkelt that is now imminent.

And not all the human receptacles into which the awfulness of the
battle for the two towns is poured are soldiers. A few dozen local
civilians have been trapped by the sudden explosion of war. Like people
living on the slopes of a dormant volcano that suddenly erupts shower-
ing death and destruction all round, their fear is compounded by utter
shock. Until dawn on *Null Tag*, they lived in the comforting belief that
the war in the west had passed them by. Now this. Those who have not
been able by December 16 to flee will spend three frightful days cowering in basements, praying and worrying in sequence. Most will survive;
a few will not, killed by exploding shells and rockets or stray bullets as
they seek food, water, medicine or tend to animals, sad footnotes to
battle.*

General Robertson, the 2nd Division commander, orders his assistant commander, General Stokes, to hold open the southern and western
exits of the two towns until the 2nd and 99th division soldiers and those of
the units working with them have made their escape safely ("repositioning"
it is termed) to the Elsenborn high plateau. To accomplish this, the 38th
Infantry and its supporting men and arms must grapple *Hitlerjugend* to
the mat all over the eastern and southern reaches of the two towns
through December 18 and most of 19 and maybe even longer. At dawn
December 18 no one can know in the American camp. And north of
Rocherath in the hilly, deeply forested Rocheratherwald, the 277th *VGD
Grenadiers* must be kept out of the battle in the dual towns. That is the
responsibility of MacKenzie's 395th Regimental Combat Team.

Müller, the *Kampfgruppe* leader, sends his power against the American defenses in what General Robertson will later term "successive
impulses." Whether this tactic is by design or necessity is not known.
The awful traffic conditions on and around the forest roads west of
Hollerath, Germany, certainly have not made it easy for the *Hitlerjugend* commanders to get their men and machines to the start line in
one mass force ready to go at the Americans, as we know. Whatever
the reason, the "successive impulses" dissipate and spread out the hitting
power of the armor and make the *Panzergrenadiers* more vulnerable to
hostile infantry in and on the perimeter of the dual towns.

After dawn on December 18, the *SS* captain whose armored patrol

---

* Cavanagh gives some details on the civilians' plight. Documentation, Volume 1, Master
List.

spread so much mayhem the night before around Colonel Mildren's 1st Battalion command post near the big stone church makes a break for the eastern edge of Rocherath and the road east to the Todeswald. He remembered, "We looked at the edge of the forest. There we saw tank after tank emerging in wide formation." However, Lieutenant Colonel Norris' 2nd Battalion riflemen remembered this as resembling a long train with cars in a row moving inexorably toward them.

The lead company of *Panther* tanks that has come down on McKinley at Lausdell crossroads is soon followed by another company of *Panthers* and after an interval, two companies of *Panzer IVs*. Some forty-five fighting tanks (*Panzerkampfwagen*) will be fed into the assault on the dual towns.

In the American camp, by late morning, the equivalent of five platoons of Sherman tanks, a company of M-10 tank destroyers, and a company of 3-inch tank-destroying long-guns are either in place or getting there.

After daylight December 18, the defenders of the dual towns and the road to Wirtzfeld from Krinkelt are lined up as follows from north (left) to south (right).

—On the far left wing, Colonel MacKenzie's 395th-393rd (2nd Battalion) infantry still occupy the dark, wooded, snow-covered hills and valleys. They have taken a few casualties from their own and enemy guns, are thoroughly confused, but remain intact, in order, and capable of fighting.

—Stokes has asked Robertson for the two rifle companies of Lieutenant Colonel John Hightower's 1st Battalion, 23rd Infantry that survived the Mürringen-Hünningen combat. (Volume 1, Narrative V, Part 5) They will go into position north of Rocherath between MacKenzie's 99th Division men and Norris' 2nd Battalion but, will not move in until Monday evening December 18.

—The 2nd Battalion (38th) by noon is in position on the eastern edge of Rocherath with a picket line of riflemen, machine gunners, bazookamen, and 57mm antitank guns. Jack Norris, its CO, also has emplaced a platoon of five Shermans and some M-10 tank destroyers at hidden locations behind the line. However, "G" Company is manning strong points around Boos' command post several hundred yards to the west.

—The 38th Infantry's Antitank Company brings a variety of weapons and techniques for killing armor and will use them all. Its nine 57mm AT guns and crews are seeded through Boos' MLR but will do most of their work in the center of the line supplemented by each battalion's three AT guns. One AT Company platoon is with Mildren's battalion round the church.

—On the right, where Rocherath meets Krinkelt, Colonel Mildren's 1st Battalion troops have suffered the most egregious damage of all the night before. So Mildren's "line" is scarcely more than a series of hedge-hogs made up of clusters of riflemen and machine gunners occupying houses and other buildings in the vicinity of the church and in foxholes to the east of the main road through the towns. With them here and there are antitank guns and a few Shermans and M-10 tracked tank destroyers.

—To Mildren's right a half mile south of the church along the road to Mürringen, Colonel Barsanti's 3rd Battalion riflemen and their gun supports are primed and ready. Close by are two rifle platoons plus the machine guns and mortars of "L" Company, 23rd Infantry driven out of the Todeswald the previous day.

—Southwest of Krinkelt in the direction of Büllingen and Wirtz-feld, two depleted battalions of Robertson's 9th Infantry and one of the 23rd Infantry are in place, holding a defensive line protecting the Krinkelt-to-Wirtzfeld road.

As SS Major Müller's *Panthers* and *Panzergrenadiers* run over McKinley's trenches, dugouts, and gun nests around Lausdell cross-roads and move on toward the edge of Rocherath, the 2nd Division's artillery observers transmit urgent messages to their fire direction centers to move the howitzer fire west to the edges of Rocherath. The rounds come in, exploding close to the hedgerows separating the houses and barns on the edge of Rocherath from the fields around Lausdell.

Panthers are not deterred by concussion and flying metal unless hit in a vital place such as the road wheel-track assembly or motor housing or hit topside rear deck by a 155mm shell. Not so their human compan-ions, the young SS soldiers. They leap from the decks of the big machines to burrow into the melting snow covering the ground to save themselves from the lash of flying metal. Yet they don't flag at all. They use the intervals between barrages to keep moving forward.

A group reach the 38th Infantry 2nd Battalion picket line and charge at Company "E" occupying the northeast side of Rocherath. They split into two groups and race across both flanks of this rifle company. Figures leap about in the fog and smoke of the sullen morn-ing. The sound of the Americans' M-1 rifles and light machine guns and bazooka rockets mingle with the abrupt ripping sound of the *Panzergrenadiers'* machine pistols and assault rifles and the whoosh-crash of *Panzerfäuste*.

Aided by the artillery, which drops exploding metal around the attacking Germans with wondrous accuracy, and their own bullet fire, the "E" Company men are getting the best of it. Then the *Panthers* arrive. Five of the massive, lumbering death machines come up on the right flank of the Americans' foxholes and slit trenches. They send a few 75mm rounds screeching at the American line, then follow up with a quick hosing of machine gun fire. The "E" Company men beat a retreat to the shelter of some stone houses and barns on the east side of Rocherath.

But the tank commanders' have bigger game in sight. They keep going. In fact, are homing in on the forward command post of the 38th Infantry leader, Colonel Boos himself. This is the nerve center of the dual towns defensive operation, rallying place for all the leading 2nd Division commanders, including their tank and tank-fighting units.

Boos orders out his 38th Regimental HQ troops: clerks, drivers, cooks, communication people, etc. They are to take the part of riflemen for the morning, reinforcing Norris' "G" Company and the antitank crews stationed there the night before. At the same time, he orders the commanders of the American armor in Rocherath to send some gun power without delay.

Twelve M-10 armored and tracked tank destroyers are within striking distance. They move to confrontation. As the five *Panthers* reach a point along the road three hundred feet from the house occupied by Colonel Boos and his staff, a fight erupts.

One M-10 emerges from a side street, levels its long 3-inch diameter gun at the sloping rear of the hull covering a *Panther's* engine and lets fly with two quick armor-piercing shots. They strike vitals. The machine bursts into fire. The commander's cupola lifts and a black-clad soldier crawls out and drops the ten feet to the ground. When he tries to get up and run off, he is shot dead by a sniper. As the remainder of the crew take their leave of the burning machine and try to save themselves, they meet the same fate: death by bullet fire. It is a hard end for brave men, but one that the infantry usually deals out to enemy tankers.

A second *Panther* on the road falls victim to a lone soldier from one of the M-10 destroyers. He jumps from the open crew compartment armed with a bazooka, hides behind a wall, loads and fires. The little explosive rocket breaks loose one of the interleaved road wheels that support the monster's chassis. It limps to a halt down the way. Few of the crew escape as Americans swarm around setting it afire with gasoline.

The three surviving *Panthers* speed south along the road heading for the church yard, vanguard of the many fighting *Panzers Kampfgruppe* Müller will bring against the 2nd Division men and their allies this day (December 18) and the next.

The captain of the 38th Infantry Antitank Company has located his own CP in a large, stone farmhouse-barn on the eastern boundary of Rocherath. His nine 57mm (diameter) guns are supposed to give the regiment protection against tanks. A lucky shot of HE (high explosive ammo) in the undercarriage or track-suspension mechanism or engine might stop a *Panzer*. But the 57 crew that tries to stand against a *Pzkw* IV or V almost always will be delivered to their maker by the *Panzer's* guns, while their little 2.3-inch diameter shots bounce off the armor. So the tactic is to emplace the guns in hidden recesses, behind walls, in stout buildings (The large doorway of a barn is most desirable.), in defilade behind a hedgerow, and to try to take hostile armor from the flank and rear.

Fortunately for the 2nd Division cause, the 38th Antitank Company men have other arrows in their quiver. They are trained in using "daisy chain" mine devices, using bazookas on vulnerable parts of enemy machines, sluicing gasoline on hot engine parts, fast handling of thermite grenades.

Not long after the brawl around the 38th Infantry CP, *Panthers* clank and pound into view along a main street in Rocherath near the AT Company command post. One halts at a crossroads nearby. Two M-10 tank destroyers and a Sherman are in the vicinity, guns erect for action, or so it seems. The AT captain leaves the shelter of his stout building to fetch the M-10s. Their commanders have orders not to engage, or so they say. (They are also well aware of what the 75mm *Panther* gun can do to their machines.)

In some disgust, the captain moves down the muddy street to the Sherman. The tank commander agrees to attack the German. His tank creeps in, track churning, bogies squealing, and stops. The turret whirs 180 degrees so the gun points off to its rear, taking aim at the *Panther* now two hundred and fifty feet away. Two armor-piercing shots explode from the Sherman's gun, plowing through the rear armor of the *Panther* and reaching into its vitals. The machine smokes up, the hatches fly open, the black-uniformed crewmen still alive climb out, drop to the ground and try to run off. A fusillade of rifle fire kills them all.

The Antitank Company possesses eighteen bazookas at the start of the dual towns battle. Each gun crew has two; headquarters the rest. On the afternoon of December 18, their supply sergeant will drive up with a surprise: a load full of new-type bazookas and ammunition—rockets with rounded noses for better penetration of armor. During the forty-eight hours plus of mayhem, the AT gunners work these rocket-firing tubes more than they do their 57mm guns.

Danger and excitement energize the unlikeliest soldiers. A cook's helper obtains a bazooka. Hiding in a farmhouse where the Antitank Company kitchen is located, he fires away at tanks going by. After dark a *Panzer* comes up behind one immobilized earlier in the day and halts, a perfect target. The cook's helper takes aim, strikes the under-carriage with an explosive rocket, and immobilizes the tank.

He crouches deeper in the room under a window, reloads and waits. Soon a *Jagdpanzer IV* sounds in the night along the road, is blocked by the two tanks in front of it. The cook's helper kills it also.* The crewmen escape into the dark fields alongside the road. A thin but persistent rain is falling. The German armor, so gross and invincible a few hours earlier, sit on their broken track assemblies, mounds of scrap metal in the dark.

Other AT Company soldiers also fire bazookas from the upper story windows of stone houses they occupy on the edge of Rocherath at hostile armor passing by. "If the German tank gunners," the captain said after the battle, "had used armor-piercing ammunition against those upper stories, all hell would have broken loose, because they (sic) had a tracer in them. All the back of the upper stories where we were were filled with hay and could have set all of those houses on fire. Instead they used HE (high explosive) shells. These would shake us up. We would be deaf for a while. But they wouldn't pierce that masonry—walls two feet thick. Our guys upstairs took very few casualties."

The forward observer for a 99th Division artillery battery caught up in the melee in Rocherath is flabbergasted at the performance of Boos' mud soldiers. "We had to go to (the dual towns) and get our radios changed over to the 2nd Division frequency as we were sup-posed to work with their artillery...the Germans had tanks in the towns and there was fighting all over the place....One thing that amazed me was the way men in the 2nd Division fought. The whole thing was a big game to them. They would argue as to whose turn it was to take a bazooka and knock off another tank. It made me feel rather ashamed to see their spirit and compare it to mine."

---

* The source for this anecdote is the commander of the 38th Infantry AT Company and his unit's after-action report. (See Documentation for this narrative.) However, so many hunters armed with bazookas were in action on the streets of Rocherath the night of December 18, the probability is high that another bazooka-armed soldier or even an antitank gun or artillery shell fragment did some of the damage attributed to the cook's helper. Winkling out the truth from the available records and recollections, here as elsewhere, must be a judgement call that goes with the most plausible, best-documented account.

A game of sorts but as deadly to the hunter as to his prey. The roving 2nd Division bazooka teams run multiple risks: being cut down by the rapid-firing machine pistols of *Panzergrenadiers* or sniped at by a hostile rifleman. Caught in the fierce beams of a *Panzer's* headlights and torn apart by machine gun fire. Run over. Mistaken by friendly soldiers for the enemy and shot dead.

Mistaking the bulky, looming form of an armored machine as enemy when it is friend is the saddest risk of all. As a big M-10 American destroyer goes clanking and squealing down a darkened street, open turret crowded with crewmen, the destroyer's commander, a sergeant, is on his feet guiding it. An American infantryman mistakes the machine for a German tank, fires off a rocket that explodes against the turret and does terrible damage to the sergeant. Learning of his mistake, the soldier rushes over to his victim waiting on a stretcher to be taken away and begs his forgiveness.

Colonel Mildren's Company "C" soldiers have clung throughout the night of December 17-18 to their little fortress of a house across the road from the one occupied by *Hitlerjugend* infantry and their American prisoners. (Part 2, this narrative) Their captain comes dashing in after daylight to the amazement of his men. They have written him off as lost.

He takes in the scene: his soldiers sleeping, manning the windows and doors, the men from other units in the basement with the terrified local civilians. No doubt a believer in Marshal Foch's principle that when things are most dire the time is ripe to attack, he orders the lieutenant in charge to retake the house across the street held by the *Hitlerjugend Panzergrenadiers*.

The soldiers of one rifle squad go running across the wide space. They are met by bullet fire and the explosion of a potato masher grenade hurled by the lieutenant who commands the *SS* men. Several of the attackers are knocked down with wounds. The others get close enough to the windows of the building to toss in grenades and rapid fire their rifles into the rooms, a death-defying piece of work. To their astonishment, the *SS* men and boys begin to emerge *Hände hoche*. But not their lieutenant. Although wounded, he fires off two red flares denoting he is in trouble and needs rescue by his armored comrades.

The "C" Company haul is fruitful: thirty *Panzergrenadiers* and as many American prisoners that they have been holding. The attackers also find eleven young Germans dead in the house and around it. Four Americans are wounded in the action, including the "C" Company captain. As he watches the attack go in, he is hit by a ricocheting rifle bullet, which zips open his leg. The Americans who have been held prisoner in the house scatter away to find their platoons and companies somewhere out there in the chaos engulfing the dual towns.

By midmorning the "C" Company men have hardened their two little fortresses with weapons picked up in the neighborhood. They will need them all and more. A street south of the two houses that they occupy starts filling with *Panzers*. Each carry on the deck six or seven infantrymen wearing the characteristic camouflage smocks of the *Waffen SS*.

The platoon lieutenant acting for his wounded captain picks four men. They are to take two bazookas and the small number of rockets available and go out *Panzer* hunting. Simultaneously, the rest of his little power will put down a screen of bullet and grenade fire, actions certain to poke up the Germans fearfully, especially the gunners down in the guts of the tanks peering through their scopes for targets.

As the bullet fire comes at them, the excited young soldiers riding the tanks leap off the decks and scatter behind walls, in ditches, and into farm buildings to await the destruction of the "C" Company men by the armor. A *Panther* sends an explosive shell at the second story of one house. It shakes the men inside to their boots and blows plaster off the walls. But it does not bring down the structure. With other objectives in mind, no doubt, the tank commander moves his machine south along the street, the *Panzergrenadiers* trailing along.

The "C" Company fighters take stock and look to the lieutenant for some saving order. It is obvious to all that only friendly armor in large numbers can even try to stand up to the powerful German machines. Their weight, size, ferocious long guns, and busy machine guns make up death's own caravan going by. As a few U.S. Shermans and M-10s appear just to the north of the "C" Company enclave, the lieutenant orders his men to evacuate their besieged building by back doors and windows and reassemble around the command post up the way.

In the afternoon, Norris' 2nd Battalion line on the left flank comes under an intense attack again.

Colonel Norris' operations officer has ordered Company "E" to move from the buildings they were driven into earlier. They return to the hedgerow and foxholes two hundred yards to the east that they abandoned under the *Panzers'* fire that morning. It is not long before a dozen or more of the same come lurching and grinding out of the fog, machine guns working madly. The "E" Company captain is hit; the operations officer takes over. The *Panzers* push across the flanks of "E" Company, running over some of the riflemen's foxholes with their wide steel tracks.

They are getting behind the "F" Company foxhole line also. The captain orders his men to rise out of the muck of their shallow holes and the depressions behind hedgerows to fall back to another hedgerow a few hundred yards closer to town.

The rush to a new position is fatal to some of the "F" Company soldiers. A medical corpsman serving with the company comes upon a lieutenant with what appears to be a fatal bullet wound and a sergeant trying to help and comfort him. The medic gives the sergeant some bandages and goes off to the "F" Company command post for litter bearers to carry the lieutenant out. "The command post was gone. The German infantry was there. I was captured."

Two main streets connect the two towns, Rocherath and Krinkelt. There also are an abundance of dirt side roads, turn arounds, crossovers and cul de sacs, ample opportunities for the German tanks to take wrong turnings, set themselves up for ambush. And everywhere, it seems, is a wall, a building, a hedgerow for the treacherous American bazookamen to hide behind as they work. A rise in temperature on December 18 plus rain have turned the fields into bogs, slowing tanks to a crawl. Their commanders are forced to channel down the main roads, another hazard.

In Rocherath, as confusion makes his masterpiece this Monday in December long ago, the men, their arms, and their armor are engaged in a deadly game of hide and seek. Encounters explode into disconnected pocket battles.

The long gun of an M-10 tank destroyer is pointed away from a brace of *Panzers* staging for an attack only yards away. The crew can't make their big open turret revolve in order to get their gun pointed in the right direction. Their leader tells his driver to charge ahead and ram one of the *Panzers*. Sure death. The destroyer crashes into the side of a *Panther* with the sound of a massive wrecking ball slamming against an equally massive steel girder. The destroyer is ruined, comes to a halt, and the shaken crew bail out and run for another one of their machines to find shelter. The *Panther* crew buttoned up in their steel shell are shaken to their bowels. They wonder what horrible new weapon the *Amis* have brought to the battlefield, put their machine in gear and go scuttling off, one set of road wheels and one wide track creaking and cranking with the sound of ruin.

Two Shermans undergoing repairs, sit immobile in a space sheltered by stout walls of buildings. When the warning comes down "Tigers coming," the gunners climb into their immobile machines, load the guns with armor-piercing rounds and wait. Shortly, a *Panther* rumbles by. Their shots plow through the side below the turret. As the screaming high-velocity *Panzer* guns come after them, the tank men scramble out of their Shermans and run away.

A historian of the dual towns combat wrote later that German armor was usually killed by some combination of hunters. "One gains a sense of the interplay of arms (from unit reports). There were tank-bazooka, bazooka-gasoline, tank destroyer-tank (combinations)."

Kampfgruppe Müller's problem is that within the confines of the two towns its armor can't find the wide open spaces necessary to bring to bear the massed weight of its high-velocity guns that can chew up *Ami* armor and their rapid-fire machine guns that can sweep through *Ami* infantry with the killing force of a prairie fire.

The big stone church on the border of the two towns is surrounded by a large open space, but the main roads south and west that the German machines must capture come up in front of the church. Buildings flank the roads, and Lieutenant Colonel Mildren's 1st Battalion men are well ensconced in them. They also have allies: the Reconnaissance Company of the M-10 tank destroyers, antitank gun crews, several Shermans.

Just before noon December 18, five *Panthers* all in a row enter the space around the church along a main street through the two towns. They have brought *Panzergrenadiers* also, riding the decks and dog trotting alongside.

Colonel Mildren's motley power of 1st Battalion HQ troops, stragglers, orphan units, 99th Division pick ups watch from behind windows of houses, walls, the shields of antitank guns. They no longer feel the bite of the cold and the depression of the drizzling rain. Their minds and bodies are tensed and focused on this powerful enemy mass. They will challenge the beasts but are harrowed by fear. At the same time, they experience a rush of excitement. Paralyzing fear and wild excitement make war in their breasts.

The morning's mayhem begins with bullet fire. The riflemen and machine gunners at the windows and other gun "ports" go after the *Panzergrenadiers*. The *Panther* turrets whirr, their long guns rise and explosive shells come crashing from the muzzles aimed at the stone houses and barns. The night before opposing shooters were working blind. Now targets are visible but distorted by the fog, and blanket of clouds hanging low over the steamy landscape.

A *Panther* moves down a road hard by the abattoir occupied by Mildren and his headquarters people, heading in their direction. It runs down an American jeep whose occupants just about escape from the vehicle before it is flattened. The impact jams the traversing mechanism of the *Panther's* turret. The driver is forced to waste time and gasoline careening around, banging the barrel of the long gun against utility poles to try to free the locked turret machinery. Watching soldiers assume the tank's driver has gone mad.

But the crazy maneuver works, as crazy maneuvers often do on the battlefield, which after all is the ultimate madhouse. And the *Panther* resumes its march toward the abattoir. Within a few yards of the building, it halts and fires a 75mm round that screeches from the muzzle and explodes against the second story, tearing off the roof and most of the wall there. Mildren remembered it more succinctly: "A tank came down and decapitated my command post."

This violence impels his communication officer to find a bazooka and a few rockets and go after the German machine, which now stands rumbling, preparing to finish off the big, stone abbattoir. He sneaks up on the rear. At near-point-blank range, he fires a rocket that digs through the armor and explodes. The *Panther's* engine begins to smoke. The huge vehicle clanks to a halt. It is no longer a tank but a steel pillbox whose crew may continue to shoot but are doomed.

The officer backs off and begins to load his bazooka tube with another rocket, not noticing that his prey has pointed its fearful long gun in his direction. Before he can shove a rocket into the tube, the tank gun goes off knocking him unconscious. A fragment of the exploding shell chops away a piece of his neck. Two soldiers drag the officer back into the abattoir, blood covering his neck and running in streams over his field jacket. "Bleeding like the devil," remembers Mildren, who wonders how to get the wounded man through the violent chaos raging outside to a place where he can receive aid.

No front line exists in the dual towns. The Americans' MLR (main line of resistance) consists of knots of resistance made up of a few fighters who may fragment at any minute in a burst of machine gun fire, the blow from a potato masher (grenade), or the concussion and burst of shell fragments laid on them by a *Panther* gun. The usual command arrangements and echelons go by the board. The ops officer of Norris' 2nd Battalion remembered, "The CO, the executive officer, and I functioned in independent combat groups. Normal coordination was impossible."

Hitlerjugend troops and machines are seizing ground, occupying houses. As a result, the fighters of both sides can't know as they go about their deadly business whether they are safe or not in seeking out a building, yard, or piece of hedgerow to find cover.

A lieutenant from the M-10 destroyer battalion's reconnaissance unit takes one of his men to load rockets and goes out with a bazooka. Working from the farmyard in front of a big barn, they hole one tank. They then run up to three or four more machines moving down a street into the battle, get within one hundred and twenty feet, and fire off more rockets, an act certain to bring retribution. One of the wounded

Panthers vomits machine gun fire from hull and turret. The lieutenant is hit; but his teammate manages to spirit him away.

Another bazooka team, this one from Mildren's antitank platoon (57s), stalk a *Panther* until they can send a rocket below the skirt (steel plates attached to the hull covering the road wheels and tracks). It explodes among the wheels. The machine can move no farther, but its crew stays down in the steel innards working the guns. They continue to boom high-explosive shells and hammer a stream of bullets in the direction of Mildren's command post.

Armor-piercing rounds fired by the *Panzers* drill holes in the thick stone walls as they enter and exit the building. Fighters crouching under windows or spread over floors escape all but direct blows. Not so if the *Panzer* gunners load with high explosive shells whose concussion and steel fragments can do awful things. But these shells also blow apart when they hit the thick stone walls and do little damage. The *Panzer* gunner must place his round through a window, not easy to do when he is peering through a narrow gun sight and his platform is rumbling and shaking and at any moment likely to move or be moved by hostile action.

The 2nd Division has been able to meet *Hitlerjugend* with a power that surprises and discourages its leaders. They expected to march through the dual towns unimpeded; they are caught now in a fiery web formed by determined 2nd Division tank-stalking infantry, tanks, antitank weapons, artillery, and mortars.

The commander of one of the two *Panther* companies has put his command post in a house northeast of the church square, within sight of the chaotic armor-infantry battle. He is discouraged at the destruction of so many of his *Panthers* and their crews. One of his tank commanders recalls the battle from the German side:

"I had to abandon my hopeless position and tried to pull (my *Panther*) back behind the crossroads. It was clear the American antitank gun had anticipated this maneuver and was ready to fire on the crossing. This is just what it did. The first shot missed. The second hit the track (of my tank) and the hull on the side. No one (of the crew) was killed but the radio was destroyed. The track was almost unusable. Then the track came off on one side, and the road wheels sank in the mud...

"The whole attack had come to a standstill. Near our new position, we saw about twenty *Amis* under a tarpaulin, then saw them quickly emerge. So they were still there in the various houses in the part of (Krinkelt) we already occupied. Some of them ambushed a comrade while he was trying to camouflage a tank with wooden planks."

"It was an absolute death trap for *Panzers*."

On the right (southern) flank facing Mürringen, Colonel Barsanti's 3rd Battalion is covering a large part of the crescent-shaped defensive line round the southeast boundary of Krinkelt. The 3rd Battalion has lost a company to shore up the defenses north of the church but has gained some seventy 99th Division men straggling through from the fighting in the Todeswald. Barsanti adds two heavy machine guns to this number and puts them under the command of his weapons company captain.

They go into the hole in the line made by the loss of the rifle company. They are immediately attacked by two platoons of *Hitlerjugend* Reconnaissance Battalion soldiers coming at them from the south. The heavy machine guns go to work as do the captain's heavy mortars, and the attack fizzles out, leaving behind dead and wounded German boys lying on the melting snow covering a field on the edge of Krinkelt, their cries for help muffled by the indifferent wind.

A parade of 394th Regiment vehicles pulling back from Mürringen passes through Barsanti's lines. (Volume 1, Narrative V, Part 5) On their heels come seven American trucks that seem to be behaving erratically to the pickets along the outpost line. The antitank gun working with them fires a shot well above the lead truck as a warning. A patrol goes out to learn what the little convoy is all about. The patrol takes fire from several of the vehicles, which seem to contain a hundred or more German soldiers wearing a combination of German and American uniforms, no doubt, a ruse to enter the *Ami* lines unmolested. Barsanti's men attack the column with bullet, mortar, and howitzer fire. The young, ill-suited Germans abandon the captured trucks and flee into the woods.[*]

Around 4 p.m. the number of artillery and mortar shells coming down on Barsanti's line of riflemen and machine gunners and on his rear emplacements begins to increase ominously. Within an hour, more lethality has been added by the German gunners and cannoneers and more variety as well: 150mm howitzers, 88mm long guns, 120mm mortars, *Neblewerfer* rocket tubes in abundance.

Immediately, all wires go out within platoons, among platoons, among companies, and to battalion headquarters. Barsanti's wire section

---

[*] This incident is one of the many throughout these narratives that are reported differently by observers. The captain of the 3rd Battalion's Heavy Weapons Company remembered that the column of trucks approaching Barsanti's lines contained American prisoners whom a *Hitlerjugend* officer wanted to exchange for some of his own. Colonel Barsanti would not speak with him and ordered his mortars to drive them off.

chief recruits men of the battalion, including some 99th Division soldiers resting around the 3rd Battalion command post, to splice and re-lay wire, even if this means working amid the explosions and flying metal. These already have killed a mortar crewman and wounded the other five in his crew.

After dark the shelling, rocketing, and mortaring slacken. Given the circumstances, it is an ominous sign. Barsanti's pickets can see by the light of flares fired by their 60mm mortars a skirmish line of infantry in camouflage clothing moving toward them, with some kind of *Panzers* just behind. Barsanti's artillery liaison officer and forward observers radio their guns for help.

The howitzer crews go into action immediately. The *Panzer* commanders don't want to hazard their undercarriages, tracks, and suspensions, and reverse directions, seeking safety behind a forested draw. The young *Panzergrenadiers* try to stay the course, as ordered. A few dozen reach Barsanti's line where they engage in a muzzle-to-muzzle fight with his riflemen, men and boys on both sides banging away in the dark night, ankle deep in melting snow, at what they believe to be enemy shapes and sizes. A few prisoners are taken by the Americans. The young Germans unwisely mouth off about "being in Paris by Christmas." Their cold, tired, angry captors can't decide whether to shoot them or pat them on the head for their touching faith in their leaders' promises.

Part 4: The Germans' Sterile Victory

As the battle rages in the dual towns, the high commanders in both the American and German camps are busy examining options and making plans, even though the fate of General Robertson's 38th Regiment and the other Americans there is still to be determined by the outcome of a battle that has yet to climax. At 1:30 p.m., December 18, he and Generals Lauer and Clift Andrus, acting commander of the U.S. 1st Infantry Division, gather at Robertson's headquarters at Camp Elsenborn. In the 2nd Division commander's words, "general concurrence on the accepted plan of action was agreed on," bloodless soldier language for a monumental undertaking fraught with the utmost peril to all involved. The plan includes these "boundaries and zones of responsibility" and missions:

—Robertson's 38th Infantry will hold off *Hitlerjugend's* attacks at Rocherath and Krinkelt until all other American troops and such rolling stock and cannons remaining in the area and not being used in the battle have moved west to the new defensive line on the Elsenborn heights. Robertson believes that by dark on December 19th, his fighters and their armor will be able to start disengaging.

—Lauer's three 99th Division infantry battalions in the Rocherather forest between the Wahlerscheid crossroads and the Rocherather Baracken will hold fast until such time as the 38th Regiment begins its move, lest the Germans push through the area north of Rocherath, get behind the regiment, and block its exodus to the west. However, the 99th Division soldiers fighting with Robertson's men inside the towns will be relieved this day (December 18) to rejoin their division on the heights of Elsenborn. Robertson has assured Gerow, the 5th Corps commander, this will be done.

—General Andrus is to afford all possible priority to his 26th Infantry to harden with earth works, armor, and antitank guns the Wirtzfeld-Dom-Bütgenbach-Weywertz angle on the right (south) flank of the Elsenborn plateau line and to move in the remainder of the 1st Division as it arrives from the north. Time's passing is the menace here.

At the conference, the three division commanders apparently also discuss the alternative of trying to hold the dual towns as a kind of massive hedgehog that will continue to impede 1st *SS Panzer* Corps' drive on the right flank of Dietrich's army. The idea is quickly dropped. Robertson commented later, "It was obvious that my defensive position (there) was untenable. Both flanks were in the air (a soldier expression meaning they have no friendly forces on either side). The position could not be properly linked to 9th Infantry Division moving in on my north flank or the 1st Division moving in on my south."

A few hours after this meeting, at 5 p.m., General Gerow issues an order placing the 99th Division under Robertson's command and naming General Lauer as his deputy commander. (Narrative VII, Part 2) The 5th Corps leader thereby makes official what has been true on the battlefield of Elsenborn for some hours: Robertson and his immediate subordinates are controlling the action. Whether the proud Lauer takes his subordination with equanimity is not on record. Probably not.[*]

---

[*] After the war, General Lauer will write that the American line from Wirtzfeld was extended "farther west and the (line) on Elsenborn Ridge (was) selected by me under whom the defense was being coordinated during the 16th to the 18th of December."

Well, yes, but the reality was that General Gerow's 5th Corps staff and Generals Robertson and Andrus and their subordinates had more to do with organizing the total Elsenborn Ridge-north shoulder defense from Kalterherberg to Weywertz than did

Ironically, the German commanders on the other side of the hill, as soldiers call the enemy camp, also are preparing to withdraw the 12th *SS Panzer* Division from the battle for the dual towns. Throughout December 18, General Dietrich's headquarters has been harassed by increasingly urgent messages from Field Marshal Walter Model, commander of Army Group B, and supported by OB-West's (von Rundstedt) chief of staff. Why is Dietrich's northern wing drooping on the crucial Monschau-to-Bütgenbach sector? What are the plans and schedules to bring forward Dietrich's power there and open up the front east of Liege? By this time 6th *Panzer* Army's infantry is supposed to be far west of the Elsenborn high plateau spread across a blocking position at Eupen. (Volume 1, Narrative II, Part 1)

As the reader knows, in the original march plan of the War Lord's headquarters (OKW), Colonel Kraas' 12th *SS Panzer* Division was to lead the march of all General Dietrich's legions to and beyond the Meuse River. Impractical in the extreme, this was nonetheless a shining prospect in Hitler's fervid imagination: the youth of the Third *Reich*, as symbolized by *Hitlerjugend* Division, carrying its banner at the front of an avenging *Wehrmacht* that would sweep his enemies in the West to the sea.

On December 18 the reality on the streets of the dual towns is something else again. Kraas' lead battle group is caught up in an unforeseen major action immobilizing for the time being the armor and the one regiment of armored infantry he has been able to bring to the field.

And the importance of the Monschau-to-Bütgenbach sector is becoming starkly evident by the hour, as large forces of Americans inexorably build on the heights of Elsenborn. It is a long, high rampart that can prevent 1st *SS Panzer* Corps from seizing the roads through the wilderness of the Haute Fagnes to respectively, Eupen and Verviers, Belgium, gateways to Liege.

All high commanders in 1st *SS* Corps know intimately the power of the American howitzer and long-gun battalions and what damage they may cause to the communication lines of 6th *SS Panzer* Army if allowed to work unmolested off the Elsenborn-to-Weywertz position. Freedom of movement for traffic along the N-32 high road will be impossible if these deadly engines of destruction are permitted to take hold on the Elsenborn heights.

General Lauer. In fairness to the 99th Division commander, during this three-day period he had all he could possibly handle gaining control of his own cruelly battered infantry and artillery battalions and seeing to their emplacement on the heights of Elsenborn.

So und so, as the Germans say, the vital road must be captured and the overhanging heights cleared of *Amis* simultaneously.

Dietrich's chief of staff, *SS* Major General Fritz Kraemer, wants 1st *SS* Corps to get moving on *Rollbahn C*, and seize Malmedy on the N-32. General Priess, 1st *SS* Corps' leader, is to order *Hitlerjugend* south by way of the international highway to Losheimergraben crossroads, now a repair, supply, and staging center for the division. From there it is to go farther south, bypassing the Bütgenbach hedgehog the Americans are building up and moving on to the N-32 in the vicinity of Weywertz or even farther west.

Priess, his chief of staff *SS* Colonel Rudolph Lehmann, and Colonel Kraas, *Hitlerjugend* Division, do not think much of this order. To entangle the armor, troop carriers, artillery, and other rolling stock of *Hitlerjugend* along the cart tracks and unpaved farm market roads south of Büllingen on the N-32 and the secondary road Colonel Peiper's machines already have turned to muck and mire is to doom them to immobility. Priess believes that Bütgenbach, the gateway west on the N-32, must be forced and occupied and the road opened thereby. His staff exchanges heated messages with Dietrich's during the late hours of December 18, then they arrive at a compromise.

Opening *Rollbahn C* along the Losheimergraben-to-Malmedy axis will henceforth be the major mission of Kraas' division. *Hitlerjugend* will seize Bütgenbach and march west with all deliberate speed on the N-32 to Malmedy. General Engle's 12th *Volksgrenadier* Division will join with Kraas' 12th *SS Panzer* in breaking open the way to Bütgenbach.

Simultaneously, a new power will enter the lists the night of 18-19: Major General Walter Denkert's 3rd *Panzergrenadier* Division, which will take over the battle for the dual towns, with the aid of Viebig's 277th *VGD*, and push on and over the Elsenborn ridge. This will open the entire north flank of 1st *SS Panzer* Corps, driving the murderous American cannons from the heights, and screen both *SS Panzer* divisions (1st, 12th) from American attacks. (Narrative X, Part 1, this volume)

To the soldiers of both sides stalking each other on foot and in armored machines in the fiery cockpit of Rocherath-Krinkelt December 18, this palavering among the generals and field marshals is of little consequence. The urgent minutes of terror they are enduring here and now and the eternity of oblivion that may be waiting for them round every corner, behind every wall, down every street, is of great consequence. The period from afternoon December 18 to noon December 19, when repositioning the contending forces begins to take hold, will be witness to some of the most ferocious fighting of the three days.

The survivors of Colonel Mildren's "C" Company still cling to their houses. (Part 3, this narrative) About four in the grey, drizzling afternoon, December 18, a passing *Panther* stops. Its long gun blasts a shell that explodes against the front wall of the easternmost house but only knocks off some stones, leaving the wall intact. Thereupon, the turret whirrs, the gun swings out of the way, and the *Panther* charges full throttle into the wall, bringing it down and the stairs to the second story with it.

The "C" Company squad manning the house scramble for ditches and other hiding places in the farmyard outside. Their company commander remains scrappy despite his wounds (leg) and hurts (shoulder, from a beam that fell on him). He orders the lieutenant and his men to get back into the rubble of the building and hold fast to it, taking on all comers. (They are armed with a light machine gun, a Browning Automatic Rifle, and their M-1 rifles.)

Near midnight the first of the comers arrives: four *Panzer IV* tanks heave into sight. An American Sherman leads them. It is a shill, a captured machine operated by a German crew. But once more the "C" Company valiants of Mildren's battalion are spared. The hostile Sherman and *Panzer IVs* trailing behind move off toward Krinkelt.

By dark December 18 a variety of German armor is infesting the two towns. (Footnotes, pps. 92, 115) When the black, foggy, and drizzling Monday night comes down on the towns and the fields around, Müller's *Kampfgruppe* leaders adopt the tactic of trying to light up the battlefield wherever they can with flares and other illuminations. Strong lights mounted up front on some of the *Panzers* are used in diabolic ways to blind, confuse, unnerve *Ami* foot soldiers and armor crews. Working with the *Panzers* are *Panzerfäuste*, *Raketenpanzerbüchse*, and fire-making teams of *Panzergrenadiers*. The latter set fires up and down the black streets to illuminate their prey; the former creep round the walls of buildings, searching into farmyards, sneaking up to barns, ferreting out the Shermans and M-10s.

Four Sherman tanks have taken up a position around a crossroads. After dark, the crews heat up a dinner of sorts using improvised stoves. They are warming water for a little post-prandial coffee. A quarter of a mile off to the east a hill suddenly comes alive with hostile *Panzers* as their headlights go on, flooding the American tank position. Flares whoosh into the sky and come floating down over the scene, further illuminating the American tankers and their machines as though they are sitting at high noon. Before the last of the flares touches ground, the *Panzer* guns crash forth, sending armor-piercing shots shrieking by. The Sherman crews disappear into the innards of their tanks pulling the hatch covers down after them and spurring the machines away from the murderous light.

At dawn, December 19 the *Panzers* leave their hill and come after the Shermans, which have been reinforced with a few more of their kind, plus a stray M-10 tank destroyer. The tanks of both sides now enter upon a deadly, if awkward, game of hide and seek: behind walls, around buildings, in and out of barns, back and forth across the hedgerows. Billows of smoke from a burning building give cover to the Americans as they seek places of concealment so their 75mm and 3-inch guns can shoot at the flanks of the German machines. The M-10 doesn't make it. It takes an armor-piercing shot in the body which touches off the ammunition. The explosion and fire that follow turn the machine and its crew into skeletons.

A Sherman forced into a head-to-head with a *Panther* sends four shots straight at the front and turret of the beast. They bounce off. Another *Panther* batters down a stone wall in its rush to devour a Sherman. Nearby lurks another Sherman, concealed. Its gun booms several rounds into the side of the German tank, which lurches to a halt, smoke billowing up rapidly. The hatches fly open, the crew scramble out and run off before the Sherman's machine guns can kill them. The German armor backs off, preferring to engage Shermans out in the open.

The fate of soldiers on both sides who become prisoners of war (POWs) may balance on the point of fleeting circumstance at the moment they are taken: the whim of the captor, his passing spasm of anger and desire for revenge, fixation on his own survival, fanaticism, indifference to the suffering and death of others.

Not all of the prisoners killed out of hand are American. At first, remembered a 2nd Division riflemen, POWs were "passed on to battalion. Later reports of enemy (atrocities) caused us to change our tactics." A wounded German tank commander is left under guard while a mortar squad go out to stalk another *Panzer*. When they return, the prisoner lies dead. The guard "had shot him through the head," recalled one of the squad.

No small number of 2nd Division soldiers are busy supplying the fighters. They obtain their ammunition, boxes of "K" rations, medical goods, and the rest from ordnance and quartermaster dumps to the west of the Elsenborn plateau then haul their loads across the clotted Wirtzfeld road to the dual towns. Enemy cannoneers and rocketeers keep bombarding the road and Wirtzfeld itself with harassing fires. Occasionally, a *Luftwaffe* pilot makes a lucky bomb drop through the layer of clouds over the area to obliterate a rear-echelon emplacement, garage, food dump. Even more destructive, a V-1 flying bomb may flame out, nose down, and explode close to a supply or repair facility. The 2nd Division service troops take their losses.

Boos' fighters also have stumbled on an unexpected source of supply in the dual towns: the stores of food, ammunition, clothing, boots, medical supplies, and officers' liquor rations left behind by units of the 99th Division. Company "L" (23rd Infantry), for example, discovers the liquor ration for the officers of a regiment (probably Colonel Jean D. Scott's 393rd) in the basement of the house it has moved into. The captain distributes bottles to his four platoons then uses the remainder to barter. Parts of local cattle freshly butchered by this or that 99th Division kitchen crew hang in barns. Second Division soldiers turn them into steak dinners with French fries (using local potatoes) washed down with a few shots of the gift whiskey. As they dine destruction, blood, and massacre rage outside.

Colonel Boos' 38th Regimental command post is in a large stone farmhouse with barn attached in Rocherath just north of two roads much favored by the marauding *Panzers*. The walls are a foot and a half thick but the high peaked roof is now missing most of its tiles and the stout walls are pock marked by flying shell fragments. More to the point, it is located in a treacherous place sure to go under as the front moves south.

At 4:30 p.m. December 18 Boos decides it is time to relocate. Records, communication equipment, map cases, extra weapons and the rest of the impedimenta of a stripped-down forward command post under fire and periodic assault are loaded on jeeps and moved to Krinkelt.

When the 38th Infantry command post group departs, Company "G" of the 2nd Battalion, which has been acting as security at the town square where the CP has been located, is free to move by a circular muddy road to shore up Jack Norris' 2nd Battalion defense line at the northeast corner of Rocherath. With the return of these men, Norris late on December 18 will have fighters of eleven companies operating under his command. Mixed in with them are three hundred or so 99th Division infantrymen, survivors of the war in the Todeswald on *Null Tag* who have found their way to Rocherath—and even more war.[*]

---

[*] The operations officer of 2nd Battalion recalled, "I positioned two of my best sergeants on the main road and 'invited' 99th Division soldiers moving south to join us. Most did willingly and were a tremendous help for a day or two. I wound up with a force of three to four hundred (of them)." (Farrell, Documentation, this volume, Narrative VIII.)

Among the formations helping defend Norris' position is Colonel Barsanti's "L" Company that has been sent there as reinforcement. The riflemen and machine gunners occupy a six hundred-foot strip of stone house, barn, and slit trench line north of the 38th Antitank Company and south of Colonel Norris' "E" Company.

No sooner have the "L" Company fighters got their feet and guns on the ground than two platoons of *Panzergrenadiers* (about seventy men) working with two *Panzer IVs* come over a rise six hundred feet to the east. The tanks stand off and their long guns flash and crash while the infantry with them move in spurts over the fields patched with snow to attack. Friendly artillery and mortar fire plus streams of machine gun and automatic rifle bullets force the young Germans to back off. They are further discouraged when a bursting artillery shell tears off the track of one tank *IV* and the other leaves the field.

Shortly, an M-10 tank destroyer comes by, halts, and backs into a hiding place between walls that a few days previous were part of two stone houses. The crew loads and fires, loads and fires. Armor-piercing shells go screeching across a field at the crippled German. Chunks of armor fly off, its long gun is wrecked, and the machine soon smokes up and quietly smolders to scrap. The crew vanishes, not even leaving charred bones behind.

A thousand and thirty (1,030) wounded soldiers will move through the 2nd-99th divisions' medical stations during the three days of battling in the two towns. "So many wounded," wrote a 2nd Division historian, "that jeeps and ammunition trucks had to be commandeered for use without the benefit of Red Cross markings. Shells blew down walls of aid stations. One hit an ambulance broadside in Krinkelt but did not explode. The men used foot paths, back roads, trails to get the wounded through."

What to do with enemy wounded when your side scarcely has facilities and supplies sufficient to take care of your own is a question the fighters and more than a few of the medical corpsmen in the American camp find irrelevant. Seldom before on the Western Front in World War II have so many soldiers of both sides flailed away at each other in so small a space as is the dual towns and been exposed to so many different kinds of instruments and engines of death.* The wounds

---

* Numbers of men on both sides in the 56-hour long battle of Rocherath-Krinkelt can only be estimated. Assuming a plus or minus deviation, as statisticians call it, of 10 percent: 6,100 American and 5,200 German soldiers were engaged at some point in the melee. This included 4,400 2nd Division men, 1,000 in support units, such as armor and antitank, and an estimated 700 99th Division assisting the 2nd in some capacity.

are as varied and dreadful as the causes and in too many cases fatal unless treated immediately. Neither side can spare much attention for enemy wounded when their own are so numerous and chilling to the senses.

At least the 2nd Division medical battalion supply unit is able to move morphine, bandages, plasma, and other goods and medicines needed by the doctors at the aid stations and the medical corpsmen roaming the streets and fields treating the men freshly violated by steel and fire. But in the chaos of the rapidly turning and returning battles neither the battalion, nor General Stokes, nor God himself can make provision for safe sites away from the mayhem to emplace these stations and provide sufficient litterbearers to carry all the wounded to them.

In the church at Krinkelt, the litters filled with wounded lie side-by-side on the icy stone floor, with scarcely space left for the doctors and their aides to move about. Hurting *Hitlerjugend* infantry and tankmen are taken in and attended to by and by, but they are not welcome. Unless they can get to the aid stations under their own power or are helped along by comrades, few even reach there. The 2nd and 99th division medics can find but few soldiers to supplement the litterbearing squads of the medical detachments. Everyone is either fighting for his life or working himself to death hauling ammunition and supplies for the fighters.

And being brought to an aid station guarantees no salvation for the hurting men, even if the violation of flesh they have suffered is not fatal. General Robertson has ordered that ambulances have absolute priority use of the Wirtzfeld road to the west. However, this road is such a crucial lifeline for the 2nd Division that Robertson's priority order is often breached in the urgent reality of moving truckloads of ammunition (second priority), replacement armor, or other items east along the road and into the fight.

What hope for a *Hitler Jugend* lying behind a broken wall in the muck of a farmyard watching his life's blood drain from the jagged hole in his abdomen as a storm of bullet and shell fire sweeps overhead and friends and enemies rush madly to and fro? What hope for the American crewman of an antitank gun out in the fields along the picket line to the east of Rocherath hit when the initial enemy assault swept through as the broil of battle moves on into the town and he is left alone with the biting wind and his own pounding heart?

Virtually all German participation was by the 12th *SS Panzer* Division, *Hitlerjugend*. Estimated numbers of armored fighting vehicles have previously been given.

The lieutenant of a Sherman tank platoon recalled, "Wrapping a bandage around the hand of one of my tank commanders (a sergeant) who had been hit by artillery. The flesh was cleaned down to the bone on the end of his fingers. He wanted to know where the medics were. I told him they just weren't available. At least, I got his fingers covered so he couldn't see them. I don't believe evacuation was available."

The houses, barns, and other buildings of the towns are rapidly being turned into rubble by the ordnance of both sides. However, they still provide shelter from the intermittent icy rain and watery sleet. Fighters will do a stint in the sloppy trenches or on the slushy streets. When the battle moves elsewhere they go shelter in a house to dry their water-logged wool clothing, obtain dry socks, and scrounge some food and coffee.

Robertson orders that the 99th Division soldiers serving with the 2nd Division in Rocherath and Krinkelt be released by nightfall, December 18, for return to Lauer's command and movement west to the Elsenborn heights, as he told Gerow he would. The loss of these men removes a part of the American power needed in a battle still building to its climax. Colonel Mildren, at his 1st Battalion CP across from the church, is shocked by the order. "Awful. Sixty of my men (gone)," he remembered later.

Just as serious to the 2nd Division commanders is losing the 99th Division troops serving in support units scattered among their men and performing essential duties: artillery forward observers, medical corpsmen, truckers, mechanics accidentally caught up in the cockpit but making the best of it.

Yet the loss of the 99th Division men who have been taking part in the broiling battle inside Rocherath and Krinkelt is as nothing compared with the shock to General Stokes and Colonel Boos late in the afternoon December 18 when Norris informs them that friendly troops seem to be gone from the Rocheratherwald north of the dual towns. This sector is the responsibility of MacKenzie's 395th Regimental Combat Team now attached to Boos, as we know. It seems MacKenzie and his power—some eighteen hundred men—are gone from the woods. Boos' left flank and in fact the whole American defense in the dual towns is wide open to a violent and possibly overwhelming attack by the Germans from the north.

About the time Colonel Boos is telephoning this news to General Robertson, General Lauer at his barracks command post nearby is receiving the same news in the flesh: MacKenzie and his executive officer, Lieutenant Colonel James S. Gallagher have jeeped over in advance of their soldiers, who are this very hour slogging and mushing their way out of the Rocheratherwald west to the Elsenborn high plateau. MacKenzie enters Lauer's CP and asks what disposition is to be made of his three battalions.

Lauer is dumbstruck. MacKenzie's men are supposed to be in the forests along the Wahlerscheid road covering the north flank of the 38th Regiment. Taken aback, the colonel asks why was he sent an order in code at 2 p.m. this day instructing him to leave his position and move his combat command cross country to Elsenborn. Lauer says no such order originated with him. The colonel is to get back in his jeep and return to his command as fast as battlefield conditions permit, faster even, turn the three rifle battalions around, and reoccupy the positions in the Rocheratherwald.

To the end of his days, General Lauer will insist no such message originated with his headquarters and MacKenzie has been misled by a German intelligence unit operating on the front with a captured U.S. Signal Corps radio and code. Not likely. If German signals intelligence originated the message, General Viebig's 277th *Volksgrenadiers* working the north flank of the 12th *SS Panzer* Division in the Wahlerscheid area would immediately have rushed into the woods and fields abandoned by MacKenzie's men and marched across the rear of the 38th Infantry regiment fighting in the dual towns. Viebig's division makes no such move. In fact the Germans are not reacting at all to the 395 RCT's movement out of the forest the afternoon and evening of December 18. They apparently do not even realize it is happening.

How then explain the "ghost message" received by MacKenzie, which could have produced a catastrophic situation for the defenders of the dual towns?

Given the chaotic battlefield conditions at the time; the fact that MacKenzie was moving his CP west, closer to the border of the Rocheratherwald; confusion over who MacKenzie reported to, Lauer or the 2nd Division's Boos; confusion and lack of information round Lauer's forward CP at Camp Elsenborn—it is no mystery that such a message might have been sent and received in good faith.[*]

Since Colonel Viebig's 277th *Volksgrenadiers* make no move to

---

[*] Lieutenant Colonel Gallagher asserted years later that he "fought (MacKenzie) all the way back to Elsenborn....I said he was wrong as he was exposing the rear of 2nd Division but he would not listen." This may be true, but the fact remains that the 395th RCT commander did receive an order from Lauer's command post to pull his three battalions out of the Rocheratherwald. (Quote, Cavanagh, p. 170. Documentation, this volume, bibliography)

exploit the mishap, nothing is lost. However, the mud soldiers of MacKenzie's RCT still pay a price. While MacKenzie is on a slow, perilous jeep journey back to his command post in the Rocheratherwald, General Robertson, who has learned of the mix up, radios Colonel Boos to order the three commanders whose battalions form the rifle strength of the 395 RCT to return their men to the slit trenches, holes, and gun nests in the forest and fields that they abandoned a few hours earlier.

At the time of this order, these battalions are spread all the way from deep in the Rocheratherwald to the heights of Elsenborn, four miles distant slogging along in long columns of tired and hungry men, bundled against the cold and tormenting drizzling rain, backs and shoulders loaded down with every single weapon in their arsenal (except antitank guns and vehicle-borne machine guns).

When Colonel Boos' message is received to reverse direction and force march back east across the snowy fields into the forest again and occupy the same positions as before, two of the three battalion commanders serving MacKenzie stoically inform their rifle and heavy weapons captains by radio and messenger. The commanding officer of his 2nd Battalion refuses to take his men back to the evil woods fearing what may happen to them and even more urgently to himself. The battalion's executive officer assumes command and leads the men into their old positions.

A rifle company captain with the 2nd Battalion, 393rd Infantry expresses the confusion of all in MacKenzie's command: "Some time after dark I received orders to abandon our position. The battalion was withdrawing back to the Elsenborn area. We marched out sometime about midnight and joined the column moving toward Elsenborn ridge. I don't remember how long we marched. I remember being in some grassy meadows when the column was stopped. We were told to go back and occupy the positions we had recently abandoned. I remember thinking, 'What the hell is going on.'"

Confusion over who controls the Rocheratherwald is fatal to some infantrymen. After dark December 18 a platoon of the 2nd Battalion's heavy machine gunners make a place for themselves in a shallow bowl under some high fir trees; a platoon of riflemen are nearby. Both are filled with dead-beat, cold, and hungry men trying to scrounge some poor comfort out of the unyielding, implacable environment of the winter night.

Just before dawn comes a rising screaming in the trees above, which shake, quiver, break, and flash bright with explosions. The men trying to sleep or watching at their guns are lashed by bursts of hot steel that tear awful holes in their flesh, smash their bones, crush away their young lives. Forty or so endure the horror, which lasts scarcely five minutes. Two are dead; twelve wounded. Their lieutenant suffers no hits but is ruined nonetheless by the destruction of his men. Nearby, the rifle soldiers suffer worse damage: seven dead, five wounded. The deed has been done by American M-10 tank destroyers firing from the northern edge of Rocherath, misinformed about an incipient attack of enemy moving in from the north.

The evening of December 18, Colonel Kraas' 12th *SS Panzer* Division makes one of its last heavy forays against General Stokes' power in the dual towns. About 6:30 p.m., in the center of Colonel Norris' 2nd Battalion, five *Jagdpanzer IVs* come rumbling down the road from the east in the dark, and clank and clamor through the "F" Company perimeter.

One of the low-slung machines reaches the "F" command post located in a deep dugout, which is roofed over with timbers taken from destroyed houses. The dugout is occupied. Yet even with its headlight illuminating the scene, the *Panzer's* driver can't quite hit it straight. A track catches the edge and scatters the roof timbers but misses the breathless men cowering inside.

The captain telephones for rescue by American tank destroyers known to be in the area. Whether their crews don't get the message or do but don't respond is not known. What is known, the M-10s don't show up. The *Hitlerjugend* machines lurch about, grinding over foxholes, blowing down walls, and machine gunning any poor infantryman caught in their headlights. A "B" Company platoon assigned to "F" Company (both 38th Regiment) is slivered. The few survivors join with men from several other platoons to help defend Norris' battalion command post from the inevitable infantry action that almost always follows such a successful *Panzer* run over.

On the left flank, "G" Company has put together a hasty defense, having been released a few hours earlier from its security duties around Boos' regimental HQ. The company occupies another of the many dangerous places to be this climactic night: the junction of the roads from Lausdell crossroads (east) and the Rocherather Baracken (north). The riflemen occupy buildings and shallow foxholes. Their machine guns and mortars are dug into suitable places. To defend against enemy coming along the two roads, they also have a .50caliber machine gun on a jeep located to shoot north, and a Sherman (Or armored car of the tank destroyer battalion, the report is not clear.), its gun pointing east.

In the early hours after dark, the rifle-soldiers take comfort in the almost ceaseless pounding by 2nd and 99th division artillery and heavy mortars to the front of their crossroads. They spell each other in using such floor space as remains in the broken houses to crawl into sleeping bags seeking warmth and rest, if not sleep.

A few hours before dawn, the pickets in the holes and slit trenches around the "G" Company perimeter detect movement along the road from the Baracken. A dozen ghostly figures are coming down the road. Wearing white winter camouflage suits and firing machine pistols, they surprise the Americans, but are soon put down by a storm of bullet fire from the hedgerow foxholes and the windows and doorways of houses on both sides of the road.

But the invaders are not alone. Within a few minutes, the "G" Company men are ducking and dodging streams of bullets coming at them from the dark. More Germans in white suits and capes are running over the fields, unnatural-looking creatures leaping around in the dark in front, seen and then not seen as the fog swirls about them. They bring several of their rapid-fire machine guns (*Maschinengewher*). These cover the rush toward the American line by the German rifle and machine-pistolmen.

In the first skirmish, Company "G" has lost most of its light mortars to "potato masher" grenades but still has four light machine guns and plenty of ammo belts. As the Germans get within a half-football-field length of where their foxholes are, they send a wall of bullet fire at them. And their captain is on his radio to battalion calling for artillery rounds to be put down on the very place occupied by his men, again the ultimate defense seen so often during the Elsenborn battles. The murderous steel soon comes whistling in to explode around the "G" Company riflemen crouching in their foxholes or sheltering behind the walls and broken roofs of nearby houses.

The machine gun fire and exploding shells drive off the Germans, who leave a dozen of their dead and wounded on the field. The survivors move north and west trying to reach round Company "G." They soon come into the perimeter of 1st Battalion, 23rd Infantry, two of whose companies have come in west of the Rocherather Baracken. Unable to take more from their *verrückt* enemy, the surviving *Grenadiers* give up.

As the grey morning of December 19 comes over the landscape in front of "G" Company, "The field in front...was littered with white-clad German infantry," one of its riflemen recalled. "It was not long before some of our men were out hunting for souvenirs." Survivors of the original dozen-man enemy patrol that started the melee have taken refuge in a barn attached to a house occupied by two platoons of "G" Company, a most unwise choice. "It took some time to clear them out.

No prisoners were taken."

During the early hours of December 19, some *Panzers* of *Hitlerjugend* have continued to roam the dual towns, but the burden of maintaining the still bitter fighting seems now to have shifted almost entirely to the German infantry: soldiers of *Hitlerjugend's* 25th *Panzergrenadier* Regiment and the arriving 3rd *Panzergrenadier* Division.

SS Colonel Hugo Kraas and his lieutenants in their bunker near the Hollerath road are busy disengaging their *Panzers* and *Panzergrenadiers* from the dual towns and moving them east and south. Second Division soldiers in the shattered buildings, basements, foxholes, machine gun nests along the tree lines and the hedgerows around and about the towns sense the battle has climaxed and its dynamics have changed. German infantry and armor continue to probe and search for weak points to push through but they look different, act different, and fight different. The eager teenagers of the *Hitlerjugend* and their determined NCOs in the billed caps or camouflaged helmets and mottled smocks over uniforms are being replaced by infantry of *das Heer* and new types of armored fighting vehicles.

American tank destroyer crews, who have been bobbing and weaving and sometimes running with their M-10s for nearly two days trying to kill *Hitlerjugend's* heavily armored death engines and avoid being holed by their ferocious long guns are considerably relieved to see them go.[*]

Yet the German soldier is ever diligent; his war machine always deadly. The grey-clad, big-helmeted men of 3rd *Panzergrenadier* get right to it in the dual towns: They start emplacing their deadly *Maschinengewehre*. They climb into the German tanks left over from the battle and not yet burnt by the Americans, and try to put the machine guns to work on their enemies. And they bring with them in their first lunge at the Americans several of the deadly little *Sturmgeschütze* tracked assault guns.

At 1:45 p.m. December 19, General Robertson sends a message to General Stokes and Colonel Boos from his forward command post in Camp Elsenborn: At dark (5 p.m. or shortly thereafter) Colonel MacKenzie's 395th Regimental Combat Team will leave the woods north of Rocherath and move west to Elsenborn. The 38th Regiment and accompanying 23rd Infantry companies, armor, and tank-fighting guns, and

---

[*] Colonel Boos has been told by Norris that some of the M-10 tank destroyer crews have not exhibited the kind of do-or-die posture that 2nd Division infantry commanders believe necessary to besting the enemy. Late in the battle, the colonel calls in the TD company commander for a little chat.

all their supply, medical, engineer and other 2nd Division helpers will start moving to Wirtzfeld, where they will be directed to positions south of Elsenborn and to Berg and Nidrum nearby.

Boos is informed that the division's 9th Infantry Regiment (less 1st Battalion and "K" Company) and a battalion of the 23rd Regiment will hold the Germans south of Wirtzfeld and the escape route to Elsenborn long enough for his command to get out. He is instructed to "Destroy all German and American equipment starting at once. Leave no equipment that the Germans can use. Execute all demolitions as (you) retire."

This dry, soldierly expression masks some dangerous work: Teams of 2nd Division soldiers must go out on the streets, byways, and fields still perilous with falling rockets and rounds and hostile infantry, find the immobilized armor of both sides, and take the time and trouble to set it afire with gasoline-oil mixtures and spike the gun barrels by inserting thermite grenades therein. Mishandling the volatile stuff can set the user afire.

As the word filters down to the battalions and companies to ready themselves to withdraw from the dual towns, Boos' survivors are befuddled. With the slackening of the heat of death and destruction in the towns and the evident retreat (as they see it) of the powerful *Hitlerjugend*, they believe they have won: They can hold Rocherath and Krinkelt indefinitely with a reasonable number of replacements for their dead and wounded and sufficient supplies of food and ammunition.

As happens frequently in battle, the men doing the fighting have little knowledge of conditions surrounding it, the threats from elsewhere, the place of their little war in the larger war being managed (or mismanaged) by their generals and field marshals. "We didn't know how bad off we were," said the captain of Boos' tank-fighting company. "...we were practically surrounded."

Part 5: An Infernal Parade

The ferocious little fifty-six hour battle of the dual towns between the U.S. 2nd Division and its allies and the 12th *SS Panzer* Division is coming to a close. The U.S. Army historian quoted before (p. 129) described the tactics used by General Stokes, Colonel Boos, and their subordinate commanders to frustrate Colonel Kraas' power:

"Tanks and tank destroyers were used to counter enemy armor. ...Our armor took up firing positions alongside the approaches and placed their (sic) fire on the flank and rear of enemy tanks....Enemy armor (was) taken under fire with medium artillery before it reached our lines. Then individual tanks were hit from the flank by our tanks, tank destroyers, and antitank guns. (They) and bazooka teams mopped up infiltrators." A concise summary of all the reader has seen in this narrative.

Having received the message to withdraw from the dual towns, Colonel Boos and his staff at their new forward command post near the western edge of Krinkelt now face the task of doing it. The battalion under the worst threat will leave first, moving south through friendly troops who will protect their rear. Then the latter will leave, their backs covered by the battalion that preceded them. In short, a leap frog of battalions.

Boos has almost four companies of armor (minus their losses) to act as a rear guard. No large movement will commence until after nightfall December 19, the dark being an enemy but also a friend. In this case more of the latter than the former.

With enemy artillery shells and rockets exploding here and there in the towns and *Panzers* still roaming about, Boos brings together his battalion commanders to go over the withdrawal plan. All know without saying that its success is hostage to many whims of fortune: German determination to press the attack after dark. The capacity of the narrow swampy road from Krinkelt to Wirtzfeld to carry the huge numbers of tracks, wheels, and boots that will burden it the night of December 19-20. The ability of commanders right down to platoon and even squad level to keep control of a mass of men and vehicles moving through the night and constantly harassed by shell and rocket fire. Whether the *Luftwaffe* has the ability to put bombers in the air over the road and blow it and all using it to smithereens. And on and on. However, the soldiers planning the risky exodus fret themselves only with probabilities they might be able to do something about in advance. None of the above falls in that category.

There are important things they can do something about before the parade begins to move after dark: Putting in place a well-gunned rear guard. Directing their artillery forward observers (those who haven't been killed or wounded, that is) and liaison officers to work out the schedule and placement of interdictory fires that will keep the enemy away from the withdrawing American columns. Seeing to the spreading of antitank and antipersonnel mines (booby traps) along the thoroughfares that carry traffic through the two towns. Destroying tanks, trucks, guns, ammunition that the Germans might be able to use.

The 2nd Battalion's CO, Colonel Norris, tells an engineer sergeant, "What I want you to do is to help me get rid of a lot of German tanks that are sitting here in town." The sergeant suggests "the best thing is to set 'em on fire—run up, throw a can of gasoline on, light a match, then get out of there." But German snipers are working and "everything else. It was hotter than a fire cracker there." A thermite grenade to touch off the gasoline is safer and more effective.

The winding streets, cart tracks, and farmyards of the dual towns are littered with the carcasses of armored vehicles: the *Panzer IVs* and *Vs* (*Panthers*) turrets knocked askew, cannons melted through, tracks spread around in the mud, spaced armor (skirt plates) hanging loose; the Americans' more compact Shermans and M-10 tank destroyers sitting broken and useless behind walls or hedgerows. And these are only the big numbers. Here and there, also, can be found carcasses of *Jagdpanzers*; broken mobile assault guns, barrels askew, steel guts spread across the ground; crushed armored cars of both sides; and a few others. (After the war, Belgian scrap metal dealers will discover an El Dorado in Rocherath and Krinkelt.)

As the Americans leave the dual towns, the rear guard consists of tanks and squads of riflemen working with them to fend off roving bands of German *Panzerfausters* bent on cutting out a laggard machine much as jackals would a wildebeest lagging behind the herd.

A third component of the rear guard is a platoon of 2nd Division engineers doing demolition work in Rocherath. They have the suicidal job of putting down antitank mines—"daisy chains" of the powerful explosive devices strung together, then pulled across the road at the last moment—before departure in the hope that the onrushing vehicles will drive over them in the dark and be destroyed.

The platoon is working close to the Germans. The engineers are not encased in armor shells waiting to respond to moves of enemy infantry or armor. They are baiting the monster, scrambling about in the fire-lit dark, mining the roads in the teeth of the German guns.

As he runs from the big six-by-six truck parked behind a shattered wall that contains the supply of mines, one engineer is struck by bullet fire coming out of the dark. The rounds put him down, wreck his legs. No matter. He goes on with the task, crawling forward, dragging a string of the big, round, devices. Tracer fire leaps through the dark, tearing out the soldier's stomach. He is now beyond hope on this earth. Other engineers in the platoon drag his body, gushing blood, to the shelter of a building. Then they go back into the night and continue to put down mines, knowing full well they may join their comrade in death at any instant.

The surviving engineers escape more damage, are out of mines, find their way to their six-by-sixes, whose drivers are frantic to get going, and hustle aboard. As the big workhorse trucks grind south and east toward Wirtzfeld, they become locked in traffic and are brought to a halt. The lieutenant in charge orders his two dozen men to disembark lest the trucks be blown apart and all lost.

Lieutenant Colonel Norris' 2nd Battalion pack up their weapons, load the few workable vehicles available, and prepare to move south through 1st and 3rd battalions and over the engineers road to Wirtzfeld. They are the first of the battalions to go, moving out, about 5:30 p.m. in an already dark night lit by the candles and torches of the battlefield: flares, muzzle flashes, long skeins of tracer fire, exploding shells. These survivors of one of the most violence-concentrated tank-infantry battles of the Western war, go quietly, in files. They are too numb and worn down to dwell much on what has happened to them, oblivious even to the treacherous night and biting wind.

The troops of Colonel Mildren's shattered and scattered 1st Battalion, 38th Infantry, pick up their guns and what remains of their sleeping bags, blankets, spare ammunition, boxes of rations, and gather with Mildren and the few survivors of his HQ Company. His few remaining officers assemble them near the now destroyed abattoir that has served as the 1st Battalion command post, last ditch fortress, and shelter for wounded and deliver march orders.

Mildren's "A" Company, which has survived the march down the forest road from Wahlerscheid and the two days and nights of war in the dual towns with fewer losses than have the other four companies of the battalion, is the last to leave. One of its rifle platoons and a light machine gun section move at the very end of the column, allowing the battalion to put distance between itself and such enemy as may be lurking in the dark waiting to pounce.

For the medical soldiers shepherding the wounded and disabled, chance and the randomness of artillery strikes and marauding *Grenadiere* in the night present agonizing dilemmas. Few of their charges can move on foot. Some will surely die unless quickly delivered to the collecting company facility where emergency surgery can be done. Some are delirious, others in shock.

By late night December 19 most of the ambulances and jeeps equipped with racks for litters have been disabled or have disappeared carrying wounded soldiers west. The few 2nd Division Medical Battalion vehicles still operating in the two towns can carry only a fraction of the wounded men remaining in the collecting stations. The six-by-six trucks, lighter trucks, jeeps, even gun-carrying halftracks, must be pressed into service to carry out the wounded, not always with their drivers' happy agreement.

A 99th Division medic caught in the melee described what was a commonplace experience for the men of his trade. "Our collecting company was set up in a small school building near a crossroad. ...December 19, vehicles and trucks stacked with men began to evacuate over the road out of Krinkelt. The aid station personnel loaded into our last remaining vehicles and joined in the evacuation.

"Another (medic) and I volunteered to stay behind with the remaining wounded. We were finally able, with the aid of a major (from somewhere) to stop one of the trucks speeding by. (But) after loading the remaining wounded in the truck, there was no room for the sergeant or me. We proceeded out of the village on foot, walking in the vehicle tracks when possible, not knowing which areas were mined."

A most dreadful fate awaits some wounded soldiers, American and German, who have been lost to their comrades and lie in the streets and cart tracks or are on their feet hobbling along. Unseen in the dark, formless in the confusion, they are ground into the slushy muck and melting snow or knocked aside by trucks and tanks rushing by.

On the southern edge of Krinkelt, Colonel Barsanti's 3rd Battalion and the 23rd Infantry's "L" Company with them are the last large infantry contingent to depart the dual towns. As they start their march, Barsanti's 3rd Battalion is attacked by a few *Sturmgeschütze* tracked assault guns of 3rd *PzGD* and two platoons of armored infantry. The colonel orders one company to stay and fight them off, while his artillery liaison officer calls on the 2nd Division artillery to get involved. Friendly howitzers once again join the battle, keeping the Germans from sending in reinforcements, and driving off the *Sturmgeschütze*, which are fat targets for the howitzers.

The rear guard of Barsanti's riflemen and machine gunners plus an M-10 and a Sherman or two hold open the roads until the 3rd Battalion has departed. And some 2nd Division engineers spread more of their chains of mines, then leap on the armor, clinging hard to the wet, icy steel.

A platoon of five Sherman tanks clank along, motors laboring, tracks grinding, bogies squealing, decks thick with infantry and engineers. Smoke from smoldering buildings and burning vehicles mixes with the ghostly fog to create the ultimate dark and dismal scene. Yet, no enemy emerge from the fire-created shadows and dark spaces along the streets to menace the escaping Americans.

However, in another part of Krinkelt, two Shermans smash into a road block unseen in the black. It was put in place earlier by some of Boos' infantrymen, is nothing more than rubble and splintered house beams piled up to conceal the antitank mines underneath. The two tank crews have neither time or equipment to drag this aside, then probe for the antitank devices. Instead, they try to drive their big machines round the obstacle by leaving the road and moving on to the field next to it. Immediately their machines bog to the top of their tracks. There is nothing for it now except to torch the two Shermans and escape on foot, which the ten tank soldiers do posthaste.

The leader of the last platoon of Shermans to depart halts his machines just before the crossroads at the southwest edge of Krinkelt. The commanders climb from their turrets as do some of their crewmen. They unload their remaining antitank mines and spread them across the space where the two roads come together. Swathed in tanker coveralls and headgear resembling football helmets, they spring back into the ice cold, stinking innards of their tanks. The drivers gun the motors, the infantry on top scrunch down and hold on, and they are gone, taking with them the last American presence in the dual towns.

The reader will recall that a mile of soggy road separates Krinkelt and Wirtzfeld. From Wirtzfeld to Elsenborn, the principal town on the high plateau, the distance is about 2.5 miles along another farm road. Only there is no road part of the way, as General Robertson, the 2nd Division leader, remarked. (Narrative VII, Part 2)

By the time Colonel Boos' regiment and the armor, mobile guns, supply vehicles, and the rest start their exodus from Krinkelt, "the engineers' road" (Justly named, since they built it in two days from virtually nothing.) already has been burdened by large numbers of 99th Division trucks and walking men making their way from the borderland forests and Losheimergraben-Buchholz to the Elsenborn crest. And the road also will need to hold up after all of the dual towns defenders have moved over it as well. Some men and machines of the three 2nd Division battalions and the gun company south of Krinkelt and Wirtzfeld guarding the road will also use it to make their escape from the Germans attacking from the east and south.

As the parade passes over the road, the 2nd Division engineers of "A" Company are out and working with picks and shovels, trucks, dozers, vehicles equipped with winches, even when the bursting shells and the flights of enemy rockets threaten to kill them or burn them alive. And if the explosion doesn't lay them low, it flings muck and shattered logs in the air that must immediately be replaced so the pushing, crowding vehicles can keep moving forward.

The job of "A" Company is so impossible, so awful, it produces a perverse euphoria among the engineers doing the work scarcely expressed by the dry report of their company clerk following the effort. "(The road) was kept passable by pioneer work in spite of melting snow and drizzling rain..."

During the night of December 19-20, the "engineers' road" becomes the scene of an extraordinary event: A seemingly endless parade of grinding, groaning engines and doggedly walking men moving through the dark and the winter drizzle, blind beyond a few feet to front and rear, surrounded by shadowy shapes and presences like themselves, threatened all the way by fiery explosions of shells and rockets ahead, behind, off to one side, which like strobe lights reveal for an instant the chaos along the road, then go dark; the soldiers' objective, to reach a village in front of them that is being saturated from the air by shells and rockets and is burning like a pyre.

The infernal journey goes on from dark December 19 to the following morning. The mass of men travelling along the miserable but precious road have little time or desire for palavering: the usual mindless, always ribald joking and japing that accompanies every gathering of soldiers or the gallows humor of those in mortal danger.

Those unable to stay on their feet because of wounds, injuries, and gross fatigue are somehow stuffed in the trucks and jeeps or spread out on the decks of tanks and held in place by other soldiers, not always successfully. A rifleman of a company in Mildren's battalion, remembered, "We had two trucks, one for the wounded, one for the dead."

As usual, few of the officers and none of the men in the companies, platoons, gun and tank sections know what the situation is: Are enemy armor and infantry about to spring from the dark on the slowly-moving column? Is a battle raging in Wirtzfeld that they are expected to join? If not, where will they halt, obtain food and ammunition for their guns, a night's sleep under shelter out of the biting air and icy muck before the next blood-letting starts?

In the confusion and dark, the leaders' task of ordering ranks and controlling units in the ragged column is moot. Movement proceeds and panic is suppressed through a kind of mass will to persevere, a stubborn determination to reach a destination whatever and wherever it may be. The road is scarcely the width of two six-by-six trucks. Walking men frequently stumble upon each others' heels. Vehicles sink into soft patches and must be manhandled out to move on or if inoperative be pushed over the shoulder of the road into the fields on either side. Even the dullest soldier in the parade has the sense to know that forward motion no matter how difficult must be maintained.

While the Germans' incessant artillery fires do the most damage to the soldiers, the storms of rockets shrieking and firey in the black sky inflict the most fright. Veterans of this night's infernal parade will remember to their end what everyone calls the screaming meemies "bracketing the road." "Fired in clusters, getting so close it would make your hair stand straight up, if you had any." "Never heard a screaming meemie 'till then, what a scary noise, no (shell fragments) just combustion..."

When they arrive at Wirtzfeld, the 38th Infantrymen and other soldiers on the road find no haven but a maelstrom of fire and brimstone much of it caused by these very same "screaming meemies," which are 8.4 to 12 inches in diameter. By now—the third night of the 2nd Division's struggle to hold the line east of Elsenborn heights—the German cannoneers and rocketeers have the tactically important little village southeast of Elsenborn well targeted. So many fires are going that the Americans believe *Luftwaffe* aircraft are overhead dropping incendiary bombs (Not so, but it doesn't matter.)

Picking their way through the village, Colonel Barsanti's 3rd Battalion march group takes a barrage of rockets, which screech in, explode, and cause "the battalion to become somewhat disorganized in the darkness." Five men of the 3rd Battalion Headquarters Company and an artillery forward observer party are injured.

Barsanti's grim and silent troops continue their way along the main road leading west out of the village. Nearby is a burning jeep and trailer filled with mortar rounds. One after another the rounds are blasting off in a belch of flame and smoke, spraying a hundred deadly shards of steel at passers by. Barsanti's men are like so many bedraggled Dante Alighieris being led past awful sights ever deeper into Hades. By 1 a.m. December 20, he and his survivors find themselves standing around in a dark, snow-covered open field a half mile northwest of Wirtzfeld in an eerie, unnerving silence wondering what happens next.

Colonel Hirschfelder's 9th Infantry, (minus 1st Battalion) and the 23rd Infantry's 2nd Battalion are to stay well dug in south of the Krinkelt-Wirtzfeld life line until it is no longer needed and can be abandoned to the Germans.

At 8 p.m. December 19, the parade along the escape route a few hundred yards to the north continues thick with men and machines. The commander of a company of towed antitank long guns (3-inch diameter), which is spread across the picket line south of Wirtzfeld, is called to Colonel Hirschfelder's 9th Infantry HQ in that town. The colonel's executive officer informs the antitank captain of the plan for a general withdrawal from the defenses protecting the escape route:

At 10 p.m. the three 2nd Division battalions in the fields south and east of Wirtzfeld will move through that town to little Berg 1.8 road miles to the west and Nidrum and Camp Elsenborn northwest of Berg. The antitank gun company captain asks the exec where his men and twelve towed guns will be located in this withdrawal. He takes no comfort in the answer. His company will bring up the rear after the infantry have departed. Thus, his men will stay emplaced with their guns in the dark hills south of Wirtzfeld while the protecting infantry goes west. At the end, the captain's gunners and their weapons will be as vulnerable to the *Volksgrenadiers* armed with *Panzerfäuste* and their vicious *Maschinengewehre* as weary stags to packs of ravenous wolves.

The captain protests—more vigorously than is wise. His men are being assigned what amounts to a suicidal role in the withdrawal. Even if the enemy infantry should bide their time behind the curtain of the night as the American riflemen and machine gunners leave, they most certainly will not do so as the captain's men struggle to displace their big, awkward guns. A formula for disaster, says the captain. Too bad. The order stands, and he returns down the trail from Wirtzfeld to his command post and the unpleasant task of phoning his platoons around the infantry line that they have been assigned the supreme honor of being the 9th Infantry's rear guard.

The 2nd Division infantrymen south of the exodus road rise from their icy holes, gun nests, and command bunkers, diligently scooped out since their arrival there thirty-six hours previous. They load themselves up with sleeping bags and blankets, weapons, ammunition, and whatever else they can carry and start mushing northwest toward Berg in the dark before dawn. Some of the companies, now well-down from their authorized strength, go through the fires of Wirtzfeld; some go round the southern edges of the village.

The fires and flame ups in the night make silhouettes of the plodding soldiers. Yet the enemy does not appear. What the Germans send instead are powerful attacks of artillery and rocket fire. Apparently, 12th *VG* Division regimental and battalion commanders are without dependable intelligence of the American forces in front of them, their intentions, and capacities. Not wanting to waste any more of their manpower until daylight, they decide to let their howitzers, 88mm long rifles, and rocket-throwing machines carry the battle for the night.

Experienced and disciplined mud soldiers, the men of the 9th and 23rd regiments do not break ranks under the pounding as they go west in widely spaced files across the patches of snow dotting the hilly fields.

Encumbered with their twelve awkward long rifles, the crews of the rear-guarding antitank company experience the worst of it. When their captain receives the signal from 9th Infantry command that they may displace, his men go to work frantically. They manhandle the awkward gun carriages weighted down by an armor shield as well as the long gun to a hauling position, move up their halftracks in the soft snow and muck, hitch the guns, climb aboard and take off.

In spite of the cold, the drivers sweat that they won't drive into a depression, sinkhole, or foxhole from which their vehicles and trailing cannons can't be extracted. However, the opportunistic attacks and harassments by German infantry that the tank-fighting crews feared do not materialize. Engle's 12th *VGD Volksgrenadiers* and *Füsiliers* are lying low for the night, or so it seems. The company of twelve crews and twelve long guns reach safety in the Berg area by 3 a.m., December 20. One man only is lost.

Instead of hazarding the crowded "engineers' road," some officers and NCOs of platoons and companies going west take their men cross country. Frustrated by the slow-moving traffic and bunched-up walking men, the captain of the M-10 tank destroyer company that has fought with Robertson's men in the dual towns decides to chance moving his surviving machines cross country.

The M-10s roll forward onto the dark fields, rising to Berg and Elsenborn, grinding and lurching, diesel engines groaning. Many times during the journey, the crews must climb out and hunt tree branches and building material to spread under a track that turns but can't get a purchase on the spongy ground. The tank destroyer men cover three miles in thirteen hours. Some are so exhausted at the end, they pull into the shelter of random patches of woods and sink into sleep in their open turrets, oblivious to the danger of the killer tree bursts that may find them.

Shortly after noon, December 19, Colonel Boos released Colonel MacKenzie's 395th Regimental Combat Team to return to Lauer's command now positioning on the high plateau east of Elsenborn. The route of 395th RCT is several miles north of the Krinkelt-Wirtzfeld-Elsenborn road. Here, for once, the poor mud soldiers have an advantage. They are not road bound as are the troops riding carriers, trucks, half-tracks, tanks, armored cars, and the rest. The infantry can move on its legs, which if not injured by shell fragments, bullets, icy water, or frost, will carry even hungry and exhausted young men a remarkably long way over uneven and unforgiving ground.

Nonetheless, it is up hill all the way, with everything carried on backs and shoulders. A machine gunner remembered trying to carry two boxes of .30caliber ammunition as he plodded up the hill "stumbling and staggering along trying to keep up. A lieutenant told me to get rid of the ammunition...throw it in the ditch and leave it....'We need you more than we need it.'..." Not an uncommon breach of discipline up and down the ragged columns of 99th Division soldiers.

When things began to turn ominous *Null Tag* afternoon General Lauer, it will be remembered, sent two companies of his combat engineers into the forest on the left (north) flank of Colonel Jack Allen's 3rd Battalion, 393rd Infantry. These two companies depart the forest

December 19, having lost connections with Lauer's headquarters and MacKenzie's RCT as well. They move to Elsenborn on their own, ignorant of what is happening to the 99th Division elsewhere and unwilling to risk being left alone in a dark woods infested with hostile wraiths.

The masses of soldiers climbing the eastern slopes of the Elsenborn plateau move through the deeply echeloned American defensive line forming between Lac de Bütgenbach and Kalterherberg. They enter upon another confusing scene. Infantrymen and combat engineers are digging in the fields. Trucks, large and small, lurch over the few usable slush-impacted mud roads, cart tracks, and cow paths trying to bring up ammunition and supplies.

In the towns of Elsenborn, Berg, and Bütgenbach and in Camp Elsenborn, officers are jeeping up and down the streets or walking about in the melting snow. They bear the burden of making order out of rank disorder. The essential foundation for a military operation: organization, control, clear lines of command has been shaken and cracked. Companies either no longer exist or are down to less than a third of their size. Several may be mixed together and are controlled, if controlled at all, by officers who are strangers to the men.

General Lauer's infantry commanders on the move west with their surviving troops or occupying posts in Elsenborn believe that their battalions should be moved off the line for rest and rebuilding before taking any more punishment up front. Five of them are down to only a few full platoons of riflemen, have lost most of their machine gunners, and not a few mortarmen and pioneers and antitank crews as well. The 393rd Infantry has taken 1,200 known battle casualties, almost all of them in two battalions (Colonel Allen's 3rd and Major Legler's 1st.). The 394th, 1,100 spread across all three battalions and headquarters troops. The 395th, 422 due to the fighting at Höfen and the attack south of the Wahlerscheid crossroads.* What these bloodless numbers mean is that at least twenty-three of Lauer's forty-five infantry companies must be restocked with men and officers and resupplied with weapons.

This restocking will not be accomplished, as all field and company COs hope, in some distant rear-area campground well away from the

---

* As might be expected, casualty estimates vary. Cole estimates the number of casualties sustained by the 99th Division as 2,442, all but 10 percent in the Elsenborn battles from December 15 to month's end. (The Ardennes, Battle of the Bulge, p. 123. Volume 1, Documentation, Master List) Lauer gives the number of casualties for his two hard-hit regiments as 1,357 (393rd), 1,198 (394th). (Battle Babies, p. 69. Same Doc.)

killing ground but right here, up front, in the melting snow and muck of the Elsenborn heights under the cannon and bullet fire of the attacking enemy. The 99th Division can not be removed from the line. U.S. Fifth Corps can not provide a relief division. Every soldier being sent to General Gerow by U.S. 1st Army is needed to harden and extend west to Malmedy and beyond the *cordon sanitare* being put down to wall off the Germans rampaging east of St. Vith and Malmedy. General Lauer's survivors must cope as best they can.

His officers are confronted in Elsenborn by those of the 2nd Division early on the 20th. The latter inform them the 99th is now commanded by General Robertson. Lauer is his deputy. And their men (or what is left of them) are expected to move on to the hilly fields east of Elsenborn, hollow out foxholes and gun nests and be ready to fight off German attacks at once.

The officer who commands Robertson's headquarters company has the job of setting up "straggler control points." He described the experience: "(I) was to collect all personnel, regardless of what unit or division, and organize fighting units with an officer in charge and send them to the Hoke Line" (referred to below). He sends the stragglers from a variety of 2nd, 99th, and other units to a building used in peacetime as a theater in Elsenborn. Here they are sorted out according to their branch of service (infantry, artillery, etc.).

Not all of the soldiers that Robertson's officer gathers up are eager to join an irregular force up front that is commanded by officers they don't know. "About the time I had a hundred or so men organized, there came a lone enemy airplane that dropped a bomb on the building. The lights went out. Everyone started for the open doors for some safety, emptying the building completely. I tried to get the men together afterward who were not 2nd Division men but many 'escaped.' (After the dust settled) I ended with about half the original number to send to the Hoke Line."

Major Frank Hoke, one of Robertson's officers, is in charge of vacuuming up every spare soldier who can fire a gun in the vicinity of Berg and Wirtzfeld. By the evening of December 19, his mixed power of fighters and nonfighters (made instant ones) is manning a line from Lauer's right flank to the left flank of the U.S. 1st Division south of Lac de Bütgenbach. The soldiers caught up in the Elsenborn-Wirtzfeld-Berg confusion start calling this force "Task Force Hoke."

An example of what it is made of are the service and supply soldiers of a tank destroyer battalion attached to the 2nd Division. This scratch force consists of clerks from the personnel section, maintenance men, and cooks; the officer in charge of the battalion's repair facilities is named commander. These instant infantrymen go marching off to dig holes and man guns in the muddy fields down the slopes from Berg. This is a bold new role in the war for these rear-echelon soldiers and one that does not at all inspire them to dreams of glory. Strayed 99th Division men are found among Hoke's power, 2nd Division headquarters people out of Wirtzfeld, antiaircraft crews without gun wagons, ammo handlers, mechanics, artillerymen—a grab bag of the American forces gathering around the Elsenborn heights.

A 2nd Division NCO in charge of collecting stragglers announces that they will be sent off to Paris for a week of R and R (rest and recreation) if they identify themselves and the units they belong to and climb aboard his truck, which will take them rearward. Those who take the bait are despatched to their companies in the fields east of Elsenborn-Berg for more of the same.

These incidents reveal the anxiety of leaders of both the 2nd and 99th divisions to emplace and garrison an armed front that can hold back what they know will be immediate, frantic, last-ditch efforts by the Germans to seize the heights of Elsenborn and the paved roads west of there that carry traffic to the Meuse River valley. It also reveals in a sad sort of way the understandable reluctance of mud soldiers to go back once again where killing and maiming rule and reign. (How many times will the terrible courtesan, Fortune, lavish her favors on a man who keeps trying her patience?)

Only forty-four men and officers of Company "B" 393rd Infantry, 99th Division remain. One platoon sergeant and one lieutenant are in charge. In the Todeswald fighting(Volume 1, Narrative III), 22 men have been killed outright, 34 wounded, and 60 bagged as prisoners of war. When they straggle into Elsenborn early on December 18 all receive a quick examination for evidence of frozen feet and other incapacities. Those unlucky ones who pass the examination get their gear together and march out of the town a few hundred yards east to "a bare ridge on Elsenborn crest in hip-deep snow," as one described it later. (However, a thaw has melted the snow on the crest. Calf-deep mud would be more accurate.)

The sergeant and officer in charge come upon General Lauer's assistant division commander, General Hugh Mayberry. He is harassed, out of temper, tells these remnants of "B" Company to start digging a defensive position. The place the general chooses is on a point with ravines on each side. Bad for defense. They have no spades to dig with, but the artillery shells falling here and there encourage ingenuity. The little band of men use bayonets and hunting knives to chop out chunks of mud and frozen turf, which they scoop away with their helmets.

Some stragglers from the 394th Infantry battalion that fought in the battle of Losheimergraben crossroads (Volume 1, Narrative V, Part 4) reach Elsenborn a few hours before dawn December 19. They are exhausted but take some pride in having held off a strong German infantry power for a few hours. "(We) thought the battle was over for us and another outfit would come in and control things while we rested," remembered one of the soldiers. "We learned there was no relief, and we were going back into the battle." They receive a cooked meal, their first in three days and nights, then move to the fields northeast of Elsenborn where they dig holes under a grey sky threatening rain.

Another 394th Infantry rifleman recalled that after his depleted platoon finally made its way to Elsenborn having survived a hundred trials the men were certain they "would have to be there for days to get re-equipped before we could even think of going on the line." After a night of sleeping in barns and a cooked breakfast eaten as they stand around a farmyard filled with slush and manure, the men of the platoon are ordered to put together such gear and weapons as they have brought back and prepare "to move out."

The tired, unhappy soldiers mush along a street through Elsenborn to the edge of the town. There they move on to a gravel road running down the slopes and up the flat hills east of town. Their objective is a large hill covered in thawing snow and bare of trees and bushes that will be the setting for many bloody scenes in days to come. (Narrative X)

It is not only the poor, long-suffering infantrymen of the 393rd and 394th regiments who have survived so much carnage and brute travel for the last seventy-two hours who now find themselves going back into the monster's lair. The men of General Lauer's combat engineering battalion expected some billeting and assignments behind the front, interspersed, of course, with the usual combat engineers' mine laying tasks in front of the front. Not here, not now. The engineer company on hand and the two believed lost in the Rocheratherwald (Part 4) that have miraculously escaped to return to the fold are ordered to drop their shovels, picks, and axes once again, seize their rifles and machine guns, and take their place on the line east of Elsenborn next to the infantry companies.

Colonel MacKenzie's 395th Regimental Combat Team will not find their way to the heights north of Elsenborn until after daylight December 20. Lieutenant Colonel McClernand Butler's 3rd Battalion (395) will not be able to clear the town of Höfen at the Gatepost (Volume 1, Narrative II, Part 1) for another day or so. Therefore, during the night of December 19-20 the forward slopes and hills east of Elsenborn will be occupied by a patched-together power consisting of stragglers reworked into the line, survivors of the two 99th Division infantry regiments (393, 394th), the division's engineers, and odds and ends of rear-area soldiers dragooned to play the infantry part.

To stand fast along the Wahlerscheid-Rocherath-Krinkelt-Wirtzfeld line from the evening of December 16 to early morning December 20 in conformance with General Robertson's plan and order (Narrative VII), the infantry, engineers, tank-fighting crews and other soldiers of the 2nd Division have paid a fearful price more crushing even than the one laid on the 99th in its three days of death and destruction in the towns, villages, and hilly woods and fields of the borderland country.

In the 9th Infantry Regiment, Lieutenant Colonel Higgins' 2nd Battalion comes to the Elsenborn heights with barely a third of its riflemen and machine gunners. (They let much blood and were also brought down by the elements in the attack toward the Roer River dams just before December 16.) (Volume 1, Narrative II) McKinley's 1st Battalion consists of 217 officers and men total—HQ, supply, mortarmen, and perhaps two dozen riflemen and machine gunners. One entire rifle company ("K") of the 3rd Battalion is gone. The other two have been taken down severely. The battalion's ammo and pioneer platoon, also gone.

In the 23rd Infantry, Lieutenant Colonel Tuttle's 1st Battalion has lost all but a few squads in Companies "I" and "K." Company "L" lacks one platoon. Company "B" of Lieutenant Colonel Hightower's 1st Battalion comes back with its captain and only a few of his men. The colonel's two remaining rifle companies have been reduced by about a third each.

In the 38th Infantry, Mildren's 1st Battalion is without two-thirds of its officers and men on the morning of Wednesday, December 20, having taken hits from the rifle squads to the HQ back-area troops. Norris' 2nd Battalion, which held the point at the brutal northeast corner of Rocherath, and the 38th Antitank Company working with them, have been halved. Barsanti (3rd Battalion) sent one company to fight off attacks on the regimental command post and lost another platoon to enemy air. He comes through with two rifle companies intact (more or less) and his heavy machine gunners, mortarmen, pioneers, and antitank platoon still substantially present and accounted for, as soldiers say, in spite of their hellish journey back.

The 2nd Division Combat Engineer Battalion has lost 25 percent of its men. The signal company, medical battalion, and artillery forward observers also have suffered egregiously.[*] Eight Sherman medium tanks

---

[*] Accurate casualty figures, as observed before, are always hard to come by. Even official regiment, division, etc. reports may not give an accurate picture. The 38th Infantry

have been lost to *Hitlerjugend* guns and rockets; three more scuttled by their crews to prevent capture. Two big M-10 tank destroyers also have fallen to enemy guns (or *Panzerfäuste*). And eight of the twelve crews armed with 3-inch (diameter) antitank guns have had to spike them to keep them out of the *Hitlerjugend* arsenal.

For all the confusion, suffering, and wastage, General Robertson's plan for holding off 1st *SS Panzer* Corps in front of the Elsenborn high plateau seems to be succeeding. Nonetheless, during the night of December 19-20 many threats still lurk round his and Lauer's formations in the east and south.

Third *Panzergrenadier* has taken over from the 12th *SS Panzer* Division in the dual towns, as we have seen.

Colonel Viebig's 277th *Volksgrenadiers*, which have been probing the 395th Regimental Combat Team in the woods north of the dual towns, is girding up its loins for new attacks.

This unknown mass of infantry and armor can be expected to move out of Rocherath, Krinkelt, and the Rocheratherwald immediately and attack toward Elsenborn and Kalterherberg.

Just to the south, Colonel Kraas' division (12th *SS*) and General Engle's 12th *Volksgrenadiers*, whose blood is up after taking Losheimer-graben crossroads and Mürringen-Hünningen, are preparing to move in great force and power on the pivotal town of Bütgenbach. West of Wirtz-feld, Third Parachute Division is south of Bütgenbach-Waimes and can be expected to join the action.

Gerow's defensive line angles toward Malmedy, eight miles by air to the west. On the morning of December 20, this position is the key to the Germans' dissolving the entire north shoulder of the breakthrough area. Gerow and his lieutenants are desperately trying to harden this shoulder as a barrier line against 6th *Panzer* Army. If the armor and infantry of 1st *SS Panzer* Corps overrun Elsenborn, the Bütgenbach rampart is lost; if they overrun Bütgenbach, Elsenborn will be taken from the rear.

For all these threats and for all he has experienced and coped with

---

monthly report showed 334 enlisted casualties in the 1st Battalion; 204, in the 2nd; 95, in the 3rd (including nonbattle) for December 16-20. Also the regiment suffered 27 officer casualties in this time. The 23rd Infantry report for the period December 17-20 listed casualties as 231, 1st Battalion, including officers; 102, 2nd Battalion; 361, 3rd Battalion. The 9th Infantry's 1st Battalion took an estimated 500 casualties from December 13 to 19th, the 2nd and 3rd, 400 total. These numbers include dead, wounded, missing in action and evacuated due to illness, etc. They do not include units not in these infantry battalions.

these last few days, General Robertson maintains his equanimity and control, his posture since the afternoon of *Null Tag*. The captain of the 38th Infantry Antitank Company brings his survivors into Camp Elsenborn early on December 20 driving a jeep and transporting a wounded 99th Division soldier. He has left some twenty-five of his men dead in the dual towns, but brought out all of his wounded. He is weary, tired, and hungry, but somehow elated over the job his men have done on the nightmarish streets. The captain encounters Robertson's aide-de-camp, who beckons him into the general's command post in a cold, battered Belgian Army barracks (much like Lauer's). The 2nd Division leader and his chief of staff, Ralph Zwicker, are drinking coffee. They offer the captain some, and Robertson asks him to "tell (his) story." He listens quietly, remembers the captain, not anxious or agitated.

After the battle, Robertson will acknowledge with a touch of pride what he and his soldiers have accomplished. Withdrawing two regimental combat teams extended far to the northeast and on the attack while enemy columns drive upon both flanks, then wheeling them into position to combat a powerful new armored assault by an enemy determined to rampage through his lines "It was a pretty good day's work for any division. The Army War College would say this was a maneuver that couldn't be done. I don't want to have to do it again."

He even has the good grace to make reference to how significant was the role of the 99th Division's soldiers in the defense against 12th *SS Panzer*: "(By) the end of the action, approximately two thousand men from the 99th Infantry Division had been incorporated into the combat elements of the 2nd Division.* (They) fought like veterans and provided the manpower to maintain my units at effective combat strength." This is an uncommon thing for a commander to say about soldiers of another division, especially the commander of a division made up of regiments whose military pedigrees go far back in U.S. history and whose motto is "second to none."

---

* Estimate no doubt includes the 395 RCT in the Rocheratherwald.

WE WERE THERE

The Engineers' Terminal Task

"The company commander came to me and said, 'Carl, we have to go up and mine all the roads around Krinkelt so that the infantry can pull out. So take your platoon.' I complained a little bit. I said, 'Look, my men are tired as everybody else. Haven't had any sleep for two days.' So he gave me a squad out of the first, second, and third platoons." (AN: Therefore the lieutenant had to take only one of his squads instead of his entire platoon.)

"I went back up to Krinkelt and reported to Colonel Boos (commander of 38th Infantry fighting in the dual towns). We parked (our six trucks) right on the edge of Krinkelt up against some buildings. We sat there practically all day. (December 19) I'd go down to Colonel Boos and I'd say, 'What do you want me to do.' He said, 'We're waiting. We're getting in contact with the battalions. Getting it all (evacuation of the dual towns) squared away. We'll give you the word as soon as we can.'

"Well, they didn't give us any word until about dark. We stayed there that night, and we were supposed to mine these roads as the infantry pulled out....It was a difficult problem because you never knew when the last man was gone and we were pulling daisy chains across the roads (AN: strings of antitank mines tied together to blow up on-coming enemy traffic). I sent my people different places to lay the mines across the roads. That's where Truman Kimbro got the Medal of Honor, but he got killed. One of my men."

"As we went through Wirtzfeld, it was like the 4th of July (with all the shooting, firing, buzz bombs, etc.). We stopped because the road was clogged with vehicles ahead of us. I yelled for all my men to get off the trucks because I thought they might get hit out there (near) a big stone building. It was just full of wounded men. They were groaning and they were moaning. They had their aid people (medical corpsmen), but everybody (else) was pulling back and leaving."

Carl T. Oran, platoon leader, Company "C,"
2nd Division Combat Engineer Battalion

Escaping the Irons of Wrath

"When we got into Rocherath and Krinkelt, the twin towns, we took up a position in a house on a ridge. When we looked to the east we could see tanks and armored vehicles going parallel to our front."

"This German tank stopped about fifty feet in front of the building, and its turret swung around and the gun pointed right at the house. I was sure it was pointing right at me. The thing fired. The concussion of that—I couldn't hear for the next couple of hours....The shell, I think was an armor-piercing shell, and it went right through the building and exploded in the back. If it had been a high explosive shell it would have wiped out everybody in the house."

"We went to a different position and were looking out of the building in which we had taken shelter. The German tanks with infantry on them came toward us, not to attack the building—I don't believe they knew a lot of troops were there—but they came down that street. Our infantry was firing at these troops. A German soldier fell off this lead tank and was lying in the road moving his arms and legs. The next tank that came along drove right over him. Frightening."

"Later that night, we were told to evacuate to Elsenborn. We went down a narrow road, deep ditches on either side...really clogged with American troops...and received some rocket fire, which bracketed either side of the road. All I could think of was we're moving really slowly and the next rounds—they are going to land right on the road—and I'm going to be there."

"It seemed to take hours and hours. I remember seeing a ridge line, bushes and trees there, and as we were approaching we saw rifle barrels point out. My reaction was 'My God, we've walked into a trap.' But it turned out to be Americans."

Frank C. Grapuner, forward observer, lieutenant, Battery A, 38th Field Artillery Battalion, 2nd Division

Death Rides with the *Panzer* Crews

"We had orders to retreat from our (105mm) gun positions at Krinkelt....We moved back through the town and pulled off at the side of a building with our three-quarter-ton weapons carrier and was (sic) prepared to dig in or whatever. Artillery fire was coming in and also small arms fire, from the Germans on our left in Krinkelt, so we abandoned our truck and took cover."

"When we went in this building in the basement, there were five other (Americans) there....We stayed in this basement during the night. (AN: probably December 18)"

"Next morning we found there was still some (American) infantry in the town. They had got cut off like we had got cut off....This guy I don't know where he came from or who he was. All I remember about him he was a short Mexican-American from San Antone (sic) or somewhere down the line in Texas. He had hand grenades, and he had bazooka ammunition, and he knew where a bazooka was, and he went and got the thing. He took that bazooka, and this tank was on the corner a hundred yards from where we was (sic) in this basement, and he said if you guys will cover me I'll see if we can get him.

"This tank was trying to go around the corner and the tank driver had turned just enough that when (this soldier) fired the bazooka he hit the tracks, and knocked it off. Either the engine died or they shut it down. But (this soldier) dropped the bazooka, and he had a hand grenade hanging on his field jacket, and as the German tankers opened the turret (hatch) on the tank and they come out of there—the Germans—he jumped up on the back part, pulled the pin and dropped it down in the turret. It killed the gunner and tank driver."

Charles A. Heilman, gunnery sergeant, Battery A, 370
Field Artillery Battalion, 99th Infantry Division

"A Heck of a Good Time"

"We had nine 57mm antitank guns, three in each platoon. Two platoons on the north and northeast. First platoon was in the south supporting Colonel Mildren's 1st Battalion around the church."

"That Sunday (December 17) morning we started engaging the tanks, but for the most part we didn't use the 57s because of the restrictive fields of fire and the fact that the tanks came in from directions in which the 57s were not facing.

"The majority of tanks we knocked out in that fight were done with bazookas. We had about eighteen. Two per gun squad and some in company HQ. My gun crews were running around with bazookas and firing from second floor windows because that's where they could get a better shot in Rocherath and Krinkelt both."

"Major source of our casualties was tank machine gun fire. Very little artillery fire. We stayed in the houses, well protected. But by the end of the first day, it was obvious our 57mm guns were not doing the job for us. They were too low down (to the ground). They were not maneuverable enough.

"Sunday night (December 17) things were really fluid. It was really confused. Guys were coming back (AN: from other 2nd and 99th division units). They were obviously confused. I said, 'Well, here, join up with us, we're fighting.' As a matter of fact, when we got the order to withdraw, we didn't want to withdraw. We were having a heck of a good time.

"We didn't know how bad off we were. Apparently we were practically surrounded."

James W. Love, commander, Antitank
Company, 38th Infantry, 2nd Division

The Confusing Adventures of Some Shermans

"Company 'B's 2nd (tank) Platoon was posted in the northern part of Rocherath by the afternoon of December 17. (AN: five Sherman medium tanks each bearing a 75mm high-velocity gun) Some tank gun fire was received and returned mainly from north and east of (the town).

"The platoon settled down in defensive positions as it got dark while we were setting up road blocks with some American tank destroyer vehicles.

"During the night, German tanks penetrated into the town. They were stopped mainly by tank fire, but they didn't go away. The Sherman tank gun's armor-piercing rounds bounced off the front of the German tanks. My tank was hit by a high explosive round and my crew evacuated."

"It was a very confusing situation in the town during December 18 and 19. Our tanks were behind houses and would move and fire at enemy fire. They played the same game. Our infantry had strong points in houses. Liaison was poor between infantry and tanks, but we complemented each other and were effective."

"When we were released to withdraw, we started our tanks up and went down the road to Wirtzfeld. Mine was the last tank out. I had a bunch of antitank mines in the rear deck, and every once in a while I would stop and put four or five mines on the road."

"We arrived at our company command post located in Berg, Belgium. The next day we set up a defense on a big hill outside the village facing south."

> Robert L. Dudley, lieutenant, platoon
> leader, 741st Tank Battalion

How the Medics Experience War

"The church (on the border between Rocherath and Krinkelt) became the aid station for the men being wounded all around it. The entire first floor of the church was covered with wounded.

"We insisted that all rifles and other arms be stacked in the vestibule of the church so that when the Germans arrived, as we fully expected them to do, we would be treated as medics, rather than combatants. We could hear the German soldiers shouting, '*Hände hoch*,' just outside the church all during the evening. Our litter bearers went out into that terrible night and brought the wounded to our doctors."

"Our people—and that includes riflemen as well as medics—performed magnificently. The slightly wounded were eager to go back into the black cold to help wherever they could. Aid men and litter bearers, absolutely defenseless, would rush in with wounded and return to the maelstrom again and again. It seemed to me that no one knew who was where."

"Of course, we in the church saw nothing of the outside events. To us, the battle, and it was all around us and just on the other side of the walls of the church, was just sounds of cries, machine guns, burp guns (machine pistols), and the sights of the wounded, standing, lying, leaning, and sitting."

> Francis J. Leone, sergeant, litterbearer platoon,
> Company "B," 324th Medical Battalion,
> 99th Division

They Shake Off Sleep, Death's Counterfeit, and Look on Death Itself

"Late December 18, 'G' Company was given a new mission. We headed out of Krinkelt in the same direction we had come from (i.e. northeast). We were ordered to occupy a road junction... considered vital as friendly troops were still trying to withdraw toward (the town)."

"My platoon (the 2nd) and 'G' Company headquarters people occupied the house and ground on the west side of the road. As night closed, the 2nd Platoon...was ordered to send out a patrol... to contact other friendly forces believed in the area."

"During the early hours, the men dug in around the perimeter of the (company) area, taking advantage of hedges and tree lines to conceal their positions....Only about one third of the men stayed in the foxholes, while others manned windows that overlooked our front. The balance of the men dropped off to sleep."

"We detected some movement coming down the road from the north....Our outposts thought that the men coming in were either our returning patrol or members of the 99th Division. It was not until this group had penetrated our position that their true identity was determined. (AN: Fifteen enemy soldiers have pushed into the 'G' Company camp. They shout for the Americans to surrender, then fire wildly with their machine pistols and assault rifles.)"

"The German automatic fire must have been a signal for the rest of the enemy troops, as extremely heavy small arms fire covered the (company) area. All the sleeping men jumped from the first floor windows and made their way to the foxhole system."

"...As the battle progressed, the company commander called for artillery fire. As a last resort, he directed this fire on our own positions. This probably saved the day."

"But 'G' Company had taken many casualties. Corporal Norman Martz, who manned the foxhole with me, had been struck in the head and was dead; others along the foxhole line were also dead and wounded. The patrol sent out never returned. Its three men were later reported dead."

John Savard, Browning Automatic Rifle team, Company "G," 38th Infantry, 2nd Division

"The Most Humiliating Moment of My Life"

"When the Germans attacked that morning (December 17), we had to fall back and as darkness came on, Dietrich, Lieutenant Flaim, a soldier whose name I can't remember, and I went into a barn a little way from the house. (AN: This house and barn were near the Lausdell crossroads a half mile east of Rocherath where the 1st Battalion and 'K' Company of the 38th Infantry Regiment were trying to establish a defense against *Hitlerjugend*.)

"When the fighting quieted at dark, we had an idea to spend the night in the dry hay in the barn. Dietrich and I went up a short ladder and had a pretty sheltered spot. Sparky and the other soldier stayed at ground level. After a pretty good while, all hell broke loose. A Tiger had idled up about one hundred yards. (AN: *Hitlerjugend* Division used no *Panzer VI* Tiger tanks in this action. It was probably a *Jagdpanzer* tank destroyer, which was frightening enough for a poor infantryman to encounter.) It opened up with a machine gun on the barn and house. Tracer bullets, (i.e. illuminated rounds) were coming through the barn so thick I don't see how we could escape being hit. But we got out, but fast. Lieutenant Flaim and the other soldier I never saw again. We were protected from the Germans attacking (by the American artillery), but our own shells would surely get us.

"Suddenly from a small basement window, someone said, 'Quick, in here.' We didn't have to be told twice....In the cellar was Captain Jack G. Garvey, 'K' Company, 9th Infantry and about fourteen of his men."

"Things quieted down, but when daylight came (December 18) we could see the Tiger (see previous note) out front with his 88 (millimeter gun) practically sticking in the front door. German troops were poking American soldiers out of holes all around. Our artillery sounded way off. No shells were falling.

"Captain Garvey knew it was only a matter of time before the Germans came to search the house, so he ordered one of his group who could speak a little German to stand by the front door (and ask a soldier to bring an officer to whom he could surrender).

"In the meantime, Captain Garvey told us to dismantle our weapons, scatter the parts, and destroy any paper we were carrying. We were marched out with our hands up. It was the most humiliating moment of my life."

Henry D. Albin, sergeant, Company
"I," 23rd Infantry, 2nd Division

Fortune Smiles on an American Tank Crew

"(The five tanks of) my platoon were in defensive positions commanding views of the roads leading into the town of Rocherath on the northeast. My tank and crew were backed into an old barn having thick stone walls..."

"...that night, after it was pitch dark, we heard a German tank clanking and creaking slowly coming down the alley directly toward us. A German on foot, apparently (guiding) the tank driver, shouted 'halt' to a cow that moved in the alley (next to us), and fired a short burst from his burp gun (machine pistol).

"I told my gunner to load a round of high explosive shell in the gun and point (the gun) where he thought the German tank was. And I told my driver to be prepared to start the engine after we fired and get the hell out of there.

"We did just that. The high explosive went off against the front of the German tank....My driver had to pull out of the barn toward the south, then make a 'U' turn to the north. In negotiating the turn, he had to back up and our tank came close to bumping the *Panzer* (we had shot at).

"As we moved north and then northwest, the German tank fired its big gun and blew off the east wall of the barn (we had been in). We moved about a half a block, pulled alongside another building and faced the tank to the southeast. The German didn't follow. I don't know why.

"Later that night, we learned our infantry (the 38th Regiment) was going to pull back and leave us alone. The plan was to get the infantry several miles down the road (to Wirtzfeld), ...then we would pull out. Fortunately nothing happened the rest of the night."

Joseph H. Dew, lieutenant, platoon leader,
Company "C," 741st Tank Battalion

Confusion's Masterpiece

"Fragments I remember of my battalion's three days of wandering in the forests north of Rocherath while the 38th Infantry and its armor were battling *Hitlerjugend* Division in the dual towns.

- - -

"The night of December 18-19, we slept in the fields and ditches near our mortars. Shortly after dawn, a dozen of us went to a nearby woods and helped carry out some of our machine gunners and riflemen who had been struck down during the night by tree bursts of high-velocity 3-inch shells fired by American tank destroyers. One machine gunner, who begged me to help him, lay in a shallow, wet slit trench, his thigh opened from groin to knee, oozing dark blood. A litter-bearing jeep appeared—just one—to take the wounded out. It could carry four plus one on the hood, able to sit. We had maybe two dozen lying around the woods, suffering."

- - -

"A long line of us had stopped at the edge of a forest on a low-lying bluff overlooking the shallow valley leading into Rocherath (i.e. Laudsell crossroads). The night was blacker than black. No one in the line of several hundred officers and men seemed to know which way to go or what to do. Doing something was urgent because to the left, down a long slope at a distance of perhaps one mile, the most awful battle had erupted. The very farm fields and marshes of the valley seemed on fire, with eerie light that rose and fell against the sky. Long streamers of tracer bullets floated lazily through the smoke and flame. From time to time, explosions shook the valley with the sound of gigantic hammers brought down on the earth. The *Panzer* guns were letting go with their violent, urgent screech-bang. But it was the obscene, laughing chatter of machine guns that struck the deepest fear of all into our hearts."

- - -

"Everyone in the battalion column was ground down by three days of confused marching; stumbling through the woods; nasty cold; sleet and rain; snowy mush underfoot; enemy bullet fire, now here now there; sudden violence from the wild artillery barrages when we arrived at night in the silent streets of a town that appeared to be safe. We followed each other down the streets, expecting in the end to be billeted in the dark and empty houses or barns sheltered at last from the hateful cold. The column did not even miss a step as it reversed direction, moved out of the town, and headed once again for the east toward the Rocheratherwald and more of the same. It was inhuman, but then everything was."

An "H" Company ammunition bearer,
393rd Infantry, 99th Division

Blood Has Bought Blood and Blows Have Answered Blows

"After the fog lifted in the morning (December 18), we formed up in ranks. The *Panther* (tank) companies preceded us in pushing into the town of Rocherath. (AN: His company was equipped with *Panzer IVs*.) My company was at the end of the formation. I thought I noticed some movement in a section of woods on our right and suspected an enemy antitank gun. In order to see better, I opened the turret hatch (of the tank) and pointed my binoculars toward the edge of the woods. Instantly I was struck by a bullet fired by an infantry rifle. I called Lieutenant Pucher on my radio and passed the command to him."

> Gotz Grossjohann, captain, commander of
> 6th Company, 12th *SS Panzer* Regiment,
> 12th *SS Panzer* Division

- - -

"The forested terrain was blown to bits by artillery fire. We received bad news: The attack did not advance and the losses were great. There were several wounded soldiers and disabled tanks."

"The leader of the 3rd Platoon (2nd *Panzer* Company), Sergeant Bierau, had fallen. We put him in our *Volkswagen* and drove back with him to the supply lines. He had been hit in the head.

"Behind the front, things were not moving along. New units pushed forward. Time and again, engineers had to (stabilize) the mud of the road so that tanks would not sink in further.

"We had to wait about two hours in the forest until we got through. We were standing close to the road (AN: The poorly maintained forest road from Hollerath, Germany to Rocherath, Belgium.) underneath the fir trees. We were cold through and through and walked around a bit. Behind us the troop carrier (*Schützenpanzerwagen*) of a *Panzerjäger* company (AN: He means *Panzergrenadier* company) was being pushed by several comrades. The motor had been damaged and could only be fixed by the repair detachment."

"I allowed two American prisoners of war to sit on the radiator (of the *VW*). We were all freezing. It was cold and wet (in these) winter woods. Our shoes were wet. We all were hungry. I cut a thick piece of lightly frozen black bread, covered it well with pork grease from a tin can and offered it to the Americans, but they declined. They looked at us with astonishment as though to say, 'How can you eat (here in the forest) among all the dead bodies?'"

Alfred Schulz, sergeant, 2nd *Panzerjäger* Company, 12th *SS Panzer* Regiment

- - -

"The tank of Captain Jurgensen is (parked) next to the door of a building (in Rocherath). Next to the building, the commander (AN: Jurgensen is CO of the *Panther* tank battalion of the 12th *SS Panzer* Regiment.) is talking to some officers and men of the battalion staff.

"I report to him. His face mirrors defeat and resignation. The unsuccessful attack and the heavy losses, especially those of the 1st and 3rd companies obviously weigh heavily on him.

"He instructs me not to change positions for the time being... since I will best be able to rejoin the battle from there. Now I can also see the main road. The disabled tanks of our company are a terribly depressing sight.

"(As we talk) a single tank approaches the division's command post. At a distance of only one hundred meters (three hundred and thirty feet), it turns into a burning torch. Shortly, the commander of this tank, Sergeant Freiberg, appears with a bandage around his head. He reports, 'I saw a woman at the door to a house waving with a white cloth. As I turned my attention to her, wondering what this was about, I was hit and my tank immediately burst into flames.'"

Willi Engle, lieutenant and tank commander, 3rd Company, 12th *SS Panzer* Regiment

- - -

"During an attack in Krinkelt on December 19, we received a direct hit. It tore a hole about one meter into our armor. Our driver, *Sturmann* (AN: No equivalent U.S. rank, roughly a corporal.) Karl Heinz von Elm, was torn to pieces. Our radio man, *Sturmann* Gottfried Opitz, lost his left arm...the legs of *Sturmann* Hannes Simon were full of splinters.

"I was sitting in the turret and had put my legs up, so I got away with just the fright of it. Hannes and Gottfried were protected in the tank as we went to the medical aid station; the tank then was towed to the repair company (of the regiment) at Losheimergraben. We buried Karl Heinz there."

Max Solner, tank gunner, 6th Company,
12th *SS Panzer* Regiment

- - -

"Krinkelt-Rocherath was an absolute death trap for armor. In the lead were the *Panzers* of 1st Company. Then came our company with Captain Kurt Brödel in command. (My tank) was positioned behind Sergeant Johann Beutelhauser, my platoon commander.

"As I reached the church (in Krinkelt), I was given a foretaste of the dire events to come. Beutelhauser caught it right in front of me. ...He succeeded in getting out and reaching a place of safety, but his gunner was hit by rifle fire as he got out.

"I moved my tank behind a house where it could not be seen or fired on, without at that moment knowing what would happen. Near me Brödel's tank was burning gently (sic) with Brödel still sitting lifeless in the turret. In front of me further along the road more (of our) tanks had been put out of action and were still burning."

Willi Fischer, tank commander, 3rd Company,
12th *SS Panzer* Regiment

Some Quick Views of a Tank Destroyer Leader's War

Following are selected entries from the diary of the commander of the company of twelve tracked and armored American tank destroyers (M-10s) with 38th Infantry in the dual towns:

"German tanks overrun Kilgallen's (tank destroyer). Sergeant Olivetti is wounded by a bazooka shell fired by an American. Murphy's tank destroyer is hit and abandoned. (Three of us) go up and recover it, take it to Wirtzfeld, pick up another, and take it back (to Rocherath). Everyone is worn out. Go to bed late, after midnight, in crowded basement of 38th Infantry command post."

"Losgar and I drive up past the church (AN: On the border between Rocherath and Krinkelt) and abandon jeep in front of a *Panther* tank.

Scramble on hands and knees past house and through a field while we are shelled. Report to Colonel Boos (38th Infantry commander), who says *Panther* was knocked out yesterday. We go back and inspect it, and get shelled with *Neblewerfer* rockets. (Abandoned) jeep has a flat tire. Find another jeep and get a spare. Eat 'K' rations (AN: boxed processed canned meat, eggs, cheese and crackers) with some infantrymen. Put a tank destroyer in position near the church. Sergeant in charge is scared."

"Colonel Boos says Colonel Norris (2nd Battalion) is not satisfied with (performance) of tank destroyers. I talk with Colonel Norris, then a guide takes me to the 38th Infantry Antitank Company command post. We shoot at Germans from upstairs. There is a huge hole in the side of the house. One of (my) tank destroyers is shooting at a German tank located among some houses but hits a squad of Americans in one."

"One of the tank destroyers hit. Karpiak and Lee badly wounded. Hughes killed. Problem of how to evacuate them."

> Harlow F. Lennon, captain, Company "C," 644th
> Tank Destroyer Battalion (Self-propelled)

Miserable Terrain, Horrible Sights, Grim Prospects

(AN: Major General Walter Denkert, CO of the 3rd *Panzergrenadier* Division, which moved into Rocherath-Krinkelt after noon on December 19, went forward during the morning along the forest road from the West Wall west of Hollerath to Rocherath.)

"The forest road west of Hollerath, Germany, leading through the Dreiherrnwald and the Krinkelterwald (AN: that part of the Todeswald defended by Lieutenant Colonel Allen's 3rd Battalion, 393rd Infantry on *Null Tag*) was extraordinarily difficult because of the nature of the terrain, steep slopes and marshy ground, and the bad weather.

"Vehicles that had been upset or were stuck fast—especially those of *Hitlerjugend* Division—blocked every means of passage, particularly because buried mines made it impossible to leave the road."

"Before long, driving (toward Rocherath) became impossible. I was compelled to continue my reconnaissance on foot. It therefore took hours before we reached the west border of the forest.

"There were signs of heavy fighting, especially at the intersections of the forest roads."

"The experience of this march—in damp, cold, slushy weather, wading in mud above the ankles, past destroyed or stuck vehicles, and weapons of all kinds that had been put out of action or had broken down while corpses (of dead soldiers)—some of whom were terribly mutilated—were constantly in sight—belongs to (my) most horrible war remembrances.

"This part of the reconnaissance for one thing showed up the difficulties that would handicap bringing up (my) division. Second, they made me realize the severity of the coming battles.

Walter Denkert, Major General, commanding
officer, 3rd *Panzergrenadier* Division

KEY TO NARRATIVE IX

Bütgenbach-Dom Bütgenbach (Area A on Map)

CONTENDERS: U.S. 26th Infantry Regiment (Colonel John F.R. Seitz), 1st Infantry Division (Brigadier General Clift Andrus), Battalion COs of 26th: 1st, Lieutenant Colonel Frank J. Murdoch; 2nd, LTC Derrill M. Daniel; 3rd, LTC John Corley. Companies of M-10 self-propelled, 3-inch antitank guns and M-36 SP 90mm AT guns; company of medium (Sherman) tanks. Company of towed 3-inch AT guns. German 12th *SS Panzer* Regiment (*SS* Major Herbert Kuhlmann) of 12th *SS Panzer* Division, *Hitlerjugend*, (*SS* Colonel Hugo Kraas); four *Panzergrenadier* (armored infantry) battalions of 12th *SS*; *Schwerpanzerjäger Abteillung* (heavy tank destroyer battalion). Companies of mobile antiaircraft guns, field artillery, antitank guns, and pioneers. These *Panzer*, infantry, and other units are organized into two battle groups (*Kampfgruppen*): *Kampfgruppe* Kuhlmann and *Kampfgruppe* Krause (Bernhard). Companies of 3rd *Fallschirmjäger* (parachute) Division. (Major General Walter Wadehn).

ISSUE: The 2nd *SS Panzer* Corps (*SS* Lieutenant General Willi Bittrich) has taken over responsibility for breaking through the U.S. 5th Corps defensive line on the Elsenborn-Bütgenbach high plateau. Twelfth *SS Panzer* Division (still part of 1st *SS* Corps) is to attack the Bütgenbach-Dom Bütgenbach part of the line held by the 1st Division. Significance: If successful this attack will open the Belgian highway N-32 west to Malmedy (the all-important *Rollbahn C* in the German plans) and clear other roads west of interdiction by American artillery fire. It may also force the 99th and 2nd divisions holding the Elsenborn high plateau from Kalterherberg south to Berg to withdraw west to a new defensive line.

LOCATION: The southeastern Belgian town of Bütgenbach and the hills, fields, and marshes to the south and east of it and of the nearby reservoir (Lac de Bütgenbach); the manor house, farm buildings, and dependencies of Dom Bütgenbach, a local farm estate a mile and a half southeast of Bütgenbach on the N-32. The village of Morschheck a mile to the south and the Bütgenbacher Heck, a woods south of Bütgenbach. The town of Büllingen, staging area for 12th *SS*, 1.5 miles se of Wirtzfeld. The Schwarzenbückel hill between Dom B and Büllingen.

Wirtzfeld-Lac de Bütgenbach (Area B on Map)

CONTENDERS: U.S. 26th Infantry, 3rd Battalion (Corley), platoon of Sherman tanks, 26th Infantry headquarters company troops, platoon of M-10s. 38th Infantry, 2nd Battalion (Norris); 3rd Battalion (Barsanti). German Infantry and pioneer companies of reserve *Grenadier* and *Füsilier* regiments of 12th *Volksgrenadier* Division (Major General Gerhard Engle). Company of *Sturmgeschütze* assault guns.

ISSUE: The German plan for seizing Bütgenbach and clearing away the 1st Division troops holding the N-32 west of Büllingen calls for simultaneous attacks by the two 12th *SS* battle groups (above) and the infantry of Engle's 12th *VGD*, a pincer movement with the former striking from the south and southeast, and the latter from the east. Significance: This will put intolerable pressure on the U.S. 26th Infantry Regiment by forcing the 26th to resist attacks on two fronts simultaneously.

LOCATION: The hills between German-held Wirtzfeld and the Lac de Bütgenbach reservoir; the single-track railroad south of the reservoir running from Büllingen to Bütgenbach.

Weywertz-Waimes (Area C on Map)

CONTENDERS: U.S. 16th Infantry (Colonel Frederick W. Gibb) of 1st Division; provisional battle group of division service and other troops; company of M-10s, platoon of light tanks (Stuarts). Defense of Weywertz commanded by LTC Charles T. Horner, CO of 3rd Battalion, 16th Infantry. German Companies of 3rd *Fallschirmjäger* (parachute) Division (General Wadehn).

ISSUE: 3rd *FJD's* mission is to attack from Schoppen and capture the towns of Waimes and Weywertz. Significance: If successful, these attacks will put German infantry at the rear of the 5th Corps' divisions east and south of Elsenborn and threaten their all-important artillery installations. The 3rd *FJD* attack is to go forward simultaneously with the attacks of 12th *SS Panzer* and 12th *VGD* (above).

LOCATION: The open fields and single track railroad line and the N-32 road south of Weywertz and east of Waimes. Weywertz is 1.5 miles northwest of Bütgenbach and 2.5 miles northeast of Waimes, partially occupied by 16th Infantry, 2nd Battalion.

MAP FOR THESE KEY PAGES: 190-191.

NARRATIVE IX: THE BLOODY ANGLE

Part 1: *OKW* Discovers the Elsenborn Plateau

The tactical threat of the Elsenborn heights as a place where the Americans might be able to take a stand to wall off and constrict 6th *SS Panzer* Army's drive west seems not to have been considered a serious matter in the planning for *Wacht am Rhein*, certainly not one needing intensive consideration in the plan.

Field Marshal Walter Model's inspiration a week or so before the German attack December 16 into the Ardennes to put glider troops down on the heights (Volume 1, Narrative II, Part 1) must have come out of a nagging concern about this sector. But a drop of glidermen (paratroops, as it turned out) was not part of the original *Oberkommando der Wehrmacht* (*OKW*) plan. In the event, the paratroops were woefully inadequate to the task.

However, by December 19 all levels of the German high command, from Hitler's headquarters (*OKW*) to the infantry and *SS* armor division leaders in the cockpit east of the Elsenborn high plateau, are awakening to the rising threat the Elsenborn heights represent to the aims and ambitions of 6th *SS Panzer* Army. The Americans in large numbers are escaping west to take new positions there. The angle at the south end of the heights in the Bütgenbach area is being powerfully shored up by the U.S. 1st Division, well known and feared by the Germans. Aerial reconnaissance and spies have made clear the frantic efforts of the Americans to fortify and harden the entire area with the vast array of howitzers and long guns described before.

The sacrifices since early *Null Tag* of Lauer and Robertson's men and the armor and gun soldiers with them have done what the *Führer's* planners did not expect: bought time for the fortification of the heights east and south of Elsenborn.[*]

---

[*] To save the reader's backpaging to find other references to this critically important terrain feature in our story, following is a summary: If you stand at the eastern edge of Elsenborn, Belgium near the road to Kalterherberg and Monschau, you look over what appears to be a vast panorama of hilly fields and patches of woods descending to a distant valley and forested hills beyond. From Kalterherberg on the north to Büllingen on the south is eight miles (as the crow flies). Elsenborn is between the two.

The heights of Elsenborn are nineteen hundred feet above sea level, but so gradual are the slopes to the east that some of the little towns located there—Wirtzfeld, Krinkelt-Rocherath, Mürringen—are scarcely less elevated. The town of Bütgenbach, two miles south of Elsenborn is at the southern terminus of the heights. Between the two towns are

Lieutenant Colonel Peiper's armored anaconda (Volume 1, Narrative V, Part 2) has reached twenty-five miles west of its starting point, but needs reinforcements, fuel, food, ammunition. Yet the high ground at the southern end of the Elsenborn plateau commands the N-32 west, the most useful route to reach Peiper.

More ominous still, General Hasso Eccard von Manteuffel's 5th *Panzer* Army has made a sizable breakthrough south of Peiper's column in the Schnee Eifel and is striking for St. Vith, Belgium, eleven miles south of Bütgenbach. So long as the vast staging and supply area of the Americans in the Eupen-Verviers-Malmedy triangle, which lies directly behind the Elsenborn heights, remains unconquered, von Manteuffel's power is at risk from the direction of its northern (right) flank as it advances west.

OKW has released the 3rd *Panzergrenadier* Division from its reserve to replace 12th *SS Panzer* Division in the march from the dual towns, Rocherath-Krinkelt, to the Elsenborn high plateau. (Narrative VIII, Part 5) Twelfth *SS Panzer* is now to concentrate its still formidable power on seizing the N-32 high road and the small but important city of Malmedy, thereby unhinging the right wing of the U.S. 5th Corps barrier line across the plateau.

As we know, (Narrative VIII, Part 4) General Kraemer, 6th *SS Panzer* Army chief of staff, wants the division to execute this mission by marching south from Büllingen as the least costly way of reaching Malmedy. First *SS* Corps commander, General Hermann Priess, is of the opinion this southern route is an impassable morass. He persuades Kraemer to go along with the original plan and pass *Hitlerjugend* over the N-32 by way of Bütgenbach. Given road conditions and other circumstances, Priess is probably correct, but his intended maneuver will bring only grief for the German cause.

Hitler is pressuring Field Marshal Model and General Dietrich to push 6th *SS Panzer* Army forward. Twelfth *SS Panzer* will break through to the west at Bütgenbach-Malmedy immediately. Simultaneously, 2nd *SS* (*Das Reich*) and 9th *SS* (*Hohenstauffen*) *Panzer* divisions of 2nd *SS Pz* Corps will drive west to nourish the 5th *Panzer* Army's breakthrough, reinforce *Kampfgruppe* Peiper, and push through the hardening

---

the tiny villages of Nidrum and Berg, where a municipal reservoir for the area is located. The Elsenborn high plateau acts as a natural rampart guarding the way west to Verviers (18 air miles) and Liege (28 air miles).

American defenses on the north flank of the breakthrough area.[*]

Late on the 19th, Dietrich's 6th *Panzer* Army HQ at Bad Münstereifel near Euskirchen, receives visitors from on high. Officers of both Hitler's *OKW* operations staff and von Rundstedt's *Ob-West* as well have travelled all the way from the Bad Nauheim area north of Frankfort, Germany to ascertain what has gone wrong on the Elsenborn front, why a mission that was to consume no more than a day still has not been accomplished near the close of the fourth day of the *Riesenanschlag*.

The leaders of 6th *Panzer* Army are told the roads available to their troops, armor, and vehicles are not being kept up properly, thus exacerbating the already awful traffic jams impeding forward movement from the bases in Germany. This is true. But the formation responsible for making the roads passable is the *Todt* organization, a *Nazi* Party labor appendage that Dietrich and his headquarters have little authority over.

A second cause of the failure of 6th *Panzer* Army in front of the Elsenborn high plateau, according to the visiting officers, is the quality of the soldiers who fill out the infantry and armor divisions. They have been inadequately trained, as if their commanders didn't already know this. Vigorous, aggressive leadership will correct the problem, the *OKW-Ob-West* staff officers assert.

Reflecting these views and pronouncements, the "war diary" of von Rundstedt's headquarters for December 19 states firmly that the 6th *Panzer* Army must obtain "room for maneuver" by seizing the Elsenborn plateau using the five divisions available there, and "with proper leadership this goal can be reached." Regardless of what is officially recorded in the *Ob-West* war diary, the high German commanders directing *Wehrmacht* operations in the Ardennes are turning their attention to fundamental changes in the *Wacht am Rhein* plan and objective.

Field Marshal Model wants to pass the *Schwerpunkt* of the Ardennes

---

[*] The exploits of the two *Panzer* divisions (2nd *SS*, *Das Reich*, and 9th *SS*, *Hohenstauffen*) in the Ardennes offensive are referred to only incidentally in our narratives. The original plan for Dietrich's two *Panzer* corps was for the 2nd *SS* Corps to move behind the spearhead *Kampfgruppen* of the 1st *SS* Corps as the second wave of armor, cross the Meuse River south of Liege, and take the lead in the climactic march to Antwerp, Belgium. By December 20 this plan was moot, even if Hitler did not admit it. Nevertheless, both divisions of the 2nd Corps became involved in fierce fighting along the northern flank of the 5th *Panzer* Army and in the case of *Hohenstauffen* at Bastogne also. From the beginning of the campaign, both experienced severe shortages of gasoline and ammunition. See also Appendices item on "Bulge" history.

counteroffensive to the *Panzers* of Manteuffel's 5th Army. Upon reaching the Meuse River they would then wheel north accompanied by Dietrich's army as a flank guard and support. At the same time, the German 15th Army, until now inactive in the counteroffensive, would make a drive on Aachen, Germany, then wheel southward to meet Manteuffel and Dietrich's divisions coming up from the south. This huge force of armor and infantry—three armies' worth—would thereby unhinge the American power on the Malmedy-to-Julich, Germany line, i.e. Hodges' U.S. 1st Army. They would destroy 1st Army's ability to wage aggressive war for some months if not for good. It is the "small solution" reborn. (Volume 1, INTRODUCTION, p. 29)

Adolph Hitler will have none of it. He countermands an order of Field Marshal von Rundstedt alerting the 15th Army to prepare for action. This plan would not realize the *Führer's* impossible dream of laying siege to Antwerp, Belgium. What Model, Manteuffel, Kraemer or any other subordinate believes might pluck the flower of partial success from the mess of nettles that *Wacht am Rhein* is becoming matters not. The *Führer* has spoken. And that ends it. Once again, as often before in this, the Second German War, Adolph Hitler tries to overcome the hard realities of the battlefield by will alone, to the despair of his commanders and the sorrow of his soldiers.

In the American camp on December 20, the high commanders, from General Eisenhower at Versailles, France, to General Gerow at Eupen, Belgium, are also busy making plans and trying to juggle their powers to meet minute-by-minute challenges, dangers, and changing circumstances across a battle area that will eventually expand into a mammoth wedge some two thousand five hundred square miles in size.

Gerow's responsibility has grown to six infantry divisions, two armored combat commands, and a cavalry group. Fifth Corps soldiers stand as far north as Simmerath, Germany, west of the German 15th Army's most southern point, and extend around the long curve of Elsenborn heights to Waimes, Belgium, four miles east of Malmedy.

General Ralph Huebner, who has led the U.S. 1st Division from the Normandy invasion to the Hürtgen Forest, takes up quarters in Eupen as Gerow's deputy, bringing along his chief of staff, Stanhope Mason. (The reader may recall their role in persuading Gerow that all was not well with the 99th Division on *Null Tag*. Volume 1, Narrative V, Part 1) Mason remembered later the arrangement worked well. "Never any rough spots so far as command was concerned....Gerow asked and used Huebner's opinion (but) there never was any question it (holding the Elsenborn position) was Gerow's fight, Gerow's decision."

Fifth Corps officers at Eupen are working under the handicap that

General Hodges and his 1st Army headquarters contingent have moved out of Spa, Belgium to a location less endangered by the onrushing German columns.

The little city of some eight thousand people (prewar) has been inundated with nearly ten thousand American soldiers. They requisitioned mansions, hotels, and houses of this ancient watering place of faded elegance. They became permanent fixtures since moving in early in October 1944, the major business and industry of Spa and its surrounding province.

Most of these installations in and around Spa have by December 19 been closed down, the movables hauled off, and the residue made secure, that is, if troops can be spared for the purpose. There is a gradual slipping away of trucks, officers' jeeps, ambulances, heavy engineer equipment, antiaircraft gun motor carriages. Spa teems with soldiers but none are fighters—combat men such as infantry, tankers, tank fighters. The city will be left essentially undefended.

The American military historian, Charles MacDonald, believed Hodges and his staff made the evacuation calmly and methodically. In fact, he wrote, they waited around most of December 18 to brief arriving American parachute officers. "(It) hardly looked like panic," wrote MacDonald.

To the citizens of Spa, however, panic is precisely what it looks like. Most *Nazi* sympathizers living in the little city have long since moved east with their German friends. The population remaining is committed to the cause of Allied victory and has openly collaborated (as the Germans would put it) with the Americans since their arrival, including informing on *Nazi* sympathizers who have gone underground. Now the Americans are leaving hurriedly without even a by your leave, and the inhabitants of Spa are frightened and angry.

An official of the city government who served as liaison with General Hodges' civil affairs unit remembered the reaction of his fellow citizens: "By 2 p.m. the 1st Army headquarters already had left, hurriedly. All the other units were doing the same thing. It was rather precipitous. We were truly appalled. There was even much bitter talk among us....The Americans have left us stranded. The prospect of seeing the Germans again at Spa would be more terrible than in the invasion of 1940. The people had talked much, given the names of resistants. Others had spoken highly of their exploits (fighting the Germans) or testified against those who collaborated with the Germans. And the German troops marching on Spa were the elite *SS*..."

"By the morning of Tuesday, December 19th...there remained no more than a U.S. military police detachment at the Hotel du Louvre and a few guards in 1st Army headquarters offices."

Three of Field Marshal Bernard Law Montgomery's liaison officers drive into Spa and enter the building where Hodges' staff have worked. "We found it deserted," one of the Brits remembered. "The Christmas tree was decorated in the dining room. Luncheon (was) laid out. Telephones were in all the offices. Papers were all over the place. But there was no one left."*

Hodges and his entourage move first to Chaudfontaine, Belgium, a few miles southeast of Liege, where his rear headquarters are located. However, if 6th *SS Panzer* armor and infantry reach Spa, with little more effort they will also reach Chaudfontaine. He decides not to remain in this little resort town for long. He orders a final move of his headquarters to Tongres, Belgium, west of the Meuse River and well out of the danger zone.

The confusion and lack of dependable communication caused by Hodges' two-step displacement undoubtedly makes more difficult General Gerow's task of shoring up the Elsenborn-Bütgenbach position. Fifth Corps must stand to, holding the Elsenborn heights ramparts alone until General Hodges and his large entourage settle in, hook up their telephone lines, and come to understand the volatile battle being managed by Gerow and the needs of his divisions for fresh artillery, armor, and air support.

For the Supreme Commander of the Allied Forces, General Dwight D. Eisenhower and his staff and advisors on December 19 the Elsenborn high plateau is merely one of several sectors of grave moment in the Ardennes-Eifel. Their pressing concern is the breakthrough area to the south of Malmedy and the inexorable movement west of the infantry and armor of Manteuffel's 5th *Panzer* Army.

Although temporarily handicapped by the extreme paranoia of his security staff over the possibility that the arch fiend Skorzeny has sent battalions of assassins to Paris to wipe him out, Eisenhower is being drawn into what British Field Marshal Montgomery calls "the land battle." He is taking control of the front. (Many in the British camp and some in the American would say it is about time.) He meets December 19 with his senior commanders at Bradley's rear U.S. 12th Army Group

---

* After the war, General Bradley wrote, "As though to compensate for the indignity suffered when 1st Army was forced to evacuate its command post at Spa, (General Hodges') staff afterward excerpted (sic) its record to 'prove' it had been clairvoyant in predicting the German offensive, but that its predictions had been disregarded at (my headquarters). (This) is pure nonsense. First Army was just as neatly hoodwinked as was the rest of the Allied command." Soldier's Story, p. 462, Documentation, Volume 1, Preface.

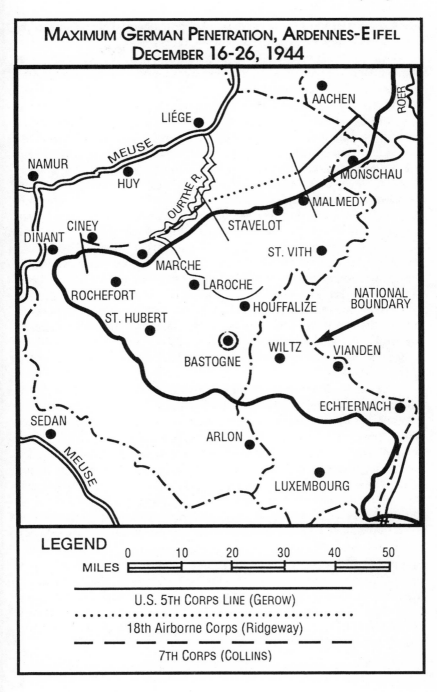

MAXIMUM GERMAN PENETRATION, ARDENNES-EIFEL
DECEMBER 16-26, 1944

ROER

AACHEN

LIÉGE

MEUSE

NAMUR

HUY

OURTHE R.

MONSCHAU

MALMEDY

CINEY

STAVELOT

DINANT

ST. VITH

MARCHE

LAROCHE

NATIONAL
BOUNDARY

ROCHEFORT

HOUFFALIZE

ST. HUBERT

WILTZ

VIANDEN

BASTOGNE

ECHTERNACH

SEDAN

MEUSE

ARLON

LUXEMBOURG

LEGEND

0   10   20   30   40   50

MILES

U.S. 5TH CORPS LINE (GEROW)

18th Airborne Corps (Ridgeway)

7TH CORPS (COLLINS)

headquarters in Verdun, France, a sad, ironic place to choose given the terrible slaughter that occurred there in World War I.

However, the most dramatic decision by General Eisenhower December 19 comes after the Verdun strategy conference when he returns to Versailles, his headquarters outside Paris. He divides the command on the Ardennes-Eifel front into two groupings: Field Marshal Bernard Law Montgomery will be in charge of the defensive battle north of a west-to-east line starting at Givet, France, and extending to Prum, Germany; and General Bradley, of the battle south of the line. This means Montgomery will command the U.S. 9th and 1st armies. In the latter is Gerow's 5th Corps, Major General Joe Collins' 7th Corps, and Major General Matt Ridgeway's 18th Airborne Corps. Bradley will command only Patton's 3rd Army and Middleton's badly torn 8th Corps. Also, Monty's air officer will control the U.S. 9th Tactical Air Command, which along with the British 2nd TAC is the principal shield and buckler in the air against the reawakened *Luftwaffe*. (Narrative X, Part 2 describes Montgomery's short but influential command of these large American forces.)

Eisenhower endorses this radical concept, then takes great pains to smooth the fur of all of his American commanders, from General Bradley (especially General Bradley) on down by reiterating that it will hold only until the Germans have been pushed back to their start line in the Eifel-Ardennes.

The mud soldiers in the melting snow and muck of the Elsenborn-Bütgenbach diggings know scarcely anything of what has happened except what each of them has actually experienced. The plans and tactics of the high commanders on both sides, indeed the reasons for the sudden eruption of their enemies from the east, are simply mysteries.

Those fortunate enough to lay their hands on the latest issue of the soldier newspaper, The Stars and Stripes, learn to their astonishment that all of the bleeding, dying, terror, and misery since Saturday at dawn have been caused by a massive German attack all along the line separating the Eifel from the Ardennes region. A mortar crewman of the 393rd Infantry remembers his squad's passing riflemen frantically digging foxholes east of Elsenborn, Wednesday, December 20. They hold up a copy of the newspaper with the fat headline, "*Panzers* Break Through in West." It is the first information he and his comrades receive of what has been going on for the last hundred hours across fifty-five miles of front line, the northern end of which their division has been defending at great cost.

Part 2: Deadly Preliminaries

Since mid September, the U.S. 1st Infantry Division has endured a literal hell of fighting, first in the siege and capture of Aachen, Germany, which Hitler demanded be defended to the absolute last living German soldier there, then into the northern reaches of the Hürtgen Forest to join what unquestionably has been the most costly, frustrating, and pointless major battle fought by U.S. forces in Western Europe to that time. These two awful combats came at the end of a long trail of fighting and dying for the infantrymen of the 1st that began in North Africa in November 1942 and carried through the capture of Sicily, the invasion of Normandy in the first wave at Omaha Beach, the bloodiest of all the invasion beaches, the subsequent battles there before the Allied breakout, and the march across France and Belgium.

The fighting spirit and formidable warcraft of the 1st Division is in the keeping of a cadre of officers, NCOs, and veterans in the ranks who train on the job a ceaseless parade of replacements in the rifle companies. By the end of the war, the 1st Division will have sustained 19,500 casualties in the European theater alone, not including those men carried off due to sickness, exposure, and other nonbattle causes, and those made prisoners of war.

On *Null Tag*, December 16, the call comes down late in the morning from U.S. 7th Corps headquarters (Major General Joe Collins) to the acting commander of the 1st, Brigadier General Clift Andrus, that his power is to stand by for immediate action. The division is in a bivouac area in and around Verviers, Belgium, a few miles south of Aachen. The soldiers are enjoying their first relief from the killing grounds in months. They have been there nine days. Many of the veterans, both officers and men, are off recreating in the flesh pots of Liege, Brussels, and Paris. Others are simply ensconced in local billets reveling in the food, warmth, and safety of the "rear." The rifle companies can scarcely muster more than one hundred men each; holes in the ranks created in the Hürtgen have not yet been filled.

No matter. The division's leaders (if not the poor, bewildered replacements coming in) take pride in bearing the worst burdens of battle and the most outrageous demands upon them. Sending the 1st Division back into the bloody crucible when its fighters have scarcely had more than a week to recover from a combat (the Hürtgen) that has devoured them in the thousands is just another example of the same.

Lieutenant Colonel E.V. Sutherland, acting commander of the 26th Infantry, 1st Division, is told to prepare his soldiers to go south to Camp Elsenborn. He will come under General Gerow's 5th Corps and

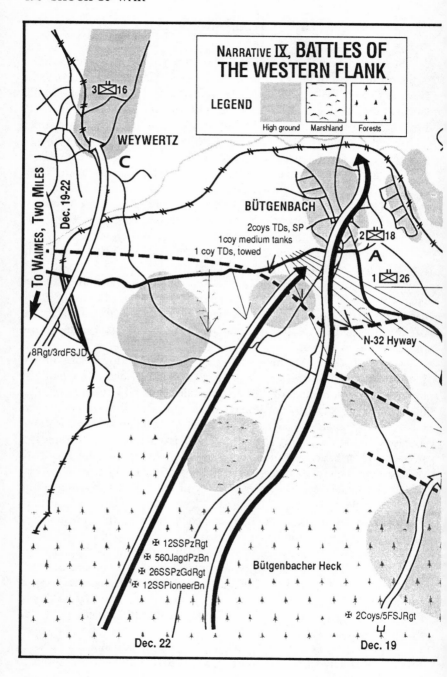

NARRATIVE IX, BATTLES OF THE WESTERN FLANK

LEGEND

High ground   Marshland   Forests

3 ⊠ 16

WEYWERTZ

C

BÜTGENBACH

To WAIMES, TWO MILES

Dec. 19-22

2coys TDs, SP
1coy medium tanks
1 coy TDs, towed

2 ⊠ 18

A

1 ⊠ 26

8Rgt/3rdFSJD

N-32 Hyway

☦ 12SSPzRgt
☦ 560JagdPzBn
☦ 26SSPzGdRgt
☦ 12SSPioneerBn

Bütgenbacher Heck

☦ 2Coys/5FSJRgt

Dec. 22

Dec. 19

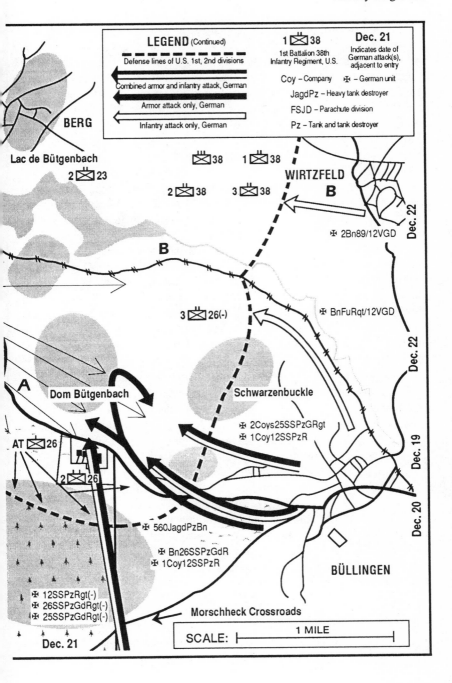

LEGEND (Continued)

– – – – – Defense lines of U.S. 1st, 2nd divisions

◄━━━━━ Combined armor and infantry attack, German

◄━━━━ Armor attack only, German

◄━━━ Infantry attack only, German

1 ⊠ 38
1st Battalion 38th
Infantry Regiment, U.S.

Coy – Company   ⊞ – German unit

JagdPz – Heavy tank destroyer

FSJD – Parachute division

Pz – Tank and tank destroyer

Dec. 21
Indicates date of
German attack(s),
adjacent to entry

BERG

Lac de Bütgenbach

2 ⊠ 23

⊠ 38   1 ⊠ 38

2 ⊠ 38   3 ⊠ 38

WIRTZFELD

B

Dec. 22

⊞ 2Bn89/12VGD

B

3 ⊠ 26(-)

⊞ BnFuRqt/12VGD

Dec. 22

A

Dom Bütgenbach

Schwarzenbuckle

⊞ 2Coys25SSPzGRgt
⊞ 1Coy12SSPzR

Dec. 19

AT ⊠ 26

2 ⊠ 26

⊞ 560JagdPzBn

⊞ Bn26SSPzGdR
⊞ 1Coy12SSPzR

BÜLLINGEN

Dec. 20

⊞ 12SSPzRgt(-)
⊞ 26SSPzGdRgt(-)
⊞ 25SSPzGdRgt(-)

Morschheck Crossroads

SCALE: ├────── 1 MILE ──────┤

Dec. 21

be attached, as soldiers call it, to General Lauer's 99th Division.

It is 2:30 a.m., December 17, when Sutherland's columns of troops and guns, plus a battalion of light howitzers and one of antiaircraft gun wagons, start moving across the black, night-shrouded landscape of the Hohes Venn. Their journey is punctuated by strange lights, antiaircraft gun fire, rattling V-1 flying bombs overhead, dancing flares in the sky, and other celestial spirits and phantoms. The colonel stops at Eupen, 5th Corps HQ, to learn from General Huebner what is going on. (He doesn't learn much.) Then he is off to Elsenborn to meet with his temporary commander, General Lauer, and receive his orders.

The meeting does not fill Sutherland with confidence. Present are the three 99th Division generals: Lauer; Mayberry, ADC; and Black, the artillery leader, and a variety of other staff and headquarters officers, "all crowded into a pub in Elsenborn," as Sutherland put it.* They seem to have little knowledge of what conditions are a few miles down the road in Bütgenbach (the 99th's former headquarters), where the enemy is, or what can be done to stop his rampaging. Mayberry orders the 1st Division colonel to "go down there and destroy the bastards." However, Sutherland will not take his soldiers anywhere until he has reconnoitered the area they are going into. A young 99th captain is produced from somewhere to guide him and his jeep driver south to Bütgenbach.

Meanwhile, the men of the 26th Infantry are huddled in open six-by-six trucks scratched and bitten by the icy night, totally ignorant of where they are going and what they are to do when they arrive. The trucks creep along the slushy roads south toward Robertville and Elsenborn, four miles to the east. Machine gunners are placed at the ready throughout the column to guard against paratroops who are rumored to be dropping from the skies in vast numbers.

A soldier of the 1st Battalion's Headquarters Company remembered a "...cold, dark night. It looked like the whole 1st Division was moving up....We could hear artillery getting louder and louder as we drove on slowly. We could hear buzz bombs (V-1s) rattling overhead and then suddenly stop. Then a large light would appear and a huge explosion as it landed....We could hear (German) planes overhead. It was obvious we were getting into something big."

---

* This account of the meeting is based on Brigadier General Sutherland's recollection written long after the event (see Documentation for this narrative). However, Lauer may not have been present. His forward command post at the time was moving to Camp Elsenborn, 1.5 miles west of Elsenborn.

A communications sergeant in Company "K" remembers the cold and confusion. "Open trucks came up at 2:30 a.m., December 17. All we were told was that the Germans had started a big drive and we were to stop them. We hadn't been issued winter clothes and it was very cold in the open trucks. My morale was the lowest it had ever been. I had been set for a thirty-day rest and there I was on the way back to combat....We met a lot of trucks and equipment going the other way. It didn't make sense to me. If there was an enemy breakthrough why weren't these other outfits going back (to the front) like we were?"

Lieutenant Colonel Derrill M. Daniel, commander of the 26th Regiment's 2nd Battalion, has not the luxury of worrying about any "outfit" but his own. He is responsible for moving six hundred men into a bivouac area at Camp Elsenborn (or so his orders have it) but is utterly confused as to where this is and how to reach there. His column comes to a fork in the road going south where they are to meet a guide. No guide. He decides to take the right fork, which does go to Camp Elsenborn, where his column arrives near daylight December 17.

He and his men wait around wasting precious time until they are given orders what to do and where to go. Daniel's battalion is supposed to be the last in the regimental line and in a reserve position. But the other two battalions are nowhere to be seen. As it turns out, the 3rd (Lieutenant Colonel John Corley) halted its march to chase von der Heydte's paratroopers (Volume 1, Narrative II, Part 2); the 1st Battalion took a wrong turn in the road.

An order comes down by messenger to take up a defensive position around some hills southeast of Bütgenbach at an estate called Domaine-Bütgenbach. Daniel recalled, "I had not been briefed as well as the other two (battalion commanders of the regiment). I knew nothing of the enemy or anything else. As I remember it, I didn't even have a road map...when we got to Dom Bütgenbach there was nobody there. We didn't relieve anybody."

The world of the battlefield is not only brutal and bloody but also capricious. Things do not usually turn out as planned. Formations programmed for one task are pushed into another altogether. Intended as the regimental reserve, Daniel's 2nd Battalion is instead stepping into the most dangerous place in General Gerow's defense line.

Dom Bütgenbach's manor house and dependencies are located one hundred yards up the rise of a high hill 1.5 miles southeast of Bütgenbach. The N-32 highway crosses the estate north of the manor house and another important road from the south meets the N-32 there as well. German-held Büllingen is scarcely more than a mile east along the N-32. The area is studded with hills covered with pastures and clumps of hedgerows, trees, and scattered marshland. One of the hills is called *Schwarzenbückel* (Black Hump) by the locals. A tactically important piece of real estate, the "hump" rises on the north side of the N-32 between Dom and Büllingen. The town is the staging place for 1st *SS Panzer* Corps' all-or-nothing drive to seize Bütgenbach and break the American's hold on the N-32 and the Elsenborn heights. Daniel's men are marching into the very maw of the Moloch.

However, in the afternoon and evening of December 17, the Domaine is quiet, although the 2nd Battalion men can plainly see the unnerving parade of enemy armor, mobile guns, troop carriers and other vehicles going south from Büllingen. These are part of Colonel Joachim Peiper's *Kampfgruppe*. Daniel's men can't know, of course, that this formidable power is not maneuvering to get behind them, then turn north to take Bütgenbach, condemning them to death or capture.

The 2nd Battalion's main line of resistance is long—nearly two thirds of a mile—and extends in the shape of a shallow curve from the *Schwarzenbückel* west to the edge of a forest, the Bütgenbacher Heck, south of the manor house. Their outposts, fighting holes, gun nests, and dugouts cross the N-32 highway, blocking all hostile traffic going west, so long, that is, as the riflemen and machine gunners who man them are able to survive.

Included in the 2nd Battalion defense are their three 57mm (diameter) antitank guns and another four from 26th Regiment Antitank Company. The crews of these 57s are each armed with a dozen rounds of British Army "sabot" ammunition. This consists of a hard steel armor-piercing projectile encased in a plastic ring, making for a tight fit in the gun barrel and greater velocity and hence penetrating power when it strikes armor.

When Corley's 3rd Battalion arrives, his men will move in on the left of Daniel. Colonel Sutherland takes a gamble and keeps his 1st Battalion in Bütgenbach as a reserve, even though his right flank is wide open, with a gap four miles long, all the way to Waimes on the N-32. Another 1st Division regiment, the 16th, will close the gap by and by. Sutherland can only hope the Germans do not find this long stretch of uncovered landscape in the meantime and turn his flank. General Andrus is sending in a scraped-together task force to hold the ground until the 16th arrives.

For all the miserable, confused, cold journey south and the reception by leaders of the 99th Division in Elsenborn that can best be described as irrelevant, the soldiers of the 26th Infantry experience a few good things at the end of their journey. Colonel Peiper's march away from the Bütgenbach sector is one. Another is the dogged fight of

the 38th Infantry and its allies at the dual towns to delay the march of
1st *SS Panzer* Corps armor and infantry across the Elsenborn high plateau, thereby purchasing time for the 26th Infantry to reach the N-32
high road and prepare positions to defend it and the pivotal town of
Bütgenbach.

Also, the two battalions programmed for the firing line—Daniel's
2nd and Corley's 3rd—have been dropped into terrain well suited for
defense. The muzzles of their gun barrels stare across open fields toward
an enemy whose troop carriers are confined to the road and cart tracks
because of the thawing snow and spongy ground. Or their guns are
emplaced on the reverse slopes of the hills, programmed to surprise
men and machines coming over the crown, a common tactic of infantry
and antitank men on the defense. And the landscape is also dotted with
hedgerows and tree lines well suited to hide guns and gunners.

However, what the men of the two battalions don't have as they file
to their allotted places are white camouflage suits and helmet covers.
Nor do they have suitable clothing to keep out the cold and icy wet, nor
shoe pacs to protect their feet, nor snow shoes and sleds to help them
move themselves and their supplies around.

The 26th Infantry's soldiers are gifted with half of December 17
and all of Monday, December 18, to build their icy fortress whose building blocks are log-covered holes in the mucky earth. Daniel is a young
reserve officer, stern and saturnine, whose combat experience stretches
back to North Africa, two years previous. He doubts not the enemy will
send his armor up the N-32 from Büllingen and along the road that
comes down hill from the Bütgenbacher Heck and joins the N-32 near
the manor house.

Daniel places five Shermans working with his battalion on a reverse
slope near the manor house, four M-10s of a company assigned to the
26th Infantry behind walls and hedgerows, and his little antitank guns
on the foxhole line. Two of these guns take the dangerous role of respectively right and left flank guards. He keeps one shorthanded rifle
platoon and the Shermans as a mobile reserve.

His men dig, dig, and dig again and cover over the diggings with
logs and mixtures of snow, mud, branches of fir trees and long marsh
grass so they will not be seen. Even the two rifle companies ("E," "F")
that are loaded with replacements for the men and officers who disappeared without a trace in an armed enemy village in the depths of the
Hürtgen Forest—even they instinctively know without urging what they
must do to get ready.

Simultaneously about 1.5 miles northwest on the N-32, in Bütgenbach, Sutherland's regimental headquarters is settling in. Bütgenbach

not only has been the headquarters of General Lauer's 99th Division but also a Quartermaster truck head and supply center. The incoming 1st Division people discover to their delight large supplies of spare clothes and food and all sorts of vehicles and other equipment that can be expropriated for their needs, including hauling ammunition and evacuating wounded.

The sergeant in Company "K" quoted before said, "As we got to the edge of Bütgenbach, I was expecting most anything to happen. What we did find was a surprise. We saw American vehicles of all kinds, gasoline, and rations, all abandoned. We moved on to the east edge of town and stopped to eat some rations we found in an abandoned ration dump."

"We were fortunate in one way that the GIs (Americans) in Bütgenbach did take off so fast and leave so much of their stuff behind. I don't know how I could have made it without the clothes I found (there) and put on."

On the other side of the hill, as soldiers term it, i.e. in the enemy camp, the 12th *SS Panzer* Division, *Hitlerjugend*, on December 17 and 18 is, of course, caught up in the murderous hurly burly that the battle for Rocherath and Krinkelt has turned into. It will be recalled, the tanks and infantry of the division start disengaging after nightfall December 18 to be replaced by the 3rd *Panzergrenadier* Division. Twelfth *SS Panzer's* new mission is to go south by various roads and open the N-32 to the west, as we know.

Following the immolation of armor on both sides in and around the dual towns, *Hitlerjugend* still can field some 100 tanks and tank destroyers, about three-quarters of those brought to the Ardennes-Eifel on the eve of *Null Tag*. Not all would agree with this estimate.* Whatever the numbers, the surviving *Hitlerjugend* armor adds up to a potential load of *Schrecken* for arriving soldiers of the 26th Infantry Regiment:

A hundred *Panthers*, *Panzer IVs*, and *Jagdpanzers* plus at least three times this number of mobile artillery guns; gun-bearing armored personnel carriers; and *Flakwagens*. And in contrast with the dual towns battle, these death machines will operate mostly in the open where no

---

* An Army historian who studied actions in the dual towns estimated 111 *Hitlerjugend* "tanks" were destroyed there. This seems far too high but is closer to the mark than the 139 kills claimed by American units. (Thompson, p. 11. Documentation, this narrative) Many ruined *Panzers* were counted twice by American units fighting in the dual towns. And some that were merely disabled were dragged back to the field repair shops and made whole again to go into action at Bütgenbach and elsewhere. Also, some of the claimed kills were not tanks but other AFVs, *PAK* guns mounted on a tank chassis, armored antiaircraft wagons, etc.

walls or basements shield the bazookamen and the American armor must expose itself as well.

During the night of December 18 and early morning and afternoon hours of December 19, the armor formations of *Hitlerjugend's* 12th *SS Panzer* Regiment not already in Büllingen are making their way there to assemble for the second round of violent battle with the Americans. The division's second *Panzergrenadier* regiment (26th *SS PzGr*) is moving west by way of Scheid, Losheim, and Losheimergraben on to the N-32 to take over the attack through Dom Bütgenbach and on to Malmedy.

Hitlerjugend's leaders are not able to mobilize for the new drive with despatch due to the entanglement in the dual towns, the condition of the roads and terrain, inexperience, and ignorance of what they face at Bütgenbach. The saga of the 3rd Battalion (*Panzer IVs*) of the tank regiment is typical:

At midnight, December 18 these tanks withdraw from the dual towns and reach the international highway in the Krinkelterwald. They need to be refuelled and restocked with ammunition. At 5 a.m., December 19, the battalion is ready to move along the international highway, south to Losheimergraben, then west along the N-32 to Büllingen. However, because of the confused traffic moving in all directions trying to reach the battlefield and trying to escape it and the delays gassing up and being resupplied with shells and machine gun bullets, the *Panzer IVs* do not start their march to Büllingen until close to noon, December 19, seven hours later.

SS Major Kuhlmann, who commands the force of armor, armored infantry, and, self-propelled artillery that will make the initial drive to open the N-32 orders combat patrols to probe the *Ami* line at Dom and the *Schwarzenbückel* north of Büllingen.

At 2:00 a.m., December 19 a few armored troop carriers, move through the black and fog-bound night carrying thirty or forty *Panzergrenadiers* swathed against the cold in long coats and camouflage smocks. They halt near a patch of fir trees on the "Hump."

An artillery observer up front with Daniel's "F" Company calls for some light—star shells—to illuminate the murky, foggy landscape. These are followed rapidly by a short, punishing barrage of 105mm howitzer shells. The *Panzergrenadiers* scatter, if they can. One carrier blows up and burns fiercely in the dark; two others are knocked on their sides.

Close upon their heels comes a parade of twenty or so troop carriers. They grind and clank along a mud and gravel road parallel to the N-32 that runs from the northern edge of Büllingen to the *Schwarzenbückel*. The light mortars (60mm) of Company "F" send a shower of

flares over the front. Again the young Germans are caught in the
yellowish, fog-reflected and amplified light. Again the artillery forward
observers call for shellfire from the battalion of twelve 105mm howitzers working with the 26th Regiment. The gunners go into frenzied
action, delivering explosive steel and the cruel phosphorous. A battery
of the 1st Division's 155mm (6-inch diameter) howitzer battalion also
joins the shoot.

The young soldiers of *Hitlerjugend* find themselves plunged into a
bath of exploding metal and flying pieces of burning phosphorous, a
bright little hell surrounded by black night. They try to burrow into the
folds of the earth, marshes, under the hedgerows seeking places to
make themselves small and covered over.

The explosions kill and maim some, the phosphorous burns others.
Some of the surviving *Grenadiers*, dogged and diligent, continue up the
rise of the Black Hump going for the Americans' outposts and artillery
observers. They meet small arms fire—machine gun and rifle bullets—
and endure the whump-whump pounding of the mortars. By and by, the
pre-dawn landscape falls silent, except for the sighs, groans, and shrieks
of the wounded Germans lying in the melting snow in the black before
dawn.

At about 10:30 a.m. two heavied-up combat patrols emerge, one
along the N-32 road from Büllingen; the other from the south toward
the woods (Bütgenbach Heck), three quarters of a mile south of Daniel's
command post at the Dom manor house.

On the left, about one hundred *Panzergrenadiers* come marching at
"F" Company near the base of the *Schwarzenbückel*. Shrouded by swirling fog and misting air, they make elusive targets. The "F" Company
men at the outposts see armor with the marchers also, but whether it
consists of tanks or tank destroyers and how many machines are moving
in the fog they can not tell.

However, the landscape begins to clear under the grey cloud
ceiling. The company's machine gunners and riflemen have long fields
of fire in front of them. Two 57mm antitank guns are with them and not
far away one of the M-10 tracked tank-destroying machines bearing its
long, high-velocity gun. Bogies squealing, 75mm (diameter) long guns
erect and waggling, the *Panzers* grind along the N-32 straight into a
trap. Spurts of flame leap from the hedgerow. Three-inch rounds from
the tank destroyer gun screech in also. The lead Panzer is hit and hit
again. Crewmen able to save themselves scramble from inside and run
off.

The others back away leaving their *Panzergrenadiers* to overcome
"F" Company's riflemen, machine gunners, and light mortarmen. The

company is short handed, scarcely more than three dozen on the firing line, new soldiers, replacements for the dead and wounded of the Hürtgen Forest. Nevertheless, they stand fast, in foxholes, behind hedgerows, at the opening of gun nests, delivering bullet fire at the young Germans in their splinter camouflage smocks. They go down, slither round in the muck and melting snow, run forward in spurts and stops, their machine gunners trying, futilely, to send covering fire at their tormentors on the slopes above. It's all over quickly. Crouching and crawling, the *Hitlerjugend* boys flee the field, no matter the exhortations of their NCOs.

A rush of shell fire and rocketry comes down on the manor house where Daniel and his staff are working and on the other buildings in the compound. However, it damages only bricks and mortar; the 2nd Battalion leaders and their aides scramble into basements and are safe from the pounding and fire-making.

When the German guns and tubes go silent, a column of *Fallschirmjäger* emerges to march down hill on the road from the Heck leading to the manor house. They are accompanied by a tank destroyer and a *Puma* (armored car). The latter travels on eight rubber-tired wheels, carries a 50mm cannon and a machine gun in a revolving turret.

A four-man crew at one of the 57mm antitank guns watches from a shallow pit behind a fence row as the *Puma* and *Jagdpanzer* leave the road and come bouncing and clanking over the uneven fields patched with snow. When they come in range, the men at the gun send three rapid shots at them. One explodes in the undercarriage of the armored car. The other two penetrate the *Panzers* front armor filling the innards with exploding steel. Both machines come to a halt.

Several teams of attacking Germans are armed with rocket launchers. One worms its way close to the American 57mm gun crew and lets fly with one, then another explosive rockets. Two of the Americans at the gun are killed instantly by fragments. The third takes hot metal in his eyes. The fourth stops functioning, is walked off the killing ground by a medical corpsman.

The enemy cause here is as hopeless as in front of "F" Company on the right. Spread out in a line of skirmishers, the *Fallschirmjäger* try to get across the "G" Company outpost line under cover of the fog. They are about fifty yards away, when the inevitable storm of American artillery shells and mortar bombs comes out of the sky and crashes all around. The attack kills some, wounds others, sends the survivors scurrying over the fields to the west. There they come into the gun sights of Daniel's "E" Company riflemen, who fire from deep cover, finishing the bloody work the artillery started.

After the weak attacks of midmorning are crushed, cryptic messages back and forth from the three battalions to Sutherland's 26th Infantry command post in Bütgenbach tell a story of ceaseless juggling of men, guns, and machines to harden the front for what all know is coming.

Murdoch (CO of 1st Battalion) reports, "Company 'A' is going to move down on Hill 569 where 'K' Company is now, (which) will move over to a nearby hill."

Daniel calls for "another tank destroyer here right away."

He tells Sutherland's operations officer (S-3). "If everything is quiet at 11:46, 'E' Company will move up and 'G' will move on its right."

Toward the close of December 18, General Andrus received a most welcome message from his artillery HQ. Fifth Corps has assigned a field artillery group to shoot with the 1st's forty-eight howitzers. The group will bring destructive power to the defense: two battalions of, respectively, 155mm, and 4.5 inch guns, and a battery (four pieces) of 8-inch howitzers.

And this is not all. General Robertson's 2nd Division artillery command post has moved some batteries from the dual towns battle, repositioned them around the village of Berg by the Lac de Bütgenbach (reservoir), and they are available for demolition work on the towns occupied by the enemy staging for the action at Bütgenbach and elsewhere.

Well before dawn, December 19, the guns get to the work of breaking up the German bases. The division artillerists have perfected the murderous time-on-target technique. They use it now to devastate Büllingen, Honsfeld, even Moderscheid in the south, one of *Kampfgruppe* Peiper's long-range bases. Throughout the morning, sudden storms of shellfire pour death and destruction from the dark and low-hanging clouds, coming and going without warning, hitting with the power of a hundred giant explosive hammers striking as one, killing and wounding men, smashing vehicles, burning up stores, bringing down buildings.

All this violent and unexpected opposition from the Americans south and east of Bütgenbach has no doubt had an impact on the hearts and minds of Colonel Kraas, Major Kuhlmann, and other *Hitlerjugend* officers at Büllingen.

Around noon, December 19, the officer commanding the *Panzer IV* battalion of the *Panzer* Regiment finds his way to the division's command post in Büllingen. There he encounters a captain of the 26th *SS Panzergrenadier* Regiment and the commander of its reconnaissance unit. "In spite of my suggestion to penetrate to Bütgenbach without delay lest the enemy gain time to bring up reserves and establish a strong line of defense, I was stopped," he recalled. One of the staff officers explains, "The enemy has strengthened himself continually during the preceding day." It is obvious to the *Panzer* commander that the decision has been made to wait until more tanks and tank destroyers are brought out of the dual towns melee and the remainder of the 12th Regiment's armor arrive on the borderland battlefield.

Other factors are taking a hand in *Hitlerjugend's* battle plan also. Sixth *SS Pz* Army's plan is to attack simultaneously from many different directions in a carefully choreographed assault across Gerow's Kalter-herberg-to-Waimes main line of resistance on the Elsenborn high plateau. Aside from 12th *SS Panzer* Division, four other divisions are expected to join in the coordinated move on the heights: 227th and 12th *Volks-grenadier*; 3rd *Fallschirmjäger*, and 3rd *Panzergrenadier*. None of the four are in place and ready to strike hard December 19.

The two *VGDs* are variously incapable, especially 277th, which is short of officers, NCOs, and replacements.

Third *PzGD* is arriving at the dual towns, but its trains and artillery are still strung out eastward beyond the German-Belgian border.

Third *Fallschirmjäger* is well stocked with bodies but is weakly of-ficered and poorly equipped.

Overarching all is what seems to be a fatal command confusion. Three corps (67th *Infanterie*, 1st and 2nd *SS Panzer*) are to have a part in the action to break the forty-five mile long Gerow line. Yet the 6th *SS Pz* Army commander, "Sepp" Dietrich, and his chief of staff, Kraemer, are increasingly preoccupied with what is happening to the spear-heads they have sent forth into the Amblève and Salm river valleys far to the west. Fronting the Gerow line the five German divisions lack a central coordinating control and command. Willi Bittrich's 2nd *Panzer* Corps is running three unrelated divisions: 3rd *Panzergrenadier*, 12th *Volks-grenadier*, and 3rd *Fallschirmjäger*. Priess' 1st *Pz* Corps has one horse only in the race: 12th *SS Panzer*, the crucial element. Hitzfeld's 67th will field the much-battered and bruised 277th *VGD*. It is all a recipe for failure: unified command lacking; control fragmented.

At midday December 19, General Clift Andrus, acting commander of the 1st Division, and his staff at Sourbrodt are juggling troops and the guns and armor moving in to work with them. Most of the 26th Infantry Regiment has now relocated to Bütgenbach, Dom Bütgenbach, the *Schwarzenbückel*, and other hills in the vicinity.

However, Andrus and his staff have other sectors of a wide and rough terrain to account for and mixed defensive tasks to perform. On the north the 1st Division's 18th Infantry is protecting 5th Corps instal-lations at Eupen. Companies of this regiment on the 19th of December also are busy chasing the remnants of Colonel von der Heydte's *Fall-schirmjäger* around the trackless Hohes Venn west of Monschau and

Höfen. (Volume 1, Narrative II, Part 3) Andrus hopes to relieve the 18th of this wearisome mission for one much more exciting, the defense of the Bütgenbach salient.

The 16th Infantry Regiment is on the move south and west toward Robertville and Waimes, to plug the wide gap in the 1st Division defense line four miles east of Malmedy of which the village of Waimes on highway N-32 is the right boundary.

At midmorning, December 19, Waimes is occupied by a scratch task force of 1st Division headquarters men, the reconnaissance company of a tank destroyer battalion, and a platoon of 75mm motorized gun carriages of a tank battalion. The officer in charge reports to Andrus' headquarters, "The situation here (Waimes) is building slowly. This task force is not strong enough to stop either a strong infantry attack or a small tank attack." The 16th Infantry Regiment commander, Colonel Fred W. Gibb, radios division, "Tell them to stay there. We are coming with reinforcements."

By 3 p.m. his 3rd Battalion and part of the 2nd is in Waimes and spreading a rifle-machine gun line. General Wadehn's 3rd *Fallschirmjäger* Division has the mission of breaking into the hardening American line at Waimes. Whatever prospect this large but untrained and badly led mass of ex *Luftwaffe* ground mechanics, clerks, supply troops, etc. may have had of accomplishing the mission is evaporating by the hour in the fogs and mists as the 1st Division infantry, armor, and artillery build up on the Waimes-Bütgenbach line.

As Colonel Kraas' mobile artillery and rocket-throwing machines move into position south and southwest of Büllingen, the 6th *SS Panzer* Army artillery corps guns come up as well, and General Engle's 12th *VGD* artillery regiment positions its guns around Wirtzfeld, they go to work on Bütgenbach. An intelligence officer with the 1st Division remembers "The shelling of Bütgenbach was perhaps the heaviest our (26th) regimental command post had (experienced) up to then in Europe. One evening as the chow (food) was brought up, the men refused to get near the chow line because of the frequent incoming shells. Some of our people felt the shelling was being directed from a church in the northeast part of Bütgenbach."

The officer investigates, finds the church filled with "countless sick and wounded women and children being taken care of by nuns." The mother superior assures him no German soldier or hostile civilian is in the high stone tower observing for the German gunners. That settled, 'She blessed me (and added) she would welcome any assistance with medical supplies.'"

Part 3: "Fight and Die Here"

By nightfall, December 19, *Hitlerjugend's* two armored infantry regiments are mustering around the town of Büllingen. Its armored fighting vehicles are gathering there also. And the *Werfer* batteries and companies are emplacing their tubes all round the area. The enemy build-up at Büllingen is a monstrous presence growing in the fog and sleety atmosphere under the prolapsed winter clouds. The probes into the 26th Infantry line of December 19 have been claws of this inchoate beast feeling for objects to devour. Or so it may seem to any watching 1st Division soldier cursed with an imagination and peering into the black and foggy night from his icy foxhole. (The worst burden a mud soldier can bring to the battlefield is a vivid imagination.)

In reality the probes were what soldiers call a reconnaissance in force. *Kampfgruppe* Kuhlmann of 12th *SS Panzer* Division is assembling to drive the 1st Division off the Bütgenbach hills and open the N-32 to the west. Kuhlmann's force consists of a mixture of armor, motorized infantry, tracked cannons, *Flakwagen*, all accompanied by pioneers, signalmen, and such other troops as may be necessary to the business at hand.

A regiment of General Walter Wadehn's 3rd *Fallschirmjäger* Division is camped in the Bütgenbacher Heck south of Bütgenbach and is attached to Colonel Kraas' division. Some of these troops will join in the action this day, although their presence will make little difference to the outcome. The base of Kuhlmann's power on December 20 will be the heavy battalion (*Abteilung*) of tank-fighting *Panzers*, half riding on a *Panzer IV* chassis; half, on a *Panther* chassis and armed with the destructive 88mm (3.5-inch diameter) high-velocity rifle. This weapon can kill any machine the Americans bring against it in head-to-head combat.

After the quick but deadly combat with Kuhlmann's patrols and the punishing artillery barrage that has followed, Daniel's men have been busy. They deepen their burrows, repair field wires, haul ammunition and supplies from the N-32 to the mortar crews, machine gunners, riflemen, antitank gunners watching in deep holes near their 57s.

A three-quarter ton truckload of bazookas (antitank rocket-firing tubes) shows up at Daniel's CP. The driver has been ordered to deliver them to Colonel Corley's 3rd Battalion on the left flank of the regiment but has made a mistake. Daniel orders the tubes unloaded for his men, assuring the dubious driver he will make it good with the man's superior officer (and presumably with Corley).

Two platoons (eight guns) of M-10s have come east on the N-32 highway, and are clanking and rumbling to firing stations, a powerful addition to Daniel's defenses.

Colonel Daniel's operations officer is also busy, as he described it later, "visiting all the platoons on the line assisting in their reorganization, patting them on the back for a job well done, warning of expected heavier attacks."

He stops at the command posts (dugouts) of the platoon and squad leaders. He explains to them where the battalion stands in the scheme of Gerow's north shoulder defense; how vital is their role; how much artillery, armor, and other back-up death machines have been sent in to help and protect them.

He takes the time and trouble to counsel with individual soldiers who seem on the point of despair, or worse, are indifferent to their fate. The operations officer reminds everyone of the battalion motto ("We fight and die," adding unnecessarily, "here.") Overwrought, perhaps, but the simple truth for many of Daniel's men at the Dom Bütgenbach position.

A continuing freshet of replacements keeps flowing to the rifle companies, even while the latter are experiencing the shock of arms and the clamors of the battlefield. A first sergeant (second highest NCO rank) of artillery converted to infantry has arrived in Bütgenbach at midnight December 18 with forty other replacements in tow. One of Daniel's rear headquarters officers has placed them in a basement to shelter from the hostile shelling.

"About 36 of the 40 men going into Bütgenbach with me were retreads from branches other than the infantry," the sergeant wrote later. "Eighty percent of (the forty) had little or no infantry training. Several of the men going with me to 'E' Company did not know how to load the M-1 rifle (the basic U.S. Army infantry weapon). They had been issued four clips of ammunition when we departed the replacement depot at Givet, France. Each clip contained two rounds of tracer (illuminating) ammunition. These were immediately removed. They would have given away our positions."

The night heavy with ground fogs from thawing snow, a truck and a noncom from "E" Company show up to transport the sergeant and seven riflemen down the N-32 to the company's positions in the hills east of Bütgenbach. Not so many weeks before, some of these replacements had safe jobs in warm billets far to the rear where not even the sounds of war could be heard. Now they are making their way past dark, unknown shapes into they know not what horror. The task that Daniel's officers and NCOs have of acclimating such men and fitting them into squads, platoons, and companies fighting for their lives in the heat of an erupting battle takes no imagining.

SS Major Kuhlmann and his *Kampfgruppe* have no intention of giving the 26th Infantry additional time to make preparations.* An hour after midnight, December 20, without any artillery preparation, a small force of four or five *Panzer IVs* begin to move from Büllingen headed in the direction of the *Schwarzenbückel* hill and the outposts on Daniel's left flank. The companies of *Panzergrenadiers* supposed to move with the tanks still are assembling on the edge of Büllingen. The night is stygian and fog bound. The absence of a praetorian guard of infantry to keep their march going in the right direction handicaps the *Panzer* drivers.

The German commander of the battalion to which these *Panzer IVs* belong recalled what happened: "In the darkness, the tank point, instead of advancing in a westerly direction, advanced towards the southwest ...the infantry was still on both sides of the road about a half mile west of the road junction near Büllingen. Slowed down by the pace of the infantry, the attached paratroopers, and the (engineer) mine detector squads, the point made only halting progress."

The march against the center of the 26th Infantry's now well-constructed defenses in the early hours of December 20 runs into opposition from the start. The advanced guard of *Panzer IVs* reaching the field are savaged by what the German commander terms "exceedingly heavy artillery and mortar fire."

Working with the 26th Infantry are three battalions of howitzers, plus a battery of four 90mm diameter high-velocity long rifles, the Americans' counterpart of the Germans' ubiquitous, all-purpose 88. This artillery is supplemented by the six 105s of the 26th Regimental Cannon Company, a company of 4.2-inch (diameter) heavy mortars, and the 81mm and 60mm mortars of the battalions.

The artillery and mortar men have had ample time to plot firing zones. Their forward observers are up front and busy. They have both radio and land line connections with their fire direction centers. In the ghoulish green light cast over the hills and fields around Dom Bütgenbach by the sputtering, slowing descending flares, the rifle outposts and

---

* Apparently, the first option was to strike with power directly at Bütgenbach on the N-32, which was the 26th Infantry's headquarters and base of operations. However, this was ruled out because of road conditions and terrain in the vicinity of the Bütgenbacher Heck. The *HJ* ops officer wrote that "because of numerous boggy sections and extensive woodland, tanks could not be used. Besides, (the division) would have had to position itself in the attack zone of 3rd *Fallschirmjäger*." So another fateful decision is made: Move on Bütgenbach by way of Dom Bütgenbach estate. (Meyer, p. 443. Volume 1, reverse title page.)

artillery observers discern the *Panzer IVs* leading the attack and the infantrymen (and boys) strung out to the east in ragged files. Map coordinates and ranges fill the artillery radio net. Daniel's men watch with cold satisfaction as the ground bearing the parade of enemy vehicles seems to explode in the brilliant light of shells and mortar bombs crashing off in spouts of flame and billows of smoke.

To order the surviving machines to try to push on up the slopes where Daniel's men are hiding would be useless. "The company of (*Panzer IVs*) was withdrawn by its commanding officer and the battalion regrouped," recalled the *Panzer* leader previously quoted.

Hitlerjugend's gunners and those with the artillery corps assigned by Dietrich's HQ to supplement their fires and the *Neblewerfer* crews now take their revenge: About 3 a.m., December 20, the night sky to the southeast and east of the 26th Infantry's 2nd and 3rd battalions is splashed with reddish light. The ominous sighing, whistling, and screeching fill the air above them. The mud soldiers in their cold, damp foxholes, huts half underground, and other earthen shelters scrunch down, tensing bodies and minds against the crashing and pounding and jagged metal flying every which way above them and the balls of flame where the rockets strike. Near Daniel's manor house CP, a parked Sherman takes shell fragments in the track assembly and must be hauled off for repairs, a major loss.

His 2nd Battalion soldiers scarcely have time to help along or carry to the battalion aid station in the basement of the manor house those soldiers struck by shell fragments or burned by exploding rockets or rendered speechless by the concussions. Daniel and his staff are working on the first floor protected by the thick fieldstone walls of the building. It is obvious to all of his soldiers up front that the pounding they have taken along the foxhole line and around the 2nd Battalion headquarters buildings is merely opening music for the parade of power about to march upon them.

Kampfgruppe Kuhlmann's company of *Panzer IVs* have reorganized on the western edge of Büllingen after the failed lunge at Daniel's outpost line a few hours before. A company of *Jagdpanthers* has come up as well. And an entire battalion of *Panzergrenadiers* assigned to the *Kampfgruppe* is present. This formidable war party also includes armored and tracked howitzers and long guns and troop carriers for the *Grenadiers*.

They are about to replicate the attack forty-eight hours previous on Lieutenant Colonel McKinley's battalion in front of the dual towns. (Narrative VIII, Part 2) There is a difference at Dom Bütgenbach, however: a different *Kampfgruppe* commander; the presence of the powerfully gunned *Jagdpanthers*; a greater weight of artillery on the German side. On the American, a defense in depth built over two days and nights; more armor support from the start; 57mm antitank guns firing high-velocity British sabot ammo; an even more fearsome array of artillery and heavy mortar tubes.

The war party of *Kampfgruppe* Kuhlmann gets moving about 3:30 a.m. Ground fog lays thick over the hills whose fields are sprinkled with patches of melting snow. Kuhlmann's *Jagdpanthers* are in the lead, moving along both sides of the N-32, heard but not seen by Daniel's men on the outposts. They call for illumination. Their heavy mortars pop star ammunition over the landscape, which soon glows with the familiar eerie light.

However, so opaque is the fog that the *Jagdpanthers*, even though 23 feet long and 9 feet high, are hidden from the gun sights of the waiting Americans. A half mile east of the road junction next to the Dom B manor house, the long, long guns on a *Panther* chassis turn north to get behind the manor house.

Daniel has buttressed his "F" Company on the left and "G" in the center with six 57mm guns up front on the firing line and a platoon of four M-10 tank destroyers. The bazooka teams of the two companies fire their tubes, seldom seeing the target. The gunners at the 57s take aim on the blue flames coming from the *Panzer* exhausts.

Several *Panzers* clank and grind into the space occupied by a platoon of "G" Company. They ride down the thirty men, machine gunning every moving one and sending explosive 88mm shells straight into their holes and dugouts. The living try to scramble away in the dark. Not many do.

This onslaught opens a gap in Daniel's defense. He rushes up his reserve rifle platoon to fight its way back into the gap. They run and crouch across some low ground into a stone barn close by the N-32 on the right flank of "G" where they prepare themselves if not to die at least to move to where they expect to die.

Having done in the thirty or so men of the "G" Company platoon, the fast, low-slung *Jagdpanthers* move in the direction of Daniel's command post. The *Panzer* commanders assume no power except infantrymen, easily shot down, stand in the way. They are wrong. The four regimental 57mm antitank guns Daniel has placed on the "G" Company firing line wait in well-camouflaged pits. The crews crawl out of their muddy holes and jump to their guns.

Suddenly—almost in their faces—two violent crashes accompanied by spouts of flame boil up in the dark. The 57s' gunners are so near to the two *Jagdpanthers* that are firing they can virtually embrace them.

But the German tank crews are preoccupied with putting high explosive 88mm rounds into Daniel's command post a football field away. They don't see the dark figures scrambling around the little antitank guns, loading sabot rounds into the breech. One crew of two men, loader and aimer, send four shots screeching into the rear of a German machine. One shot penetrates the engine compartment touching off the fuel. The *Panzer* boils up in a cloud of smoke and flame.

A second *Jagdpanther* comes lurching and clanking over the muddy field searching for the men and their vicious little gun. The Americans know only that a monster is nearby and means to kill them; they can discern no shape to shoot at because of the surrounding fog and darkness lit only by the drifting flares and muzzle fires.

Suddenly, the *Panzer* emerges, its huge bulk bearing down on the two men, the machine gun barrel sticking from a ball turret in front flashing with tracer bullet fire. The men stand their ground, frantically feeding and firing their weapon. The little armor-piercing shells powered up by the sabots screech at the *Panzer*. It is hit in several places. The crew bails out and disappears in the fog.

But the brave antitank men are now at the center of a stampede of the beasts. Another bursts from the fog, machine gun blazing. All the Americans run for their dugouts but one. The loader at the gun that stopped the *Panzers* will not give way. He continues to defy the German armor, but now his gun fails him. It will not, as artillerymen say, return to battery. He can not reload. The *Jagdpanther* is within ten feet of the desperate gunner when it halts, the hatch cover rises, and its commander emerges for a better look round. Possessed by the crazy courage that will sometimes seize a soldier in the heat of battle, the American unholsters his .45caliber automatic, aims and fires at the figure standing in the hatch, then leaps for safety into the shallow pit where his gun is emplaced. Expecting this very second to be his last on earth, the gunner watches in astonishment as the *Panzer* moves forward a few feet, then back a few more feet, then slowly lumbers away.

By 6 a.m., December 20, as the heavy, minatory clouds begin to show streaks of feeble light, *Kampfgruppe* Kuhlmann's armor has broken into Daniel's perimeter where the foxholes of companies "G" and "F" meet and the platoon of "G's" valiant riflemen have been destroyed or driven off. A half dozen *Jagdpanthers* climb a hill north of the foxhole line, halt and fire explosive rounds toward the Dom B compound. At the same time, they start hosing down Daniel's infantrymen with machine gun fire aimed at their backs. Daniel sends an urgent radio message to the 26th Regimental command post in Bütgenbach. He needs bazooka ammo. He needs reinforcements. He is promised "C"

Company from the regiment's right, defending the town of Bütgenbach—if they can be spared.

By now the *Panzergrenadiers* have moved into the melee in troop carriers, on the decks of the *Jagdpanzers* and the reinforcing *Panzer IV* tanks, on foot. They join the assault on Daniel's battalion. They come on, over the hilly fields, screened by their machine gun teams whose long-barrelled, rapid-fire weapons are moved forward as the young *SS* infantry armed with machinepistols and assault rifles advance, then moved again to keep up their protective bullet fire.

As the cold light of dawn rises across the hills around Dom Bütgenbach, the soldiers and armor of *Kampfgruppe* Kuhlmann take shape: helmeted figures in splinter camouflage clothing cradling guns, potato mashers, *Panzerfäuste*; armored machines, obscenely erect guns swinging up front, machine guns hammering.

Subjected during the dark to the random and impersonal punishment of the howitzers, the *Hitlerjugend* now become targets for the shooters along Daniel's rifle-machine gun line. Despite the bullet and tank fire coming at the Americans from their rear and flanks, they stand fast, bundled up figures, swathed to shapelessness in layers of clothes that make their foxhole homes endurable. Only loyalty to their comrades and hope for safety in numbers pin them to duty as death stands off watching impassively to receive them. Their weapons are talismans, their comrades fasteners to the realm of the living.

The young Germans do a foolish thing, as Daniel will later tell it. They start yelling "surrender Yank," thus alerting (and angering) his men.

Some *Panzer IVs* that have made it through the 2nd Battalion's main line of resistance are helping the Americans. Their guns working on Daniel's riflemen from behind his front line are hurting the *Hitlerjugend* infantry attacking them. The young Germans are out in the open while the men of Daniel's three rifle companies are hidden in the earth. Also, the *Panzermen* can not discern friend from foe in the smoke and fire of the feeble dawn. Daniel's line has been sealed by the battalion's reserve platoon. The *Panzergrenadiers* find themselves forced away from their armor.

Daniel and the artillery liaison at his command post believe if the howitzers behind the hills to the west can redouble their already ferocious strikes at the attacking enemy, the morning's assault on the 2nd Battalion will be dissolved.

The curtain of 1st Division and 26th Infantry artillery shell and mortar bomb explosions comes down on the scrambling, running, crouching *Panzergrenadiers* of *Kampfgruppe* Kuhlmann darting in and out of the fog over the fields. The young soldiers are being hit not only by the flailing shell and mortar fragments but also by sniper and machine gun bullets and rifle grenades. The Americans have cover; the Germans do not. The American lieutenants and NCOs have control; the dwindling number of *Panzergrenadier* leaders, not large to begin with, are losing theirs.

By midmorning, December 20, the four to five hundred infantry that has come in with the *Kampfgruppe* is fragmenting into isolated platoons, even squads, roaming across the fields still trying to get through the 2nd Battalion's main line. Eventually they will pull back to Büllingen if not killed or wounded. (Few are made prisoners.)

For awhile the *Jagdpanthers* of the heavy tank destroyer company working with *Kampfgruppe* Kuhlmann continue to rampage through the 2nd Battalion position. The heavy-bodied machines with their ferocious 88s and their busy machine guns have done destructive business. They have breached Daniel's line, destroyed a platoon of his riflemen, lurched and clanked and blasted their way more than a half mile into his camp. By late morning eight of them occupy the hill north of the Dom B command post.

Retribution now arrives. Forward observers from the 1st Division's medium howitzer (155mm) battalion are on the field. They observe the idling, dangerous machines in position on the sloping fields of the hill, obviously intending to consolidate their gains and the tactical advantage of being behind the 2nd Battalion command post.

The FOs call for tank-killing high-explosive rounds. Some M-10 tank destroyers, well sited and camouflaged, send three-inch (diameter) armor-piercing rounds shrieking at the *Panzers*. Teams of adventurous infantry (and other) soldiers roam the landscape armed with bazookas and rockets to bedevil them. Three of the eight beasts go down.

Formidable though they are, the *Jagdpanthers* are cursed with two fatal impediments: They are without *Panzergrenadiers* to fight off the bazookamen. Their murderous 88mm cannon is not seated in a revolving turret. In the midst of their battle for survival on the hill, the *SS* captain in charge can be heard on his radio cursing this lack of a turret that would allow him and his fellow *Panzermen* to blast and machine gun targets behind and to the side, targets that if not taken out can and do kill their machines.

Later in the day Corley's 3rd Battalion on the left gets a smell of the *Jagdpanthers*. A half dozen come charging through companies "I" and "L" trying to reach a safe haven at Büllingen before they run out of ammunition, fuel, and luck. In the 3rd Battalion space, they are forced to run another gauntlet, but five of the low-slung speedy *Panzers* are able to escape.

First Division headquarters has shown concern throughout the 20th that the seam between the 1st and 2nd divisions remains unsealed, vulnerable to flanking attacks. At 5 p.m., the 2nd moves its 38th Infantry outposts west of Wirtzfeld back to the edge of the Lac de Bütgenbach reservoir. Corley, on the left flank of the 26th Infantry establishes a connection along the stream feeding the reservoir. This sector will henceforth be defended by soldiers of these two formidable U.S. infantry divisions.

Daniel's 2nd Battalion, 26th Infantry has paid a large sum in dead, wounded, and broken soldiers this day. The aid station at Dom B has been the scene of suffering and sorrow almost from the time the first enemy shell came down after midnight. The litter bearers deposit their burdens there. The ambulances and litter jeeps drive up to move the wounded who have a chance at life on to Bütgenbach. The "E" Company first sergeant estimates that twenty of his men have been killed or have taken wounds. Company "G" has lost an entire platoon of thirty men, and others as well. Company "F" losses are not estimated, but probably exceed those of "G," given the ferocity of battling in and around its perimeter and being run down by steel behemoths. The regimental antitank company has suffered severely, too.

Death and destruction have been early risers. By noon the battle is over except for the inevitable shelling, rocketing, and mortaring delivered by both sides and the patrols of *Hitlerjugend* infantry that keep probing nervously for soft places in Daniel and Corley's line. After dark, December 20, the enemy falls silent.

The 26th Infantry's commander, Colonel John F.R. Seitz, who has returned from leave and resumed his role, and the other leaders of the regiment are among the most battle hardened of American soldiers in Gerow's 5th Corps. They are not about to relax because their enemy has backed off. With the German foe—especially with the German foe— this is usually the prologue to an even more horrendous attack.

General Andrus and his staff at the division CP are of like mind. Late in the afternoon, they send the 2nd Battalion, 18th Infantry, down to Bütgenbach as a reserve for the coming battles. They also scrape together additional antitank guns, including more 90mm high-velocity AA guns. The division combat engineering battalion is ordered to put down mines and more mines all along the 26th Regiment's outpost line, even if this means—as it does—working in the harsh light of falling flares and well within range of enemy snipers and mortar forward observers.

At 6:35 p.m. Seitz receives a message from General Andrus, "This looks like an all-out offensive. If we stop them now, it may be the end of the war. Get it out to your men, 'Everyone stand fast.'"

Part 4: Dreams of Glory, Day of Wrath

By the night of December 20, the *HJ* reserve infantry regiment (26th *SS Panzergrenadier*) is in the Büllingen vicinity and ready to assume the main burden of carrying the battle for the N-32 at Bütgenbach. The 25th *SS Panzergrenadier* Regiment has suffered greatly in this battle and the one for the dual towns. And although its 3rd Battalion will participate in the next day's attack on the 1st Division line, the weight of the infantry role will be carried by 26th *SS Panzergrenadiers*.

The troop carriers, reconnaissance cars, *Flakwagen*, and supply vehicles of 26th *SS Panzergrenadier* Regiment have consumed a full eleven days in arriving at Büllingen from assembly areas in Germany. A fatal delay, as it turns out. Had these three thousand *Panzergrenadiers* been on the field east of Büllingen December 17th they could have marched unimpeded up the N-32 into Bütgenbach.

When they finally arrive at Büllingen, they receive their first cooked meal courtesy of the food stores left behind by the retreating Americans; ample, if temporary supplies of American gasoline for their vehicles; and a large selection of pants, coats, field jackets, and boots also left behind. The eagerness with which these and other soldiers of the *Waffen SS* and the *Heer* grab up and wear into battle bits and pieces of American uniforms probably explains the many sightings of Germans masquerading as American soldiers reported by 1st, 2nd, and 99th divisions during the Elsenborn battles.

Afternoon December 20, five days into the *Riesenanschlag im Westen*, Colonel Kraas and his officers meet in his headquarters in Büllingen. *Hitlerjugend* Division, pride of the *Führer* though it be, is being squeezed between the irresistible force of the German high command and the immovable object of the implacable U.S. 1st Division. *Kampfgruppe* Kuhlmann's armored attack earlier in the day has been torn apart and scattered across the hills and fields under the guns of the 1st Division infantry and armor and the ceaseless pounding of their artillery and mortars.

The officer of the 12 *SS Panzer* battalion having most of the *Panzer IVs* in the division noted in his combat report that during the night of December 20, "the *Panzerjäger* battalion was taken back to its starting positions, (but) refueling, repairs, and receipt of ammunition could not be accomplished in Büllingen as originally planned because of the enemy artillery (having zeroed in on the town). The battalion was taken two miles to the rear (of Büllingen)."

In fact, the constant bombarding of Büllingen by the American howitzers and long guns has caused intractable problems of supply, command, and communication for Kraas' captains. This town on the N-32 has connections north to Rocherath, south to Heppenbach, and east to the German border towns. It is a vital base for the assault against the "Gerow Line."

By nightfall December 20, scarcely a building there is intact. All business must be conducted in basements. Travel about the streets or on foot or in an unarmored vehicle requires agility, courage, and luck, mostly the latter. Even the old timers of the *Waffen SS* serving with *Hitlerjugend* Division are unnerved by the ceaseless pounding and crashing all around and the lifeless bodies and ruined machines littering the streets. The third battalion of the 26th *SS* Regiment is scarcely in town a few hours when it loses four of fifteen armored troop carriers to exploding shells.

Colonel Kraas and his staff draw up plans to invest most of the remaining power of *Hitlerjugend* in a climactic drive to destroy the 1st Division's position at Dom Bütgenbach and then march up the N-32 into Bütgenbach. The weight of the attack will go in from the Morschheck crossroads on the edge of Bütgenbacher Heck, a mile south of Dom B. It will be organized as *Kampfgruppe* Krause (SS Lieutenant Colonel Bernhard—).

During the grey afternoon, steamy with warming air shot through with fog and the cold night that follows of December 20, Colonel Daniel and his captains count their losses, evacuate their dead and wounded. He expects more murderous wrath from his enemy and has driven his captains to prepare for it.

Second Battalion's preparations began almost as soon as *Kampfgruppe* Kuhlmann's armor and infantry withdrew. Colonel Seitz sent Daniel a rifle company ("C") from Murdoch's 1st Battalion in Bütgenbach. And about noon the captain in charge of the 26th Regimental Antitank Company was ordered to send three more 57mm antitank guns. The captain and Daniel's operations officer endured bombs from a light mortar as they walked the main line of resistance selecting suitable sites for the guns. Daniel's MLR is so far into the bend of the bloody angle that anything moving there is fair game—for both sides.

A company of 1st Division engineers comes up late December 20 bringing antitank mines. They drive down the N-32 from Bütgenbach in their big trucks, well spaced along the road to dodge enemy shell explosions, pull up near the 2nd Battalion command post at the manor house. As soon as night descends, they plant the platter-shaped devices in front of 2nd Battalion outposts along the road to Büllingen and the slope of the hill crossed by the road to Morschheck, the two gateways for armor marching on Dom.

"During the remainder of the night," wrote Daniel's operations officer, "the enemy ceased his artillery and mortar fires. A strange lull rested over the battalion's positions. This quiet was merely a calm before the severest attack of all."

In Büllingen in the basement of a farm house a few hours after midnight, a half dozen German boys, some as young as sixteen, none older than seventeen, are lying about bundled in their uniforms and such other bits and pieces of clothing, including some American, they have been able to find to try to stay warm. Some sleep; others are awake but lie or sit in a cold-induced stupor. They are *Panzergrenadiers* belonging to one of the companies that will once again try to drive the Americans from the heights southeast of Bütgenbach. Six months before, they were swinging along the roads of springtime Germany reveling in the comradeship of the Hitler Youth organization.

The door to the cellar bangs open and two *Unteroffiziere* come down the stairs to rouse the young soldiers for the day's work. They have already experienced terror and despair inflicted by American howitzers, mortars, and machine guns. They have seen comrades no older than themselves die of awful wounds as they lay in the snow and muck. The young *SS* boys are not what they were at the start of the march by *Hitlerjugend* against the Americans: eager for adventure, full of enthusiasm for the *Riesenanschlag* that would save the *Vaterland*, proud to be numbered among the heroes of the *Waffen SS*. The Belgian farmer whose house it is hears the sharp commands of the NCOs. He watches as the boy soldiers file up the stairs toting their machine pistols and assault rifles into the pitiless night. The grimy faces of some are streaked with tears.

Sad and fearful though they be, these teen-age *Hitlerjugend* soldiers are nonetheless cogs in a formidable power that Major Krause, the *Kampfgruppe* commander, plans to send this day December 21, against Daniel's 2nd Battalion.

Kampfgruppe Krause will field three battalions of *Panzergrenadiers* riding armored troop carriers, some of which are armed with cannons and machine guns. They bring the usual lethal tools: machine guns, machine pistols, standard and assault rifles, potato masher and egg grenades for close-in mayhem, *Panzerfäuste* and *Raketenpanzerbuschse*, the latter two to cripple the *Amis'* antitank guns and tanks.

Working with them (and vice versa) will be four companies of *Panther* and *Panzer IV* tanks of 12th *SS Panzer* Regiment plus the remaining two *Panzerjäger IV* companies. Waiting in the wings (reserve) will be one company of the heavy *Jagdpanthers* that carried the armored weight of the attack the day before on Daniel's battalion. In all, at least fifty-five big, armored machines, each bearing a devastating high-velocity long gun and one or two machine guns. Several companies of combat engineers, *Racketenwerfer*, mobile antitank guns and howitzers, and *Flakpanzers* will be moving into battle with the *Kampfgruppe* as well.

Three battalions of the 12th *SS* Artillery Regiment will also be firing in support of the march against the 1st Division and a battalion of *Neblewerfer* vehicles each carrying a fasces of 6-inch diameter rocket tubes. These guns and rocket-throwing vehicles and towed machines are emplaced around Büllingen, Hünningen, and Honsfeld.

Kraas and his lieutenants also expect General Engle's 12th *Volksgrenadier* Division troops and armored assault guns (*Sturmgeschütze*) to at last make a strong march against the left flank of the 26th Infantry (Corley's 3rd Battalion) defending the sector northeast of Daniel. This could be decisive by drawing off men and guns from the focus of the day's armored-infantry assault on Dom B and the N-32.

The 26th Infantry commander, Colonel Seitz, takes stock of his assets the evening of December 20. He does not yet have at his command as many tanks or tracked and armored antitank guns as does his enemy. Daniel has been supported by two platoons of M-10 tank destroyers (eight) and a platoon of Shermans (five). Another platoon of M-10s and the remainder of the Shermans (ten) are spread around the regimental main line south of Bütgenbach.

A small stable compared with the number of powerful armored machines, including two companies of *Panthers*, that remain available to Colonel Kraas, *Hitlerjugend* commander, even after the terrible blasting and burning and wasting of his armored fighting vehicles since *Null Tag*. However, 26th Infantry is being sent a company of the new American tank destroyers (officially, gun motor carriages) that bear a destructive 90mm diameter high-velocity gun. The vanguard of these brutes already is clanking down the muddy streets of Bütgenbach, a glorious sight to the hard-pressed infantrymen.

Seitz's regiment contains scarcely eight hundred *bona fide* riflemen plus an unknown number of machine gunners, light and heavy. However, in the 1st, as in the 2nd Division, everybody fights. The colonel will routinely call on his back-area men: clerks, ammo haulers, messengers, repair men, wiremen, etc. to take their places beside the shooters if the need arises. Also, the 2nd Battalion of the division's 18th Infantry has arrived at Bütgenbach (Part 2), settled into the icy houses and barns, been placed under Seitz, and is waiting a call to action, an excellent hole card for the colonel and his staff.

The artillery power that Colonel Seitz's 26th Infantry soldiers can call upon outmatches that of their enemy. Before the battle is done this day (21), seven battalions of 1st, 2nd, and 99th Division artillery will have joined in the shoot, plus three battalions assigned by 5th Corps: 144 light and medium howitzers and long guns in all. The ceaseless fire of these tubes will be supplemented and reinforced by all sorts of other guns and mortars: the regiment's Cannon Company, a 4.2-inch mortar company, mortars of the infantry, armored tank and tank destroyer guns firing in an artillery mode. The boys of *Hitlerjugend* have cause to weep.

SS Colonel Kraas's recon patrols have been active after dark, December 20 probing for weak places in the middle of the 26th Infantry main line of resistance west of the manor house, where the foxholes have been stretched out over a dangerously wide space.

It will take some doing to assemble and maneuver a mass of armor and infantry of the size described before in the blackest night in this hilly and unfamiliar country while friendly artillery rages at the enemy. Whether the one or two officers available in each *Panzergrenadier* company are up to the job remains to be seen.

December 21 comes to the Bütgenbach hills cloudy, foggy, and quiet. An occasional shell explodes with a spurt of reddish, smokey light somewhere on the landscape where the 1st Division men, guns, and machines are ensconced. Flares sputter here and there in the opaque sky. A machine gun chatters, then goes silent. It is the archetypal all-quiet-on-the-Western-Front battlefield setting that would have been familiar to soldiers of the 1st Division twenty-six years before in France. What comes next would have been familiar too.

About 3:30 a.m., a flight of artillery rounds come down and explode among the buildings near the manor house, Daniel's command post, and on the hill behind it, sending up gushers of muck mixed with snow. A quick shoot by the *Hitlerjugend* gunners to help them find the range, adjust the fire.

A few minutes go by. Daniel's soldiers in their holes, dugouts, and basements lay low. Their comrades shivering at the outposts in front of the main defensive line peer into the night. The old soldiers (in hard experience, not age) among them can sense the killing power crouching in the darkness off to the east, waiting. They see a flame leap up here, then there, then everywhere as the horizon seems to be catching fire. The booms and rumbles of the guns and weird moans of the rocket-throwing machines roll toward them. The deadly birds heard so many times in these pages come shrieking, whistling, and crying through the night, this time in flocks so thick they seem to shake the sky.

The howitzers, long guns, mortars, and *Werfers* operating along the

N-32 from Büllingen to Hünningen work over Colonel Daniel's 2nd Battalion for two hours. Close in and well camouflaged by night and terrain are the mobile high-velocity *PAK* guns, 75s and 88s, operating in an artillery mode, their fire adding maniacal shrieks to the general bedlam of noise pressing down on the battlefield.

In the manor house, Daniel and his staff keep working by oil lights and electric torches. They depend on the thick stone walls, two stories above, and sturdy roof to shelter them from the rain of steel and fire. The other buildings of the manor are not so durable. Fires from exploding rockets take hold in the roofs and hay lofts of two barns that are part of the estate. They blaze up in the wind blowing around the night, lighting a demonic scene.

In one of these barns is the spillover of wounded men from the manor house basement waiting for ambulances to take them west. Some walk, others hobble, more are carried by comrades to new shelter by the light of the fires and the sound of explosions. (Another tableau from The Inferno, another in which the poor tormented souls have done no wrong and deserve no such punishment.)

Daniel's heavy weapons company (mortars and machine guns) has its headquarters in the other barn. The captain and his aides, messengers, communication people dodge through the explosions to a nearby building where "E" Company headquarters is located and crowd in.

Two Sherman tanks parked along a road leading out of the compound take hits, so does one of the big M-10 tank-fighting vehicles down the road toward "G" Company's line. The three machines, vital to Daniel's defense, are lost to the battle.

His artillery liaison officer works the big SCR (radio) connecting the 2nd Battalion with their howiztors, its only hope for rescue from this overarching malignancy that is about to devour every last man of the battalion. The artillerymen also are trying to obtain usable information from a light and sound observation battalion to identify targets for counterbattery fire that will suppress the enemy howitzers, long guns, and rocket-throwing machines.

But these are located over a wide space. And *Hitlerjugend's* mobile gun crews keep moving the tubes that are mounted on tracked, armored vehicles. The *Werfer* machines are, of course, nothing more than a collection of light barrels mounted on two-wheeled carriages or self-propelled vehicles. And so many *Hitlerjugend* guns have joined in the pre-dawn shoot December 21 that sufficient numbers can not be put out of action to make a significant difference.

The massive array of American howitzers and long guns send thousands of shells down on the towns and villages to the east along the N-32, but still the enemy rounds and rockets keep smashing at the dugouts, foxholes, and half-buried hutments of Daniel's men and on his own headquarters compound as well.

The 26th Infantry's telephone network is coming apart. Wire connections carefully laid and connected in the previous forty-eight hours are being shot to pieces. The platoon, company, and battalion radio nets are either silent or transmitting confusion. Some of the 2nd Battalion's dugouts and foxholes up front that sheltered their occupants throughout the armored attacks of December 20 are disappearing under the cascade of fire, smoke, and exploding metal. Whether the soldiers who inhabit these holes are dead or no longer have means of communication can not be known at the company and battalion command post during the German bombardment.

Just before dawn, the German gunners slake their fires. Daniel's survivors emerge from their holes and dugouts and basements and prepare for what they suspect will be a ground attack as horrendous as the one from the air they have just endured.

But first the victims of the artillery and rockets must be found, wrapped in blankets, and gotten out least they fall into shock and die in the cold and wet. The job must be done quickly for the enemy is coming. Not all the wounded are found; some will lie dying and suffering in crushed holes throughout the day's battle, others have been obliterated. The dead men perform their last service by being beyond help. They are therefore of no bother to their harassed and desperate comrades scrambling in the pale, icy light of dawn to evacuate the damaged and prepare for what is coming.

Colonel Kraas and his officers have programmed the assault on the 26th Infantry for the immediate time when their *Artilleriereschlag* slacks off. However, it soon becomes obvious to the *Hitlerjugend* commanders that the *Panzergrenadier* battalion assigned the lead role is hopelessly disorganized. None of the four assault companies can be located in the night and fog and the radio net used by Krause's *Kampfgruppe* seems to be down.

Kraas goes forward to the little crossroads village of Morschheck, about a mile south of Dom B. After conferring with Lieutenant Colonel Krause, he makes the only decision possible: He postpones the attack until his officers can remedy matters, put their men in position, and synchronize their planned march with that of the armor. Kraas orders a renewal of artillery and rocket fire on the Americans.

With the greyish dawn light now up and illuminating the landscape, *Kampfgruppe* Krause begins moving on the American line at last. It is a sight to stop up the heart and shrivel the soul of the most valiant soldier: A company of twelve 44-ton *Panther* tanks in the lead followed by *Panzer IVs* and *Jagdpanzers*, a battalion of *Panzergrenadiers* riding troop carriers, tracked in the rear, wheeled up front, some armed with light cannons, close behind. "As far as your eye could see, German tanks were coming over the rise..." as a "C" Company soldier described it.

The parade moves down the slope from the Heck, along the Morschheck-to-Dom road. As they reach the northeast edge of the woods, the armored machines and troop carriers following behind disgorge their loads, and armor and dismounted troops. They fan out toward the west and north, aiming to engulf the command post of Daniel and obliterate what remains of his main line of defense after the artillery-rocket pounding earlier and the ground attack the day before.

Considerable remains of it, as the *Hitlerjugend Panzergrenadiers* and *Panzermänner* soon learn to their sorrow. Except for the two Shermans and M-10 tank destroyer disabled by shellfire, the American armor and antitank guns spread around Daniel's perimeter and on the tree line by the slit trenches and fighting holes are present and ready for action. The crews of the tanks and destroyers emerge from their basement and dugout hiding places and climb into their machines.

Had *Kampfgruppe* Krause's troops been organized and ready to march when their artillery and rocket throwers had ceased firing before daylight, they would have encountered an enemy groggy and beaten down by the awful pummelling they had just endured. Now, they will march upon men who have shaken off their numbness of mind and body imposed by the guns and *Werfer* tubes, are angrier than ever, and determined to get their own back.

The lead *Panthers* move parallel to the line of trees that mark the main defenses of Daniel's forward positions in an otherwise barren winter landscape of fields and hedgerows. This movement was to take place at night. There's nothing for it now except to call for smoke to mingle with the fog. Soon the hill across from Daniel's positions is draped with curtains of dirty, whitish smoke obscuring the oncoming German power. However, the dawn air is quick and snappish with gusts of cold wind that drive away the curtains, leaving the *Kampfgruppe's* vanguard to hide themselves as best they can in the ground fog suffusing the hill.

One of the German tank commanders remembered: "There was a row of tall spruce running parallel with the direction we were taking. These stood on the highest point of the meadow, with a slope leading up to them but with nothing to be seen on the other side. It was in this area of dead ground that the object of our attack had to be lying. ...Instinctively, as if in response to an order, all the turrets swung around to the row of trees on our right flank...we sent one or two bursts into the trees with our machine guns by way of initiating the fight against an imaginary enemy. We sensed, however, that there was an enemy somewhere out there, excellently camouflaged, watching us through the eye-pieces of his antitank gun sights."

The *Panzer* leaders are prescient. In the tree line are two antitank gun crews. As the huge *Panthers* clank, rumble, and pitch across the hilly fields, the crews load armor-piercing rounds into their guns and shoot, aiming at the road wheels and rear of these machines where they are most vulnerable. One *Panther* is struck in the engine housing and spews forth a stream of fire. A second is hit also and flames up, the black-uniformed survivors among the crew dropping to the ground and running for their lives.

Opening their muzzles has exposed the American crews to the fearsome 75mm long guns mounted on the *Panthers*. These blast away with high-explosive shells at the tree line, spraying shell splinters in every direction. Several men among the gun crews are hit. Others scurry away.

Daniel's artillery liaison officer radios for harassing fire on the woods to the left of the Morschheck road where the mass of *Panzergrenadiers* are moving into the attack. The companies of infantry are to work in teams with the *Panzers*, but the ceaseless shelling makes for disorder in the ranks.

Company "E" of Daniel's battalion occupies the right flank. The company's foxholes and machine gun nests stretch west from the road to Colonel Murdoch's 1st Battalion line, now emplaced south of Bütgenbach.

Standing with the riflemen are four 57mm antitank guns of the 26th Infantry Antitank Company. Two infantrymen of "E" Company armed with Browning Automatic Rifles were assigned to protect the crews of the 57s from attack by infantry. However, they were victims of the night's storm of fire and steel and have been carried off to the battalion aid station. The gun crews will have to act as their own security even as they try to stop the armored machines of the Germans.

Shouting as they emerge from the woods, an entire company—some one hundred men and boys—clad in camouflage smocks over great coats, steel helmets down over their ears, rifles and machinepistols at the ready, are running at the American gunners. Their aim is kill them or drive them off, then destroy their antitank guns, thus protecting the *Panzers* moving along with them. *Maschinengewehr* teams are also on the field sending streams of bullet fire at the "E" Company line.

The American artillery action accelerates. Shell explosions blossom among the *Hitlerjugend* soldiers. They churn soil into the air, blow smoke, flash red in the grey light of morning. The flying shell fragments hit one, then another, then more, dropping them into the melting snow and muck. But the mass keeps coming with the armor.

Enemy infantry are now within a few hundred feet of the antitank gun positions. The sergeant in charge of the first gun uses a wounded infantrymen's automatic rifle to try to hold them off while a crewman frantically prepares the gun for action, shoving a round into the breech just in time to fire at a *Panzer IV* lurching toward him. The shell strikes a front sprocket, ruining the track assembly on one side, forcing the machine to limp away, its rear exposed to the gun. The *Ami* gunner shoves another shell into the breech, then another, holing the tank fatally. It smokes up, then explodes in fire; no one emerges from the burning carcass.

Another *Panzer IV* tank runs at the American gun crew on the far right flank, road wheels rumbling, both machine guns hammering. The antitank gunner is able to get in two shots. A round strikes the gross machine, but it brings along the usual swarm of infantry. They press hard, are held off for the moment only by a desperate amount of small arms firing by the 57mm gun crew, using an automatic rifle, two M-1s (rifles), and a bag full of fragmentation grenades.

Crazy men, thinks the NCO in charge of the *Panzergrenadiers*. Better to wait them out until their ammunition is gone. It is, and soon, whereupon a German bazookaman moves close, sends a rocket screeching at the antitank gun, which shatters the breech mechanism. By some battlefield miracle the three Americans are able to fade into the tree line and get away as the *Hitlerjugend* infantry swarm over the gun site moving north to reach the N-32 west of the manor house.

Three more of the little 57s and their six-man crews are strung out along the "E" Company front, interdicting the road to Morschheck. The regiment's Antitank Company captain is not comfortable with his men and weapons' being so far up forward, but Daniel insists this is where he wants them, and this is where they are. Both officers are right: Daniel, because the sturdy little guns and sturdier men with their British sabot ammunition slow the rush of German armor into his perimeter; the captain, because, as he anticipated, his gun crews are being destroyed.

About 9:15 a.m., several *Panthers* come raging at these gun crews, wide treads propelling them, forty-four tons of armored machine rumbling and lurching along at close to thirty miles an hour, long gun feeling its way forward, machine guns hammering. Two men at an antitank gun try to stop one of the armored beasts coming down on them. A burst of machine gun fire from the hull of the *Panther* smashes the recoil mechanism of their gun. The gunner is also armed with a bazooka and a few rockets. He and another crewman try to use it on the machine. He is hit by bullet fire from somewhere, becomes an easy prey for the *Hitlerjugend* infantry now swarming over the scene.

The two crewmen are bagged and sent south as prisoners of war. They had expected to be shot. But the *Panzergrenadier* NCOs seem to respect enemies who put up a fight, as these two certainly have. And the gunner is not hurt so badly that he can not walk. Were he on his back and immobile, his fate might have been different.

The next gun in line to the east is manned by a shorthanded crew, three of the normal six having been struck down in the bombardment earlier this day. Through waves of fog and smoke, they see what appears to be an enemy tank behaving in an odd way: standing off and cannon-ading Daniel's headquarters compound a few hundred yards north.

This gives the tank-fighting crew a chance. They load and fire one round after another at the big machine scoring some hits. Flames begin licking round the tracks. Five soldiers emerge, and go off, unnerved, not wanting any more encounters. (The "tank" turns out to be a 150mm (diameter) howitzer mounted on a *Panzer III* chassis.)

Not one hundred and fifty feet to the left, almost on the shoulder of the Morschheck road, the corporal gunner who did so much damage to the *Panzers* and their crews with his 57mm gun and his pistol the previous day (Part 3) once again enters the beasts' cage. His assistant gunner is gone, wounded by a shell explosion earlier. The corporal is working alone, decides nonetheless to take aim at a *Panzer IV* roaming about. His first shot hits the tank in the rear causing thin wisps of smoke to rise from the ventilators. He shoves another shell in the breech. The tank halts, swings its turret around. The machine gunner has the corporal in his sights and fires a burst that kills him.

Friendly artillery—the 155mm guns mainly—have this morning smashed five of *Hitlerjugend* armored machines. They stand where struck, sending wavy pillars of smoke toward the grey, clotted clouds. But the American Shermans and M-10 tank destroyers simply are not present in sufficient numbers to supplement the artillery and keep the rampaging enemy at bay. Three Shermans are on station near Daniel's command compound. The M-10s with their powerful 3-inch guns are back of the long main line of resistance. They have taken losses, too. By 2 p.m. three have been put out of action by hostile (or friendly) artillery hits and enemy tank fire.

At 9:37 a.m. Daniel sends an urgent message to Colonel Seitz, 26th Infantry commander. He needs more tank destroyers with 3-inch high-velocity guns. He now has four rifle companies on line, three of his own and "C" from 1st Battalion. All are being drained of riflemen. They are no match for the *Hitlerjugend* tanks with their brutal long guns and their busy machine guns.

One of Daniel's men lies low in a patch of melting snow, a loaded bazooka by his side. As a *Panzer* lurches by he rises to his knees, aims the tube and sends a rocket whooshing into the road wheel assembly.

Another stands boldly, hidden only by wisps of fog. He fires a rifle grenade at a *Panzer* and some infantry coming over a rise nearby, then runs for his life.

Another in an absolute frenzy of determination stands his ground cradling a Browning Automatic Rifle, which he points at a *Panther* clanking by. He fires a clip. The bullets ricochet off the monster's skirting plates covering the tops of the road wheels. No matter. The soldier has done what he can, and disappears in the fog. The *Panther's* crew doesn't even know they have been shot at.

The howitzers, long guns, antitank guns firing in an artillery mode, and mortars backing Colonel Seitz's 26th Infantry do not spare the 2nd Battalion soldiers. The killing ground flanking the Morschheck road is drenched with fire and explosive steel that hurts them as well as their foes. Violence is everywhere and deals evenly with both sides.

The men of rifle companies directly south and west of the manor have about had enough. Singly and in small groups, they move north a few hundred yards, into and behind the manor compound. Daniel messages Seitz that "G" has about been shot away and the survivors must be relieved. At 11:30 a.m. he gets some good news: "E" Company, 18th Infantry is coming over from Bütgenbach to replace "G."

Still and all, the 2nd Battalion right flank is coming undone: A wide space of nearly a half mile is opening there, with only a few die-hard mud soldiers, machine gunners, and bazookamen to hold the ground.

In the manor house, Daniel's artillery officer is calling for more and still more action by the howitzers and long guns. Daniel wants the artillery to put high explosives and phosphorous in the Bütgenbacher Heck directly to his south. Increasingly, the *Hitlerjugend* troops and armor seem to be disgorging from these scrubby, dark woods.

Even now many of the 105 and 155mm crews shooting for the 2nd Battalion are exceeding the book limit of rounds that can safely be fired per minute. The gunners ignore the book. The howitzermen know what the infantry up front is enduring. They feel blessed to be distant from the killing ground where the searing blast of a tank gun and the bullet fire of a machine pistol are as close as one's beating heart and failing bowels. Blessed, and willing thereby to work themselves to the nub to punish the enemy threatening their infantry.

Nine tanks have survived the initial rampage this morning by *Kampfgruppe* Krause across the right flank of the 2nd Battalion. A battalion of *Panzergrenadiers* worked with them to suppress the American antitank gunners and bazookamen. However, the battle has devoured so many of these *Hitlerjugend* infantrymen (mostly boys), they no longer have the weight to go on with a consolidated attack. They disperse, some moving through the gaps in the 2nd Battalion front northwest toward Bütgenbach. Others, dead on the killing ground or dragged off wounded.

Commanders of four of the *Panzers* back their machines off to await a new supply of *Panzergrenadiers* to come up and march with them when they make the final push into the command compound of 2nd Battalion at Dom B south of the N-32. However, the leader of a platoon of *Panzer IVs* with the strike force refuses to wait. He orders an immediate rush up the slope into the compound. Not only is Daniel's command post located there in the big manor house but also spread around are other foci of 2nd Battalion command and support: the command posts of two of his companies, the battalion medical aid station, caches of ammunition and food, a vehicle park.

The five *Panzer IVs* crash their way into the perimeter. They hide in and around some farm buildings and begin to blast 75mm explosive shells at the stone walls of the manor house and barns occupied by Daniel and his people. An American M-10 tank destroyer in the vicinity shoots from over the hill north of the manor, but the rounds are far off the mark.

Two Sherman tanks move into the battle. Immediately, their crews find themselves in the kind of face-on battle with German armor so dreaded by American tankers. The Shermans strike first, damaging one of the *Panzer IVs*, but the armor skirting plates protecting the sides of the German tanks frustrate them. Their shells penetrate the plates but not the hull.

Now it is the Germans' turn. Two of the *Panzers* blast high-velocity 75mm shells at the Shermans, penetrating one, which smolders, then begins to show fire round the chassis. The other reverses directions and goes off.

The *Ami* tanks out of the way, the five *Panzers* return to the task of taking apart the buildings in the compound. Their 75mm guns attack them while their machine guns (hull, turret) shoot down every American soldier who moves in front of their muzzles.

Meanwhile, several companies of *Panzergrenadiers* work their way up the slope and across the 2nd Battalion's line. Dogged sniping and machine gunning by the surviving soldiers of Daniel's rifle companies and other 26th Infantry troops bedevil the attackers. A few *Schützenpanzerwagen* stuffed with young soldiers even make it as far as the N-32 highway west of Dom Bütgenbach.

Panzergrenadiers appear in the command compound also, take up firing positions behind piles of stone and wood caused by shellfire, put bursts of assault rifle and machine gun fire into the windows and doors of the buildings. With fatal determination, several of the invaders rush the manor house, no doubt intending to kill or capture Daniel and his staff. Three of his men armed with automatic rifles watch from hiding until the young Germans are well within range, then kill them all.

Enemies at the heart of the 2nd Battalion defense make for logistical problems: How to get officers, messengers, and others in and out of the buildings without sacrificing them to enemy machine guns and pistols? "All movement thereafter was made by crawling or running past the danger areas," in the words of a battalion report.

Late in the morning Daniel once again sends a message to Colonel Seitz, the 26th's Regiment commander in Bütgenbach. Seitz knows that enemy infantry have reached the N-32 west of Dom, and Daniel's command post is invaded. The two commanders discuss the unthinkable: 2nd Battalion's retreat (withdrawal) to positions a half mile to the northwest on the edge of Bütgenbach.

Seitz authorizes the move if necessary. In the meantime, he will try to scrape up more rifle reinforcements and direct a platoon of M-36 tank destroyers mounting 90mm (diameter) long guns that are "down there somewhere where the tanks broke through" into the fight for the manor house.

By noon, December 21, the 2nd Battalion is dying hard in place. Colonel Seitz believes the entire regiment is facing catastrophe. If the battalion is destroyed, as seems likely, the regimental front will sag open for three miles at the very center of the 26th's main line of resistance. Near 3 p.m. he sends a dire message by teletype to General Andrus, the 1st Division's acting commander:

"This thing is still going. Hitting us from all sides with tanks and infantry...the companies are getting very small. 'F' is down to two 10 man platoons (AN: table of organization strength in each platoon is 36). Company 'E' way down. 'G' Company, practically nothing. Possibly may have to draw back one thousand yards due to shortage of manpower. What we plan to do is pull back to hill just north of Bütgenbach and go from there north and east to lake. (AN: Lac de Bütgenbach reservoir)"

The CO of the 3rd Battalion, Lieutenant Colonel Corley, learns of the plan and protests to Seitz: "I don't think it is feasible. I can show you the lay on the ground and the good features of it. If we do that (i.e. pull back), we will lose all of the high ground."

At the Dom B perimeter, Daniel and his officers and men have had to put by for the moment a plan of retreat or any other tactical movement of any kind. They are preoccupied with survival here and now.

The battalion command group has moved into the basement of the manor house, which is serving as the battalion aid station and bunker for survivors of the mayhem up on the battalion's MLR. More miserable and disorderly conditions for managing a last-ditch defense can scarcely be imagined: the huge dark, dank basement, the shapes of prone and sitting wounded men, shadowed and silhouetted in the light of lanterns and electric torches. From time to time the building shudders from the hit of an explosive round and hostile machine gun bullets rattle against the doors, remaining windows, and walls with the sound of hail striking wood and brick.

A detachment of medics are assigned to Daniel's battalion. Four of them have been sweating in the cold fetching the wounded from the killing ground south of Dom B and carrying them down and up the slopes to the aid station. About midday the 1st Division medical battalion sends in eight more soldiers to help with the litters, a stark measure of the carnage that the 2nd Battalion is suffering.

The rifle reinforcements that Colonel Seitz has promised Daniel arrive in the form of the captain of a company of the 18th Infantry Regiment. Daniel tells him to take his men up the hill behind the manor house close by the N-32, dig foxholes, stay alert, and stand by for orders.

Daniel and his captains know it is imperative to get rid of the armored incubus that threatens to suck away his headquarters, which is to say kill him and the other officers there. Such a happening would doom the 2nd Battalion companies in the battle to dissolution. And all waging the fierce little battle for the manor compound know it.

The young lieutenant running the Sherman tank platoon assigned to the battalion slips into the manor house. He is very nearly a commander without a command. Three of his machines have been put out of action. Daniel tells the officer to maneuver his surviving two tanks to a position from which they can do harm while avoiding the dangerous bite of the *Panzer IVs'* high-velocity guns.

The plan is to try to root out the German armor with 81mm (diameter) mortar rounds fired by Daniel's heavy mortar platoon. Their pits and dugouts are on the reverse slope of the hill north of the compound. The exploding mortar bombs will goad the tanks from their hiding places. When this happens, the tank destroyer, antitank guns, and Shermans in and around the compound will kill them with armor-piercing shells. Or so goes the plan.

Forward observers from the mortar platoon radio aiming points to the gunners that will allow them to put their bombs down somewhere near the German tanks. Soon the destructive things are hitting round the farm sheds and buildings near where the *Panzer IVs* are hiding. It can not be a pleasant experience for the crewmen squeezed into the gritty, cold, foul-smelling compartments behind the armored walls to be rocked and shaken by the explosions all round. But they do not move their machines.

The battalion HQ company commander next tries bazooka teams, two men armed with rocket-propelling tubes sneaking up on the hostile tanks. With their machine guns still up and ready and the *Panzer-grenadiers* still loose in the compound, this is dangerous business.

Two teams work their way along the walls and near enough to two of the *Panzer IVs* to bring them into the crude sights of the bazookas. In the fastest possible time, they fire off seven of the vicious little hollow-charge rockets. Five miss but the other two hit; one a dud, the other not. It penetrates a vital part of one machine, setting it afire and driving out the crew. They escape into the countryside but are bagged later.

Three *Panzer IVs* remain, and the crews inside their armored bellies will not give way. They continue to inflict damage in the compound with their long guns and machine guns; by and by they will exhaust their ammunition but not yet.

The 26th Regiment Antitank Company commander has come into Daniel's basement. He radios to the 26th Regiment operations officer in Bütgenbach to send some of the M-36 tank destroyers without delay. At about 3:30 p.m., four of them come clanking and rumbling down the icy N-32 behind a screen of smoke fired by friendly guns to hide their approach. The lieutenant in charge of the big machines dodges the bullet fire to find his way to the battalion command post. Daniel gives him a simple order: kill the three *Panzer IVs* or drive them away.

The arrival of the M-36s with the 90mm gun seals their doom. Two M-36s stand by a small house on the edge of the compound at the junction of the Morschheck road to discourage reinforcing German armor from coming in from the south. The other two grind slowly down a mud road in the compound and take a position near the manor house. From there the long guns can bracket the machinery shed that two of the *Panzer* crews are using as a cover for their shooting.

The M-36 crews load with armor-piercing rounds, each 3.6-inches in diameter. They start banging away, one at one side of the shed, the other at the other side, searching for the range. As the shells go screeching by, the two German tank commanders know a new thing has come into the battle for the Dom Bütgenbach compound. Also, they have nearly fired away their ammunition.

They order their drivers to start their engines and fast forward out of the compound. One of the *Panzers* hurtles itself over a hedgerow and breaks for the woods to the southwest. Several 90mm shells hit the machine, penetrating the spaced armor around the turret and the skirt plates and going into the crew compartment. They end the life of the *Panzer* and its crew. The other meets a similar fate. Caught on the run, hit, and destroyed.

The last of the five *Panzer IVs* that have given Daniel and his headquarters men so much grief this day, sits still, not firing, not reacting until the evening fog and winter dark begin to move across the manor. Through some battlefield miracle, its crew and their tank manage to slip to safety from what is now a bear pit of hostility.

Even before the showdown with the *Panzers*, the few surviving *Panzergrenadiers* who infiltrated the compound sought cover, not for more sniping but to hide until nightfall when they hoped also to escape. Their choice of a hiding place could not have been more of a disaster for them: a large tent that a week before was used by a medical company evacuating wounded from the 99th Division front line.

The antitank company captain remarked afterward, "Why (they) thought they had any security behind the thin walls of the tent, I will never know. Perhaps they thought we hadn't seen them." Several of Daniel's HQ soldiers take up automatic rifles, creep up on the tent, and send streams of bullet fire through the canvas. The brave but hapless *Hitlerjugends* crouching in the tent have no chance. They don't even take an American or two with them in the end. The sad skirmish also ends *Kampfgruppe* Krause's bold attempt to destroy the brain and nerve center of the 2nd Battalion—for now at least.

At 5 p.m. in the darkening afternoon of December 21, Colonel Seitz, the 26th Infantry commander, orders Colonel Corley to send a company of his 3rd Battalion riflemen to the N-32 between Dom and Bütgenbach where several platoons of *Panzergrenadiers* have got round Daniel's right flank on foot and in their *Schützenpanzerwagen*.

The Company "K" captain moves his headquarters to the southeast edge of Bütgenbach. Teams of its riflemen hunt through the early evening to kill the invaders or drive them off. They don't see much action. Most of the young *SS* soldiers have fled.

In the afternoon, artillery strikes by the American howitzers and long guns against the Bütgenbacher Heck and the hills to the east impose an absolute reign of terror on the infantry of *Kampfgruppe* Krause mustering there for a yet more powerful assault. The few *SS* officers and NCOs leading the platoons and companies are unable to organize their boys and men under the ceaseless falls of 105mm, 155mm, 4-inch shells and mortar bombs.

The *Panzer* company leaders with Krause's *Kampfgruppe* are unwilling to send more of their machines at the 26th Infantry perimeter unless they are accompanied by *Panzergrenadiers*. But the men and boys of *Hitlerjugend's* 26th and 25th *Panzergrenadier* regiments are being hurt this afternoon even before they sort themselves out with their armor and begin the last-wave attack to cross the N-32 highway west of Dom and seize Bütgenbach.

Colonel Kraas, the *Hitlerjugend* commander, is on the scene at the Morschheck crossroads on the edge of the Heck. He knows what his men are going through and accepts the inevitable. The big push will be postponed until the next day with a march vectored directly from south to north into the heart of the town. The blockage at the Dom Bütgenbach manor will be bypassed.

It is a fatal mistake. For the only possibility of *Kampfgruppe* Krause's breaking through is now, late in the afternoon, when the 2nd Battalion and its added rifle companies have been punished so severely after three days of mayhem that its men are at the breaking point. As often happens on the battlefield, Krause's opportunity comes and goes with the swiftness of a shell fired from a high-velocity gun. It is now gone this day, December 21, for *Hitlerjugend*.

An estimated ten thousand shells and mortar bombs have been put down on the fields and woods by the American artillerymen firing off the Elsenborn heights in the direction of Dom Bütgenbach, the Heck, Büllingen, Wirtzfeld, and the cannon company and mortar crews closer to the action. At 4:30 p.m. Daniel signals Seitz, "I don't know where (our) artillery got the ammo or when they took the time out to flush their guns, but we wouldn't be here now if it wasn't for them."

How many boys and men of *Hitlerjugend* have been struck down this day under the torrents of fiery metal is not known. The victims are intermixed with those put down by bullet fire, canister, rocket explosions, grenade fragments, mortaring. Few die well who die in battle. The young Germans who have died on these cold, desolate fields, in creek bottoms, under the bushes and trees of the Heck, by muddy tracks and country roads, have died exceedingly awful deaths.

Once darkness arrives, Daniel's staff and captains bustle about the blasted front of the battalion engaged in "extensive reorganization of the companies," as the operations officer put it. The battalion's leaders face an arduous and depressing task in this reorganization. The 2nd Battalion's four rifle companies up front are down by nearly two-thirds: (A fully manned rifle company consists of 193 soldiers.) Company "E" has 75; "F," 75; "G," 55; "H," 80; "C," 75. These survivors are mostly in the weapons platoon and company HQ, or replacements who have come in since the mayhem started on the 19th. *Hitlerjugend* also wrecked or disabled four Sherman medium tanks, five 57mm guns, and three M-10 tracked antitank guns in Daniel's sector.

He shortens his main line of resistance, moves some squads and platoons about, orders in four squads (forty-eight men) of the 18th Infantry company on the hill, repositions such armor as is still behind the manor house, on the field and working.

All this bustling about in the night and sleety cold of December 21 may be for nothing. Later—at 8:30 p.m. to be precise—Colonel Seitz calls a meeting of his number two, Colonel Sutherland, his staff, and the commanders of his three battalions. The topic is withdrawal to more defensible positions, as proposed earlier. (Above, page 225) Colonel Murdoch, 1st Battalion CO, is there, but Corley and Daniel send deputies: They are too busy shoring up their dikes to travel even the few miles west and north to Bütgenbach, where Seitz is headquartered in a large stone house.

The colonel reviews his power, especially in the center of the regimental line, Daniel's pounded and battered sector. Fifty more replacements are being sent to 2nd Battalion, scarcely a replenishment. Additional Sherman tanks are not to be had. However, the lightly wounded Sherman is being repaired and will go in again, plus some 3-inch gun replacements for the lost 57mm antitank guns of the 26th regiment. Heavy machine gun sections of "H" Company have disappeared. Replacements are not available.

Intelligence on *Hitlerjugend* seems sketchy round the table in Seitz's command post. The regimental S-2 (Intelligence) officer estimates that two battalions of *Panzergrenadiers* have been sent against the 26th Regiment. Little, if anything, has been received from division intelligence on the enemy formations coming at them. They have not captured enough prisoners (or brought them in alive) to identify which units make up these formations.

Colonel Murdoch is concerned over giving up ground and the defenses built there by the regiment in the past three days, including putting down some one thousand mines. Someone reminds the group that the 18th Infantry is arriving, but Seitz's operations officer says that Andrus does not want its battalions committed in force "unless in case of emergency." Colonel Corley has two companies "I" and "L" on "good ground," from the reservoir to Daniel's left flank. More discussion, then Seitz bites it off. "We stay," he says and rises, closing the meeting.

Part 5: *Hitlerjugend's* Violent Farewell

SS General Willi Bittrich, 2nd *SS* Corps commander, was a World War I flyer and thereafter a career military officer. He early on committed himself to the *Nazi* cause (as did more than a few of the younger career officers of the *Heer*). However, in recent months Bittrich has become disillusioned, "sick and tired" of Hitler's interference with military operations and disgusted with the toadyish bureaucracy that has grown round the War Lord. The 2nd *SS* Corps commander also has been shocked by the execution of his old chief, General Eric Höpner, who was involved in the July 1944 plot to kill Hitler.

Yet Bittrich for all his disillusionment sees no other way than to go on with it—to the bitter end. He is well aware, as are Colonel Kraas, 12th *SS* Division commander, and Krause, leader of the *Kampfgruppe* now spearheading the attack at Bütgenbach that time is running out, their armor is being ground down, and their men and boys are being winnowed by the American artillery, mortar, and automatic weapons fire. Also, Bittrich is turning his attention to happenings farther west. The fall of St. Vith has opened a way for his 2nd Corps to join the struggles in the river valleys southeast of Huy Belgium on the Meuse. (Appendices, p. 408) The "Bütgenbach problem" must be resolved post haste.

To insure that the 1st Infantry Division is well occupied while Krause's power is sent against Bütgenbach, Bittrich orders General Wadehn's 3rd *Fallschirmjäger* Division to attack the 1st Division's 16th Infantry Regiment holding the right flank at Weywertz, two miles northwest of Bütgenbach; and General Engle's 12th *Volksgrenadier* Division to attack along the southern edge of the Lac de Bütgenbach to the eastern edge of the town. This will drive away Colonel Corley's 1st Battalion and isolate what is left of Daniel's 2nd Battalion.

General Wadehn's 3rd *Fallschirmjäger* Division has been probing the front of the 16th Infantry all the while Daniel's battalion has been fighting off the columns of *Hitlerjugend* at Dom Bütgenbach. The paratroopers have been ineffective. Wadehn's officers seem unable to conceive of tactics other than the salami kind: sending one or two companies or even platoons at the *Amis* with little artillery preparation, poor coordination among them, and no strong second thrust coming on top of the first. The experienced leaders of the U.S. 16th Infantry have handled these incursions with dispatch.

On December 20, for example, one of the *Fallschirmjäger* battalions made an attack up the railroad track from Faymonville to Weywertz. The defenders were well ensconced in holes, houses, and bunkers. Only two companies of paratroopers came filing up the track bed. They circled to the east intending to sneak up on the infantrymen of Lieutenant Colonel Charles T. Horner's 3rd Battalion. They formed a line of skirmishers at the eastern edge of Weywertz. But Horner's men had the paratroops in their gun sights all the way. They sent bullet fire at the approaching enemy soldiers and dropped mortar bombs on their heads, killing some, wounding more. Surrender seemed the wisest move to the captain in charge.

The third company of the paratroop battalion was programmed to nourish the attack once it breached the American line and moved into Weywertz. It did not appear. Forward observers of the 1st Division artillery harrowed the company with 105mm shells, and it never even started up the railroad track.

On December 21, platoon-size (thirty or so men) combat patrols continued to pick at the defenses around Weywertz, even penetrating the outskirts of the town. Hopelessly ineffectual for the magnitude of their mission, the German paratroops shot wildly with their *Maschinenpistolen* and *Sturmgewehre*, but Horner's infantry were deep in holes, behind walls, in basements, in the second stories of buildings. For those not so unlucky as to take a wound, it was rather a game.

Late in the day, the paratroops tried to storm an outpost of the 3rd Battalion located in a house across a field from the edge of Weywertz. By happenstance Horner was visiting. He rallied his men, most of whom were replacements recently come to the 1st Division. "It was necessary for me to provide the necessary vocal incentive to get (my men) to fire their rifles and also to alert a tank destroyer outside of the house," he recalled.

On the left flank of the 26th Infantry line, the actions of General Engle's 12th *Volksgrenadier* Division were equally ineffectual. On December 20, the day 12th *SS* Division sent a powerful *Kampfgruppe* at Daniel's 2nd Battalion in front of the Dom Bütgenbach manor, Engle's men were expected to march simultaneously on Bütgenbach from the east by way of Wirtzfeld. However, 12 *VGD's* vanguard columns had scarcely reached and consolidated their hold on the latter by nightfall. (Narrative VIII, Part 5)

The three towns and villages, Bütgenbach, Berg, and Nidrum, form a small but tactically important triangle just behind the angle at the southern pivot of the Gerow line. General Engle's objectives include

Berg and Nidrum and, in conjunction with *Hitlerjugend*, Bütgenbach
also.

However, when Engle's captains finally took possession of Wirtzfeld, the jumping off place, as soldiers call it, for their attack toward
these places, they discovered an unpleasant geographic feature: The Lac
de Bütgenbach reservoir east of Bütgenbach split their assigned field of
action in two parts. Engle would need to divide his power, with one
regiment going north of the reservoir at Robertson's 38th Infantry; the
other south at Andrus' 26th. Coordination and communication, two
absolutely essential elements of a successful military operation, as Engle
and his staff most certainly knew, would be difficult, if not impossible,
to attain.

On December 21, early, large combat patrols of *Grenadiers* accompanied by a few *Sturmgeschütze* (tracked assault guns) moved out of
Wirtzfeld toward the reservoir. Artillery and mortar forward observers
with Colonel Corley's battalion and rifle companies of Colonel Boos'
38th Infantry alerted their batteries and sections. Engle's patrols came
under intense shell and mortar bomb falls from the dawn skies, as did
the mobile assault guns moving with them. These *Sturmgeschütze* were
especially tasty bites for the 155mm howitzers firing from behind Nidrum
on the heights.

Those *Grenadiers* who survived the artillery-mortar pasting, soon
reached within bullet range of the American main line of resistance.
(MLR) The *Amis* fired from hidden recesses in the ground, along the
hedgerows, ensconced in farm houses and out buildings here and there
on the barren fields. The *Grenadiers* were out in the open and confused
as to who was shooting at them and from where. Their attacks petered
out except for brave gestures here and there by platoon-size teams trying to work their way into the American lines to gain a foothold for
subsequent penetrations.*

---

* For an historian of the Elsenborn battles, the recollections of Major General Gerhard
Engle, 12th *VGD* commander, can be confusing. He wrote of a joint attack December
22 by 12th *SS* and his own division on both Dom Bütgenbach and Bütgenbach. However,
the objective of 12th *SS* and 12 *VGD* on December 22 was an attack directly against the
latter town only. The General also wrote of 12th *SS* being subordinated to (i.e. under)
his command in this operation, an unlikely arrangement. *SS* Colonel Kraas was running
the 12th *SS*. However, in a combat interview December 27, 1947 with a representative
of the U.S. Office of Chief of Military History, General Engle did summarize in factual
terms the attacks of his division on December 22, 1944 as described later in this
narrative. Meyer questions the accuracy of Engle's memory concerning the date things
happened. *Kriegsgeschichte*, p. 448. (Volume 1, Acknowledgements, obverse, title page.)

December 22, a Friday and last day of the first week of the *Wehrmacht* offensive in the Ardennes, brings the climactic attack by 12th *SS Panzer* Division to overrun the Americans at Bütgenbach and open the way west on the N-32. The action this day will come out of the Bütgenbacher Heck south of the town and aim directly for it. Most of the 3rd *Fallschirmjäger* Division have cleared out of the woods, and apparently the *HJ* leaders believe the miserable roads (cart tracks, really) and marshy terrain south of Bütgenbach can be mastered. In any event, they see no hope of breaking through at Dom B, and with good reason.

Before daylight, the young soldiers of the 3rd Battalion, 26th *SS Panzergrenadier* Regiment, climb into their troop carriers (*Schützenpanzerwagen*) and other vehicles. They and their machines are setting out on an approach march, as it is called, to where they will assemble for the day's work.

After the thaw of the last few days, the pre-dawn temperature has again dropped to near freezing. The ugly wind has taken on a sharper edge. Snow showers are whipping around in the black as the parade moves south and southwest from Büllingen. Undetected by the American pickets around Dom B, they soon arrive at their assembly point, a clearing in the Bütgenbacher Heck. The troop carriers lurch and squeal to a halt along the forest road. The soldiers in those not armed for battle take up their weapons and belts of ammunition, descend to the ground, and start walking north.

All round in the dark are the hulking *Panzers* fueled up and filled with ammunition after the rampages of the previous morning. A mixed bag: sturdy, dependable *Panzer IVs*; formidable *Panthers*; *Jagdpanthers* with long guns out front that thrust way beyond the glacis plate; *Jagdpanzer IVs*, compact, close to the ground; armored cars; powerful guns mounted on a *Panzer III* chassis.

Individually, these are killer machines, but they are built for different missions and have different capacities, from the bone-crunching, all-round destructiveness of the *Panther* to the tank-destroying and assault gun roles of the *Jagdpanzer*.

From different companies and battalions, they will be difficult to meld into a well-coordinated attack, especially when so many *Panzergrenadiers* are working with them. The radio operators in the tanks can expect problems with codes and frequencies and will not be able to communicate with the tank destroyers at all. (However, in the *Waffen SS* it is a mark of pride that courage and esprit overcome technical problems.)

Just before midnight, the town of Bütgenbach undergoes a fierce but short storm of artillery fire, some four hundred 105, 150, and 210mm rounds. They set roofs afire, damage buildings, and boil up clouds of orange-tinted smoke that blow across the hills round the town. Colonel Seitz's rear-echelon soldiers and those of other units are protected by stout walls, deep basements, and wine and food storage cellars. All expect this to be merely the prologue.

They are wrong, one of the few occasions in the Elsenborn battles when the American defenders' worst fears do not prefigure even worse events. For whatever reason, the powerful aggregation of German cannon and rocket tubes strung out along the N-32 all the way to the Losheimergraben crossroads on the border do not repeat their midnight attack. At 1 a.m.. December 22, Seitz's operations section messages General Andrus' forward command post at Sourbrodt, "Everything quiet for the present." At 5:30 a.m. the signal is still, "All quiet."

Not quite. About this time the *Panzergrenadiers* of 3rd Battalion, 26th *SS PzG* Regiment a mile or so south of Bütgenbach, sit shivering in their *Schützenpanzerwagen* or are scrambling up the sides of the *Panzers*, taking precarious perches on the decks, clinging to the sides, holding fast to such projections as can be found. To lose a grip or a foothold and fall off the machine is to hazard being ground into the frost of the fields beneath the wide, cruel tracks.

Shortly before streaks of iron-grey dawn appear in the sky, outposts and artillery forward observers on the right of Colonel Daniel's position detect rumbling motors, squeaking road wheels, grinding tracks turning. They call for time-on-target shooting by all guns working with Seitz's battalion. What results is capsulated in the matter-of-fact report afterward of the 1st Division artillery HQ:

"At 6 a.m. (we) are firing on tanks...points south of Bütgenbach and west of Büllingen brought under fire by all battalions at once. Infiltration of infantry fired on (in this manner)." Five battalions of howitzers (sixty in all), the 26th Infantry Cannon Company (six howitzers), and a 90mm diameter gun battalion (twelve) take part, filling up their tubes and blasting off as rapidly as the overheated metal will allow. High-velocity guns of the tank destroyers also join in the shoot.

The first strike threatens the vanguard of *Hitlerjugend* before it even reaches what soldiers call the zone of advance. The young *Grenadiers* leap off the tanks and out of the troop carriers. Their machines and armor move down into the draws. Several tanks bog down, settling to the top of their tracks in the sink holes and wet bottom land. Others come to a halt to wait out the barrage. Still others reverse direction, returning up the slopes into the Heck. It is not an auspicious beginning.

For this big push on Bütgenbach, General Engle's 12th *VGD* is to march from Wirtzfeld once more and drive into the town from the west as *Hitlerjugend* takes it from the south.

The fight put up by the 99th and 2nd division infantry and artillery at Losheimergraben crossroads, Hünningen, and Wirtzfeld eliminated some of the armored *Sturmgeschütze* assault guns Engle's division started with. He has pleaded for replacements in order to heavy up the Bütgenbach assault. Sixth *SS Panzer* Army HQ has assured Bittrich and Engle that a contingent of *Sturmpanzer IVs* will soon arrive at Wirtzfeld to reinforce the *Sturmgeschütze*. *Panzer* soldiers have nicknamed this monster *"Brummbär,"* i.e. grizzly bear. (The Germans have a penchant for giving their armored machines the names of fierce animals: "Panther," "Leopard," "Tiger," "Puma," etc., a practice that seems to please the *Führer* no end. In contrast, the Americans name theirs after Civil War generals.)

The *Brummbär* is frightening: 100mm thick armor at the front, weighing nearly 30 tons, standing over 8 feet carrying a powerful 150mm (6-inch) diameter cannon and in some models a machine gun. It is designed to put itself in the face of enemy machine gun nests and antitank gun emplacements and blast them to oblivion. Unfortunately, *Brummbärs* are in short supply. Scarcely four hundred exist in the *Wehrmacht*. Engle was once the War Lord's adjutant. (Volume 1, Narrative IV, Part 1) But he is realistic enough to know that this old connection is unlikely to produce the *Brummbärs*.

It doesn't. The night of December 21-22 passes without the armored grizzlies making an appearance at Wirtzfeld. No doubt, General Engle and his regimental commanders are not surprised. In the *Riesenanschlag* almost anything can go awry: The *Brummbärs* may have run out of fuel or come under bombardment by large caliber enemy guns or been reprogrammed by Dietrich's staff for a sector more in need of emergency cannon power or—the possibilities are limitless.

No matter. Engle has his orders from II *SS Panzer* Corps. The staff of 12th *Volksgrenadier* now confronts the tactical problem of bad geography described before: the Lac de Bütgenbach reservoir lies across their line of advance.

The reserve *Grenadier* regiment of 12th *VGD* will debouch from Wirtzfeld toward the hamlet of Berg on a hill just north of the reservoir. On the south side of the reservoir, Engle's *Füsilier** Regiment

---

* *"Füsilier"* means "soldier armed with a light musket." In the German infantry division, the *Füsilier* unit was expected to travel light, move fast, and strike swiftly. They sometimes included bicycle troops. Most of the newly minted *Panzergrenadier* divisions had only a few companies of *Füsiliers* for recon work and special missions. General Engle's *Füsiliers* have been seen in action before. (Volume 1, Narrative IV, Part 2)

will move along the railroad track from Büllingen to Bütgenbach, overawe Colonel Corley's weakened 3rd Battalion, and go into the town, there to meet the vanguard armor and infantry of *Hitlerjugend*. A classic pincer movement but one that will depend for its success on the hardness and power of the pincers and the weakness of the enemy to be pinced.

Staging the attacks to reinforce each other also is critical—and nightmarish, given the situation: 12th *VGD* cut in two by the reservoir; *Hitlerjugend* operating four to five miles west and pretty much on its own, not in Bittrich's corps at all. General Engle divides his remaining twelve or so *Sturmgeschütze* armored guns between his north and south columns. As the light comes up to illuminate the woods and fields along the slopes leading up to the Elsenborn plateau, his foot soldiers start west in clouds of fog and a driving wind laced with snow. Some walk; some ride the decks of the tracked and armored *Sturmgeschütze*.

Lieutenant Colonel Frank J. Murdoch, Jr.'s 1st Battalion, 26th Infantry, is defending the south edge of Bütgenbach, its main line of resistance bisecting several rough farm roads leading into the town. However, he controls two rifle companies only, "A" and "B." His third company ("C") is with Daniel at Dom B. Murdoch's attenuated line extends from the boundary of the 16th Infantry on the right flank to "K" Company on the southeast edge of Bütgenbach.

Company "K," it may be remembered, was sent by Colonel Corley to close the gap on the right flank of the 2nd Battalion. (All this is confusing. But it shows how many moves and marches rifle companies of the 26th Infantry have had to make to shore up breaks and fissures in the line for the last seventy-two hours.) It is the fate of companies "A" and "K" this day to be astride the march route of *Hitlerjugend's Kampfgruppe* Krause.

The 26th Infantry has already been through a ringer of blood and fire. Some of the replacements who came in early in the battle already have been killed or wounded and sent off to the hospital, their places taken by a second contingent of replacements who even now are awaiting their own time on the rack. The old timers—battalion and company leaders, both officers and NCOs—take pride in standing up to anything and everything. How much longer they can do so remains to be seen.

Brigadier General Andrus, the 1st Division's acting commander, has husbanded his trump card: the 18th Infantry Regiment, one of whose battalions is occupying buildings in Bütgenbach and is assigned to Seitz's command. The other two battalions have arrived in Sourbrodt, the division forward HQ, a few miles northwest of Bütgenbach. Should the *Panzers* and *Panzergrenadiers* succeed in putting down the 26th Infantry, they will then come up against the 18th Infantry Regiment and the tanks and tank destroyers working with it.

Kampfgruppe Krause restarts its march north, this time moving in three parallel columns. Infantry clad in white capes and smocks, helmets covered with white cloth follow close behind. Several *Panzers* splashed with white-camouflage paint come pressing at the seam between "A" and "K" companies.

Black-clad commanders stand boldly in their cupolas as the bright front lights illuminate prey. The attackers put their weight against the foxholes and automatic weapons dugouts of "A" Company's left platoon. Its riflemen try to fight back with Browning Automatic Rifles, bazookas, rifle grenades. Friendly tank destroyers stationed on the N-32 on the outskirts of Bütgenbach fire at the *Panzers*, but they are distant and their shells explode uselessly.

Two *Panthers* rumble and clank up to the holes and dugouts where the *Amis* crouch, their machine guns spewing bullets. The "A" Company men not ripped and holed by the machine gun fire are immediately confronted by the gun muzzles of the *Panzergrenadiers* coming in behind the tanks. They are (or seem) a multitude, firing their *Maschinenpistolen* and *Sturmgewehre* wildly.

The melee continues no more than ten minutes, long enough for the "A" Company platoon to fall into one of those battlefield black holes that swallow unlucky soldiers caught up in ferocious combat. Some die instantly, others slowly without being found; some are taken and if able to walk, marched away by their captors. (Three months after the battle, Seitz's HQ will still list all but a few men of this platoon as missing in action.)

On the left flank, a platoon of "K" Company also is being eaten quick by the same mass of *Hitlerjugend* men and machines. The company commander of "K" in a farm house on the edge of Bütgenbach tells his communications sergeant to try to reach his platoons by phone or radio. He knows something bad is happening to them but not what. The sergeant remembered, "All of our phone lines were out (due to the earlier barrage), but I did get the lieutenant (3rd Platoon) on the radio. He said the tanks had gone right over their holes, and when they had passed (his men) had come up and taken on the infantry. He had lost some men and guns but was holding on."

However, as the day before at Dom, *Kampfgruppe* Krause has ruptured the 26th Infantry line, opening a gap eight hundred feet wide directly south of Bütgenbach. Stormed at by the American howitzers, long guns and mortars, several platoons of *Panzergrenadiers* moving with the a company of *Panthers* on foot or in *Schützenpanzerwagen* drive through the gap and into the town.

A quarter of a mile north of the road junction where the hostile machines and infantry are moving into the outskirts of Bütgenbach, Colonel Seitz, 26th Infantry commander, receives some good tidings by teletype from General Andrus. The 18th Infantry of the 1st Division will start moving in, first to reinforce his 1st Battalion, then to take over the Bütgenbach front. Andrus adds, "The Germans want the road (the N-32) to Malmedy. If we pull back we will be giving it to them. Must hold."

Seitz has no intention this day of not holding. The decision has been made. (Part 4, this narrative) Yet at midmorning even more tanks and infantry of *Hitlerjugend* are moving across the 26th's main line of resistance and into Bütgenbach. Five *Panzers* have ground and clanked up the hill into the town well behind the infantry line a few hundred yards south.

Three have not made it. Snow and sleet now are drumming across the fields. They are softening the ground, and these *Panthers* sink to the top of their tracks. The drivers rock them, gun the powerful motors to near destruction, but the steel monsters stay stuck. They are seen by the artillery forward observers. Retribution is swift. Not only the tank-killing 155mm shells but also high-velocity armor-piercing rounds from the tank destroyers in the vicinity that are with the 1st Division. The struggling *Panthers* lose tracks, take gun damage, sustain ruptures in armor, their crews chopped up, burned, or, if luck is with them, sent packing across the countryside.

A quarter of a mile to the north the vanguard of *Kampfgruppe* Krause is moving into the center of Bütgenbach. Several *Schützenpanzerwagen (SPWs)*, the armored troop carriers armed with a machine gun or small cannon, each carrying *SS Grenadiers* loaded up with weapons, ammo belts, *Panzerfäuste*, and the rest have made it in with the *Panthers* under cover of fog and confusion. The *Panthers* take stations and start blasting away at the buildings sheltering Colonel Seitz's command post and the other vitals of his command and those of other units working with the 26th Infantry. The *Panzergrenadiers* take leave of their *SPWs* as quickly as they can to form little fighting hedgehogs and wait for reinforcements: more *Panzers*, more infantry. It is Dom Bütgenbach of the day before repeated, only on a grander scale.

The 26th Infantry's operations officer informs 1st Division forward CP at Sourbrodt that "everything is under control. I think we can take care of it." A bully posture given the angry presence of *Panthers* on the streets outside the building he is telephoning from.

Seitz orders Colonel Murdoch, the 1st Battalion commander, whose own headquarters is in a house nearby to send his "B" Company into the wide space created by the German breakthrough, seal it, and eliminate the *Panzergrenadiers* moving through.

1st Division HQ also orders him to move some parts of his front line north, in other words, to shorten the line, as soldiers term it. Colonel Daniel's position at Dom B is especially at risk, his supply line in danger of being cut, and his thin line of survivors out front, of being on the enemy side of the mayhem.

While this is going on at Bütgenbach, three miles to the east on the fields west of Wirtzfeld, General Engle's 12th *Volksgrenadier* Division has started forward with a two-regiment attack to enter Bütgenbach from the north and east side. It is the complementary action that the *Hitlerjugend* commanders are counting on to force the 1st Division defenders to fight on two fronts.

The forward column of *Volksgrenadiers* tries to follow a meandering farm track over sparsely wooded hills to the vicinity of Berg. They wear long, grey overcoats covered with white snow capes, carry a variety of rifles, machine pistols, grenade throwers, *Panzerfäuste*. Serving as outriders are a half dozen of the low-slung *Sturmgeschütze* assault guns, machine gun on top, cannon up front, crew sheltered by the armor plating, sturdy little *Panzer III* track assembly churning away.

It is down hill from Wirtzfeld and up hill to Berg. On the slopes that the *Grenadiers* are marching toward, infantry outposts and artillery forward observers of Colonel Boos' 38th Regiment are hunkered down in their cold holes and dugouts, watching. They call for artillery and mortar rounds. Most of the 2nd Division artillery battalion and other guns working with them get in on the shoot. The sloping fields heave up muck and slush, pounding explosions echo across the landscape, the fog and smoke glow orange and red.

The 12th *VGD's* four battalions of artillery guns are not sufficient to suppress those of the Americans'. Also, because of road and traffic problems, some of the German howitzers remain too far east to be of assistance. Also 2nd *SS Panzer* Corps lacks intelligence on the American gun positions on the heights and have not the means of acquiring it.

The *Grenadiers* moving toward Berg are ordered to burrow in, hold their ground, and await further orders. Their medical corpsmen busy themselves trying to locate the wounded before their injuries, the misery of the cold, and fright over their condition destroy them.

A half mile to the south, a battalion of the division's *Füsilier* regiment moves west along the single-track railroad line that connects Büllingen and Bütgenbach. It is located just south of the Lac de Bütgenbach. The two rifle companies of Colonel Corley's 3rd Battalion ("I,"

"L") blocking their way have had several days to deepen and harden their positions. Their light and heavy machine guns are rooted in logged-over bunkers with gun ports that allow firing across a half circle of front; their heavy mortars are preregistered on likely target sectors and connected by telephone line and radio to their forward observers. "I" and "L" are forward of a large clump of woods south of the reservoir. Corley has no reserve, having sent his "K" Company to first battalion.

Engle's *Füsiliers* exhibit uncommon courage moving along the railroad tracks just north of the *Schwarzenbückel* in lines of skirmishers shooting as they come with their machine pistols, assault rifles, machine guns. The American automatic weapons hammer back; the mortars whomp round after explosive round down on them; and the always-present artillery tears at them. The *Füsiliers* go down, first a few, then more, then entire lines. But they do not give way until close to Corley's gun line where an ugly muzzle-to-muzzle melee ends with the survivors going back east along the railroad or south toward Büllingen.

"Our attack collapsed," remembers Engle, "because our infantry lacked striking power, being short of assault guns essential for support. And also because of the enemy artillery firing at us from the Elsenborn area."

Shortly after noon, December 22, he orders the *Grenadier* and *Füsilier* assault companies to return to their positions at the start of the day's action. For all their courage and doggedness, the *Landsers* of this well-regarded division of the *Heer* have accomplished little in 6th *SS* Army's urgent mission to seize Bütgenbach and open the N-32. As it tries to enlarge its gains this day, *Hitlerjugend* is on its own at Bütgenbach.

By late morning December 22 the battlefield in and around that town is splintered into disparate areas of deadly action and reaction. General Andrus sends a teletype summary of the situation to General Gerow, U.S. 5th Corps commander at Eupen: "The 26th *Panzergrenadier* Regiment of the 12th *SS* Division closed right in on us. Between companies 'A' and 'K,' 26th Infantry, is a gap. Enemy have got through to Bütgenbach. 'B' moving...to close the gap. First Battalion, 18th Infantry moving to recapture positions companies 'A' and 'K' held." And he might have added, at least five *Panther* tanks are loose in Bütgenbach threatening everything and everybody on the American side.

By early afternoon, fires are burning in many of the Bütgenbach houses and barns. American vehicles hit by shells and rockets stand smoldering on the streets. Smoke hangs over the town permeating the falling snow and making the furtive moves of the enemy tanks and infantry even more treacherous to the 1st Division soldiers engaged in the dangerous task of hunting them down.

However, as in the Dom Bütgenbach battles, Sherman tanks and tank destroyers—both tracked M-10s and M-36s—are taking down the *Hitlerjugend* armor attempting to get through the gap in the 1st Battalion line and grind their way into Bütgenbach to reinforce the *Panzers* there.

Next to the "K" Company command post on the edge of the town, an M-10 waiting between the buildings lurches forward from time to time to send one of its high-velocity 3-inch diameter rounds screeching across the field in front where a half dozen *Panzers* are moving inexorably forward.

By early afternoon, the Germans are in trouble. The *Panzers* sending shell and machine gun fire at the buildings where Colonel Seitz and his staff are trying to run the confused battle find themselves bombarded with bombs fired by 81mm mortar crews. The *Panzer* drivers try to move their big machines away from the danger only to be confronted by the high-velocity guns of the American tank destroyers. And the stealthy teams of bazookamen are out hunting with their tubes and bags of armor-piercing rockets.

Major Krause, the *Kampfgruppe* commander is well aware that his *Panthers* and *Panzergrenadiers* in Bütgenbach must be reinforced. About midafternoon, a powerful parade starts moving north from the Bütgenbacher Heck toward the town. It consists of a dozen or so *Panzers*, several tracked field and antitank guns, *Flakwagens*, companies of *Panzergrenadiers*, some riding troop carriers, some on foot. The sky is heavy with clouds, the snow showers thickening to a blizzard.

Once again, the American artillerymen on the heights outdo themselves. They lash at the marchers from the time they come out of the woods to their arrival at the 1st Battalion line south of Bütgenbach. "An almost indescribable hail of fire from the American artillery," remembered a commander of one of the *Hitlerjugend* tanks.

Some of the machines in the march take direct hits and explode or flame up, stagger to a halt, and blaze away; others are driven to seek escape in the fields away from the roads where they sink immobile in the muck. Others take the blast of 155mm shells in the chassis and track assemblies, bringing them to a halt. The black-clad crews can only flee their crippled and burning machines and trust in God or the *Führer* that an exploding shell or hostile machine gun bullet will not find them. However, for the commander of *Hitlerjugend's Panther* battalion it is too late to try to come out of the turret hatch and escape his burning machine. The fire already has engulfed him.

The young *Panzergrenadiers* moving with the armor have the worst of it. Their flesh is naked to the blasts of shell fragments and concussions. Those in the tracked troop carriers can only hunker down and yearn that their vehicle will not take a hit; those on foot rush to find some mud hole or fold in the earth to hide in or slither under an immobilized tank or troop carrier. Yet with incredible determination in the vivid presence of death and hurt all around, they rally to the whistles and calls of their leaders and press on toward Bütgenbach.

About a third of a mile directly south of the town, the *Panzergrenadiers*, some riding, some running, strike into the improvised hedgehogs that Lieutenant Colonel Murdoch's 1st Battalion captains have tried to wedge into the breach in the 1st Division line. Each of these strong points is made up of a machine gunner or Browning Automatic Rifle shooter and the few riflemen of "A" and "K" companies who have survived the morning.

Several *Schützenpanzerwagen* (*SPWs*) troop carriers grind and lurch over the roads across the *Ami* foxhole line, their up-front cannons flailing away with 20mm (diameter) explosive rounds, their *Panzergrenadiere* shooting wildly from behind the sloping armor plates of the passenger compartments. Others are following the *SPWs* in, running and shouting and firing wildly also.

The attackers penetrate to a hill in the rear of the 1st Battalion main line of resistance that dominates an entrance to Bütgenbach. The young Germans run straight into a line of skirmishers, coming to the aid of Murdoch's two depleted companies, "A" and "K." These are his reserve company ("B") sent in to beat back the *Panzergrenadiers* and restore the line, as soldiers put it. The *SPWs* overflowing with the *Hitlerjugend* soldiers charge through. But those on foot go to ground under the fire of the newly arrived *Ami* reserves.

It is now 4 p.m., December 22. The landscape is darkening, the wind rising, and the bursts of snow coming closer together. Pointless and suicidal for the "B" Company officers to try to drive into an enemy of unknown size and power under these conditions.

The *Grenadiers* who have crossed the 1st Battalion MLR need some of the *Panzers* they started out with to help them bull their way into the town to reinforce the strong points established earlier. The big armored machines don't appear. Few in the drive up the hill to Bütgenbach have made it this afternoon. They have fallen victim to shell explosions, anti-tank guns firing armor-penetrating rounds, the swamp-like terrain, confused orders over unintelligible radio transmissions, drivers blinded by the swirling snow.

Every minute of delay in getting more troops and armor into

Bütgenbach and building more strong points is a defeat for Colonel Krause's *Kampfgruppe* this waning afternoon of December 22. The armor that has reached Bütgenbach either has been driven out or is hiding. The 1st Battalion of the 18th Infantry Regiment is mustering to relieve the dwindling number of Murdoch's riflemen and machine gunners.

As nightfall arrives, *Hitlerjugend's* window of opportunity, such as it has been, is gone. Two rifle companies of the 1st Battalion are already on the field. Some of the *HJ* troop carriers that reached Bütgenbach have already withdrawn. An NCO in charge of one remembered, "We had to pull back because the *Panzergrenadiers* did not reinforce us. We moved (south) to the entrance (to Bütgenbach) and found a more secure place."

About one hundred fifty of *Kampfgruppe* Krause's infantry still menace "B" Company and what is left of "A" and "K" companies on the hill. However, the German boys are boxed in, with no hope of being reinforced, menaced by the ceaseless explosions all round of artillery shells and mortar bombs. They will either use the cover of night to make their escape south to the Bütgenbacher Heck or they will die.

Not only is their situation perilous; it is irrelevant as well. Even before dark, the foothold their tanks and *Panzergrenadier* comrades seized before noon in Bütgenbach has slipped away. The *Panthers* in the town have worked their way to the single track railroad line on the northern edge. They have taken cover behind the walls of a large hospital compound. The *Panther* commanders believe they can hold on until more friendly armor and foot soldiers arrive. None do, and the little foxy *Ami* bazooka teams come darting in and out of the shadows, let fly hissing rockets, then disappear to do the same from another place. Hostile tank destroyers are hunting too.

Most serious of all, the beleaguered *Panthers* are running low on fuel and shells for their long guns and bullets for their machine guns. Useless to stay only to meet the fate of *Panzermen* evacuating stranded machines in the presence of hostile infantry: instant death by bullet fire. As the dark comes down amid thickening snow, the three *Panthers* still mobile, rev up, plunge from behind the walls of the hospital grounds, and pound and grind at top speed south to friendly lines, resembling in the blizzardy night, locomotives run amok.

They leave a few of their infantry still hiding here and there in Bütgenbach. But they are a dwindling number. By late afternoon they have been hunted down or have slipped away. The "K" Company headquarters men bag three of the last of the *Kampfgruppe*: young boys, wearing clothing parts taken from the American stores in Büllingen, trying to save themselves with their school-boy English.

A soldier with Murdoch's Headquarters Company recalled the vile odor in the town: "Fires were breaking out all over town. The smell of smoke, gun powder, and dead bodies was all over the place. Bodies in German tanks were burning, and the smell of burning hair and flesh was prevalent."

The 1st Division has been grappling with the *Wehrmacht* for two years. Nothing in their foe's pattern of conduct leads the division's reigning officers to believe that the German forces attacking their men will now give up.

The night of December 22, at Sourbrodt, Bütgenbach, Weywertz, Robertville and elsewhere, they prepare for more of the same:

—On the east, what is left of Colonel Corley's 3rd Battalion, 26th Regiment is moving its main line closer to Bütgenbach.

—Four hundred rifle replacements for men lost in the past few days have arrived and are finding their way to the rifle companies they will live and die with.

—The 18th Infantry Regiment is taking over from the survivors of the 26th Infantry.

—The powerful new M-36 tank destroyers are being collected in Bütgenbach for assignment the next day where needed.

—First Division engineers working with the regimental pioneer battalions are spending the night putting down belt after belt of tank destroying and man-maiming mines in front of the 16th Infantry line from Bütgenbach to the 30th Infantry Division boundary east of Malmedy.

At 4 a.m., December 23, Andrus receives a disconcerting message from Gerow's headquarters that 1st Army (Lieutenant General Hodges) fears a gas attack. Troops up front will "carry gas masks at all times." How the 1st Division staff and subordinate commanders take this is not recorded.

Down in the cold, icy holes and dugouts under the snow where the surviving infantry soldiers have just endured spasm after spasm of deadly tank and bullet fire and sporadic artillery and rocket pounding, an order to first find then strap on a gas mask as they stretch out on a mud-caked shelter half or blanket or hunch over a tiny fire in a can seems so irrelevant to their condition it is beyond risible. Most simply ignore the order.

At 10 a.m., Andrus' HQ is still insisting the gas mask order is to be obeyed; at 3 p.m. Gerow's 5th Corps informs 1st Division that a mistake has been made: Gas masks are merely to be available at rear depots for distribution if necessary. The soldiers in the snow and mud knew it all along.

What the 1st Division leaders do not know is that after dark December

22, the principal axis of the German advance into Belgium and Luxembourg has shifted to the south and west, away from the Monschau-Büllingen sector originally assigned to Dietrich's 6th *SS Panzer* Army in Hitler's plan. Dietrich's armored divisions, including 12th *SS Panzer*, are moving out. About midnight Kraas receives orders to rally what remains of his division around Moderscheid and Schoppen south of the Bütgenbacher Heck and await orders.

It has been *Hitlerjugend's* malignant fate since December 17 to grapple with two of the most warrior-like infantry divisions in the U.S. Army, the 1st and the 2nd, whose officer and NCO superstructure is comparable in bloody battlecraft and determination to that of even the most hardened *SS* or *Heer Panzer* Division.

Hitlerjugend Division, for all its destructive power and *Nazi* youth indoctrination and elan, has been doomed from the time of its organization in 1943. (Narrative VIII, Part 1) First in Normandy, now in the Ardennes, the infantrymen and tankers of the division—mostly youth 17 to 19 years of age—have been wasted in suicidal last stands and attacks against superior forces. About their four days of driving *Panzers* and *Panzergrenadiers* at the U.S. 1st Division at the bloody angle, the operations officer of *Hitlerjugend* wrote long after the war, "The result (was) disappointing....An attack with insufficient strength is better not made."*

Disappointing, yes, and devastating to the men and boys in the *Panzergrenadier* companies. On December 8 when the division assembled in the borderland towns of Germany for the march on the dual towns and Losheimergraben, Büllingen, Bütgenbach, 23,244 officers and men were on the division's role. By the end of December the number

---

* And better not made unless your side can suppress the enemy's artillery and mortars. *Hitlerjugend* and corps and army gunners tried but were never able in four days of battle to silence the terrible American guns no matter how much fire and steel they put down on the gunners. First Division artillery HQ estimated that its four battalions plus added battalions assigned by 5th Corps plus tank destroyers and antiaircraft long guns firing in a field artillery mode executed 896 firing missions during the 4 days of the Bütgenbach battle. Each of these consumed scores if not hundreds of 105, 155, 90mm, and 3- and 4-inch shells. The total weight of steel put down on *Hitlerjugend* is incalculable. One 155mm battalion working with 1st Division artillery fired 5,096 shells weighing an estimated 242 tons.

Colonel Seitz said afterward, "The position could not have been held save for the intense, unstinting, and accurate fire support rendered by the artillery." Mortars also did terrible things to the *Hitlerjugend* infantry. Colonel Corley's 3rd Battalion heavy (81mm) mortar section, for example, fired from 600 to 900 rounds each day of the fight, a prodigious expenditure of high explosives.

had dropped to 19,657.* And this number includes men and boys who have come in as replacements and returnees from hospitals since the Ardennes-Eifel action began in mid December. Probably two-thirds of these losses were taken in the dual towns and Bütgenbach battles.

Several of *Hitlerjugend's* field leaders were among the casualties sustained south of Bütgenbach and the reservoir: the commanders of three companies of *Jagdpanzers* and *SS* Major Arnold Jurgensen, commander of the *Panther* battalion of 12th *SS Panzer* Regiment. (It was he who was burnt in his fiery machine in the last attack on Bütgenbach, December 22.)

How many armored fighting vehicles 12 *SS Panzer* abandoned on the hilly fields enfolding the N-32 south of Lac de Bütgenbach, north of the Bütgenbacher Heck can not be known for certain.

After the fight, Colonel Seitz's staff estimated that 44 enemy tanks, 15 troop-carrying vehicles, 1 armored car, and 1 amphibious scout car, had been damaged so badly they could not be salvaged or were abandoned because hostile fire cut down any salvage crew from the *Hitlerjugend* tank-retrieval unit trying to get at them. As in the dual towns, the "tanks" probably included *Jagdpanzers* (tank destroyers), mobile howitzers and PAK (antitank) guns riding on old tank track assemblies, and *Flakpanzer* armored antiaircraft wagons. These losses in armored fighting vehicles must be added to the losses sustained in the two-day battle for the dual towns.

On the American side, an accurate count of casualties taken by 1st Division in the four-day battle is even more difficult to come by. The medical company working for Seitz's regiment reported 457 men treated during the battle and 450 of these sent west for more care. This doesn't include the men killed outright on the battlefield or bagged as prisoners by *Hitlerjugend*, some after being wounded. A few of the soldiers patched up by the 1st Division medics were men and boys of the two *Kampfgruppen* that struck the 26th Infantry. But it takes little imagination to know their numbers were few.

As to the material losses, the regiment's estimate of the two Shermans and four of the 26th Infantry's little 57mm antitank guns is without question unrealistic. At least fifteen Sherman tanks were in the melee, plus tracked and armored tank destroyers of at least two companies. One company of M-10 destroyers reported it lost three machines. Given

---

* These numbers are from Luther, Appendix table 6, p. 254. (Documentation, biblio., this volume.) The author's numbers seem somewhat inflated. However, the loss ratio seems reasonable.

the three days of blasting back and forth at each other by the armor on both sides, this, too, appears to be on the low side.

Dawn, December 23, comes up in the usual grudging, grey, and icy way of winter in the Low Ardennes. The snowfall of the day before has softened the awful sights down the slopes and in the folds of the hills south of Bütgenbach and the reservoir: tanks and other vehicles strewn about, some lying on their sides, others upended, others sunk in the snow; weapons and pieces of clothing; shapeless bundles covered with new-fallen snow, the human detritus of battle.

A few hours before in the dark, a patrol has gone out from the 18th Infantry now taking over the battlefield from the 26th. The soldiers pick their way across the hill where the Germans tried to hold out after battling "B" Company to a draw. The patrol finds "quite a few American and enemy dead. They were unable to identify them."

The soldiers of the 26th Infantry Regiment still alive and on the field and the combat engineers, tankmen, tank fighters and others of the fraternity of the sharp edge have won a decisive battle in the *Wehrmacht's* last great offensive of World War II. They don't know this, of course. They know only that they are cold, tired, hungry, and need a rest away from the cruel guns and the murderous enemy before they are summoned out for the next round.

WE WERE THERE

How to Determine Morale

"(On the 20th of December) the Jerry (German) tanks, maybe seven or eight of them, broke through our lines. It was kind of foggy that day and cold as a witch's tail. (AN: When soldiers in World War II used this expression, they made reference to a different part of the witch's anatomy.) The tanks busted through the fog like ghosts, their machine guns blazing. One tank started pulling up alongside our foxholes, dropped that long barrel right down into the openings and blasted the holes and the men together.

"One man kept firing a machine gun into a tank as it kept coming. He fired two boxes of .30caliber machine gun (bullets) at the openings (AN: probably at driver's and machine gunner's periscopes). But the tank didn't stop. The muzzle swung toward him and blasted him out of his hole. Some of us got out of the foxholes and started running and got away even though some were wounded."

"We stayed up on line for three days, then moved back into reserve for three days. 'Reserve' was a joke. We weren't out of range of Jerry (German) artillery and mortar fire. You never knew when it was coming in on our position. It was worth your life to crawl out of your hole."

"Twice morale was reported in the (company) morning report as 'poor.' The soldier who reported it said he didn't think it was approved policy to record morale as anything lower than 'fair,' but being conscientious and being two miles behind the (front) line he arrived at an accurate estimate of the morale of the front by dividing his own morale by two." (AN: The company clerk was in the rear HQ in Bütgenbach.)

> Loren W. Gast, rifleman, "G" Company,
> 26th Infantry, 1st Division

"Not a Very Wise Move"

"I received word of the second tank attack on the 2nd Battalion (AN: Daniel's battalion, 2nd-26th Infantry) about 7:30 a.m. on December 21....My (antitank) company command post was about a mile and a half from the 2nd Battalion. The 26th Regimental command post was also there..."

"About 8 a.m. when the situation seemed stabilized, I decided to drive up the road to see what was happening. It was not a very wise move. As I left the edge of Bütgenbach, the road wound around to the right and then curved left in the countryside. I could see no infantry anywhere on either side of the road. Three tanks were burning on the ridge to my right and two or more seemed disabled.

"I told my driver to keep on going. I had a very eerie feeling that I was in the wrong place....The 2nd Battalion command post suddenly appeared out of the morning mist on the right. We turned off the main road onto the small road to the farmhouse. (AN: location of the command post). I told the driver to slow down.

"Instead his foot hit the accelerator, which turned out to be fortunate, for at this time a German tank not one hundred feet away behind one of the stone barns fired a machine gun at us. I was nicked in the back; the driver, in the neck. Had he slowed down as I told him to, we would have caught the burst in its full blast."

"When I reached the first floor of the farmhouse, I found the situation was rather critical....Three enemy tanks were within fifty yards of the battalion command post building, one behind each of the long stone barns and one to the right in the tree line. They were only kept in check by three of our (Sherman) tanks on the reverse slope of the hill to our rear. Every thirty minutes one of the German tanks would fire a round at the end of our building. We weren't too sure just how long it would be before the next round would come into the room we were occupying."

Donald E. Rivette, captain, commander,
Antitank Company, 26th Infantry

Shaken Up Some

"My place in the defense was in a house on the southeast side of (Bütgenbach). There wasn't much left of the house, but it had a basement where we went when not on guard to try and get warm.

"Early on the morning of December 22, the Germans opened up with a very heavy artillery barrage on us. It was one of the heaviest barrages I had been under for a long time. We had taken cover in the basement and felt the house take hit after hit...

"When the artillery let up some, we ran upstairs because we knew that after a barrage like that there was sure to be an attack.

It was still dark, but what I saw shook me up some. There were German tanks and infantry all over our front. The tanks were painted white and the infantry wore white capes. The tanks had spot lights and the (tank) commanders were standing up in the open turrets, using them to pick out targets.

"One of our tank destroyers was between our house and the next one. He did a whale of a job that morning. He would pick out a German tank, pull out between the houses, blast the tank, then pull back in again. I have no idea how many he got that morning, but he sure helped save our necks.

"After the tanks stopped, we were able to handle the infantry 'OK,' in our part of town."

> Leroy N. Stewart, communications sergeant,
> Company "K," 26th Infantry

A Fatal Passion for the Fire-eyed Maid of Smoky War
All Hot and Bleeding

"Half of the right-hand drive wheel of our *Panzer IV* was shot off and we rolled out of the line. Now we couldn't move. A row of trees and a hedgerow about one hundred and fifty meters distant were occupied by the American infantry. We managed to keep them at bay with rounds from the turret gun and the machine gun.

"For two hours, we played 'dead man,' because of the heavy artillery fire. The meadow (we were on), which had been snow-covered white, was now blackened (AN: due to the many places where artillery rounds had exploded).

"During a pause in the firing, I ran to the *Panzer* that was closest to mine and asked (its commander) to pull my tank. Unfortunately his was disabled, too. All of the other *Panzer IVs* (in the company) as well as the self-propelled gun carriages with them also had suffered the same fate. Most of them had to drop out because of damage due to artillery and antitank fire."

> Willy Kretzschmar, sergeant, *Panzer IV*
> commander, 12th *SS Panzer* Regiment

- - - -

"It was our first day in action after we received replacements (AN: for *Panzergrenadiers* who had been killed or wounded). Our advance went through a sparse forest on a rising terrain. Suddenly, the artillery barrage started. There was uninterrupted cannon fire. We looked for cover immediately.

"My corporal and I jumped into a ditch on our right front, which ran in the direction of the enemy and was about a meter in depth. We were lying next to each other. Then the shells hit the forest. In the first ten minutes, a shell hit on the right in a tree and fragments hit both of us in the ditch. My corporal must have been hit in the chest and suffered lung damage. He breathed a death rattle and died soon afterwards."

> Karl Leitner, sergeant, troop carrier commander,
> 6th Company, 26th *Panzergrenadier* Regiment

- - - -

"Lieutenant Schittenhelm had just reached the border of the woods when a spurt of flame shot from the rear of his *Panzer V* (*Panther*) as though it had come from some spectral hand. The *Panther* was hidden by thick, black smoke mushrooming up. Two men got out.

"Captain Hills gave the order to get ready for action. He was standing in the open turret (hatch) studying his map to make an exact check on his position. He fired a flare to indicate the direction of the attack. The flare died away down the sloping terrain. We waited for the order to march into the attack (with the *Panzers*).

"Nothing happened. I looked at (Hills') tank. The turret was burning and there was no sign of him. His crew were abandoning the tank. I could recognize the driver, Corporal Bunke, and the radio operator, whose name I didn't know. But I had to accept the fact that the rest of the crew, including Hills, his gunner, Lorentzen, and gun layer, Krieg, had become casualties. Then an almost indescribable hail of fire from the American artillery began..."

> Unnamed *Panzer* commander, 3rd Company,
> 12th *SS Panzer* Regiment

The Snow and the Dead Frustrate the Machine Gunners

"We did manage to get into our positions. We had ample time to dig in quite well, particularly my (heavy) machine guns...the mortars were able to register. It was a real fine defensive position.

"On the 20th we really started getting attacks. We were attacked up to about five or six times a day. They didn't penetrate our lines, but they got very close.

"Some of the machine gun positions in front of the 3rd Battalion—we'd have stacked up bodies in front of those positions. In some of the places during the lull in the battle, my machine gunners would actually have to go out and pull (the dead) aside so they could continue to have their fields of fire.

"One of my sergeants called me on the telephone and wanted to speak to me personally about it. I told him that all he could do was...pull them aside so they wouldn't conflict with the fields of fire because some of the Germans in the attack would get behind the bodies and use them as protection.

"We also had a problem with snow. It was snowing most of the time we were in that position. The snow was getting quite deep, and many times the men had to go out in front of their positions and clear snow so they could get good fields of fire.

Walter Nechy, captain, "M"
Company, 26th Infantry

A Little Quad Four Wagon Rescues Some Medics

"The battalion went into position in the Weywertz (Belgium) area with the railroad on our left and an abandoned dump in the right rear of our front line, which was forward of the road from Bütgenbach to Waimes. (AN: The N-32 highway.) My command post, as I remember, was in the priest's house on the right side of the road looking south.

"On the following day I went on a reconnaissance with my driver. We were riding down the road to Waimes when an ambulance loaded with casualties heading towards Bütgenbach stopped us. They told me the hospital they just came from (in Waimes) was in German hands, and its personnel were being prepared to be evacuated to Germany as prisoners of war.

"With an AAA halftrack (AN: motorized multiple gun carriage mounting four .50caliber machine guns) we preceded to Waimes and found the enlisted personnel of the 99th Division Clearing Company (which operated the casualty evacuation unit for the division) and the U.S. 47th Field Hospital being held in a school yard by about three or four German soldiers.

"A few bursts from the quad 50s on the halftracks put them to flight. I directed the medical units to leave their equipment and go to Elsenborn, which they did. Later in the day, tanks and tank destroyers with the 2nd Battalion (16th Infantry) were sent into Waimes. A few members of the 1st *SS Panzer* Division (*Leibstandarte Adolph Hitler*) were killed or captured."

Charles T. Horner, lieutenant colonel, commanding officer, 3rd Battalion, 16th Infantry

KEY TO NARRATIVE X

This narrative covers the final phases of the U.S. 5th Corps (Major General Leonard T. Gerow; after January 15, Major General Ralph Huebner) operations, defensive and offensive, on the north shoulder of the "Bulge." These include: (1) Countering the final attacks by the Germans to break through the corps' defenses. (2) Improvement of these defenses, front and rear, against the enemy, the weather, and artillery, rocket, and mortar fire. Controlling Allied strategic and tactical air power to bear on enemy installations and communications. Preparing for the 5th Corps counteroffensive against German positions south and east. (3) The counteroffensive, which begins January 15 and continues to February 5, to recapture ground lost in the first week after the Germans began their offensive December 16 and to drive the remaining enemy east of the West Wall fortifications.

Phase 1, First Attack
(Part 1 in Narrative) (Map 1)

CONTENDERS: <u>U.S.</u> Infantry divisions: 9th (47th Regiment), 99th (393rd, 394th regiments; 324th Combat Engineer Battalion; 99th Reconnaissance Troop), 2nd (38th Regiment). Supporting artillery, heavy mortar, armor, antitank and other units. <u>German</u>: 277th *Volksgrenadier* Division, 3rd *Panzergrenadier* Division (Major General Walter Denkert). Sixty-seventh Corps and 6th *SS Panzer* Army artillery and *Werfer* units.

ISSUE: The 3rd *PzGD* and 277th *VGD* advance against the 99th Division and 47th Regiment lines takes place December 20 to 22 simultaneously with attacks by other German divisions against the U.S. 5th Corps defenses. (See Narrative IX Key.) The 3rd *PzGD* attack, which is supported by the 277th *VGD*, is intended by the German command to bring armor and infantry power to bear on the right wing simultaneously with that applied by 12th *SS Panzer*, 12th *VGD*, and 3rd *FSJ* divisions (Narrative IX) on the left wing. <u>Significance</u>: This is the last major effort by the German high command to execute the original plan contained in *Wacht am Rhein* of rolling up the American defenses between the Meuse River and Elsenborn. The objective is to open out the front of 6th *SS Panzer* Army's northern (right) wing and free the roads south of the Elsenborn plateau for German traffic moving west.

LOCATION: Hills east of Elsenborn and Kalterherberg occupied by the 99th Division and 47th Infantry.

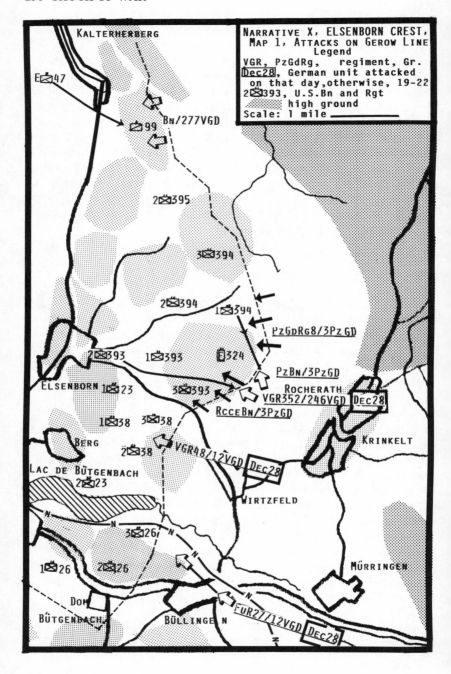

NARRATIVE X, ELSENBORN CREST,
MAP 1, ATTACKS ON GEROW LINE
Legend
VGR, PzGdRg,   regiment, Gr.
Dec28, German unit attacked
on that day, otherwise, 19–22
2393, U.S. Bn and Rgt
    high ground
Scale: 1 mile

Phase 1, 2nd Attack
(Part 5 in Narrative) (Map 1)

CONTENDERS: U.S. 393rd and 394th infantry regiments; 38th Infantry Regiment, (Colonel P.D. Ginder); 26th Infantry Regiment. German: 246th *Volksgrenadier* Division (Colonel Peter Körte), 12th *Volksgrenadier* Division. (One regiment of the 246th and two of the 12th *VGD* will participate.) ISSUE: To flatten out the projection in the U.S. 5th Corps line east of Elsenborn and Berg and south of Dom Bütgenbach. Significance: This would eliminate a potential jumping off place for U.S. 5th Corps troops when they counterattack.

LOCATION: Hills south and east of Elsenborn; open space a mile to the south between Wirtzfeld and the Lac de Bütgenbach; single track RR from Büllingen to Bütgenbach south of the Lac.

Phase 2, Occupation of Elsenborn-Bütgenbach High Plateau
(Parts 3, 4, 5, 6 in Narrative) (Map 2)

CONTENDERS: U.S. 9th, 99th, 2nd, and 1st infantry divisions and one artillery battalion assigned by 5th Corps, antiaircraft battalions, a 4.2-inch (chemical) mortar battalion, tank destroyer battalions, two tank battalions, additional corps and Army troops, including combat and construction engineers. 9th Army Air Force Tactical Air Command (Brigadier General Elwood R. Quesada) and 9th Bombardment Command; British 2nd Tactical Air Force. German: 326th *Volksgrenadier* (*VGD*) Division; 277th *VGD*, 3rd *Panzergrenadier* Division (replaced December 27 by 246th *VGD*); 12th *VGD* (replaced January 5 by 89th *VGD*). Corps artillery and heavy mortars, cannons, *Werfer* and *Flak* guns; *Luftwaffekommando* West, 2nd *Jagdcorps*, 3rd *Jagdivision* (Major General Walter Grabmann) plus specialized reconnaissance and bomber aircraft.

ISSUE: "The Gerow Line," which extends from Monschau south to the Lac de Bütgenbach, then west to Waimes a few miles east of Malmedy, is the hard north shoulder against German advances into U.S. 1st Army command, control, and supply centers, and bases east of Liege on the Meuse River. After the German attacks to overrun the American defenses here peter out in late December, the two sides engage in a war of attrition. Artillery, mortar, and aerial attacks are frequent. Patrolling across the lines, especially by the Americans, is the mode of combat. Significance: By December 25, 1st Army has so much power on the Elsenborn high plateau that the danger of a German break through there is nil. Gerow's forces prepare to counterattack as part of the general 1st Army drive from the north to liquidate the "Bulge" while 67th Corps (General of Infantry Hitzfeld) digs in to hold back the Americans as long as possible.

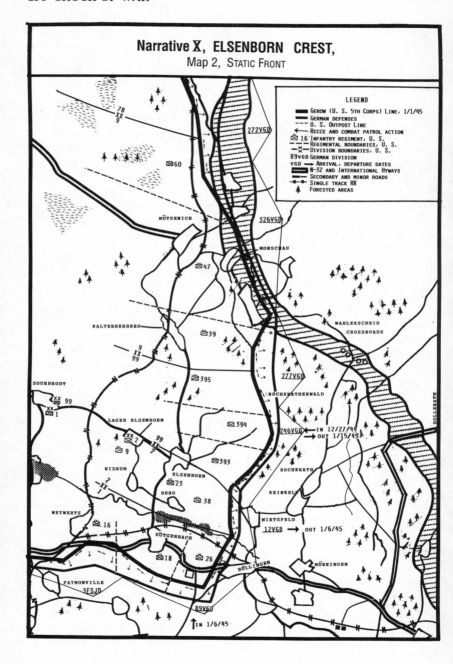

Narrative X, ELSENBORN CREST,
Map 2, STATIC FRONT

LEGEND

Gerow (U. S. 5TH CORPS) LINE, 1/1/45
GERMAN DEFENSES
U. S. OUTPOST LINE
RECCE AND COMBAT PATROL ACTION
16 INFANTRY REGIMENT, U. S.
REGIMENTAL BOUNDARIES, U. S.
DIVISION BOUNDARIES, U. S.
VGD GERMAN DIVISION
ARRIVAL, DEPARTURE DATES
N-32 AND INTERNATIONAL HYWAYS
SECONDARY AND MINOR ROADS
SINGLE TRACK RR
FORESTED AREAS

LOCATION: The hills, plains, marshes, creek bottoms, patches of conifer woods, and towns that make up the terrain between the Elsenborn and Bütgenbach high ground and the Monschauwald to the northeast and Bütgenbacher Heck to the south.

Phase 3, The American Counteroffensive
(Part 7 and 8 in Narrative) (Map 3)

CONTENDERS: U.S. Same as Phase 2 plus additional battalions of artillery including 240mm howitzers and 8-inch guns assigned by corps and army. German: Same as Phase 2 except that *Jagdcorps* fighter bomber operations are severely curtailed.

ISSUE: The U.S. 1st Army drive from the northern face of the breakthrough area made by the German counteroffensive begins January 2 as first, 7th Corps; then, 18th AB Corps; then, 5th Corps push south and east. The purpose of this operation is to roll the Germans out of the northern part of "the Bulge" beginning at their westernmost penetration and extending in sequence to the Elsenborn high plateau (north shoulder). When nothing more is to be gained by keeping their three armies in the breakthrough area, the German Army Group B plan of withdrawal is to hold the Americans out of important road junctions and communications centers and away from vital roads until first, the *SS Panzer* divisions; then, the regular *Panzer* divisions; then, the most viable infantry divisions are extricated. Significance: How successfully each side performs its respective missions will determine how much or little of the *Wehrmacht's* power will escape to build a new defensive line between the West Wall and the Rhine or move to the Eastern Front.

LOCATION of counterattack of U.S. 5th Corps: South of Waimes, Belgium toward Faymonville, Schoppen, the Ondenval Pass and Ebertange (U.S. 23rd and 16th regimental combat teams). South and east of Bütgenbach through Bütgenbacher Heck (woods) to Heppenbach and Honsfeld (18th RCT). South and east of Dom Bütgenbach and Lac de Bütgenbach to Büllingen, Hünningen, and Mürringen (26th RCT). East of Berg and the Lac to Büllingen, Wirtzfeld, Krinkelt/Rocherath (the dual towns), and the Wahlerscheid crossroads (38th and 9th RCTs, later 23rd RCT also). From hills east of Elsenborn to Rocheratherwald, (393rd Infantry). From hills east of Elsenborn north to road from Rocherath to Wahlerscheid crossroads in the Monschau woods (394th Infantry). From vicinity of Kalterherberg east through Monschauwald (39th RCT, battalion of 395th).

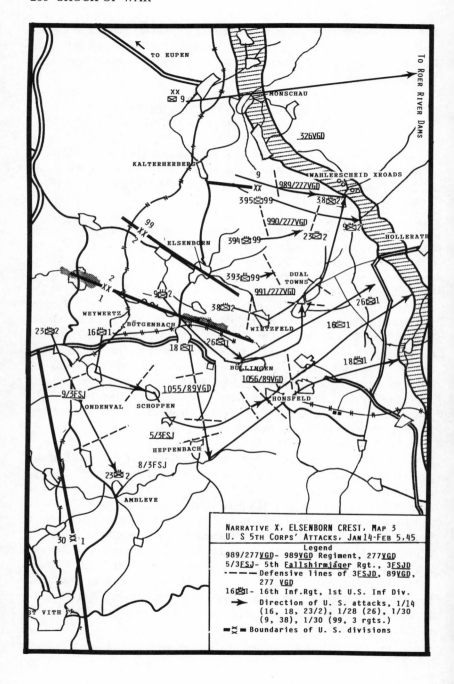

NARRATIVE X, ELSENBORN CREST, MAP 3
U. S 5TH CORPS' ATTACKS, JAN 14-FEB 5, 45
Legend
989/277VGD- 989VGD Regiment, 277VGD
5/3FSJ- 5th Fallschirmjäger Rgt., 3FSJD
———— Defensive lines of 3FSJD, 89VGD,
     277 VGD
16⊠1- 16th Inf.Rgt, 1st U.S. Inf Div.
➔ Direction of U. S. attacks, 1/14
   (16, 18, 23/2), 1/28 (26), 1/30
   (9, 38), 1/30 (99, 3 rgts.)
◼◼xx◼ Boundaries of U. S. divisions

TENTH NARRATIVE: THE LAST TRIAL: FIRE AND ICE

Part 1: A Second Lunge at the 99th

A few days before *Null Tag*, General Walter Denkert, commander of the 3rd *Panzergrenadier* (armored infantry) Division, is ordered to report to Field Marshal Walter Model's headquarters. Denkert is stunned to learn of plans for the Ardennes offensive from Model's chief of staff and that his division is assigned to Hitzfeld's 67 Corps.

Model is present but says nothing at first. After the briefing he quizzes the 3rd *PzGDivision* commander with his usual thoroughness and acerbity on how well the division is prepared to fight and what is the condition of its supplies, especially fuel for its vehicles. Doubtless, Denkert did not describe the true situation: 3rd *PzGD*, as he would report later, "was not fit for offensive tasks."

Like countless other units of the *Wehrmacht* in the five years of war, 3rd *PzGD* has been destroyed, resurrected, battered again to near destruction, rebuilt, and sent one more time into the breach or breaches opening everywhere in the east and west in summer and fall, 1944. It was in the heat of the early battles (Salerno, Anzio) in Italy, stopped off in France to rebuild, then joined in the to-the-last-man defense of the German city of Aachen, and helped hold the Roer River line against U.S. 9th Army in November.

During late November and early December, 3rd *PzGD* has been off the battleground, absorbing large numbers of replacements. Almost all of these new men are from such noninfantry service as antiaircraft units, naval stations, and other places and parts of the vast *Wehrmacht* establishment. Whether the new men and boys are impressed with the fact that General Denkert once served as commander of the *Führer's* palace guard is not recorded. Third *PzGD* was classified as Army Group B reserve, and hoped to remain so for some time. As Denkert put it, "(We) did not reckon with an early commitment but hoped for a period of freshening up."

The division is armed with nothing like the weight of *Panzers* that was normal for the armored infantry divisions of earlier days. It will bring to the Nordeifel only fifteen *Sturmgeschütze*[*], the core of its armored

---

[*] To repeat: This lethal little armored machine rides on a *Panzer III* chassis, is armed with a 75mm or 105mm gun in a fixed mount (no turret). It is designed to move right in with the attacking infantrymen and to blast defending enemy soldiers from their holes, dugouts, and gun nests. Usually, a machine gunner will ride the deck to keep hostiles at bay. It is not an assignment with much longevity.

hitting force. The division's artillery regiment is equipped with thirty-eight 105 and 150mm tubes. The 105s ride on tracks; the 150s on wheeled carriages that require pulling by a truck or prime mover. There also is a battalion of 75mm high-velocity tank-fighting guns, part of which ride on tracks. A battalion of *Flak* guns including twelve 88mm high-velocity pieces also have been assigned by 6th *Panzer* Army to Denkert's division. The weather-rotted roads and general congestion leading through the Krinkelterwald to the dual towns will keep some of this armor and artillery out of the battle. Nevertheless, the 3rd *PzGD* will still move on the 99th Division east of Elsenborn with ample motorized killing power.

On December 18, General "Sepp" Dietrich's 6th *SS Panzer* Army headquarters orders General Denkert to move his men and machines into the Krinkelterwald (Todeswald) to take over the role of *Hitler-jugend* Division, which is moving south and west. (Narrative VIII, Part 4)

Third *PzGD's* march during the night is not a pleasant one. It starts around Kall, Germany, then moves to Hellenthal and Hollerath. Denkert and his reconnaissance troops lead the way. The dark is ruptured by the pyrotechnics of V-1 flying bombs belching fire overhead on their way to Liege and Antwerp, flares sputtering above the forest, and the occasional excrescence of flame and smoke from a bursting shell. Once in the woods west of the international highway, Denkert and his officers are forced out of their vehicles because of what he called "dismal weather. The forest road west of Hollerath was extraordinarily difficult," he went on, "because of the nature of the terrain and the bad weather. Before long, driving became completely impossible, compelling us to continue the reconnaissance on foot."

General Denkert finds his way back to Hollerath and a bunker of the West Wall just west of the town. Here he meets with his staff and captains. They learn for the first time what is happening and what is expected of their soldiers. Third *PzGDivision*, Denkert tells them, is to march the next day (December 20) on the Americans occupying the high ground west of Rocherath. They will do so with part of the division artillery still strung out along the roads all the way east to Hellenthal: the battalion of medium (150mm) cannons and two batteries—eight guns—of light artillery.

In the icy and dismal hour before dawn December 20, the 3rd *PzGD* captains who will lead the attack meet on a hill just east of Rocherath. All around is dreadful evidence of the battle between the U.S. 2nd Division and *Hitlerjugend* forty-eight hours earlier. The awful killing field of Lausdell crossroads is nearby still populated by the unfound dead and the burnt-out hulks of armored machines. (Narrative VIII, Parts 1-2)

A hill 1.7 miles southeast of Elsenborn called by locals the Rodel-höhe (sledders' hill) is the first objective of the day; Elsenborn itself, the second; Camp Elsenborn a mile and a half to the west, the third. The right attacking column will consist of infantry of Denkert's 8th *Panzergrenadier* Regiment plus some of the *Sturmgeschütze*. On the left, the division's reconnaissance battalion riding *Schützenpanzerwagen*.

Denkert believes the morale of his troops is "quite high because of the reports of success received so far. Their readiness for action, praise-worthy."*

Fronting Denkert's "action ready" soldiers are the battered infantry battalions of General Walter Lauer's 393rd and 394th Infantry regiments, 99th Division. The division's boundary on the left traverses some treeless hills 3.5 miles south of Kalterherberg. The right boundary is a bend in the farm road from Wirtzfeld to Elsenborn near the Rodelhöhe. Lauer's left flank is made secure by a battalion of the 47th Infantry, U.S. 9th Division, and his own reconnaissance troop; 1st Battalion 23rd Infantry (LTC Hightower) is on the right. Or what is left of it. The battalion lost a company at Mürringen. It was taken down more in the subsequent fighting to hold the dual towns and the fall back to Wirtzfeld and Berg. (Volume 1, Narrative V, Part 5) It will soon be relieved by 3rd Battalion, 38th Infantry (LTC Barsanti).

No doubt with General Gerow's assent, Robertson and his 2nd Division staff have carved out the narrowest possible front for both the 99th and his own three regiments to defend. The contrast between the front that the 99th defended before the *Riesenanschlag* erupted and that assigned here on the Elsenborn high plateau is notable: twenty-two miles then; three miles now.

Even so Lauer's fighting troops—riflemen, machine gunners, mortar-men, antitank gunners, etc.—appear at a disadvantage when compared with General Denkert's *Panzergrenadiers*. The former have been worn down by four days of mayhem and marching without sleep worth the name. The clothes they wear are icy damp and penetrated by muck and the raff of field and forest. Their boots have long since been marinated in snow, slush, and watery muck. And, as has been reported (Narrative VIII, Part 5), their numbers are down severely from the normal 836 soldiers per infantry battalion.

---

* As reported elsewhere, the German high command intended a coordinated assault on the Gerow line beginning early on December 20, from Kalterherberg on the north around to Weywertz on the southwest. The 277th *VGD*, 3rd *PzGD*, 12th *VGD*, 12th *SS Panzer*, and 3rd *Fallschirmjäger* (parachute) divisions were to move in concert initiating this massive attack. For reasons we have seen, and will see, the plan was neither massive nor well coordinated in execution.

All night long December 19-20, 1st and 3rd battalions of Lauer's 393rd Infantry are frantically digging in at the Rodelhöhe on the left flank of 3rd Battalion, 23rd Infantry. Three battalions of the 394th Infantry are a half mile to the north. These are the same five battalions of the 99th division that took the blast of war full force on *Null Tag*. The numbers they bring to the Elsenborn ridge show this starkly. Colonel Allen's 3rd Battalion (393) can muster scarcely 16 officers and 372 enlisted men, most of whom are not up-front fighters. Major Matt Legler's 1st Battalion (393) consists of 20 officers and 260 EMs. Scared and confused replacements are trickling in to fill the holes in the rifle platoons. They are too few and too untried to make much difference.

The captain of Company "B" makes one of his few surviving NCOs the company first sergeant. His first duty is to prepare an accurate count of officers and men present and accounted for, as the expression goes: one officer and thirteen enlisted men, down from 190 total on *Null Tag* dawn.

To reinforce these battered and put-upon infantrymen, General Lauer once again—the second time in four days—orders the commander of his combat engineer battalion to convert his troops into temporary infantrymen and send them forward. The two companies of engineers that escaped from the Rocheratherwald less than a day before are to insert themselves between the 393rd and the 394th regiments, on the hills east of Elsenborn, put aside once more the "engineer" part of their duties and take up the "combat" part. The 99th Division's engineers were lucky in the Todeswald. They escaped from the killing machine with little damage. Now the machine will have another go at them.

However, Lauer's infantry and engineers will be able to call on powerful helpers: M-10 tank destroyers and Sherman medium tanks; also, some part of the four hundred artillery and heavy (4.2-inch) mortar tubes massing across the heights of Elsenborn and seen in action at the Bloody Angle. (Narrative IX)

They are grouped into sixteen divisional artillery battalions; plus six battalions assigned by corps and 1st Army; plus twelve regimental cannon companies; and one 4.2-inch mortar battalion. General Hinds, artillery chief of 2nd Division, has the complicated task of coordinating the action of all these guns to insure they deliver the maximum amount of death and destruction when and where needed.

The artillery batteries and mortar companies backing Gerow's infantry line are being fed by a steady stream of ammunition brought to the front by countless numbers of the workhorse six-by-six (two and one half ton) and larger trucks. Their drivers and the supply battery soldiers riding with them risk serious injuries on the icy roads as they race back and forth between the ammunition supply dumps in and around cities such as Liege and their gun batteries a few miles behind the front.

Some of the iron river of shells being trucked in are tipped with proximity fuses. Also called variable time (VT) fuses, these diabolic little devices are new to the battlefield and until now top secret. They sense targets on the ground by means of a mini radar. The returning signal explodes the shell and the target beneath is sprayed with jagged steel, another giant step forward in killing men in battle.

The German artillerymen possess no VT fuses, and their supply of ammunition for the guns, although large even by standards prevailing in the early years of the German war against the Soviet Union, is not moving as planned to the batteries supporting the offensive.

The 6th *SS* Army chief of staff, Fritz Kraemer, described the battle-field cost to his troops. "We had to live from hand to mouth. It frequently happened that a tactical success could not be exploited because the gasoline or ammunition supplies did not arrive in time or in too small quantities."

On the front of Colonel Jack Allen's 3rd Battalion, 393rd Infantry a mile north of Wirtzfeld, the fields are bare of trees, cut by shallow ravines filled with brush and sword grass covered with patches of melt-ing snow. "A lonely, snow-covered land on the edge of the (borderland) forest," as an operations officer of Legler's 1st Battalion described it. On the left flank are two battalions of Colonel Riley's 394th Infantry: the remains of Major Moore's 3rd and Colonel Douglas' 1st.

The few squads of riflemen and machine gunners that make up "K" Company (3rd Battalion) are up front working frantically to carve out fighting holes and position the few weapons they have been able to salvage from the fighting in the Fateful Triangle. (Volume 1, Narrative IV, Part 2) Their place of work is a treeless sloping field that falls off to a thick evergreen forest a mile to the east (the Rochratherwald).

During the night (19-20) a company of *Volksgrenadiers* emerge from the forest and plod up the hill toward the "K" Company outposts. An artillery forward observer with the company calls for star, then high explosive, then the terrible phosphorous. The 99th's cannons saturate the field with exploding metal and chunks of hissing phosphorous, bursting smoky orange in the black night.

The distance between friend and enemy is narrow and the time for close calculation short. Some of the blasts occur inside the American perimeter. Three "K" Company men are hurt. Their captain makes the best of it. "Many rounds landed on our front line. They made larger and better foxholes than (my) men had been able to dig in the rocky ground with their limited number of entrenching tools." (Folding shovels carried by each mud soldier but in limited supply just then in the company.)

The poor *Landser* of Viebig's division have not even shallow holes to flatten themselves in. Their flesh is torn and burnt. For the remainder of the night, the "K" Company soldiers will lie awake in the icy wet of their grave-shaped trenches listening to the cries and screams of the German wounded.

In the plan of the 3rd *PzGD* staff, first blood December 20 will be drawn at the Rodelhöhe (hill) just north of the gravel and dirt farm road leading from Wirtzfeld to Elsenborn. The division's armored reconnaissance battalion will make the attack, the troops riding *Schützenpanzerwagen* or moving on foot accompanied by tracked artillery and antitank guns. If their action shows promise, a battalion or two of the division's 8th *PzG* Regiment accompanied by a dozen *Sturmgeschütze* assault guns of the division's *Panzer* battalion will push through to Elsenborn. Only Allen's (393-3) Battalion and two companies of the 99th's engineers stand in the way.

Daylight arrives slowly and grudgingly in the manner now familiar in this grey, bleak, and icy December in the Low Ardennes. The temperature has risen; fog lies on the landscape. Between the 99th engineers and Colonel Allen's battalion, a wide depression (draw) formed by the base of several low hills extends southeast toward Wirtzfeld.

About 9:30 a.m. the outposts in front of Allen's main defense line detect some movement in the draw a hundred yards down slope. A half dozen *Panzergrenadiers*, machine pistols and rifles slung round their shoulders are moving there. Several are waving large pieces of white cloth on sticks. Close by are at least a platoon of their fellows, arms also slung.

Allen's HQ sends forward a soldier who speaks a little German to try to express the idea that so long as the *Grenadiers* cling to their weapons their flags of presumed surrender will not be honored. Either they do not understand or the whole maneuver is a ruse to keep the battalion's guns silent until the remainder of Denkert's recon force is prepared to strike. In the event, neither side moves for an agonizing half hour whereupon Allen instructs his artillery liaison officer to put shell fire on the Germans milling around in the draw.

The *Grenadiers* scramble to escape from the explosions that pummel the ground between the hills with crashing, fiery, exploding steel. But the 3rd *Panzergrenadier* Division also has howitzers and high-velocity antitank guns, rocket-firing tubes, and 120mm mortars. These now are heard, driving Allen's soldiers and the engineers deep into their holes and slit trenches. When they emerge, several armed troop carriers with tracked cannons following can be seen lurching through the fog and early morning shadows across the snow-patched ground toward them. Each carrier is armed with a small caliber cannon or a machine gun. *Panzergrenadiers* encumbered with supplies, ammunition, and weapons for a long fight also are moving on foot in loosely organized squads and platoons.

After surviving the Todeswald (Volume 1, Narrative III, Part 2), Allen's men once more seem on the cusp of a violent end, as though they have been singled out by the malevolent dark angel of battle to be pursued until destroyed. However, this time the 3rd Battalion riflemen and machine gunners have clear fields of fire and foreknowledge of the kind and intentions of the hostiles they are facing. Also, from which direction they are coming and in how much strength. And those powerful allies referred to above are at hand. As the *Panzergrenadiers* materialize, Allen calls for artillery and armor instantly, at once, and now.

A half dozen batteries of 99th Division and Corps artillery respond, some firing rounds tipped with VT fuses. The heavy, 4.2-inch and 81mm "M" Company mortars mix their bombs with the barrage and the heavy machine guns of this company hammer away to pile on the death and destruction. Two platoons of five Sherman tanks each start grinding their way east from the vicinity of Elsenborn and Berg toward the Rodelhöhe. Four M-10 tracked and armored tank destroyers bearing 3-inch diameter long guns are on the field and moving to the infantrymen-engineers' hill, also.

In this first lunge of these 3rd *PzGDivision* troops, the storm of artillery rounds and mortar bombs is their ruination. The draw they are using for the attack is narrow and the terrain treacherous. They go to ground or mill about and start double timing back down the draw. The tracked guns bang away at the *Ami* line but soon back off also, fleeing the 155mm rounds that can (and do) smash them totally. Two of the M-10 tank destroyers that have clanked and lurched their ungainly bulks down the slope let fly a few high-velocity shells at the retreating German guns and *Schützenpanzerwagen* to hurry them along.

However, the retreat of Denkert's reconnaissance soldiers does not endure in spite of the punishment they've taken. By midmorning, 3rd *PzGD* has regrouped, as the military term has it, and are ready for a more determined march against the 3rd Battalion and the 99th engineers.

The vanguard of a reinforced battalion of *Panzergrenadiere*, armed *Schützenpanzerwagen*, and artillery and antitank guns mounted on a tank chassis push into the wide seam between Allen's infantry and the company of combat engineers on the left. The Germans dismount, fan out and soon spread their action into the perimeters of the two 99th Division companies at the seam. They use their machine pistols and assault rifles on some of the defenders; snatch others here and there as prisoners of war. Their tracked cannons and assault guns are booming shells and hammering machine gun bullets across the American positions.

Yet the armor is unable to prevail against the Americans' killer shells falling all around. The 99th Division's 155mm batteries are in action and their rounds do fatal damage to the thin-skinned motorized German guns and their track assemblies. (These are not *Panzer IV's* or *V's*, able to sustain shell fragments hitting their thickly armored skins.)

The terrain is no friend either. "Extremely difficult," Denkert would call it later. "There were roads (across the high plateau to Elsenborn), but some had completely turned into mud, rendering the terrain impassable." Some of his armor on the field has fallen victim to the American guns, some has bogged to the top of the tracks in the icy muck, some is in retreat.

With these friendly machines falling away, the *Panzergrenadiers* in and among the 99th's infantry and engineers are in trouble. They face a rising tide of bullet fire from their enemy's machine guns, automatic rifles, and grenade launchers and artillery. By 1 p.m., four hours after the morning's attack has started, Denkert's infantry are dwindling, looking for ways to escape from the American perimeter lest they die there.

The pressure is on Denkert and his captains at Rocherath this waning December 20 afternoon to push aside the 99th Division and get into Elsenborn. At Dom Bütgenbach a few miles to the south, *Hitlerjugend* Division is grappling the 1st Division's 26th Infantry (Narrative IX, Parts 3 and 4) in a fierce combat. If Denkert's men and armor can drive to the rear installations and artillery batteries, *Hitlerjugend's* march north will receive aid, and Gerow's divisions may be forced to withdraw west.

Third *PzGD* will make a second attempt before day's end to fight their way to Elsenborn. This time the *Panzergrenadiers* and their armor will move on the 394th Infantry's 1st Battalion (Lieutenant Colonel Douglas) and the engineer company on their right flank. A second attack will strike again at the seam between Allen's 3rd Battalion 393rd and the engineers. The two streams of *Panzergrenadiers* and their armored guns will meet behind the 99th main line of resistance and march as one on Elsenborn, or so goes the plan.

With a dozen of the *Sturmgeschütze* assault guns moving in and among them, the *Panzergrenadiers* on the right debouch from the woods in the brittle twilight and move doggedly, methodically over the fields and hedgerows toward the right flank rifle company of Douglas' battalion and the engineers.

Infantry soldiers armed with machine guns, assault rifles, and machine pistols ride the squat assault guns. When the machines rumble across the American line, they leap off and go to work on the Americans' holes and trenches.

They fight back, the engineers slamming away with their .50caliber machine guns operating like venomous snake mouths whose long, fiery tongues shatter flesh and bone where they strike. A half dozen or so of the engineers also have risen from their foxholes to stalk the German gun machines with bazookas. However, the *Sturmgeschütze* keep pressing.

An artillery lieutenant assigned to the engineers gets caught up in the dangerous euphoria of the blood letting and this most dangerous game of man vs. machine. He and an engineer soldier lurch across a muddy field after a *Sturmgeschütz*, load a rocket into a bazooka and fire it. The small hollow-charge missile strikes the side armor but does not explode. The machine retaliates, turning on the bazooka team, halting, and firing a high-velocity 75mm shell that explodes near the two soldiers. The artilleryman is hit by shell fragments. A medical corpsman comes out of his hole, impervious to the lethal creature nearby, intent on helping the wounded lieutenant. The gun of the *Sturmgeschütz* blasts forth once more with a belch of smoke and flame killing both men quicker than they can draw a breath.

Several 57mm (diameter) tank-fighting guns are stationed near the main line of resistance. However, their crews are not armed with the sabot-boostering shells seen in the Dom Bütgenbach fight. (Narrative IX, Part 2) The rounds that they send screeching at the rampaging 3rd *PzGD* armor strike the machines, then bounce off.

One of the battalion's heavy (81mm) mortar gunners participates in the battle but does not see the enemy's face. His mortar is behind a hill. He and his crew take orders from their forward observer up front in the maelstrom. "The attack lasted about two hours. (We) fired furious mortar missions (while) heavy artillery was coming in and machine gun tracers were going overhead. I did not see a German soldier during this entire period." Lucky mortar guy, as the rifle soldiers would put it.

The left attack column of 3rd *PzGDivision* moves in parallel toward the 99th line, trying to strike through the seam between the engineers and the infantry, the same maneuver as seen earlier. Company "L" (3rd Battalion) along the seam is armed with a few light machine guns, Browning Automatic Rifles, and rifle grenade-launching devices, but far too few of any. Scarcely one hundred soldiers are scattered around the

company perimeter on the forward slope of the Rodelhöhe to use these
weapons. A few 57mm antitank guns also are working with the battalion. The engineers on the left flank have their .50caliber guns.

The dark line of *Panzergrenadiere* obscured by the dimming light,
dog trotting and riding the decks of their tracked and armored assault
guns push through sporadic bullet fire and into the perimeter of "L"
Company and the platoon of engineers next in line to them on the hill.
The young Americans crouch in their diggings trying to see the young
Germans come to kill, maim, or capture them.

Company "L" is outnumbered and soon taking the worst of it:
machine gunners and riflemen banging away in the gathering night only
to be shot, dragged from their trenches, forced to surrender or fall back
up the ridge toward the rear and LTC Matt Legler's 1st Battalion,
which is manning the second line of resistance. A rifle soldier remembered the frenzy of the young Germans attacking Allen's battalion. "By
now they were practically on top of us. You could hear them screaming
to each other, calling names of their men. You could hear the fear in
their voices..."

Sturmgeschütze assault guns grind around on the muddy, uneven
ground. The machine gunners and riflemen riding the decks shoot
wildly in the semi-dark. Two of the machines lurch on up the hill to
reach behind "L" Company and lead the way through the 99th position.

What finally forces the *Panzergrenadiers* and their machines to give
over and abandon their late afternoon attack is once again the American
artillery. Barrage after barrage on and over the American defenses down
the Rodelhöhe add fiery explosions and smoke and glowing fog to the
jumping tracers of machine guns, and muzzle blasts all around of high-
velocity *Panzer* guns. Decades later one terrified infantryman still remembered how the artillery forward observer (FO) he shared his slit
trench with seemed determined to bring rounds down on even those
Panzergrenadiers within leap-frog distance of the trench.

"Artillery was pouring in like it was never going to stop. The FO
kept repeating, 'Cut twenty-five.'" (AN: call the artillery fire in twenty-
five yards closer to the American line) "He said that over and over as
(the Germans) came in on us. You couldn't talk to be heard. You had
to scream. We were like two peas in a pod....I said lieutenant what are
you doing? (The shells) are falling on us now and you are still cutting
twenty-five. He lifted his head like a turtle, listened, and said, 'No,
that's their artillery coming in' and went right back to his radio and 'cut
twenty-five.'"

A 393rd Infantry Headquarters Company communications man also
remembered this afternoon as one terrorized by the storms of artillery

fire: "On December 20 the Germans came within fifty yards of my position." (He is operating a telephone switchboard in the forward command post of Scott's 393rd Regiment.) "I had to keep operating the switchboard so that calls for supporting artillery fire could get through. Our artillery, which fired practically on top of our foxholes, was what saved us."

Speaking for all the 3rd Battalion survivors, the rifleman who shared his trench with the forward observer said, "I'm not sure which was worse, the morning of December 16 or the evening of December 20." (The reader may remember the morning of December 16 was *Null Tag*, the day that 3rd Battalion was struck by a mighty artillery barrage, two battalions of *Grenadiers*, and later armor and *Panzergrenadiers* of *Hitlerjugend's* 12th *SS* Division. [Volume 1, Narrative II] It can't get much worse than that.)

Confronting increasingly bad news, General Denkert decides to back off for the day. "The enemy infantry defense had become greatly intensified. The artillery increased to considerable strength. (I) gave the order to cease attacking and to change to defensive operations."

During the night (20-21) in the 99th Division sector, more new men (and boys) coming in from the replacement depots and men from back-echelon units pressed into temporary and uneasy service as riflemen find their way east to the hills occupied by the fighters up front.

The 99th Division resistance is thin, the soldiers depressed and exhausted after five days of concentrated mayhem and unmitigated hazard. Should 3rd *Panzergrenadier* Division come forward the next day (December 21) with a powerful infantry-armor assault, it could be all up with Lauer's survivors, even if the Shermans and M-10s hold off the *Sturmgeschütze* and tracked artillery and the American howitzers once again saturate the ridge line they occupy with defensive fires.

To some of the rifle company captains up front, placing their men on the forward slopes of hills such as the Rodelhöhe puts them at greater risk than need be. General Denkert's antitank (PAK) guns and howitzers that move on tracks can be brought in close to the 99th's main defensive line to rake the infantrymen's holes, gun nests, and dugouts. The 88 and 75mm high-velocity rifles are being fired flat out by gunners looking straight at their targets on the opposite hill. The day's mayhem has produced bloody evidence of this. One captain asks permission to move his riflemen and machine gunners back to dig in on what soldiers call the reverse slope, i.e. the back of the hill. He is ordered to stay put.

Meanwhile, this night, General Denkert's captains gather on the edge of the Todeswald east of Rocherath at "Sherman Corner"* and plot out their tactics for the next day (December 21). Two batteries of their light (105mm) guns have yet to arrive from the tangle of traffic in and beyond the woods and through the West Wall. However, the battalion of medium guns (150mm) have finally shouldered their way through the traffic and will be present to add their considerable weight to the shooting this day.

Their arrival gives Denkert and his captains some heart. For their plan is to move their tracked and armored cannons and PAK (antitank) guns close to the 394-393rd and engineers' diggings on the hill, send a curtain of shells at them, then make a vigorous charge by *Panzergrenadiere* on foot and in *Schützenpanzerwagen*. The assault guns will suppress enemy rifle-machine gun opposition; the hard-charging infantry, with the *Schützenpanzerwagen* up front, will carry through the 99th line to Elsenborn.

The 3rd *PzGD* tracked gun machines have been hiding on the edge of Rocherath and along the firebreaks in the Rocheratherwald to the north occupied a few days before by Colonel MacKenzie's 395th Regimental Combat Team. (Narrative VIII, Part 4) Before light December 21 a vanguard have moved down hill as close as is prudent to the holes and dugouts on the slopes a quarter of a mile away. About dawn December 21 the gunners in the *Panzer* crew compartments start sending shells flat out toward the ridge.

On the left flank of Lauer's front line where the sparsely wooded hills, pastures, and brushy knobs of the Elsenborn high plateau stop and the deep borderland forest begins, Denkert's machine gunners and their sharp shooters have secreted themselves among the trees in covered holes or in depressions in the earth. The 80 and 120mm mortar crews working with them have located their tubes to bomb the ridge as well. "Visibility was good," recalled a 394th Infantry captain. "(This) gave the enemy excellent observation of our front line position from the high ground in the woods."

All seems in order on the 3rd *PzGDivision* side for one more powerful march up the hill and through the depleted and sorely tried mud soldiers of the 99th Division, crouching in their holes and slit trenches. (The captain commands only 71 officers and men, for example, less than half the normal strength of 193.) High-velocity enemy

---

* So named by Denkert's staff because nearby stand the burnt carcasses of the two U.S. medium tanks killed a few days before by *Hitlerjugend's Panzer* guns. (Volume 1, page 321)

guns send explosive shells screeching at them and the howitzer and mortar shells fall from the midmorning sky to explode with a whump and a blast of fire, smoke, and jagged steel.

Shortly after noon about two battalions (a thousand plus) of Denkert's 8th *PzGD* regiment muster for the action. The vanguard moves from the woods north of Rocherath. Back at Camp Elsenborn General Hinds' artillery staff has alerted no less than eight battalions of howitzers for the day's shoot. Every one of the near one hundred angry throats is prepared to bellow in unison as Denkert's infantry make their move.

However, third *PzGD* staff seem unwilling to sacrifice any more of the irreplaceable *Sturmgeschütze*, even though they were to be up front in their plan to finally break the 99th Division line on the hills east of Elsenborn. In contrast with the previous day's action, these murderous little machines are not with the *Panzergrenadiers*. They hold back, firing at the *Amis* on the hills while the infantry go forward into the attack. Between the forest and the hills, General Black's 99th Division cannons find the lines of men in their *Feldgrau* overcoats and bulbous helmets cradling machine pistols and assault rifles doggedly plodding forward. Find them and kill many of them. Denkert described it in the matter-of-fact way of soldiers, "On account of the considerably increased enemy artillery fire, (our) attack broke down."

The general orders both men and machines back to a sketchy defensive line whose terminus on the left flank is a point deep in the Rocheratherwald and on the right, a hill five hundred yards north of Wirtzfeld. At this stage of the war, the *Landser* do not show sufficient heart on the killing grounds unless accompanied by *Sturmschütze*, Denkert will say later.[*]

His captains after December 21, are content to move only small combat patrols against the 99th Division's battalions on the Rodelhöhe, plus the now-persistent direct shooting by the 3rd *PzGDivision's* mobile guns. Both tactics harass and threaten Lauer's mud soldiers up front clinging to their icy holes and wondering how much more cold, snow, muck, and imminent death they can endure, but they make no difference tactically.

---

[*] How important the *Sturmgeschütze* assault guns were to the Germans and feared by the Americans was shown by the efforts made by the former to salvage the little monsters disabled on the Elsenborn battlefield and by the latter to destroy them. Lauer's men go out in darkness to locate the broken *STGs* and dynamite them; Denkert orders a salvage crew back to the Elsenborn front after the division has departed to try to locate and haul them back to a repair shop. The Americans succeeded in blowing up two or three; Denkert's salvage crews were chased off by arty fire and returned to their division *sans Sturmgeschütze*.

274 SHOCK OF WAR

The dawn of Friday, December 22, brings falling temperatures and snowfall across the Elsenborn high plateau. This day, the seventh in the *Wehrmacht's* Ardennes-Eifel Counteroffensive, also brings the anticlimax of 6th *SS Panzer* Army's bloody, expensive attempt to shake loose its northern wing for the march over the Elsenborn high plateau to the Meuse River. It is a day of ultimate humiliating failure for the Germans.

Twelfth *SS Panzer*, Division will withdraw the few *Panthers* that have shot their way into Bütgenbach, regroup its surviving infantry and armor, and prepare to move to another killing ground in the Ardennes. Twelfth *VGD*ivision has pulled back into its Wirtzfeld defenses after several attempts to take Bütgenbach from the east. (Narrative IX, Part 5)

In the west, General Wadehn's paratroops (3rd *Fallschirmjäger* Division) make an ineffectual lunge for Weywertz, once again after being driven off earlier. (Narrative IX, Part 5) They will continue for the next few days to try to rupture the 16th Infantry's main line of resistance, generally returning to the railroad as the vector of these attacks. Platoon after platoon will disappear under the ferocious U.S. 1st Division artillery and automatic bullet fire. They have tried to do their duty, but their influence on the final stage of the Bütgenbach campaign will be nil.

On the north (right) flank of the German offensive, Colonel Viebig's 277th *Volksgrenadier* Division has drawn the unenviable task of attacking the U.S. 5th Corps defense line anchored by strong points on the hills east of Kalterherberg. In terms of terrain, timing, support, purpose, and prospects of success the task seems utterly useless, not to say wasteful of young German bodies.

Opposing them in the hilly woods north of Riley's 394th Infantry are the cavalrymen of General Lauer's Reconnaissance Troop buttressed by the entire 47th Infantry of General Louis A. Craig's 9th Division on their left. (These 47th Regiment soldiers are the equal of General Robertson and Andrus' scarred and steely 2nd and 1st division veterans.) General Lauer's little cavalry contingent is attached to the 47th until the components and commands are able to sort themselves out along the Elsenborn high plateau.

The 99th Reconnaissance Troop consists of 6 officers and 150 men equipped with 12 armored cars, 4 halftracks (gun motor carriages), and 30 jeeps. The troop is spread along the wooded hill above the bank of a creek southeast of Kalterherberg. This would be difficult terrain to defend even by a well-weaponed and fully manned infantry company. The cavalrymen can only emplace their vehicles in locations that their captain and his three subordinate officers believe attacking troops might choose as likely strike points.

Their orders are to stand fast. Thus their strong suit, mobility, is rendered useless. They possess lethal weapons. Their M-8 armored cars are armed with 37mm (1.5-inch diameter) cannons in revolving turrets, and .30caliber machine guns. Half the jeeps carry .30caliber machine guns in mounts that permit fast and easy operation. The halftracks mount .50 caliber machine guns. But the 99th Recon Troop's role, as its men like to say, is to seek, see, and report, not to play the infantry part.

Before dawn December 22 pioneers of Colonel Viebig's *VGD* pick their way through the forest and brush, across the creek on to the high ground occupied by the troop. They wear snow clothes and blend well into the white of the ground and the white flying around in the air. The 99th cavalrymen know the enemy is coming at them. However, the night is black and the thickening snow showers hide movement over the ground. Neither attacker nor defender can see his enemy, although the jeeps, armored cars, and halftracks of the two cavalry platoons on the main line of resistance bulk large to mark their positions as the German infantrymen move around their foxholes and dugouts near the vehicles.

Shooting starts. Machine guns saw and hammer away, sending flashes of tracer fire round and about the dimly lit, snow-clouded fields at the top of the ridge. Here and there a grenade explodes. Now and then the little cannons of the armored cars send flashes of flame into the night. But the gunners find it near impossible to see targets to shoot at. And all the troopers fear the unseen hostile *Grenadiers* stalking through the dark.

By midmorning, at least two companies of Viebig's infantry are in among the recon troops and their vehicles. The marauding figures in white camouflage suits have cut out small numbers of cavalrymen and surrounded them. However, they are intent on moving west to sever the road connecting Kalterherberg and Elsenborn. After putting bullet fire and grenades into the vehicles they take, they lose interest in their prisoners.

The two reconnaissance platoons try to disengage and fall back to a more secure line. One is surrounded and fends off the *Grenadiers* until well after dark when the troopers not killed or bagged as prisoners dodge their attackers west to safety. The platoon leader and his soldiers even manage to drag along a prisoner or two and carry two of their wounded with them.

General Craig's soldiers (47th Infantry) have by now come into the fight. Company "E" joins the troopers' headquarters group and the reserve platoon to put an end to the 277th *Grenadiers'* threat to the recon troop and the vital road from Kalterherberg to Elsenborn. At first, the Germans put up a nasty fight. Company "E" is engulfed. Only the ferocity of a few riflemen of the company force them to back off.

As afternoon shadows begin to flow up the hills from the ravines and draws and the bursts of snow thicken, the 9th Division infantrymen, now reinforced by even more of their companies, chase down those enemy soldiers who have reached the road to Elsenborn. They also have sealed off the break in the recon troop's line, thus ending whatever dreams of glory and triumph Viebig's *Grenadiers* may have had as they moved through and around the formers' defensive hedgehogs a few hours before. Later, General Lauer will assert "over fifty" of the 277th attackers lie dead on the field.

The attack on Lauer's recon troop has been one of several attempts December 22 by Viebig's division to drive through the 99th-9th defenses south of Kalterherberg and gain the road to Elsenborn. The other tries are weak in number, buttressed by no armor, half hearted and eventually collapsed by the fearsome *Ami* artillery and mortar fire.

The offensive capacity of the 277th *VGD* and its right flank neighbor, General Erwin Kaschner's 326th *VGD*, is now at an end. Both have been major players in our story. (Volume 1, Narratives II and III; Volume 2, Narrative VIII, Part 4) Their condition after a week of mayhem in the icy Low Ardennes-Nordeifel is summed up by a U.S. Army historian; "(After December 22) the 277th no longer possessed the strength to make a real effort against the north wing of the Elsenborn line. The 326th *VGD*, its northern neighbor, had given no hand in this fight, not surprising in view of the punishment taken at Höfen and Monschau. Both divisions now fell out of the drive to widen the way west." (However, Viebig's survivors still have plenty of capacity to inflict pain, suffering, and death on Lauer's soldiers, as we shall see.)

After dark on December 22, Lieutenant Colonel Allen's 3rd Battalion occupying the forward slopes of the Rodelhöhe and fronting the assault guns and mobile artillery of the 3rd *PzGD* is relieved by Lieutenant Colonel Ernest C. Peters' 2nd Battalion, 393rd Infantry. A rifleman in the latter's "G" Company remembered it well: "The wind was blowing and the snow beginning to drift. When we reached (the 3rd Battalion's line) two miles from our starting point (on the edge of Elsenborn), the gaunt-eyed survivors we were relieving, many without coats or even bedrolls, scrambled out of their foxholes and filed past us to the rear....There seemed to be far more foxholes than needed by the departing troops, a sign of a high casualty rate from enemy fire."

General Denkert, the 3rd *PzGD* commander said that the attacks of December 20-22 in front of Elsenborn failed because of "the extremely lively activity of the enemy artillery and the tenaciously fighting enemy (infantry). The Americans at Elsenborn crest were truly worthy of our soldierly esteem."

Part 2: Saint George and the Persistent Dragons

Late December 19 General Eisenhower made his controversial decision to turn the American power north of the Ardennes rupture over to Field Marshal Bernard Law Montgomery, commander of the British and Canadian 21st Army Group. (Narrative IX, Part 1)

This means a British officer is in command of Simpson's 9th Army and three corps of General Hodges' 1st Army. He is responsible for the defense of the entire northern flank of the rupture area, from Monschau, Germany, all the way west to the banks of the River Meuse at Dinant, Belgium.

This addition to Montgomery's 21st Army Group command would be awesome under any battlefield circumstance. Now it comes at a time of crisis in the Allied camp caused by the *Wehrmacht's* counteroffensive. Yet the assignment does not appear to disconcert the feisty little British soldier in the least. Monty's supreme (some would say outrageous) self-confidence is based on the respect shown him by the British people and the men in the ranks, his standing with Field Marshal Alan Brooke, chief of the British Imperial Staff, his broad experience of command at many levels in both World War I and II, and his victories in North Africa and Normandy. (Monty commanded all of the Allied forces on the ground in the Normandy invasion and subsequent battles in France. It was gall and wormwood for him to give up this position to General Eisenhower September 1.)

He starts out from his HQ in a modest house in Zonhoven, a small town twenty-five miles northwest of Liege, in the fog and cold rain to visit his new subordinate commanders. To characterize Montgomery's feelings at the time as "gleeful" would be an exaggeration; "supremely self confident and vindicated" would be closer to the mark.[*]

As briefly noted (Volume 1, INTRODUCTION), from the break-

---

[*] The literature on Field Marshal Montgomery's role in the containment and reversal of the German Ardennes counteroffensive of December-January 1944-45 is voluminous. To an uncommon degree, it is also influenced by partisan, nationalistic, and personal prejudices. Montgomery was not one to deny his own greatness. He also couldn't control the habit of criticizing and second guessing the American high commanders in Europe, some of whom he considered inexperienced, if not incompetent, soldiers and battle leaders. He caused genuine pain to them in his pronouncements and writings after the war, and Generals Bradley and Patton, in particular, reciprocated. Fortunately for us, this book is not about the Field Marshal, his defenders and attackers. Readers interested in learning more about his role in the Ardennes battle and views of his soldiership and leadership are referred to titles listed in the documentation for this narrative.

out in Normandy on Montgomery has been a thorn in Eisenhower's side. It is the Field Marshal's belief, repeated over and over again on every possible occasion, that either Bradley or he should assume command of what he calls "the land battle." Eisenhower should confine himself to the high-level administration and politics of Allied Expeditionary Forces management and external relations. Allied resources should be concentrated on an overwhelming drive across the plains west and north of Cologne on the Rhine and not wasted in simultaneous assaults by several armies.

The German counteroffensive in the Eifel-Ardennes has obviously dumbfounded the Americans, from General Bradley down to the soldiers up front. Monty believes his philosophy of war making and his criticisms have been vindicated: The Americans have been complacent; underestimated the power of their enemies; spread their forces too thin; refused to consider the Western Front as a seamless construct of Allied power demanding one overall command intelligence on the scene to control and coordinate both offense and defense. General Eisenhower has allowed Bradley and Patton too much rope and neglected Hodges' serious failings. The massive German counterattack is the result.

For all his self-satisfaction, Montgomery exuded pessimism in messages to London after his designation as Allied commander on the north. On December 19 he informed Brooke that the "American forces have been cut clean in half and the Germans can reach the Meuse (River) at Namur without any opposition." A signal to Brooke the same evening: "There is a definite lack of grip and control (on the U.S. side). No one has a clear picture as to the situation.…There is an atmosphere of great pessimism in 1st and 9th armies due I think to the fact that everyone knows something has gone wrong and no one knows what or why."

As Montgomery sets out from his HQ at Zonhoven December 20 for General Hodges' new forward command post in the Hôtel des Baines, Chaudfontaine, Belgium, an all-points warning has gone out in the Allied camp that Colonel Skorzeny's saboteurs are hunting for Eisenhower, Bradley, and Montgomery with murderous intent. Montgomery is not one to be restrained by vague prospects of being bushwhacked and killed. He rides in his well-travelled Rolls Royce, is accompanied by one or two armored fighting vehicles and that is all.

By prearrangement General Simpson, U.S. 9th Army, also is at the des Baines for the council of war. Monty strides in, "Saint George come to slay the dragon," as an American historian will describe his posture throughout the Ardennes campaign. He is perturbed by how tired and worn Hodges appears and what he considers the confusion and drift pervading his headquarters. Following the meeting, Montgomery sends another of his lengthy reports to London: "Neither army commander had seen Bradley or any of his staff since the battle began. There are no reserves anywhere behind the front. Morale was very low. They (Hodges and Simpson) seemed delighted to have someone to give them orders."*

Montgomery's first order of business is to travel round the northern flank of the breakthrough area visiting his corps and on occasion division commanders. His second is to obtain American General Joe Collins' 7th Corps for the defense of the western reaches of the breakthrough area and to increase its armored and infantry power. His third is to see to the strengthening of Ridgeway's Airborne Corps. (Only the 82nd Airborne Division makes up the "airborne" part.) Ridgeway's corps will occupy the center of the 1st Army defensive line, between Collins' 7th Corps on the right (western) flank and Gerow on the left. Monty's fourth order of business December 20-21 is to order up the powerful 30th Corps from his own army to guard the crossings over the Meuse River to the west.

When he assumes responsibility on December 20, the fighting in the bulge made in the American line and along its edges is still volatile, threatening, and dangerous in the extreme to the whole of Hodges' 1st Army. Major General Middleton's U.S. 8th Corps, which has remained under General Bradley's control, is being engulfed right and left by the driving power of von Manteuffel's 5th *Panzer* and Brandenberger's 7th *Infanterie* armies. (Appendices, p. 407)

Also, Gerow's 1st, 2nd, and 99th divisions may not be able to sustain more attacks by the right wing of Dietrich's army. After visiting Gerow's HQ at Eupen December 23, Monty messages Brooke, "A disturbing factor which is coming to light as I visit American formations is the weak state of most divisions...the four divisions of (5th Corps) in

---

* The perceptive reader will have noticed that the Field Marshal's messages and reports invariably bolstered his position that the Americans needed a firmer hand and a clear objective to guide them to victory, both during the crisis of the German breakthrough and later when the Allies had once again seized the initiative.

However, for the record it should be noted that by afternoon December 20, when Monty strode confidently into the U.S. 1st Army headquarters, General Eisenhower had already sent two armored and two paratroop divisions to 1st Army. Hodges had ordered in the 1st Division and also all available artillery, engineers, and special troops to harden Gerow's critically important Elsenborn line. He also had asked Eisenhower to send the 30th Infantry Division from U.S. 9th Army to Ridgeway's new 18th Airborne Corp. All of this and more are not precisely evidence of confusion and drift.

However, Montgomery's concerns over General Hodges' flagging energies and morale and the shortage of reserves in the American infantry regiments were well taken.

the line are together deficient seven thousand men, mostly infantry..."
To Montgomery, with his cautious approach and sympathy for the mud
soldiers he commands, it is simply irrational to expect these divisions
directly in the path of Dietrich's still formidable power to hold out for
long unless more troops come in to carry some of the bloody burden.

He believes some retrograde repositioning of troops and shortening
of defense lines may be necessary. The Field Marshal is not alone in
this. In these early days as the Germans pour west in the center of the
breakthrough area, even the American leaders nervously contemplate
pulling back here and there. Eisenhower signals Montgomery on December 20 "on the possibility of giving up, if necessary, some ground
in order to shorten our line and collect a strong reserve."

In his usual irrepressible manner, General Patton advises Eisenhower
to allow Model's Army Group B legions to run "all the way to Paris,"
after which they would be "cut off and chewed up." As usual it is difficult
to know whether the 3rd Army leader is serious or is simply blowing
smoke to impress the gallery.

Monty's own 30th Corps commander, Lieutenant General Brian G.
Horrocks, suggests that the German armies be allowed to cross the Meuse
River whereupon his men and the Americans would meet them on the
fields of Waterloo and bring them low. Montgomery orders him to go
on leave in England for a week or two to rest his mind and curb his
imagination.

General Hodges, the commander most threatened, is opposed to shortening 1st Army's front. However, soon after the enemy strike into 1st
Army's 5th and 8th corps, his supply troops got busy moving heavy
equipment, gasoline, and ammunition across the Meuse. (He and his
staff would soon follow.)

On December 23 General Hodges' G-2 (Intelligence section chief),
Colonel Dickson, issues an ominous estimate of German capabilities that
surely gives Hodges and his chief of staff, General Keane, more worries
than they already have and may have influenced Monty as well: 24
enemy divisions already on the field in the Ardennes-Eifel offensive; 13
more in reserve, 4 of which are armored; a possible 9 more divisions
in reserve; and 12 more in Germany within travel distance of the vast
killing ground. In short, more enemy infantry and armored divisions
waiting in the wings than are actually on the stage.

Whether Montgomery has in fact taken Dickson's intelligence
estimate seriously or even knows about it is not known. However, in
the first week after he has assumed command on the north of the huge
wedge-shaped rupture in the American line, the Field Marshal is indeed
preoccupied with the likelihood of a powerful enemy attack west of

Malmedy against either Ridgeway or Collins or both.[*]

As an experienced war manager and self-styled master strategist, Monty knows in his bones that having been blocked at the Elsenborn high plateau and having opened a route over St. Vith-Vielsalm the Germans will now send a large force—including the *SS Panzer* divisions—at the northern and western face of the breakthrough area.

Bastogne in the far south is an important road junction and communication center. However, it is too far from the planned Meuse River crossings near Liege to constitute a prime objective of overwhelming importance to the Germans. So far as Montgomery is concerned, the city and its defense are secondary; the river valleys southeast of Liege are primary. These include the valleys of the Amblève, Salm, and Ourthe rivers and of the Meuse itself near Huy, Belgium.

Henceforth, Montgomery reasons the weight of enemy armor and infantry will be drawn to these valleys, the places of decision within the twenty-five hundred square mile Ardennes-Eifel breakthrough area. At the start of the second week of struggle, Monty sees 5th *Panzer* Army "tapping in against 7th Corps (Collins) and trying to overlap to the west." Sixth *SS Panzer* Army, frustrated at the Elsenborn high plateau, also appears to be moving west by way of St. Vith to attack Manhay, Belgium, in Ridgeway's 18th Airborne Corps sector.[**]

The two American corps (7th, 18th) will soon total eight full divisions, including some of the most combatative aggregations of men and machines in the U.S. Army in Europe (2nd Armored, 82nd Airborne, 30th Infantry, for example). And working with them will be a large array of medium and heavy artillery, fifteen battalions in Collins' command alone, assigned by corps and army.

Montgomery is concerned that Collins and Ridgeway's power will be dissipated in premature, piecemeal actions in the named river valleys

---

[*] The reader is again advised to consult the Appendices item on the progress of the *Wehrmacht's* attack during the early days after dawn on December 16, p. 407.

[**] Curious to report, Montgomery implied that the unmovable American hedgehog at Bastogne proved its importance only after the German forces had failed to break through along the northern side of the bulge in the American line. After the first week of January 1945 "the enemy tried to shift his main weight further west and southwest. Essential to this redisposition, however, was the capture of Bastogne and its road net. The dogged and indeed aggressive defense of Bastogne by the Americans continued to attract enemy divisions away from the northern sector until by 6 January there were no less than ten divisions, including three *SS*, fighting round the place." (Normandy to Baltic, p. 284. Documentation, this volume)

and therefore unavailable to stop the Germans from marching north from these valleys to river crossings near Liege. He also is critical of Bradley and Eisenhower for encouraging Patton to sally forth in snow and ice with too few divisions (one armored, two infantry) to lift the siege of Bastogne.

The German assault on St. Vith (December 19-22), an important road junction ten miles south of Bütgenbach, has been successful. Montgomery orders the entire position liquidated and the surviving armor and other soldiers to escape behind Ridgeway's line to the north.*

To Eisenhower, the Field Marshal may be a thorn in the side; to Bradley "an arrogant, stubborn little fellow," as his aide de camp and chronicler put it; and to certain other senior U.S. commanders a wet blanket and spoil sport who doesn't even try to hide his disdain for their rear-area diversions.

To the fighters and leaders near the front, however, Montgomery seems one of their own in spite of his high-pitched voice, odd mixture of uniforms (or nonuniforms), and British accent and mannerisms. Even U.S. commanders such as Joe Collins and Lieutenant General William Simpson, 9th Army Chief, are impressed with his professionalism and obsession with preparedness and his concern for the mud soldiers, tankers, and others who do the suffering and dying.

And the Field Marshal exhibits surprising reasonableness when dealing with field commanders faced with difficult battlefield situations and tactical dilemmas. During the December 23 visit to General Gerow's 5th Corps HQ at Eupen (above), Montgomery meets with Major General Clarence Huebner, Gerow's deputy and designated successor. (Volume 1, Narrative V, Part 1) He informs Huebner that he intends to order the withdrawal of the 5th Corps infantry divisions from the Elsen-born crest to avoid unsustainable losses should the Germans strike hard again.

Huebner convinces Monty that the most defensible place to block the enemy is right there. The fighters have done their digging. The

---

* The premier historian of the Ardennes-Eifel counteroffensive, Charles B. MacDonald, does not accept the standard interpretation that Field Marshal Montgomery overruled General Ridgeway to release the American defenders from their untenable position in the St. Vith "goose egg" December 23. He writes Ridgeway was very much involved in the decision and in the end believed it the only possible one to save some twenty thousand American troops to fight another day. (Trumpets, pps. 479-80. Documentation, Volume 1, master list) However, Major General Robert W. Hasbrouck, who commanded the 7th Armored Division at St. Vith, is on record that Montgomery alone saved the Americans to fight another day. He prevented "a debacle that would have gone down in history." (Letter to General Bruce C. Clarke, quoted in The Bulge Bugle, February 1994, p. 9.)

cannons are massed. The powerful 12th *SS Panzer* Division has been stalemated at the dual towns and Bütgenbach and is departing for the west. It would be a disaster to abandon it all, especially since the Elsenborn line has been constructed and defended at such a terrible cost in men and material.

The Field Marshal is a complicated character: egotistical and utterly sure of himself and his grand strategic ideas among his peers but flexible and open to ideas and suggestions from his subordinates. He finally agrees that 5th Corps may stay where it is but he wants the heavy equipment—large trucks, wreckers, tank retrievers, etc.—moved out to clear the roads west just in case. The following day, General Hodges' 1st Army staff prepares a plan and order to carry out Monty's wishes.[*]

The German tide in the Ardennes has yet to turn; however, a week after it started running, the tide has not the force and inevitability of the first days. Gerow's valiants on the ridge are stronger than ever. Bastogne is out of irons. Patton is grinding north. And the American and British air forces are able to fly again as the weather improves.

Generals Eisenhower and Bradley want to hurry along the day when the Americans—and British—take the initiative away from the Germans. They want a drive from north and south that will pinch off most of the three German armies within the breakthrough area. They want, in the words of an American military historian, "to exploit the opportunity created by the enemy in the Ardennes to destroy the German Army west of the Rhine..." The two U.S. chiefs want Montgomery to bring up the British 30th Corps, which is standing to on the River Meuse, to assist in this massive operation.

However, Montgomery, is simply not focusing on this objective for now. His concern is first, the moves of 5th and 6th *SS Panzer* armies toward the middle (Ridgeway) and right flank (Collins) of 1st Army, which by Christmas eve are plain for all to see; second, the preservation of American and British power for the real war, i.e. the drive across the Cologne Plain into the Ruhr, the liver and lights of the *Reich* after the *Wehrmacht* is finally driven from Belgium and Luxembourg.

He wants Collins' and Ridgeway's 7th and 18th Airborne corps to stand fast as Model's men and machines break against them, then be forced back and hounded to their end by the merciless *Jaboes*. Only then, will he let loose Collins, Ridgeway, and Gerow to start marching upon German-held positions within the Bulge. His own 30th Corps will

---

[*] For Colonel Mason's recollections of this important meeting and its aftermath, see the "We Were There" anecdotes following this narrative.

not join the action at all but stand as a reserve on the Meuse River line or at most contribute a guards division or two. (Montgomery most especially wants to preserve this power for the climactic push into Germany.)

The difficult situation of General Gerow's 5th Corps troops on the Elsenborn high plateau is again at the forefront of Montgomery's overview of the contest. Map exercises by staff officers in warm and secure (and usually elegant) old buildings far from the killing grounds might dictate that U.S. 1st Army should drive in from the north and 3rd Army, the south straight across the base of the vast wedge that Field Marshal Model's three armies have thrust into the Ardennes-Eifel, thus trapping them all. The textbook solution, sure enough: If the fox is in the bag, draw the strings. Do not keep punching at the sides as he (or she) scampers out the opening. Certainly, the American commanders on the scene are also well schooled in the principle.

However, staff officers and textbooks rarely have a grip on the reality of the killing grounds. Commanders on the scene do. Montgomery's grasp of the realities of the battlefield and the men who live, hunt, and are hunted there is enhanced by his network of young officers who inhabit every division HQ, have access to the front line, and report to one commander only: his own self.

Montgomery has no intention of supporting an action late in December that tries to fling Gerow's battered and undermanned divisions twenty or more miles south across a wild, icy Golgotha studded with hostile mines and guns to try to meet up with General Patton's troops coming north from Diekirch in Luxembourg. (Patton has suggested this jump-off place to Bradley.)

So we see Montgomery's influence again in deciding the fate of Gerow's 5th Corps and the American divisions—Andrus' 1st, Robertson's 2nd, Lauer's 99th—that are the protagonists of our story. It needs to be added there is no evidence Gerow, his successor Huebner, or Hodges or General Bradley, for that matter, show any Pattonesque enthusiasm for an attack into the base of "the Bulge" either, regardless of what they believe is theoretically the boldest solution.

Montgomery invites Bradley to his headquarters in Zonhoven on Christmas day for a spot of (nonalcoholic) punch and a chat about the Ardennes battle, past and future. It will be the first meeting the two Allied officers running the Ardennes battle have had since the Germans struck December 16. Bradley accepts the invitation in spite of the dangerous journey by air round the western reaches of the breakthrough area it will entail. He hopes the meeting will be productive of understanding and decisions necessary to future operations.

It is not. Montgomery in the presence of his peer and quondam rival takes on his stern, righteous, schoolmasterish persona. Resplendent in a fresh uniform alive with campaign ribbons, he proceeds to lecture Bradley on SHAEF's (read, American) strategic mistakes and command disorganization that, he asserts, have produced the Ardennes disaster. Furthermore, he does not know when his power on the northern face of the bulge area will be ready to attack. "It (is) quite clear that neither of us (can) do anything without more troops." The Germans "have given us a real 'bloody nose.'"

Bradley departs after a half hour with one thought only: Montgomery was "more arrogant and egotistical than I had ever seen him." The meeting has been an unpleasant Christmas surprise whose bitter memory the 12th Army commander will take to his grave.

Eisenhower soon learns of it from Bedell Smith, his chief of staff, to whom Bradley has confided, mincing neither words nor wounded feelings. The Supreme Commander is troubled by Montgomery's continuing reluctance to start driving into the breakthrough area from the north. He also is annoyed by Monty's obvious opportunism in using the chaos and danger of the massive *Wehrmacht* breakthrough to bore in again with his strategic plans and ambitions, which, rightly or wrongly, Ike is by now sick to death of.

He decides he must confront Montgomery, take his measure, and try to obtain his commitment to start driving on the Germans from the north. This means he will have to play the subordinate and travel to the Field Marshal's lair rather than vice versa since Monty will not come to him. Bad weather and concerns of his large security detail delay until December 28 Eisenhower's journey from Versailles to Hasselt, a nondescript Belgian town south of Montgomery's HQ at Zonhoven. The Supreme Commander travels in a heavily guarded train. When it arrives, he is embarrassed and his host amused to witness platoons of heavily armed soldiers piling from the train to surround the station with enough armed might to fight off a battalion of *SS* troops.

The meeting takes place in one of the cars of the train and consists of two participants: Ike and Monty. Things seem to go well. Eisenhower shares with Montgomery the latter's concern over the amount of power Field Marshal Model can still bring up for new and weighty attacks against the northern and western margins of the breakthrough area. And he acknowledges that Patton's 3rd Army will need reinforcing, probably by ordering U.S. 7th Army south of Patton to give up some troops. Montgomery commits himself to unleashing Joe Collins' 7th Corps from the vicinity of Marche and Hotton on the Ourthe River on January 3 if the Germans have not shown signs of bringing in new forces for a major new assault by that date.

The British Field Marshal can not, however, allow the meeting to end without once again insisting that a new field commander for the Western Front be appointed. He leaves no doubt who that commander should be. Eisenhower is noncommittal; Monty thinks he is committal and favors the arrangement. Some demon (or imp) urges him on to message the Supreme Commander the very next day (December 29) in effect directing the latter to sign an order without delay giving Montgomery "full operational direction, control, and coordination" of the Allied armies on the Western Front.

For Ike the message is just too much, coming as it does after long months of annoyance and badgering by the Field Marshal and at a time of extreme peril for his U.S. 1st Army and indeed Bradley's 12th Army Group. Eisenhower decides to lance the boil once and for all by informing the Allied Joint Chiefs of Staff, the U.S.-U.K. military leaders of the Allied coalition, that a choice will have to be made: Monty or he.

Eisenhower knows, of course, what their choice will be should it come to that. Monty's leaving would be a temporary break in Allied command force continuity and solidarity. Ike's leaving would be a disaster signaling to all the world, friend and foe alike, that Hitler's Ardennes-Eifel counteroffensive has done grave damage to the Anglo-American coalition against him and put their plans for breaking into the trans-Rhine *Reich* at risk. Furthermore, without Eisenhower, Bradley and Montgomery, two soldiers who disdain each other in equal measure, would be in charge, at least temporarily. The result would impair the Allied fighting capacities all the way down to the command posts of the infantry and armor.

The storm passes as quickly as it has blown up. Monty's chief of staff makes it painfully clear to him that his message to Eisenhower not only has roused the Supreme Commander's legendary temper but also has precipitated a crisis in command. (The Brits on Eisenhower's staff also consider Monty's initiative to be unsoldierly, insubordinate, and in extremely bad taste.)

The Field Marshal is hurt, believing, as he has since September, that his cause is just and must be heard: Eisenhower and Bradley are wasting lives, especially American lives, with their benighted strategy and unfocused command arrangements. Nevertheless, he apologizes profusely to Ike and swears eternal and undying loyalty in all matters great and small.

Eisenhower has a generous heart toward comrades in arms. He regains his tolerance of the prickly Field Marshal and will even accord him a prime role in the plans for leaping the Rhine. By the 1st of

January, 1945 both soldiers have made up and turned their full attention to excising the enemy carbuncle at the center of the Allied front.

In the German camp, the high commanders in the field—Model, Dietrich, Manteuffel, Brandenberger (7th *Infanterie* Army, south of Bastogne)—are burdened with no such worries over squabbles among their leaders. They have one only, Adolph Hitler, and he has undying faith in the superiority of his genius for war over all others.

As we have seen (Narrative IX, Part 1), the *Führer* overruled his Western Front commander, *Oberbefehlshaber West* Gerd von Rundstedt concerning the immediate use of the German 15th Army east of Aachen, Germany. Von Rundstedt believed the army could break General Gerow's 5th Corps' hold on the Elsenborn high plateau and join with Dietrich's 6th *SS Panzer* Army in a massive pincer to crush all of 1st U.S. Army.[*]

By December 23 it is coming plain even to the *Führer* that Dietrich's *Panzers* will not accomplish their original mission on the northern (right) wing: Peiper's once mighty *Kampfgruppe* is done for, trapped and ground down in the river valleys west of Stavelot, Belgium. Gerow's valiants have repelled the repeated attacks of enemy armor and accompanying infantry, as has been seen.

General Bittrich's 2nd *SS* Corps HQ and support echelons took a hand in the climactic actions December 20-23 along the Elsenborn-Bütgenbach line (Narrative IX, Part 2), although his two *Panzer* divisions: *Das Reich* (2nd *SS Panzer*) and *Hohenstauffen* (9th *SS Panzer*) were not involved. By the close of the Bütgenbach battles, both of these powerful, albeit understrength and underequipped divisions, had moved west on the right flank of General Manteuffel's 5th *Panzer* Army. *Hitlerjugend* (12th *SS*) will follow behind *Hohenstauffen* as a reserve. Hitler still expects 6th *SS Panzer* Army to lead the way to and over the Meuse. But to the professionals running the battle of the Ardennes-Eifel—Model, Kraemer (Dietrich's chief of staff), Manteuffel, even *Generaloberst* Alfred Jodl, operations chief of *OKW*—it is obvious that after December 23 Fifth *Panzer* Army has the ball and Dietrich's power will henceforth run interference only.

---

[*] What was just one more ill Hitlerian wind for his generals blew 5th Corps commander Major General Gerow and his four divisions some decisive good. Gerow's 5th Corps position on the Elsenborn high plateau almost certainly would have been rendered untenable by an attack of the German 15th Army on its left flank simultaneously with the determined assaults on the right that did indeed take place December 19-22. The *Führer's* overruling his *Ob-W* commander in the matter of putting 15th Army into play saved the Americans on Elsenborn ridge from a battlefield crisis of serious proportions.

Twelfth *SS Panzer* Division, now filled with *Panzergrenadier* replacements and lacking 40 percent or so of its armored fighting vehicles, is under orders to leave the Bütgenbach area early on December 24. With the departure and dispersal of the four *SS Panzer* divisions of Dietrich's Army into the great wedge in the American line, the forces of *das Heer* besieging the Elsenborn-Bütgenbach heights are transferred to General Otto Hitzfeld's 67th *Infanterie* Corps.

Model, Dietrich, and their subordinate commanders can not simply shut down the German initiative at the Elsenborn high plateau and send Hitzfeld and his battered *VG* divisions elsewhere. For one they have expended too much blood and steel getting there. For another, the Americans holding the position represent a major threat to the movement of men and material into the breakthrough area. For a third, the Elsenborn high plateau at the northeastern-most angle of the Bulge is a likely jumping off place for a march from the north across the wide base of the breakthrough area.

Although the *Waffen SS* presence is no more at the Elsenborn high plateau, ample infantry of *das Heer* plus the still-dangerous 3rd *Panzergrenadier* Division of General Denkert remains in place around the 5th Corps perimeter from Kalterherberg on the north to Weywertz on the southwest. Field Marshal Model still expects this power to push through to Elsenborn and the American installations to the west of the heights. His staff has drawn up a plan for Hitzfeld: His infantry and the armor of 3rd *Panzergrenadier* Division will attack north and south of Wirtzfeld to flatten out the salients of Gerow's front that are close to this town. Then they will penetrate west to overrun the *Ami* artillery positions that interdict the roads along the southern reaches of the Elsenborn heights. A bold plan, but lacking bold resources.

General Hitzfeld calls his division and artillery commanders together the day following Christmas. They meet at his headquarters, a large house in the small village of Kronenberg, Germany, a dozen miles east of Losheimergraben and the international highway, scene of so much blood letting by both sides on *Null Tag*.

Hitzfeld presides at a map exercise whose purpose is to arrive at tactics for eliminating salients and running over designated artillery positions. General Denkert's 3rd *Panzergrenadier* Division will supply the hitting force; Viebig's 277th and Engle's 12th *VGDs* will attack simultaneously on right and left.

This time 3rd *Panzergrenadier* will strike farther north, midway between Kalterherberg and Elsenborn, march over Camp Elsenborn to the west, and seize Sourbrodt, three miles west. Corps and division artillery and rocket throwers will precede the march with a violent barrage of fiery steel and obscuring smoke. Given the circumstances and conditions, this is an objective so unattainable with the power available to Denkert and Hitzfeld that even the hard professionals of *das Heer* round the table at Kronenberg must have blanched.

Midway in the council of war, the door to the conference room swings open and a short, compact soldier enters. His face is like flint concealing fire, and he wears a field marshal's collar tabs. The soldier is, of course, Model, Army Group B commander. His visit is probably no surprise to the officers present. He is in the habit of prowling the front, dropping in on his subordinates, and even lending his volcanic temper to moving things along.

However, what he has to say is a surprise, an unpleasant one: General Denkert's 3rd *PzGD* will not participate in the attack on the Gerow line that they are planning. Sixth *SS Panzer* Army needs all available mobile forces in their march through the Amblève River valley to attack U.S. 17th Airborne Corps (Ridgeway). Hitler has personally ordered the removal of 3rd *PzGD* Division to that sector immediately. In fact, Denkert is to depart this very moment with his advance guard, leaving his operations officer behind to organize the move. Once again, a direct order of the War Lord has saved the Americans on Elsenborn high plateau from another spasm of blood letting. (See footnote page 287.)

No doubt Hitzfeld and the *Volksgrenadier* division leaders in the room have one thought only at this news: Are our men expected to drive through the *Ami* lines at Elsenborn-Kalterherberg without even an underequipped armored infantry division leading the way? Model is a realist, but his subordinates know him also as a harsh taskmaster little inclined to compromise. To their great relief, this time the realist prevails. Model tells Hitzfeld to redo the attack plan and establish a more limited objective: Try to eliminate the Bloody Angle, the salient at Wirtzfeld-Dom Bütgenbach, then stand fast and stop any move of the enemy to march south into the base of the breakthrough area.

Even such a minor action may not be possible. Unless sufficient friendly cannons and *Luftwaffe* fighter-bombers can be brought into the attack to suppress the terrible *Ami* artillery working off the fields behind Elsenborn and Bütgenbach, Hitzfeld's infantry will be eaten alive by the insatiable guns. This the 67th Corps officers know. They have witnessed the very scene over and over for nearly a week.

Part 3: The Ground Assembles; the Air Emerges

Major General Leonard T. Gerow's long defensive line on the Elsenborn high plateau is ideal for defense: from Kalterherberg south of Monschau to Bütgenbach east of Malmedy, high ground covered with hedge-rowed fields, pastures, and marshland drops off gradually to the hills, stream valleys, and battered towns of the borderland country now occupied by the Germans.

By the close of General Denkert's 3rd *Panzergrenadier* drive December 22 into the 99th Division positions southeast of Elsenborn (Part 1), the Americans have succeeded in making the Elsenborn high plateau, front and back, impregnable to all but the most massive and determined armored assault by Dietrich's 6th *SS Panzer* Army. And the time has long since gone for that.

To recapitulate contenders and positions: On the north (left) flank is General Craig's 9th Division, well stocked with replacements ("reinforcements") led by officers and NCOs who are among the most battle experienced in all the armies on either side. Lauer's Reconnaissance Troop and a battalion of his 395th Infantry are temporarily attached to the 9th and are on its right.

Next in line to the south are the two regiments of the 99th Division (393rd, 394th) that were nearly consumed in the Todeswald and at the Fatal Triangle, then fought 3rd *PzGD* to a draw. The remains of Krinkelt are within view on a clear day; Wirtzfeld is scarcely more than a mile to the south.

General Walter T. Robertson's 2nd Division occupies the ground to the right of the 99th. The terrain occupied by the support units is hilly and contains Berg, a village that makes an excellent aiming point for enemy gunners, and the north shore of the Lac de Bütgenbach reservoir. Two battalions of Colonel Boos' 38th Infantry are up front, the outposts a mile from German-held Wirtzfeld. Colonel Lovless' 23rd Infantry is at their rear, Colonel Hirschfelder's 9th Infantry is in reserve to the northwest around the town of Nidrum.

Around the bend of the Gerow line, northwest of German-held Büllingen, the 1st Division's 18th Infantry has moved into the holes, dugouts, and emplacements south of Bütgenbach. Colonel Seitz's 26th Infantry has squeezed left along the railroad track leading into Bütgenbach on the 2nd Division left flank.

Adjoining the 18th Infantry on the right, or "refusing the flank" as soldiers say, is the division's 16th Infantry, seen in action at Weywertz. (Narrative IX, Part 5) The 16th is responsible for the remainder of the Gerow line, which adjoins Ridgeway's 18th Airborne Corps a few miles east of Malmedy.

At the backs of the infantry, armor soldiers, wire men, forward observers, medical corpsmen, etc. up front on the Gerow line is the vast military metropolis of the rear echelon described before. (Volume 1, Narrative 5, Part 1) It is anchored on innumerable small towns and villages in the Belgian district of Malmedy and borderland Germany, not only Monschau, Kalterherberg, Elsenborn, and Bütgenbach but also Camp Elsenborn (a Belgian military post), Nidrum, Berg, Robertville, Sourbrodt, Weywertz. By December 23 all have been tied together by a web of snow-heavy communication wire and newly bulldozed or snow-cleared roads and are humming with military business.

On the other side of the hill, Field Marshal Model wants to transfer General Hitzfeld's 67th Corps to the 15th Army's control. This army is on the right (north) of the 67th. It makes military sense. The *Waffen SS* men and armor have moved west into the breakthrough area. The *Heer* fronting the Gerow line is in a holding posture, not an aggressive one. The divisions there no longer belong in Dietrich's aggressive 6th *SS Panzer* Army. Hitler, once again, overrules his field commander. Hitzfeld's *Infanterie* Corps will remain with Dietrich's Army, complicating command and control for both leaders.

General Hitzfeld leads a group of *Volksgrenadier* divisions that are without sufficient officers or NCOs, and their ranks have been depleted in the battles since *Null Tag* or are filled with ill-trained *Landser*.

On the right (north) flank opposing Craig's 9th Division is the 326th *VGD* of Major General Erwin Kaschner, whose *Grenadiere* took severe punishment in their attacks on Höfen and Mützenich. (Volume 1, Narrative II, Parts 2 and 3)

Its neighbor on the left flank, Colonel Wilhelm Viebig's 277th *VGD*, has let blood steadily since attacking General Lauer's two 393rd Infantry battalions on *Null Tag* in the Todeswald. The division in January will receive fifteen hundred new men and boys to fill up the ranks of its six depleted infantry battalions. Viebig will be less than impressed. "(They were) scraped together from the bottom of the cadre formations of the *Luftwaffe*. These men were unable to operate their personal weapons. (They) had no knowledge of infantry warfare." (His opinion of his troops aside, Viebig is promoted to major general about this time.)

To fill the hole created in the 67th Corps' order of battle by the loss of 3rd *Panzergrenadier* Division, *OKW* sends Hitzfeld Colonel Peter Körte's 246th *VGD* about December 27. In the course of the war on both the Eastern and Western fronts, the infantry regiments of the 246th have been destroyed, and rebuilt several times. After being smashed once again in the terrible fight for the city of Aachen in October-November, the 246th *VGD* was combined with another division and thereupon joined the killing in the Hürtgen Forest. By the end of November, the 246th *Grenadier* battalions had scarcely a hundred men each.

A flood of untrained *Luftwaffe* ground troops came in to fill the ranks. Thus renewed and reinvigorated, the 246th *VGD* has taken its place in the snowy wastes east of Elsenborn where the *Ami* have devised a mantrap that would break the spirit of the most stalwart old veteran of the *Wehrmacht's* struggles in Russia.

Next in line, at the Wirtzfeld-Büllingen angle, General Engle's 12th *VGD* remains temporarily in the order of battle here. Of all the German infantry power remaining in the campaign to seize the Elsenborn crest, Engle's men, armor (*Sturmgeschütze*), and guns are the most likely to do damage to the Americans in any line-straightening exercise Hitzfeld might try. Engle's troops have been in costly fighting since *Null Tag*. However, the 12th *VGD* started with nearly fifteen thousand men. By late December, it still consists of three regiments of infantry (*Grenadiers* and *Füsiliers*), a company or two of *Sturmgeschütze*, and a regiment of horse-drawn artillery not dependent on dwindling supplies of petrol. Unfortunately, *SS* General Bittrich wants the division in the Amblève River Valley and soon. About January 3 the 89th Infantry Division, an underequipped, manned, and officered unit from the 15th Army will be assigned to the 12th *VGD's* place.

West of the 12th *VGD* General Walter Wadehn's 3rd *Fallschirmjäger* (parachute) Division still is in place from Faymonville-Waimes to the front south of Bütgenbach. Third *Fallschirmjäger* is well stocked with *Luftwaffe* ground troops but is poorly equipped and led. Officers who have survived other battles try to instill "the old parachutist spirit and soldierly bearing," as one puts it. But truth to tell, this formerly elite division is little better than are the others manning General Hitzfeld's 67th Corps front on at the close of December.

Although Hitler's headquarters (*OKW*) is unwilling to invest any more armor in futile aggressions here on the north shoulder, howitzer, gun, and rocket power is on the scene to hold the U.S. 5th Corps at bay, keep its infantry and artillery suppressed, and menace its rear bases. The three divisions, 277th, 12th *VGD*, and 3rd *PzGD*, have brought nearly one hundred 105 and 150mm cannons to the battle. These numbers are increased by division artillery of the newly arrived 246th *VGD*. Also, the howitzers of a *Volksartillerie* corps, rocket-throwing machines of a *Volkswerfer* brigade, and an unknown number of *Luftwaffe* antiaircraft 88 and 120mm guns are present, and off to the east, the railroad cannons assigned by *OKW* to Dietrich's army. However, ammo deliveries to the guns and *Werfer* tubes are erratic.

The towns and villages occupied by Hitzfeld's regiments and battalions—Honsfeld, Rocherath-Krinkelt, Mürringen, Hünningen, Büllingen, Wirtzfeld—have been smashed not only by intensive and ceaseless harassing artillery fire but also by the violent combat between the men and machines of the two sides that has taken place there. Few buildings

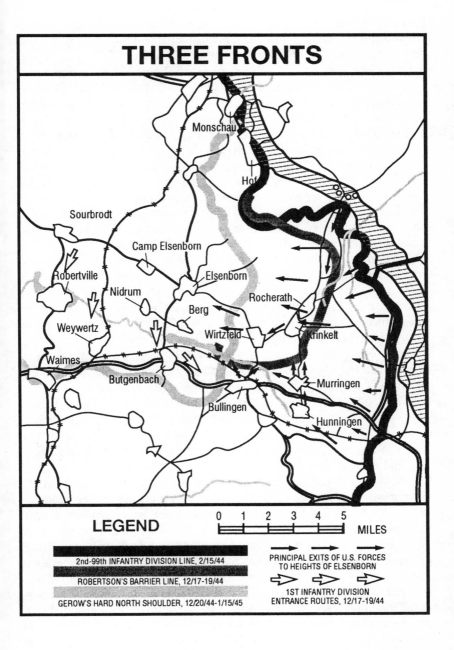

THREE FRONTS

Monschau

Hof

Sourbrodt

Camp Elsenborn

Elsenborn

Robertville

Nidrum

Rocherath

Berg

Weywertz

Wirtzfeld

Krinkelt

Waimes

Butgenbach

Murringen

Bullingen

Hunningen

LEGEND

0   1   2   3   4   5

MILES

PRINCIPAL EXITS OF U.S. FORCES
TO HEIGHTS OF ELSENBORN

2nd-99th INFANTRY DIVISION LINE, 2/15/44

ROBERTSON'S BARRIER LINE, 12/17-19/44

1ST INFANTRY DIVISION
ENTRANCE ROUTES, 12/17-19/44

GEROW'S HARD NORTH SHOULDER, 12/20/44-1/15/45

remain standing and those that do lack all or part of their roofs, windows, and a wall or two. Basements, cellars, improvised stone and timber dugouts made from debris—these are the dwelling and working places of the rear-echelon soldiers of General Hitzfeld's divisions.

They also must endure (or ignore) the unnerving presence of many silent neighbors: the dead. American, German, and a few civilian bodies lie about the farm yards and back streets, under debris in the broken houses, scattered in the fields nearby. The *Landser* occupying these towns have not the time or inclination to undertake the task of collecting these bodies and burying them or bringing them to a central place shielded from the eyes of the living. However, the vast deep freeze that is the Nordeifel-Low Ardennes in winter makes immediate burial unnecessary. The snows of late December and January cover over the bodies. Not only can they not be seen but are also indistinguishable from all the other debris of war lying about.

December 22, the weather across eastern Belgium brings severe cold and driving snow. This bodes ill for the poor mud soldiers of both sides trying to endure up front in holes and dugouts. Yet the next day, December 23, the weather curses the Germans with an even more ominous change, one the commanders from Model down to the platoon leaders have been dreading: A "Russian High" sweeps across northwest Europe. The ground fogs are chased away by the icy air and the bitter winds. The huge belly-like cloud formations move off that have blotted out the sky above and cast a grey pallor over the landscape below.

The hated and feared *Jaboes*, American and British fighter-bombers, can fly again, not now and then, not here and there on suicidal missions, not for a few hours on this or that front to take advantage of a temporary break in the weather but for all the daylight hours every day and everywhere.

Vignettes of the air war in the Ardennes-Eifel up to December 23 have appeared in the preceding narratives. However, the "Hitler weather" of the first seven days of the Ardennes-Eifel battle permitted only sporadic air missions and raids. Even so the young and in many cases ill-trained pilots of the *Luftwaffe* seemed hell bent on storming their way through the massive clouds and searching for openings in the ground fogs to make wild, often suicidal attacks on American columns and positions. In the three days, December 16-18, GAF tactical air flew 1,669 battlefield sorties (one plane, one mission) compared with 1,166 by Allied pilots. And the Germans, equipped for and experienced in night fighting, also made about two hundred sorties over the battlefields after dark.

The clearing skies bring the U.S. 9th and British 2nd air forces into the battle *en masse*. These two destructive air powers are armed with fighter-bombers and medium bombers. On one day alone, December 24, the 9th and 2nd pilots fly 1,138 sorties. About half are aimed at helping American ground fighters hold off the enemy. The *Luftwaffe* pilots are able to fly nearly as many that day: 1,088. The sky is alive with dog fights, an event rarely seen before in 1944 on the Western Front.[*]

The *Luftwaffe* fighter pilots flying off bases in Germany are overwhelmed with demands: ground attack, interdiction of American supply trains, supporting friendly infantry and armor operations, reconnaissance, high-altitude attacks on the big American bombers, combating the *Jaboes*, and on and on.

Over the 5th Corps' Gerow line on the north shoulder of the breakthrough area, fighter-bombers and reconnaissance and photographic aircraft of both sides will work the skies and strike at the ground from December 23 to the dying days of the German counterattack. However, clouds and snow storms, thawing and freezing, and ground fogs will return from time to time to discourage flying. (On December 28, for example, heavy snow eliminates flying everywhere across eastern Belgium and Luxembourg.)

The skies over the Ardennes-Eifel are the scene of two distinctly different air wars. One takes place four, five, or six miles in the air. Its combatants are the big American bombers and the fighters of both sides.

---

[*] The air war in the Ardennes-Eifel between December 15, 1944 and January 31, 1945 is among the least recognized major combats of WW II. One writer called it, "the Unknown Bulge." By December 20, 1944 the *Luftwaffe* had approximately 2,400 aircraft of all types in the formations active over and near the battlefield and nearby protecting the supply routes from Germany. (At any one time, 30 percent of these were not in service.)

The U.S. 9th and British 2nd air forces had 2,500 fighters and another 1,400 medium bombers available, 85 percent serviceable, but not all committed to the Ardennes. Also, heavy bombers of the U.S. 8th Air Force in England and France attacked seventeen *Luftwaffe* bases in Germany being used by aircraft aiding *Wehrmacht* ground troops in the Ardennes. (Parker, Winter Sky, table 1, p. 54; table 6, p. 134; page 517. Full reference in Documentation, this volume. Quote also found in Parker, Preface, p. 9.)

Numbers of aircraft on both sides do not entirely reveal the *Luftwaffe's* disadvantage. Fuel supplies for training and operations were a chronic problem. Also, many of the German pilots were young, poorly trained substitutes for the *Luftwaffe* warriors who fell to their deaths in vast numbers on many fronts throughout the war. It removes no star from the shining record of the American, British, and Canadian flyers to acknowledge the courage of these young Germans, who, ill-trained, ill-prepared, knowing the odds against them, nevertheless took to the unforgiving winter skies.

For the groundlings occupying the Elsenborn high plateau the aerial brawls, come as something of a diversion: a ringside seat at some of the most ferocious high-altitude combats of World War II in the West, even if brave men (and boys) die in circumstances of unalloyed terror. One such combat occurs on December 24 as two thousand plus heavy bombers of the U.S. Eighth Air Force lift from their airdromes in England and Scotland and move over Holland and Belgium toward targets in western Germany, particularly enemy airfields.

One box of B-17 bombers passing over Liege and Aachen is without the usual fighter escort because of weather in England. They are attacked by German fighters east of Liege, which kill four bombers and cripple five more. The B-17 crews fight back with their thirteen .50caliber machine guns and win some kills of their own. Then their fighter escort of sleek, P-51 Mustangs finally catches up with them. The *Luftwaffe* fighter pilots now are in serious trouble. Thirty-five Germans from another *Gruppe*, including *Focke Wulf* 190s and *Messerschmidt* 109s, ascend to the high battle to feed on the bombers. They encounter instead nearly as many bottle-shaped, workhorse P-47s, which have come up from Belgian airdromes to press them away.

The battle among the distant specks trailing vapor trails, fire, smoke, pieces of aircraft, and an occasional parachute is visible from the ground in the Malmedy-Eupen-Elsenborn triangle. Broken and burning machines can be seen falling in a slow, corkscrewing descent or dropping straight, like a rock. A few shed the remains of air crew as they fall, a sight that chills even the most hard-bitten mud soldier watching from below.

The other air war in the Ardennes-Eifel involves fighter aircraft, ground attack aircraft, low-level bombers. It takes place in space that seldom extends more than two thousand feet above the ground and often dips to tree-top and church-steeple level. For the groundlings, this air war is rousing, immediate, awesomely violent, and deadly to many of those in the aircraft and on the ground unfortunate enough to be caught up in the melee. It is a war in which the men on the ground, up front and in the rear, are as likely to be hurt by friendly aircraft as by enemy ones. And Allied pilots are occasionally sent to their doom by the ubiquitous American antiaircraft gun wagons.

On December 27, for example, seven P-47s, their wings prickly with rockets, come charging over the high plateau at Elsenborn hunting German howitzers. They find the howitzers right enough. Unfortunately they belong to the batteries of the 99th Division. A sharp, ground-air battle among friends follows. The destructive rockets come whooshing down to strike round the gun pits. Several five-hundred-pound bombs raise geysers of fire, steel, and frozen earth all around.

The little cannons and machine guns on the AA gun motor carriages near the arty's emplacements send forth a tide of bullet and 37mm shell fire at the swooping, wheeling machines in the air overhead. One goes out of control, wings over, and hits the earth with a shattering roar; another is holed several times, but the pilot manages to land it safely on a nearby field. He is hurt and is carried off to the nearest battalion aid station protesting that he and his fellows have been misinformed on the location of the enemy. Three 99th artillerymen are dead; ten wounded.

In fact, in the last days of December confusion seems common among 9th Air Force pilots concerning the location of German attacking columns and positions south of Gerow's 5th Corps and Ridgeway's 18th Airborne Corps defensive lines. On December 23, A-20 Invaders of the 9th Bombardment Command appear in the skies over Bütgenbach, headquarters of Colonel Seitz's 26th Infantry, and let go eight bombs. Fortunately only half explode, and casualties among the groundlings are few. General Andrus, the 1st Division acting CO, sends Gerow a cryptic message: "Mediums are bombing Bütgenbach. We have troops in there."

The same day, Malmedy, Belgium, only a few miles west of 16th Infantry positions (1st Division) is attacked by a half dozen B-26s. First Division sends in a task force to determine what is going on. They report, "The town of Malmedy is *kaputt* (done for). Thirty killed and twenty wounded in the 120th Infantry (U.S. 30th Division). Town is in flames." Not *kaputt* enough apparently. On Christmas eve, eighteen heavy U.S. bombers (B-24s) strike the already outraged city and utterly ruin its center. The day after Christmas, four 9th Bombardment Command B-26s on another misplaced bomb run administer the *coup de grâce*.

The 1st Division soldiers are becoming acclimated to air attacks from both sides. On the 24th, 16th Infantry HQ informs Andrus HQ at Sourbrodt, Belgium that large bombing aircraft—they believe them to be B-17s—"are dropping markers and bombs while (over) our front lines."

The day before, U.S. antiaircraft gun wagons around Weywertz (16th Infantry) engage in a fight with a U.S. P-47 that persists in strafing the area. The AA artillerymen fire parachute flares to warn off the dogged American, but he continues strafing and they continue shooting.

December 25 the antiaircraft soldiers working with the 1st Division find more action. A vicious little dog fight between Allied and *Luftwaffe* fighters concludes with three speedy *Focke Wulf* 190s chasing a P-51 Mustang, the best fighter plane in the U.S. air stable. The AA men report to 1st Division: "Three FWs shot down, also P-51. We got them all. Pilot of the P-51 was dead."

This deadly and confusing air war fought close to the ground by tactical aircraft of the USAF and the Royal Air Force and the fighters of the *Luftwaffe*—is, of course, infinitely more than mistaken targets, confused bomb runs, and ground-air fights in which American groundlings engage American pilots. Although painfully frequent, these are aberrations. The vast bomber armadas and fighter-bomber cavalries of American and Royal Air Force machines do round-the-clock harm to the enemy on the ground and in the air for the entire six weeks of the *Riesenanschlag*. And the mud soldiers love them for it. Their role in the Ardennes campaign is not decisive, as some airmen to this day assert, but it certainly is indispensable.

Part 4: Snow Dogs

Of all the malevolent spirits that torment the soldiers manning the now-static defense lines on the Elsenborn-Bütgenbach crest, the unending and random falls and strikes of explosive artillery rounds and mortar bombs cause the most agony and anxiety.

And the worst of it is the stream of direct fire from German high-velocity tank destroyer and antiaircraft guns operating in a ground mode. They are easily moved from place to place around the mostly treeless hills and shallow valleys of the Elsenborn plateau. They are capable of direct line-of-sight shooting. They can be, and now and then are, directed at individual soldiers running from hole to hole, two-man carrying parties bringing water or food up front, or a lone engineer sweeping a mine detector across the snow.

"We tried to have a fire in one of the holes," writes the lieutenant of an antitank gun platoon to his parents. "Everything worked out fine except they shot our stovepipe off twice, real quick. That ended that. You can't imagine how we appreciate being in a hole. As long as you are in a hole, the enemy artillery has got to lay it right on top of you to get you. Sometimes, our hole vibrates like a fiddle string, but so far they have only hit close. There is more danger in a fire fight. But one can ease his nerves by doing some of the same (AN: shooting back). Artillery, you just have to sweat it out. It bothers us more than anything."

The shell fire spreads diverse kinds of death and destruction. "Some holes suffered near hits in which cave-ins were caused," a rifleman of the 393rd Infantry remembered. "(This) resulted in suffocation of the men in these holes. Most of the open-top holes had shell fragments and splinters entering quite frequently. Covered holes were better. But even these were vulnerable."

The commander of the 3rd *Panzergrenadier* Division, General Denkert, (Part 1) best expressed the condition of flesh-and-blood man versus crashing, fragmenting steel: "The artillery on both sides controlled the situation during the following days. No matter whether one was at the "Sherman Corner" (footnote, p. 272), inside Rocherath, on the main road leading from (there) to the north, or in the forest west of the road, there was always artillery fire. When (I) visited the command post of the 8th *Panzergrenadier* Regiment in the northern part of Rocherath, the house in which it was located was put to ruin by a surprise fire of the enemy artillery..."

Rocketry is mixed with the German artillery: 5 and 8.4-inch diameter explosive rounds fired from cheap little five- and six-barrel launchers (*Nebelwerfer*) on two-wheeled carriages. The command post of a tank destroyer battalion with the 2nd Division is near Berg. The building can be seen from German lines east of Lac de Bütgenbach. It is attacked several times by flurries of rockets, which come streaking in with their characteristic otherworldly moan and smash into the ground with a roar and a blast of smoke and flame.

After every shelling and rocketing, wiremen swarm across the snow-covered ground repairing breaks in the telephone and telegraph lines. The assignment takes them away from holes and dugouts and basements for hours on end, struck through with cold, savaged by the wind, and in constant danger of being just one more unimportant victim of enemy (or friendly) guns.

In the vast military "metropolis" of the Elsenborn-Bütgenbach high plateau, there are two classes only. They have nothing to do with military rank, family origin, money in the bank, education, or any of the other measures by which people are categorized back in never-never land, i.e. the States. Here what determines your class is your location: Are you in the rear or are you up front?

The soldiers of the rear—officers and men—generally inhabit shelter of some kind, be it an abandoned house or barn, a hastily thrown together hutment, a prefabricated building of metal, or a tent near to a dugout or cellar they can flee to when the shells and mortar bombs come in.

With some exceptions, the soldiers of the rear are outdoors most of the time performing the countless tasks necessary to maintaining the men confronting the enemy up front. However, when their day's work is done, they usually return to a place to sleep that is warmed by some kind of fire, feeble though it be. They also regularly eat warm food cooked in real pots and pans on a genuine cook stove.

They are by no means unthreatened by war's malevolent vengefulness. The big guns assigned to 6th *SS Panzer* Army and *Heersgruppe*

B, which throw shells weighing a quarter ton or more into the near and distant rear of the American positions, may strike sudden as a Jovian thunderbolt. Men of the headquarters company of a tank destroyer battalion working with Robertson's 2nd Division have been up front on the firing line as surrogate riflemen filling in for the division infantry. Late on December 20 they are released to return to their HQ located in Sourbrodt northwest of Elsenborn and six miles distant from the front. They have filed into a large meeting room of the Sourbrodt town hall for their first cooked meal in four days and nights.

As they noisily and happily trencher away, there comes to all ears what sounds like a locomotive bearing down on the hall. It is the last sound some of them will ever hear. A quarter ton, nine-inch diameter, shell from a German railroad gun east of Monschau strikes dead on, blowing apart the hall and injuring or killing half the men there.

Among those soldiers of the rear located or forced to work around prime targets such as large artillery concentrations, supply centers, communication facilities, the odds increase they may fall victim to the guns or one or more fighter-bombers may sweep in bombing, machine gunning, rocketing.

And, of course, there is always the possibility the enemy will overwhelm the up-front fighters of the "other" class and spread havoc in the rear, as Peiper's *Kampfgruppe* did at Büllingen. (Volume 1, Narrative V, Part 4)

The men and officers of this other class on the high plateau, i.e. the soldiers of the front and near front, don't dwell on top of the earth in structures built for the purpose. They dwell under the earth in holes and dugouts. Few of these are large enough for even a makeshift stove. They rarely receive a meal that has been cooked and is still warm on arrival. And they dare not gather above ground to eat the meal for fear enemy snipers or cannoneers will make it their last.

Of course, what really distinguishes the up-front class of soldiers is the all-pervading danger that they live with night and day. A nature writer has described prairie dogs on the Western Plains of the U.S. as living in "a violent and unforgiving world...continually beset by predators of one kind or another." The animals are hunted and eaten quick by black-footed ferrets, snakes, coyotes, hawks.

The "snow dogs" up front in the hills of the Elsenborn high plateau and Bütgenbach are hunted and eaten quick by sniper and machine gun fire, hostile patrols, mortar bombs, howitzer and rocket fire, direct high-velocity gun fire, the wild shooting or stray bombing of an aircraft hunting prey below, immersion or frozen feet, pneumonia and dysentery, and gross, unshakable depression.

Unlike the little animals of the Western Plains, the snow dogs can not stick to their deep burrows. From time to time they must go on patrol, sallying forth to confront the beasts and predatory birds, or work above ground hauling water, supplies, and ammunition; patching wire; making living holes and gun nests more secure and less intolerable to shelter in; moving from one position to another; carrying messages.

After one of the frequent, all-night snowfalls across the Elsenborn-Bütgenbach hills, even the landscape occupied by the men up front resembles that of a prairie dog colony in winter: closed, empty, with scarcely any sign of man or beast in the snowy wasteland until first one, then another, then scores of figures slither out of their holes, and break through the snow to go about the day's business. And of course the predators become active also. Shells and mortar bombs come in. A hostile machine gunner in the patch of woods below lets fly a stream of bullets their way. The 88mm gun in the valley cracks, sending a shell shrieking by to explode with a crash—somewhere.

The analogy must not be carried too far. Prairie dogs are cute little fellows that threaten no other animal; the snow dogs of the American infantry divisions occupying the Elsenborn-Berg-Bütgenbach sector have long teeth and sharp claws and plenty of dangerous friends and give better than they get to their enemies.

And it needs to be added that many soldiers manning the Gerow line are denizens of both the rear and the front. Artillery forward observer teams are typical of this group. They spend a few days in unpleasant and dangerous foxholes and dugouts at the absolute front of the rifle line then return to their batteries in the rear for a few days.

With some exceptions, their gun crews are hole dwellers also, although not near the enemy. Some get lucky. Their piece, as they call it, is placed near a broken house with a basement or strong walls that will protect them from the invariable counterbattery fire and wild *Luftwaffe* bombing.

Soldiers of the combat engineering battalions that are part of Gerow's 5th Corps infantry divisions or add-on units also inhabit both worlds. When they are not actually engaging the enemy as substitute infantry, (Part 1), they are somewhere doing mine laying, mine lifting, barbedwiring, construction, road building, or whatever job division orders their officers to get done. Skilled in putting things together, the engineers usually fashion snug and warm dwellings for themselves if occupying rear echelon sites. But they spend much time outside suffering all of the wrath of the cold and the malevolence of random shellfire.

And just behind the main line of resistance manned by the infantry and their reserves, can be found diggings of the soldiers there to help the riflemen stop the enemy from marching over the high plateau. They occupy mortar positions, forward CPs, armor parks, medical aid stations, antitank gun sites, communications switchboard dugouts, etc.

Even the riflemen and machine gunners fronting the enemy may on occasion be sent to the rear, even the deep rear (Eupen, Verviers) for a bath, a warm, dry bed, and a day or two of cooked food eaten at a table.

A few are blessed by the unimaginable good fortune of a transfer to a job in a company or battalion headquarters or service section in one of the towns. A soldier with "H" Company, 393rd Infantry has drawn the dangerous job of repairing wire running from the platoon's 81mm mortars to the rifle company forward command posts a few dozen yards behind the main line of resistance. Every time a flight of enemy artillery shells land, they blow the wire into fragments. So the mortar man spends his days and nights in the snow hunting for wire ends to splice. High-velocity cannon fire rages over the snowy fields as he works.

Someone on high decides the soldier needs a job change. He is assigned to the company's motor park (pool) as a jeep driver. He goes to live in a battered farmhouse in Elsenborn with the other drivers. They sleep on the floor, endure icy nights punctuated by explosions of large caliber shells here and there. Nevertheless, he has stepped into another world. He has joined the soldiers of the rear.

A Company "G," 394th rifleman is plucked from a snow-impacted, freezing hole on the rifle outpost line and sent to Elsenborn to be the company mail clerk. "It was so wonderful to be in a warm building again," he remembered years later. "I sat on the sofa by the fire an hour just enjoying it all." (No doubt the sofa has been punctured in several places and is caked with mud from many boots. The fire is in a fireplace whose flu is cracked, broken, and draws badly.)

The shortfall of 2nd lieutenants (lowest commissioned officer grade) to lead the rifle platoons is so serious that senior NCOs can sooner or later expect to be offered a battlefield commission, as the promotion is called. Not all offers are accepted. Rifle platoon leaders receive a liquor ration and more pay. But they live as meanly as do their men and can look forward to an even shorter tenure.[*]

Except for candles sent from home, the only light and heat up front is derived from saturating a dirt-filled can with gasoline, pushing a rag into a bottle half-filled with gasoline and igniting same, or putting a match to a can of "dubbing," a greasy material used to waterproof shoes.

---

[*] A total of 10,898 battlefield commissions were issued in the European Theater in WW II. (Source is John C. Angier, National Order of Battlefield Commissions)

The improvised stoves and lights easily tip over or explode, inundating their users with flame, which in the close confines of the foxhole can be fatal. Yet the cans and bottles give off precious little heat or light. The foxholes are scarcely warmer than is the bitter air above.

Generally, two men inhabit one hole (mutual protection, companionship, body warmth, misery loving company, etc.). Two "E" Company, 393rd Infantrymen move to a new location and find a hole, "fully covered," and including an entryway at right angles to the sleeping quarters, good protection against shell fragments. However, "It had the usual failing: The entry was only large enough for one man to fight from (i.e. shoot from)....We set about converting the hole to our requirements. We...lined the (bottom) and walls with blankets and hung another one in the entrance to keep in light and keep out cold and wind and snow."

Upon arrival in position, the infantryman's first digging is minimal, just sufficient to obtain protection from the exploding shell and mortar fragments and a place to lay one's head until better can be done. The soldier sent to the rear to be a mail clerk (above) remembered decades later the grave-like dimensions of his first two-man foxhole: four feet deep; three, wide; seven, long. "We improvised a roof to keep out the snow with branches and a shelter half."

East of Berg and north of Lac de Bütgenbach, Colonel Boos' 38th Infantrymen hasten the process of making foxholes and dugouts. They plant blocks of dynamite in the frozen crust covering the top soil. Following the blow out, they go to work with shovels to improve things. One of the improvements is a network of what soldiers call "communication trenches" connecting holes and dugouts within the regiment's defenses. By the close of January the 38th's sector resembles a World War I trench line in minature.

On all fronts to protect against direct hits, the burrows are covered over with as many logs, boards, or other debris of the battlefield and town as can be found and the walls will bear. This offers some protection against nearby explosions but not, of course, direct hits. When covered with closely packed and frigid snow, the roof also offers some protection against the elements. Not when the sun shines, however, as it sometimes does in January. Then the snow melts as does the hoar frost on the inside walls. Water begins to seep in from countless places. Thaws also weaken the mud walls, which may collapse under the weight of the roof, burying the hole dwellers.

The outposts of the rifle companies and forward observer posts of the artillery battalions and recon units are located in the very maw of the enemy. Two soldiers man the rifle company outposts (OPs). By night they watch for enemy stealing upon them to reconnoiter the ground or snatch a prisoner to drag back for interrogation. One watches fused to the field telephone; the other snoozes, or tries to. By day the two rifle soldiers watch for signs the enemy is stirring for an assault, large or small. By and by, if something hasn't gotten them, they rotate west to the company perimeter and another team plods through the snow to the OP, so isolated, far down the sharp edge, and close to the enemy.

When the brief spell of warming weather and accompanying thaw comes to an abrupt end December 22, winter, the deep winter of the Nordeifel-Ardennes, arrives to take hold of the Elsenborn high plateau and its environs. Snow falls, not watery and sporadically as before but icy and crystalline in day- or night-long blizzards that pile up in smothering layers. Many nights the temperature drops to near zero (fahrenheit) and only occasionally rises above freezing at high noon under a pale winter sun. The wind bites, not now and then on a nasty day or bitter night, as experienced by the soldiers of the 99th and 2nd divisions in the past month, but continuously and rising at times to gale-like force that sucks the breath from men forced to work or fight in the open, turns the blood in their veins to slush, and solidifies the very marrow of their bones.

The miserable holes in the ground are a protection of sorts from the bite of the wind. Clothing is another protection—of sorts. But truth to tell, the U.S. Army is simply unprepared for a Russian-style winter environment not only here on the Elsenborn-Bütgenbach position but throughout the Ardennes-Eifel. Nowhere is this more obvious than in the clothing and footgear available to the ever-exposed fighters up front.

The captain of "K" Company, 394th Infantry, complained after the campaign that 80 percent of the men of his company were without proper footwear or clothing for the conditions. Neither repelled water and they were inundated with water from beginning to end in the form of rain, sleet, snow, and ice.

Captain Ben Legare, who took over the 394th's 2nd Battalion when its commander fell apart (Volume 1, Narrative III, Part 2), agreed: "The troops of the 99th Division were ill-equipped to withstand the rigors of the bitterly cold December weather....(The standard winter uniform) proved woefully inadequate in the deep snow and winter cold."

The executive officer of the 1st Division's Quartermaster Company wrote, "One fact is clear: American lives were lost and the war in Europe prolonged as a direct result of the lack of needed winterized clothing and equipment for the combat troops."

The officer may have exaggerated. Yet the reality of the life among the men and officers in the holes and dugouts on the Elsenborn high plateau is that no matter how much they improvise and invent they are not able to keep the cruel cold and frost at bay. They pull and push on to their bodies every scrap of clothing they can find, but it is never enough to banish the stasis of body and soul, like a drug, that the cold of the Elsenborn Ridge in late December 1944 and January 1945 inflicts upon them. They dwell in a massive tank of cold that turns even the simplest task into misery.

A "K" Company, 26th Infantry, soldier remembered his wardrobe: "I had a sheepskin-lined helmet on my head under my steel helmet that I had found in a house before we went into the Hürtgen Forest. I had on a pair of wool long johns (underwear) and two Army-issue sweat shirts. Next (were) a wool shirt and pants and a wool sweater that was sent me from home. Over this went an Army-issue sweater. Over the wool pants I had a pair of wind-and almost waterproof pants that had been issued to us. Finally, I had a field jacket and wool overcoat and a wool scarf around my neck that I could pull up over my face (for wind protection)."

Takes little time in the holes, dens, and dugouts up front to turn a sharp, young, handsome lad of a soldier into a creature of the nether-world: bulky in his layers of dirty clothing; bearded face blackened by soot from smoke given off by the gasoline-fueled lights used in the holes; eyes hollow from lack of sleep and the omnipresent danger.

Feet are the Achilles heel, so to speak, of the American defense. If too many riflemen, machine gunners, and other infantry soldiers up front are laid low by immersion (water-logged) or the more serious frozen feet and must be taken off the field, the gaps opening across the MLR can be fatal even if the enemy is weak in power and aggressiveness.

Officers down to platoon level are held strictly accountable for the condition of their men's feet. Too many losses due to foot ailments and the officer in charge receives a court martial. It's that serious and that simple. (This order is not strictly enforced: Company grade officers can be spared from the ridge even less than riflemen can.)

In their campaign against bad feet, the commanders are up against two realities difficult to deal with, one sad, the other infuriating. The first is that driven to distraction by all the furies biting at them, some men decide the loss of a toe or two is a price worth paying to get away. Deliberately or not, they ignore the gradual deterioration of their feet until the day comes when they no longer even know they have feet because the damp frost inside their boots has blotted out all feeling and the flesh of the soles is as white as bone and already blistering.

The infuriating one is the footgear itself. The standard Army-issue leather boot alone is always water logged. Encased in galoshes it is serviceable and protective if the wearer maintains dry pairs of socks to substitute for the constantly wet ones; he has plenty of waterproofing for the boots; he is not immersed in calf-high water or snow for long; and if he can obtain galoshes that fit. (One company receives a shipment of size twelve galoshes only.)

By and by the U.S. Quartermaster Corps ships in Shoe Pacs, i.e. the Maine hunting boot with rubber bottoms and leather uppers. These are an improvement but also must be carefully programmed: The inner sole (insert) becomes damp with perspiration, freezes. If not changed it soon infects the wearer's feet with frosty cold. So soldiers lucky enough to be issued Pacs, the minority at the front, must maintain dry insoles and make changes periodically. Of course, the Shoe Pacs don't always arrive with inserts, and as with the galoshes one size is often supposed to fit all.

The battalion medical officer and his men spread through the companies are cursed with the responsibility of handling the immersion and frost-bitten foot plague. From the doctors to the hard-pressed medics in dugouts among the infantry foxholes, they search out the incipient cases and send the most serious ones west. The 395th Infantry Cannon Company captain is appalled after one such inspection. "The young medic with my company said 'Captain, I got to look at all the damn feet.' He knocked out about thirty of my men because he could take his fingers and just rub the flesh off the outer edges of the feet."

Diarrhea is not the problem for the commanders that bad feet are. Not because this misery is not as prevalent on the plateau as is immersion foot. Diarrhea is more prevalent, in fact. However, few soldiers of the front are sent to a battalion aid station because they are suffering this ailment. They cope as best they can, enduring the nasty cramps, slithering out of their foxholes in darkest night, if necessary, to defecate. Not always making it. It helps not that several layers of clothing must be peeled down for the job, the wind is so cold that flesh begins to freeze after a few minutes of exposure, and an enemy gunner may just at that time decide to send over a mortar bomb or artillery round. The medics (medical corpsmen) use up almost as many bottles of Kaopectate as of aspirin.

The battalion medical aid station is usually located a half mile to a mile away from the mayhem up front. Most battalion medics don't work at the station, however. They work close with the front line fighters of all units, infantry, armor, antitank, engineers, etc. They man the forward collecting station of the battalion medical detachment, as it is called. They are an integral part of the infantry and other fighting platoons.

As we have seen, red crosses inside a white circle decorate their helmets. They wear arm bands with same. However, these are no talismans insuring their wearer safety on the battlefield, as we have also seen. (Narrative VI, Part 2) The medics' flesh is as vulnerable to harm from artillery, mortar, and rocket fire as is that of any fighting soldier up front. And if the enemy sniper or machine gunner with a red cross in his sights is especially vindictive, it offers an excellent aiming point.

The iciness and sub-zero gales of the Elsenborn-Bütgenbach sector lay unusual demands upon the medical soldiers. Cold hurries shock in wounded men; shock kills. Blood plasma fed into a vein helps to fight off shock, but the plasma must not freeze and thaw before use. The same for the blessed, pain-killing, sleep-inducing morphine. Once frozen it is useless. The medics with the infantry companies go to uncomfortable lengths to prevent these substances from freezing. They take the bottles and syringes into their sleeping bags with them, tape them under arms and between legs.

Battalion surgeons establish "drying rooms," as they are called at their aid stations to treat slight cases of immersion foot and respiratory infections, another common affliction. And after the first desperate week on the plateau, the regiments raise warming tents and other shelters to give their fighters a few hours respite from the wet, dirt, cold, and mental and spiritual grinding down of the front.

Also causing empty spaces at the guns up front are the sad and difficult (for everybody) cases of breakdown: soldiers who simply won't and in most cases can't take it anymore—it being all the terrors and miseries we've described. The breakdown assumes many awful forms: ignoring an ailment such as advanced immersion foot, pneumonia, or worse that will force the medics to move the afflicted soldier out; loss of control over bowels and bladder; putting a bullet through the flesh (but not the bone) of an arm or leg; gross craziness or refusal to follow an order, even one entailing no danger; attempts sometimes successful, to kill oneself.

The official records are vague. NBI (nonbattle injury) or NBC (nonbattle casualty) is generally the designation. In the old-line regiments, such as those of the 1st and 2nd divisions, there is a reluctance even to acknowledge such breakdowns occur.

Enduring endless days of cold, shelling, nightmarish patrolling, and misery in a static position seems to grind down men more than does the kind of wild and violent mayhem we have seen in the Todeswald, at Losheimergraben, in the dual towns, at Dom Bütgenbach. If you survive such battles intact, you feel a perverse sense of triumph; surviving a day on the Elsenborn front line means nothing more than that you survived another day. And tomorrow or the next day or the next may be the one you don't survive.

The "I" Company, 394th Infantry, captain wrote in his memoirs: "A few men broke under the strain, wetting themselves repeatedly or vomiting or showing other severe physical symptoms. Only with a raging fever was a soldier deemed sick enough for temporary relief from duty. Otherwise the cure-all aspirin tablets had to do. Men began to wound themselves to get away from the front line....Nor were all intentional. Many were the result of negligence born of fatigue and misery."

On Christmas eve, a BAR (Browning Automatic Rifle) soldier with "G" Company, 393rd Infantry, returns to his two-man foxhole. He discovers the member of his BAR team with whom he shares the foxhole "bobbing up and down on his knees." After slashing his wrists with a razor blade, the boy has tried, not very successfully to hang himself from a pole supporting the roof. "I can't stand it anymore," he tells the BAR man. A medical corpsman and his foxhole mate escort him to the rear. He is not seen again by the men of "G" Company.*

Not far away at about the same time on Christmas eve on the reverse slope of the Rodelhöhe (Part 1), four soldiers of the 2nd Battalion, 393rd Infantry, heavy (81mm) mortar platoon, settle down for the night as best they can in a large dugout they have excavated. They have slung a few tree limbs and timbers over the big hole and covered these with pup tent (shelter) halves and ponchos, (a form of rain cape), piling on dirt and snow for protection.

The rule is two-man foxholes only. For some reason the mortarmen have been able to ignore it and hack living space from the frozen ground that is longer and deeper and more accommodating. The black night has taken hold. The temperature is below freezing. The start of a snow storm is riding the bitter air.

The soldiers are preparing to make of Christmas eve what they can in their new diggings. Suddenly, they are inundated by a violent light and a mighty concussion accompanied by chunks of hot steel flailing everywhere in their small space. The shell fragments destroy the face and head of one soldier, the spine of a second, the rib cage of a third.

---

* In more than a few such cases, the prognosis is not as dire as the reader might imagine. For the up-front soldier who has endured all he can but is still rational, a place may be found in the rear, washing pots, stacking ammo, unloading trucks, felling trees, etc. However, if the soldier is so far gone he can not even tolerate the sound of distant artillery fire, and appears literally driven mad by fear there is nothing for it but to get him out of the combat zone, and quick.

The fourth man suffers a mangled foot that will be amputated later. No surgery can save the others, who die within the hour.

Christmas time, as a matter of fact, seems perversely fertile with such awful happenings typical of life on the Elsenborn high plateau during late December and January. Awareness of the contrast between the generous spirit of Christmas and the evil animus of war lies heavy upon all but the most obtuse mind.

The mess sergeants and their crews across the plateau are ordered to get a hot turkey dinner to all troops on Christmas no matter what the effort or risk. The Army Quartermaster supplies the turkeys, thousands of them. The company cooks roast them, mash potatoes, open countless cans of cranberry sauce, even cream some onions or other vegetables.

All available hands exert their souls to move the food to the men in the foxholes. Vehicle breakdowns occur. Impassable cart tracks and trails force carrying parties to move the large cans of rapidly cooling food forward. Shell and mortar explosions stop a few kitchen trucks and helpers dead in their tracks (literally). Other mishaps occur. Yet most of the soldiers on the fighting line receive a Christmas dinner, cold though the turkey, mash potatoes, creamed onions may be. They are grateful.

The chilly turkey and little surprises contained in the few boxes received from home are about it in the way of yuletide merriment for the up-front fighters. A small opportunity for fun in the holes is opening the boxes from the folks and the girl friend. The candy, cookies, and liquor disguised as cough medicine are shared out. Some of the gifts are so inappropriate they generate real laughter among the recipients, the best gift of all.

One small group of infantrymen don't enjoy themselves much on Christmas day opening packages from home. The packages are addressed to the men of their companies lost since *Null Tag*. The sad duty is done in the living room of the house occupied by their battalion chaplain in Elsenborn. The NCO in charge of the "detail," as soldiers call it, still remembered forty years later: "We were to take all of the perishable foods. The valuables were sent back to the families in the states. Most of (my) company was dead, captured, wounded, and evacuated. So we (survivors) had a lot of food....Our departed buddies' gifts were a big help in feeding us under dire conditions."

For some of the men at the front, Christmas passes with scarcely a thought, so tense, preoccupied, and time indifferent are they in their struggle to cope and survive. It is just another working day, meaning killing and being killed day. This is starkly set forth in the log of a rifle company occupying the Rodelhöhe position ("G" 393rd Infantry): "25 Dec 1944: A seven-man reconnaissance patrol departed company command post, encountered the enemy and returned to the command post. Clary killed by sniper. Schuerger and Clayton killed by tank destroyer." (AN: presumably a German one but perhaps not)

In the other part of the huge American military encampment on the Elsenborn high plateau, the part where the soldiers live under shelter in the towns and villages, an effort is made to celebrate the hour if not the day. Chaplains hold religious services. Command posts and rear headquarters are decorated after a fashion. Boxes from home are opened in warm rooms not smoky holes in the earth. Beer and wine is procured. Above all, the food is hot and plentiful. And carols can be carolled without fear of giving the enemy's sound and light artillery observation teams a marker to shoot at. However, even here war has a way of dropping in to ruin the day.

—In a parish house in Weywertz, Lieutenant Colonel Charles T. Horner and his staff of 2nd Battalion, 16th Infantry (Narrative IX, Part 5) are sitting down to Christmas dinner in a room decorated with what the colonel calls "a beautiful Christmas tree." Artillery rounds explode near the house and drive them all into the basement where they hunker down as the turkey cools and the creamed onions coagulate.

—American AA artillery gun wagons working with an M-10 tank destroyer battalion assigned to the 2nd Division (Narrative VIII, Parts 2-4) disable a *Focke Wulf* 190 over Elsenborn. The pilot jumps from his burning aircraft, his parachute opens, and he comes floating down. A captain with the battalion has to make loud noises to prevent his men from killing the pilot in the air, a nice Christmas gift for the German.

—At 11:00 a.m. Christmas morn, the 9th Tactical Air Force liaison officer with the 1st Division HQ in Sourbrodt informs the operations officer that Royal Air Force Typhoons, Tempests, and Spitfires and USAF Lightnings (P-38s), Thunderbolts (P-47s), and Mustangs (P-51) will be operating in the skies, bombing and strafing and hunting *Luftwaffe* machines to shoot down, a big gift to the Americans on the ground, so long as they are not mistaken for enemy by the friendly pilots.

—About the same time, a light artillery battery of the 2nd Division firing from positions on the outskirts of Elsenborn takes a flurry of enemy shell fire. The large pyramidal tent sheltering the battery kitchen is cut loose from its moorings, and the wind sweeps it away. The supply and communications sergeants are hit by shell fragments.

In the German camp, Christmas brings as much unhappiness and danger to the *Landser* as to the Americans and considerably less food and passing cheer.

The Germans at the front dwell underground just as does their enemy across the line. They must make do with clothing and footwear even less suitable to winter conditions and eagerly search for parts of uniforms and shoes taken from dead Americans, prisoners of war, or discarded on the killing grounds. Their bases are in towns and villages that now resemble ruined, ice-covered charnel houses.

The *Landser* of the five divisions in General Hitzfeld's 67th Corps receive less food and fewer mail deliveries. These divisions now have only second-level priority in the German Army Group B scheme of things. The precious "Otto" (gasoline and diesel fuel) can not be wasted bringing Christmas dinners and good cheer from home to their troops. Their *Landser* will make do with routine rations and, if they are lucky, an extra cup of the blessed, reality-changing *Schnapps*. One remembers that their Christmas treat is to be fed their first meal in three days (probably bread and stew washed down with *Schnapps*). "A sad Christmas," he remembers.

General Denkert's 3rd *Panzergrenadier* Division infantry is holed up on the western edge of the Rocheratherwald. Early on Christmas, the American howitzers begin to pound and pound their foxholes and dugouts, making movement almost impossible. They take casualties—deaths and wounds—and endure a day with little food and no Christmas spirit at all.

Muffled sounds of revelry and song drifting across no man's land from the German camp are greeted with artillery strikes if the American gunners can locate the source. Outposts of the 1st Division northwest of Büllingen, for example, detect music—"voice and instrument"—from a gathering of Germans outside the town. Division artillery puts paid to the party with a murderous time-on-target barrage.

A *Landser* up front sits in his foxhole reading an old letter from his mother. "I pulled a shelter half over my foxhole and lit a candle stump. I shoved my bayonet into the side of my foxhole and stuck the lit candle on the handle. 'My dear son,' my mother wrote. 'We are very sad that you could not spend Christmas with us this year. The New Year is at the door—and we hope.'" His reverie is interrupted by an exploding mortar bomb nearby, which blows out the candle.

Part 5: *Der Führer* Wills It

A few days after Christmas—December 28th, to be precise—General Hitzfeld's 67th Corps make their move to push in the nose of the Gerow line along a curving front that extends east of Elsenborn, west of Wirtzfeld, and northwest of Büllingen. General Denkert's third large and semiarmored *Panzergrenadier* Division was to play the *Schwerpunkt* role in this operation. But Denkert's men and machines have departed.

Colonel Peter Körte's 246th *VGD* (Part 3), which has replaced the 3rd *PzGD*, is in no condition to *schwerpunkt* anything.

Major General Gerhard Engle's 12th *VGD Grenadiers* and *Füsiliers* on the left will march with Körte's *Grenadiers* this day against the Gerow line. The two German powers are supported by 105 and 150mm howitzers of their artillery regiments, ample mortars, artillery and rocket-throwing battalions of 67th Corps and *Luftwaffe* antiaircraft batteries armed with high-velocity 88mm diameter guns firing in a ground mode. And on the right flank, General Viebig's 277th *VGD* will make a demonstration, as soldiers say.

Hitzfeld's staff, if not the 67th Corps leader himself, and Körte and Engle must surely know their soldiers are setting forth on a hopeless mission that will cost many their lives. But in the way of *das Heer*, they go on with it, faithful to orders that no longer have much relevance.

The German commanders try to give their *Landser* assistance at the start line by ordering up a powerful artillery-rocket-mortar attack on the infantry and artillery of the three U.S. divisions. An artillery observer on the foxhole line with Lieutenant Colonel Peters' 2nd Battalion, 393rd Infantry, on the Rodelhöhe southeast of Elsenborn arrives well before dawn at his position next to a heavy machine gun nest. The rifle fighters and machine gunners up front seem anxious, he notices. They are expecting the Germans in some form this day. A football field away and down the slope is a large patch of woods where enemy soldiers (Körte's men) seem to be present. The 2nd Battalion fighters let fly streams of machine gun and automatic rifle bullets in their direction.

Suddenly, muffled by the wind comes the familiar whoosh and whine of artillery shells: Some are the 6-inch diameter medium rounds that spread death and destruction wherever they hit. The artillery observer hears screams around him.

"(The Germans) must think they are going to blow us off this hill," shouts the "F" Company first sergeant. The pummelling is intense but short. However, when it stops, the 246 *VG* soldiers in and behind the woods do not move. Colonel Peters' men don't know what the reason is, but being pessimists (an occupational necessity in the infantry) they think the worst.

At 7:30 a.m. under grey skies heavy with incipient snow, more hostile artillery fire saturates the Rodelhöhe with explosive steel blackening the fresh snow. "If there were hundreds (of rounds) in the first shelling, there were thousands this time...no man in the sector ever thought he would live to see another day," the artillery FO later wrote, no doubt exaggerating for effect. ("Thousands of rounds" is a powerful lot.) He manages to reach his battalion by radio with a request for all the medium (155mm) shells they can put down on the map coordinates he names (in code). "The light artilleries (105mm battalions) had the same idea."

The 99th guns now go to work in earnest, dropping a curtain of shells across all the space Colonel Körte's soldiers must traverse this morning. Heavy mortars join the shoot. Once again, the American artillery and mortars put paid to the enemy action. Patrols go out to find many dead *Landser* lying in the shell-pocked snow and nearly as many wounded or wanting to surrender. They tell the 99th's POW interrogation team that they were promised *Sturmgeschütze* (assault guns) to work with them but none appeared.

On the left Lieutenant Colonel Douglas' 1st Battalion, 394th, is in front of the 246th *VGD's* attack also. A 394th machine gunner recalled how unprepared for combat the young Germans appeared to be. "(They wore) grey overcoats with huge packs on their backs." They walk in file down a hedgerow toward Douglas' picket line. When they reach the end of the row, smoky orange explosions swallow them up, and their brave but sad advance comes to a halt.

General Engle (12th *VGD*) has chosen his 48th Regiment to march upon the 2nd Division defensive line at its most southern point outside Wirtzfeld where the 38th Infantry is located. The pre-attack barrage on the 2nd Division reaches beyond the infantry's lines and outposts to Berg and Nidrum north of Lac de Bütgenbach.

The black sky is slowly beginning to grey with streaks of dawn light when a battalion of *Grenadiers* moves from Wirtzfeld to the high ground on the right flank of the 38th position, a mile east of Berg. Not encumbered by heavy pack rolls, wearing white capes, armed with machine pistols, assault rifles, and machine guns a small force worms its way through the outposts. They occupy the hill as the outnumbered 2nd Division pickets move west toward their main line.

Once again the American artillery frustrates the attacking German infantry. The hill and all to the east of it on up to the gates of Wirtzfeld are racked with shell fire, driving the vanguard of Engle's infantry off the hill and forcing the follow-on companies to go to ground. By early afternoon Robertson's 38th Infantrymen have returned to their outposts, this time with reinforcements.

South of the hill is Company "L" of Colonel Corley's 3rd Battalion, 26th Infantry, and on its flank other companies of the regiment. Its sector is more narrow than during the running battle with *Hitlerjugend* a week before. Yet so severely has the regiment been taken down by these battles that all three battalions are on the line.

Shortly before dawn, apparently in sync with the barrages against the 99th and 2nd divisions, German 105 and 150 artillery pieces, 88mm long guns, and *Werfer* tubes go into action against the 26th. Colonel Seitz's soldiers are deep in the frozen earth in roofed over foxholes. The moans, whistles, and shrieks of the arriving rockets, howitzer rounds, and high-velocity gun shells fright the souls of even the few surviving old soldiers up front but harm them little.

When the last of the fiery orange explosions and waves of smoke blow away, the pre-dawn blackness closes over the killing ground once again. In the darkness, a light battalion—four hundred or so white-clad *Füsiliers*—leave Büllingen and move northwest along the single railroad track toward Bütgenbach. ((Narrative IX, Part 2) The artillerymen of the 1st Division are covering every square yard of ground south and east of the Lac de Bütgenbach, including the ground being traversed by the *Füsiliers*. One intense pounding about dawn is sufficient to ruin their march against the 26th Infantry. All but a few of the *Füsiliers* retreat in disorder south over the hilly, snow-covered fields toward Büllingen.

One company and some combat engineers with them in the vanguard has reached the 1st Division lines by means of a shallow depression between two hills. But they are boxed in and remain immobile and impotent throughout the day. After dark, they manage to escape the 26th's patrols hunting them down and get back to Büllingen.

They take with them the last embers of what two weeks previous were the flaming hopes of Adolph Hitler that Sepp Dietrich's powerful 6th Army would pace the *Wehrmacht's* march to the River Meuse and beyond by storming out of the borderland forests and crossing the Elsenborn high plateau to the Hohes Venn, Malmedy, Spa, Eupen, Verviers, and the banks of the Meuse. All German military operations fronting Gerow's 5th Corps line at Kalterherberg-Elsenborn-Bütgenbach will henceforth be defensive only.

By the end of December, the focus of decisive action in the Ardennes-Eifel region has shifted far to the west and south. It is becoming apparent to the professionals of Army Group B (Model) as well as those at *Ob-West* (von Rundstedt) headquarters near the War Lord's *Alderhorst* that the game is up in the Ardennes-Eifel.

—General Patton's 3rd Army is pushing north across the waist of the pyramidal breakthrough area.

—Major General Joe Collins' 7th Corps is preparing a powerful offensive from Marche, Belgium to meet Patton.

—General *der Panzertruppen* Hasso von Manteuffel's 5th *Panzer* Army has failed to get the Americans out of the critical communication center of Bastogne or to stop up the supply routes into the city.

—St. Vith has been taken by Manteuffel. However, the aggressive

SS Panzer divisions (1st, 2nd, 9th), have been unable to reach through the American defenses at Trois Ponts and Mahay, Belgium, to gain the Meuse River.

—The 30th British Corps, the most formidable in the British Army, has massed its armor on the west side of the Meuse from Masstricht, Holland to Namur, Belgium.*

—And to administer the *coup de grâce* to German hopes, the Allied *Jaboes*, medium bombers, and heavy bombers are out in all their destructive force and power.

The senior field commanders of the *Riesenanschlag*, Model, Manteuffel, Dietrich and their staffs are even losing confidence that the "small solution" should be tried. This is the alternative plan to seize space on the east bank of the Meuse River behind Hodges' 1st Army with the intention of surrounding and devouring this army. It was proposed to Hitler during the planning period for *Wacht am Rhein* in November. (Volume 1, p. 29) The German field commanders are fixing their attention instead on extricating their legions from the winter wasteland and charnel house that the Ardennes-Eifel is becoming for their troops.

General Manteuffel, who only a week before was a leading advocate of the "small solution," asks Hitler for permission to begin a general withdrawal of his 5th *Panzer* Army. Permission is refused. At Christmas the irrepressible Sepp Dietrich, commander of 6th *SS Panzer* Army, told a visitor to his HQ at Meyerode north of St. Vith that his armored divisions would soon push through to the Meuse at Huy, then wheel north. A week later his euphoria is no more. The 2nd *SS Panzer* Division has been driven from Manhay, a defining defeat for Dietrich. After the war, he will tell his U.S. Army interrogators, "I didn't think it was possible to get through. As far as I was concerned, the offensive was completely stalled."

Von Rundstedt, supposedly the grand commander of the Ardennes-Eifel Counteroffensive, left the train long before. "I wanted to stop (it) at an early stage when it was plain that it could not attain its aim..." he told an interviewer after the war.

No matter (again). Adolph Hitler holds fast to his unshakable faith in a principle that has served him well in his rise to supreme power in Germany and all of Europe from the Bay of Biscay to the gates of Moscow: Regardless of the odds, victory goes to the adversary whose will to win is most unbending. He refuses to recognize that lengthening

---

* See the Appendices, pps. 407-410 for a bare-bones chronicle of the fighting in the Ardennes outside of the areas covered by our ten Narratives.

shadows of disaster are falling across his three armies in the Ardennes-Eifel. He will not give way there. He orders his field commanders to destroy Collins' 7th Corps south of Marche and capture Bastogne as well, thus eliminating a base for Patton's operations in the south. The conditions for more aggressive action will then be ripe. These are fantasies.

Even Dietrich, the *Altekampfer*, recognizes how remote from reality his *Führer* has become. He tells Albert Speer, who pays him a visit on New Year's eve, that Bastogne can not be taken. The Americans are not as Hitler imagines, not pushovers, not Italians. They are "tough opponents, good as our own men....Besides our supply routes have been cut."

The orders for renewed aggressiveness in the Ardennes-Eifel are not all. Hitler has additional plans that he believes will ease the badgering and bedeviling his troops are being subjected to everywhere in the Ardennes breakthrough area. He will open another front. He will go forward with a second attack (code name *Nordwind*) on New Year's eve against Lieutenant General Jacob Devers' dangerously spread out 6th Army Group on the Upper Rhine.

And on New Year's day the *Luftwaffe* will smother the American and British airfields in Belgium, France (Metz), and Holland with attacks by one thousand and three hundred aircraft. The purpose of this extraordinary *Luftflotteschlag* whose code name is *Bodenplatte*, is to destroy on the ground a goodly part of the Allied fighter-bombers and medium bombers that are swarming over the killing grounds, machine gunning, rocketing, and bombing every German thing that moves and much that doesn't.

On December 28 the *Führer* meets at the Alderhorst with von Rundstedt and the commanders who will lead the *Nordwind* operation. Shaky on his feet, his bomb-damaged arm scarcely usable, hollow eyed, with the look of doom about him, the War Lord nevertheless retains enough of his old characteristic fire, brimstone, and mesmerizing aura of power to impress the generals and colonels (all save one, that is, von Rundstedt).

Hitler tells the assembly that the *Wehrmacht* must not go on the defensive. "Only the offensive will enable us to once more give a successful turn to the war in the West." The enemy is weakest in the Alsace area (Devers' sector). An attack there will force the Allied high command to draw power from the Ardennes, thus setting the stage for a renewed drive to the Meuse.

Not a foolish plan but like *Wacht am Rhein* to be carried out by forces inadequate to the mission. Furthermore, the Americans know all about what is coming and are prepared to parry it. This time their intelligence services have done their job. Just as important, Devers' headquarters instructs the U.S. 7th Army "to be prepared to yield ground rather than endanger the integrity of its forces." This gives the commanders on the ground leeway to use their judgment in responding to the German threat, even if it means drawing back a few miles.

In *Wacht am Rhein*, a massive *Luftwaffe* attack on Allied air fields was to be an important element of the surprise strike of the *Wehrmacht* December 16, *Null Tag*. A pre-dawn attack on the U.S. and British tactical air force airdromes in Belgium and the Netherlands was to disable these two dangerous powers for at least the first critical week of the German ground attack in the Ardennes-Eifel. As with other important parts of *Wacht am Rhein*, it didn't happen. Ironically, the "Hitler weather" that the War Lord desired (and got) forced his *Reichsmarshal* and *Luftwaffe* chief, Hermann Goering, to cancel the strike at the Allied bases. The plan now (late December) has been revived, much to the anger and frustration of the senior *Luftwaffe* commanders: too late, too risky, too potentially wasteful of their precious machines and their even more precious pilots.

OKW invests eight divisions in *Nordwind*, the assault on U.S. 7th Army and French 1st Army[*] in Alsace. After nearly a month of icy combat, many days of it in driving snow, the Germans gain twenty miles of unimportant ground, kill and wound a few thousand Allied troops, and come near to retaking the city of Strasbourg, France on the Upper Rhine. But the operation drains scarcely any American power from the big war in the Ardennes-Eifel. And this sideshow costs the eight German divisions twenty-five thousand dead, wounded, and missing.

As to *Bodenplatte*, the young *Luftwaffe* pilots once again show extraordinary courage in the presence of the most dreadful hazards. They must come in low to avoid being detected by Allied radar and picket aircraft roaming the dawn skies. The majority are ill-trained youngsters whose lack of flying skill is supposed to be compensated for by their *esprit*, not to say foolhardiness.

Their bombs, machine guns, and rockets do damage at the seventeen Allied air bases in the Netherlands, Belgium, and France that they

---

[*] Both U.S. 7th and French 1st armies, which made up the U.S. 6th Army Group, were operating under severe handicaps when *OKW* initiated *Nordwind* on New Year's Day, 1945. U.S. 7th had given up divisions to Patton's 3rd Army and also was forced to send contingents of new divisions coming in straight to the front as replacements either in Alsace or the Ardennes. French 1st consisted mainly of French colonial regiments that were far below authorized strength. Furthermore, they presented "a serious morale problem," because they lacked qualified officers. (Source: 7th U.S. Army <u>Report of Operations</u>, pages 496, 509.)

target. A close student of the air war in the Ardennes wrote that the German pilots destroyed "at least" three hundred Allied aircraft on the ground and another seventy in the air. A proud bag for one day's shooting.

However, the *Luftwaffe* pays in precious coin for this success: Three hundred aircraft lost (eighty-five of these due to *Luftwaffe* anti-aircraft crews who mistake them for *Jaboes*). More devastating is the loss of pilots: two hundred and fifty killed, missing, and injured. Thus, close to 30 percent of the men and machines that have raided the Allied air fields this climactic air war day, January 1, 1945, are lost to Hitler's cause and are irreplaceable at this stage of the war. The American and British aircraft destroyed on the ground are easily replaced, however. Nor is the Allied loss of pilots even a third that of their enemy.[*]

With *Bodenplatte* and *Nordwind*, Hitler has once again wasted precious assets to no purpose.[**]

---

[*] The quotation and loss numbers are from Parker, pps. 447-448. Documentation, this narrative.

[**] For the record, *Nordwind* did cause the long-suffering General Eisenhower another heartburn over the attitude of his allies, this time the French. He intended to order a tactical withdrawal from Strasbourg on the Rhine to the edge of the Vosges Mountains. When the Provisional President of the French Republic, General Charles de Gaulle, and his defense minister learned of the plan, they protested vehemently. De Gaulle even threatened to remove French forces from Eisenhower's command unless the latter reconsidered and kept enough fighting soldiers in the city to defend it. Ike made plain to *le Grand General* how totally the French Army was dependent on the U.S. Army for every bullet its soldiers fired and every boot they wore. Having used the stick, the Supreme Commander then extended a carrot, offering a compromise de Gaulle accepted grudgingly.

A week after the start of *Nordwind* and the flap with de Gaulle over Strasbourg, Ike's other ally, British Field Marshal Bernard Law Montgomery, struck again. He held a press conference eagerly attended by what seemed to be every British correspondent on the continent. In a long, schoolmasterish discourse on the Ardennes-Eifel campaign, Monty impressed his audience with the absolutely decisive role he as a leader and British troops as a resource played in overcoming the attacking Germans. The British press was delighted, as delighted as the American commanders were appalled and angry, especially General Bradley.

A weary Eisenhower and no doubt amused Churchill eventually put matters right, aided by a contrite and apologetic Field Marshal and a stirring speech by the Prime Minister in the House of Commons, who gave full credit to the Americans for turning back the *Wehrmacht*. "Their greatest battle of the war." (Quoted in John Eisenhower, Bitter Woods, p. 392. Documentation, Volume 1.) However, during the first week of January 1945, Eisenhower must have muttered at least once, "With allies like de Gaulle and Montgomery, who needs enemies like Hitler."

The Americans at Elsenborn take scant notice of these two anticlimactic operations. Allied airdromes in Belgium that are targets of the raiders are well west of a line Liege-Aachen or far to the north in Holland. However, on New Year's day at first light, aircraft of at least one *Jagdgeschwander* (fighter squadron) almost certainly passed over the Elsenborn ridge on an attack path aimed at a base near Asch, Belgium.

Operation *Nordwind* has made no impression whatsoever on them. In fact, isn't even known by the men up front and those busy with their tasks in the rear until they read about it in a week-old <u>Stars and Stripes</u>. In an oblique way, however, *Nordwind* may have saved the four U.S. divisions holding the north shoulder of the Bulge and all of their supporting arms and units from even more grief.

The *Führer's* pursuit of this diversionary action in Alsace has used up eight irreplaceable *Wehrmacht* divisions that might have made a decisive difference in the 6th *SS* Army operations in the Elsenborn-Bütgenbach area during the critical days, December 19 to 24. Or if used in an attack by 15th Army toward Aachen, they might have enabled this army to flank the Americans on the north. Monty's nervousness over opening escape routes (Part 2) can be attributed to his concerns that something like this might happen. Hitler instead chose to pursue the ephemeral *Nordwind* in Alsace, nearly two hundred airline miles to the southeast.

Part 6: The Most Dangerous Game

As we know after December 28, General Gerow's 5th Corps divisions are defending a sector that has lost its priority in the plans and strategies of staffs in both warring camps. However, the hazards we have seen that haunt the waking and sleeping hours of the men in the holes up front are no less for that.

"Going on patrol" is among the ultimate tests of the rifleman's willingness to put his life at awful risk, not occasionally, as happens when his regiment is making a serious attack on the enemy, but again and again for the entire time his company is in a defensive position, as here along the Elsenborn high plateau.

Among the twelve infantry regiments defending the north shoulder in December and January, recon patrols become something of a deadly game that the riflemen, machine gunners, forward observers, medics play because they are ordered to and a few welcome in order to break the monotony of a static front, even though it may cost them their lives.

A reconnaissance patrol seldom exceeds fifteen soldiers including an officer. They slip past their outposts usually in darkest night, thread their way through friendly mine fields into no man's land, pick their way through the enemy minefield, and enter upon his outpost line.

The purpose of the patrol is to reconnoiter, ascertain where the enemy has placed his main defenses, what he appears to be up to (digging in, withdrawing men, bringing more in, etc.). Sometimes the mission is simple enough: seize a German or two, silence him with a blow or a gag, drag him back to your lines for interrogating.

To step out on patrol in the raven night, two feet or more of snow underfoot, shivering cold all round, harrowed by fear, is an experience only those who have endured it can describe.

— "We continued toward the German lines for about another five hundred yards before making contact (with the enemy). We surprised two German soldiers at an outpost....I had the sergeant give me cover while I jumped them with my carbine. Their eyes popped wide open, wondering where the hell I came from."

— "The time you had to wait before patrol duty was very hard on the nerves....I was on several patrols with instructions to bring back prisoners. Once or twice we just went out and hid until morning, then came back in." (AN: To avoid this understandable lapse in discipline, battalion commanders of the 99th Division begin requiring recon patrols to be made up of men and officers from different companies.)

— "...we made a right turn and seemed to be following a fence running parallel to the German lines. It was one of those clear, brittle cold nights when sound carried easily through the air and it seemed to me that the crunch of our boots in the snow must be heard for miles. Suddenly we heard a command barked out in German, 'Kommen sie raus.' (AN: 'Come out of there,' spoken by one of the Americans on the patrol to a scared *Landser* cowering in his foxhole. 'Kommst du raus' might have produced better results.) All up and down the fence line, I heard the sharp metallic click...of safeties being snapped off on the weapons of our patrol....I waited for the expected tongue of flame from a German machine gun opening up on us."

— "A squad of us was sent out to locate a unit that disappeared into a wooded ravine....We came down (another) ravine into a heavy wooded area at the bottom. Once we got down the hill, the Germans in the woods opened fire on us with mortars and machine guns. The lieutenant caught a direct mortar round, killing him instantly. They slaughtered us, killed all but me and one other guy. We laid low, playing dead, then slowly worked our way to the top of the hill."

— "(The sergeant) was making up a twelve-man patrol....I would take up the rear as the get-away man to provide fire cover (for the patrol) while returning....The ice on the trees and bushes of the hedgerows on either side of the lane (into the enemy position) rattled in the wind, helping to conceal our approach and whispered commands. ...Suddenly I sensed that I was all alone. Get-away man indeed. Somebody hadn't passed the word (to me to pull back). Voices sounded from the German position about fifty yards away. Then a burp gun (*Maschinenpistole*) opened up, followed by the heavier pounding of a machine gun." [*]

Even these recollections do not capture all of the deadly inevitability and feeling of resignation and fatalism that blackens the spirit of an up-front soldier as he steps out on a patrol. Nor do these stories reveal all of the special hazards of this most dangerous game.

<u>Mines</u>, for example. Just as the Americans do, the Germans bury antipersonnel mines in the earth beneath the snow in front of their outposts, mostly *Schrapnellminen*, Bouncing Bettys, as they are called by the Americans. A patrolling soldier who steps on the top-side igniter sets off the mine. It leaps four or five feet into the air, exploding with a flash and a roar and spraying shrapnel (small steel balls) at bullet-force in all directions. The explosion not only kills and maims but also alerts enemy pickets that a hostile patrol is trying to come through.

<u>Camouflage</u>: When the infantrymen of the U.S. divisions occupying the high plateau established themselves (December 18-21), a general thaw in the borderland country melted the snow cover to patches. When the cold returned and the snow started in earnest, about December 22, however, their olive drab overcoats, jackets, and pants made excellent targets against the white background, especially when illuminated by enemy flares and star shells. Once again the fighting men and their service companies in the rear have to improvise. Sheets, white table cloths, even bolts of muslin are stripped from Belgian homes and sent forward to be fashioned into capes and helmet covers. They are made to serve, although awkwardly. However, the muslin won't do, as some 1st Division men discover. It wicks up moisture that promptly freezes, turning the camouflage robe into cardboard.

<u>Frozen weapons</u>: Knives, Browning Automatic Rifles, light (.30 caliber) machine guns, M-1 rifles, carbines, tommy guns and grease guns stolen or bartered from troops equipped with them, even *Maschinenpistolen* and *Sturmgewehr*, fast-firing and accurate, taken from prisoners or the dead, and hand grenades are weapons of choice when going patrolling. However, when the temperature drops below freezing, as it

---

[*] The five patrols described took place on the front of the 99th Division in the period December 20 to January 20, 1944-45. Sources of quotes may be found in the Documentation for this narrative.

almost always does on the hilly plains below the Elsenborn-Bütgenbach heights, the firing mechanism of some weapons tends to lock if moisture has been allowed to accumulate there. What is most distressing, a weapon that shoots on the journey out may be frozen up when the enemy is met with or on the way back when fire is needed to discourage pursuit.

Night lights: Among the multiple terrors of patrolling at night is the threat to the soldiers silently filing across the snow toward the enemy outposts that the dreaded pop-hiss of a flare will sound and the sky overhead suddenly glow with garish light. The patrollers can only stop dead in their tracks, praying the bed sheets covering their layers of clothing will blend them into the snow. But they can not hide their shadows. Inevitably the machine gun fire comes rattling at them and the mortar bombs explode nearby.

Unrelieved: Every night during the 5th Corps occupation of the plateau, the patrols slip past their outposts, through the mine fields, and into the German positions in the Bütgenbacher Heck; in front of Büllingen and Wirtzfeld; on the wide, flat slopes and low-lying hills east of Elsenborn; in the forests east of Kalterherberg.

Occasionally, as in the 99th Division sector on the night of January 10, a patrol simply vanishes. The ten men who go out are killed or captured. However, so far as their comrades back at the rifle company are concerned, they have walked off the edge of the earth. Few recon patrols vanish totally as this one has. Most of the patrollers return to slide into their foxholes and toss down shots of whiskey (if a company officer has been generous with his liquor ration) and smoke cigarettes. They also try to put out of their heads the certain knowledge that the day after tomorrow or the day after that or before a week has passed or soon again anyway, the familiar call will come down from their company's forward command post nearby, "Three men from first squad, three from third..."

With the New Year (1945), the commanders of fighting troops holding the high ground at Kalterherberg, Elsenborn, Berg, Bütgenbach, Weywertz know the time is coming soon when they will be ordered to start them driving east and south to push Hitzfeld's 67th Corps from the borderland hills and woods.

General Lauer moves his headquarters from Camp Elsenborn to a large manor house, Dom Ruhrhof near Sourbrodt, Belgium. General Andrus' 1st Division forward command post also is located in this village. Dom Ruhrhof makes for considerably more pleasant surroundings than does the ugly, drafty, inconvenient barracks of Camp Elsenborn. Walter Robertson and his 2nd Division CP stay at the camp, however.

The ranks of the three divisions continue to fill up with replacements, newly minted riflemen who departed embarkation camps in the States after the *Wehrmacht's* Ardennes counteroffensive began and men culled from various services—Army Air Force ground troops, surplus antiaircraft gun crews, Quartermaster depot workers, and so forth—converted to infantrymen by a few weeks of drill and target practice and sent forward. A thin stream of the recovered wounded and victims of exposure also flows back.

Field Marshal Montgomery's estimate that Gerow's four divisions are short a total of seven thousand men (Part 2) is about half accurate. From December 25 to the end of January, the 99th Division will alone absorb 4,300 new officers and men and hospital returnees. Most are sent into the nine infantry battalions. The 2nd Division's replacement numbers are close to this. When the 1st Division's three regiments moved into position south of Bütgenbach, the rifle companies already were down to scarcely 100 soldiers each (from 196). The vicious tank-infantry-artillery brawling there eliminated most of those in the 26th Infantry Regiment rifle companies.

Each division has its routines for trying to give the new men and boys a minimal amount of preparation for the dreadful things they will soon experience. The 2nd establishes training programs in the rear operated by no-nonsense veterans from the up-front class who impress upon them that mistakes bring death. The static front in late December and part of January makes this possible.

In the 1st Division, patrols (above) run by veterans are made to serve as a training exercise: They give the many new riflemen coming into the regiment a taste of the teamwork and terror of combat. "A deadly training ground for our high percentage of new men," as the 18th Regiment's monthly report for December puts it.

Time on the Elsenborn high plateau also enables the armor commanders and the 1st Army supply depots to improve their machines and guns. The tank battalion with the 2nd Division converts its Shermans to a model with better suspension, wider tracks, and a long gun that (at last) is capable of holing all but the thickest enemy armor.

The antitank battalion with the 2nd Division that is armed with towed 3-inch (diameter) long guns and has sustained serious losses in the borderland and town fighting of December 16-20 is sent to an armor depot near Verviers, Belgium. Here its men dispose of the wheeled guns and towing vehicles (halftracks) and acquire M-18 tracked tank destroying machines ("gun motor carriages" they are called). Each is armed with a 76mm high-velocity gun and is fast on its treads. A mammoth improvement over their wheeled 3-inchers.

The attacks against the 99th Division in the first thirty-six hours of the *Wehrmacht's* counteroffensive; the often chaotic fall-back from the borderland woods and towns; the desperate attempt to get new positions established on the Elsenborn heights, pressing into service the battered survivors of all this bloodletting—all have taken their toll on the 99th's field commanders:

The major who commanded the 2nd Battalion of MacKenzie's 395th Infantry and refused to return his men to the Monschauwald the night of December 18 (Narrative VIII, Part 5) sends himself to the hospital.

The lieutenant colonel who became a burden to his 2nd Battalion, 394th headquarter's officers in the retreat from the Todeswald (Volume 1, Narrative III, Part 1) is relieved by Brigadier General Hugh Mayberry, Lauer's second in command, but only after the colonel's officers insist it be done.

Lieutenant Colonel Jack Allen (3rd Battalion, 393rd) and newly promoted Lieutenant Colonel Matt Legler (1st Battalion, 393rd) will soon be gone, both having suffered serious wounds.

By mid-February, Lieutenant Colonel Jean D. Scott, commander of the 393rd Infantry, Colonel Don Riley of the 394th, and Colonel Alex J. MacKenzie will also have departed their commands. Riley and MacKenzie have had enough; Scott is reassigned in the division. War is a brutal business even for the field commanders who run things and are seldom in the gunsights of the enemy's infantry.

On January 3, 1945 Field Marshal Montgomery starts the drive from the north side of the Ardennes to herd the Germans east and meet with Patton's 3rd Army coming from the south across the waist of the German-occupied area. (Part 2)

Montgomery orders Collins to start attacking southeast from the line Dinant-Marche, Belgium. General Ridgeway's 18th Airborne Corps is soon to follow. Gerow's four infantry divisions on the high plateau are to stand fast but drive large combat patrols into the German positions opposite them up to and even behind the main line of resistance.

"Combat patrols" are different in size, kind, and purpose from the deadly night-time prowls into the enemy positions described above. They usually consist of at least one platoon of riflemen, led by one or more lieutenants. They take with them the irreplaceable medics, light machine gun and mortar sections, an artillery forward observer and his radioman. To communicate with the battalion commander's forward command post, the patrol leader brings along a soldier carrying a radio.

These patrols also are backed by howitzer batteries and mortar sections (81mm, sometimes 4.2-inch) off to the west. The crews on these guns are clued into the patrol's mission and area of operation, and prepared on radio or telephone order to deliver explosive steel, phosphorous, smoke as needed to help the struggling infantry do their mission. Sometimes they succeed.

Most of these fighting patrols go out in daylight or just before dawn. Their purpose is to provoke, harass, and delude the Germans, as well as to gain information on their defenses. As the 5th Corps directive to the division commanders puts it, "to lead the enemy to believe an attack in force is underway or in prospect."[*]

The soldiers of a combat patrol are engaged in a small-scale attack on the enemy but without either the means or the staying power to follow through and without strong friendly powers on either flank. Men inevitably die, are wounded, taken prisoner, or lost for all time on these patrols; whether what is gained compensates for these losses is for soldiers to debate. For the divisions in Gerow's command, the question is irrelevant to the business at hand. Sending large fighting patrols at General Hitzfeld's lines to create havoc and uncertainty is the order of the day in the first weeks of January.

On January 3 soldiers of 2nd Battalion, 394th Infantry, are occupying foxholes and dugouts to the west of the regiment's main line of resistance on the forward slope of the Elsenborn crest northeast of the Rodelhöhe. Their new commander, Major Robert L. Kriz, receives an order to march three heavied-up rifle platoons into the woods north of Rocherath to harass *Grenadiers* of General Viebig's 277th *VGD*, who are well dug in there. The 277th may be ineffectual on the offense. Not so on the defense: Its men and boys are well rooted in the forest in many hidden places.

Each rifle company of the 2nd Battalion furnishes one platoon for the action. Each platoon (thirty to thirty-six soldiers) is led by an officer and includes a light machine gunner, a light mortar, an artillery forward observer team, medical aid men, a radio operator.

The hilly fields, hedgerows, and brush land west of the forest are obliterated by two and three feet of snow, and the icy air makes movement

---

[*] This rather superficial description of infantry patrolling is not meant to imply that recon patrols do not get into some ferocious shooting matches, albeit on a small scale. Or that combat (fighting) patrols do not bring back prisoners and information in addition to roughing up the enemy. Nor is it meant to imply that only infantrymen and their helpers go out on these missions. Dismounted cavalrymen, battalion and regimental special troops, even combat engineers, for example, can be found playing this most dangerous game as well. And especially aggressive commanders may even order out their HQ and other behind-the-line troops on occasion just to give them an idea of what the mud soldiers up front go through all the time.

painful as the three platoons mush past their battalion's outposts shortly after dawn January 3. The lead platoon (from "E" Company) takes two casualties right at the start from a sudden flurry of artillery shells they believe has been fired by American howitzers shooting toward the woods. The platoon's principal sergeant is one of them. No matter. They must be on their way. In three files the soldiers move east, cross a creek frozen hard to its bottom and obscured by snow, and fan out toward the woods (Rocheratherwald).

The men wading through the snow are easily seen by the enemy outposts on the edge of the woods. When the lead squad reaches a point in the fields about fifty yards from the woods, two machine guns strike from right and left, forcing the men to burrow into the snow. Several slither on their bellies toward the woods line to direct fire from their mortar, automatic rifles, and light machine gun at the unseen Germans.

Their weapons fail: ice in the firing chambers, wet mortar bomb propellants. They lie shivering and wondering what next. Suddenly a young soldier gets to his feet and motions his companions forward. At the start of this patrol, he "expressed a growing feeling of doom and misery," remembered a companion. He is bounced to the snow by a rush of bullet fire, and death snatches him up.

On a hill a hundred yards to the west, the "E" Company executive officer, who is leading the patrol, orders the artillery observer team travelling with him to saturate the forest to the front with 105mm shells. They soon come in. The woods flash and smoke with explosive rounds hitting high in the branches. However, the Germans are deep in their logged-over holes. The artillery attack matters little. It does, however, goad the Germans into retaliating.

The three squads of the combat patrol spread around in the snow on the fields west of the forest are soon bracketed by enemy 105mm artillery and mortar rounds coming down with muffled whumps and crashes in the deep snow. Nor does the bullet fire from the woods slacken.

The "E" Company exec passes the word among his three squads to withdraw from the ring of fire and stand fast while he tries to devise a different tactic for getting into the woods. As his men execute the move, crawling, crab walking, running, and flopping, and running again, always immersed in snow, to a safer position, the enemy machine gunners send streams of bullet fire at them. And to their shock and dismay, some of it is coming from their backs, from the direction where their outposts are located. A dozen or so *Grenadiers* have moved out of the woods and found positions to strike the patrol from its rear.

The patrol leader radios to Kriz standing by in his forward command dugout north of the Rodelhöhe to obtain permission to bring his survivors back. The major grants it. He has little alternative. Four hours after coming out of their lines early that morning, the "E" Company men move west through the deep snow of a ravine amidst the pop-pop-popping of rifles and the bur-rurp-ping of machine pistols and the vicious sawing of *Maschinengewehre*. All reach safety except one young rifleman at the rear of the column. He is hit with bullet fire, sinks into the snow, and is never seen again dead or alive.

Major Kriz's second patrol of the day ("F" Company soldiers) reach the woods but is immediately attacked from all sides and must withdraw. The third ("G" Company soldiers) have great success, if the prisoners and reports they return with are any indication. Reaching the dark Rocheratherwald, they rampage through a company of *Grenadiers* whom they surprise, killing some, bagging others. When the mayhem grows intolerable, the patrol leader signals for artillery rounds straight down on the scene. The patrol brings out five of their wounded from the woods; leaves two behind who are too badly injured to move; captures thirteen *Landser*; claims to have left thirty-five more dead in the forest. Probably an exaggeration, but the "G" Company men are entitled.

The 2nd Battalion infantry soldiers on these patrols are largely newcomers. It is the same battalion that was left behind in the Todeswald the day after *Null Tag*, made a confused and costly withdrawal, fought in German-held Mürringen, and took tragic losses under American artillery fire on the way to Krinkelt. (Volume 1, Narrative V, Part 6)

However, in the infantry every day is a new day for fighting and dying. And the soldiers of the battalion, newcomers and veterans alike, have just experienced one of them. Two men have been killed, one dies later of wounds as a prisoner of the Germans, nine have been wounded. Small toll for such a treacherous piece of work (except to the dead and wounded).

South of this action at the same time, January 3, the 2nd and 1st divisions also send forth large combat patrols at the 89th *Volksgrenadier* and 3rd *Fallschirmjäger* divisions.

Company "G" of Colonel Norris' 2nd Battalion, 38th Infantry makes a raid on German-held Wirtzfeld with a seventy-man patrol from the 2nd Battalion. They take along light mortars, light machine guns, the usual SCR 300, an artillery forward observer team, medics. Light field artillery, tank, and tank destroyer batteries and platoons have been alerted to deliver shell fire on order. This large fighting group is expected "to drive into the enemy outpost line, fix the enemy main line of resistance, secure information of enemy strength and positions."

At 7:15 a.m. in the same harrowing cold and deep snow that afflicts the 99th's men a few miles to the north, the reinforced rifle squads depart their lines along the northern shore of the Lac de Bütgenbach. They move down a ravine to the edge of Wirtzfeld. Here they fan out for shooting, which develops immediately as they come in sight of the shattered buildings of the little town where only two weeks previous their division made its headquarters.

All during daylight (8 a.m. to 4 p.m.) the 38th infantrymen provoke fire fights with the Germans. So intermixed are the hostile sides that the patrol leaders make little use of the friendly guns waiting along the northern side of the Lac to help them. Running brawls alive with small arms fire erupt across the length and breadth of the narrow town, first one side then the other having the advantage.

Early winter twilight is creeping across the ruins of Wirtzfeld and the cold, exhausted soldiers still brawling there when the word comes from the 38th's forward command post behind a hill west of Wirtzfeld to disengage and move back to safety. The survivors do, bringing prisoners with them and five of their wounded. As the lines of 38th Infantry soldiers slog across the snow-covered fields, patrols of *Grenadiers* move out of Wirtzfeld and follow them west, shooting machine guns and rifles. A platoon of "E" Company comes up to hold off the Germans. The day's score: 10 *Grenadiers* dead and 17 bagged as POW, including six medical aides captured with their ambulance coming up the road from Büllingen to Wirtzfeld. The cost to Norris' men has been serious, 25 dead and wounded.

As the long, icy days and even longer dark nights go by on the crest, the misery, danger, and frustration begin to seep into the souls of the soldiers most at risk. The run up to the climactic attacks after January 15 to drive the Germans back behind the West Wall demands even more reconnaissance and fighting patrols. These place a sword over the head of every single rifleman, a sword that at any time may drop and split his soul from his body.

The Army newspaper, The Stars and Stripes, gives ample coverage to atrocities committed against American soldiers and Belgian civilians. Rogue officers and NCOs of the *Waffen SS*, most of whom are members of 1st *SS* Division and the *SD* squads travelling with it, are responsible. But the men in the miserable holes under the ceaseless pounding and rocketing make no distinction: A German is a German is a German. All deserve the severest punishment.

The sight of enemy POWs shuffling past them toward interrogation centers and cages in the rear infuriates some of the fighters up front. They appear so dirty, unsoldierly, ragged. What evil lies in their genes to impel them to condemn themselves and everyone else to the hellish imprisonment of this icy war? Why waste food and care on them? Even the thinking soldier has by now little room in his mind or heart for either rationality or sympathy. A lieutenant in headquarters company of Major Legler's battalion writes his parents, "We are the ones that know the German and what he will do. I hope there is never another Germany."

Nasty things happen. Not all German prisoners of war survive the journey from capture to interrogation center in the rear. The unarmed enemy pilot floating to the ground makes a tempting target. Dirty, cold, dead beat, and unarmed *Landser* mushing through the snow to surrender in the night and fog are assumed to be hiding guns and are shot before they reach the American lines. Enemy dead are found now and then on the killing ground with .45caliber bullet holes stark between their iced-over, staring eyes. Natural born killers, of which every infantry battalion has a few, must be watched carefully around prisoners, more so now than before.

By means of The Stars and Stripes, the men at the front also know the Soviet Army has finally put its monster killing machine in action to break the *Wehrmacht's* lines in the East. The lieutenant quoted above writes, "We are quite joyed by the Russian situation. I can't see why the big shots in Washington don't trust the Russians more....As long as they kill Germans, we love them." The mortar man assigned to his platoon's motor park (Part 4, this narrative) writes home that "We hear of a Red (sic) drive in the East. All our hopes and hearts are with the Russian soldiers. Most of the news we hear is later proved false, and what is true is days old. The Russian news is good. I hope it is true."

By mid-January 1945, the 2,500-square-mile bulge in the American front line is rapidly shrinking. Even the immovable War Lord himself seems willing at last to face reality. He orders Field Marshal Model to put the four *SS Panzer* divisions into reserve near St. Vith and to take a stand east of Houffalize with 5th *Panzer* Army. All know, including Hitler, that these moves are preliminary to liquidating *OKW's* huge and disastrous investment.

In the Allied camp on January 17, Field Marshal Montgomery relinquishes his command of the three corps of Hodges' 1st Army and all of Simpson's 9th Army on the left flank. (Part 2, this narrative) They go back to Bradley's 12th Army Group, from which, in Bradley's opinion, they should never have strayed. At Eupen General Leonard T. Gerow is finally able to depart 5th Corps to organize a new army. He is succeeded by Major General Ralph Huebner, former leader of the 1st Division and Gerow's second throughout the containment battle on the north shoulder of the breakthrough area.

The powerful American ground attacks supplemented by several British divisions or parts thereof are closing on the German forces in the Ardennes battleground in what amounts to successive waves rolling in from the south and north. Huebner's 5th Corps divisions (1st, 2nd, 9th, 99th) are to join in after Ridgeway's 18th Airborne Corps on the right flank gets started.

Huebner's infantry will be marching on Hitzfeld's 67th *Infanterie* Corps, which by mid-January consists of 326th, 277th, 89th, *Volksgrenadier* and 3rd *Fallschirmjäger* divisions. They are of mixed quality. However, it scarcely matters at this stage of the Ardennes battle. What matters is their potential on the defense, to delay and punish Huebner's infantry regiments as they begin their march across the hills of the high plateau east and south toward the West Wall and beyond. After mid-January the order of the day for Hitzfeld's power, received from Field Marshal Model's headquarters and passed down the chain of command to the smallest squad of machine gun and rifle soldiers on the outposts of the five divisions: "Hold at all costs."

An intelligence summary prepared by the 1st Division G-2 section summarizes Army Group B's tactics for withdrawing men and machines from the Bulge. It points out how important are Hitzfeld's barrier lines at Elsenborn-Bütgenbach-Weywertz against 5th Corps attacks: "By mid-January the enemy no longer had the initiative of attack. His most pressing concern, in fact, was to get what he could of his indispensable *Panzer* divisions off the hook. To accomplish this, it was imperative that the shoulders of his original salient be held firm. He could not allow any reduction of the mouth of the Bulge since his road nets, clogged with traffic and blocked with snow, were already carrying capacity movement. The loss of any roads at all would be disastrous."

From long instruction in war, the German commanders know that even third-rate infantry can be made to stand and deliver punishment to the last so long as a few determined and veteran NCOs are present and the soldiers have plenty of weapons and ammunition and well-protected, hidden places to shoot from. The dogged fight put up by the men and boys of *das Heer* against the American patrols of early January and the aggressive way they follow the lines of Americans falling back to their positions (above) foreshadows grim journeys for Huebner's divisions in the coming American offensive.

Part 7: Walking with the White Death

At the conclusion of our story, it would be gratifying to report that the American survivors of the fighting in the borderland forests and towns and the siege of the Elsenborn-Bütgenbach high plateau are to be rewarded with a safe, easy, and rapid passage to accomplishing their part in eliminating the German presence in the Ardennes.

It is not to be. In war as in peace, fate is indifferent to who lives, who dies; who gets his or her just rewards; who does not. Fate grinds on inexorably. And so it does with the soldiers of General Huebner's 5th Corps as they start walking through the masses of snow, whipped and burnt by winds that reach 40 degrees below fahrenheit, to overcome the well-prepared defenses of Hitzfeld's 67th Corps. The men of the 1st, 2nd, and 99th divisions will spend as much time—two weeks—taking back the fields, forests, villages, and towns of the Belgian district of Malmedy as they did fighting to hold them in the last two weeks of December. And some of their infantry companies will shed even more blood.[*]

General Huebner's plan for the January counteroffensive against the Germans in the borderland and northern Losheim Gap areas of Belgium is to send regimental combat teams of 1st, 2nd 9th, and 99th divisions in three waves rolling from west to east. One will follow the other in sequence from the right to the left flank of the corps until the men and machines of Hitzfeld's divisions opposing them are either eliminated or driven back east and south behind the West Wall.

General Hodges' 1st Army and Huebner's corps headquarters have ordered in batteries of twelve additional battalions of howitzers and long guns to supplement the arsenal of cannons already on the field. An officer present recalled later "Most of (this) was squeezed into the general area in the vicinity of or east of Sourbrodt, Belgium. Just how, I'm not quite sure."[**]

On January 15 in icy darkness the 1st Division starts moving against General Wadehn's 3rd *Fallschirmjäger* occupying fields, towns and villages south of Weywertz and Bütgenbach. Two regimental combat teams (RCTs) of the division (16th, 18th) plus Colonel Lovless' 23rd RCT, which is attached to the division, are in the attack. Each of the three brings armor and engineers with it. Each is backed by light and medium artillery.

---

[*] The December 16, 1944-January 14, 1945 fighting is the subject of our ten narratives. The counteroffensive of the U.S. 5th Corps from January 15 to February 3 to recapture lost territory in the Low Ardennes-Eifel region and upper Losheim Gap can only be described in summary. However, the reader should be aware that these "unknown battles" also witnessed much individual heroism, death, and suffering on both sides. They too deserve a special place in the annals of American military history.

[**] Some of these batteries departed after the 6th Army attacks of late December petered out and now have been returned for the 5th Corps offensive. See also Documentation for this narrative, "Units referred to in Text but not Identified by Number, Field Artillery-U.S."

Wadehn's paratroops have not been taken down in the fighting as seriously as have the *Volksgrenadier* divisions. Still and all, they manifest the handicaps described before. (Volume 1, Narrative IV, Part 1) These have been made worse by a month of winter warfare on poor rations. However, they have been stiffened by new leadership at the regimental level. And they are defending a critical sector that Field Marshal Model and von Rundstedt want held until the last. If 3rd *FSJ* fails to block the American counterattack here, south of the line Waimes-Bütgenbach, Model's plan for the northern escape routes of the *Wehrmacht* divisions in the breakthrough area will fall apart. "Our watchword is strong and true for *Führer* and *Reich*," says a newly assigned regimental commander.

The 1st Division G-2 (Intelligence) report quoted before (Part 6, this narrative), describes conditions on the right flank of the 5th Corps attack, January 15 to February 1. The description applies as well to the center and right where the 2nd and 99th divisions will be marching east and south during the same period:

"An element that aided the enemy in his delaying defense (though it also operated against him by increasing his losses) was the bitter weather. Terrain that would have been a minor problem in supply and evacuation during the summer presents almost insoluble problems under a two-foot cover of snow. The progress of the infantrymen through this obstacle was painfully slow. Points (AN: riflemen-scouts at the front of attacking columns) had to be changed every seventy-five to one hundred yards. Machine gunners and mortarmen were barely able to move at all.

"The temperature added its weight to the difficulties. Frostbite and freezing were common. Radio mouthpieces froze and broke. Laying wire was extremely difficult and repairing a break almost impossible. A wire crew from the 16th Infantry worked for six hours to locate a break in one thousand yards of wire buried under four feet of snow. Evacuation of the wounded was equally serious when only a Weasel was able to cover the ground. (AN: unarmed vehicle riding on tracks and used for general hauling) Mines were hard to locate. In one case an invaluable Weasel was destroyed travelling over a cleared road.

"Since most of the terrain covered by the 1st Division in its advance was open ground, there were no villages or houses to shelter the troops. Many of the advance companies spent two or three successive days with no more shelter than they could dig for themselves in the frozen ground. Altogether, the month's operations were as difficult as any in the 1st Division's campaigns."

For more than a month, General Wadehn's paratroops have occupied the ground that the three U.S. regimental combat teams are moving toward in their attack. Wadehn's men have the advantage of deep bunkers, foxholes, gun nests tactically well placed to administer the maximum punishment to their enemy in field, forest, and village. Likely routes of attack are well covered with "Hitler saws" (*Maschinengewehre*), mortars, and cannons. The position of the contending forces are now reversed: the attackers have become the defenders and vice versa. War's everlasting turn and turn about.

In this operation, Colonel Lovless' 23rd RCT (of Robertson's 2nd Division) will drive for a tactically important pass through the forested hills south of Waimes, Belgium; the 16th RCT, for the German base of Faymonville, two miles to the northeast; the 18th RCT, for a cluster of hills near Schoppen, Belgium, three miles south of Bütgenbach.

The 1st Division-23rd Infantry march south drags out for five terrible days of snow, wind, blood, and fire. The infantry companies of the three RCTs suffer from the furious winter gales and the below-freezing temperatures and from the dogged defense put up by the 3rd *FSJ* Division.

The pass between the high, forested hills at Ondenval south of Waimes is the key to St. Vith, Belgium, ten miles to the south. And St. Vith is the assembly area and port of exit from the Ardennes for the four armored divisions of Dietrich's 6th *SS Panzer* Army, or what is left of them. The 23rd RCT is marching on the left flank of the U.S. 30th Division, also engaged in opening the way to St. Vith for a U.S. armored-infantry seizure of the city. Field Marshal Model and General Dietrich are laying heavy hands on Generals Hitzfeld and Wadehn to keep the Americans out of the pass no matter what.

By nightfall January 15, the 23rd RCT's 1st and 2nd battalions have reached their initial objective. The infantry has shed blood and the armor has lost machines (two new model [M-18] tank destroyers, one new model Sherman). A battalion is taken away from the 18th RCT and assigned temporarily to Lovless' team because the going has been so difficult.

In a forest flanking the Ondenval Pass on the east, the *Fallschirmjäger* are well dug in, are bolstered by a half dozen *Sturmgeschütze* (tracked assault guns), have just been reinforced by one hundred and fifty replacements. Lieutenant Colonel Paul Tuttle's 3rd Battalion and Lieutenant Colonel John Hightower's 1st spend most of a bloody, terrifying, and confusing day and night trying to dig them out of the woods with shell fire, mortar bombs, automatic weapons, bazookas, grenades, bayonets, and shovels. Both battalions are filled with new men. (One company commander in Tuttle's battalion hasn't even been granted time to welcome the one hundred he will take into battle. He is not unique.) The fighters of each side scarcely ever see who or what they are shooting at as they lie or crouch in the snow under the black conifers.

Late in the battle a freezing rain falls, followed by sleet, then snow. Men die unattended and unseen. By the next day, January 18, there are almost as many evacuations from frozen limbs and feet as from shells and bullets. However, the German paratroops don't have the reinforcements that Lovless does. They move, stubborn and malign, south to one of the several villages in the area where they join 3rd *FSJ* troops already there.

To seize these villages, the 2nd Division soldiers must first pick their way through undetectable *Schützenminen*, (The charge is housed in wooded boxes to make mine detectors useless.), then confront *Sturmgeschütze* along the streets and *Fallschirmjäger* holed up in the houses and basements. However, friendly howitzers and heavy mortars dump such a huge load of murderous high explosives and phosphorous on the villages, the Germans are forced out.

Wadehn's men don't back off. They keep jumping from village to village near the Amel (Amblève) River. The 23rd Infantry accompanied by Shermans, slipping and sliding every yard of the way, must go in and root them out. In two of these villages, Ebertange and Montenau, *Panzer IVs* loaned by one of the *SS Panzer* divisions assembling in St. Vith are working with the paratroops and must be put down by Shermans, M-18s, and artillery fire. As ever, the Germans are dying hard.

Late on January 19, under cover of snow-saturated gales, the surviving paratroops start moving out of Ebertange, hurried along by barrage after barrage of American howitzer fire. Montenau also falls this day referred to in the 2nd Division history as one of "indescribably adverse weather conditions." In fact, the mayhem in an all-encompassing white landscape with winds blowing at gale force and the chill factor dipping to 40 degrees fahrenheit below zero is as close as American soldiers in the war will come to fighting and dying in the glacial conditions of deep winter on the Russia steppes.

In the center of the 1st Division counteroffensive, the 16th Infantry's 1st and 3rd battalions go south from Weywertz January 15 to capture the town of Faymonville, northeast of the Ondenval Pass. The 3rd Battalion is commanded by Lieutenant Colonel Charles T. Horner and has been seen before in these pages. (Narrative IX, Part 5; Part 4, this narrative) The weather frustrates their march and so do Wadehn's paratroops. Horner's battalion clears them from woods north of Faymonville but encounters dozens of machine gun-hardened strongpoints in the town, man-maiming mines in front of it, and hostile artillery fire everywhere. The fire fight and artillery exchanges go on for the whole day. By nightfall, the Germans are still rooted in half of Faymonville. They slip away southward during the night. By midmorning January 16, the 16th Infantry's 2nd Battalion comes up to take the point.

Their objective is Schoppen, two miles southeast of Faymonville. The battalion's attack on Schoppen "aborted," as Horner put it. Third *Fallschirmjäger* troops made more deadly by *Sturmgeschütze* 75mm high-velocity guns, hull deep in the earth and snow, send death and destruction at the 2nd Battalion riflemen from front, side, and rear. Friendly armor tries to come in but the roads are made impassable by piles of drifting snow. The 2nd Battalion falls back to its start line.

On the 19th Horner's battalion takes up the baton, moving out in what he terms "the worst weather encountered by the (regiment) during all its campaigning in World War II." The sky is still black and bitter. The air burns like dry ice. The snow is coming down in tidal waves. This time, however, the 1st Division engineers have managed somehow to get a road cleared for the American armor. No artillery softening up is done. Horner's men and machines barrel into Schoppen before Wadehn's troops know what is happening. The blizzard helps; the Germans can't believe the *Amis* would try to move on them under such conditions.

Horner's victory is pivotal for the 16th RCT. Its men continue south against flagging opposition, as Wadehn's division begins to withdraw from the sector.

South of Bütgenbach the 18th Infantry RCT is moving on the left of the 1st Division attack. As the lead battalion (3rd) goes southeast over the wide snow-covered fields and hedgerows, the troops are harassed by bullet and artillery shooting from hills in the vicinity even though they are moving in darkness. One rifle company ("L") crosses a field as the dull and foggy daylight of the winter morning comes up.

The light is quite enough for Wadehn's paratroops in their firing holes at the other end of the field to see the riflemen moving heavily toward them over the snow and uneven terrain. The *Maschinengewehren* saw away unmercifully. By the time the "L" Company soldiers get back to safe ground, twenty-six are wounded, forty-three missing. The missing have been taken prisoner or more likely hit and covered up by layers of snow. They are found later frozen to death, if found at all.

At dawn the following day, another rifle company ("K") crosses the field to climb the hill beyond. As they struggle through the snow, they see dead Americans all around. "Strewn with our predecessor's casualties," as a "K" Company man described the field. He and his fellow riflemen expect to join them. But the paratroops have departed. The company's harm this day (January 16, 1945) is caused by mortar bombs and fragments of bursting shells.

The 18th RCT (less one battalion) also has drawn the nasty job of driving the 89th *VGD* from the now snow-impacted Bütgenbacher Heck south of Bütgenbach and west of the Morschheck crossroads. The 89th is filled with troops scraped up from hither and yon. But sufficient veteran noncommissioned officers are present to shape them up. And they have had time to root themselves in holes and bunkers under the trees and brush.

In the teeth of intense bullet fire from snipers and machine gunners, plus hostile artillery pounding on the entrances to the brushy woods, the 1st Division infantry slogs doggedly forward. They root the 89th *Grenadiers* and *Füsiliers* from a half-mile of woods on the north. As seen before, combat in such dark woods is uniquely terrifying. The adversaries seldom see or hear each other until they feel the bullet or grenade fragment tearing through their flesh. The battle in the Heck ebbs and flows. However, by January 23, the *Grenadiers* and *Füsiliers* of the 89th are being methodically destroyed by the ceaseless artillery and mortar pounding and the shooters of the 18th Infantry's rifle companies.

The following day on the left, Colonel Seitz's 26th Infantry, 1st Battalion moves on Morschheck crossroads, defended by a complex of dugouts guarding the road in from Dom Bütgenbach. Riflemen of 1st Battalion go in at 3 a.m. in what one describes as "the coldest weather I had ever experienced in my lifetime." They take the crossroads, are then saturated with hostile artillery fire.

Having broken the German defenses around the crossroads, the Americans move south to Moderscheid, unhinging the fall-back defensive line of the 3rd *Fallschirmjäger* from the Amblève River north to this village. The Germans move south and east to Heppenbach.

The die-hard German commanders will not give up Heppenbach without making the 1st Division expend even more flesh and blood. The 89th *VGD Grenadiers* and Wadehn's *Fallschirmjäger* again are aided by the weather. Another opaque snow storm on January 28th blankets the killing ground. When the storm stops, the 18th Regiment infantry accompanied by Shermans, slipping and sliding forward behind tank dozers, shoot their way into Heppenbach. The German troops move, northeast toward Honsfeld, where so many Americans were bagged by Colonel Peiper's *Kampfgruppe* just six weeks previous. (Volume 1, Narrative V, Part 2)

Hitzfeld's 67 Corps strongholds south of the 1st Division are falling one by one. And those of his infantry troops there who have survived death, wounds, capture, and freezing are falling back across the northern reaches of the Losheim Gap toward the West Wall. And what is happening on their right wing is hurrying them along.

On January 28 Colonel Seitz's 3rd Battalion starts for Büllingen a mile or so south of their outpost line. It is 2 a.m. The ground is up and down and the snow drifts in places are five feet deep. Shortly after the attack begins, the weather clears, the black clouds part, and the moon shines forth to help the German machine gunners on the forward defenses of Büllingen.

Seitz's men flatten themselves in the snow. They wear camouflage covers made out of bed sheets. Still the bright winter moon hanging over the crystalline snowy fields acts as a malevolent eye in the heaven, a huge celestial star shell. And when the 1st Division men try to work their weapons at the Germans on the edge of the town, they find many of them locked up with ice.

However, the 26th's leaders are as experienced by now as any in the war. They strike at several places, confusing Büllingen's defenders, most of whom are the 89th *VGD Landser* new to the front. Seitz and his captains also are using tanks: Shermans equipped with snow plows up front. After the usual deaths and wounds on both sides, Büllingen's defenders are overwhelmed. Two hundred German prisoners bagged; at least that many killed and wounded.

As soon as the 1st Division soldiers are in full occupancy, the howitzers of 89th *VGD* take their revenge with a sustained barrage of 105 and 150mm shells plus rockets plus mortar bombs. Twenty-six Americans are wounded in one company alone ("K") in the morning's shooting and shelling, nineteen serious enough to be evacuated.

With the fall of Büllingen, a German base and stronghold throughout the siege of the Elsenborn-Bütgenbach heights, the way is open for a general assault by the two regimental combat teams of the 2nd Division: Ginder's 9th and Boos' 38th. The mission of these two regiments on January 30 is to retake ground lost in the withdrawal from the borderland and the towns and villages there in the first week after the German counteroffensive of December 16 started. As are the 23rd and 26th infantries, both regiments are filled with replacements in the ranks.

In the forty-eight hours before they start their attack, the 2nd Division engineers strain themselves and their machines to clear roads to the start lines at Nidrum, Berg, and newly won Büllingen. One engineer company has worked twenty-four straight hours in the blinding snow and numbing cold to open the N-32 into Büllingen. As they tankdoze away four feet of snow and countless stalled and burnt-out machines of war, they lose several vehicles (and crews) to mines; the day that the infantry goes forward, several more.

The 2nd Division action begins at 3 a.m., January 30, under the most abominable conditions imaginable: the thermometer hovering around 15 degrees fahrenheit; the wind whipping across the slopes south and east of Berg and the frozen Lac de Bütgenbach reservoir, the snow descending and blowing simultaneously; the night, raven black, obscuring all.

Colonel Ginder's 9th Infantrymen march south and east from Nidrum, their base on the high plateau, toward newly "liberated" Büllingen. There they assemble for an attack on Krinkelt from the south.

About the same time (3:30 in the morning), Boos' 38th Infantrymen push off from Berg to force the 89th *VGD Grenadiers* and assorted other 67th Corps troops out of Wirtzfeld. By now it is a snow-covered rubble hiding uncounted dead men. Colonel Boos needs Wirtzfeld as a base for his soldiers' march cross country to take Rocherath.

Wirtzfeld is infested with mines under the snow and rubble, hidden in abandoned vehicles, under corpses, in doorways and basements. Boos' men die and are maimed. No matter. After a hot meal, the riflemen and machine gunners accompanied by their ever-faithful medical corpsmen, are moving north across the broad, treeless fields toward the dual towns. The unit journal of 2nd Battalion describes the operation:

"There was nothing to break the cold, icy wind that swept across the open fields. The falling snow and sleet formed a frozen sheen on every part of the men's clothing and weapons. The whining of incoming and outgoing artillery shells, the diffused red glow of the sky over burning Krinkelt made this slow, difficult trek back into Rocherath almost as memorable as our exodus from it a month before." (Narrative VIII, Part 5)

When the vanguards of the 2nd Division reach Krinkelt, they find that buildings and basements "are filled to capacity with (Germans), some surprised, some happy to be prisoners, some wounded, and some still willing to fight." Boos' regiment is soon pushing north into adjoining Rocherath where they find more Germans in the same mental and physical conditions.

An engineering construction battalion assigned by 5th Corps works round the clock January 30 to install bridging over the badly deteriorated road used by the 99th and 2nd division troops five weeks before to withdraw from Krinkelt to Wirtzfeld. (Narrative VIII, Part 5) That night the driving snow turns to driving sleet then to rain and the little farm cart tracks and farm-to-market roads in the area start falling apart. Huebner's order to Robertson is to keep herding the Germans east, weather be damned. Several companies of Colonel Lovless' 23rd Infantry returned from the fight at the Ondenval Pass (above) and Ginder's 9th Infantry start plowing through the now almost impenetrable Rocheratherwald toward the Wahlerscheid crossroads where all of the death and destruction of the Elsenborn battles started six weeks before. (Volume 1, Narrative I)

One grim tale remains to be told. In the 5th Corps action to push back the Germans that began January 15, General Lauer's 99th Division has drawn what appears to be a privileged part. It is assigned the relatively secondary task of clearing General Viebig's 277th *Grenadiers* from the Rocheratherwald, the deep, dark conifer forest north of Rocherath and east of Höfen. When this is accomplished, his attacking force will be "pinched off," as soldiers put it, by the advance of the 2nd and 9th divisions on, respectively, the right and left flanks and will then return to their start lines on the Elsenborn high plateau.

Lauer's intelligence officers inform him that not more than eight hundred hostiles are defending in the woods "counting reserves and everything." In fact, he and his staff appear to be more concerned over movement in the terrible winter weather than about the opposition that the assault companies may face. (The experience of the combat patrols described in Part 6 above should have taught a different lesson.)

Two regiments, LTC Scott's 393rd and Colonel Riley's 394th, will do the job. (Riley is indisposed and will soon leave the front. He takes no part in the operation [Part 6, this Narrative.]) By order of General Lauer, the fighters in the companies assigned the point are not told of the dangerous and difficult mission until January 29, a few hours before they are to go. The tactics to be used, it seems, are those of surprise and stealth, a predawn march into the woods and a rapid suppression of the surprised and outnumbered enemy. General Black, Lauer's artillery chief, is concerned over the miserable roads, snow and ice storms, and traffic as obstacles to displacing his guns forward to support the march into the woods. However, given the tactics of surprise and stealth this concern seems irrelevant, at least on the 393rd front.

On the eve of the action, LTC Ernest C. Peters' 2nd Battalion, 393rd Infantry is occupying the right flank of the 99th Division line on the Rodelhöhe (hill) at the north side of the road from Wirtzfeld to Elsenborn. Its men have endured this dangerous, exposed, and bitterly cold position for five and one half weeks. They are being rewarded for their endurance by drawing the lead role in the march of the 99th Division's right wing (393rd Infantry) into the Rocheratherwald.

Peters' men start up a low hill in the moonless night of January 29-30 at 2:30 toward the place where the assault platoons will assemble for the advance a mile or so north of Wirtzfeld. All three rifle companies of the 2nd Battalion are closing together on the assembly area, but "E" is to take the point when the action starts this night.

The assault platoons move forward in the dark but soon pause at a line of trees while their leaders try to come to grip with things. Time is slipping by. Already the sky shows faint skeins of dirty grey light. But when full dawn comes, Company "E" remains under the trees.

A dozen or so 105mm shells from the 393rd Cannon Company guns two miles to the rear whisper overhead and strike the dark woods and the field west of it. The riflemen and machine gunners assume these are target and range-finding shots and will be followed by an annihilating barrage. Nothing follows: No light or medium howitzer rounds, no 8-inchers from the big 1st Army guns, no 4.2 mortar bombs, not even a flurry from their own battalion "artillery," the 81mm mortars.*

The three platoons of "E" Company are ordered to put their bayonets on their rifle barrels (fix bayonets) and go forward into their assault immediately. As they near the woods where the enemy waits, the plan is to form what soldiers call a line of skirmishers, prepared to engage in what they also call "marching fire."

It is now full light, an icy, grey day with lowering clouds dipping to the tops of the conifer-covered borderland hills. "Just out from the tree line," remembered one of the rifle soldiers, "we walked into very deep snow. Some of it hip deep, all of it thigh deep."

Company "E" is walking with death. Every man jack of them has death as a companion this morning. Some will shake the fellow; many will not. The company is stumbling forward in the snow into a cul-de-sac, the open end of a horseshoe formed by the irregular line of the woods. On each arm of the horseshoe the *Grenadiers* of 277 *VGD* are waiting in hidden nests under the trees behind the killer machine guns (*Maschinengewehre*), the "Hitler saws."

As the line of thirty or so men of the lead platoon push their way through the drifts into the wide opening of the horseshoe, the machine gunners go to work. The approaching riflemen are in plain sight. The machine gunners have only to draw a bead on them. Not one of the attackers can hide. "(They) had us exactly as they wanted us," remembered the riflemen quoted above. First one, then another, then a third machine gun grinds away, putting all but a few of the attackers down in the deep snow, dead, wounded, or dumb with cold and fear. The skirmish line never even gets formed.

---

* An officer of "G" Company who was there wrote, "Artillery was called in (during the attack) but it was not forthcoming. The regimental commander (Scott) refused the request....The 2nd Battalion could well have used 4.2-inch mortars of a 5th Corps battalion that were within shooting range as part of its contingency plans. (Or) it should have considered using its own heavy weapons company with its three sections of 81mm mortars and two platoons of heavy machine guns." (Niedermayer, pages 127-128, Documentation, Volume 1)

In his history of the 99th Division in WW II, General Lauer asserts "heavy concentrations of artillery fire were poured into that German position (but) the (2nd Battalion) troops remained pinned down." (Battle Babies, p. 139, Master List, Documentation, Volume 1.) Not true.

Before this iced-over, bloody day ends, it will be demanded of the "E" Company soldiers that they repeat their doomed maneuver twice. The whole time, they never once see the German gunners who are distributing so much death and suffering among them as they try to reach their objective in the Rocheratherwald.

They are joined by "F" Company, 2nd Battalion. Its men, too, move the same way up the sloping hill, forward into the horseshoe formed by the wide arms of the sinister woods on either side. They too are naked to the streams of machine gun fire spewing from the edge of the woods and the mortar bombs exploding in the snow around them.

In making the second and third attempts to reach the *Grenadiers* at the edge of the woods, the "F" and "E" company soldiers must pass by the bodies of their slain comrades. These are frozen in grotesque positions, ice sculptures already frosted over, spreadeagled or half rising or standing straight up in snow drifts, sightless eyes open. The men moving forward one more time toward the woods are giving their companion, death, one more opportunity to snatch them up. They need only glance left or right to see where the journey leads.

It can not go on. As the blood-spattered snow and corpse-strewn landscape between the tree line and the forest edge begins to darken, the 393rd Infantry commander, Colonel Scott, calls a halt before every single remaining rifleman, officer, and medic in the two companies has been killed, wounded, or frozen to death. In fact, few officers remain and the "E" Company commander is dead. His duties have been assumed by a second lieutenant commissioned a few weeks before at Elsenborn.

The suffering of his men this day have crushed LTC Peters, the 2nd Battalion commander. After dark Matt Legler, the 1st Battalion CO, stops at his dugout southwest of the deadly woods line where so many died. West Pointer, tough veteran of early battles in the war with Japan, Peters is scarcely able to converse.

Lauer is being pressed by General Huebner to keep moving lest the 9th and 2nd divisions on the left and right expose their flanks to the Germans as they go forward with their own attacks. Colonel Scott's new plan is to go on with the 393rd's operation two hours after midnight the following day (January 31). However, this time it will be done right, or as right as possible given the abominable conditions. Preceding the attack will be a powerful artillery onslaught against the near side of the Rocheratherwald and the 277th *VGD* positions therein. Following that at 2 a.m., January 31, the surviving 2nd Battalion riflemen and light machine gunners will move obliquely toward the big woods, with the reserve company ("G") in the lead this time. Third Battalion, commanded by a new CO who has replaced Allen, will enter the woods from the right flank. This tactic will place in a nutcracker the 277th *VGD* machine gunners and riflemen who have inflicted so much suffering on the 2nd Battalion.

The maneuver is scarcely necessary. This time the howitzers of 99th Division and 5th Corps do their work. Scott's angry infantrymen spoiling for a no-quarters brawl find only German corpses, lying at the bottom of firing holes, behind brush, sprawled on the ground, the trees above them turned to mammoth splinters. And God save any *Landser* who has survived the barrage and is lurking about.

However, the War Moloch still menaces the infantrymen who have finally gained the woods. The "E" Company rifleman quoted before remembered that with daylight January 31 he and his fellows in the woods saw that "the forest was liberally laced with mines and booby traps, mostly the little egg-shaped concussion grenades (*Eierhandgranaten*) wired craftily between trees and on fallen logs."

North of 2nd Battalion, Lieutenant Colonel Matt Legler's 1st Battalion (393rd) is slogging through the same forest herding the stubborn 277th *VGD* rear guard to the east. They also are menaced by hidden mines every tortuous step through the trees, into the ravines and up the hills of the nearly impenetrable Monschauwald. A dozen men moving close together is devastated by the explosion of a *Schrapnellmine* (Bouncing Betty) when one trips over a hidden wire. Most are hit by shrapnel; several die.

In the pale light of the Nordeifel dawn, awash in fog floating up from the ravines to cover the hills, the woods must seem to Scott's cold, hungry, worn-to-death men to be infested with unseen grotesques, chimeras from a Hieronymus Bosch painting. Nevertheless, they settle down as best they can and await orders.

Late in the day, the order comes down to Peters' 2nd Battalion to be ready to move immediately back to the hills of Elsenborn four miles to the west, their start line thirty-six hours before.

However, it is not until a few hours before midnight when they begin moving over the vast expanse of white that is the hilly, snow-impacted fields and hedgerows between the woods and Elsenborn. They walk in long files, dead beat, some asleep on their feet, dirty, bearded, draped in filthy uniforms, clammy with frost and damp, feet sore or without feeling at all.

And their nemesis, the vile weather, plays them one last vile trick: The temperature rises. The air becomes saturated with a fine, misty rain. The deep snow across the plateau starts to melt. The trails and cart tracks become slick. The detritus of battling over this ground since December 18 poke through the snow: broken guns, discarded ammo boxes, bits of uniforms, and equipment, burnt-out armored vehicles, dead *Landser* frozen at the bottom of outpost and fighting holes on what was their main line of resistance. The men in the long files even pass corpses of their own killed in the brutal attacks of January 30 and waiting to be gathered up and transported to temporary burial sites.

The trails and narrow roads that the infantrymen are using have been cleared of mines or marked (for the most part) by the engineers and the vanguard of the infantry companies. But in the night and fog, it is an easy thing to wander from the trail or slip in the wet snow and mud off to the side where the hidden killers wait.

Legler is walking at the head of his 1st Battalion. He leaves the path a few paces, is lifted and slammed down by a violent explosion that mangles his leg and renders him unconscious. Ignoring the danger of also being eaten quick by a mine, his men leave the marked path to find their wounded colonel in the dark. The litter on which his men lay him down becomes one more of several being carried along by the walkers in the night. They contain men too badly hurt, or worn out, or numbed by fear and misery to keep going. Legler will live, but his military career is over.

The 99th Division infantry companies coming back from the Rocheratherwald on February 1 are to return to their diggings on the low hills east of Elsenborn until their next move. There they will be safe from harm except for the occasional attack by a die-hard *Luftwaffe* fighter-bomber pilot bent on revenge more than victory or the impact of a monster shell from a German railroad gun far off to the east behind the West Wall.

The quondam foxholes and dugouts of the 393rd Infantry fighters may be safe. They are also unusable. The thaw and persistent drizzling rain has ruined most of them. Mud walls, sturdy when frozen, are collapsing. Log overs and other roofs of scrap lumber are falling in. Scarcely any of the holes are without three or four inches of water at bottom. The fighters of the 393rd have just survived two days of the most ghastly combat in the seven weeks of Elsenborn battles. They are not now about to slither down into the ice water at the bottom of these holes encased in disintegrating mud walls.

The bolder ones keep walking west into Elsenborn, cursing all the way. There they push into the billets of the rear echelon men (Part 5, this narrative), whether invited or not to crash on floors, couches, shelves, hay racks of barns. They will not return to their fellows up front until they have slept warm and dry one time.

Those who stay in the open under the cold rain on what was the Rodelhöhe and the nearby hills try to sleep on the ground, covered with whatever they can find to separate them from the snow and muck: shelter halves, rain capes, blankets over old wooden doors. The shelter halves even find their intended use: to make a little "pup" tent for two men to slide into. Few go back into the foxhole graves-for-the-living.

And they build open fires, an unheard of breech of security. The officers of the 99th permit it in their desire to do something for their long-suffering men. Jerry cans of gasoline are hauled in, logs and scrap lumber and old doors are piled up, doused and set afire. First a few, then many, then a multitude of great bonfires fountain in the night, fog, and drizzle around the hills east of Elsenborn.

In the warmth and light of the bonfires, the weary soldiers come alive in body and spirit. The heat drives away the bitter cold and dries their layers of clothing. The fires even bring a touch of gaiety, of all things, to the gatherings around them. And if someone, officer or NCO, can produce a bottle, the gaiety rises. The soldiers draw their sleeping arrangements as close to the flames as is safe, closer even. From afar the figures silhouetted by the bonfires appear phantoms, long-gone Belgae warriors camping out on the eve of a battle with Roman legionnaires or putting out votive fires to appease the spirits of their dead.

In the way of infantrymen, the soldiers gathered there put from their minds what horrors tomorrow or the day after or the day after that may bring. The war in Europe will last ninety-six more of these days. Some of the men warming themselves at the fires, joking and japing with their fellows, speaking of their dead friends, talking of home, will not be alive when the war ends. Others will be in military hospitals recovering from wounds that will make their lives harder to bear and will test their courage not for a few hours on the battlefield but for every waking moment. No matter. This night of the blessed fires, they are alive and whole and thankful for that.

WE WERE THERE

Field Marshal Montgomery Takes Charge

"Early in the affair, when U.S. 5th Corps was doing all right holding the north shoulder (AN: the Monschau-Bütgenbach-Malmedy line at Elsenborn Ridge), but before the German effort was under control, we learned of the new top command set up, with Montgomery taking over north of the breakthrough. (This narrative, Part 2)

"Monty, as was his habit, soon visited our (5th Corps) command post at Eupen. He either brought along or had sent previously one of his communication units, which were called Phantoms, small unit— maybe a couple of vehicles, a couple of junior British officers and a few radio operators. No problem developed. They functioned smoothly within the staff.

"When Monty arrived, Huebner (AN: Major General Clarence R., acting as General Gerow's deputy preliminary to taking over 5th Corps) ushered him in....Huebner had me along to listen and take notes. The conversation (with Monty) was easy, a discussion of the big and little picture, not controversial. Monty said that he was planning a withdrawal on the northern shoulder to shorten the lines, improve logistics, take steps to avoid heavy loss in case the north shoulder couldn't hold with poor road and weather conditions for a forced fall back.

"Huebner, with convincing logic and confidence, assured Monty that 5th Corps could and would hold; that the shoulder position, which we were very successfully holding, was the best defensive position we could find without going all the way back to the Meuse River; that we had paid dearly to take all this ground and that he did not want to give it up.

"Apparently Monty was favorably impressed, so after a bit more easy chatting on the subject Monty told Huebner that he could stay on the Elsenborn heights but would he please get everything but combat forces out of the corps sector and forward area and back in our rear so in case of necessity our roads would be more capable of handling the fall back. Huebner readily agreed, turned to me and simply said for me to see that General Montgomery's and his agreement was executed. Monty left and all was pleasant and smooth.

"Twenty-four hours later Huebner asked me in passing whether I had executed the evacuation order. He knew very well what I had done. I had been his chief of staff so long, I knew what he wanted me to do....So I told him very seriously and in a staff report manner how I had moved all the Red Cross clubmobiles back to the rear, evacuated some USO (United Service Organization entertainers), a few bits of odds and ends—to make it sound impressive....With a completely straight face, he told me to report to 1st Army that we had evacuated all excess in the sector. And that ended our withdrawal from Elsenborn..."

> Colonel Stanhope B. Mason, acting chief
> of staff, U.S. 5th Corps, 1st Army

Excellent Opportunities for Advancement

(AN: This rifle company of the 393rd Infantry was in reserve until December 23, when it is moved up front a mile and a half southeast of the town of Elsenborn.)

"Casualties began to pick up significantly."

"Duffy, our squad leader, was killed. Mike Kelly, a little bantam Irishman from Boston, took over the squad with me as second in command..."

"Nelson and Sutphen had taken over the 2nd Platoon: a buck sergeant (AN: the lowest sergeant rank) and a private first class taking the place of a second lieutenant and a technical sergeant (AN: third highest NCO rank in the WW II Army)."

"Lieutenant Green had been carted away from the 3rd Platoon with multiple wounds."

"Our platoon sergeant from Camp Maxey, nicknamed the Desert Rat, had been wounded and his place had been taken by the platoon guide, a staff sergeant named Moore.

"(Moore) in turn was killed the first day on Elsenborn ridge and the platoon was taken over by Hugo Degamo, one of the better squad leaders. (He) lacked excessive ambition and was generally liked by all."

"The 1st Platoon sergeant's position was taken over by a private first class from Joliet, Illinois, Bob Stella. (He) later served as platoon leader when Lieutenant Womack was killed."

> Francis N. Iglehart, rifleman, "G"
> Company, 393rd Infantry, 99th Division

"We Made It Again, but It Can't Go on Forever"

"Early a.m. January 13, we had a combat patrol into the enemy lines. A large lieutenant, whose name I can't remember led (the patrol). For some reason, we skirted to the right across the enemy front....A machine gun opened up from the woods above us. They shot flares into the sky, which parachuted slowly down as they fired at us with the machine gun....

"Arnold Owens ('Akie') and I stayed back and dragged out the lieutenant (AN: Apparently wounded. The narrator does not say.). We probably killed him, dragging him out. He weighed more than two hundred pounds and we were in twenty inches of snow. It was a job getting him back into the lines where a litter team met us..."

"As 'Akie' and I wended (sic) our way back to the company command post, we went down a little draw....'Akie' placed his right arm around my waist lightly and said, 'Well, Mac, we made it again, but it can't go on forever.'"

"(Two days later), another patrol. We were to be on it. Before departure that night, I went into my foxhole for a bit of sleep. I died in my sleep. I had a dream and saw myself in a bed with a sheet up to my chest. I decided right then that I was going to make it home, but that I had no idea what was under that sheet."

"We crossed no man's land (the distance between the German and American lines) and penetrated five hundred yards, destroyed a machine gun nest, then headed back toward our lines. The Germans closed in on us from both flanks and opened up. We took a perimeter (AN: circle of riflemen) defense...and radioed back for artillery support, but nothing came.

"I was hit in the hand, and called to 'Akie' to take charge. In just seconds, I was hit twice more, through the left shoulder and knee. 'Akie' called back, 'Mac, I'm hit bad.' His last words. Firing ceased and we surrendered. I did not see his body. We feared artillery bombarding us, so we moved hurriedly into captivity."

"(After the first patrol) I felt that my wonderful, wonderful buddy had a very definite premonition of things ahead. I've grieved over 'Akie' more than anything in all my life. We were practically residents of each other's bodies.

> Clifford E. McDaniel, rifleman, Company "L,"
> 394th Infantry Regiment, 99th Division

Two's Company and Four's Even Better Company

"I was ordered out to find an observation point from which to register the (155mm howitzer) battalion and fire upon any targets of opportunity. (AN: Artilleryman's term for enemy targets that appear unexpectedly.)"

"We parked the jeep some two hundred yards from the crest of the hill."

"We began to dig furiously because it looked as though there was going to be a little battle taking place....In a short while, Russo had about six inches (sic) dug, wide enough for the two of us to fit in. Seconds later (a 88millimeter round) came over, landing much short of some tank destroyers (a quarter mile to the rear) and much closer to us. We began to dig with our hands (AN: The ground is frozen but thawing.).

"By this time the tank destroyers had begun to fire back at the German tanks....In the interim Russo took a reel of wire and ran it down to Wallace to set up the remote control so that we would be able to contact the battalion.

"Minutes after Russo returned, another burst from the German tanks sent us all scurrying for safety. Two doughboys (infantry-men) who had carelessly left their own foxholes instinctively jumped in ours, one landing on Russo and the other on me. There was barely room for us, much less two more.

"We didn't complain. In fact, it felt very comfortable, so comfortable that when the firing subsided, Russo warned the two fellows that they should stay a little while, because no one knew when the firing would start up again. (AN: The two infantrymen not only brought body heat but also protection against shell fragments.)

Armand J. Duplantier, Jr., lieutenant, forward observer,
372 Field Artillery Battalion, 99th Infantry Division

A Shoot Out with Howitzers

"Christmas day we were knocked out of our gun positions by counter-battery artillery fire at Elsenborn. The colonel (battalion commander) finally came up. I said we've lost one gun. We've lost our wire sergeant. We've lost our supply sergeant. We've lost our kitchen. It was blown off the face of the earth. The pyramidal tent went up like a balloon. (AN: Field kitchens would often be sheltered in such a tent.) The colonel finally said pull back a half mile to that line of trees back there."

"I'm sure the (German gunners) were pinpointing our positions with civilian observers. Who they were I'll never know....I'm sure there were civilians in American uniforms reporting our positions because the German counter-battery fire would not have followed us back to our next position along the tree line.

"We got shelled real badly and lost several men there. Finally they quit shooting at us. They thought they had knocked us out because there were several direct hits right in our gun stations. Lieutenant Kenney—he was my assistant—and I dug a hole and a round hit right in the hole and killed him."

"We kept firing back at them. We didn't give up. As long as we got orders from headquarters to shoot, we're going to shoot. Some of the chiefs of (gun) sections had to pull their men out of the holes, they were so scared to shoot back because artillery fire was landing on us and we were shooting back at them (at the same time)."

John P. Wakefield, captain, executive officer, Battery "A," 38th Field Artillery Battalion, 2nd Division

The 277th *Volksgrenadiers* Start Touching Bottom

"Even after the attack had ceased (AN: He probably means his division's attempt to break through to the Kalterherberg-Elsenborn road December 22.) due to the general replacement situation, it was impossible to even approximately replace the losses in officers and enlisted men.

"The replacements, about fifteen hundred men, that the division received during January (1945) consisted for the most part of forces scraped together from the bottom of the cadre formations of the *Luftwaffe*. They could scarcely operate their small arms (machine pistols, rifles, etc.); still less did they possess any experience in infantry warfare.

"In spite of all efforts by the replacement battalion of the division behind the front, it was impossible to make any full-fledged fighters out of these replacements within a short time."

"Under the circumstances, the division awaited the expected American counterattack, which did take place at the end of January."

Wilhelm Viebig, major general, commander,
277th *Volksgrenadier* Division

The Inglorious Tale of a *Landser* in the Elsenborn Battles

(AN: The following excerpts are from a diary taken from an infantryman of General Viebig's division whom the U.S. 99th Division captured east of Elsenborn in January 1945.)
"In close contact with the neighboring regiment. Something big in the making (December 14). Relieved. By motor to Hollerath, Germany. Everyone is on the alert. This might be the decisive phase of the war (15). We are ready to attack. Concentrated artillery fire. Bitter forest fighting. Many casualties (16). Slow progress with many heavy losses. Forest mopped up. At night we take the village. We are surrounded in the village waiting for relief (17). All around are Americans. Our tanks break through to us. *Hitlerjugend Panzer* Division cooperates with us....Many *Panthers* and *Panzerjäger* (18). Continuous artillery fire. Snipers in every building. Our attack is stalled. *Neblewerfer* (rocket-throwing unit) arrives. We are relieved during the night (19). Near Rocherath. Dead bodies everywhere. Spent the night in a house there. Heavy artillery fire (22). Only a few men left in the battalion. My feet are frozen (23). A sad Christmas. No food (24). Still no food. The only water we have is from a foxhole. Very cold (25). Some food arrives (26). Back to Rocherath (from the front). Command post in a house, finally a warm place (27). Another unit on the attack on Elsenborn hill. Badly beaten (28). We go over to the defensive (30)."

Unnamed rifleman, 991 *Volksgrenadier*
Regiment, 277th *VG* Division

Anatomy of a "Small Unit Action"

"The 1st Battalion was assigned the mission to capture and hold the Morschheck crossroads. (AN: The important road center a mile south of Dom Bütgenbach. Narrative IX) The attack was to take place on January 24."
"Captain Donald Lister, Company 'C' commander organized a

patrol for the night of January....The patrol returned with the information (that) the snow in some places was four feet deep. (The Germans) had a series of dugouts, which were probably used as strong points, approximately one hundred yards north of the (road to the crossroads)."

"The 1st Platoon was assigned the point. They were to attack straight down the road...the point consisting of one squad and a second out as flank protection. (Their snowsuits blended in perfectly with the snow as they moved down the road....They were met with fire from two machine guns and about a squad of (German) riflemen. They very quickly gained fire superiority, killing four of the enemy. Six were taken prisoner."

"The 2nd Platoon in the meantime ran into enemy around the house....After a brief fire fight two (enemy) were killed, five more captured. Additional Germans were caught in their dugouts and surrendered without firing a shot....It was a textbook attack. Everything broke right.

"(The company) quickly started to dig in, using the half pound block of TNT each man carried to help break up the frozen ground. The TNT threw up heavy black smoke...(and) the enemy quickly began to rake our positions with heavy concentrations of artillery fire. We began to sustain heavy casualties.

"At 4 p.m. the Germans launched a counterattack in battalion force...(AN: presumably on his entire 1st Battalion front) The 2nd Platoon (took) the brunt of (it). One of the two machine guns (AN: of heavy MG sections attached to 'C' Company) was still operable. But only one gunner remained. He was hand feeding the ammo from a broken belt, and he almost single handedly held off the Germans. Our artillery and mortars took care of the rest, catching them out in the open. In the meantime, reinforcements were being sent to the 2nd Platoon. They were able to plug the gap, and the day was saved.

Rollo J. Moretto, rifleman, Company
"C," 26th Infantry, 1st Division

The Stoics

"In our attack on Büllingen (in mid-January 1945), we took an underground cement structure just south of town on a small rise. It looked like it might have been used to hold water for the town at one time but the Germans had been using it for a command post.

"While a couple of our platoons were cleaning out the rest of the town, some of us thought we better look after our casualties. When a guy got hit out in the cold, he didn't last long because he would go into shock.

"The Germans were starting to throw a lot of artillery on us, and if the cold didn't get the wounded the artillery would. It looked like the closest and best place to take the wounded was into the cement deal (sic)."

"It always amazed me how calm most men were after they got hit. I found one man that was hit real bad and was lying near some trees. He had lit up a cigarette and was laying there smoking while shells were landing all over. I couldn't carry him in the deep snow so I had to drag him to the (structure).

"It was hard on some of the wounded getting them inside but we didn't have much choice. After we got all inside, that we could find, we started to patch them up the best we could. There was only one aid man (medical corpsman) there, so some of us helped. We used all the wounded men's first aid packs and all of our own.

"After Büllingen was cleared and the tanks got through with the snow plows, I suppose (these) wounded were taken back. I was on the other side of town then and don't know how this was done."

Leroy N. Stewart, sergeant, communications section,
Company "K," 26th Infantry, 1st Division

A German Officer Slips Through Death's Net

"I was in the northern-most house along the road to Rocherather Baracken (AN: The date is January 31, 1945. The Baracken (barracks) is a half mile north of the then German-held town of Rocherath on the road to Wahlerscheid crossroads.)

"It was a small, timbered house, heavily damaged. During the afternoon, heavy snow. No contact with our artillery fire control or infantry.

"We were in the cellar when through the cellar window we saw the first American go by. I ran up the stairs with my assault rifle (*Sturmgewehr*) and bumped into an American. (AN: from the 2nd Division) Completely surprised, we fired at each other. I hit him."

"In front of the house, (I) saw twenty Americans approaching at a distance of 30 meters (33 yards). I fired the full clip of bullets in my weapon, then returned to the cellar."

"I called our fire control for artillery shells on our own position. Several salvos came in but there were no hits on the house. The Americans tossed three hand grenades in the cellar windows, but none came in where we were (hiding)."

"Towards evening, the Americans left and after dark so did my men and I. We moved down the road to Rocherather Baracken. (It) was under fire, but late in the night we reached our positions."

Heinz Thieleke, captain, commander, 11th Battery,
artillery regiment of 277th *Volksgrenadier* Division

A Parachute Commander Tries to Revive the Old Spirit

"Order of the Day, January 7, 1945 to the 8th Parachute Regiment, 3rd Parachute Division:

"As of today, I am again in command of the regiment. (AN: holding the front against U.S. 1st Division) I greet you in old comradeship, mindful of the old spirit and soldierly bearing, that you displayed in so many actions as parachutists. With proud memory, I think of the many officers, NCOs, and enlisted men who died for the freedom and future of Germany."

"I particularly expect the 'old men' of the 8th Regiment to carry on the traditions of the regiment and also that the new men will fit themselves into the unit. They owe that spirit to the many who have died for the flag in the course of their duty. With the old parachutist spirit, we will fight on, master the difficult, and achieve the impossible.

"I expect strict discipline in all men of my command. I expect everyone to bear responsibility for his command down to the letter."

"We are a community of battle-hardened men. We look with confidence to the new year. Our watchword is strong and true for *Führer* and *Reich*."

Colonel Liebach, commander, 8th Parachute
Regiment, 3rd *Fallschirmjäger* Division

"No Ordinary Digging In"

"...we started pushing the Bulge (AN: the German penetration into U.S. 1st Army lines) back slowly. We would move forward a short distance and dig in, advance again and dig in, and so on, sometimes three or four times a day, if memory serves.

"This was no ordinary 'digging in.' It was bitterly cold. The ground was frozen so deeply and so hard it was almost impossible to penetrate. We carried quarter pound blocks of TNT with detonators to loosen the frozen crust. With a pickaxe we would dig a small hole to accommodate the TNT, set it off, then proceed to dig our foxhole. We carried picks and shovels to expedite the digging. And since we were fighting in deep forest we carried axes and crosscut saws....It was necessary to put a cover of logs and soil over our holes (to protect against tree bursts)."

"Everyone's most vivid memories are of the numbing cold. ...Just staying alive took all of one's ingenuity. I remember being on an outpost right in front of the German lines where the choice seemed to be between moving and being shot or lying perfectly still and freezing to death. Somehow we survived..."

"One of my saddest memories is of seeing German prisoners of war carrying bodies, both American and German, out of the woods. Most were frozen in such grotesque positions, it was difficult to keep them on a stretcher. They had frozen stiff in the exact positions in which they had died."

Bert H. Morphis, rifleman, Company
"B," 26th Infantry, 1st Division

A RECKONING—THEN AND NOW

By mid-February 1945, the three *Wehrmacht* armies that attacked the U.S. 1st Army on December 16, 1944 had withdrawn from the Ardennes.

Their infantry, armor, and other units had been taken down drastically. Many of the *Volksgrenadier* and *Panzergrenadier* regiments were scarcely more than a battalion in size or less. *Panzer* regiments were reduced to a few tanks and other armored fighting vehicles. Artillery and *Werfer* battalions lacked sufficient means of hauling their weapons from the battleground.

Mobile artillery and antitank pieces had suffered a particularly severe attrition. Not only had ferocious combat taken its toll but also the *Jaboes* and medium bombers of both American and British air forces had pounded the German supply and combat columns unmercifully with fire and steel, making useless junk of what were formidable tanks and guns. By one estimate, in mid-January, when the Germans began withdrawing, 6th *Panzer* Army had only 143 "operational armored vehicles;" 5th *Panzer*, 167; and 7th *Infanterie* Army, 39.

Nevertheless, the retreat of the Germans from the vast breakthrough area gouged out of the American line in December could not be termed a rout. In a few sectors where there were rivers to cross, the *Jaboes* caused spasms of panic. However, for the most part the German hegira from the Ardennes was methodical, grudging, a fighting retreat. And as we have seen (Narrative X, Part 7), countless small units of the *Heer* engaged in near suicidal last stands against the overwhelming force of the surging American columns.

Also, as in France after the Allies broke out of the beachhead, the German commanders managed somehow to keep in hand a nucleus of men, NCOs, and officers. (Volume 1, pps. 18-19) And the four *SS Panzer* divisions salvaged sufficient materiel and soldiers to serve as a basis for refitting and moving to Hungary.

The three U.S. infantry divisions whose bloody fortunes we have been following these many pages did not retire from the scene after closing on the borderland towns and forests at the end of January, 1945. Not at all.

In the first week of February, Andrus' 1st Division, with the aid of the 395th Combat Team from Lauer's 99th, pushed into the forests and pillbox (West Wall) line from east of Losheimergraben crossroads to the Hellenthalwald, north of Hollerath, Germany, which had been used by the Germans as a staging and communications center for their attack December 16.

The remainder of Lauer's infantry marched south to the towns and villages along the N-32, relieving the 82nd Airborne and 1st Division troops there.

After driving deep into the Monschauwald west of the Wahlerscheid crossroads fortress that caused so much grief in early December, Robertson's 2nd Division infantry reached the headwaters of the Urft River a few miles north of Schleiden, Germany. Craig's 9th Division and the U.S. 78th Division thereupon moved in to seize, finally, the Urft-Roer river dams.[*]

By the third week of February 1945, the three divisions were granted a small reward for their bloody labors of the previous two months. They moved out of the line of fire: the 99th, around Aubel, Belgium; the 2nd in the Höfen-Kalterherberg sector; the 1st, at Aywaille, Belgium in the Amblève River valley. Their short stay away from the killing grounds was barely long enough to do more than clean and oil their weapons, repair and replace vehicles and guns, and provide harsh instruction to the streams of replacements arriving to flesh out their infantry ranks. Some of these replaced replacements obtained during the December-January blood letting and already dead or wounded. The rifleman's hard way in war.

By the last week in February, Andrus' men were back in action, as were Robertson's and Lauer's a week later, joining the 1st Army's attacks all along the line to destroy the *Wehrmacht* on the ground in the Rhineland, make landfalls on the east bank of the Rhine, then go on to march across Germany to the Elbe River, the demarcation line between the forces of the Western Allies and the Soviet Army.

The ground forces of the *Wehrmacht* died hard. Each of the three divisions, as well as Craig's 9th, which defended the northernmost position on Elsenborn heights, fought deadly running battles as they made their way into the *Reich* and were involved in some of the most ruinous actions for the German cause.[**] Riding trucks or the decks of tanks,

---

[*] All of the sacrifices going back to early December 1944 made by the American infantry to seize the dams before the German engineers could sabotage the water-control machinery went for naught. Bradley wrote, "Before quitting (the dams) the enemy dynamited their flood gates. (A) torrent of water sluiced down the Roer Valley. The river washed three feet above its muddy banks." (Soldier's Story, p. 499. Volume 1, Documentary.)

[**] See Appendices, pps. 430-434 for a bare-bones account of the progress of the three divisions and General Craig's 9th Division in the last three months of war in Europe. Also, the fate of the *Wehrmacht* divisions that opposed them in the Elsenborn battles. This account will also provide the reader with a general idea of the Allies' final operations in Germany and Austria leading to the Germans surrender at midnight May 8, 1945.

infantry of the four divisions made incredibly long journeys (nearly three hundred miles in one case) amid scenes of a great nation's disintegration and despair not witnessed in heartland Europe since the religious wars of the early 17th Century.

About the *Wehrmacht's* resistance on German soil, the English military historian, John Keegan, wrote, "As if by symbiosis, (an) extraordinary spasm of final combat...convulsed Germany in late March and during April, 1945. Ten thousand German prisoners were captured by the Americans and British every day in March, and the figure rose to 30,000 a day during April. But those Germans still at liberty battled on, fighting and dying at every river line between the Rhine and Elbe, counterattacking when they could, and compelling the enemy to turn into rubble every other provincial town they approached."

The casualty figures are grim evidence of the truth of Keegan's observation. In March 1945, the period of heavy fighting in the Rhineland, the Remagen bridgehead, and the Rhine crossings, 53,209 casualties were sustained by the U.S. Army in the European Theater of Operations. This was slightly more than three quarters of the January number when the fighting in the "Bulge" was blazing away.

What effect the Ardennes campaign and the sizeable German losses there had on these climactic battles in Germany remains to this day, fifty plus years later, a question for military historians to argue about. Some say the losses in men and materiel made it impossible for Hitler's generals to mount a meaningful defense thereafter on either the Eastern or Western fronts; others, that the check of the momentum of the Allies administered by Hitler's *Riesenanschlag* prevented an invasion of the Rhineland by U.S. 9th and 3rd armies and the British before the end of 1944 and also the capture of even more enemy troops and materiel than actually occurred west of the Rhine in the early spring.

However, considering how fiercely German units fought on their own soil right up to the day of surrender in May, 1945, it seems certain that had Hitler allowed the *Wehrmacht* to husband its resources for a last-ditch defense in the Rhineland instead of wasting them in the Ardennes, the cost to the Allies would have been much higher and the total Allied losses much greater.

It is always more expensive in men and materiel to fight on the offense rather than the defense. German war craft and determination might have built formidable bastions throughout the Saar and Rhineland. Not only would the men and materiel lost in the Ardennes-Eifel been available but also the German commanders, from the crafty von Rundstedt down to the regimental commanders, could have devoted planning and training time to this end rather than to the pursuit of the *Führer's* dreams of marching to Antwerp.

The expenditure of human lives and suffering on both sides in the Ardennes was large: Some two hundred thousand battle casualties. At least half again that number of men and boys removed from the battleground because of physical or mental afflictions and the ubiquitous frozen and immersion foot, all of which were caused by the unbearable cold and wretched conditions and the ferocity of the fighting.[*]

The opinions of military historians concerning the importance of the Elsenborn battles described in our ten Narratives have changed since the close of World War II. As we reported (Volume 1, pps. v-vi), they have come to be recognized as pivotal in changing the course of the *Wehrmacht's* last great offensive of the war ("Ruining Adolph Hitler's plan for a second *Blitzkrieg* in the West" as our subtitle has it.). They also are a set-piece example of the military adage that even the most obscure and isolated combat may set in motion a chain of events that will turn the course of a great battle. And they are an illustration of the difference an outstanding field commander (in this case, the 2nd Infantry Division's Walter M. Robertson) can make by gathering up the reins of friendly forces that are sore beset everywhere by an aggressive enemy and concentrating these forces to accomplish a nearly impossible mission.

The Elsenborn battles did not change the outcome of the German's counteroffensive in the Ardennes-Eifel. A German defeat and withdrawal were foreordained. What they did accomplish, however, was a fatal change in the missions of the two *Panzer* armies and an even more fatal change in the direction of the German attack and its sustainability. From the time *Wacht am Rhein* emerged from the early deliberations of the

---

[*] General Eisenhower gave a figure of 120,000 enemy killed, wounded, missing, and taken prisoner. This is 30,000 higher than German commanders' estimates. The correct number is probably somewhere in between.

The Americans also suffered grievously although not so decisively. Eisenhower gives 77,000 as total American casualties, of whom 8,000 were killed and 21,000 captured or missing. Charles MacDonald is probably closer to the reality of the cost on the American side: 105,102, of whom 16,000 were killed; 3,058, missing and later declared dead; and 23,554, captured. The British had fourteen hundred casualties, two hundred of whom were KIA.

In just the two-month period December-January, 1944-45, 26,586 Americans were killed in battle or died of wounds in the entire European Theater of War (which did not include Italy). To put this two-month ETO toll of dead American soldiers and airmen in historical perspective; it is equivalent to 50 percent of the American dead in all of World War I; 75 percent, in the Korean War; 56 percent, in the Vietnam War. And these three conflicts lasted, respectively, 22, 36, and 96 months. (The latter, the eight years when virtually all of the casualties were sustained.)

German commanders and the veto by Hitler of all "small solutions," as von Rundstedt called them, the borderland from Monschau, Germany south to the Losheim Gap was always front and center as the main gateway to the ultimate objective, Antwerp, Belgium.

As we know, Hitler assigned what he considered his most powerful army to that front, Dietrich's 6th *SS Panzer*. He made certain it would have sufficient infantry to break the way for the *Panzers*, plus a mighty weight of cannon and *Werfer* pieces to support both infantry and armor as they marched west to the Meuse. Hitler's two favorites, 1st and 12th *SS Panzer* divisions, were assigned the most important armor routes (*Rollbahnen*) of the two attacking *Panzer* armies.

It was crucial for Dietrich's infantry to drive the Americans out of their defensive positions without delay on *Null Tag* so the *Panzers* of 1st and 12th *SS* divisions could leap forward on their five *Rollbahnen*. (Vol. 1, p. 150, footnote) Even a few hours lost could be fatal by giving the stunned Americans in the command centers to the rear time to react and order in reinforcements.

And in the *OKW* plan, both *Panzer* divisions had to make the break for the west together, for one complemented the other: If 1st *SS Panzer's Kampfgruppen* were stymied at Losheim, the left flank of 12th *SS Panzer* would be vulnerable to multiple American attacks as its *Kampfgruppen* tried to move over the N-32 highway to Malmedy and the Elsenborn heights toward Spa, Belgium. In similar fashion, if 12th *SS Panzer* were stymied on the right, 1st *SS Panzer* Division's movement and supply would be menaced by blocks and flanking attacks.

The experience of 1st *SS Panzer* Corps' attack and operations during the first week of the counteroffensive proved how right the *OKW* planners were—to their profound sorrow. The powerful *Kampfgruppe* Peiper of 1st *SS Panzer* Division broke loose (after a twenty-four hour delay); the *Kampfgruppen* of 12th *SS Panzer* did not. And this made all the difference. Not only did 12th *Panzer* fail to fulfill its absolutely crucial mission of rolling across the Elsenborn-Bütgenbach hills but also Peiper's power was ground to extinction in the Amblève River valley because its right flank was unprotected and its supply line, interdicted.

Twelfth *SS Panzer* (*Hitlerjugend*) failed for four reasons:

First, the 99th Division's infantry battalions at Höfen, in the woods east of Krinkelt-Rocherath and at Losheimergraben, Buchholz Station, Hünningen, and Lanzerath buttressed by two battalions of the 2nd Infantry Division, held off for nearly thirty hours the *Volksgrenadiers* responsible for opening the way.

Second, this gave 2nd Infantry Division leaders, from Robertson down, time to get the mass of their men, guns, and armor into a blocking position at Krinkelt-Rocherath.* Here the *Panzers* and *Panzergrenadiers* of 12th *SS* Division became bogged down for two days in pointless, time-consuming fighting.

Third, the quicksand pit that 2nd Division devised at the dual towns for the *Hitlerjugend Kampfgruppe* trying to force its way in enabled the 1st Division on the right, a few miles south of Elsenborn, to construct and man a block that prevented other *Kampfgruppen* of 12th *SS* from turning the flank of the 99th and 2nd divisions.

Fourth, while all this bloody business was going on, General Robertson's plan could be implemented to withdraw the 2nd and 99th divisions and their armor, howitzers, antitank guns, pioneers, etc. from the borderland forests and villages west to the Elsenborn crest. Along with the 1st and 9th divisions, they then sealed off the Monschau-Elsenborn-Bütgenbach front against further enemy attacks.

Thus was lost to the Germans in the Ardennes offensive the most important and direct pathway to the Meuse River, as set forth in the *Wacht am Rhein* plan. And this was not all. By failing to push through to Eupen from Monschau, over the Elsenborn high plateau to Spa, Belgium, and along the N-32 at the base of the plateau to Malmedy, 6th *SS Panzer* Army infantry divisions were unable to interdict the U.S. reinforcements coming south from the vicinity of Aachen, Maastricht, and Liege. In the first week of the German assault, these reinforcements—7th Armored Division, which went to St. Vith; 30th Infantry Division, to Malmedy; 82nd Airborne, to the Amblève River valley—crushed the powerful *Kampfgruppe* Peiper, tangled up the 5th *Panzer* Army's northern flank; and hardened the northern face of the Ardennes "bulge."

The containment of Adolph Hitler's 6th *SS Panzer* Army and chosen instrument for leading the parade of the *Wehrmacht* to Antwerp and the sea was completed by U.S. 18th Airborne Corps between the Ourthe and the Salm rivers southeast of Liege, using these three divisions and other U.S. forces.

The British military historian, B.H. Liddell Hart put it concisely: "Sepp Dietrich's right-hand punch was blocked early by the Americans' tough defense of Monschau (AN: He means the entire Elsenborn sector.). His left-hand punch (Peiper's *Kampfgruppe*) burst through and bypassing

---

* As the reader knows (Narrative VII, Part 1), not the least hair-raising aspect of this hair-raising story is that for some twenty hours of this precious time, General Courtney Hodges, U.S. 1st Army commander, refused to give the order that would allow Robertson and his lieutenants to do what they had to do.

Malmedy, gained a crossing over the Amblève River beyond Stavelot.
...But it was checked in this narrow defile (between the Ourthe and the
Salm rivers), then cornered by an American countermove."

The course and eventual outcome of Hitler's last great offensive of
World War II was thereby wrenched from its original plan and purpose
and put in the hands of Manteuffel's 5th *Panzer* Army. The offensive
wasted away in that army's endless battering of Bastogne and fending
off the ceaseless blows of Patton's army and Collins' U.S. 7th Corps.

The German commanders soon realized the mistake they had made
by not succeeding at Elsenborn. An officer on Jodl's staff at *OKW* said
later, "Elsenborn crest was the doorpost." So long as the U.S. 5th Corps
clung to it, the door could not be swung open for Dietrich's army.
Another *OKW* officer said "the decisive factor" was the failure to secure
the Elsenborn heights. "General Jodl saw great danger from that direction."
SS Colonel Rudolph Lehmann, 1st *SS Panzer* Corps chief of staff, wrote
after the war, that the town of Büllingen at the southeast corner of the
Elsenborn-Bütgenbach line on the all-important N-32 highway "was the
crunch point" of the offensive.

Unfortunately for the German cause, the American infantry, artillery, and armor on the Elsenborn-Bütgenbach heights did the crunching and
not *Hitlerjugend* Division and its *Volksgrenadier* and *Fallschirmjäger*
allies.*

How would the course of the *Wehrmacht's* great counteroffensive
been changed if Gerow's 5th Corps had failed to stop 12th *SS Panzer*
Division and its infantry allies at Elsenborn? All is conjecture, of course.
However, the immediate military consequences seem obvious.

—For one, the Americans' attempt to form a hard shoulder, as it
was called, to contain the enemy breakthrough in the north would have
been made considerably more difficult. Certainly, the "crunch point"

---

* The U.S. War (later Defense) Department authorized an exceptionally large number of
the most prestigious awards and medals to units and individual soldiers for action in the
Elsenborn battles including the "return" battles described in Narrative X, Part 7.. Fifteen
Presidential Unit Citations were awarded to units—from battalion to platoon—of the three
divisions (1st, 2nd, 99th and the attached armor, combat engineers, and cavalry). Thirty
percent of the twenty Medals of Honor, the highest U.S. award for valor, received by
Americans fighting in Belgium and Luxembourg in 1944-45 (principally the Ardennes
Counteroffensive) were earned in the Elsenborn battles. Four of the six MOH's received
by soldiers of the 2nd Infantry Division, which participated in some of the heaviest
fighting in WW II, were awarded for action in the Elsenborn battles. The one MOH and
56 percent of the Distinguished Service Crosses received by 99th Division men in WW
II were for actions in these battles as well. Major General Walter M. Robertson also
received a DSC for his leadership under fire.

of this position, as it was called, would have been pushed west at least to Spa, Belgium, the city where General Hodges had his 1st Army HQ.

—Sixth *SS Panzer's* front would have opened wide for expanded motion and mobility, and the routes and schedules of the five armored spearheads of 1st and 12 *SS PzDs* could have been maintained with some consistency. Also, the second wave, 2nd *SS Panzer* Corps' two divisions (2nd and 9th), would have experienced an easier passage to the west.

—Supply and reinforcement of all units of 6th *Panzer* Army would have been eased, with more space and roads west available that were free of American harassment on the ground (but not, of course, from the air).

—The movement of U.S. men and material described above from the Maastricht, Aachen, Liege area to shore up vital sectors and defensive hedgehogs south and west of the Elsenborn plateau and the Hautes Fagnes would have been more problematical. Roundabout ways of travel would have been necessary. Bütgenbach and Malmedy would have been occupied by enemy troops and the main north-south road to St. Vith would have been cut in several places. The delay of 5th *Panzer* Army forces at St. Vith, one of the critical engagements of the Battle of the Bulge, might not have been possible.

—The war of 82nd Airborne, 30th Infantry and 3rd Armored divisions on *Kampfgruppe* Peiper in the Amblève River valley would have had to take place elsewhere.

In sum the armored columns of 1st and 2nd *SS Panzer* Corps might still have been stopped short of the Meuse River, but they would have come much nearer to this goal than they did.

U.S. 5th Corps' failure to hold the Elsenborn high plateau and the military setbacks that followed from this might also have nurtured undesirable political consequences for the Western Allies. In unveiling his plan to the *Wehrmacht* commanders for a grand offensive in the Ardennes, Hitler made plain that he was after political as well as military objectives. In fact, the former would flow inevitably from the latter.

Reaching Antwerp and the North Sea would discourage the British Government from investing the lives of any more young men on the continent; widen the fissures among the various Allied commanders; force Roosevelt and the other American war leaders to reappraise their priorities in a global conflict; strengthen Roosevelt's critics in the U.S. Congress; shock the American public into an awareness that a long, hard, deadly row had still to be plowed in Europe.

These were Hitlerian fantasies, but not altogether. The shock of the German attack in the Ardennes-Eifel region, under-manned and -armored and ineptly managed as it was, nevertheless produced serious controversies and strained relations in the Allied Camp, as we know. (Narrative X, Part 2, and footnote p. 318) General Bradley wrote long after the war of "the high-level <u>political</u> and strategic battles that the German attack precipitated. These battles violently shook and very nearly shattered the Allied High Command." (underline added)

In England, Field Marshal Montgomery's supporters in the press and Parliament used the opportunity to rail against the wasteful war strategies of SHAEF and the urgent need for an approach to war making on the continent that would not continue the American-led policy of attrition, as they put it. Also, the British were running out of manpower; the Canadians, too, had suffered serious losses and were unlikely to have the will or means of making up the difference.

The German counterattack and its progress in the first two weeks had more of an impact on the minds and hearts of American leaders than was admitted at the time. The respected war correspondent, Drew Middleton, writing in <u>The New York Times</u> of December 21, 1944, worried that, "the offensive has lost its local character. It now affects the security of more than one U.S. army and the whole character of the war in the West."

The military analyst of <u>The Times</u>, Hanson W. Baldwin, was even more pessimistic. In a column December 20th he wrote, "The capture of the important communication network of Liege...might force the withdrawal of U.S. 1st and 9th armies from the Roer-Aachen area or even the capture of Antwerp or penetration to the sea (by the German armies)." (AN: He obviously did not realize this was the ultimate German objective.)

The American commanders on the scene were either noncommittal publicly, or in General Eisenhower's case, upbeat. In an order of the day soon after the Germans struck, he said, "by rushing out from his fixed defenses, the enemy has given us the chance to turn his great gamble into his worst defeat." In secret messages to the Joint Chiefs in Washington, however, the Supreme Commander expressed more concern. For example on January 7, 1945 he cabled, "I have no doubt that the Germans are making a supreme and all-out effort to achieve victory in the West in the shortest possible time."

Secretary of War Henry Stimson seemed especially shaken by the unexpected power of the "beaten" *Wehrmacht* and pessimistic over what it might mean. On December 27, 1944 he discussed his fears with Chief of Staff, General George Marshall. Marshall too expressed concern over the threat to Antwerp and uneasiness over the *Wehrmacht's* progress.

Stimson wrote in his diary, "(Marshall) said that if Germany beat us in this counterattack and particularly if the Russians failed to come in (i.e. attack in the East), we should have to recast the whole war. We should have to take a defensive position on the German boundary. He believed we could do (this) with perfect safety, and then have the people of the U.S. decide whether they wanted to go on with the war enough to raise the new armies which would be necessary to do it. But that was a problem he (Marshall) did not believe would arise."

Eisenhower and Churchill made a vigorous effort to persuade ("beg" might not be an exaggeration) Marshal Stalin to accelerate his planned spring offensive against the German armies in the East. This, too, seems to show how concerned the two leaders were over the Ardennes-Eifel battles.

On January 6 Churchill wrote a personal note to Stalin, "The battle in the West is very heavy....I shall be grateful if you can tell me whether we can count on a major Russian offensive during January. I regard the matter as urgent." Eisenhower did, too. A week later, his deputy, Air Chief Marshall Tedder, arrived in Moscow, met with the dictator, and learned to his considerable relief that the Soviet Army already had started their spring offensive.

Stalin took great satisfaction in being magnanimous toward his allies. The American military historian, Forrest Pogue, wrote, "The fact that Roosevelt and Churchill had sought Stalin's help gave him a basis for claiming later that he had saved the Western Allies from a defeat at German hands." Yet Pogue's colleague, Charles MacDonald's opinion was that, "The Russian offensive did nothing to ease the situation for American forces in the Ardennes. By the time (it started) the issue (in the West) was no longer in doubt....Born out of an unjustified concern (not far from panic), the call for help from Stalin was ill-considered and unnecessary. It was to help put Stalin in a strong bargaining position a few weeks later at Yalta....The Red Army's drive, proclaimed Stalin, 'resulted in breaking the German attack in the West.'"

All of this ancient history, of the deep concern "not far from panic," as MacDonald termed it, is included here to show that Hitler's Ardennes initiative was not the mere footnote to World War II that it has become for some military historians.

Had things turned out differently. Had the powerful 6th *SS Panzer* Army, which Eisenhower described as "the strongest and most efficient mobile reserve remaining to the enemy..." stormed across the Elsenborn high plateau and reached the environs of Liege on the Meuse River, pulling forward the northern (right) flank of Manteuffel's 5th *Panzer* Army in its wake, the "panic" in the Allied camp might have been more menacing.

What difference would this have made in the political dynamics of the war in the West? The military and the political are intertwined, as Hitler knew well and used well during his rise to power. (The defeat of France in 1940 was, after all, due to political factors both inside the French military and in French society at large.) If 1st *Panzer* Corps had overrun the Elsenborn high plateau and carried Dietrich's army to the banks of the Meuse, several political consequences might have followed more serious than those described above that did arise.

At the December 28 meeting, referred to before (Narrative X, Part 5) Hitler told commanders of units participating in *Nordwind*, the strike in Alsace, that the Ardennes Counteroffensive already had achieved much. "The enemy has had to abandon all his plans for attack," Hitler said. "He has had to re-group all his forces....His operational plans have been upset. He is enormously criticized at home. Already he has had to admit there is no chance of the war being decided before August, perhaps not before the end of next year."

As often before *Der Führer* exaggerated. However, there was enough truth in what he told his officers to make us wonder how much "upset" there might have been in Allied plans and how much delay in the spring offensive into the Rhineland and the Saar and criticism at home if matters had gone worse for the Allies. Another year or even eight months of fighting in the West would certainly have given German industry time to produce more jet aircraft, snorkel-equipped submarines, destructive V-2 rockets, and V-1 flying bombs; and given Marshal Stalin a good reason to keep the Red Army leashed while his enemies and his friends in the West savaged each other a little longer.

General Dietrich's 6th *SS Panzer* Army on the Meuse in force might have transformed a serious but ultimately ineffective German counteroffensive into one that threatened Allied plans and preparations for the push into the *Reich* in the spring, provided the Soviet Union with even more opportunities for post-war mischief, and caused Churchill and a gravely ill Roosevelt political troubles at home they didn't need on the eve of the tripartite Yalta Conference.

However, 6th *Panzer* did not reach the Meuse on even one of the *Rollbahnen* allocated to it by Hitler. In the words of Hugh Cole, "(It) had begun the Ardennes Counteroffensive with two distinct missions in hand: The first, to cross the Meuse between Liege and Huy as a prelude to the seizure of Antwerp. The second, to wheel a cordon of divisions onto a blocking line extending due east of Liege to cover the depth of the advancing army and to deny incoming Allied reinforcements the use of the highway complex southeast of Liege....Sixth *Panzer* Army failed to achieve the momentum and maneuver room requisite to the assigned missions."

This failure was caused in large part to the blockage of 1st *SS Panzer* Corps' right wing in the battles described in our ten Narratives. The American soldiers who fought these battles could not have known— and would not have cared much—what consequences, great or small, might follow the bloody combat they had been plunged into. They were too busy fighting for their lives, maintaining a manly front although riven with terror, following orders, in many cases, to the death. As ever in war, the fighters at the sharp edge existed within a closed world of death and destruction. All else was of little consequence to them.

The European part of World War II ended at midnight May 8, 1945, according to terms of surrender agreed to by General Jodl on behalf of Admiral Doenitz, Hitler's successor as head of the now defunct Third *Reich*. At war's close, the 1st Division occupied ground in and around Karlsbad, Czechoslovakia; the 2nd, Pilsen, also in Czechoslovakia; the 99th, Landshut on the Isar River northeast of Munich, Germany.

For the 1st Infantry Division, May 8 marked the end of a terrible, long journey that had begun with the invasion of North Africa in November 1942. During that journey, the 1st's three regiments (16, 18, 26) logged 292 days of combat on the European continent alone and suffered 19,488 casualties there, not including missing and never found and prisoners of war later returned.

The 2nd Division landed in Normandy the day following D-Day and got caught up in sustained battling in Normandy and Brittany until the end of September, 1944, long after other U.S. units had moved east toward Germany. By war's end, the 2nd had been in combat 303 days and sustained 16,273 casualties not including missing and returned POWs.

The 99th arrived at LeHarve, France on November 6, 1944 and immediately marched east by truck to the front. In 151 days of combat, this neophyte Army reserve division carried its weight in three of the most important and bloody combats of the war in Europe: the blockage of 1st *SS Panzer* Corps at the Elsenborn high plateau, the Remagen bridgehead, and the closing of the Ruhr Pocket. The 99th also took sharp losses scarcely more than a week before the Germans surrendered when several of its companies were savaged trying to cross the Danube River. The 99th sustained 5,311 casualties, not including 33 missing and some 1,000 POWs, several of whom died in the camps.[*]

---

[*] It is an injustice to the men who suffered the misfortune of being taken prisoner by the Germans in the Elsenborn battles that our history has virtually ignored their experiences in and getting to the camps for *Kriegsgefangenen* in Germany. An estimated one thousand three hundred soldiers of the three divisions were taken prisoner during December 1944 and January 1945. Probably three quarters of these were 99th Division men bagged in

With the Japanese surrender early in August, the urgency of moving units to the U.S. for combat in the Far East was replaced by the urgency of moving every soldier to the Zone of the Interior (U.S.) who wanted out. Congressional pressure on the War Department to bring the boys home immediately if not sooner was intolerable. The Army attempted to play fair by giving priority to those with the longest and most decorated service. This was the famous or infamous "point system."

The procedure produced a vast exchange of men among U.S. units on the continent as those designated for rapid repatriation to the states received "high point" men and those held back for temporary or indefinite occupation duty received the low pointers. (Some officers and senior NCOs came to long for the simplicity of fighting the Germans.)

After the dust had settled, the 1st Division, now filled with low-point men and replacements, became among the first of the permanent occupation divisions. The 2nd Division, which had been selected for the invasion of Japan, began its move to the States in July. It was eventually assigned to Fort Lewis, Washington (state) as a permanent part of the standing Army. However, by then most of the senior officers prominent in our story, including General Robertson, had moved on to other duties. The 99th Division, filled with high-point men from other units, returned to the States in September 1945. It was thereupon deactivated, its colors, pennants, and battle streamers folded away.

For the 1st and 2nd infantry divisions the long decades of so-called Cold War that followed, involving the U.S. and its allies, East and West, and the Soviet Union and the other Communist nations, East and West, were anything but cold.

---

the woods east of the dual towns, at Losheimergraben crossroads, Buchholz Station, the rest camp at Honsfeld, and Büllingen. More than a few were taken only after being wounded, which increased the odds they would not survive the camp experience.

By this time, the *Wehrmacht* was running short of food and supplies, even for its own soldiers in the ranks. There was little to spare for the enemy prisoners in the camps. Red Cross packages kept many of the Americans alive, and God help those who didn't receive the packages and had to depend on the meager rations doled out by their keepers. Also, soap and other cleaning products were almost nonexistent for allocation to the POWs. Vermin infested their clothes and sores and abscesses caused by dirt and insect bites plagued them night and day. And for most of their stay in the camps, their barracks were nearly as cold as the winter outside. The German guards seemed not to mistreat them as a rule, although misbehavior or escape attempts were severely punished, and the escapee hazarded a bullet in the back as he ran or hid.

And all of this followed the most miserable and terrifying journey by rail in locked freight cars (goods wagons) in which the POWs were jammed cheek by jowl and subject to intermittent bombing by Allied air force pilots who, of course, could not know the long freight train crawling along below was stuffed to the walls with American POWs.

In July 1950 the 2nd Division was rushed to the Korean Peninsula and the desperate and completely unexpected battle to keep the North Korean Army from occupying all of South Korea. For the next forty-five years, to the time of this writing (1996) in fact, the 2nd would be closely identified with Korea: first, instrumental in helping keep the peninsula at least half free, second, in permanently fronting an always unpredictable and hostile North Korean Army along the famous 38th Parallel demilitarized zone. During the shooting part of the Korean experience, 1950-53, the 2nd was immersed in some of the bloodiest fighting there was up and down the peninsula not only with the North Korean Army but also with the Chinese Army after it stormed en masse across the Yalu River.

The 1st Division remained in Germany for ten years, until June 1955, becoming an important part of the evolving U.S.-Western European defense structure. On returning to the U.S. and its base, Fort Riley, Kansas, the 1st served as a primary combat-ready unit rated for immediate movement and action. In 1965 its then three brigades went to Vietnam and straight into some of the most costly, frustrating combat of that costly, frustrating war.

By 1971 it was back at Fort Riley undergoing the kind of total reorganization (reflagging) that characterized the post-Vietnam Army experience when it became imperative to reinvigorate a severely damaged military organization. The 1st Division (mechanized) fielded two brigades in the Gulf War.

A strange footnote to the post-World War II saga of the three "Elsenborn divisions" is that in 1967, the Army decided to reactivate the 99th Army Reserve Command, a lineal descendant of the reserve unit that had formed the nucleus of the 99th Infantry Division a quarter of a century before. Ninety-ninth ARCOM is a reserve of various support and supply units available for quick mobilization in emergencies to support regular combat units.[*]

---

[*] Such an emergency was the Gulf War and such a unit was a quartermaster company of 99th ARCOM responsible for water purification, generally an operation well to the rear of the fighting front. Made up principally of men and women from the vicinity of Greensburg in Western Pennsylvania, the company arrived in Dhahran, Saudi Arabia, set up shop and were using a large local warehouse as a barracks. The night of February 21, 1991 most of company had bedded down in the makeshift barracks or were getting ready to when a SCUD missile scored a direct hit, killing 28 and wounding another 98.

Ironically, the SCUD was not that much different from the V-1 flying bombs that menaced the 99th's soldiers in the borderland woods along the Monschau-to-Losheimergraben defense line forty-five years earlier. The SCUD was a rocket but an imprecise

The Army of today (1996) has four light divisions (light infantry, airborne, and assault) and six heavy ones (mechanized infantry, armored). The newly reflagged 1st and 2nd are mechanized infantry divisions. Their organization and weapons are of course, much different than were those of their counterparts fifty-two years ago. Also, women soldiers are found in almost all subunits, something more than a few grizzled veterans of the grim days on the Elsenborn plateau find disconcerting.

The traditional infantry regiments of World War II do not exist anymore. Battalions bearing numbers of the old regiments are the building blocks, heavied up, as necessary with armor, helicopters, armored artillery, and whatever else is needed to form the fighting brigades that now make up divisions. The killing power of the latter, as was seen in the Gulf War, is equal to if not greater than that of an entire infantry division of World War II, even powered up as they were with armor and antitank and antiaircraft guns.

Changes in unit designations, reorganizations, and reflaggings over the past few decades make it a rather pointless exercise to try to identify the lineal descendants of the famous old infantry regiments of the 1st and 2nd infantry divisions that fought in the Elsenborn battles.

The 2nd Infantry Division (mechanized) has returned to Korea. In 1996 it consisted of five infantry battalions: 1st and 2nd battalions, 9th Infantry, are with the division in Korea; 1st Battalion, 23rd Infantry is at Fort Lewis, Washington. These are the only battalions in the 2nd at present still carrying the old numbers.

As to the 1st Division (mechanized), the 1st Battalion, 26th Infantry and 1st Battalion, 16th Infantry, are on station at Fort Riley, Kansas. Two additional battalions formerly with an armored division are in Germany serving under the 1st Division flag.

Although few are among the living and those alive have long since retired, a large number of the field and company grade commanders seen in action in our Narratives made important contributions to the combat, training, readiness, and diplomatic missions of the U.S. Army from 1945 to 1975. Commanding an infantry battalion or regiment in the 1st and 2nd infantry divisions in World War II seemed to be a giant step toward becoming a general if the post-war experience of the officers who figured prominently in our Narratives is any indication. At

---

weapon of terror and mass destruction; the V-1 was a large bomb powered by an outboard rocket motor, also an imprecise weapon of terror and mass destruction. Strange echo of mayhem across four decades for the 99th.

least eleven of them were promoted to that rank after the war.[*]

The senior commanders who led the three infantry divisions went on to diverse careers before and after retiring from the Army. Walter M. Robertson left the 2nd before war's end, was promoted to command of 15th Corps and after retirement ran California's civil defense program.

Walter E. Lauer briefly commanded another division in Europe, then retired in 1946 and went to work for the United Nations Relief and Rehabilitation Agency. Afterward he lived in Monterey, California, opening his doors to one and all 99th veterans passing through.

Clift Andrus, acting CO of the 1st at the time of the Elsenborn fighting, received a promotion to major general and command of the division. Later he headed the Field Artillery School and was director of the Army's General Staff, Organization and Training Division.

Clarence R. Huebner, who left the 1st in mid December to become the 5th Corps commander, rose to lieutenant general and eventually became CO of U.S. Army forces in Europe. After retiring, he was head of New York state civil defense.

Illustrative of the myriad interesting (or difficult) post-war experiences and events in the lives of soldiers, high and low, who played a part in our story are the following:

The men of LTC Frank T. Mildren's 1st Battalion, 38th Infantry it will be recalled, came through fire (literally, a *Neblewerfer* attack) to defend the church square in the dual towns. After the war, Mildren, who became a four-star general, held progressively more important commands: 3rd Infantry Division; 7th Corps; deputy CO, U.S. Army, Vietnam; commander, Allied Land Forces, Southeast Europe.

Another impressive move up the Army ladder after the war was that of Thomas Sams Bishop, a major and assistant operations officer of the 99th Division, quoted in a footnote on page 57. In forty-four years in the Army he went from underage enlistee to major general.

Lieutenant Lyle J. Bouck, Jr.'s little Intelligence platoon held off part of a German parachute regiment for one entire daylight period at Lanzerath, Belgium (Narrative IV, Part 3). After release from a German POW camp and return to the U.S. he became a chiropractor. More relevant to this story, he vowed to get his men the recognition they deserved. Bouck spent much of his free time for the next thirty-five years pushing against closed doors to do so. He succeeded finally in interesting the late Senator Jacob Javits, New York. A Congressional

---

[*] See Appendices item p. 434-35 for post-WW II careers and ranks of infantry leaders featured in our story.

hearing was held. The media got interested. And the Defense Department, with some reluctance, did the nearly unprecedented thing of awarding the platoon a Presidential Unit Citation thirty-five years after the action. Four members of the platoon received Distinguished Service Crosses, also.

It will be recalled, General Robertson, and his chief of staff, Colonel Ralph W. Zwicker spent the night of December 16-17 working out the plan to hold the dual towns and clear the borderland woods and villages of U.S. troops. (Narrative VII, Part 2) Following the war, Zwicker went on to reach the rank of major general. Along the way he served as commander of Camp Kilmer, NJ. In the course of routinely approving a batch of promotions he signed one for an Army dentist who it was later alleged had been a member of the Communist Party, or associated with members, or something.

This routine action brought General Zwicker before the Congressional subcommittee of Senator Joseph McCarthy, who at the time (1954) was hunting Communists and alleged Communists in the Army. In questioning Zwicker, the Senator went out of his way to humiliate him, asserting among other things that he did not have the mental capacity of a five-year old and was not fit to wear the uniform. Senator McCarthy's televised performance shocked the military community and disconcerted some of his close political associates in the Congress. It was the first in a chain of entanglements with the Eisenhower Administration and rebuffs by his Senatorial colleagues that finally brought the Senator low.

Captain Frederic J. McIntire was the surgeon of the 3rd Battalion, 393rd Infantry who would not leave the wounded and was therefore taken prisoner on December 17 in the Todeswald. (Volume 1, page 187)[*] Like all Americans interned in Germany he served hard time. After the war, McIntire trained as a specialist and practiced medicine in Lynn, MA, but not for long. By 1957 he was dead of cancer at the age of forty-three.

Some eight million veterans of World War II were still alive in 1996. Some who endured and survived the battles described in our ten Narratives are active in their respective infantry division associations and those of the attached battalions of armor, engineers, antiaircraft artillery, antitank guns, etc. that helped the infantry form and then hold the Gerow line on Elsenborn heights.

---

[*] In early editions of Volume 1, McIntire was erroneously reported as dying in a German POW camp.

And even if the Defense Department has dispensed with the infantry regiment in modernizing the fighting divisions, the veterans of the regiments that fought in World War II under the flags of the 9th, 38th, 23rd, 26th, 18th, and 16th infantries still meet to reminisce and honor the acts of the past and long traditions of these regiments.

Proof of how young many of these old soldiers (and those of the 99th Infantry Division) were fifty-two years ago is the fact that even in 1996 there is an abundance among them of men in their early seventies, the "young old," as the euphemism of the day has it. They and the older survivors still functioning are willing and able to recall the details of experiences they have long since put behind them but never quite forgotten.

It is a sobering experience to attend one or another of their annual meetings and encounter veterans who fifty-two years ago "walked with the white death," or "endured mayhem in dark places," or stood fast at "the Fateful Triangle," or fashioned "a death trap for the *Panzers*" in the dual towns, or fought at "the Bloody Angle" as these horrendous events are labeled in this history.

A decade from now, most will be gone but for now (1996) they are alive, feisty, and quite willing to express their views on what has been written about the battles they participated in (including this history).

Their yearly gatherings invariably include a small memorial service honoring the dead of long ago. Many veterans of the three divisions have returned to the old killing fields, forests, and villages of the borderland southeast of Liege, Belgium. They invariably pay a visit to the military cemetery at Henri-Chapelle, Belgium where are buried hundreds of the men and boys they served with. They walk beside the crosses seeking those bearing familiar names.*

Until the Americans arrived in October 1944 and the Germans attacked in December, the Belgian district of Malmedy had escaped the war, except politically. In 1940 it was detached from Belgium and re-attached to Germany, not an easy change for the many natives opposed to becoming citizens of the *Reich*. Among other doleful results was to put young men in the area at risk of being drafted into the *Wehrmacht*.

Although not all the natives in 1944 were delighted to see the Americans arrive, there was relief that the war had moved east and they

---

* A few 99th Division veterans have organized a project to find the remains of the thirty-three men of the division lost in the borderland area whose bodies were never recovered. With the help of some interested young Belgians and a U.S. Army "mortuary affairs" team, they have discovered six sites containing identifiable remains since 1990.

were quit of it. Where permitted, the local farmers, householders, and small business people began returning to rebuild their lives. Even in those towns where the Americans requisitioned most of the housing and public space, the kind of utter destruction visited on cities like Aachen to the north had blessedly been avoided.

Then at dawn on December 16 the *Wehrmacht* attacked. The most destructive and murderous war imaginable was visited upon the Malmedy district and Germany's Monschau-Mützenich area nearby. The contending forces laid a weight of artillery, bomb, mortar, and rocket ordnance upon the fields, forests, and towns sufficient to obliterate roads, utilities, buildings, dams, even stream banks, and acres upon acres of the high-standing conifer trees.

By early February when the armies moved east, a large part of the Malmedy district and the Monschau area (but not Monschau itself) was a wasteland. The places seen in our Narratives—Höfen, Mützenich, Elsenborn, Bütgenbach, Wirtzfeld, the dual towns, and the rest—were charnel houses of death and destruction: buildings leveled or reduced to rubble; once impressive old churches, lacking steeples, their thick stone walls gouged by shellfire; huge holes torn in the few paved roads; the others churned to muck and mire. And everywhere the detritus of war: broken guns, tanks smashed and burnt, vehicles damaged and immobile in the muck, the dead horses of the German infantry, the dead cattle of the Belgian farmers.

U.S. burial teams roamed the area hunting bodies under the rubble in the villages and towns, deep in foxholes and shell holes and log bunkers in the fields and forests east and south of the heights of Elsenborn, the grisly task hampered by deep snow, day-time thaws, and night-time freezes.

Fifty-two years later, the borderland country shows scarcely any trace of war damage or wastage. In the deep forested areas along the border, the disturbing ruin of a West Wall pillbox squats here and there on the forest floor covered with moss and lichens. Bordering pastures near the international highway east of the dual towns, the weathered concrete "dragon teeth" antitank barriers still stand, resembling the crudely carved lintel stones of a prehistoric religious site, mute evidence that something strange went on there long ago.

Only the 1st Infantry Division memorial, a modest obelisk covered with names of the dead, at what once was Dom Bütgenbach, and the 99th Division memorial, a large grey and pink marble headstone across from the new church on the boundary of Krinkelt and Rocherath, would lead the passerby to believe that once, long ago, soldiers fought and died here.

The Belgian Army *Lager* (camp) two miles west of Elsenborn is still a military post whose troops use some part of the sloping fields east of Elsenborn as a firing range, much to the disappointment of visiting 99th Division veterans. (They are unable to search out the places where they built their underground bunkers and foxholes.)

The eastern half of the Malmedy district and Monschau have evolved from their pre-war economic and physical condition of being a remote small farming and logging area distant even from the provincial cities of Malmedy and Eupen. Tri-country (Netherlands, Belgium, Germany) tourism and recreation plus public investments in international highways and reconstruction have transformed the area.

The natives are bilingual if not trilingual (French, German, Dutch). Hunters and fishermen roam the hilly municipal forests described so many times in these pages or dip lines in the many lakes, reservoirs, and streams: Skiers are attracted to the runs cleared through the forests at such places as the two-thousand foot high Weisser Stein, also referred to before in these pages. Weekenders and honeymooners put up at the many little inns and hotels that have never been more prevalent or pleasant in the small towns and villages. And the restaurants, a few of which certainly deserve a star, are patronized as a special treat by people who motor in from Aachen, Stolberg, Schleiden, Verviers, and Liege. The surviving dairy farms and municipal logging operations give the area an air of authenticity it would not otherwise have as merely a place where people go to recreate.

If the terrible battles that were waged in the borderland country fifty years ago are mostly unmarked and, truth to tell, unknown locally, the U.S. military cemetery at Henri-Chapelle a few miles west of Eupen could not be more devastating as a signifier of war's appalling waste. Henri-Chapelle's indescribably sad and beautiful landscape of grass and white crosses that seem to extend to infinity is austere, elegant, ordered, stoic in its expression of how inevitable is tragedy in the lives of men.

At first sight of the cemetery, the visitor can feel his heart break. He is overwhelmed by sorrow over the lives unlived, girls unloved, children uncreated, work undone, careers unpursued, pleasures unexperienced, sorrows unplumbed and overcome that are the leavings of the War Monster. At Henri-Chapelle the ghosts are always in attendance, not ghosts of the dead under the crosses and the sweet-smelling grass but of the living who might have been. The visitor may find what solace he can in three texts:

"God be praised that to believing souls gives light in darkness, comfort in despair."*

"(To) honor those who died for freedom and in the name of liberty...commemorating their service to mankind."**

"The hero who dies in his life's bloom,
Lives in men's regret and women's tears,
More sacred than in life, more beautiful by far,
Because he perished on the battlefield."***

Or having walked between the crosses the visitor to Henri-Chapelle may put aside the need for solace and bravely bear the wound inflicted upon him by such sadness.

---

* Shakespeare, Henry VI, Part II, Act 2, Scene 1.
** Inscription on 99th Infantry Division memorial across from the church, Krinkelt, Belgium.
*** Tyrateaus' anthem for fallen Spartan warriors, quoted in Edith Hamilton, The Greek Way, W.W. Norton Co., NY, 1983, p. 143.

DOCUMENTATION

The reader is referred to Volume 1, pps. 360 to 364, for an explanation of what is meant by primary and secondary sources as used here, also "MacDonald file" and "Hill correspondence." In addition, on pps. 361-363 of Volume 1 is found a master list of secondary sources that were useful in the preparation of both volumes. Since Volume 1 was issued additional books have been published on the German Counteroffensive of December 1944 in the Ardennes that may be of interest. These include:

Trevor N. Dupuy, et. al., Hitler's Last Gamble, The Battle of the Bulge, December 1944-January 1945, Harper Perennial edition, NY, 1994.

D. Goldstein, et. al., Nuts, The Battle of the Bulge, story and photographs, Brassey, London, 1994.

James R. Arnold, Ardennes 1944, Hitler's Last Gamble in the West, Osprey Military Campaign Series 5, London, 1994. A compact, well-illustrated history of the Ardennes fighting. The author finds space to describe the struggles of the 99th-393rd Infantry with the 277 Volksgrenadier Division in the Todeswald.

Charles Whiting, The Last Assault: 1944, The Battle of the Bulge Reassessed, Sarpedon, NY, 1994. The author has written numerous histories of World War II battles and events. This one is controversial because he argues that General Eisenhower with the cooperation of Bradley and Middleton (U.S. 8th Corps commander) plotted to allow a serious breakthrough by Wehrmacht troops and tanks on the 8th Corps front in order to get them out in the open where American and British air power could destroy them. American reviewers have been critical of his argument. However, the U.S. intelligence failure before the German attack and complacency in the presence of their troop and tank buildup raise questions that probably will never be answered to the satisfaction of all historians, professional and amateur. (See pps. 29-33 of Volume 1 and item on enemy sightings in the Appendices of this volume.)

Danny S. Parker, To Win the Winter Sky, Air War Over the Ardennes, 1944-45, Combined Books, Conshocken, PA, 1994. A well-researched, detailed history of the countless air combats over the Ardennes and adjoining areas that made up, in effect, a second, "Battle of the Bulge."

Roland Gaul, The Battle of the Bulge, December 1944, An Historical Collage on the Ardennes in two volumes, Schiffer Military History, West Chester, PA, 1995.

George Winter, Freineux and Lamormenil, The Ardennes, Fedorowicz, Winnipeg, Ontario, 1995.

Roscoe C. Blunt, Jr., Inside the Battle of the Bulge, A Private Comes of Age, Greenwood, 1994.

In addition to these histories concerned entirely with the German Counteroffensive and the many histories and related works described or cited in the Documentation, Volume 1, pps. 366-367, the following references were consulted in the preparation of Volume 2:

William C. C. Cavanagh, "Dauntless," A History of the 99th Infantry Division, Taylor Publishing, Dallas, TX, 1994. Among the most detailed and candid of all the WW II unit histories. Invaluable reference.

Geoffrey Perret, There's a War to be Won, The U.S. Army in World War II, Random House, NY, 1991.

Albert Speer, Inside the Third Reich, Avon Books edition, NY, 1970.

Id., Spandau, The Secret Diaries, Pocket Books edition, NY, 1977.

(General) J. Lawton Collins, Lightening Joe, An Autobiography, Louisiana U. Press, Baton Rouge, 1979.

James Lucas, Das Reich, the Military Role of the 2nd SS Division, Arms and Armor Press, London, 1991.

Russell F. Weigley, History of the U.S. Army, Indiana U. Press, Bloomington, 1984.

Richard Brett-Smith, Hitler's Generals, Presidio Press, 1977.

Craig W.H. Luther, Blood and Honor: The History of the 12th SS Panzer Division, Hitler Youth, 1943-45, Bender Publishers, San Jose, CA, 1987. This is a well-researched and illustrated history of the division. However, it does not cover the role of Hitlerjugend in the counteroffensive. Hubert Meyer's History does, however. (See Acknowledgements, obverse title page, Volume 1.)

Felix Gilbert, ed., Hitler Directs His War, Octagon Books, NY, 1982.

Samuel W. Mitcham, The German Army Order of Battle, World War II, Stein and Day, NY, 1985.

Otto Skorzeny, My Commando Operations, The Memoirs of Hitler's Most Daring Commando, Schiffer Military History, West Chester, PA, 1995. Included is an interesting section on Operation Griffin.

John Strawson, Hitler as Military Commander, Barnes and Noble, NY, 1971.

Tom Bird, American POWs of World War II, Forgotten Men Tell Their Stories, Greenwood, 1992.

David Johnson, V-1, V-2, Hitler's Vengeance on London, Stein and Day, NY, 1981.

For readers curious to know the names of some of the references to arms and weapons used by the author in the preparation of Volumes 1 and 2, following is a partial list:

W.J.K. Davies, German Army Handbook, 1939-45, Arco, NY, 1981. A compact, well-illustrated little volume that tells everything the nonspecialist needs to know about the arms and organization and basic battle tactics of the Wehrmacht ground forces.

Terry Gander and Peter Chamberlain, Weapons of the Third *Reich*, An Encyclopedic Survey of All Small Arms, Artillery, and Special Weapons of the German Land Forces, 1939-45, Doubleday, Garden City, NY, 1978. Is indeed encyclopedic, and every weapon described is pictured.

Tony Wood and Bill Gunston, Hitler's *Luftwaffe*, Salamander Military Press, London, 1990. An oversize, colorfully illustrated encyclopedic reference covering the principal aircraft and their development history.

Simon Forty, American Armor, 1939-45 Portfolio, Ian Allan Ltd, London, 1981. Well-illustrated little handbook with stats on the basic machines.

Ian V. Hogg, Fighting Tanks, Grosset and Dunlap, NY, 1977.

Id., The Guns: 1939-45, Ballantine Books, NY, 1977. A compact well-illustrated little volume on artillery types and use in WW II on the Western Front.

B.T. White, Tanks and Other Armored Fighting Vehicles of World War II, Peerage Books edition, London, 1975. Well-illustrated, detailed, good coverage of U.S. and German armored fighting vehicles.

Christopher R. Gabel, Seek, Strike, and Destroy: U.S. Army Tank Destroyer Doctrine in World War II, Leavenworth Paper No. 12, U.S. Army Command and General Staff College, Leavenworth, KS, September 1985. Details of WW II tank destroyer types and models, including towed guns, and the rocky history of the weapon and its performance on the battlefield.

USAAF, The Official World War II Guide to the Army Air Forces, Bonanza Books reprint, NY, 1988.

Kenneth Munson, Fighters and Bombers of World War II, Peerage Books edition, London, 1969. An air companion to the B.T. White book on armor. However, not as complete on U.S. and *Luftwaffe* aircraft.

G.M. Barnes, Weapons of World War II, Van Norstrand, NY, 1947. Another well-illustrated, encyclopedic reference work.

John Keegan, Encyclopedia of World War II, Bison Books, London, 1977. Contains numerous entries on weapons and arms used by all combatants in the war.

The compact (generally under fifty pages) booklets issued by Osprey Publishing Company, London covering a large variety of weapons, arms, branches, etc. of both sides are well-illustrated and informative. Excellent for quick reference.

Also, on the weapons and arms used by U.S. Ground Forces in World War II, the standard histories of the war and its countless battles contain much excellent and objective information on their merits and demerits. The reader is referred, for example, to Volume 1, Documentation: MacDonald, Hürtgen, Mighty Endeavor, Trumpets; Weigley, Eisenhower's Lieutenants; Cole, Ardennes; O'Neil, Democracy; Parker, Battle of the Bulge. Also, this documentation Weigley, U.S. Army History and Perret, War to be Won.

Finally, War Department tables of organization and equipment and technical manuals containing full descriptions of weapons and arms and ammunition of the period can be found in U.S. Government archival collections.

<u>Some notes on citations and cross references
used in the documentation for Volume 2.</u>

—Primary sources as defined in Volume 1, pps. 360-61, have also been used extensively in preparing Volume 2.

—The numbers in parenthesis following the referenced quotation indicate the narrative part where the quote will be found. ("...enemy troops..." [4] means Part 4.)

—If the citation is not followed by a quote, the source was used for general information but did not in addition provide a quote.

—Some 250 veterans of the Elsenborn battles were interviewed or corresponded with during the research for the two volumes of THE SHOCK OF WAR, mostly in the period 1980-1985. Their addresses as of that period are given. Some of these have changed in the years since; and sadly but inevitably, some of these veterans have died since our contact with them.

—Many times a primary or secondary source is given that has previously been cited. To save the reader's searching through lists of sources to find the first citation, we use the following system to inform the reader where it is to be found:

For printed works: <u>name, brief title of work, place in documentation where found</u>. (Pallaud, <u>Then/Now</u>, p. 123. Vol. 1, intro., doc., master list, which means the quotation or other reference can be found on page 123 in the book by Jean Paul Pallaud, <u>The Battle of the Bulge, Then and Now</u>, described in the master list of secondary sources in the introduction to the documentation for Volume 1.

For individuals: <u>last name of source, narrative, documentation where original citation can be found</u>. (Burgen, nar. II, doc., which means Charles Burgen, whose address can be found in the documentation for Narrative II, Volume 1. The same is used for cross references to sources named in official materials. (Duffin, nar. III, doc., which refers to Captain Lawrence H. Duffin, combat interview with Captain William J. Fox, 1/27/45. This citation is found in Volume 1, Documentation for Narrative III.)

<u>We Were</u>, above, refers to a source of one of the personal stories at the beginning of the documentation for the narrative. If a different narrative, the number is given. (<u>We Were, nar. VII, doc.</u>)

—Some abbreviations used: ltr., letter to author; interview, taped interview with author; dash (—) preceding unit name stands for U.S.; OCMH, Office of the Chief of Military History; ms., manuscript, i.e. written recollections of enemy officers for OCMH; ETHNIT, European Theater interviews with enemy officers for OCMH; AAR, after-action report; bk., book; bibl., bibliography; CB, <u>Checkerboard</u>, newspaper of 99th Infantry Division Veterans' Association; do., the same.

Narrative VI: HOWITZERS' WAR

<u>Primary Sources</u>

<u>We Were There</u>:

Trice, 2150 Old Shell Rd., Mobile, AL, <u>CB</u>, 10/92.
Press, deceased, <u>CB</u>, 5/90.
Ryals, 317 Ivy Lane, Hewitt, TX, ltr. with enclosures, 3/15/83. Five audio cassettes containing taped recollections by separate cover.
Denhart, 109B Knoll Court, Noblesville, IN, <u>CB</u>, 9/90.
Smith, quoted in Cavanagh, <u>Dauntless</u>, p. 82. Vol. 2, doc., bibl.

<u>Other personal stories and recollections that contributed to narrative</u>:

Clifford D. Lawrence, 20641 Damon St., Harper Woods, MI, <u>CB</u>, 7/83. "...seeing, hearing flashes." (1)
Armand Duplantier, Jr., nar. V, doc. "...bursting all around." (1)
Denhart, <u>We Were</u>, above. "...a miracle..." (1)
Orville A. Morgan, 905 Overbrook Rd., Baltimore, MD, <u>CB</u>, 7/92. "...out all day." (1)
Press, <u>We Were</u>, above. "...can't hit what can't see." (1) "Germans surrounded..." (1)
Curtis Killen, 6813 Whitehall Rd., Norfolk, VA, ltr. to Hill, 2/20/83. "A terrific artillery..." (1)
Ray Hutchinson, 45 Crestwood Rd., Leicester, MA, interview, 7/15/82. "...stay and stay..." (2)
Matt F.C. Konop, 2714 School St., Two Rivers, WI, ltr., 5/5/81. "...noticing several shells land." (2)
Elwood J. Hill, 44 Brookside Rd., Philadelphia, PA, <u>CB</u>, 12/91. "A half hour later..." (2)
Henry B. Dewey, 8 Fenimore Rd., Worchester, MA, <u>CB</u>, 12/91. "Very late in the evening..." (2)
Byers, nar. IV, doc. "...much less seen..." (2)
William Mahaffey, 711 Blucher St., Falfurrias, TX, <u>CB</u>, 1/91. "...sad bunch." (2)
Guy W. Duren, 4707 S. Irvington Pl., Tulsa, OK, <u>CB</u>, 8/88. "Go west and fast..." (2) "Hit the street hard." (2)

Richard H. Folmar, Rt. 16, Box 312-1, Sante Fe, NM, <u>CB</u>, 6/93. "...189 charge
one..." (1) "Everyone was in a state..." (2) "...raked from front to back..."
(2)

Glen Warkentier, interview, 7/22/82. "German training planes..." (2)

Trice, <u>We Were</u>, above. "I was twenty-three..." (1)

Young B. Johnson, Goldthwaite, TX, deceased, <u>CB</u>, 9/87. "...firing over
open..." (1)

Charles V. Romani, 502 Hena St., Greenville, IL, ltr. to Hill, 8/28/82. "Infantry
and artillery...in disarray." (1)

Ryals, <u>We Were</u>, above. "...did run low..." (1) "limit of physical endurance..."
(1)

Id., nar. V, doc. "First information we had..." (1)

Francis Haskins, 820 Robert Rd., Lincoln, NE, <u>CB</u>, 12/90.

Andrew H. Weston, 410 Chieftan Dr., Fairdale, KY, <u>CB</u>, 5/87.

John R. Riley, Route 10, Glasgow, KY, interview, 7/15/82.

Interviews, annual reunion of 2nd Infantry Division veterans, Harrisburg, PA,
7/22/82: Frank C. Graupner, Battery A, 38th Field Artillery; Robert Dent,
Battery A; John P. Wakefield, Battery A, 37th FA; Earl Hurt, Battery B,
32nd FAB.

Charles P. Biggio, Jr., (Colonel-Ret., USA), 6411 22nd St., N. Arlington, VA,
ltr. 7/15/95 correcting ms.

<u>U.S. Official Materials</u>:

—371st Field Artillery Battalion, morning reports for 12/15-19/44, reproduced in
<u>CB</u> 12/91.

—Headquarters, 2nd Infantry Division, "Commendation for 37th Field Artillery
Battalion," 2/14/45, MacDonald file. "An extremely high rate..." (1)

—99th Infantry Division, AAR, 1/1/45 for period 12/1-31, 44, Section IV-
Division Artillery Report.

—393rd Infantry Regiment, AAR, 1/4/45.

—394th Infantry Regiment, AAR, 1/1/45.

<u>Secondary Sources</u>

<u>History of the 12th Field Artillery Battalion in the European Theater of
Operations, 1944-45</u>, Graph Kunstanstalten, J.J. Weber, Leipzig, 5/45.

<u>D+106, The Story of the 2nd Division</u>, forward by Walter M. Robertson, no
date, no publisher.

<u>Second Division History</u>, "The Ardennes Forest," nar. I, doc.

Lauer, <u>Battle Babies</u>, pps. 18, 42. Vol. 1, doc., master list. "...are all
nervous..." (1) "Germans had captured plenty..." (1)

Field Artillery (F) and Antiaircraft Artillery (A) Battalions
Referred to in Text but Not Identified by Unit Number
(Attached battalions generally provided a battery or two only.)

370 (F) working with 393rd Infantry.

371 (F) do., 394th Infantry.

924 (F) do., 395th Infantry.

372 (F) mediums, generalized support for three 99th Division regiments.

37 (F) working with 9th Infantry.

38 (F) do., 38th Infantry.

15 (F) do., 23rd Infantry.

12 (F) mediums, generalized support, 2nd Division.

776 (F) mediums attached to 99th Division by 5th Corps.

987 (F) 155mm long guns, self-propelled, attached to 2nd Division.

200 (F) mediums attached to 2nd Division.

955 (F) do., 2nd Division.

535 (A) automatic weapons attached to 99th Division.

462 (A) do., 2nd Division.

602 (A) gun battalion, in vicinity for anti-robot bomb (V-1) work.

86th Chemical Battalion (4.2-inch mortars), one company attached to 2nd Division.

German artillery units:

Artillery regiments and attached mortar battalions of six attacking divisions plus supporting artillery, mortar, *Flak*, and *Werfer* batteries, battalions, regiments assigned by 67th *Infanterie* Corps, 1st *SS Pz* Corps, 6th Army. *Luftwaffe Jagdkorps*, 3rd *Jagdivision*.

Narrative VII: TO HOLD RUIN AT ARM'S END

Primary Sources

We Were There:

Konrad, 8977 Linville Ave., Livonia, MI, ltr., undated, about 1981, enclosing wartime diary.

Konop, 2714 School St., Two Rivers, WI, wartime diary enclosed with ltr., 1/29/81.

Homan, 303 Henry St., Lexington, SC, interview, 7/22/82.

Perryman, nar. I, doc.

Mildren, interview, 7/22/82, Harrisburg, PA.

Other personal stories and recollections that contributed to narrative:

Konop, <u>We Were</u>, above. "Everything you can..." (2)

Eisler, nar. V, doc. "Our first friendly contact..." (3)

Robert D. Bass, ltr. to parents, 1/5/45, Center for Military History, Carlisle, PA. "For two days and two nights..." (4)

Irving A. Hinderaker, 25 1st Ave., Watertown, SD, diary enclosed with ltr., 12/29/82. "Pancakes with an egg on top..." (2)

Stanley Sorrell, 4112 Central Ave., Middleton, OH, ltr., 2/2/81. (4)

E.F. Graham, Jr., 4139 High Sierra, San Antonio, TX, ltr., 1/30/82. (2) CO of 644 TD Bn.

Harold F. Lenon, 7344 SE 45th Ave., Portland, OR, ltr., 6/2/82, enclosing wartime diary. (3) CO of 644 TD Company.

Ralph V. Steele, 2613 Main St., La Cross, WI, ltr., 9/29/81, enclosing personal recollections entitled "Eyewitness Account of Events Leading up to and Details of the Battle of the Bulge." (3)

Victor Schnee, Ben Salem, PA, interview, 7/22/82. (4)

Official Materials:

Robertson, nar. I, doc. "...use own judgement." (2); "...defensive position..." (2); "...cut to pieces..." (2); "I told (General Gerow)..." (4); "It was generally agreed..." (4); "...bottomless mud." (2)

John H. Hinds, "Summary of Action in Vicinity of 2nd Division Artillery Command Post," 12/17/44. MacDonald file. "...could not believe eyes..." (3) "...the soft ground..." (3)

—OCMH mss. for German commanders' recollections: Priess, Kraemer, Kraas, Kaschner, Viebig, Engle. (1) Numbers in series for interviews with these officers cited elsewhere.

—1st Army, "Report of Operations, 8/1/44 to 2/22/45," pps. 98, 103-104, 107. (1) Pps. 103-108. (2)

Antitank Company, 9th Infantry Regiment, AAR, part II, 12/17/44. (3)

"Commendation," 37th Field Artillery Bn., nar. VI, doc. (3)

Kemp, p. 14. Nar. II, doc. (3)

—38th Infantry AAR and Colonel Boos' Appendix, 1/1/45. (4)

—2nd Engineering Combat Battalion, 2nd Infantry Division, AAR, 1/4/45. (4)

—23rd Infantry "Unit History," pps. 4-6. (3)

1st Battalion, 9th Infantry, AAR. (4)

2nd Battalion, 9th Infantry, AAR undated, "Upon arrival, the full meaning..." (4)

Fritz Kraemer, OCMH ms., A-924. "Extremely difficult country..." (1)

Hugo Kraas, OCMH ETHNIT series, 5/1/47. "Camp Elsenborn group..." (1)

—5th Corps "Combat Interviews," February-March 1945, conducted by Captain
Francis H. Phelps, Jr. with following:
Wesley Knutsen, 3rd Battalion, 9th Infantry, Ammunition and Pioneer
Platoon Commander, 3/18. (4)
George Adams, platoon leader, "C" Company, 38th Infantry, 2/25. (4)
Lloyd Crusius, platoon leader, "B" Company, 38th Infantry, 2/27. (4)
Olinto M. Barsanti, commander, 3rd Battalion, 38th Infantry, 3/15. (3)

Secondary Sources

2nd Division History, nar. I, doc.
Lauer, Battle Babies, p. 36. Vol. 1, doc., master list. "My staff felt..." (2); p.
62, "During the 16, 17, and most of the 18th..." (2)
Speer, Inside Reich, pps. 529-530. This doc., bibl. (1)
F.H. Hinsley, British Intelligence in World War II, Volume 3, Part II, Cambridge
U. Press, p. 444. (1)
Liddell-Hart, German Generals, pps. 278-279. Vol. 1, intro., doc. (1)
Bennett, Ultra in West, pps. 209, 212. Vol. 1, intro., doc. (1)
MacDonald, Trumpets, p. 189. Vol. 1, doc., master list. "Situation...well in
hand." (1) P. 193, "Everything has changed..." (1)
Cole, Ardennes, pps. 46-105. Vol. 1, doc., master list. (1)
Eisenhower, Crusade, chapter 18. Vol. 1, preface, doc. (1)
Bradley, Soldier's, chapter 21. Vol. 1, preface, doc.
Id., General's Life, chapter 38. Vol. 1, preface, doc. (1)
Wilmont, Struggle for Europe, p. 592. Vol. 1, intro., doc., bibl. (1)
John Eisenhower, Bitter, p. 221. Vol. 1, master list, doc. "Probably the most..."
(2)
2nd Battalion, 38th Infantry in World War II, pps. 21-23, mimeo unit history
written by soldiers of the battalion. "...eerie sense..." (4)
23rd Infantry History, pps. 4-6, origin as previous entry. (3)
Cavanagh, Krinkelt-Rocherath, p. 75. Vol. 1, master list, doc., quoting Robert
W. Bricker. "He wanted to know the type of guns..." (3)
Id., Dauntless, vol. 2, bibl., doc., quoting Thomas B. Bishop. "The remainder
of the command..." (2 foot)

Units Referred to in Text but Not Identified by Number
(Wirtzfeld area only. Generally only part of the battalion present.)

644 Tank Destroyer Bn. (self-propelled)
612 do. (towed)
462 Antiaircraft Bn. (automatic weapons)
741 Tank Battalion
37 Field Artillery Bn., 2nd Division
372 do. 99th Division

Narrative VIII: MORTAL ENGINES

Primary Sources

We Were There:

Oran, 2222 5th Ave., Kearney, NE, interview, Harrisburg, PA, 7/22/82.

Graupner, Reading, MA, interview, 7/22/82.

Heilman, 1624 S. 7th St., Chickasha, OK, interview, Chicago, IL, 7/12/80.

Love, 400 Rainbow Dr., Staunton, VA, interview, 7/22/82.

Dudley, 305 S. Cherry Grove Ave., Annapolis, MD, undated ltr. enclosing completed questionnaire.

Leone, 54 Terrace Ave., Albany, NY, ltr. to Larry Taylor, quoted in CB, 4/87.

Savard, 2106 Radatz Ave., N. St. Paul, MN, ltr. enclosing ms. 3/13/81.

Albin, 16027 Avenue "C," Channelview, TX, ltr., 9/4/81, MacDonald file.

Dew, 11051 W. Baldwin Rd., Gaines, WI, ltr., 4/4/81.

"H" Company, 393rd Infantry, mortar squad: the author.

Recollections of 12th *SS Panzer* Division veterans quoted in Meyer, *Kriegsgeschichte*, vol. 1, acknowledgements. Grossjohann (p. 430), Engle (432) Solner (434), Fischer (431), Schulz (425).

Lennon, 7344 SE 45th St., Portland, OR, ltr. enclosing diary, 6/2/82.

Denkert, OCMH, series B-465, 4/47.

Other personal stories and recollections that contributed to narrative:

Hubert Meyer, operations officer, 12th *SS Panzer* Division, ltr. to Hill, 8/10/83. "They could not be trained..." (1)

Herbert P. Hunt, #3 Shamrock Court, Macon Rd., Dublin, GA, "A Rifle Company that Would Not Budge," unpublished memoir, MacDonald file. "Made no sense." (2)

Harry S. Arnold, Rt. 1, Box 745, Roper, NC, ltr., 8/1/81. "Existed as separate..." (2)

Harry Rutledge, 981 Shorecrest Ave., Deltona, FL, interview, 7/22/82. "We had no cover..." (3)

H.E. Coffinger, 1226 Bronx Ave., Kalamazoo, MI, ltr. enclosing questionnaire, 3/81. "All up hill..." (3)

Sorrell, nar. VII, doc. "Take our men..." (3)

H.W. Hankel, "Operations of Company 'M' in Vicinity of Krinkelt, Belgium, December 17-20, 1944." MacDonald file. (3, 4, 5)

Lenon, nar. VII, doc., ltr., 10/5/82. (3-5)

Clarence L. Hiner, Route 2, Moravia, IA, ltr., 4/6/82. "The command post was gone." (3)

Graham, nar. VII, doc., ltr. (3-5)

Roy C. Mullins, 7800 Mockingbird Lane, 177, Fort Worth, TX, ltr., 6/4/82. "Had shot him..." (4)

Ronald R. Mayer, 1409 Meadowbrook Ave., Racine, WI, ltr., undated. (3)

Love, <u>We Were</u>, above. "If the German tank gunners..." (3) "...tell his story..." (5) "We were practically surrounded..." (4)

Robert White, <u>CB</u>, 4/92. "We had to go to the towns..." (3)

John B. Savard, <u>We Were</u>, above. "...passed on to battalion..." (4) "The field in front..." (4)

Edward L. Farrell, 42 Grand Ave., Newborough, NY, ltr., 5/5/96. "The CO, the executive officer, and I..." (3)

Joseph H. Dew, <u>We Were</u>, above. "...wrapping bandage around..." (4)

William R. Smith, 6306 Harlan Dr., Klamath Falls, OR, undated ltr. "Sometime after dark..." (4)

William P. Tucker, 1009 Castleton Way, S. Lexington, KY, <u>CB</u>, 7/92. "Our collecting company..." (5)

Mildren, <u>We Were</u>, nar. VII, doc. "A tank came down..." (3) "Bleeding like..." (3) "Awful, sixty of my men..." (3)

Oran, <u>We Were</u>, above. "What I want you to do..." (5) "The best thing is..." (5)

Zenas H. Hoover, Box 1, Indiana, PA, undated ltr. "We had two trucks..." (5) "What a scary noise..." (5)

Graupner, <u>We Were</u>, above. "Bracketing the road..." (5)

F.J. Topham, Jr., 4200 Carey St., Fort Worth, TX, ltr., 6/4/82. "...fired in clusters..." (5)

R.H. Brannon, 2009 Chesterfield Square, Apt. 1, Columbia, SC, <u>CB</u>, 1/85. "...stumbling and staggering..." (5)

Ben Nawrocki, nar. I, doc. "A bare ridge on Elsenborn crest..." (5)

Robert Newbrough, 7209 Airline, Des Moines, IA, <u>CB</u>, 7/80. "We thought the battle..." (5)

Donald H. Mehus, nar. III, doc., <u>CB</u>, 3/83. "...would have to be there..." (5)

Konop, nar. VII, doc. "(I) was to collect all..." (5)

Ryals, Jr., <u>We Were</u>, nar. VI, doc. Source of story concerning ruse to gather stragglers at Elsenborn ridge for the front. (5)

Bass, nar. VII, doc. (5)

Dudley, <u>We Were</u>, above. (3)

Lennon, nar. VII, doc. His diary is source for Norris' criticism of tank destroyer performance.

Edward L. Farrell, Jr., 42 Grand Ave., Newburgh, NY, ltr. 5/5/96. "The CO, the executive officer, and I..." (3) "I positioned two..." (foot., 4)

Official Materials:

Phelps' combat interviews, nar. VII, doc.

    Carl G. Patterson, platoon sergeant, Company "B," 38th Infantry, 2/26/45. "With the exception of seven men..." (2)

    Wesley Knuston, commander, Ammunition and Pioneer Platoon, 3rd Battalion, 9th Infantry, 3/18/45. (2)

    George Adams, platoon leader, Company "C," 38th Infantry, 2/25/45. "During the rest of the night..." (2) Information from this interview also used for parts 3 and 4.

    Barsanti, 3/15/45 and John H. Murphy, captain, Company "L." (3, 4, 5) Barsanti: "The battalion came to be somewhat..." (5)

—Fifth Corps "Combat Interview" conducted by Captain William J. Fox with Captain Carl S. Swisher, HQ, 2nd Battalion, 393rd Infantry, 1/19/45. (4, 5)

—Unidentified interviewer, combat interview with Lieutenant Colonel William D. McKinley, commander, 1st Battalion, 9th Infantry, MacDonald file. (2, 3)

Roy Allen, 1st, Lt., "B" Company, 9th Infantry, statement concerning combat of his company with *Hitlerjugend Panzers* and *Grenadiers* east of Rocherath. No other reference given. MacDonald file. (2, 3)

John T. Fisher, "Testimony to court convened by G-1 Division, SHAEF, 2/4/45 to examine alleged atrocities committed by 12th *SS Panzer* Division (*Hitlerjugend*) troops in Krinkelt, Belgium. MacDonald file. "He said leave him..." (2)

Kraas, nar. VII, doc. (2, 4)

Viebig, nar. III, doc. "By December 19 the division had lost..." (4)

U.S. 2nd Infantry Division materials:

    Robertson, nar. I, doc. "Successive impulses..." (3) "It was obvious..." (4) "...general concurrence on the accepted..." (4) "Maps showed a road..." (5) "By the end of the action..." (5) "A pretty good day's work..." (5)

    38th Infantry, AAR, 1/4/45, with appendix containing comments of Colonel Francis H. Boos, commanding officer. "It was the last element..." (2) "My third battalion..." (2) "...boundaries and your..." (4) "Destroy all German..." (4)

    23rd Infantry, Unit History for December 1944. (2, 5)

    9th Infantry, 1st Battalion, Unit History, do. 2nd Battalion, do.

    Extract from report, "Operations of Antitank Company, 9th Infantry, 13-20 December 1944, part II, December 17." MacDonald file. (2, 5)

    2nd Combat Engineering Battalion, AAR, nar. VII, doc. "The road was kept passable." (5) Battalion history including citation on occasion of posthumous award of Medal of Honor to Truman Kimbro. (See Part 5, Narrative VIII for engineers' spreading mines and Kimbro sacrifice.)

—741st Medium Tank Battalion, AAR, 12/44. (3, 4)

Kemp, nar. II, doc. (5)

Nelson, C. Works, Jr., "Antitank Guns in the Ardennes," Rpt. No. 2, Operational Research Section, 21st Army Group, undated. (3-5)

Royce L. Thompson, "Tank Fight at Rocherath-Krinkelt, Belgium, 12/17-19/44," OCMH, Washington, DC, 2/13/52. (2-4). "One gains a sense of interplay..." (5)

—395th Infantry AAR, 1/4/45 for 12/1-31/44. (4, 5)

Secondary Sources

MacDonald, <u>Trumpets</u>, p. 383. Vol. 1, doc., master list. "Reach out for God..." (2)

Ibid. "Strenuously engaged..." (2)

Id. <u>Company Commander</u>, p. 139. Nar. III, doc. "Wake up captain..." (2)

"We'll Never Go Overseas, the Story of Vitamin Baker" (Company "B," 741st Medium Tank Battalion), privately printed, undated, pps. 61-76. (3-5)

<u>2nd Division History</u>, p. 104. Nar. I, doc. "So many wounded." (4)

<u>2nd Battalion, 38th Infantry in World War II</u>, nar. VII, doc. (3-4)

Lauer, <u>Battle Babies</u>, foot p. 63. Vol. 1, doc., master list. "...and the line on Elsenborn Ridge..." (4)

Pallud, <u>Then/Now</u>, pps. 94 and 97. Vol. 1, doc., master list, quoting Meyer, op. cit., below. "...promptly engage" (2) "The first sign of..." (2) "We looked at the edge..." (3)

Cavanagh, <u>Dauntless</u>, p. 170. This doc., bibl. "...fought him all the way..." (4)

Meyer, <u>Kriegsgeschichte</u>, vol. 1, acknowledgements, reverse of title page.
     p. 393. "Today was our..." (1)
     p. 422. " Their attack got stuck..." (2)
     p. 425. "...only three antitank units..." (2)
     p. 425. "...east of Rocherath together..." (2)
     p. 425. "Some of this battalion..." (2)
     p. 421. "A very small village..." (1)
     p. 429-30. "...So we left the position..." (1)
     p. 425. "...only three antitank units..." (2)
     p. 431. "I had to abandon..." (3)
     p. 429. "...destroy the enemy..." (1)

Luther, <u>Blood and Honor</u>, p. 57. This doc., bibl. "The *HJ* Division will fight..." (1) Data on division's losses in France in 1944 also from Luther.

<u>Units Referred to in Text but Not Identified by Number</u>
<u>(Some battalions, only one or two companies or batteries in this action.)</u>

105mm Field Artillery Battalions:
    15th, 37th, 38th, 370th, 924th
155mm FA Battalions:
    12th, 955th, 776th, 987th self-propelled guns
2nd Infantry Division units other than artillery:
    Signal Company
    Combat Engineering Battalion
    Medical Battalion and regimental medical detachments
    Quartermaster Company
    Ordinance Company
    Reconnaissance Troop
462nd Antiaircraft Artillery Battalion (automatic weapons)
86th Chemical Mortar Battalion.
612th Tank Destroyer Battalion (towed guns)
644th do., (self-propelled guns)
741st Medium Tank Battalion
989 and 990th *Volksgrenadier* regiments of 277th *VGD*
12th *SS* Reconnaissance Battalion (motorized), 12th *SS* Engineer Battalion.
8th Motorized *Grenadier* Regiment of 3rd *PzGD*
Artillery regiments of 12th *SS PzD*, 277th *VGD*, and 3rd *PzGD*
Batteries of *Volksartillerie Korps* and *Volkswerfer* brigades. Heavy mortar
    batteries of 6th *SS Panzer* Army.

Narrative IX: THE BLOODY ANGLE

<u>Primary Sources</u>

<u>We Were There</u>:

Gast, 604 Park Ave., Prospect, OH, ltr., 9/11/81.
Rivette, 3338 Breton Circle, Atlanta, GA, ltr., 5/10/82.
Stewart, 116 W. 2nd St., Washington, KS, ltr. 2/17/83.
Meyer, <u>*Kriegsgeschichte*</u>, vol. 1, reverse title page, quoting Kretzschmar (p. 445),
    Leitner (445), unnamed *Panzer* commander (444).
Nechy, 1204 Hillcrest Rd., Odenton, OH, audio tape sent to author, no date.
Horner, 2322 S. Pierce St., Arlington, VA, ltr., 4/7/82 enclosing unpublished
    ms. "Comments on the Battle of the Bulge as Viewed by a Battalion
    Commander."

<u>Other personal stories and recollections that contributed to narrative</u>:

Author's recollection, *"Panzers* Break Through..." (1)

Stanhope Mason, 2500 Crest Rd., Birmingham, AL, ltr., 7/9/82. "Never any rough spots..." (1)

E.V. Sutherland, Box 809, Amagansett, NY, ltr., 10/18/81. "All crowded into a pub..." (2) "Go down there..." (2)

George Cataldo, 12 Unity Ave., Revere, MA, ltr., 11/4/81. "Cold, dark night..." (2) "Fires were breaking out..." (5)

Stewart, <u>We Were</u>, above. "Open trucks came up..." (2) "As we got to the edge..." (2) "All our phone lines..." (5)

Thomas J. Gendron, "Operations of the 2nd Battalion 26th Infantry at Dom Bütgenbach, Belgium, December 18-21, 1944. Personal Experiences of a Battalion Operations Officer," Advanced Infantry Officers' Class, No. II, 1949-50, U.S. Infantry School, Fort Benning, GA, p. 32. "Extensive reorganization..." (4) "Visiting all the platoons..." (3) "During the remainder of..." (4) (See also Gendron, Official Materials.)

William Boehm, 5319 Murdock Ave., Sarasota, FL, ltr., 1/1/82. "The shelling of Bütgenbach..." (2)

Vaughn E. Manning, 8623 Starcrest St., San Antonio, TX, ltr., 6/18/82. "About thirty-six of the forty men going..." (3)

Derrill M. Daniel, 1626 NW Baytree Circle, Stewart, FL, answers to questionnaire enclosed with undated ltr. early 1982 (deceased). "I had not been briefed..." (2) "Surrender Yanks." (3)

Rivette, <u>We Were</u>, above. "Why they thought..." (4)

Horner, <u>We Were</u>, above. "It was necessary for me..." (5)

F.G. Prutzman, Box 850, Jackson, MS, ltr. to BG A. H. Hinds concerning artillery emplaced on Elsenborn heights in December 1944-January 1945. MacDonald file. (1)

Rollo J. Moretto, 35-21st St., Long Island City, NY, memoir enclosed with ltr., 5/17/96. "As far as your eye..." (4)

<u>Official Materials</u>:

U.S. 1st Army, Report of Operations, 8/1/44-2/22/45. (1)

—1st Infantry Division materials:

"G-3 (operations section, division staff) Report," December 16-23, 1944. (2-5)

G-2 (intelligence section, do.) "Selected Intelligence Reports, December 1944-May 1945," 6/6/45. (p. 23) "In spite of my suggestion..." (2) "In the darkness..." (3) "The company of *Panzers*..." (3); (p. 24) "...exceedingly heavy artillery..." (3) "The *Panzerjäger* Battalion was..." (4)

AAR, Excerpts for Period December 16-31, 1944, Phase III, "Restoration and Defense of the Bütgenbach-Weywertz-Waimes, Belgium Sector." (p. 7) "Situation building..." (2) "Tell them to stay..." (2); (pps. 19-20) "At 6 a.m. we are firing..." (5); (p. 17) "The Germans want the road..." (5) "The 26th Regiment..." (5); (p. 21) "Carry gas masks..." (5); (p. 19) "Quite a few American and German dead." (5)

—26th Infantry Regiment materials:

"S-2 (intelligence section, regimental staff) Report for December 16-22, 1944." (2-5)

"Unit Journal" for each of following days, December 16-24, 1944. Pages unnumbered. (December 19) "Company "A" is going to move..." and other details on changing position of companies. (2) (December 19) "Want to inform you..." (2); (December 20) "This looks like..." (3); (December 20) "I don't think it is feasible..." (4); (December 21) "This thing is..." (4) (December 21) "...unless in case of..." (4) "Down there somewhere..." (4) "Everything quiet..." (5); (December 22) "Everything is under control..." (5) Journal for December 21 contains report of Colonel Seitz's meeting to decide whether to withdraw north of Bütgenbach or not.

—OCMH ms series B-733, Major General Gerhard Engle, 12/12/47. "...bogged-down offensive." (4)

Author not identified but apparently Gendron, this doc., loc. cit. "Operations of the 2nd Battalion, 26th Infantry at Dom Bütgenbach, Belgium, December 16-21, 1944," Library of Congress MS. Division, p. 15. "All movements thereafter..." (4)

"Extract of History of the 18th Infantry, December 1944." (5)

Colonel J.F.R. Seitz, "Commendation of 955th Field Artillery Battalion," quoted in Bulge Bugle, publication of Veterans of the Battle of the Bulge, February 1995, p. 4. "This position could not have been held." (5) Also firing record of 955th FAB from this article. (5)

Secondary Sources

Meyer, *Kriegsgeschichte*, vol. 1, reverse title page:

p. 437, "With proper leadership..." (1)

Gunter Burdack, troop carrier, 26th *SS PzGD* Rgt., quoted p. 448. "We had to pull back..." (5)

p. 448, "The result was disappointing..." (5)

p. 437, "...room for maneuver..." (1)

p. 444, "There was a row of tall spruces..." (4)

Also for background information, pps. 443, 445, 449, Anlage 19.

This author is also the source of evidence on what we term "the fatal command confusion" in the northern wing of 6th *SS Pz Armee* during the critical days December 20-22. He quotes (p. 442) the *Ob-West* morning report for December 20, 1944. This puts the 277th *VGD* under 67th *Infanterie Korps*; 3rd *PzGD* and 3rd *FSJD* under 2nd *SS Pz Korps*; and 12th *SS PzD*, still under 1st *Korps*. Yet these units were to march on the Gerow Line in unison in a well-coordinated action designed to overwhelm the Americans defending it.

Luther, <u>Blood and Honor</u>, table p. 254. This doc., bibl., for personnel strength of *HJ* Division before and after 12/16.

Cole, <u>The Ardennes</u>, pps. 128 and 603. Vol. 1, doc., master list; MacDonald, <u>Trumpets</u>, pps. 426-27, do.; for changing German views of the Elsenborn ridge position. (1) Model killed himself shortly before the war ended and therefore could not be interviewed by representatives of the OCMH office.

MacDonald, p. 132, quoting LTC Daniel, "I don't know where..." (4)

Ibid., p. 419, "Hardly looked..." (1) Also p. 406 for anecdote re. distraught young *Hitlerjugend Grenadiere.* (4)

George R. de Lame, <u>Spa et les Americains</u>, Editions Soledi, Liege, Belgium, undated, pps. 102-103. "By 2 a.m. 1st Army HQ already had left..." (1)

Hinsley, <u>Intelligence</u>, pps. 442, 444-446. This vol., nar. VIII, doc. (5) (1).

Alistair Horne with David Montgomery, <u>Monty, the Lonely Leader</u>, 1944-45, Harper Collins, NY, 1944, p. 302. "We found it deserted..." (1)

Donald E. Rivette, "Hot Corner at Dom Bütgenbach," <u>Infantry Journal</u>, October 1945, p. 19-23. (2-4)

Smith, <u>Hitler's Generals</u>, p. 161. Bibl., above. "Sick and tired..." (5)

Pallud, <u>Then and Now</u>, p. 104. Nar. VIII, doc. "Our attack collapsed..." (5)

Works, "Antitank Guns in the Ardennes," sheets 3-6. Nar. VIII, doc. (5)

Units Referred to in Text but Not Identified by Number

Field artillery battalions of 1st and two battalions of 2nd divisions.
955 and 200 FABs (mediums)
406 Field Artillery Group (four medium battalions, not all batteries)
103 and 414 AAA battalions (automatic weapons)
745, 741 medium tank battalions
634th, 703 self-propelled tank destroyer battalions (latter with 90mm guns)
801 tank destroyer battalion (towed 3-inch diameter guns)
86th Chemical Mortar Battalion (4.2-inch diameter), one company
On German side, in addition to regiments of 12th *SS Panzer (Hitlerjugend)* Division, the following: 560 *Pantherjäger* Battalion; *Füsilier* Regiment 27 and *Volksgrenadier* Regiment 89, 12th *VGD*; 8th *Fallschirmjäger* Regiment of 3rd *FSJD*; Artillery regiments of 12th *SS PzD*, 12th *VGD*, and 3rd *FSJD*, and batteries of *Volksartillerie Korps* and *Volkswerfer* brigades. Heavy mortar batteries of 6th *SS Panzer* Army.

Narrative X: THE LAST TRIAL: FIRE AND ICE

Primary Sources

We Were There:

Mason, nar. IX, doc.

Iglehart, 307 W. Allegheny Ave., Towson, MD, CB, 7th issue, 1994.

McDaniel, 1610 S. Madison Ave., Albany, OR, ltr. to Robert Cigoy, 909 E.
214th St., Euclid, OH, enclosed with ltr. 6/81.

Duplantier, vol. 1, nar. V, doc.

Wakefield, 5650 W. 57th Ave., Des Moines, IA, interview, 7/22/82.

Viebig, vol. 1, nar. III, doc.

Unnamed rifleman, 277th VGD, quoted in Lauer, Battle Babies, p. 88, vol. 1,
doc., master list.

Moretto, nar. IX, doc.

Stewart, We Were, nar. IX, doc.

Thieleke, quoted in Cavanagh, Dauntless, p. 246. This vol., doc., bibl.

Liebach, quoted in "2nd Division Intelligence Rpts.," p. 38. Nar. IX, doc.

Morphis, ltr. to editor, The Bulge Bugle, August 1990.

Other personal stories and recollections that contributed to narrative:

Walter Hochwald, 6 Canyon Ridge, Irving, CA, CB, 4th issue, 1995. "On
December 20 the Germans came within fifty..." (1)

Simmons, nar. IV, doc., "Many rounds landed on..." "...visibility was good..."
"This gave the enemy excellent observation..." (1). Nar. IV, doc. Source of
observation re. poor foot gear of "K" Co. 394th Infantry. (4)

Newbrough, this vol., nar. VIII, doc., ltr., 7/31/80. "The attack lasted about two
hours." (1)

Iglehart, We Were, above. "The wind was blowing." (1) "...bobbing up and
down." (4) "The sergeant was making up..." (6)

Sil D'Alisera, 92 N. Fulton St., Bloomfield, NJ, CB, May 1985. "They were
practically on top..." (1) "Artillery was pouring in..." (1) "I'm not sure
which was worse..." (1)

Chester Hansen, quoted on National Public Television "American Experience"
series broadcast on most stations in December 1994. "...arrogant, stubborn,
little fellow." (2)

Guy W. Duren, 4707 S. Irvinton Pl., Tulsa, OK, CB, 10/92. (4)

Horner, nar. IX, doc. "A beautiful Christmas tree..." (4) "Aborted..." (7)
"...worst weather..." (7)

Mehus, nar. III, doc. "We improvised a roof to keep out..." (4) "We decided to
make the hole..." (4) " It was so wonderful..." (4)

Charles P. Roland, "GI Joe, Citizen Soldier," nar. IV, doc. "A few men broke under the strain..." (4)

Herbert B. Allen, 606 Waterloo Drive, Clarksville, TN, interview, 7/16/82. "The young medic with..." (4)

W.G. Hawkins, 50 Kenosha St., Albany, NY, ltr., 6/10/92. "One fact is clear.." (4)

Johnson, nar. VI, doc., ltr. to parents, 1/21/45, enclosed with ltr. from son 5/25/95. "We have tried to have a fire..." (4) 1/23/45, "We are the ones..." (6) 2/10/45, "We are quite joyed..." (6)

Sidney Salins, 10 Beechvue Court, Silver Spring, MD and author's recollection. Sources of story re. 393rd Infantry mortar crewmen killed on Christmas eve. (4)

Karl Heinz Franke, quoted in Cavanagh, Dauntless, p. 196. This doc., bibl. "I pulled a shelter half..." (4)

Nawrocki, nar. I, doc. "We were to take all..." (4)

Stewart, We Were, above. "I had a sheepskin-lined helmet..." (4)

Arnold, nar. III, doc. "The Way It Was" (unpublished ms.) p. 61 "...fully covered. It had the usual..." (4); p. 52. "Some holes suffered..." (4) All quotes for part 7:
   p. 76. "Just out from the tree line..."
   p. 86. "The open holes..."
   p. 90. "...exactly as they wanted..."
   p. 92. "...the forest was liberally..."

Duplantier, diary, pps. 24-31, nar. V, doc. "If there were hundreds of rounds..." (5) "The light artilleries..." (5)

Daniel A. Spenser, 3524 Ascot St., Kettering, OH, diary enclosed with ltr., 9/95. "The Germans must think..." (5)

James R. McIlroy, Highway 289, Celina, TX, ltr., 3/11/81. "The time you had to wait..." (6)

Frank J. Peck, 841 N. 24th St., Allentown, PA, CB, 4/86. "We continued toward the German lines for..." (6)

Truman K. Jenkins, Apt. B, 1076 Neil Ave., Columbus, OH, CB, 3/90. "A squad of us was sent out..." (6)

Ernest McDaniel, 4251 Black Forest Lane, W. Lafayette St., IN, CB, 9/91. (6) "...made a right turn and seemed..." (6)

Author, ltr. home, 1/26/44. "We hear of a Red drive..." (6)

Prutzman, nar. IX, doc. "Most of this artillery was squeezed..." (7)

Neil W. Burd, Suite 1207, 1315 Walnut St., Philadelphia, PA, ltr., 2/2/82. "...strewn with our casualties..." (7)

Official Materials:

Denkert, nar. VIII, doc., all quotes for part 1: "Extremely difficult…roads…" "The enemy infantry defense…" "…the extremely lively activity…" "…dismal weather…" "(Their) morale was quite high…" "…we did not reckon with…" "…was not fit for offensive…" "…on account of the considerably…" "The artillery on both sides controlled…" (4)

—5th Corps combat interviews:

    Howe with Douglas, nar. IV, doc., re. 5th Corps arty. hitting 394th Infantry on 12/20/44. (1)

    Fox with McElroy, nar. III, doc. "…lonely, snow-covered land…" (1)

Kraemer, nar. III, doc. "…we had to live from hand to mouth…" (1)

—1st Division, AAR, nar. IX, doc., all quotes for part 3:

    p. 22, "Mediums are bombing Bütgenbach."

    p. 24, "…are dropping markers and bombs…"

    p. 25, "The Town of Malmedy is *kaputt.*"

    p. 27, "Three Focke-Wulfs shot down…"

Liebach, We Were, above. P. 38 of reference. "The old parachutist spirit." (3)

Viebig, nar. III, doc. "(They were) scraped together…" (3)

"G" Company, 393rd Infantry, "Daily Journal," copy enclosed with ltr. from William Smith, nar. VIII, doc. "25 December 44, One seven man…" (4)

Legare, nar. III, doc. "The troops of the 99th Division…" (4)

—1st Division, AAR, p. 29. Nar. IX, doc. "…musicals, voice and instrument…" (4)

SS General Josef (Sepp) Dietrich, OCMH, ETHNIT 15. "I didn't think it was possible…" (5)

—7th Army, "Report of Operations, France and Germany, 1944-45," p. 499. "To be prepared to yield ground…" (5)

—18th Infantry Journal for December 1944, p. 2 of extract. "A deadly training ground…" (6)

—1st Infantry Division, "G-2 Reports," p. 26. Nar. IX, doc. "By mid January, the enemy no longer…" (6)

Ibid., p. 33. "One element that aided the enemy…" (7)

Ibid., p. 38. Liebach, We Were, above. "Our watchword is…" (7)

Secondary Sources

Lauer, Battle Babies, p. 76. Vol. 1, doc., master list. "…over fifty…" (1)

Cole, Ardennes, p. 134. Vol. 1, doc., master list. "After December 22 the 277th no longer possessed…" (1)

"Forever Forward, History of 99th Recce Troop," compiled by enlisted members, undated, 1945. (1)

Field Marshal the Viscount Montgomery of Alamein, <u>Normandy to the Baltic</u>, Houghton-Mifflin, Boston, 1948, re. Bastogne importance. (foot, part 2)

Eisenhower, <u>Crusade</u>, p. 350. Vol. 1, preface, doc. "...the possibility of giving up..." (2) "...all the way to Paris." (2)

MacDonald, <u>Trumpets</u>, p. 611. Vol. 1, doc., master list. "St. George come to slay..."; p. 595, "...full operational direction." (2)

Chester Wilmont, <u>The Struggle for Europe</u>, Carroll/Graf edition, NY, 1952, p. 595 for Colonel Dickson's estimate 12/22/44 of potential German strength. (2)

Weigley, <u>Eisenhower's Lieutenants</u>, p. 545. Vol. 1, intro., doc., additional reading. "...to exploit the opportunity..." (2)

Nigel Hamilton, <u>Monty, Final Years of the Field Marshal, 1944-1976</u>, McGraw Hill, NY, 1987, all quotes for part 2:

p. 17, foot, Hansen, Sylvan diaries ref.

p. 198, "American forces have been cut clean..."

p. 199, "There is a definite lack of grip and control..."

p. 213, "Neither army commander had seen..."

p. 232, "...finds that the four..." "Tapping against 7th Corps..."

p. 243, Sylvan diary, quoted. (William C. Sylvan was aide de camp to Hodges, 1st Army CO.) Reference to Hodges' plan to move heavy equipment.

p. 247, quoting M., "It (is) quite clear..."

p. 255, For source of story on General Horrocks' plan to fight the Germans on the plains of Waterloo, Belgium. M. is quoted as saying, "I am sending Horrocks back to England for a few days. He has gone mad."

Bradley, <u>General's Life</u>, p. 369, vol. 1, preface, doc. "...more arrogant..." Also pages 350-387.

Additional references re. Montgomery's relations with Allies, plans and policies, and leadership initiatives and performance:

MacDonald, <u>Trumpets</u>. Vol. 1, intro., master list, pps. 415-430; 587-604.

Eisenhower, <u>Crusade</u>, loc. cit., pps. 342-366.

Wilmont, <u>Struggle</u>, loc. cit., pps. 580-603.

Weigley, <u>Lieutenants</u>, loc. cit., pps. 445-566.

Perret, <u>War to be Won</u>, 397-415. This vol., doc., bibl.

David Irving, <u>War Between the Generals, Inside the Allied High Command</u>, Congdon and Weed, NY, 1981, numerous references to Monty conflicts. Difficult to separate wheat from chaff in this book.

J. Lawton Collins, <u>Lightening Joe, An Autobiography</u>, Louisiana U. Press, Baton Rouge, 1979, 281-298.

Horne, <u>Lonely Leader</u>, nar. IX, doc.

Elstob, pps. 46-48, 272-5, 261-4, 457-66. Vol. 1, intro., doc.

Bernard Law Montgomery, <u>Memoirs</u>, Collins, NY, 1958.

Essame, <u>Battle for Germany</u>, pps. 92-138. Vol. 1, intro., doc.

Parker, <u>Winter Sky</u>, p. 9. This doc., bibl., above, all part 3. Also pps. 60-66, tables 2, 3, 4; appendix, pps. 515-520; pps. 248-252, source of high altitude aerial battle described part 3. Parker's book provides a detailed account of the air war over the Ardennes, December-January 1944-45.

Cole, <u>Ardennes</u>, pps. 660-663. Vol. 1, doc., master list. (3)

Lauer, <u>Battle Babies</u>, p. 88, quoting unnamed *Landser*, "a sad Christmas..." (4)

William K. Stevens, <u>NY Times</u>, 7/11/95, "violent and unforgiving world..." (4) "...continually beset by predators..." (4)

Liddell Hart, <u>German Generals Talk</u>, p. 292. Vol. 1, doc., intro., bibl., quoting von Rundstedt, "I wanted to stop..." (5)

Cavanagh, <u>Dauntless</u>, p. 195. This doc., bibl., quoting Howard Bowers. "They wore grey overcoats..." (5)

Speer, <u>Inside</u>, p. 531. This doc., bibl., quoting Dietrich, "...tough opponents, good as..." (5)

Wilmont, <u>Struggle</u>, loc. cit., p. 605, quoting Hitler, "...only the offensive will..." (5)

2nd Bn., 38th History, p. 25. Nar. VIII, doc. "...to drive into the enemy outpost line..." (6); p. 28, "...filled to capacity." "There was nothing..." (7)

Cavanagh, <u>Dauntless</u>, pps. 201-203. This vol., bibl.; ltrs. to <u>CB</u> and other 99th Division sources for January 3, 1944 combat patrols. <u>Dauntless</u>: p. 201, "...doom and misery..." "to lead the enemy to believe..." (6); p. 235, quoting Arnold, above, this doc., part 4. "On January 29 we were told..." (7); p. 235, quoting 99th Division G-2, "...counting reserves and everything..." (7)

Units Referred to in Text but Not Identified by Number
Field Artillery-U.S.

Sixteen battalions of field artillery, four each with the four divisions, 1st, 2nd, 9th, and 99th. Only those of 9th Division (26, 34, 60, 84 battalions) not previously identified. Seventy-six, 186, 196, 200, 987 battalions and one battery of 955 battalion assigned by 5th Corps during enemy attacks December 19-22. Afterward all but 200 battalion and 955 battery of self-propelled 155mm guns withdrawn west until January 1945 buildup for attack. About the second week of January, the withdrawn artillery battalions began moving back into the Elsenborn Ridge sector. They were supplemented by batteries of seven additional battalions assigned by 5th Corps plus batteries of 1st-Army assigned 79th FA brigade.

86 Chemical Mortar Battalion (4.2-inch tubes).

Antiaircraft Artillery-U.S.

103 Automatic Weapons Bn.
535 do.
462 do.
602 Gun Bn.

Armor and Tank Destroyer Battalions-U.S.

741 Medium Tank Battalion
745 do.
634 TD Bn. (self-propelled)
703 do.
644 do.
801 TD Bn. (towed guns)
612 do.

Infantry-German

989, 990, 991 *VG* regiments, 277 *VGD*
48, 49 *VG* regiments, 27 *Füsilier* Regiment, 12 *VGD* (departed last week of December, 1944)
751, 752, 753 *VG* regiments, 326 *VGD* (North of Kalterherberg.)
5, 8, 9 *Fallschirmjäger* regiments, 3 *FSJD*
352, 689, 404 *VG* regiments, 246 *VGD* (replaced 12 *VGD* at Büllingen-Wirtzfeld, departed second week of January, 1944)
1055, 1056 *VG* regiments, 89 *VGD* (Entered at Büllingen early January, replaced 246th.)
8, 29 *PzG* regiments and 103 *Panzer* Bn., 3 *PzGD* (departed December 27)

Artillery-German

Artillery regiments of divisions supplemented by:
  405 *Volksgrenadier Artillerie Korps*,
  88, 89 *Werfer* brigades,
  Batteries and companies of 6th *SS* Army guns and mortars plus railroad guns assigned by *OKW*,
  Luftwaffe AAA batteries operating in ground support.

RECKONING - THEN AND NOW
References in order of appearance in text.
Parker, Battle of the Bulge, p. 293. Vol. 1, doc., master list. "...operational armored vehicles."

John Keegan, <u>Six Armies in Normandy, From D-Day to the Liberation of Paris</u>, Penguin Book ed., Middlesex, 1983, p. 323. "As if by symbiosis..."

Re. casualty numbers for the six weeks of combat between the day the *Wehrmacht* attacked, 12/16/44 and the conclusion about 2/5/45, the reader is advised to consult several sources, e.g. Cole, <u>The Ardennes</u>, pps. 673-676; Eisenhower, <u>Crusade</u>, pps. 364-365; MacDonald, <u>Trumpets</u>, p. 618. The latter's numbers in <u>Trumpets</u> are lower than those given in a speech before annual meeting of the Veterans of the Battle of the Bulge, 12/17/81.

    The comparison of battle deaths for the two months, December-January in the European Theater of Operations is based on numbers appearing in a final report of the AGO, Statistical Branch, entitled "Army Battle Casualties and Non Battle Deaths in WW II, Final Rpt., 1953," and those appearing in table 564, "Armed Forces Personnel, Summary of Major Conflicts," p. 359, <u>Statistical Abstract of the U.S.</u>, 1993, Government Printing Office, DC, 1993. To summarize the number of battle dead: WW I, <u>53,000</u>; Korean War, <u>34,000</u>; Vietnam War, <u>47,000</u>. Killed in action and died of wounds in the European Theater of Operations, December-January 1944-45: <u>26,586</u>. Not all of these deaths were sustained in the Ardennes battles. They include USAAF pilots and crews lost elsewhere than over the Ardennes and deaths in the severe fighting across the entire front during the first two weeks of December. However, casualties in Italy are not included.

Liddell Hart, <u>Generals Talk</u>, p. 292. Vol. 1, doc., intro., bibl. "Sepp Dietrich's right hand..."

Cole, <u>Ardennes</u>, p. 578. Vol. 1, doc., master list. "...the doorpost."

Elstob, <u>Last Offensive</u>, p. 475. Vol. 1, doc., intro., bibl. "the decisive factor..." —OCMH ms. collection for Lehmann statement re. Büllingen, Belgium.

Bradley, <u>General's Life</u>, p. 361. Vol. 1, doc., preface. "...high-level political..."

Harry C. Butcher, <u>My Three Years with Eisenhower</u>, Simon and Schuster, NY, 1946, p. 134. "By rushing out..."

Alfred D. Chandler, Jr., ed., <u>The Papers of Dwight David Eisenhower</u>, Volume IV, <u>The War Years</u>, J. Hopkins Press, Baltimore, 1970, number 2226. "I have no doubt that..."

Henry L. Stimson, unpublished wartime diaries on deposit in Yale U. Library: Microfilm copy, Naval Academy Library, Annapolis, MD, reel 9, for period 5/44-9/45. "If Germany beat us..."

MacDonald, <u>Trumpets</u>, p. 605, quoting Churchill. Vol. 1, doc., master list. "The battle in the West..."

Forrest C. Pogue, George C. Marshall, <u>Organizer of Victory</u>, Viking, NY, 1973, p. 504. "The fact that..."

MacDonald, op. cit., p. 605. "...the offensive did nothing..."

Eisenhower, <u>Crusade</u>, p. 340. Vol. 1., doc., preface. "The strongest and most efficient..."

Cole, op. cit., p. 578. "(It) had begun the Ardennes Counteroffensive..."

BACK COVER

Al Boeger, 100 Quartz St., Hot Springs, AR, ltr., 1/10/96. "The confusion, terror..."

Walter S. Melford, 5 Ravine Dr., Hastings on Hudson, NY, ltr., 8/10/95. "I can hardly put down..."

John B. Savard, 2106 Radatz Ave., N. St. Paul, MN, ltr., 1/24/95. "As a member..."

James R. McIlroy, McIlroy Motors, Celina, TX, ltr., 1/27/95. "a marvelous job..."

Editorial, CB, p. 3, 1st issue, 1995. "Without the cumbersome..."

Lionel P. Adda, 5692 Burning Tree Lane, Macungie, PA, ltr., 3/2/96. "A valuable contribution..."

✠   ✠   ✠   ✠   ✠

APPENDICES

Principal U.S. Arms, Units, Other Terms Defined

Aircraft, fighters: P-47 (Thunderbolt), P-38 (Lightning), P-51 (Mustang); Medium bombers: B-26 (Marauder); A-20 (Havoc). These aircraft were employed by the three tactical air commands and the single bombardment command of U.S. 9th Air Force. (Other American and British/Canadian air forces and aircraft also participated in the Ardennes-Eifel battles.)

Antiaircraft artillery (AAA), operating as automatic weapons (AW) or gun (G) battalions. Former armed with 37mm cannons and coaxial .50caliber machine guns four to a mount; latter with 90mm high-velocity long guns.

Antitank battalion:

Self-propelled, 673 officers and men, 6 model-8 armored cars, 36 three-inch or 76mm diameter high-velocity long guns on M-10 or M-18 tracked gun motor carriages. The model-36 carried a 90mm long gun. Three gun companies plus HQ company.

Towed, 814 officers and men, 36 three-inch diameter high-velocity long guns, each towed by half-track personnel carrier. Three gun companies plus HQ.

Armored car, lightly armored, six-wheeled vehicle armed with 37mm gun or .50caliber machine gun. Crew of four.

Army Specialized Training Program (ASTP) of college-level studies for unranked enlisted men. (See p. 417)

Artillery:

Gun, firing shells long distances in a flat trajectory and at a relatively high muzzle velocity.

Howitzer, firing shells at medium muzzle velocity and in a relatively high trajectory. Each U.S. infantry division had 54 105mm (4.2-in.) diameter light (including 18 in infantry cannon companies) and twelve 155mm (6-in) medium howitzers.

Artillery battalion of infantry division, 509 to 518 officers and men; 105 or 155mm howitzers operating in three firing batteries of 4 pieces each; also headquarters battery. Non-divisional battalions under control of corps and army also were available as needed. They were armed with 240mm howitzers, 155mm howitzers and guns, and 4.5-inch guns.

Bazooka, popular name for Rocket Launcher Model 1 firing 2.36-inch diameter shaped-charge projectile. Widely used in Elsenborn battles.

Browning Automatic Rifle (BAR), fully automatic .30caliber rifle, one per infantry squad. (p. 424)

Cavalry reconnaissance squadron, lightly armored, highly mobile force for reconnaissance, fast in-and-out operations, patrolling, maneuver. Generally consisted of 41 officers and 702 men equipped with 40 armored cars, six

75mm howitzers on gun carriages, 17 light tanks, 26 armed halftracks, and 87 jeeps. Two squadrons or more made up a cavalry group.

Combat Command of armored division. Generally, armored divisions were organized for battlefield action into three combat commands (A, B, and R for reserve): tanks, armored infantry, self-propelled artillery, armored engineers, and medics. Comparable to an armored *Kampfgruppe* in the *Wehrmacht.*

Fighter-bombers, fighter aircraft (see entry "Aircraft") armed with bombs (generally one or more 500 pounders) and rockets for ground attack missions. These were in addition to the standard inboard .50caliber machine guns.

Forward observer (FO), an artillery or 4.2 chemical mortar battalion officer whose job it was to observe the enemy and transmit target information via land line or radio to fire direction centers. Artillery FOs were assisted by a radio operator and a jeep driver. The 81mm mortar platoon of an infantry battalion also used FOs.

G-1, 2, 3, 4, respectively, personnel, intelligence, operations, and supply sections of division staff, headed by a chief of staff reporting directly to the commander. Regiment, designation is S-1 etc.

Gun, antitank, a high-velocity, flat-trajectory piece used against armor. Fired armor-piercing ammunition, 57mm (2.3-in.), 3-in., and 76mm diameter, sometimes enhanced with sabots for greater punching power, as well as high explosive and other ammo. An infantry division had fifty-seven 57mms spread through its regiments and battalions. (See also Antitank Battalion and p. 425)

Gun Motor Carriage, Model 10, referred to in text as "tracked tank destroyer," armored, open-turreted vehicle riding on Sherman tank chassis, armed with 3-in. diameter high-velocity antitank gun and a .50caliber machine gun. Crew of five. (See also "Antitank")

Halftrack personnel carrier and multiple gun motor carriage, all-purpose, lightly armored vehicle with drive wheels in front, tracks in back. Used for transporting cavalry, armored infantry troops. Also as mount for guns, mortars, howitzers, quad-four .50caliber AA guns.

Infantry, echelons:

Rifle company, 193 officers and men in 3 rifle platoons, 1 weapons platoon, headquarters. Usually commanded by a captain.

Battalion, 836 officers and men in 3 rifle companies, 1 weapons company (heavy mortars and machine guns), headquarters and headquarters company (antitank, mine, pioneer, recce platoons, and battalion headquarters). Lieutenant colonel.

Regiment, 3,118 officers and enlisted men, 3 infantry battalions; antitank, cannon, headquarters, and service companies; medical detachment. Colonel.

Division, 14,253 officers and enlisted men, 3 infantry regiments; four artillery and one combat engineer battalion; signal, quartermaster,

ordnance companies; military police platoon, cavalry recce troop,medical
battalion. Major general.

"Jerry" cans, metal containers holding five gallons of fluid, usually gasoline or
water.

Machine guns (See Arms Compared, p. 425)

Medical detachment, 136-man unit attached to each infantry regiment, which
provided medical personnel for battalion aid stations and medical corpsmen
for infantry companies.

Mortars, smooth-bore tubes firing bomb-like projectiles for close (200 yards to 3
miles) support of combat troops; common size used by U.S. 60mm (2.4-in.),
81mm (3.24-in.), 4.2-in. diameters.

Noncommissioned officer (NCO), ranked enlisted soldier, corporal though master
(senior) sergeant.

Piper Cub, light, single-engine aircraft of artillery battalions to spot targets,
perform other recce functions.

Recon or recce, reconnaissance unit of infantry, cavalry, tank formations.

Regimental Combat Team (RCT), infantry regiment-size command that included
artillery and engineers and such other arms and units as necessary to do the
mission. Comparable to *Kampfgruppe*. (See German terms.)

Rifle Model 1, semi-automatic basic infantry rifle.

Sherman Model 4 medium tank. (See p. 426)

Stuart Model 5, light tank. (p. 426)

Supreme Headquarters Allied Expeditionary Force (SHAEF), General Dwight D.
Eisenhower's headquarters.

Tank battalion, 750 officers and men, 17 light tanks (Stuart) and 59 medium
(Sherman) tanks, latter in three tank and one headquarters company.

- - - - -

Glossary of German Words Used in Text

Abteilung, detachment, usually battalion in size.

Adlerhorst, Eagle's Nest, Hitler's HQ in the Taunus Hills north of Frankfurt,
Germany.

Ami, slang word for American. *Amis* is plural.

Armeegruppe B: 6th *SS Panzer*, 5th *Panzer*, and 7th *Infanterie* armies, the group
commanded by Field Marshal Walter Model.

Das Reich, honorific title of 2nd *SS Panzer* Division.

Dritte Reich, the *Nazi* state, third German empire.

Ersatz, substitute, replacement.

Fallschirmjäger, parachute infantry of the *Luftwaffe*. (See *Wehrmacht* division
types)

Festung, fortress, as in *Festung Europa*.

Flakwagen, see *Panzer*.

404 SHOCK OF WAR

Fliegerabwehrkanone (Flak), antiaircraft gun.

Focke Wulf, many models, single-piston-engine fighter aircraft.

Führer (der), Adolph Hitler

Füsilier, light infantryman, sometimes travelling by bicycle.

GAF, abbreviation for German Air Force.

Geschütz, gun.

Gewehr, rifle.

Greif, lit. griffin, code name for sabotage operation commanded by *SS* Colonel Otto Skorzeny. (See p. 417)

Grenadier, infantry soldier, see also *Panzergrenadier, Volksgrenadier*.

Gruppe, group.

Heer (das), principal military ground formation of *Wehrmacht*, which included the *Waffen SS* and *Luftwaffe* paratroop, ground, and *Flak* divisions as well. (See also *Wehrmacht*)

Heersgruppe, army group.

Hitlerjugend (HJ), German youth organization, also honorific title of 12th *SS Panzer* Division.

Hohenstauffen, honorific title of 9th *SS Panzer* Division.

Infanterie Korps, 67th, northern wing of 6th *SS Panzer* Army. Later transferred to 15th Army. Of four divisions in *Korps*, only 326th *Volksgrenadier* attacked on *Null Tag*.

Jabo, slang word for American and British fighter-bomber aircraft.

Jagdgeschwader, fighter aircraft wing, generally one hundred or more machines.

Jagdkorps, GAF fighter command.

Jagdpanzer, lit. hunting armor, versatile tank destroyer and assault gun, several models and types.

Kampfgruppe, combat group of varied size, types of units and weapons employed.

Kaputt, done for, ruined, destroyed.

Karabiner, light rifle, carbine.

Korps, 1st *SS Panzer*, consisting on *Null Tag* (below) of 1st and 12th *SS Panzer* divisions; 12th and 277 *Volksgrenadier* divisions and 3rd *Fallschirmjäger* Division.

      2nd *SS Panzer* Corps, consisting of 2nd and 9th *SS Panzer* divisions. In reserve on *Null Tag*.

Landser, common soldier.

Leibstandarte Adolph Hitler (LAH), honorific name of 1st *SS Panzer* Division. (See p. 413)

Luftwaffe, air force, also *GAF*.

Maschinengewehr, machinegun. (See p. 425)

Maschinenpistole, type of submachinegun. (do.)

Messerschmitt Bf 109, many models. Together with the *Focke Wulf* 190, the workhorse fighter aircraft of the Luftwaffe.

Mine: antitank, *Tellermine*. Antipersonnel, *Schrapnellmine, Schützenmine* of plywood, and *Glasmine* of glass.

Mobelwagen, lit. moving van, antiaircraft gun mounted on *Panzer IV* chassis. Also *Wirbelwind* (below).

Nazi, commonly used abbreviation of *National Sozialist Partie* or member thereof.

Nebelwerfer, rocket-firing machine, also *Racketenwerfer*.

Null Tag, literally zero day, attack day, December 16, 1944.

Oberbefehlshaber West (Ob-West), commander of all *Wehrmacht* forces on the Western Front. In December 1944, Field Marshal Gerd von Rundstedt.

Oberkommando des Heeres (OKH), commander of the Army, Adolph Hitler. Also used for *das Heer* HQ and staff thereof.

Oberkommando der Wehrmacht (OKW), commander of the German armed forces, Adolph Hitler. Also used for *Wehrmacht* HQ and staff thereof.

Otto, slang word for gasoline, diesel fuel.

Panzer, literally armor, armored-fighting vehicle, many models and types. See individual entries.

Panzerabwehrkanone (Pak), antitank gun.

Panzerfaust, recoilless launching tube fitted at front with a 100 or 150mm diameter armor-piercing projectile.

Panzergrenadier, infantry transported in mobile troop carriers, trained to work with tanks.

Panzerkampfwagen (Pzkw) IV, V (Panther), VI and *VII (Tiger)*, principal battle tanks of *Wehrmacht* in 1944.

Panzerspähwagen, armored scout car.

Raketenpanzerbüchse, rocket launcher similar to U.S. bazooka.

Racketenwerfer, machine for launching rockets.

Reich, the German state.

Reichsführer SS, leader of the state protective organizations, Heinrich Himmler.

Riesenanschlag, heroic action or blow, Ardennes Counteroffensive.

Rollbahn, march road of armor units.

Schlag, blow or hit.

Schurzen, apron, spaced armor or skirting plates. Shields of armor bolted or welded to *Panzer* hull and turret for added protection against armor-piercing weapons. Sometimes steel mesh was used.

Schützenpanzerwagen, lightly armored troop carrier armed with cannon or machine gun.

Schutzstaffel (SS), lit. protective echelon, security organizations of the *Nazi* state. (See p. 413)

Schwerpunkt, the place of armor concentration in an attack.

Sicherheitsdienst (SD), security service of the *SS*.

Stalhelm, helmet worn by German soldiers; paratroops wore a modified version.

Sturmgeschütz, armored and tracked assault gun.

Sturmgewehr, rapid-fire assault rifle with features of both rifle and machine pistol.

Todt Organization, paramilitary formation of labor units supporting *Wehrmacht*.

Unteroffizier, noncommissioned officer.

Vergeltungswaffe 1 (V-1), literally, revenge weapon; flying bomb, "buzz" bomb, propelled by outboard rocket motor.

Vergeltungswaffe 2 (V-2), a true rocket missile with greatly expanded range and destructive power.

Volksdeutsch, citizen of an area outside the pre-war *Reich* considered to be racially German.

Volksgrenadier, lit. peoples' infantryman, soldier of streamlined infantry division organized after September 1944 or of a division awarded this honorific term. (See *Wehrmacht* division types.)

Volksturm, locally organized collections of under- and overage males lightly armed for a last-ditch defense of the *Reich*.

Volkswerfer, Volksartillerie, etc. As in the case of *Volksgrenadier*, a widely applied honorific meant to imply *das Heer* had become a "peoples' force" of volunteers, an outpouring of fighters who would vanquish the enemies of the *Reich*.

Wacht am Rhein, a code name for the Ardennes Counteroffensive plan.

Waffen SS, lit. weaponed protective echelon, the military formation of the *SS*. The four armored divisions identified in the text were *Waffen SS* divisions. (See p. 413)

Wehrkreis, one of the eighteen districts (home bases) for units of the *Feldheer*.

Wehrmacht, armed forces of *Reich*, including *das Heer*, *Luftwaffe*, *Waffen SS*, *Kriegsmarine*.

Wehrmacht division types seen in action in Narratives:

Fallschirmjäger: three parachute (infantry) regiments; artillery regiment; other support and armor attached when in ground combat role, their usual employment.

Infanterie: three rifle regiments of three battalions each; artillery regiment; antitank and recce battalions; supporting units.

Panzer: one armor and two armored infantry (*Panzergrenadier*) regiments of three battalions each; artillery regiment of self-propelled and motor-towed guns and howitzers; antitank, recce, and antiaircraft battalions, plus supporting units.

Panzergrenadier: assault gun battalion; two regiments of armored infantry (as *Panzer* division); artillery regiment of self-propelled and motor-towed guns; antitank, recce, and antiaircraft battalions, plus supporting units.

Volksgrenadier: three rifle regiments of two battalions each armed with large number of *Sturmgewehr*-type weapons; artillery regiment; *Füsilier* unit; antitank battalion; supporting units. Late in the war, *Infanterie* divisions were sometimes awarded the *VGD* honorific.

Werfer, throwing machine.

Zeitgeist, prevailing spirit of the time.

- - - - -

Chronology of Battles and Other Events in the Ardennes-Eifel Region, December 16-January 31, 1944-45, Not Covered by the Ten Narratives. (Also see map, p. 187)

DECEMBER 16: One infantry and two *Panzer* divisions of German 47th *Korps* (5th *Panzer Armee*) cross Our River on U.S. 8th Corps, 1st Army front. First *SS Panzer Korps* and 66th *Korps* attack U.S. cavalry group in Losheim Gap. The 80th and 85th *Korps*, 7th *Infanterie Armee*, infiltrate front-line positions of U.S. 28th and 5th divisions (8th Corps) on the left.

DECEMBER 17: German 47th *Korps* pushes west across Clerf River toward Bastogne, Belgium. 8th Corps orders reserve armor to the city. German 66th *Korps* infantry, *Panzers* push cavalry west toward St. Vith, Belgium. *Korps* infantry also moves to rear of two U.S. infantry regiments (106th Division) occupying Schnee Eifel east of this city. 1st *SS Korps* (*Kampfgruppe* Peiper) leaves Büllingen, Belgium heading west into Amblève River valley against little opposition.

DECEMBER 18: Clervaux falls to 47th *Korps* (5th *PzA*). One *Infanterie* and one *Panzer* division of *Korps* strike for Bastogne, fifteen miles to the west. *Kampfgruppe* Peiper reaches Stavelot, Belgium. German 66th *Korps* takes Schönberg, Belgium and encircles two U.S. regiments on Schnee Eifel. Overcoming numerous U.S. 5th-28th division strongpoints, German 7th *Armee's* two *Korps* keep grinding forward west of Sauer River: 85th *Korps*, toward Wiltz, Luxem-bourg, eight miles southeast of Bastogne; 80th, toward Diekirch, north of Luxembourg City. U.S. paratroops (82nd, 101st airborne divisions), only SHAEF reserve, are on the road to the breakthrough area. Ninth *SS Pz* Division (2nd *SS Pz Korps*) starts moving toward Vielsalm, Belgium, south of Peiper *KG*, is hampered by traffic, lack of good roads for supply.

DECEMBER 19: Peiper *KG* attack by new U.S. force (30th Infantry Division) west of Malmedy. Two surrounded U.S. regiments on Schnee Eifel are forced to surrender. German 66th *Korps* moves too slowly in attack on important road junction of St. Vith. U.S. 7th Armored Division (1st Army) comes in to defend it. German 47th *Korps* is ordered to seize Bastogne, which is only weakly defended by a mixture of U.S. armor and infantry. However, 47th *Korps* infantry fails to move quickly on city; at same time, main *Panzer* unit of *Korps* (2nd *PzD*) bypasses city on the north racing for Meuse River, fifty miles west. Eighty-fifth *Korps* (7th *Infanterie Armee*) takes Wiltz in chaotic fighting and is in position to move on Bastogne from south. Eightieth *Korps* of 7th *Armee* takes Echternach near southern corner of "Bulge" as two U.S. armored combat commands withdraw. U.S. 3rd Army south of breakthrough area begins taking over defense of southern shoulder using 8th Corps (1st Army) survivors. Hard line forming against further German advances south toward Luxembourg City, U.S. 12th Army Group headquarters.

DECEMBER 20: 1st *SS Pz Korps* tries again to reinforce, resupply Peiper *KG*. Skorzeny Brigade tries to take Malmedy. Both initiatives repelled (p. 416). Both sides stage for battle at St. Vith: a *VGD* and armored brigade of 66th *Korps*; a mixed U.S. force (7th AD, a regiment of 106th ID, tank destroyers, engineers). U.S. reinforcements arrive at Bastogne (101st Airborne Division, an armor combat command, TD battalion, several battalions of artillery assigned by 8th Corps and 1st Army). German 47th *Korps* bringing in additional troops, armor, artillery for attack on city. *Luftwaffe* also active. By midnight Bastogne is surrounded. In south 85th *Korps* (7th *Armee*) moving west of Wiltz to block any attempt by 3rd Army to try to open roads into city. Other *Korps* (80th) goes over to defense.

DECEMBER 21: 1st *SS Pz Korps* makes one more attempt to reach Peiper *KG*, again repelled in vicious fighting. Skorzeny Brigade withdraws from sector. St. Vith battle joined. U.S. defense extends in wide arc east of the city. Two divisions of 66th *Korps* aided by armor drive in defense, which is then reformed for a last-ditch stand west of the city. Infantry of 47th *Korps* (5th *Pz Armee*) consolidates positions around Bastogne; American defenders dig in for siege behind wide circular main line of resistance outside city. Second *Pz* Division moves rapidly north of city toward Meuse River in vicinity of Dinant, which is forty airline miles southwest of Liege. German 58th *Korps* (5th *Pz Armee*) sends spearheads toward Houffalize, ten miles north of Bastogne. Second *SS Pz Korps* moves vanguard of two divisions (9th, 2nd) into the new German initiative to punch through the hardening U.S. defense line along the north face of the breakthrough area and take Liege from the south.

DECEMBER 22: *KG* Peiper's situation worsening by the hour. In St. Vith German traffic piles up, causing delay in forward movement, but early in the morning 66th *Korps* (5th *Pz Armee*) forces press on Americans still holding line west of city. U.S. 7th Armored Division (18th AB Corps) ordered to form a "fortified goose egg" and block the Germans' westward flow. British Field Marshal Montgomery, now commanding U.S. forces on the north face of the breakthrough area, countermands the order. South of Manhay, an important town astride the main road from the south to Liege, 2nd *SS PzD* attacks mixed U.S. force. At Bastogne U.S. artillery is running low on ammunition. Fifth *Pz Armee* troops, armor surrounding city begin to close in. USAAF transports drop supplies, ammunition. U.S. Third Army has wheeled 3rd Corps (two infantry, one armored division) 90 degrees from marching in eastern to northern direction. Corps moves off in execrable weather to relieve Bastogne. 85th *Korps* (7th *Armee*) tries to move across 3rd Army line of advance.

DECEMBER 23: Peiper moves east on foot with survivors of *KG* to reach friendly lines. St. Vith defenders withdraw from "goose egg" and move north into 18th AB Corps lines, adding power to American defenses against northward drive of 6th *SS Pz* and 5th *Pz Armee*. Second *SS PzD* drives hard against 7th AD, trying to break through to Liege road. Second *PzD* (47th *Korps*) advance units reach Celles, three miles from the Meuse River near Dinant, Belgium. Around Bastogne perimeter USAAF fighter-bombers, mediums attack German combat teams of 47th *Korps* moving on American defenders. Third Corps (U.S. 3rd Army) advances north to relieve siege slowed by terrible weather, miserable roads, attacks by 85 *Korps* (7th *Armee*).

DECEMBER 24: British armor begins moving toward Celles from Dinant on Meuse River to block 2nd *PzD* (47th *Korps*) from reaching banks of river. First and 2nd *SS Pz Korps* moving west to stage for drive north toward Liege. Road conditions, shortage of fuel for supply vehicles restricts resupply, reinforcements. Christmas Eve 2nd *SS PzD* drives through U.S. armor to take Manhay, opening the road to Liege from the south. U.S. 3rd Corps (4th AD plus infantry) continues to grind north over nearly impassable winter roads to relieve Bastogne while USAAF bombs and strafes German assault groups, supply lines on ground and its transports fly resupply missions.

DECEMBER 25: U.S. 7th Corps holding western sector of northern face of breakthrough area strikes unexpectedly with 2nd AD at 2nd *PzD* in Celles area. Exhausted U.S. 7th Armored AD (18th AB Corps) begins counterattack at Manhay. *Luftwaffe* bombs Bastogne as 47th *Korps* makes all-out effort before dawn to break through American perimeter. Western arm of attack penetrates to within a mile of city border before being stalled by last-ditch defense on ground and ceaseless USAAF pounding from the air.

DECEMBER 26: Beginning of the end for the Germans. Manhay retaken from 2nd *SS PzD*, which has been weakened by lack of supplies and failure of 9th *SS PzD* to reinforce it. Latter held up by shortage of fuel, congestion on roads west. Series of local attacks by German 58th and 47th *Korps* (5th *Pz Armee*) against towns on northern face from the Salm to the Meuse rivers are repulsed by 7th and 18 AB corps (1st Army). Spearheads of 2nd *PzD* (47 *Korps*) withdraw from Meuse vicinity, leaving behind large amounts of equipment. Third Army armored patrols open narrow passage into Bastogne.

DECEMBER 27-29: Fifth *Pz Armee* mobilizes additional power (6th *SS Pz Armee* [minus 2nd *SS PzD*] and 39th *Pz Korps*) to close 3rd Army's corridor into Bastogne and attack the American defenders there. Third Army (9th Armored AD) opens second road into city as snow piles up and temperature drops. Divisions of two *Panzer* armies engage in localized actions against 18th AB and 7th corps occupying north face of breakthrough area west of Malmedy.

DECEMBER 30-31: *Luftwaffe* opens 5th *Pz Armee* offensive to close Bastogne corridor by bombing city and defenses along perimeter. Simultaneously, U.S. 3rd and 8th corps begin powerful 3rd Army attack with several armored and infantry divisions just arrived on the scene. Ensuing battle in deep snow and bitter cold over barren terrain is one of the most costly for both sides during the Ardennes Counteroffensive.

JANUARY 1: Third Army succeeds in beating off German attacks and forcing 5th *Panzer* and 7th *Infanterie Armee* to retrench and defend against threatening encirclement of units southeast of Bastogne perimeter. *Nordwind* (Narrative X, Part 5), *Operation Bodenplatte* (same).

JANUARY 2: Commander of 5th *Pz Armee* asks Hitler to permit end of costly campaign to take Bastogne, switch his army to defensive operations in breakthrough area, begin withdrawing from Ardennes region. Hitler refuses, orders renewed effort to take the city, stop 3rd Army from marching north.

JANUARY 3: In deep snow, bitter cold, over ice-encrusted roads, U.S. 7th Corps (1st Army) begins drive from northwest into German-held positions north of Houffalize, Belgium; 3rd Army begins march north of Bastogne under same conditions to meet 7th Corps, pinch off waist of "Bulge." German 5th *Pz Armee* makes one more vigorous attempt to stalemate 3rd Army and menace defenders occupying Bastogne. The result is a series of costly running battles that get nowhere.

JANUARY 4: German 5th *Pz Armee* goes on defensive, begins to release *SS* armor for action elsewhere in shrinking breakthrough area.

JANUARY 8: Hitler permits armies to shorten lines, withdraw to defensive positions, signalling end of offensive action.

JANUARY 9-15: U.S. 7th Corps and 3rd Army continue march across the waist of the breakthrough area toward a meeting in vicinity of Houffalize. U.S. 18th AB Corps begins drive on left flank of 7th Corps to take back St. Vith. Hitler orders 6th *SS Pz Armee* to begin staging what remains of its four armored divisions (1st, 2nd, 9th, 12th) for withdrawal to Eastern Front. Advance units of 1st and 3rd armies meet on outskirts of Houffalize.

JANUARY 17-18: U.S. XII Corps (3rd Army) starts second northward drive from vicinity of Diekirch on southeast corner of breakthrough area.

JANUARY 19-31: U.S. 18 Corps (7th AD) recaptures St. Vith on 23rd as Germans accelerate leave taking. Confusion on roads leading east to German border. Our River crossings become disaster area for remnants of 5th *Pz* and 7th *Infanterie Armee* as U.S. artillery, air force pound retreating columns. Only German rear-guard, armored-infantry combat teams still fighting aggressively to allow main body to cross into Germany.

- - - - -

Anecdotal Evidence of German Preparations for Major Attack in the Ardennes

Questions concerning what the American and British commands knew about *Wacht am Rhein*, Adolph Hitler's plan for the attack in the Ardennes-Eifel region of Western Europe in late autumn 1944, will continue to fascinate professional and amateur historians so long as the Battle of the Bulge and World War II remain of interest to them. (See also Introduction, Volume 1, p. 30-32)

In the course of our research and interviewing to gather material for this history, several veterans of front-line units volunteered the information that days before the *Wehrmacht* struck in the Ardennes-Eifel, they witnessed or heard enemy activity "on the other side of the hill," which indicated unusual preparations not for hardening a defense but for taking aggressive action. A few others who served in higher commands also volunteered that at the time they too were receiving information indicating forthcoming enemy action.

Like all events recollected in tranquility forty and fifty years afterward, not all of these "sightings" and "hearings" can be accepted at face value. And as every historian knows, remembrances of participants in an event frequently are influenced by popular perceptions and opinions of the event that followed long after. Nevertheless, so many veterans of the Elsenborn battles whose stories we used for the Narratives made reference to increased enemy activity before December 16 that we decided to include some of their comments here. Explanatory notes and minor additions for the sake of coherence are not in quotes.

- - -

"I recall how we were very much aware of a change in the enemy units" (opposite us on the Schnee Eifel). "We lost some people occupying a forward outpost one of the last nights we were in position. This...indicated a more highly trained and aggressive unit opposing us than we had known in that area. Also, some of our patrols reported that the wood tank obstacles to our front had been sawed close to the ground but were still standing so as to escape detection" (as though being prepared for an attack). (Thomas H. Birch, 333 S. Cascade St., Colorado Springs, CO, ltr. to author, 4/20/82. He was with the 9th Regiment, 2nd Infantry Division.)

- - -

"I remember when we were fighting for Aachen several weeks before December 16, we exchanged intelligence with a British armored division. There were many snippets in their output that we read with interest—long trains moving even then by night into the Schnee Eifel, clusters of *Panzer* troops at the railheads, etc."

"So the intelligence was 'out.' It must have been that 12th Army Group (Bradley's HQ) and SHAEF (Eisenhower's HQ) didn't care to get exercised. Why this could have been, given the terrific (sic) use of the 'difficult' Ardennes in the early days of the war (AN: During the German May 1940 attack on Belgium) still is a mystery to me." (Sutherland, Documentation, Narrative IX, Volume 2)

- - -

"(Pilots of artillery spotter aircraft, i.e. L-2 Piper Cubs) with the battalion detected tank buildup about December 14. It was reported to battalion HQ and relayed to division." (AN: 99th Division HQ Intelligence staff) (Duplantier, Documentation, Narrative III, Volume 1)

- - -

(AN: A soldier of a 393rd Infantry company occupying a sector overlooking a German-held village before December 16.) "Germans active. We could hear them at night. Gave the feeling lots of people there doing something." (Ballard, Documentation, Narrative III, Volume 1)

- - -

"The increase in German activities during the final week before they launched their Ardennes offensive greatly increased the number and length of the daily intelligence summary we (artillery battalion forward observers) turned in on this section of the front. (AN: defended by 394th Infantry, 99th Division) The reports were bucked up to 99th Division HQ or higher..." (Byers, Documentation, Narrative IV, Volume 1)

- - -

"First Division artillery HQ pinpointed 256 batteries of enemy guns east and south of position. Each fired one or two rounds per day. They were registering in during the week preceding December 16." (Mason, Documentation, Narrative X, Volume 2)

- - -

"Our 90mm AAA gun battalion was positioned near Büllingen, Belgium, November 23, 1944. On December 11...we were visited by Colonel Hunt, our battalion commanding officer. (He) conducted a meeting. I was present with four of our officers of the battery. (The colonel told us) the Germans were gathering troops to our front, along with tanks and artillery in order to make a last desperate attack against the American lines....We were reminded that some of our radar equipment was 'secret' and had to be destroyed if capture was likely." (Edward Kapala, 134th AAA Battalion, quoted in The Checkerboard, September 1991)

- - -

(AN: Source of the following was a U.S. Office of Strategic Services [OSS] officer stationed in Ettlebruck, Luxembourg, ten miles north of Luxembourg City, General Bradley's 12th Army Group HQ. His duties were to turn German POWs and pass them in and out of Germany in the vicinity of Vianden on the Our River, a few miles north of Ettlebruck.)

"(We) picked up lots of information that in the hills above Vianden on the German side there was a tremendous amount of buildup of armor troops and fuel. This information we passed on to Eagle Tac" (U.S. 12th AG HQ).... "It was very evident from an intelligence standpoint that something large was in the making. After about three meetings in which we presented the facts as we saw them, I was very strongly scolded by the colonel at the time. (AN: presumably an officer on the G-2 staff of 12th AG HQ). ...they didn't believe this was possible."

"My (OSS) commanding officer in Nancy, France told me...to bypass Eagle Tac and let (him) have the information." (Charles L. Barnes, address to meeting of Veterans of the Battle of the Bulge, Alexandria, VA December 13, 1983. Address transcribed by author at scene.)

- - -

"Around December 11 just before the 2nd Infantry Division left St. Vith, Belgium, we became very concerned about what was going on on the German side. We directed all units to patrol actively in the hope of corroborating apparent evidence of considerable movement on the German side. We thought there was more to it than simply a relief of units. General Robertson (AN: Walter T. Robertson, 2nd Division commander) became so concerned he telephoned Middleton (Major General Troy H. Middleton, CO of U.S. 8th Corps). He told Middleton of his concern and asked for air reconnaissance or something to confirm or disallow (sic) what he thought was happening. Middleton replied, 'Robby, go back to sleep. You're having a bad dream.'" (Ralph Zwicker, former chief of staff of 2nd Division, quoted by Charles MacDonald in papers on file at U.S. Army War College, Carlisle Barracks, PA. Zwicker said he was present when Robertson phoned Middleton.)

- - - - -

Notes on 1st *SS Panzer Division (Leibstandarte Adolph Hitler)* and the Battles of its Lead *Kampfgruppe* Peiper

The *Nazi Schutzstaffel* (*SS*) got started well before Adolph Hitler and his party wormed their way to supreme power in the German state. Its purpose was to provide bodily protection for *Der Führer* and carry out such police and quasi-military duties and tasks as he and his close companion, Heinrich Himmler, might deem necessary to further the ascendancy of the *Nazi* Party in Germany.

By early 1933, when Hitler was appointed chancellor of the *Reich*, the so-called *Allegemeine* (general) *SS* had reached fifty thousand in number, volunteers hastily organized and trained to serve the *Nazi* Party within the developing National Socialist state as a protective and terroristic force. The *SS* evolved quickly into two branches to serve these respective ends: (1) physical protection of the leader and (2) impressment of political foes and unwanted minorities at home and in alien nations when subdued and brought under German hegemony. The latter organization (*Totenkopfverbande*) provided unlimited opportunities for sadists and bullies.

The protective branch in the prewar period was called the *Vergungstruppe*, a small-scale military organization. By 1938 the single regiment of carefully selected, indoctrinated, and trained bodyguards for the *Führer* (*Leibstandarte*) had grown to division size and would soon acquire artillery, transport, and light armored fighting vehicles. With the outbreak of war, Hitler decreed that the division and other *SS* military units of less than division size should participate in combat. By 1940 the *Waffen SS* or armed *Schutzstaffel* had been established as an independent branch of the German army (*das Heer*), although the leaders of the army were always wary of its role. George H. Stein (Documentation, Volume 1, Preface), a close student of the organization has written, "(It) played a role in WW II for which it was not originally intended. Conceived as the *Führer's* elite guard and militarized police force of the revolution, it became instead the elite combat arm of Hitler's *Wehrmacht*...it retained an ethos that was distinctly National Socialist." (p. 294)

As the war waxed more disastrous for the German cause and *Der Führer* became increasingly exasperated with *das Heer* and its generals, the *Waffen SS* turned into a kind of huge fire brigade: It was shoved into the most dangerous and difficult combat roles on first the Eastern Front and immediately after the Allied invasion in Normandy, the Western Front as well.

By early 1944 the *Waffen SS* consisted of thirty-eight divisions, and a variety of smaller units enrolling some six hundred thousand soldiers. By then the organization was also a truly international military force. No single *WSS* division was entirely German in nationality. According to Stein, "It is quite possible the *Waffen SS* was the largest multinational army ever to fight under one flag." (p. 287)

First *SS* Division (*LAH*), however, remained throughout the war the exemplar of the *Schutzstaffel* fighting formations: large, fully armored, led by aggressive, experienced officers, and filled with healthy young fighters well indoctrinated in the ideals and missions of the Third *Reich*. *LAH* participated in every major German campaign during the nearly six years of war. It also endured huge losses, again setting an example. Stein wrote, "The fanaticism or spirited recklessness that characterized the combat performance of the elite *SS* formations resulted in an enormous number of casualties. In fact, most of the old guard—the professionals of the prewar *SS*—died on the Eastern front." (p. 287)

LAH had a symbiotic relationship with 12th *SS Panzer* Division (*Hitlerjugend*). The latter's first commander was Fritz Witt, a much-decorated *LAH* regimental commander, and many of the cadre that went with him to build *HJ* Division also came from *LAH*.

It was no accident that Hitler assigned the absolutely crucial mission of spearheading the *Wehrmacht's* counteroffensive in the Ardennes-Eifel on December 16, 1944 to *LAH* and its "child," *HJ* Division, and insisted that both be fully manned and equipped for their mission. The War Lord put his faith in the power of these two favorites and 2nd and 9th *SS Pz* divisions to accomplish the Meuse River crossings well within the three-day time limit he laid down.

In the event, only 1st *SS Panzer* Division succeeded in the first hours of the German attack in making a clean break for the west, first at Losheim and Lanzerath-Honsfeld, then at Büllingen, Belgium, south of Elsenborn. (Volume 1,

Narrative V, Parts 2 and 3) Its formidable armored *Kampfgruppe* led by *SS* Lieutenant Colonel Joachim Peiper, a 1st *SS* Division battalion commander and highly experienced Eastern-front fighter, broke into the Amblève River valley Sunday, December 17. By late afternoon Peiper and his leading armor had moved across Baugnetz crossroads just south of Malmedy, Belgium, an important small city on the Belgian highway N-32 west of the Meuse.

Near Baugnetz two tank crews of the 1st *SS Panzer* Battalion came upon eighty American prisoners of war waiting disarmed in a field. An officer ordered the gunners to shoot them all. An armored engineer unit next in line finished the grisly job. Peiper himself learned only days later of the massacre and apparently had nothing personally to do with it. As at Honsfeld (Volume 1, Narrative V, Part 2), the killings seemed to have been ordered by keyed-up officers and NCOs determined to show how ruthless they were and how contemptible was their *Ami* enemy. (An *SD* [security service of the *SS*] unit travelling with the *Kampfgruppe* also murdered more than a hundred Belgian civilians later.)

In any case, soon after what came to be known as the Malmedy Massacre, the fortunes of *Kampfgruppe* Peiper began to turn down. The lead vehicles reached the little Belgian town of Ligneuville south of Malmedy. Here they were delayed by the narrow streets and poor roads and valiant (and suicidal) rear-guard action by a few American tank crews. Colonel Peiper had lost radio communication with 1st *SS* Division HQ and was moving blind along his pre-set *Rollbahn* course toward Huy on the Meuse River. His mighty armored column, fifteen miles long, was still essentially intact, however.

By nightfall December 17 forward elements of the *Kampfgruppe* reached Stavelot, Belgium on the Amblève River, where they halted to prepare for a river crossing at dawn. The crossing on an intact bridge was successful but American rear guards fought off the lead *Panzers* and a vast supply dump of gasoline sufficient for all Peiper's needs (and then some) was set afire by the Americans, blocking further advance north of Stavelot.

Peiper sent the bulk of his armor south along the east bank of the river to the conflux of the Amblève and the Salm at Trois Ponts (three bridges) where they planned to cross for a quick run west to the Meuse. However, an *Ami* antitank gun crew and some scratched-together bazookamen and machine gunners delayed Peiper's advanced guard long enough for teams of combat engineers (291st Combat Engineer Battalion) to blow up the bridges thus denying the *Kampfgruppe's Panzers* a means of crossing the river there. Peiper was forced north toward Stoumont where the tough U.S. 30th Infantry Division had already assembled a hasty defense line.

By this time it was Monday afternoon, December 18, and USAAF fighter-bombers were having at the forward elements of Peiper's column, delaying them long enough for the intrepid engineers to blow up another bridge that Peiper was counting on to get his column round Stoumont and the 30th Division fighters there. Peiper's forward armor supported by infantry fought its way into Stoumont early the next morning as the main body moved south to cross the Amblève River by one more bridge still standing and able to bear armor.

This two-pronged attack, so formidable in appearance and potential, depended on fuel supplies coming forward from the east. However, a battalion of 30th Division infantry, plus Sherman tanks and artillery, succeeded in cutting Peiper's supply line at Stavelot, several miles to the east on the Amblève River. His vehicles were running out of fuel.

Another blow fell that night when the Americans found a way to get a truck loaded with TNT on to the last bridge available to Peiper's force and to damage it so badly it would not bear heavy vehicles. He did, however, obtain a powerful new radio that reconnected him to 1st *Panzer* Division HQ and enabled him to inform *SS* Colonel Wilhelm Mohnke, its CO, how perilous was his position. Mohnke sent a strong relieving column of *Panzergrenadiers*, mobile artillery, and assault guns toward Peiper.

However, the American forces circling round the Amblève and Salm River valleys and towns where *Kampfgruppe* Peiper had established strongpoints also were increasing. The U.S. 82nd Airborne Division and a combat command of 3rd Armored Division joined the 30th and the combat engineers. Fierce fighting took place at Stoumont, Stavelot, Trois Ponts, La Gleize. *Kampfgruppe* Peiper was dying hard.

On its north flank, Skorzeny's brigade of scratched-together infantry, paratroops, and armor did not succeed in driving the 30th Division from Malmedy; on the south flank, the relieving column of 1st *SS PzD* (2nd *SS PzGd* Regiment) was blocked by American defense lines west of the Salm and north of the Amblève. Also a grave handicap to this powerful force was the continued occupation of the Elsenborn heights by U.S. 5th Corps, which closed off the best, fastest road west to Peiper.

The relieving force tried to go forward with a two-pronged attack to reach Peiper, from the east and south while the *Kampfgruppe* shortened its lines, hardened its defensive hedgehogs, and prepared for a last-ditch fight until the 2nd *PzGd* column could break through to it. The ensuing battles up and down the two river valleys between the three American forces (30th, 82nd AB, 3rd ArmdCC) and the 1st *SS PzD* were ferocious.

However, the *Panzergrenadiers* of the 2nd *SS PzGd* Regiment failed to force crossings to the west bank of the Amblève River that would have served as springboards to move north and relieve Peiper. The *Kampfgruppe*—or what remained of it—was driven into La Gleize for a last stand. Here, the *SS* troops fought like demons, grimly holding off infantry, tank, and air attacks.

By Saturday afternoon December 23 however, the game was up for *Kampfgruppe* Peiper. He got permission to abandon La Gleize and move back to German lines in the east, if he could find them. Peiper brought out eight hundred or so of his original force of four thousand and left behind all his armor. The mighty 1st *SS Panzer* Division would henceforth be able to field only small combat groups of combined infantry and armor in the Ardennes fighting.

Outcome of Operation *Greif* (Pages 154-159, Volume 1)

The jeep-riding commando teams of *SS* Lieutenant Colonel Otto Skorzeny did roam around the American rear cutting telephone wires, changing road signs, reporting by radio on American troop dispositions, and most effective of all spreading rumors.

Large numbers of American troops, already knocked off balance by the force of the German counteroffensive, now began to see spies and saboteurs in American uniforms here, there, and everywhere. Nervous and trigger-happy soldiers were wont to shoot first and investigate afterward. Woe betide the poor soldier who did not know or had forgotten the night's password. The Americans took extreme, time- and resource-wasting precautions from the battle line all the way back to the flesh pots and soft billets of Paris to maintain "security," and foil Hitler's army of spies and terrorists. Von der Heydte tried to separate his paratroop brigade from identification with Operation *Greif*. However, American soldiers, including not a few of their officers, were certain Skorzeny's men were dropping from the skies all across the Ardennes to do unimaginable mischief. Many "verified" sightings of parachute spies, commandos, and terrorists were reported.

The Americans showed little mercy to the jeep commandos wearing American Army uniforms and taken prisoner. Their fate was a speedy court martial and even speedier execution by musket fire. A few teams did their mischief and got away. Some simply disappeared in the melee. And a few survivors kept slipping across the lines on Quixotic missions until the Germans withdrew at the end of January 1945.

The other *Greif* element, the XYZ strike forces of Skorzeny's brigade were frustrated from the start. One did get moving with Peiper's *Kampfgruppe*, not out in front, as was intended, but as just another unit in the fifteen-mile long column, and a bizarre one at that. The other two were delayed by the 99th Division's stubborn defense at Losheimergraben and along the international highway that prevented a breakthrough for some thirty-six hours and caused a crucial delay in their schedule of operations. Skorzeny bowed to the inevitable, pulled the three armored forces together, and fought them as an armored brigade in the (unsuccessful) siege of Malmedy, Belgium, (above) under the overall command of Colonel Mohnke, *Leibstandarte* Division leader. They took heavy losses there and their fake U.S. tanks, etc. embellished with the American star did them no service.

- - - - -

The Rise and Fall of the ASTP

Companies and batteries of the 99th Infantry Division, which figures prominently in our story, were filled with former members of the Army

Specialized Training Program (ASTP). In fact, at the time it sailed for Europe nearly one quarter of all the enlisted men in the 99th had been student-soldiers in that program. In its infantry battalions 30 percent of the riflemen, machine gunners, and mortar crewmen were former ASTPers. (Volume 1, Introduction, pps. 2-7) In fact, at least twenty infantry and armor divisions fighting in Western Europe in 1944-45 were fleshed out with ex-ASTP student-soldiers in varying numbers.

The ASTP, which got underway officially in December 1942, was the result of two influences that at the time seemed compelling:

(1) The belief of university and college officials that their establishments and personnel should be utilized for college-level and professional training of Army enlisted men. (They faced the problem of large fixed costs and few students to help cover them.)

(2) The belief of the Secretary of War, Henry L. Stimson, and some of his military aides that qualified young soldiers should receive college-level preparation for future leadership and technical responsibilities in an Army and Air Force they expected would need to fight a long war.

The Army's initial goal for enrollment in the program was 150,000. These came almost entirely from the ranks of young soldiers already on active service, some of whom were performing important technical duties in the Services of Supply, the Army Air Force, or the Army Ground Forces. To join the ASTP they were required to give up their ratings. Commanders had no choice about transferring these men to the colleges. They were ordered to if the soldier passed the exam and met other requirements, important duties or not.

Eventually 223 U.S. colleges and universities played host to the ASTP units, as they were called, and 220,000 soldier-students passed through classes there. Their studies were rigidly restricted to pre-engineering, advanced engineering, language, medical, dentistry, and veterinary courses. Seventy percent of the ASTP soldiers were in the pre-engineering group. They studied advanced mathematics and physics and chemistry, with a little English and American History as leavening.

ASTP suffered from two weaknesses that turned out to be fatal:

First, no official of the Army, from Secretary Stimson down, seemed to have a clear idea of what use would be made of the student-soldiers once they had completed their basic engineering studies. Certainly the Army, including its air force, did not and would not need the number of professional engineers the ASTP seemed to be preparing for advanced study.

Vague goals had been announced that the program would lead to commissions as second lieutenants or technical job assignments requiring high levels of skill. Army-originated promotional material implied this in so many words. Yet the goals and intentions remained just that, in the realm of the promotional. Soldier-students graduating from basic engineering would still need considerable training to become specialists. As to lieutenants, the Army and Army Air Force had a surplus.

Second, the Army Ground Forces commanders, from Lieutenant General Lesley J. McNair on down, were opposed to the whole concept of the program. Throughout 1942 and 1943 they were forced to operate under a War Department policy that allocated priority to every branch and service but their own: to the Navy, the Army Air Force, the Services of Supply, the Marines. This in spite of the reality that it was the Ground Forces that would be required in the end to grapple with the enemy on the ground in the bloody battles to come.

Also, the rank and file of draftees and volunteers assigned to the Ground Forces—infantry, artillery, armor, cavalry, etc.—were, in general, those who scored lowest on the classification exams at entrance and exhibited the least promising educational and experience backgrounds. In short, the Army Ground Forces commanders believed the War Department consistently treated their branches and arms as step children in terms of quantity and quality.

Announcement of the ASTP in late 1942 and the War Department plan to withdraw from the ranks of the Ground Forces (and the other Army branches as well) something on the order of one hundred fifty thousand young soldiers with high IQ scores and good potential as noncommissioned officers and technical personnel and send them off to college campuses for some vague kind of education having no relevance to the pressing here-and-now problems of getting troops ready for combat—well, it was just too much.

McNair, not an impetuous soldier, exploded: "With four or five (infantry and armored) divisions being activated each month and preferential assignment to the Air Forces in full effect, this is the worst period of personnel shortage in the history of the Army Ground Forces....And now, with 300,000 men short, we are asked to send men to college."

Nonetheless, both President Franklin Delano Roosevelt and most Congressional leaders supported Secretary Stimson, and the ASTP went forward. But not for long. By early summer 1943, the soldiers assigned to college and university campuses began to arrive to take up their rather difficult courses of engineering, pre-engineering, pre-medical, and language studies. And soon there-after the rumors started that the ASTP was in trouble.

This did not come about because of the failure of the educators to educate or the soldier-students to pass their courses (although attrition in the basic engineer-ing program was high). It came about because by the close of 1943 war on the ground in Europe and the demand for Army divisions in the Far East to stage for the big battles there brought about a serious manpower crisis in the American war-making camp.

McNair (who would soon die under American bombs in Normandy) persuaded General George Marshall, the chief of the U.S. General Staff, that ASTP had to be severely curtailed. All those bright heads and young bodies were needed by the fighting formations being readied for the battlefields of the world. Marshall in turn took the stark Ground Forces' requirements to Stimson and Roosevelt and the Congressional committees. They did not quarrel with them.

Congress, in fact, was in an especially weak position to try to forestall ending the ASTP, no matter the pleas of some influential parents of the soldier-students and media criticism. Policies it imposed had consistently reduced the manpower base for all of the armed services: Eighteen year olds could be drafted but could not be shipped overseas until reaching nineteen. Until well into the war, fathers were exempted from the draft regardless of their age. Congress also insisted on generous deferments for workers in agriculture and critical industries. In late February 1944, the President announced that "almost five million men have been deferred for occupational reasons." This number was in addition to the nearly four million men rejected for service because of physical and mental conditions and ills.

With some nine million men and boys 18 to 45 years old removed from the nation's eligible manpower base, Roosevelt, Stimson, and Marshall brought all the pressure they could muster on the Congress to enact a national manpower law. Their aim was to force qualified men into the service or, if unqualified, into war work and to begin to mobilize womanpower as well. Congress consistently refused to pass such a law.

By early 1944 every ASTP campus in the land was rife with premonitions of the end. On February 18, 1944 the War Department announced that 110,000 (of roughly 150,000) soldier-students would be removed from their campuses and returned to duty with organized units of the various branches and arms wherever needed.

Educators, newspaper editorialists, and some members of Congress were disturbed over this "snatching away of young men undergoing (ASTP) training, a select group numbering only 2 percent of the Army, for conversion into infantry privates," as an Army historian put it. Not all were "snatched away," however. Some thirty thousand student soldiers remained in the program taking pre-medical and dental, advanced engineering, and language studies.

The overwhelming majority of student-soldiers mustered into Ground Forces combat units came from the basic engineering courses. Thirty-five infantry and armored divisions received on the average about one thousand five hundred ASTPers. However, some infantry divisions obtained as many as three thousand replacements from ASTP and a curtailed air cadet program combined. Without exception they entered at the bottom rank as buck privates.

The young soldier-students who found their home in the 99th Division were fortunate. They at least received six months of hard training before shipping out. Some ex ASTPers were sent directly to units slated for imminent shipment to battlefronts or to replacement depots at ports of embarkation. Fortunate or not in their training opportunities, a large majority of the ex student-soldiers found themselves not only in the infantry but also in the most dangerous part of it, the rifle and machine gun units. Their three-to-twelve months of college study did not come cheap.

The ASTP experience seems to have disappeared as a topic of interest even to scholars still turning over the ashes of World War II for neglected subjects that might bear sparks worth fanning into a book or monograph. The series, <u>U.S. Army in World War II</u>, <u>Army Ground Forces</u>, includes a volume, <u>Procurement and Training of Ground Combat Troops</u>, Robert R. Palmer, et. al, 1948, Office of the Chief of Military History, Washington, D.C. Pps. 15-39 and 76-85 of this volume include a concise account of the ASTP. The McNair quotation above is taken from this reference, p. 39.

The best single history is Louis E. Keefer <u>Scholars in Foxholes</u>, <u>The Story of the ASTP in World War II</u>, McFarland and Co., Jefferson, NC, 1988. The author includes a short bibliography of books and monographs. The books cited cover many aspects of WW II but refer to the ASTP in passing. Facts and figures used in the foregoing short history of the program have been derived from either Palmer or Keefer. The Roosevelt quotation is taken from Keefer, p. 169.

- - - - -

Cribbings from Shakespeare

Readers familiar with the plays of William Shakespeare (1564-1616) will recognize phrases, words, descriptions, etc. in the Narratives that have been cribbed from these plays. Following is a mostly complete list including the play, act, and scene in which they can be found verbatim or in slightly modified form, as indicated. We hope readers will take these not as acts of plagiarism but of homage to a poet whose characters spoke of war (as of every other human endeavor) with incomparable power, imagination, and understanding.

Black, fearful, comfortless night... (King John: V, 6)
Pluck the flower of success from the nettle of danger. ("Out of this nettle, danger, we pluck this flower safety." 1 Henry IV: II, 3)
Shallow fears wanting instance... (Richard III: III, 2)
Mortal engines... (Othello: III, 3)
Bottom of all their fortunes... (2 Henry VI: V, 2)
Few die well that die in battle. (Henry V: IV, 1)
Let blood... (Richard III: III, 1)
Icy fingers... (King John: V, 7)
Moles working in the earth... (Hamlet: I, 5)
To send rescue... (Richard III: V, 4)
Screw courage to the sticking point... (Macbeth: I, 7)
Rude throats... (Othello: III, 3)
Death and destruction... (Richard III: IV, 1)
Bruising irons of wrath... (Richard III: V, 3)
Steeped in blood... (Macbeth: III, 4)
Bloody instruction... (Macbeth: I, 7)
Black-browed night... (Midsummer Night's Dream: III, 2)
A murderous hurly burly... (Macbeth: I, 1)

Mortal, staring war... (Richard III: V, 3)
Clamorous harbingers of blood and death... (Macbeth: V, 6)
Die a hundred deaths... (Julius Caesar: II, 1)
Foul womb of night... (Henry V: IV, Prologue)
Broil and battle... (Othello: I, 3)
Cold comfort... (King John: V, 7)
Fire-eyed maid of smoky war all hot and bleeding... (1, Henry IV: IV, 1)
A soldier unapt to weep or exclaim on fortune's fickleness... (1, Henry VI: V, 3)
Night wanderers laughing at their harm... (Midsummer Night's Dream: II, 1)
Blast of war... (Henry V: III, 1)
Bloody strokes... (Richard III: V, 3)
Fire in the flint shows not 'till it be struck. (Timon of Athens: I, 1)
Full soldier... (Othello: II, 1)
Power... ("Will he bring his power?" i.e. soldiers, Richard III: V, 3)
Shuddering fear... (Merchant of Venice: III, 2)
No mourner for that news. (Richard III: III, 2)
Fright the souls... (Richard III: I, 1)
Shivering cold... (Richard II: V, 1)
Desperate undertakings... (Hamlet: II, 1)
Icy fangs...of the winter wind. (As You Like It: II, 1)
Wrathful, nipping cold. (2 Henry VI: V, 2)
Vast confusion... (King John: IV, 3)
Confusion now has made his masterpiece. (Macbeth: II, 3)
A thousand dreadful things... (Titus Andronicus: V, 1)
Engines whose rude throats... (Othello: III, 3)
Blood hath bought blood and blows hath answered blows. (King John: II, 1)
Shake off sleep, death's counterfeit... (Macbeth: II, 3)
Furious winter rages... (Cymbeline: IV, 2)
Harrows me... (Hamlet: I, 1)
Blind cave of eternal night. (Richard III: V, 3)
Shock of arms... (Richard III: V, 3)
Hold...at thy arms end... (As You Like It: II, 6)
Ate him quick. (Richard III: I, 2)
Bloody sign of battle hung out. (Julius Caesar: II, 2)
Into the breach... (Henry V: III, 1)
When sorrows come... (Hamlet: IV, 5)

- - - - -

Weapons Compared

Both sides brought large numbers and kinds of deadly weapons on the ground and in the air to the climactic Ardennes-Eifel battles of late December and January, 1944-45. However, only the U.S. proximity fuse had not been seen in action before. The *Luftwaffe's* breakthrough jet fighter and recce aircraft had been and were much dreaded by the USAAF.

The arsenal of each contending army was the product of the war experience of its nation up to then and, even more important, of the nation's history after World War I. Armies and their weapons are not created on the eve of great battles. The American forces that participated in the Ardennes-Eifel battles brought with them many war-making assets. They also suffered severely from many war-making liabilities. The American fighting men on the ground, the soldiers at the sharp edge of battle, as the British call it, suffered greater losses than need have been because several of their most important weapons were inferior to those of their enemy.

In late 1944 the *Wehrmacht* was entering upon its death throes. Nevertheless, this once invincible monster of a war-making machine still was able to benefit from two historical factors denied to the Americans:

1. The World War II *Wehrmacht* began taking shape as early as 1930, even before Adolph Hitler and his *Nazis* came to power, and Germany was well into a major rearmament campaign by the mid 1930s. This campaign definitely included weapons development and research, a process hurried along by *der Führer* himself who believed he was an expert in modern ground combat and the arms and weapons employed therein.

2. The most effective setting for developing new weapons is the battlefield. By mid 1944 the *Wehrmacht* had been at war with several nations and peoples for nearly five years. Three of these years had been devoted to trying to subdue the Soviet Union's army and air force over a bloody battlefield so vast and terrible that even today, fifty years later, it is difficult for Western historians and students of military affairs to fathom. After their initial easy victories in the East, the *Wehrmacht* leaders were unpleasantly surprised to find that the contemptible *Untermenschen* that their armies were beginning to encounter were difficult to budge on defense and overwhelming in numbers on offense.

More unnerving, the Soviets brought to the battlefield several important weapons superior to the *Wehrmacht's* own. Among these were large numbers of automatic rifles and submachineguns. The Russians knew something the Germans were to learn: In modern infantry warfare, lots of small-arms firepower up close is more effective than are old-fashioned rifles and carbines with which most of the German infantry was armed at the time. "...the lack of automatic rifles came as rather a nasty surprise to the German soldier in 1941." (Source at end.)

The *Wehrmacht's* highly trained and prideful professionals also were dumbfounded to be confronted in 1942 with the Soviet T34, an all-round, versatile, medium tank mounting a high-velocity gun that blew away their own *Panzer IIIs* and *IVs*.

The Germans also were stunned by the abundance and tactical use the Soviet armies made of rocketry employing a wide range of calibers that was devastating against unprotected infantry.

The proud German commanders were not too proud to set their weapons' designers and arsenals to working on improved versions of the Soviet arms and armored fighting vehicles for mass production. They also encouraged their troops to make immediate use of captured weapons and equipment.

In December 1944 the U.S. Army had not had the benefit of these two historical experiences upon which to base a weapons program: a long period of preparation for war and sufficient years of intensive battling against an inventive foe to have time to perfect old weapons, design new ones, and produce them in sufficient quantity to make a difference on the battlefield.

America was indifferent to the realities of the rest of the world in the 1920s and 30s. This indifference produced a complacent attitude toward the military. We loved our Armistice Day parades and war movies but we pushed the real military and its preparation for possible war to the margins of our concerns as a nation. Neither the money, will, or political impetus was there to prepare for war.

The political leaders of the nation, regardless of whether they were pro- or anti-New Deal (the defining attitude in those days), believed that America should stay out of foreign wars and stick to solving its many domestic problems. A small army and air force supplemented by a small reserve plus the National Guard could handle all the war emergencies the nation might face. After 1936 President Roosevelt was one of the exceptions among the politicians. His responsibilities forced him to be more concerned about events abroad and the state of the armed forces. The President's views seemed to make little difference until war came, however.

Factions in the Congress did occasionally push for more money for the Navy and Army Air Force. However, these services suffered from infighting and rivalry, which deprived both of the support they might have realized working together (an impossibility at the time). A few months before war broke out in Europe in 1939, the U.S. Army and its air force together totalled only 188,000.

The human costs of these head-in-the-sand national policies in the 1920s and 30s were paid by the American soldiers who fought in World War II.

After 1940 American designers and engineers worked frantically to improve ground and air weapons and move the prototypes from design tables to factory floors. However, they were consistently playing catch up. It was not until the last year of the war that improved armored fighting vehicles, antitank guns, and long-range fighter aircraft began moving to the battlefields. And in some departments the U.S. never did catch up: small arms, rocketry, recoilless weapons, mobile assault guns, to cite a few.

In the Ardennes-Eifel battles, the U.S. rifleman was armed with the Garand Model-1 semiautomatic rifle and the Browning Automatic Rifle (BAR). The BAR had been carried over from World War I. It was a fully automatic but cumbersome weapon developed by the French to expedite the head-on mass attacks of infantry characteristic of the trench battling of that war. It was heavy, fifteen pounds without the twenty-round magazine. The bipod used to steady the weapon added another ten pounds or so. Even with the bipod, the BAR tended to buck after every shot, throwing off the rifleman's aim. Nevertheless, it remained throughout the war the basic rifle squad automatic weapon and influenced the battlefield tactics used at that level.

The Garand M-1 rifle was superior to any other standard infantry rifle or carbine in use in the *Wehrmacht*. Semiautomatic in function, firing a disposable clip of eight rounds, accurate at even long range, the M-1 was much admired and coveted by the German *Infanterie* soldier. However, as the Germans learned in Russia, the traditional infantry rifle (except for that used by snipers) was becoming inadequate for front-line combat. The assault rifle and machine pistol firing in an automatic mode, light weight, cheaply manufactured, and distributed in large numbers throughout infantry companies were supplanting the standard rifle.

In the *Wehrmacht* this change came to full flower with the *Volksgrenadier* divisions of 1944, whose assault platoons were armed largely with *Maschinenpistolen* and *Sturmgewehre* assault rifles. In 1940 there were eleven standard infantry rifles in a German rifle company for each assault rifle and machine pistol; by the time of the Ardennes-Eifel Counteroffensive, there were more assault rifles and machine pistols than standard rifles.

The German *Infanterie* relied greatly on their model 34 and 42 light and heavy *Maschinengewehren* (machine guns). One ordnance expert called the 42 "probably the best machine gun design ever developed." It fired at a fantastic rate, fifteen hundred rounds per minute. The gun weighed only twenty-three pounds and was designed to permit a rapid and simple method of changing the barrel. This was supremely important in the heat of combat. It made unnecessary a cooling off period (not desirable when hostiles are charging at you) or a cumbersome water jacket surrounding the barrel.

The first of these design faults afflicted the Browning .30caliber light machine gun; the second, the .30caliber heavy machine gun, which were standard in the American infantry battalions. Like the BAR (above), both the light and the heavy MGs were relics of World War I, resurrected twenty-five years later by the U.S. Ordnance Department for World War II duty.

In the Ardennes-Eifel fighting, both sides made deadly use of mortars. Both used light to heavy tubes (60mm to 4.2-inch, U.S.; 60mm to 120mm, German). The 120mm was, according to the ordnance expert quoted before, "the best mortar design to emerge from World War II." (Another weapon copied from the Soviet Army.) The German infantry seemed to depend on mortars more than did the Americans. Accordingly they developed more advanced techniques for their use.

Both sides brought towed antitank guns (*Panzerabwehrkanone, PAK* for short) to the Ardennes battlefields. The Americans put more faith in these to do the job than did their enemy. They were sorely disappointed. Separate battalions of towed 3-inch antitank guns on the American side were at least armed with an effective gun. However, "organic" to the American infantry divisions were fifty-seven of the little "pea-shooter" 57mm guns supposed to stand fast at or near the firing line and ward off German armor. Only if firing sabot-powered ammunition as at Dom Bütgenbach (Volume 2, Narrative IX) were they effective.

Another lesson the Germans learned on the Eastern Front was that antitank guns mounted on wheeled carriages were disastrously vulnerable to hostile infantry and armor. This was especially true in the deep freeze of the Ardennes-Eifel winter. The wheels of the gun carriages often froze in the icy muck and could only be moved or displaced at great effort by man and machine (usually under intense enemy fire).

The Germans did all that their dwindling resources allowed to put their PAK guns on tracked platforms and surround them with at least some armor to protect the crews. They also developed a full line of self-propelled antitank and assault guns. The Americans were never able to match this effort, although they tried. (Below)

The U.S. Army equipped every unit with at least a few bazookas, tubes fitted with a battery and wires to fire off a hollow-charge finned rocket. The little 2.6-inch diameter rockets did more damage to enemy vehicles in the Ardennes fighting than they have been credited for, especially as at Rocherath-Krinkelt (Volume 2, Narrative VIII) and Bütgenbach-Dom Bütgenbach (Volume 2, Narrative IX), where the bazookas were in the hands of determined American fighters operating from good cover.

However, the *Wehrmacht's Infanterie* once again was armed with a better weapon. The ubiquitous, disposable *Panzerfäust*, a recoilless, hand-held *PAK*, in effect, delivered a powerful armor-penetrating punch. It was eagerly sought by American infantry when abandoned by the enemy. The commander of the 82nd Airborne Division remarked, "(We) did not get adequate antitank weapons until (we) began to capture the German *Panzerfäusts*. By the fall of '44, we had truckloads of them." The German version of the bazooka (*Raketenpanzerbusche*) in the 88mm size also could punch through many inches of armor. However, it was nearly as dangerous to its operator as to its target.

As described before, the *Heer* and *Waffen SS* brought a whole family of tanks and armored, tracked tank-fighting vehicles and assault guns to their second invasion of Belgium and Luxembourg in December 1944. (Footnotes pps. 92, 115) The Americans brought the little Stuart (Model-5) light tank; the Sherman (Model-4) medium tank, whose main gun was a not very satisfactory 75mm (diameter) short rifle; the Model-10 gun motor carriage (tank destroyer) armed with a 3-inch high-velocity rifle; the Model-18 TD, faster, better gunned, light on its treads; tracked and lightly armored howitzers and long guns riding a modified M-4 tank chassis. There also were armored troop and weapons carriers (personnel and multiple gun motor carriages, to use the terminology). And some units (cavalry, e.g.) were equipped with armored cars.

The U.S. tanks and tank destroyers had serious failings. The Stuart was lightly armed and incapable of standing against even the lightest of enemy armor or infantry armed with rocket tubes or recoilless weapons. The Sherman, whose crew carried the main load of armor warfare on the American side, did not have armor thick enough to withstand the punch of the fearsome, high-velocity *PAK* guns that the Germans armed their *Panther V* and *Panzerjäger* tank destroyers with. The Sherman's gun (Model-3, 75mm) could not penetrate the front or turret armor of the *Panther V*. If the *Panzer IV* was protected by spaced armor on sides and turret or mesh skirting, the 75mm might also have trouble. The Sherman crews were forced to maneuver for shots at the vulnerable spaces (for example engine housing, road wheels, sprocket wheels, periscopes, seam between turret and deck). Also the Model-4 ran on volatile high-octane gasoline and was easily set afire.

On the plus side, the machine was more reliable in performance than were many of the German models and types, which broke down frequently. The Sherman also was maneuverable. Nevertheless, the respected WW II historian, Charles B. MacDonald, wrote that the Sherman Model-4 was already "obsolescent" when the American and British armies (which used it extensively) stepped on to the continent in mid 1944.

The U.S. gun motor carriages M-10 and M-18 (tank destroyers) had one big advantage over the many tank destroyer types (*Panzerjäger*) their enemy fielded: a revolving turret. However, this turret was open to the skies, exposing the crew to fearful damage from overhead artillery bursts. Neither the M-10 nor the M-18 were protected with adequate armor to withstand shots from the German *PAK* guns aimed at the hull. The American crews were trained to hit and run. But the infantry they worked with invariably wanted them to stand fast and engage in gun battles with the onrushing enemy armor. As at Rocherath-Krinkelt and Dom Bütgenbach (Volume 2, Narrative VIII and IX) this difference in outlook sometimes produced bad blood among friends.

The Americans did not possess a version of their enemy's *Sturmgeschütz* assault guns, seen in action many places in our Narratives. By December 1944 the German infantry had come to depend on these little mobile armored 75mm and 105mm guns, supplemented by one or two machine guns firing from the decks, to force down hostile soldiers as they attacked. A shortage of this weapon and its ineffectual use hurt the German cause in front of Höfen (Narrative II), in the Todeswald (III), at Losheimergraben crossroads (IV), at Lanzerath (IV), and at Wirtzfeld (IX) and the Rodelhöhe (X).

As a poor substitute, American infantry commanders with tanks, self-propelled tank destroyers, or tracked 155mm guns attached or available otherwise would often press their crews into playing the assault gun role to blast the way forward for their riflemen. (Narrative I; Narrative X, Part 7). U.S. tanks and tank destroyers were not intended to play this role, and they suffered for it.

The *Wehrmacht* introduced the Americans to a whole arsenal of rocketry the latter did not dream could be applied in so many sizes and calibers and in such mobile, easily positioned numbers. Horse- or vehicle-towed six tube carriages and banks of tubes carried on trucks or tracked vehicles played an important role in the German assaults in the Ardennes-Eifel battles. So did their so-called Revenge Weapon 1 (V-1) which rumbled over the 99th Division positions day in and out for a week before *Null Tag* and several weeks thereafter heading for the supply centers in the deep rear.

American rocket-firing units were scarcely evident in the Elsenborn sector. The USAAF's fighter-bombers made many attacks on ground targets with wing-mounted rockets, however; and as noted before the little rocket-firing bazooka was ubiquitous.

Ground-to-ground rocketry was a weapon of terror. The Germans' launching ramps and racks and carriages could not be aimed accurately to hit targets with precision. However, fired *en masse* the often huge missiles (up to 210mm in diameter) could literally drive men mad on the receiving end with their horrible screaming, fiery explosions, and widespread devastation.

The mobility of the *Racketenwerfer* and *Neblewerfer* units in the Ardennes gave the German infantry and armored formations some close support on the attack while their artillery was often entangled in the morass of traffic along the roads or waiting for the scarce gasoline or diesel fuel to be brought up for the hauling vehicles.

Both sides brought a large arsenal of artillery pieces to the Elsenborn battles, as our Narratives have shown in detail. The standard 105mm and 155mm (150mm in German use) howitzers found in the infantry division artillery battalions of both sides were comparable in quality. The Germans made frequent use of long-range large caliber guns and mortars generally controlled by the army echelon. These included railroad guns 280mm and 340mm in diameter with ranges of 20 to 25 miles. The Americans fielded a 240mm diameter heavy artillery piece. However, with so many Allied heavy and medium bombers and fighter-bombers in the air, cumbersome guns of this size were unnecessary.

The Germans made constant and deadly use of their versatile 88 and 120mm *Flak* guns for anti-tank and anti-personnel use up front at the sharp edge of the battlefield. The extraordinary 88mm diameter long rifle was probably the most effective all-round killer of the war. The American 90mm antiaircraft gun was comparable in range, muzzle velocity, and power but not in the same league with the 88 when it came to mobility and versatility.

The armored divisions of *das Heer* and the *Waffen SS* were generally equipped with field artillery mounted on tracked carriages, as were U.S. armored divisions.

American artillerists enjoyed a tremendous advantage in the quality and quantity of ammunition they fired; its ample supply; the introduction at this time of the proximity fuse, which exploded rounds above troops and vehicles at which they were fired; mastery of fire direction technology; and synchronized firing by batteries.

Also, due to the terrain, condition of roads into the Ardennes-Eifel breakthrough area, congestion on these roads, loss of the Belgian N-32 highway running along the southern flank of the Elsenborn heights, and ceaseless attacks from the air on clear days, the German artillery units suffered extreme difficulties in displacing their guns forward to the scene of the action. After the initial chaos following *Null Tag*, the movement of U.S. guns and ammunition proceeded smoothly and an enormous concentration of tubes was brought to the battleground. The weight of American artillery helped overcome the handicap of so many infantry and armor weapons that were inferior to those of the *Wehrmacht*.

So did Allied air power, which first suppressed the *Luftwaffe's* brave attempt to resurrect its mighty fighter-bomber weapons of earlier day; then pounded the fighting formations of the *Heer* and *Waffen SS* on the ground until they and their supply troops, vehicles, and horse-drawn wagons could move only in darkest night, if then.

So did the extraordinary mobility of the American divisions and detached units on the ground and their supply trains as well. Here the superiority of hauling vehicles—from little jeep to the behemoth workhorses—six-by-six trucks, four-ton trucks, tractor trailers—made itself decisive as compared with the motley collection of mismatched hauling vehicles (military, civilian, foreign army, horse-drawn, etc.) available to the German ground units operating in the counteroffensive.

Also, at this stage of the war, the *Wehrmacht* could not supply its formations with sufficient of the weapons described, superior or not, to make a decisive difference. Once an aircraft was lost or a *Panzer* smashed or broken down due to mechanical failings (not an uncommon happening), it could not be replaced. On the other side of the hill, the Americans seemed to have an unlimited supply of aircraft, armored machines, and transport.

U.S. troops in January 1945 began receiving improved armor: A new model Sherman and M-36 tank destroyer came on the scene. Entire battalions equipped with towed 3-inch antitank guns turned them in for M-36s. (Volume 2, Narrative X, Part 6) Also, the American tankers and TD men caught on to the simple expedient of using sand bags supported in racks on turret and hull to increase resistance to high-velocity shellfire. And the TD soldiers found ways of covering over their turrets when on the defense.

Nevertheless, these new tanks and TDs were not seen on the battlefields of the Ardennes-Eifel in anything like the numbers needed; and not seen at all in some sectors. And the U.S. infantry's automatic weapons, towed antitank guns, and bazooka tubes that friend and foe alike considered obsolete or inadequate or both continued to provide their principal front-line fire power right up to the end on these battlefields. (An improved bazooka tube plus more effective rockets for it did arrive late in the game, however.)

The ground fighters of the American Army in WW II deserve recognition for doing so well in spite of being armed with many weapons that were inferior to those of the enemy they grappled with in mortal combat.

430 SHOCK OF WAR

Source of quotations:

"...best machine gun..." Peter Chamberlain and Terry Gordon, Weapons of the Third *Reich*, Doubleday, NY, 1979, p. 90.

"...lack of automatic rifles..." Ibid., p. 49.

"...best mortar..." Ibid., p. 298.

"...obsolescent..." Charles B. MacDonald, The Battle of the Hürtgen Forest, Jove Edition, NY, 1983, p. 22.

"We didn't get..." Major General James M. Gavin, quoted in Russell F. Weigley, Eisenhower's Lieutenants, Indiana U. Press, Bloomington, 1981, p. 11.

- - - - -

Final Battles in Germany of U.S. 5th Corps Infantry Divisions

The 16th Infantry (1st Division) crossed the Roer River late in February 1945 a few miles south of Düren, Germany. The division captured Bonn, Germany on the Rhine by March 7. The Rhine crossings were made on a pontoon-supported treadway and ferry in mid March. The 1st waged a hard fight using all three regiments to gain the heights of Siegen, forty miles east of Bonn. Two regiments developed a bridgehead on the east bank of the Weser River north of Kassel. The 1st was one of three U.S. divisions that assumed the task of rooting a strong, seventy-thousand-man enemy force out of the Harz Mountains northeast of Kassel. It then marched by truck to the Czech-German border and its last action at Karlsbad (Karlovy Vary) in Czechoslovakia.

After its short stay on a quiet front east of Eupen, Belgium, the 2nd Division was back in the vicinity of the well-defended Roer and Urft River dams early in March, this time a few miles to the northeast where its regiments crossed the Roer River headwaters. The 38th Regiment overcame opposition around pillboxes near the Urft River then captured Gemund, Germany a few miles southeast of the dams. Riding the decks of armor, men of the 2nd Division rifle companies rolled up enemy hedgehogs in dozens of small towns and villages as the division closed on the west bank of the Rhine River north of Remagen. The 38th crossed the Rhine on March 21, marched to the Wied River and established a bridgehead on the east side, with help from 9th Armored Division tanks. The 23rd Infantry helped enlarge the bridgehead, and the 2nd's columns now went rapidly northeast to the much wider Weser River.

The 23rd Infantry assaulted the heights east of the river and infantry and tanks followed. By April 8, the ancient German university center of Göttingen had been taken. A week later the joint armor-infantry force was pressing an attack on Leipzig. The city was taken April 19 after sharp, deadly combat involving the 2nd and 69th divisions. Thereupon, the 2nd made a mechanized forced march of two hundred miles directly south to Bayreuth and then east to Pilsen in Czechoslovakia. An assault on the city was being prepared when the war ended.

After Lauer's now thoroughly bloodied (as soldiers say) 99th Division departed their campgrounds near Aubel and Claremont, Belgium at the end of February, its first task was to seize sixty square miles of the Cologne Plain lying between the Erft Canal on the west to the Rhine River on the east. The 395th Regiment attached to the 3rd Armored Division crossed the canal February 28 to make a bridgehead. The 393rd followed close on.

In the vicinity of Düsseldorf on the west bank of the Rhine, the 99th received an order to stand to. A railroad bridge (the Ludendorff Bridge) had been taken intact across the Rhine at Remagen south of Bonn by a 9th AD patrol the afternoon of March 7. The U.S. 9th and 78th Infantry divisions had started moving across accompanied by armor. During the night of 10-11 the 394th Regiment accompanied by engineers and armor were the first of the division to cross on the bridge. The 99th was assigned the south flank of the bridgehead, the 9th the center, the 78th, the north. By this time a large force of German infantry and armor backed by innumerable large and small caliber guns and supported by a squadron of jet aircraft were pounding at the front and side of the bridgehead. However, their attacks were sporadic, and a weight of U.S. air, artillery, and armor power backing the infantry in the bridgehead was too much for them.

By March 17 the 99th was moving east to take Wetzlar north of Frankfort on the Main River. The division then made a long truck trip north to the perimeter of the Ruhr pocket. By mid-April 99th Division infantry were pushing against an enclave of German forces in a triangle formed by the Lenne and Ruhr rivers. After the Ruhr pocket was liquidated, the 99th trucked three hundred miles to the southeast to the vicinity of Bamberg, Germany, staging area for their attack to and across the Danube. The 99th occupied Landshut and Moosburg on the Isar River at the end, liberating a large number of U.S. soldiers from the POW camps around the area.

The 9th Infantry Division, which defended the Kalterherberg-Monschau end of the Gerow Line on Elsenborn Ridge, helped the 78th Division capture the Roer-Urft River dams in early February. It then crossed the Roer River north of the Hürtgen Forest and drove hard for the Rhine south of Bonn and started crossing on the Lundendorf Bridge the day after it was captured. After the breakout from the bridgehead (above), the 9th helped shrink the Ruhr pocket, then moved east to roll up the German force in the Harz Mountains (above). The three regiments eliminated resistance in towns east of the mountains. When hostilities ended, the 9th's men were encamped on the Mulde River near Dessau, close to the Elbe.

The German Divisions that Fought Against U.S. 5th Corps at Elsenborn Crest

272nd *Volksgrenadier Division*: Although second-rate, the six thousand or so soldiers of the 272nd, which held the extreme northern flank of the German 67th *Korps* above Monschau, made it difficult for the U.S. 78th and 9th divisions in the second Roer-Urft river dams campaign (above). It had little fight left after that encounter or men and equipment to fight with. However, survivors, still operating as a division, tried to harass U.S. units on their way to Remagen, then crossed the Rhine and marched into the Ruhr area. There they were bagged along with some three hundred thousand German soldiers captured after the U.S. and British forces had dissolved their defensive positions.

277th *VGD*: After rear-guarding the German exodus east of Elsenborn late in January, this division, which battled the 99th Division for six weeks, retreated to the west bank of the Rhine where its HQ was overrun and its commander, Major General Wilhelm Viebig captured. The survivors ended in POW cages in the Ruhr pocket.

12th *VGD*: After leaving the Wirtzfeld-Büllingen front, this division went west to work with the 2nd *SS Panzer Korps* in its operations along the northern leg of the Ardennes "wedge." After the *Korps* moved east (below), the division's survivors, still operating as 12th *VGD*, moved north to oppose the U.S. 9th Army along the Roer River. Its commander, Major General Gerhard Engle, had been wounded and was not with the division at the time. Following its encounters with 9th Army, the 12th was about finished. Its survivors, mostly artillery and service people of HQ units ended in POW pens in the Ruhr.

246th *VGD*: After its short stay on the front east of Elsenborn replacing 3rd *Panzergrenadier* Division, this division was sent to the German 7th Army front in the south to help hold back U.S. 3rd Army's post-Bulge offensive eastward. The division was scattered hither and yon in the Upper Rhine region after Peter Körte, the commander, died in action.

3rd *Fallschirmjäger* Division: At the end of January 1945 after its dogged stand in the ice and snow to hold off the U.S. 1st Division and 23rd Infantry (2nd Division), this *FSJ* formation moved east with a small number of remaining fighters and horse-drawn artillery to the vicinity of Koblenz on the north leg of the triangle that U.S. 7th and 3rd armies were methodically rolling up in February 1945. The division was ordered to fight a wasting rear-guard action on the west bank of the Rhine. The few paratroops who escaped over the river ended in the Ruhr pocket. There they were united with their original commander, General Schmipf, returned in time from recovering from wounds to surrender the division.

3rd *Panzergrenadier* Division: After its abrupt and unexpected withdrawal from the Elsenborn front facing the 99th Division, this armored infantry unit moved into the battle for Bastogne and by December 30 was in General Lüttwitz's 47 *Korps* pushing on the U.S. 8th Corps west of Bastogne. After the *Wehrmacht* withdrew from the breakthrough area, the 3rd found itself in more heavy combat in the Roer River sector south of Düren. Along with a *Panzer* division, 3rd *PzGD* fought to keep General Collins' 7th Corps from crossing the Erft Canal between the Roer and the Rhine. The fight was hopeless. General Denkert's dwindling men and armor marched north over the Rhine and into that graveyard of German divisions, the Ruhr pocket. Its few remaining companies of *Panzergrenadiers*, an assault gun company, and a few batteries of self-propelled artillery gave up there.

12th *SS Panzer* Division (*Hitlerjugend*): After leaving the Bütgenbach-Dom
Bütgenbach front December 23-24, 1944, the division moved west and south, one
Kampfgruppe trying to screen the remnants of *Kampfgruppe* Peiper from being
attacked from the south, the rest of the division going south to join the Bastogne
melee. By January 4 the 12th *SS* was caught up in heavy fighting on the north side
of the perimeter around the road from Bastogne to Houffalize. Hitler's
determination that the former be taken at all costs forced Field Marshal Model to
order the surviving armored power of the 6th *SS Panzer* Army into the 5th *PzA*
sector and the terrible, grinding, pointless battle for the city.

The *SS* armored divisions were the first to begin assembling for a movement
out of the breakthrough area. By the third week of January, 12th *SS PzD* was
staging for a move to the Eastern Front. After such refitting and restocking of the
Panzergrenadier ranks and replacement of lost armor as could be done at this late
stage of the war, the division moved southeast with the 6th *SS Panzer* Army to
relieve the siege of Budapest, Hungary by the Soviet Army. Martin Bormann,
Hitler's aide wrote at the time, "Our greatest asset in the West, Sepp Dietrich and
his army, is to be withdrawn and sent to the Eastern Front."

Once again the *Waffen SS* tried to do its all for an increasingly irrational
Hitler. 1st *SS Pz* Corps (1st and 12th *PzD's*) had some success in attacking the
Russians east of Lake Balaton, but its armor soon ground to a halt in the muck
and mire. The *Panzergrenadiers* were thrown in on foot but got nowhere. Dietrich
wanted to withdraw west into Austria; Hitler refused, storming that the *SS* troops
were to die to the last man.

They didn't. Instead, Hitler ordered Dietrich's army to defend Vienna, its last
major stand. Sixth *PzA's* divisions soon went their separate ways to various fates.
General Kraas surrendered 12th *SS PzD* to the troops of the U.S. 3rd Army on the
Enns River near Linz, Austria. Close to ten thousand men and officers turned
themselves in, approximately half the normal complement of the division.

1st *SS Panzer* Division (*Leibstandarte Adolph Hitler*) shared the fate of
Hitlerjugend. However, Hitler demanded even more of its soldiers and fewer
survived to surrender. The division tried to screen the 6th *SS Pz* Army's rear as
it withdrew from Hungary, then melted away to the west. Few *LAH* soldiers
captured by the Russians returned to Germany. (See also Appendix item on this
division, p. 413)

Following the surrender, the *Waffen SS* organization was condemned by the
International Military Tribunal of the Allies. Men who served in the *SS* fighting
divisions who were convicted of specific criminal acts (some five hundred cases)
were hung or sentenced to long prison terms. (*SS* Lieutenant General "Sepp"
Dietrich served ten years.)

Also, all officers and NCOs of the *Waffen SS* were kept in camps for up to
four years until their keepers could assure themselves their charges were not guilty
of such acts during the war. Following their release, these men were then hauled
before German-run denazification courts.

(Sources: U.S. Cole, The Ardennes, Volume 1, Documentation, master list; Charles B. MacDonald, The Last Offensive, OCMH, USGPO. German: Samuel E. Mitcham, Jr., Hitler's Legions, The German Army Order of Battle, World War II, Stein and Day, NY, 1985.; Messenger, Hitler's Gladiator, p. 164, for Bormann's quote. Volume 1, Documentation, bibl.; Stein Waffen SS, pps. 250-252. Volume 1, Documentation, Preface, for post-war trials of Waffen SS men.

- - - - -

Post-War Careers of U.S. Battalion and Regiment Commanders

Following are post-war ranks plus a few career highlights of U.S. infantry leaders featured in our story in addition to those described in the "Reckoning" chapter. All of the following officers have long since retired, and most are deceased. Those still alive (1996) are identified by state of residence. Abbreviations used: MA, U.S. Military Academy at West Point, NY; LTC, lieutenant colonel; Cl, colonel; G, general; B, brigadier; M, major; L, lieutenant; I, infantry; CC, armored combat command; ADC, assistant division commander; ID, infantry division; AD, armored division; CO, commanding officer; Bn, battalion; CS, chief of staff; IB, infantry brigade; G-3, operations officer; DCO, deputy commanding officer; HQ, headquarters.

1st Infantry Division

Cl Stanhope Mason, MA (General Huebner's CS, 5th Corps) MG. CO, 26thI; CO, 24th ID, Korea.

LTC Derrill Daniel (CO, 2ndBn, 26thI, Dom Bütgenbach) MG. Various posts and commands including CO, 16th Corps Army Reserve.

Cl J.F.R. Seitz, MA (CO, 26thI Bütgenbach) MG. ADC, 45thID; CO, 2nd ID, DCO, 1st Army.

LTC John T. Corley, MA (CO, 3rdBn, 26thI, east of Bütgenbach) BG. CO, 24thI, Korea; G-3, Chief of Army Field Forces staff; asst. CS, 7th Army, Europe; director, Infantry School Ranger Dept.; ADC, 2ndID.

LTC Frank J. Murdoch, Jr., MA (CO, 1stBn, 26th I, Bütgenbach) MG. CO, CCB, 3rdAD; ADC, 7thID, Korea; DCO, 4th Army Reserve Forces.

LTC E.V. Sutherland, MA (acting CO, 26thI on move to Bütgenbach) BG. Asst. G-3, Army Ground Forces HQ; Military Advisory Group, Cambodia; chairman English Department, MA. (NY)

LTC Charles T. Horner, Jr., MA (CO, 3rdBn, 16thI defending Weywertz, west of Bütgenbach) MG. CO, 1stIB; ADC, 5thID; CO, 2nd Logistics Command, Okinawa. (VA)

2nd Infantry Division

MG Walter M. Robertson, MA, see p. 370.

BG John H. Stokes, MA (ADC, 2ndID, in charge of dual towns defense) MG. Chief, Office of Military History, Washington, DC; CO, Military District of Washington (District of Columbia).

Cl Chester J. Hirschfelder (9th Infantry Regiment at Wahlerscheid crossroads) Cl., DCO, Caribbean Defense Command; CO, Ft. Sam Houston, TX.

Cl Francis H. Boos, MA (CO, 38thI, which defended the dual towns against 12th *SS PzD*) Cl. G-3, 5th Army; liaison with NC National Guard.

LTC Jack K. Norris (CO, 2ndBn, 38thI on left flank at dual towns) Cl. Commandant of cadets, NGa. State College. Practiced law in GA for ten years. (ID)

LTC Olinto M. Barsanti (CO, 3rdBn, 38thI on right flank at dual towns) MG. CO, ID, Korea.

LTC Frank Mildren, MA, see p. 370.

BG John H. Hinds, MA (CO, 2ndID artillery at Elsenborn crest) MG. Army Security Agency; deputy chief, Research and Development Board, Secretary of Defense.

LTC Paul V. Tuttle, MA (CO, 3rdBn, 23rdI, battle in Todeswald) Cl. G-3, 7thAD; CO, 34thI; head, department of military science, NC State U.

LTC William D. McKinley, MA (CO, 1stBn, 9thI, which lost five hundred men fighting off 12th *SS PzD*) Cl. Military Affairs Advisory Group, various countries; died age 41 in Seoul, Korea.

LTC John H. Hightower (CO, 1stBn, 23rdI, battle for Mürringen, north flank of dual towns, Ondenval Pass) MG. (GA)

99th Infantry Division

The 99th was a pre-war Army reserve unit. After its activation late in 1942 it was officered principally by reservists and graduates of the war-time Army schools. Most departed the Army at war's end for civilian pursuits. Those field and company-grade officers who remained in the Army served in a variety of assignments and posts characteristic of the Cold War. Others returned to civilian life.

LTC Jean D. Scott, MA (CO, 393rdI, which held against the 277th *VGD* in the Todeswald December 16; stayed with the 99th until war's end) Cl. G-1 (personnel) on staff of 15th Army and later of 1st Army; retired in 1954.

Cl Don Riley (CO, 394thI, was "at ground zero" of the German attack in the Losheimergraben crossroads area). In August 1945, CO, 11th Special Troops unit, Fort Hood, TX. Retired thereafter.

436 SHOCK OF WAR

Cl Alexander J. MacKenzie, MA (395thI, held the Höfen breakwater against the assaults of the 326th *VGD* and the woods north of the dual towns). Retired from the Army soon after the war.

LTC McClernand Butler (CO, 3rdBn, 395thI and attached cavalry squadron held off several battalions of a *VGD* at Höfen-Monschau in one of the most decisive engagements of the Elsenborn battles). Returned to the telephone business after the War. (IL)

LTC Jack G. Allen (CO, 3rdBn, 393rdI blocked enemy infantry and tank destroyers from the main road to the dual towns for thirty hours; lost an eye to shellfire soon afterward). Remained in the Army until 1946. Afterward,he was in the metal-working business, rising to president of his company. He died in 1995 at age ninety.

LTC Matt Legler, MA (CO, 1stBn, 393rdI was on Allen's right and tied up enemy infantry in the borderland forests, was badly hurt when he stepped on a mine [Narrative X, Part 7]). He intended to make a career in the Army. Instead his career was as a design engineer with a major oil company. (SC)

LTC Ernest C. Peters, MA (CO, 2nd Battalion, 393rdI, fought in the woods north of the dual towns and suffered grave losses in the attack late in January to take back these same woods). Cl. G-3 section, HQ, U.S. Army Forces, Europe; commander of HQ unit, 4th Army.

LTC Robert H. Douglas (CO, 1st Battalion, 394th, defense of Losheimergraben crossroads), career in the Army.

M Norman A. Moore (CO, 3rd Battalion at Buchholz Station, west of crossroads), LTC, career in the Army.

✠   ✠   ✠   ✠   ✠

INDEX TO NAMED COMMANDERS AND STAFF OFFICERS, VOLUMES 1 AND 2*

---

* Does not include Appendices or Documentation.

Hinds, BG John H., Artillery CO, 2nd Infantry Division. 2: 10, 16, 17, 20, 22, 23, 34, 42, 62-66, 264, 273.

Hirschfelder, Col., Chester J., CO, 9Inf (to 12/30/44). 1: 38, 44, 45, 54, 60, 62, 333. 2: 4, 6,42, 56, 63, 66, 68, 69, 155, 290.

Hitler, Adolph, *Reichschancellor* and Supreme Commander, German Armed Forces. 1: iv, v, 18, 26, 27, 29, 30, 33, 34, 86, 87, 89-91, 105, 118, 151, 152, 155, 206-208, 214, 295. 2: 1, 45, 49, f49, 50, 91-93, 135, 181-184, 189, 214, 231, 246, 286, 287, f287, 289, 291, 292, 294, 314-319, 329, 333, 340, 357-359, 361, 362, 364, 365.

Hitzfeld, LG Otto, CO, 67th *Infanterie Korps*. 1: 61, 83-85, 90-92, 96, 104, 116, 118, 127, 130, 152. 2: 4, 5, 7, 48, 201, 257, 261, 288, 289, 291, 292, 294, 311, 312, 322, 325, 330, 331, 333, 336.

Hodges, LG Courtney H., CO, 1st Army. 1: vi, 15, 20, 22, 25, 26, 39, 40, 274, 295, 304. 2: 5, 6, 50-55, 184-186, f186, 245, 277-280, f279, 283, 284, 315, 329, 331, f360, 362.

Hoffman, Col. Helmut von, CO, 9Para Rgt, 3rd*FSJD*. 1: 251, 253, 260, 261, 300.

Hoke, Maj. Frank, 2nd Infantry Division HQ. 2: 159, 160.

Horner, LTC Charles T., CO, 3/16. 2: 6, 180, 232, 254, 310, 334, 335.

Huebner, MG Clarence R., CO, 1st Division, later 5th Corps. 1: 292-294. 2: 6, 53, 81, 184, 192, 255, 282, 284, 329-331, 338, 341, 345, 346, 370.

Jodl, General Alfred, Chief of Operations, *OKW*. 2: 287, 361, 366.

Jones, Alan W., CO, U.S. 106th Infantry Division. 2: 51.

Jurgensen, *SS* Major Arnold, CO, *Panther* Bn, 12th *SS Pz* Division. 2: 247.

Kaschner, MG Erwin, CO, 326th*VGD*. 1: 61, 73, 83, 85, 91-93, 96, 100-104, 113, 115, 117-119, 121, 123-125, 127, 128, 293. 2: 4, 7, 19, 45, 47, 48, 60, 77, 276, 291.

Keane, MG William B., C/S, U.S. 1st Army. 2: 6, 51, 280.

Konop, LTC Matthew, CO, Headquarters Coy, 2nd Infantry Division. 2: 42, 61, 62, 66, 67, 84.

Körte, Col. Peter, CO, 246th *Volksgrenadier* Division. 2: 257, 291, 312, 313.

Kraas, *SS* Col. Hugo, CO, 12th *SS Panzer* Division. 1: 140, 177, 178, 184, 185, 188, 312, 313, 316, 319. 2: 4, 6,48, 88, 91-97, 110-113, 115, 135, 136, 145, 147, 148, 163, 179, 200, 202, 203, 212, 213, 215, 216, 218, 229, 231, 246.

Kraemer, *SS* MG Fritz, C/S, 6th *Panzer Armee*. 1: 89, 90, 105, 154. 2: 46, 81, 92, 136, 182, 184, 201, 265, 287.

Krause, *SS* LTC Berhard, CO, *Kampfgruppe* Krause, 12th *SS Panzer* Division. 2: 179, 213, 214, 218, 219, 224, 228, 229, 231, 237-239, 242, 244.

Kriz, Maj. Robert L., CO, 2/394 (after December 31). 2: 325-327.

Kuhlmann, _____, CO, *Kampfgruppe* Kuhlmann, 12th *SS Panzer* Division. 2: 179, 197, 200, 203, 205-210, 212, 213.

NOTE FOR RESEARCHERS AND READERS

Primary reference materials as described on pages 360-61 of Volume 1 are of two kinds: (1) personal stories and recollections and (2) official materials. The former, (1), including "MacDonald File" and Ralph Hill correspondence items, have been donated to the U.S. Army Military History Institute at Carlisle, PA for deposit in the extensive World War II collections maintained there. The latter, (2), can be found in the Textual Reference (Military) part of the U.S. National Archives, College Park, MD. A "photo annex" to the two volumes of The Shock of War is planned. Readers of Volume 1 and/or 2 will be informed when it is available.